IF FOUND, please notify and arrange return to owner. The owner of t~~~~
the Certified in Financial Management Examination.

Name of CFM Candidate _____

Address _____

City, State, Zip _____

Telephone ( )_____ E-mail _____

Additional Gleim *CMA/CFM Review* books, software, and other accounting study materials are available directly from

Gleim Publications, Inc.
P.O. Box 12848
University Station
Gainesville, Florida 32604
(800) 87-GLEIM
(352) 375-0772
FAX: (352) 375-6940
E-mail: admin@gleim.com
Internet: www.gleim.com

This is *CFM Review (for Part 2CFM only)* available for $22.95. Also available are

CMA/CFM Review: Part 1, Economics, Finance, and Management, 8th ed. $22.95
CMA Review: Part 2CMA, Financial Accounting and Reporting, 8th ed. 22.95
CMA/CFM Review: Part 3, Mgmt. Reporting, Analysis, and Behavioral Issues, 8th ed. .. 22.95
CMA/CFM Review: Part 4, Decision Analysis and Information Systems, 8th ed. 22.95

CMA/CFM Test Prep software ($35 per section) is also available to complement your study.

Other review manuals available are

CPA Review: Financial $24.50
CPA Review: Auditing 24.50
CPA Review: Business Law 24.50
CPA Review: TAX-MAN-GOV 24.50

CPA Test Prep software ($35 per section) and *CPA Review* audiotapes ($75 per section) are also available to complement your study.

Order forms for these and all of our other publications are provided at the back of this book.

Groundwood Paper and Highlighters -- This book is printed on high quality groundwood paper. It is lightweight and easy-to-recycle. We recommend that you purchase a highlighter specifically designed to be non-bleed-through (e.g., Avery *Glidestick*™) at your local office supply store.

REVIEWERS AND CONTRIBUTORS

Karen Hom, B.A., University of Florida, provided production assistance throughout the project.

Grady M. Irwin, J.D., University of Florida Holland Law Center, has taught in the University of Florida College of Business. Mr. Irwin wrote many answer explanations, provided extensive editorial assistance, and assisted with the preparation of first drafts of the outlines.

Travis Moore, M.B.A., University of Florida, is our production coordinator. Mr. Moore coordinated and supervised the production staff, prepared the page layout for the entire edition, and reviewed the final manuscript.

Nancy Raughley, B.A., Tift College, is our editor. Ms. Raughley reviewed the entire manuscript and assisted in all phases of production.

Bradley D. Smerage, M.Acc., CPA, University of Florida, provided editorial assistance throughout the project.

A PERSONAL THANKS

This manual would not have been possible without the extraordinary effort and dedication of Jim Collis, Terry Hall, and Gail Luparello, who typed the entire manuscript and all revisions as well as prepared the camera-ready pages.

The authors appreciate the proofreading and production assistance of Chad Houghton and Mark Moore.

The authors also appreciate the editorial assistance of Amy Lasris, John Higgins, Jennifer Menge, Shana Robbins, and Lisa Saltz.

Finally, we appreciate the encouragement and tolerance of our families throughout the project.

EIGHTH EDITION
CFM REVIEW

for PART 2CFM only
CORPORATE FINANCIAL MANAGEMENT

by Irvin N. Gleim, Ph.D., CPA, CIA, CMA, CFM

and

Dale L. Flesher, Ph.D., CPA, CIA, CMA, CFM

with the assistance of

Grady M. Irwin, J.D.

ABOUT THE AUTHORS

Irvin N. Gleim is Professor Emeritus in the Fisher School of Accounting at the University of Florida and is a member of the American Accounting Association, Academy of Legal Studies in Business, American Institute of Certified Public Accountants, Association of Government Accountants, Florida Institute of Certified Public Accountants, Institute of Internal Auditors, and the Institute of Management Accountants. He has had articles published in the *Journal of Accountancy, The Accounting Review,* and *The American Business Law Journal* and is author/coauthor of numerous accounting and aviation books and CPE courses.

Dale L. Flesher is the Arthur Andersen Alumni Professor in the School of Accountancy at the University of Mississippi and has written over 180 articles for business and professional journals, including *Management Accounting, Journal of Accountancy,* and *The Accounting Review,* as well as numerous books. He is a member of the Institute of Management Accountants, American Institute of Certified Public Accountants, Institute of Internal Auditors, American Accounting Association, and American Taxation Association. He is a past editor of *The Accounting Historians' Journal* and is a trustee and past president of the Academy of Accounting Historians.

Gleim Publications, Inc.
P.O. Box 12848
University Station
Gainesville, Florida 32604
(352) 375-0772
(800) 87-GLEIM
FAX: (352) 375-6940
E-mail: admin@gleim.com
Internet: www.gleim.com

ISSN: 1090-543X

ISBN 0-917539-82-6

This is the first printing of the eighth edition of *CFM Review.*
Please e-mail update@gleim.com with CFM 8-1 included in the subject or text. You will receive our current update as a reply.

EXAMPLE:

To:	update@gleim.com
From:	your e-mail address
Subject:	CFM 8-1

ACKNOWLEDGMENTS

The authors are indebted to the Institute of Certified Management Accountants for permission to use problem materials from past CMA examinations. Questions and unofficial answers from the Certified Management Accountant Examinations, copyright © 1976 through 1996 by the Institute of Certified Management Accountants, are reprinted and/or adapted with permission.

The authors are also indebted to The Institute of Internal Auditors, Inc. for permission to use Certified Internal Auditor Examination Questions and Suggested Solutions, copyright © 1980 through 1995 by The Institute of Internal Auditors, Inc.

The authors would also like to thank the following professors for contributing questions to this book: J.O. Hall, Western Kentucky University; Ruth R. O'Keefe, Jacksonville University; Alfonso R. Oddo, Niagara University; and Steven Rubin, Brooklyn College -- CUNY.

This publication is designed to provide accurate and authoritative information with regard to the subject matter covered. It is sold with the understanding that the publisher is not engaged in rendering legal, accounting, or other professional service.

If legal advice or other expert assistance is required, the services of a competent professional person should be sought.

(From a declaration of principles jointly adopted by a Committee of the American Bar Association and a Committee of Publishers.)

PREFACE FOR CFM CANDIDATES

The purpose of this book is to help YOU prepare YOURSELF to pass Part 2 of the CFM examination. The overriding consideration is an inexpensive, effective, and easy-to-use study program. This manual

1. Defines topics tested on Part 2 of the CFM exam.

2. Explains how to optimize your exam score by analyzing how the CFM exam is constructed, administered, and graded.

3. Outlines all of the subject matter tested on Part 2 of the CFM exam in 10 easy-to-use study units.

4. Presents multiple-choice questions to prepare you to answer questions on future CFM exams. The answer explanations are presented to the immediate right of the questions for your convenience.

5. Illustrates **individual question answering techniques** to minimize selecting incorrect answers and to maximize your exam score.

6. Suggests **exam-taking techniques** to help you maintain control and achieve success.

This is the Eighth Edition of *CFM Review*, which covers only Part 2 of the new CFM exam. Recall that the only difference between the CFM exam and the CMA exam is Part 2. Part 2CFM is "Corporate Financial Management." Part 2CMA is "Financial Accounting and Reporting."

Now is the time to take and pass the CFM exam. The CMA examination has been administered annually since 1972. The number of CMA candidates has increased from 410 in 1972 to a combined total of over 10,000 for 1996. The pass rate for each section of the exam averages over 40%. This higher (compared to other certifications) pass rate is consistent with the more mature CMA candidate (average age 30+) and the professional development nature of the CMA program. We expect the initial pass rates on the CFM exam to be similar.

To maximize the efficiency of your review program, begin by **studying** (not reading) the first 30 pages in this book. "Preparing for and Taking the CFM Exam" is very short but very important. It has been carefully organized and written to provide you with important information to assist you in successfully completing Part 2 of the CFM examination.

The outline format and spacing and the question and answer formats are designed to facilitate learning and readability. While this manual constitutes a complete self-study program for Part 2 of the CFM exam, CFM candidates should consider enrolling in a formal review program. Local colleges and universities as well as IMA chapters throughout the country have coordinated CMA review programs in the past and will continue to do so, as well as add CFM reviews.

Thank you for your interest in our CFM/CMA materials. We deeply appreciate the thousands of letters and suggestions received from CIA, CMA, and CPA candidates since 1974. Please give us feedback concerning this manual. The last page has been designed to help you note corrections and suggestions throughout your study process. Please tear it out and mail it to us with your comments. We request that questions about our books and software be sent to us via mail, e-mail, or fax. The appropriate staff member will give your question thorough consideration and a prompt response. Questions concerning orders, prices, shipments, or payments will be handled via telephone by our customer service staff.

Good Luck on the Exam,

Irvin N. Gleim
Dale L. Flesher

September 1997

TABLE OF CONTENTS

PUBLISHER'S NOTE:
   Please help. Use the form on pages 487-488 to send us corrections and suggestions for improvement (please send after you take the CFM). FAX the support request form on page vii or e-mail irvin@gleim.com for inquiries about errors, omissions, etc. An example of how this helps our customers can be found on page 461 in our "Addendum: Quantitative Practice Questions." Users asked for more quantitative questions and Gleim provides them.
   For updates and information on this and other Gleim books, please see our web page (www.gleim.com/updates.html), or send e-mail to update@gleim.com.

Gleim's *CFM Review* Support via FAX

If you FAX us inquiries about errors, omissions, etc., before 1:00 p.m. eastern time, we will respond by FAX the following business day. If we have trouble FAXing our response, it will be mailed. Technical support is also available via e-mail (support@gleim.com). Please include your e-mail address on the fax form below if you wish to receive a response to your request by e-mail (required if you are outside the United States).

Please photocopy this *CFM Review* FAX Support Request form. It must be completed as requested so we can address the issues and questions you have. All items should refer to a specific page number and outline letter/number or question number.

Wait until after you take the CFM exam to send us the separate evaluation form provided on pages 487 and 488. Please DO NOT duplicate items via FAX that you will be sending to us on the evaluation form.

Gleim Publications, Inc. FAX (352) 375-6940

***CFM REVIEW* SUPPORT REQUEST**

Complete this form and attach additional pages as necessary.

Your name _____ Your Fax # ( ) _____-_____

Address: _____

_____

City: _____ State: _____ Zip: _____

E-mail: _____

Inquiry: _____

_____

_____

_____

_____

_____

_____

_____

_____

_____

_____

PREPARING FOR AND TAKING THE CMA/CFM EXAMS

ABOUT THE CMA/CFM EXAMS

INTRODUCTION

CMA is the acronym for Certified Management Accountant. CFM is an acronym for Certified in Financial Management. The CFM exam is an offshoot of the CMA. The two exams are identical except that the Part 2CFM exam is "Corporate Financial Management," while the Part 2CMA exam is "Financial Accounting and Reporting."

The CMA examination has been, and the CMA/CFM exams will continue to be, developed and offered by the Institute of Certified Management Accountants (ICMA) in over 175 locations in the U.S. as well as in San Juan, Puerto Rico; Amman, Jordan; Amsterdam; Bahrain; Cairo; Dhahran, Saudi Arabia; Hong Kong; London; Taipei; and Zurich. International availability will begin May 1, 1998.

Both the CMA and the CFM are computer-administered, on-demand exams. Each part consists of 120 multiple-choice questions with a 3-hour time limit. The exam is administered at Sylvan testing centers.

CFM Review contains this 30-page introduction and 10 study units of outlines and multiple-choice questions that cover all of the material tested on Part 2 of the CFM exam. This introduction discusses exam content, pass rates, administration, organization, background information, preparing for the CFM exam, and taking the CFM exam. We urge you to read the next 26 pages carefully because they will help you dramatically improve your study and test-taking procedures.

CORPORATE MANAGEMENT ACCOUNTANTS AND FINANCIAL MANAGERS

1. Objective: Maximize the value of the firm by optimizing

    a. Long-term investment strategies
    b. The capital structure, i.e., how these long-term investments are funded
    c. Short-term cash flow management

2. Corporate financial management involves a financial manager, usually a vice-president/chief financial officer, who is assisted by the

    a. Treasurer -- cash, credit, capital outlay management
    b. Controller -- financial, cost, tax accounting

3. All accounting and finance personnel are beneficiaries of CFM and/or CMA participation.

4. The CMA/CFM tools are set forth in the ICMA's Content Specification Outlines for the CMA/CFM exams.

5. The diagram below illustrates an entity combining the factors of production into finished goods (arrows to the right) with money flowing to the left.

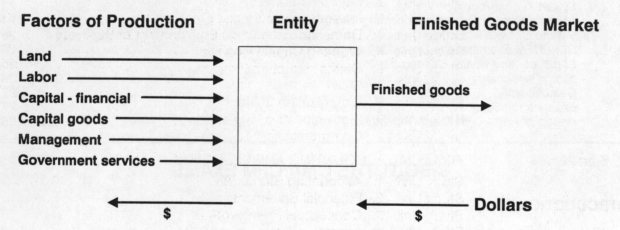

6. Put CMA and CFM in perspective of goods or services production in our capitalistic society. An entity combines the factors of production into finished goods.

    a. Note that the CMA/CFM programs focus on financial capital and the other factors of production as well as the finished goods market. The CEO (chief executive officer) has overall responsibility for the entity's operations.

OBJECTIVES AND CONTENT OF THE CMA/CFM EXAMINATIONS

The primary purpose of the CMA/CFM examination programs is "to establish an objective measure of an individual's knowledge and competence in the fields of management accounting and financial management." Three other objectives set forth by the ICMA are to

1. "Establish management accounting and financial management as recognized professions by identifying the role of the professional, the underlying body of knowledge, and a course of study by which such knowledge is acquired"

2. "Encourage higher educational standards in the management accounting and financial management fields"

3. "Encourage continued professional development"

The exams test the candidates' knowledge and ability with respect to the current state of the art in the fields of management accounting and financial management.

We have arranged the subject matter tested on the CMA/CFM examinations into 10 study units for each part. Each part is presented in a separate book. For CMA/CFM Parts 1, 3, and 4, study the corresponding *CMA/CFM Review* book. For Part 2CMA, study *CMA Review: Part 2CMA* and, for Part 2CFM, study *CFM Review: Part 2CFM*. All contain review outlines and prior CMA/CFM exam questions and answers. The 50 study units are organized as follows:

CMA/CFM Part 1:   ECONOMICS, FINANCE, AND MANAGEMENT
- Study Unit 1: Microeconomics
- Study Unit 2: Macroeconomics
- Study Unit 3: International Business Environment
- Study Unit 4: Domestic Institutional Environment of Business
- Study Unit 5: Working Capital Finance
- Study Unit 6: Capital Structure Finance
- Study Unit 7: Risk
- Study Unit 8: Organizational Theory
- Study Unit 9: Motivation and the Directing Process
- Study Unit 10: Communication

Part 2CMA: FINANCIAL ACCOUNTING AND REPORTING
- Study Unit 1: Accounting Standards
- Study Unit 2: Financial Statements
- Study Unit 3: Conceptual Framework
- Study Unit 4: Assets
- Study Unit 5: Liabilities
- Study Unit 6: Shareholders' Equity
- Study Unit 7: Other Income Items
- Study Unit 8: Other Reporting Issues
- Study Unit 9: Financial Statement Analysis
- Study Unit 10: External Auditing

Part 2CFM: CORPORATE FINANCIAL MANAGEMENT

                    Study Unit 1: Financial Statements and Annual Reports
                    Study Unit 2: Financial Statements: Special Topics
                    Study Unit 3: Long-Term Capital Financing
                    Study Unit 4: Financial Markets and Interest Rates
                    Study Unit 5: Investment Banking and Commercial Banking
                    Study Unit 6: Financial Statement Analysis
                    Study Unit 7: Business Combinations and Restructurings
                    Study Unit 8: Risk Management
                    Study Unit 9: External Financial Environment
                    Study Unit 10: Accounting Standard Setting
                    Addendum: Quantitative Practice Questions*

CMA/CFM Part 3:   MANAGEMENT REPORTING, ANALYSIS, AND BEHAVIORAL ISSUES

                    Study Unit 1: Cost and Managerial Accounting Definitions
                    Study Unit 2: Product Costing and Related Topics
                    Study Unit 3: Cost Behavior
                    Study Unit 4: Statements on Management Accounting
                    Study Unit 5: Planning
                    Study Unit 6: Budgeting
                    Study Unit 7: The Controlling Process
                    Study Unit 8: Standard Costs and Variance Analysis
                    Study Unit 9: Responsibility Accounting
                    Study Unit 10: Behavioral Issues

CMA/CFM Part 4:   DECISION ANALYSIS AND INFORMATION SYSTEMS

                    Study Unit 1: Decision Analysis
                    Study Unit 2: Cost-Volume-Profit Analysis
                    Study Unit 3: Capital Budgeting
                    Study Unit 4: Decision Making under Uncertainty
                    Study Unit 5: Quantitative Methods I
                    Study Unit 6: Quantitative Methods II
                    Study Unit 7: Information Systems I
                    Study Unit 8: Information Systems II
                    Study Unit 9: Internal Control
                    Study Unit 10: Internal Auditing

Recap: The only difference between the CFM exam and the CMA exam is Part 2. This book covers Part 2CFM of the CMA/CFM exam.

The *CMA/CFM Review* study unit titles and organization differ somewhat from the subtopic titles used by the ICMA in its content specification outlines for the CMA/CFM exams. The selection of study units in *CFM Review: Part 2CFM* is based on the types and number of questions that have appeared on past CMA and CFM exams as well as the extensiveness of past and expected future exam coverage.

*Due to candidate feedback, we have added a set of quantitative practice questions at the end of this book.

CONTENT SPECIFICATION OUTLINES

The ICMA has developed content specification outlines and has committed to follow them on each examination. Thus, each examination will cover the major topics specified below; e.g., risk management will constitute 10% to 15% of Part 2CFM on each examination.

Candidates for the CMA/CFM designations are expected to have a minimum level of business knowledge that transcends all examination parts. This minimum level includes knowledge of basic financial statements, time value of money concepts, and elementary statistics. Specific discussion of the ICMA's Levels of Performance (A, B, and C) is provided on the next page.

CMA/CFM Part 1:   Economics, Finance, and Management

    A. Microeconomics--10%-15% (Level B)
    B. Macroeconomics--10%-15% (Level A)
    C. International Business Environment--10%-15% (Level B)
    D. Domestic Institutional Environment of Business--10%-15% (Level A)
    E. Working Capital Policy and Management--10%-15% (Level C)
    F. Long-term Finance and Capital Structure--10%-15% (Level B)
    G. Organizational Structures, Management, and Communication--20%-30% (Level B)

Part 2CMA: Financial Accounting and Reporting

    A. Development of Accounting Standards--10%-15% (Level A)
    B. Advanced Topics on the Preparation of Financial Statements--50%-70% (Level C)
    C. Interpretation and Analysis of Financial Statements--10%-15% (Level C)
    D. External Auditing--10%-15% (Level A)

Part 2CFM: Corporate Financial Management

    A. Use of Financial Statements--10%-20% (Level B)
    B. Advanced Topics in Corporate Financial Management--50%-70% (Level C)
    C. Risk Management--10%-15% (Level C)
    D. External Financial Environment--10%-20% (Level A)
    E. Accounting Standard Setting Environment--5%-10% (Level A)

CMA/CFM Part 3:   Management Reporting, Analysis, and Behavioral Issues

    A. Cost Measurement--20%-30% (Level C)
    B. Planning--20%-30% (Level C)
    C. Control and Performance Evaluation--20%-30% (Level C)
    D. Behavioral Issues--20%-30% (Level B)

CMA/CFM Part 4:   Decision Analysis and Information Systems

    A. Decision Theory and Operational Decision Analysis--20%-30% (Level C)
    B. Investment Decision Analysis--20%-30% (Level C)
    C. Quantitative Methods for Decision Analysis--10%-15% (Level B)
    D. Information Systems--20%-30% (Level B)
    E. Management Controls--10%-15% (Level B)

LEVEL OF PERFORMANCE REQUIRED

All parts of the exams appear to be tested at the skill level of a final examination for the appropriate course at a good school of business. The ICMA has specified three levels of coverage as reproduced below and indicated in its content specification outlines. You will evaluate and compare the difficulty of each part of the CMA/CFM exams as you work the questions in this book.

Authors' Note: Rely on the questions at the back of each study unit in each *CMA/CFM Review* book and *CMA/CFM Test Prep* software.

Level A: Requiring an appreciation of the broad nature and fundamentals, the ability to recognize the existence of special features and problems in various business transactions, and the ability to apply this knowledge in new and concrete situations, i.e., requiring the skill levels of knowledge and comprehension.

Level B: Requiring a sound understanding of the broad aspects of practices and procedures and awareness of the problems relating to more detailed aspects, the ability to apply such broad knowledge in new and concrete situations, the ability to analyze the components of the material and their relationships, and the ability to reformulate the components into a new whole, i.e., requiring the skill levels of knowledge, comprehension, application and analysis.

Level C: Requiring a sound understanding of principles, practices, and procedures, the ability to analyze material so that its organizational structure can be understood, the proficiency to apply such knowledge to situations likely to be encountered, the ability to deal with all aspects of the situation without extensive recourse to technical research and assistance, and the ability to judge the value of material for a given purpose, i.e., requiring all six skill levels.

Authors' Note: The number of Level C questions will be relatively small, even as low as 5 to 10% because Level C questions are so difficult to construct. Thus, for example, the ICMA Content Specification Outlines indicate "risk management" in Part 2CFM at Level C with 10 to 15% coverage. Expect 12 to 18 questions on risk management, but as few as 2 to 4 might be Level C with the remainder being Levels A and B.

HOW ETHICS AND TAXES ARE TESTED

Ethics will probably be tested on every exam within the context of a specific subject area tested on that part. Appendix A beginning on page 409 covers ethics.

Federal income taxes are tested as (1) accounting for income taxes and (2) tax implications for business decisions. Accounting for income taxes including the proper treatment of deferred income taxes is tested in Part 2CMA, Financial Accounting and Reporting, and Part 2CFM, Corporate Financial Management.

The tax code provisions that impact business decisions will be contained in (1) questions that require decision analysis regarding debt versus equity issues in CMA/CFM Part 1, Economics, Finance, and Management; (2) questions in Part 2CFM, Corporate Financial Management; and (3) the decision analysis questions in CMA/CFM Part 4, Decision Analysis and Information Systems.

REQUIREMENTS TO ATTAIN THE CMA/CFM DESIGNATIONS

The CMA and/or the CFM designations are granted only by the ICMA. Candidates must complete five steps to become a CMA and/or CFM:

1. Become a member of the Institute of Management Accountants.
2. File an application for admission with the ICMA and register for the CMA/CFM examinations.
3. Pass all four parts of the CMA or CFM examination within a 3-year period. To attain both designations, CMAs in good standing need only pass Part 2CFM; CFMs in good standing need only pass Part 2CMA.
4. Meet the CMA/CFM experience requirement.
5. Comply with the Standards of Ethical Conduct.

Once a designation is earned, the CMA and/or CFM is a member of the Institute of Certified Management Accountants and must comply with the program's CPE requirement and maintain IMA membership in good standing. The certificate of a CMA or CFM delinquent in these requirements will be subject to recall.

THE INSTITUTE OF MANAGEMENT ACCOUNTANTS (IMA)

Conceived as an educational organization to develop the individual management accountant professionally and to provide business management with the most advanced techniques and procedures, the IMA was founded as the National Association of Accountants in 1919 with 37 charter members. It grew rapidly, with 2,000 applications for membership in the first year, and today it is the largest management accounting association in the world, with approximately 80,000 members and more than 300 chapters in the U.S. and abroad.

The IMA has made major contributions to business management through its continuing education program, with courses and seminars conducted in numerous locations across the country; the monthly magazine *Management Accounting*; other literature, including research reports, monographs, and books; a technical inquiry service; a library; the annual international conference; and frequent meetings at chapter levels.

Membership in the IMA is open to all persons interested in advancing their knowledge of accounting or financial management. It is required for CMA/CFM candidates and CMAs/CFMs.

IMA Dues in the USA and Canada

1. **Regular**: 1 year, $135
2. **Associate**: $45.00 (2nd year, $90.00); must apply within 2 years of completing full-time studies; automatic transfer to regular dues at end of second year
3. **Academic member**: $67.50; must be a full-time faculty member
4. **Student**: $27.00; not less than 6 equivalent hours per semester

Membership application forms may be obtained by writing the Institute of Management Accountants, 10 Paragon Drive, Montvale, NJ 07645-1760, or calling (201) 573-9000 or (800) 638-4427. A sample of the two-page form appears in Appendix C on pages 428 and 429.

THE INSTITUTE OF CERTIFIED MANAGEMENT ACCOUNTANTS (ICMA)

The ICMA is located at the IMA headquarters in Montvale, New Jersey. The only function of the ICMA is to offer and administer the CFM and CMA designations. The staff consists of the senior director, the director of examinations, and three associates (all of whom are professional accountants), plus support personnel. The ICMA occupies about 4,000 square feet of office space in the IMA headquarters. This office is where the examinations are prepared and graded and where all records are kept.

ICMA BOARD OF REGENTS AND STAFF

The ICMA Board of Regents is a special committee of the IMA established to direct the CFM and CMA programs for financial managers and management accountants through the ICMA.

The Board of Regents consists of nine regents, one of whom is designated as chair by the president of the IMA. The regents are appointed by the president of the IMA to serve 3-year terms. Membership on the Board of Regents rotates, with one-third of the regents being appointed each year.

The regents usually meet four times a year for 1 or 2 days. The Board is divided into the following committees:

1. The Promotion and Publicity Committee consults with the staff on how to promote and market the CMA and CFM designations. Three regents serve on this committee.

2. The Credentials Committee reviews the admission standards for the CFM and CMA programs. Two regents serve on this committee.

3. The Continuing Education Committee sets continuing education standards for CFMs and CMAs and advises the staff on implementation of the CPE monitoring process. Two regents serve on this committee.

4. The Examination Policy Committee is concerned with the overall content, grading, and administration of the CFM and CMA exams. Three regents serve on this committee.

5. An Examination Review Committee consisting of two regents and two outside CMAs or CFMs exists for each of the four parts of the CFM and CMA exams. The committee reviews the content specification and grading basis of each specific exam.

The managing director of the ICMA (currently Ms. Priscilla Payne), the director of examinations (currently Ms. Terri Funk), and the ICMA staff are located at the ICMA office in Montvale, NJ. They undertake all of the day-to-day work with respect to the CFM and CMA programs.

ADMISSION TO THE CMA/CFM PROGRAMS

Candidates seeking admission to the CMA/CFM programs must

1. Hold a baccalaureate degree, in any area, from an accredited college or university. (Students may apply when they attain senior standing and will be permitted to take the examination pending receipt of a degree. Degrees from foreign institutions must be evaluated by an independent agency approved by the ICMA.) Alternatively, candidates may qualify for admission if they achieve a score in the 50th percentile or higher on either the Graduate Management Admissions Test (GMAT) or the Graduate Record Examination (GRE).

2. Be a member of the Institute of Management Accountants or submit an IMA application when applying to the ICMA

3. Be employed or expect to be employed in a position that meets the experience requirement

4. Submit the names of two character references. They will be confirmed on a random basis.

5. Be of good moral character

6. Abide by the Standards of Ethical Conduct

CMA/CFM WORK EXPERIENCE REQUIRED

Two continuous years of professional experience in financial management and/or management accounting are required any time prior to, or within 7 years of, passing the examination.

1. Professional experience shall be defined as full-time continuous experience at a level where judgments are regularly made that employ the principles of financial management and/or management accounting, e.g.,

   a. Financial analysis

   b. Budget preparation

   c. Management information systems analysis

   d. Management accounting in government, finance, or industry

   e. Auditing in government, finance, or industry

   f. Management consulting

   g. Audit work in public accounting (3 years required)

   h. Research, teaching, or consulting related to management accounting (for teaching, a significant portion required to be above the principles level)

2. Employment in functions that require the occasional application of financial management or management accounting principles but are not essentially management accounting oriented will not satisfy the requirement, e.g.,

   a. Computer operations
   b. Sales and marketing
   c. Manufacturing
   d. Engineering
   e. Personnel
   f. Employment in trainee, clerical, or nontechnical positions

If you have any questions about the acceptability of your work experience or baccalaureate degree, please write or call the ICMA. Include a complete description of your situation. You will receive a response from the ICMA as soon as your request is evaluated.

Institute of Certified Management Accountants
10 Paragon Drive
Montvale, NJ 07645-1759
(201) 573-9000
(800) 638-4427

HOW TO (1) APPLY AND (2) REGISTER FOR THE CMA/CFM EXAMS

First, you are required to **apply** both for membership in the IMA (see sample application form in Appendix C on pages 428 and 429) and for admission into the ICMA (see sample application form in Appendix C on pages 430 and 431). Thus, two applications are required if you are not already an IMA member. Apply to join the IMA and the ICMA **today** -- it only takes a few minutes. Application to the ICMA requires education, employment, and reference data. The educational experience requirements are discussed on page 8. You must provide two references: one from your employer and the second from someone other than a family member or fellow employee. Character reference forms are sent by the ICMA with your application forms. An official transcript providing proof of graduation is also required. There is a $50 application fee (waived for students and faculty). Once a person has become a candidate, there is no participant's fee other than IMA membership dues.

Second, it is necessary to **register** each time you wish to sit for the exams. The exam registration form (see page 432) is very simple (it takes about 2 minutes to complete). The registration fee for each part of the exam is $80. There is an additional $40 processing fee for candidates taking the examination at an international site. But graduating seniors and full-time graduate students are charged a one-time special rate of $40 per part. Full-time faculty are permitted to take the exam one time at no cost and thereafter pay $40 per part.

A sample of the first page of the ICMA registration form available to candidates from the ICMA appears in Appendix C. Order a registration booklet and IMA membership application form from the ICMA at (800) 638-4427, extension 303.

SPECIAL STUDENT EXAMINATION FEE

Seniors and full-time graduate students may take five examination parts at $40 per part (versus the normal $80). The procedure is to apply and register at the same time. This procedure requires completion and submittal of the following:

1. Name of someone who confirms your student status
2. The standard ICMA application form
3. A completed examination registration form
4. A check for $27 (IMA membership) plus $40 per part for the number of parts to be taken

FEES FOR FULL-TIME PROFESSORS

Full-time faculty members are permitted to take five examination parts once at no charge. The fee for any parts that must be retaken is 50% of the normal fee. The $50 application fee is also waived. To qualify, a faculty member must submit a letter on school stationery affirming his/her full-time status. Faculty should sit for the CMA/CFM examinations because a professor's status as a CMA/CFM encourages students to enter the program. Full-time doctoral students who plan to pursue a teaching career are treated as faculty members for purposes of qualifying for the free examination.

ICMA REFUND POLICY

In general, fees paid to the ICMA are nonrefundable. However, a candidate withdrawing from the examination within 30 days of registration may receive a credit for the examination fee less a $25 processing charge. Failure to take the examination within the assigned 60-day authorization period will result in the loss of examination fees; there will be no refund or credit available.

PASS/FAIL AND GRADE REPORTS

For CMA/CFM Parts 1, 3, and 4 and Part 2CMA, there is a 3-month pilot testing period from December 1, 1997 to February 28, 1998, during which immediate grade reporting is not available. Grades will be mailed in April and on-demand testing will start May 1, 1998.

The IMA has set a passing score for the Part 2CFM based on 43% of the approximately 1,000 persons taking the Part 2CFM from December 1996 through January 1997. In addition to pass or fail, you are given a "scaled score" between 200 and 700, with 500 being the passing mark. This provides information about how close, above or below, you were to passing.

MAINTAINING YOUR CMA/CFM DESIGNATIONS

Membership in the IMA is required to maintain your CMA/CFM certificates. The general membership fee is $135. There is no additional participant fee.

Continuing professional education is required of CMAs/CFMs to maintain their proficiency in the fields of managerial accounting and financial management. Every 3 years, 90 hours of CPE must be completed, which is about 4 days per year. Qualifying topics include management accounting, finance, corporate taxation, mathematics and statistics, computer science, systems analysis, economics, management skills, production, marketing, business law, insurance, and behavioral science.

Credit for hours of study will be given for participation in programs sponsored by businesses, educational institutions, or professional and trade associations at either the national or local level. Programs conducted by an individual's employer must provide for an instructor or course leader. There must be formal instructional training material. On-the-job training does not qualify. An affidavit from the employer is required to attest to the hours of instruction. The programs may be seminars, workshops, technical meetings, or college courses under the direction of an instructor. The method of instruction may include lecture, discussion, case studies, and teaching aids such as training films and cassettes.

Credit for hours of study may be given for technical articles published in business, professional, or trade journals, and for major technical talks given for the first time before business, professional, or trade organizations. The specific hours of credit in each case will be determined by the Institute.

ICMA SUGGESTED READING LIST

The ICMA suggested reading list that follows is reproduced to give you an overview of the scope of each part. You will not have the time to study these texts. Rely on Gleim's *CMA/CFM Review* and *CMA/CFM Test Prep* software for complete coverage of topics tested on the exam.

PART 1 -- ECONOMICS, FINANCE, AND MANAGEMENT

Economics

An introductory economics book, such as:

Lipsey, Richard G., Steiner, Peter O., and Purvis, Douglas D., *Economics*, 10th edition, Harper & Row, New York, NY, 1993, or

McConnell, Campbell R., *Economics: Principles, Problems and Policies*, 12th edition, McGraw-Hill Book Co., New York, NY, 1993.

An international economics book, such as:

Root, Franklin R., *International Trade and Investment*, 7th edition, Southwest Publishing Co., Cincinnati, OH, 1994.

Government and Business

Frederick, William C., Post, James E. and Davis, Keith, *Business and Society: Corporate Strategy, Public Policy, Ethics*, 7th edition, McGraw-Hill Book Co., New York, NY, 1992.

Greer, Douglas F., *Business, Government, and Society*, 3rd edition, Macmillan Publishing Company, New York, NY, 1992.

Business Finance

Van Horne, James C. and Wachowicz, John M., Jr., *Fundamentals of Financial Management*, 9th edition, Prentice-Hall, Inc., Englewood Cliffs, NJ, 1995.

Weston, J. Fred and Copeland Thomas, E., *Managerial Finance*, 9th edition, The Dryden Press, Chicago, IL, 1992.

Organization and Management Theory and Communication

Books that cover organization and management theory, such as:

Griffin, Ricky W., *Management*, 4th edition, Houghton Mifflin Company, Boston, MA, 1993.

Tosi, Henry L., Rizzo, John R., and Carroll, Stephen J., *Managing Organizational Behavior*, 2nd edition, Ballinger Publishing, Cambridge, MA, 1990.

PART 2CFM -- CORPORATE FINANCIAL MANAGEMENT

Financial Management

A finance book, such as:

Ross, Stephen A., Westerfield, Randolph W., and Jaffe, Jeffrey F., *Corporate Finance*, 3rd edition, Richard D. Irwin, Inc., Homewood, Illinois, 1993.

Van Horne, James C., *Financial Management and Policy*, 10th edition, Prentice-Hall, Inc., Englewood Cliffs, NJ, 1995.

Van Horne, James C. and Wachowicz, John M., Jr., *Fundamentals of Financial Management*, 9th edition, Prentice-Hall, Inc., Englewood Cliffs, NJ, 1995.

Weston, J. Fred and Copeland, Thomas E., *Management Finance*, 9th edition, The Dryden Press, Chicago, Illinois, 1992.

Analysis of Financial Statements

Gibson, Charles H., *Financial Statement Analysis*, 6th edition, South-Western Publishing Co., Cincinnati, OH, 1995.

Financial Statements and Accounting Standards

An intermediate accounting book, such as:

Kieso, Donald E. and Weygandt, Jerry J., *Intermediate Accounting*, 8th edition, John Wiley & Sons, Inc., New York, NY, 1995.

PART 3 -- MANAGEMENT REPORTING, ANALYSIS, AND BEHAVIORAL ISSUES

Management Reporting and Analysis

A managerial cost accounting book, such as:

Horngren, Charles, Foster, George, and Datar, Srikant, *Cost Accounting: A Managerial Emphasis,* 8th edition, Prentice-Hall, Inc., Englewood Cliffs, NJ, 1994.

Rayburn, Letricia Gayle, *Principles of Cost Accounting: Managerial Applications*, 5th edition, Richard D. Irwin, Inc., Homewood, IL, 1993.

Wolk, Harry I., Gerber, Quentin N., and Porter, Gary A., *Management Accounting: Planning and Control*, PWS-Kent Publishing Company, Boston, MA, 1988.

Also:

Welsch, Glenn, Hilton, Ronald W., and Gordon, Paul N., *Budgeting: Profit Planning and Control*, 5th edition, Prentice-Hall, Inc., Englewood Cliffs, NJ, 1988.

Behavioral Issues

See appropriate material on cost, budgeting, and responsibility centers in the managerial accounting books listed above, i.e., Horngren, Rayburn, and Welsch.

PART 4 -- DECISION ANALYSIS AND INFORMATION SYSTEMS

Decision Analysis and Quantitative Methods

A managerial cost accounting book, such as:

Horngren, Charles, Foster, George, and Datar, Srikant, *Cost Accounting: A Managerial Emphasis,* 8th edition, Prentice-Hall, Inc., Englewood Cliffs, NJ, 1994.

Rayburn, Letricia Gayle, *Principles of Cost Accounting: Managerial Applications*, 5th edition, Richard D. Irwin, Inc., Homewood, IL, 1993.

A finance book that covers capital budgeting, such as:

VanHorne, James C., *Financial Management and Policy*, 10th edition, Prentice-Hall, Inc., Englewood Cliffs, NJ, 1995 (chapters on capital investment analysis).

Weston, J. Fred and Copeland, Thomas E., *Managerial Finance*, 9th edition, The Dryden Press, Chicago, IL, 1992 (chapters on capital investment analysis).

A tax reference, such as:

Sommerfield, Ray M., *Federal Taxes and Management Decisions*, current edition, Richard D. Irwin, Inc., Homewood, IL.

Also:

Bierman, Harold Jr., Bonini, Charles P., and Hauseman, Warren H., *Quantitative Analysis for Business Decisions*, 8th edition, Richard D. Irwin, Inc., Homewood, IL, 1991.

Information Systems

A business data processing book, such as:

Kroenke, David and Hatch, Richard, *Business Computer Systems*, 5th edition, Mitchell Publishing, Inc., Santa Cruz, CA, 1993, or

O'Brien, James A., *Introduction to Information Systems*, 7th edition, Irwin Professional Publishers, Barr Ridge, IL, 1993.

Also:

Cushing, Barry E. and Romney, Marshall B., *Accounting Information Systems*, 6th edition, Addison-Wesley Publishing Company, Reading, MA, 1994.

Moscove, Stephen A. and Simkin, Mark G., *Accounting Information Systems: Concepts and Practice for Effective Decision Making*, 4th edition, John Wiley & Sons, Inc., New York, NY, 1990.

Internal Auditing

An internal auditing book, such as:

Brink, Victor and Witt, Herbert, *Modern Internal Auditing: Appraising Operations and Controls*, 4th edition, John Wiley & Sons, New York, NY, 1982, or

Sawyer, Lawrence, *Internal Auditing*, Institute of Internal Auditors, Inc., Altamonte Springs, FL, 1988.

CMA/CFM TEST PREPARATION

The ICMA has developed thousands of multiple-choice questions from which each test of 120 questions will be selected. Each test will conform to the content specification outlines, which for Part 2CFM are

    A.   Use of Financial Statements--10%-20% (Level B)
    B.   Advanced Topics in Corporate Financial Management--50%-70% (Level C)
    C.   Risk Management--10%-15% (Level C)
    D.   External Financial Environment--10%-20% (Level B)
    E.   Accounting Standard Setting Environment--5%-10% (Level A)

Questions will be refined, rewritten, etc., as the ICMA gains experience with the questions. The multiple-choice questions will have four answer choices.

CMA/CFM TEST ADMINISTRATION AND GRADING

The ICMA will send you authorization to take Part 2CFM, which will have a 60-day window. A pilot period will exist for CMA/CFM Parts 1, 3, and 4 and Part 2CMA from December 1, 1997 to February 28, 1998, during which you must take your exam. The authorization will instruct you to call the National Sylvan registration office (800) 967-1100 and register for your test at a local Sylvan testing center.

After on-demand testing begins on May 1, 1998, your test will be graded by the computer as soon as you complete the test. This is **not** true for persons taking the CMA/CFM Parts 1, 3, and 4 and Part 2CMA exams between December 1, 1997 and February 28, 1998 because the ICMA wants to assess the difficulty of the test and curve the scores during this initial pilot period. We expect a high pass rate during this initial test period to encourage participation in the CMA/CFM programs and in computer-based testing.

COMPUTER TESTING PROCEDURES

When you arrive at the computer testing center, you will be required to provide positive proof of identification and your ICMA authorization to take the test. The identification presented must include your photograph, signature, and actual residential address, if different from the mailing address. This information may be presented in more than one form of identification. You then will sign in on the testing center's daily log.

Next, you will be taken into the testing room and seated at a computer terminal. A person from the testing center will assist you in logging on the system, and you will be asked to confirm your personal data (e.g., name, Social Security number, etc.). Then you will be prompted and given an online introduction to the computer testing system and you will take a sample test.

If you have used our **CMA/CFM Test Prep** software, you will be conversant with the computer testing methodology and environment, and you will probably want to skip the sample test and begin the actual test immediately. Once you begin your test, you will be allowed 3 hrs. to complete the actual test. This is 1.5 minutes per question. After May 1, 1998, a computer test report will be printed and given to you when you have completed your exam. If you take the exam between December 1, 1997 and February 28, 1998, you will receive your grade in April 1998. Before you leave the testing center, you will be required to sign out on the testing center's daily log.

During the exam, you are permitted to step out of the testing room to stretch, get a drink of water, use the restroom, etc. You will be required to sign out and then back in each time.

PREPARING FOR THE CMA/CFM EXAMS

HOW MANY PARTS TO TAKE

We suggest that you take one part at a time. Currently, you have 3 years within which to pass all four parts of either the CMA or the CFM exam. If you pass parts after the June 1997 exam, you will be given credit until 3 years after these parts were passed.

CMA/CFM Part 1:   Economics, Finance, and Management
Part 2CMA: Financial Accounting and Reporting
Part 2CFM: Corporate Financial Management
CMA/CFM Part 3:   Management Reporting, Analysis, and Behavioral Issues
CMA/CFM Part 4:   Decision Analysis and Information Systems

Parts 2CMA, 2CFM, and 3 cover many of the accounting and finance topics included in typical undergraduate accounting/finance programs. Part 1 covers the material found in management, microeconomics, macroeconomics, and corporate finance courses. Part 4 covers computer systems, quantitative methods, and statistics courses.

STEPS TO EXAM SUCCESS (THEY REALLY WORK!)

1. Study this "Introduction" carefully. Then study each of the 10 study units one at a time.

2. Using *CMA/CFM Test Prep* software, in test mode, create and answer a 20-question "assessment" test from each study unit before studying the study unit.

3. Study the knowledge transfer outline in this book for that study unit.

4. Take two or three more 20-question tests in test mode after studying knowledge transfer outlines.

5. After EACH of these 20-question test sessions, immediately switch to study mode and select questions "missed on last session" so you can analyze why you answered each question incorrectly.

6. Continue the process until you reach your desired proficiency on each study unit, e.g., 75%.

7. Modify the process to suit your individual learning process.

8. Study the "Addendum: Quantitative Practice Questions" at the end of this book. These questions were added due to candidate feedback and should prove useful in your preparation process.

9. Attend and plan on passing your CMA/CFM exams.

SELF-ASSESSMENT AND PLANNING YOUR PREPARATION

Planning is essential to a successful preparation program. After studying this Introduction to obtain a good understanding of the CFM exam, its preparation, administration, and grading, you should undertake a preliminary self-assessment to enable you to plan your preparation.

Beginning on this page is a self-assessment and study control chart that lists the study units tested on the CFM and/or CMA exams.

For each of the 10 study units in this book:

1. Answer only three to five multiple-choice questions.

2. Look over all of the remaining multiple-choice questions.

3. Turn to the self-assessment chart on the following page and rate your knowledge of the topic (circle the grade you feel represents your knowledge).

4. Spend about 5 minutes per study unit. Because there are 10 study units, you can get a good overview of the exam as well as an evaluation of your skill levels in about one hour.

After you have completed your assessment on a study unit-by-study unit basis, you will have an overall Part 2CFM exam perspective. Based on this self-assessment, you should understand the standards to which you will be held.

PRELIMINARY SELF-ASSESSMENT AND STUDY CONTROL

	Preliminary Evaluation (circle one)	Study Control (enter date completed) Outline	Questions

ECONOMICS, FINANCE, AND MANAGEMENT (Part 1)

SU 1: Microeconomics ... A B C D E ___ ___
SU 2: Macroeconomics ... A B C D E ___ ___
SU 3: International Business Environment ... A B C D E ___ ___
SU 4: Domestic Institutional Environment of Business . A B C D E ___ ___
SU 5: Working Capital Finance ... A B C D E ___ ___
SU 6: Capital Structure Finance ... A B C D E ___ ___
SU 7: Risk ... A B C D E ___ ___
SU 8: Organizational Theory ... A B C D E ___ ___
SU 9: Motivation and the Directing Process ... A B C D E ___ ___
SU 10: Communication ... A B C D E ___ ___

CORPORATE FINANCIAL MANAGEMENT (Part 2CFM) (This Book)

SU 1: Financial Statements and Annual Reports ... A B C D E ___ ___
SU 2: Financial Statements: Special Topics ... A B C D E ___ ___
SU 3: Long-Term Capital Financing ... A B C D E ___ ___
SU 4: Financial Markets and Interest Rates ... A B C D E ___ ___
SU 5: Investment Banking & Commercial Banking ... A B C D E ___ ___
SU 6: Financial Statement Analysis ... A B C D E ___ ___
SU 7: Business Combinations and Restructurings ... A B C D E ___ ___
SU 8: Risk Management ... A B C D E ___ ___
SU 9: External Financial Environment ... A B C D E ___ ___
SU 10: Accounting Standard Setting ... A B C D E ___ ___
Addendum: Quantitative Practice Questions ... A B C D E N/A ___

FINANCIAL ACCOUNTING AND REPORTING (Part 2CMA)

SU 1: Accounting Standards	A B C D E	____	____
SU 2: Financial Statements	A B C D E	____	____
SU 3: Conceptual Framework	A B C D E	____	____
SU 4: Assets	A B C D E	____	____
SU 5: Liabilities	A B C D E	____	____
SU 6: Shareholders' Equity	A B C D E	____	____
SU 7: Other Income Items	A B C D E	____	____
SU 8: Other Reporting Issues	A B C D E	____	____
SU 9: Financial Statement Analysis	A B C D E	____	____
SU 10: External Auditing	A B C D E	____	____

MANAGEMENT REPORTING, ANALYSIS, AND BEHAVIORAL ISSUES (Part 3)

SU 1: Cost and Managerial Accounting Definitions	A B C D E	____	____
SU 2: Product Costing and Related Topics	A B C D E	____	____
SU 3: Cost Behavior	A B C D E	____	____
SU 4: Statements on Management Accounting	A B C D E	____	____
SU 5: Planning	A B C D E	____	____
SU 6: Budgeting	A B C D E	____	____
SU 7: The Controlling Process	A B C D E	____	____
SU 8: Standard Costs and Variance Analysis	A B C D E	____	____
SU 9: Responsibility Accounting	A B C D E	____	____
SU 10: Behavioral Issues	A B C D E	____	____

DECISION ANALYSIS AND INFORMATION SYSTEMS (Part 4)

SU 1: Decision Analysis	A B C D E	____	____
SU 2: Cost-Volume-Profit Analysis	A B C D E	____	____
SU 3: Capital Budgeting	A B C D E	____	____
SU 4: Decision Making under Uncertainty	A B C D E	____	____
SU 5: Quantitative Methods I	A B C D E	____	____
SU 6: Quantitative Methods II	A B C D E	____	____
SU 7: Information Systems I	A B C D E	____	____
SU 8: Information Systems II	A B C D E	____	____
SU 9: Internal Control	A B C D E	____	____
SU 10: Internal Auditing	A B C D E	____	____

WEEKS-TO-GO SCHEDULE

Weeks Remaining	Study Unit(s) Scheduled	Comments
12		
11		
10		
9		
8		
7		
6		
5		
4		
3		
2		
1		
0		

Exam Date: _____   Time: _____

Sylvan Address: _____

STUDY PLAN, TIME BUDGET, AND CALENDAR

Complete one study unit at a time. Initially, budget 3 to 4 hours per study unit (1 to 2 hours studying the outline and 1 to 2 minutes each on all the multiple-choice questions).

This Introduction	2
10 study units at 3.5 hours each	35
General review	3
Total Hours	40

Each week you should evaluate your progress and review your preparation plans for the time remaining prior to the exam. The CMA/CFM calendar on page 21 will assist you in preparing for the pilot testing period which begins December 1, 1997 and ends February 28, 1998. Review your commitments, e.g., out-of-town assignments, personal responsibilities, etc., and note them on your calendar. This precaution will assist you in keeping to your schedule.

CONTROL

You have to be in control to be successful during exam preparation and execution. Control can also contribute greatly to your personal and other professional goals. Control is a process whereby you

1.   Develop expectations, standards, budgets, and plans.
2.   Undertake activity, production, study, and learning.
3.   Measure the activity, production, output, and knowledge.
4.   Compare actual activity with expected, or budgeted.
5.   Modify the activity, behavior, or production to better achieve the desired outcome.
6.   Revise expectations and standards in light of actual experience.
7.   Continue the process.

The objective is to be confident that the best possible performance is being generated. Most accountants study this process in relation to standard costs, i.e., establish cost standards and compute cost variances.

Every day you rely on control systems implicitly. When you groom your hair, you have expectations about the desired appearance of your hair and the time required to style it. You monitor your progress and make adjustments as appropriate, e.g., brush it a different way or speed up.

Develop and enforce standards in all of your endeavors. Exercise control, implicitly or explicitly. Most endeavors will improve with explicit control. This is particularly true with certification examinations and other academic tests.

1.   Practice your question answering techniques (and develop control) as you prepare answers/solutions to practice questions/problems during your study program.

2.   Develop explicit control over your study programs based on the control process discussed previously.

3.   Think about using more explicit control systems over any and all of your endeavors.

4.   Seek continuous improvement to meet your needs given a particular situation or constraint. Additional practice will result in further efficiencies.

1997-1998 CMA/CFM CALENDAR

	Sun	Mon	Tues	Wed	Thurs	Fri	Sat
SEPT		1	2	3	4	5	6
	7	8	9	10	11	12	13
	14	15	16	17	18	19	20
	21	22	23	24	25	26	27
OCT	28	29	30	1	2	3	4
	5	6	7	8	9	10	11
	12	13	14	15	16	17	18
	19	20	21	22	23	24	25
NOV	26	27	28	29	30	31	1
	2	3	4	5	6	7	8
	9	10	11	12	13	14	15
	16	17	18	19	20	21	22
	23	24	25	26	27	28	29
DEC	30	1 Pilot Testing Period Begins	2	3	4	5	6
	7	8	9	10	11	12	13
	14	15	16	17	18	19	20
	21	22	23	24	25	26	27
JAN	28	29	30	31	1	2	3
	4	5	6	7	8	9	10
	11	12	13	14	15	16	17
	18	19	20	21	22	23	24
	25	26	27	28	29	30	31
FEB	1	2	3	4	5	6	7
	8	9	10	11	12	13	14
	15	16	17	18	19	20	21
	22	23	24	25	26	27	28 Pilot Testing Period Ends

SYLVAN TECHNOLOGY CENTERS: Part of the Sylvan Learning Center Network

ALABAMA
Birmingham
Decatur
Mobile
Montgomery

ALASKA
Anchorage

ARIZONA
Tucson
Phoenix
  Chandler

ARKANSAS
Ft. Smith
Little Rock

CALIFORNIA
Fresno
Los Angeles
  Diamond Bar
  Rancho Cuc.
  Redlands
  Riverside
  Santa Monica
  Torrance
  Westlake
Orange County
  Anaheim Hills
  Brea/Fullerton
  Garden Grove
  Irvine
Sacramento
  Fair Oaks
San Diego
  La Jolla
San Francisco
  Burlingame
  Oakland
  Walnut Creek
San Jose
Santa Rosa

COLORADO
Boulder
Colorado Sprgs
Denver
  Littleton
Pueblo

CONNECTICUT
Hartford
  Glastonbury
New Haven
  Hamden

DELAWARE
Dover

FLORIDA
Daytona Beach
  Ormond Bch
Gainesville
Jacksonville
Miami Metro
  Davie
  Miami Lakes

FLORIDA (cont'd)
West Palm Beach
  Wellington
Sarasota
Tallahassee
Tampa
  Temple Terr.
Orlando
  Winter Park

GEORGIA
Atlanta Metro
  Jonesboro
  Smyrna
Augusta
Macon
Savannah

HAWAII
Oahu
  Kailua
Maui
  Wailuku

IDAHO
Boise

ILLINOIS
Bloomington
Carbondale
Chicago Metro
  Carpentersville
  Chicago
  Homewood
  Northbrook
  Westchester
Peoria
Springfield

INDIANA
Evansville
Ft. Wayne
Merrillville
Indianapolis
Layfayette
South Bend
  Mishawaka

IOWA
Bettendorf
Cedar Rapids
W. Des Moines

KANSAS
Topeka
Wichita

KENTUCKY
Lexington
Louisville

LOUISIANA
Baton Rouge
Shreveport
  Bossier City
New Orleans

MAINE
South Portland

MARYLAND
Baltimore Metro
  Columbia
  Pikesville
Bethesda
Frederick

MASSACHUSETTS
Boston Metro
  Boston
  Woburn
Springfield
Worcester

MICHIGAN
Ann Arbor
Grand Rapids
Lansing
Detroit Metro
  Troy
  Utica
  Livonia

MINNESOTA
Duluth
Minn-St. Paul
  Bloomington
  Maplewood

MISSISSIPPI
Jackson

MISSOURI
Kansas City
  Gladstone
Springfield
St. Louis
  Ballwin
  Creve Coeur

MONTANA
Billings
Helena

NEBRASKA
Lincoln
Omaha

NEVADA
Las Vegas
Reno

NEW HAMPSHIRE
Concord

NEW JERSEY
East Brunswick
Newark Metro
  Verona
Toms River
Trenton
  Hamilton Town

NEW MEXICO
Albuquerque

NEW YORK
Albany
Buffalo
  Amherst
Long Island
  Garden City
New York City
  Queens
  Staten Island
  Poughkeepsie
  Wappgrs Falls
Rochester
Syracuse
  Fayetteville
  Vestal

NORTH CAROLINA
Asheville
Charlotte
Greensboro
Greenville
Raleigh

NORTH DAKOTA
Bismarck

OHIO
Akron
Cincinnati-North
Cleveland Metro
  Mentor
  Solon
  Strongsville
Columbus
  Reynoldsburg
Dayton
Toledo
Youngstown
  Niles

OKLAHOMA
Oklahoma City
Tulsa

OREGON
Eugene
Portland

PENNSYLVANIA
Allentown
Erie
Harrisburg
Philadelphia
  Center City
Pittsburgh
  North Hills
Scranton
  North Wales

RHODE ISLAND
Providence
  Cranston

SOUTH CAROLINA
Charleston
Irmo
Greenville

SOUTH DAKOTA
Sioux Falls

TENNESSEE
Chattanooga
Knoxville
Memphis
Nashville
  Madison

TEXAS
Amarillo
Austin
Beaumont
Corpus Christi
Dallas Metro
  Arlington
  Fort Worth
  Mesquite
El Paso
Houston
  Clearlake
  West Univ.
Longview
Lubbock
Midland
San Antonio
Waco

UTAH
Orem
Salt Lake City

VERMONT
Williston

VIRGINIA
Arlington
Richmond
Roanoke
Newport News

WASHINGTON
Seattle
  Lynnwood
Spokane
Tacoma
  Puyallup

WASHINGTON, DC

WEST VIRGINIA
Charleston
Morgantown

WISCONSIN
Madison
Milwaukee
  Brookfield

WYOMING
Casper

After you register to take each part of the CMA/CFM exams and pay $80, the ICMA will send you a letter with an authorization number and instructions on contacting Sylvan to schedule your test. Call your local Sylvan testing center a day or two before your test to confirm your time and obtain directions to the testing center. A listing of Sylvan testing centers is presented on page 22.

INSTRUCTIONS TO CANDIDATES

The letter accompanying these instructions is your authorization to schedule the taking of CMA/CFM Part 4 with Sylvan Technologies. If you registered for additional parts of the CMA/CFM Examinations, information regarding these parts will be sent to you under separate cover. Questions regarding your registration with ICMA should be directed to 800-638-4427, ext. 301.

Scheduling with Sylvan Technologies

The interval dates shown on your authorization letter represent the 60-day window during which you are authorized to take CMA/CFM Part 4. To schedule your examination, please call Sylvan Technologies at 800-479-6370 at least 48 hours before you would like to take the examination. Be sure you have your authorization number from the accompanying letter handy when you call as you will be required to provide this number. In addition, please choose a Sylvan Technology Center from the list shown on the reverse of this sheet. You must schedule your examination during this 60-day period as your authorization will lapse at the end of the period, and your fees will be forfeited.

General Instructions

- Be sure to arrive at the Sylvan Technology Center on time. If you are more than 30 minutes late, you may lose your scheduled sitting and be required to reschedule at a later date.

- You will be required to sign the Sylvan Log Book when you enter the center.

- You are required to present a photo identification with signature for examination admission. Approved IDs are a passport, driver's license, military ID, credit card with photo, or company ID. Student IDs are **not** acceptable. You will not be permitted into the examination without proper photo identification.

- Lockers are available at the test centers for personal belongings. Items such as purses, briefcases, and jackets will not be allowed in the testing room.

- Small battery or solar powered electronic calculators restricted to a maximum of six functions - addition, subtraction, multiplication, division, square root, and percent - are allowed. The calculator must be non-programmable and must not use any type of tape. Memory must erase when the calculator is turned off. Candidates **will not** be allowed to use calculators that do not comply with these restrictions.

- On request, candidates will be provided with scrap paper which will be counted by the test center personnel when given to candidates and will also be counted when collected from candidates. Candidates should bring pencils or pens to the test center for use in making calculations, etc., on scrap paper.

- The staff at the Sylvan Technology Centers are not involved in grading your examination. Please do not contact them for information about your performance. Examination results will be mailed from the ICMA in April 1998 for CMA/CFM Parts 1, 3, and 4 taken from December 1, 1997 through February 28, 1998. On-demand testing of CMA/CFM Parts 1, 3, and 4 and CMA Part 2 and CFM Part 2 will begin on May 1, 1998.

MULTIPLE-CHOICE QUESTION ANSWERING TECHNIQUE

1. **Budget your time.**

   a. We make this point with emphasis. Just as you should fill up your gas tank prior to reaching empty, you should finish your exam before time expires.

   b. You have 180 minutes to answer 120 questions, i.e., 1.5 minutes per question. We suggest you attempt to answer eight questions every 10 minutes, which is 1.25 minutes per question. This would result in completing 120 questions in 150 minutes to give you 30 minutes to review questions that you have marked. (See 3.c.2) for a brief discussion of marking questions at Sylvan.)

   c. On your Sylvan computer screen, the time remaining (starting with 150 minutes) appears at the upper right of your screen.

2. **Answer the questions in chronological order.**

   a. Do **not** agonize over any one question. Stay within your time budget.

   b. It is not necessary to "mark" unanswered questions. Sylvan provides options to review both unanswered questions and marked questions.

3. **For each question**

   a. **Read the question** stem carefully (the part of the question that precedes the answer choices) to determine the precise requirement.

      1) Focusing on what is required enables you to ignore extraneous information and to proceed directly to determining the correct answer.

         a) Be especially careful to note when the requirement is an **exception**; e.g., "All of the following statements regarding a company's internal rate of return are true **except**:."

   b. **Determine the correct answer** before reading the answer choices. The objective is to avoid allowing the answer choices to affect your reading of the question.

      1) When four answer choices are presented, three of them are incorrect. They are called **distractors** for a very good reason.

      2) **Read each answer choice** with close attention.

         a) Even if answer (A) appears to be the correct choice, do **not** skip the remaining answer choices. Answer (B), (C), or (D) may be better.

         b) Treat each answer choice as a true-false question.

   c. **Select the best answer**. The answer is selected by either pressing the answer letter on your keyboard or by using your mouse. Select the most likely or best answer choice. If you are uncertain, make an educated guess.

      1) The CMA/CFM does not penalize guessing because your score is determined by the number of correct responses. Thus, you should answer every question.

      2) As you answer a question, you can mark it by pressing "M" or unmark a marked question by pressing "M." After you have answered, marked, or looked at and not answered all 120 questions, you will be presented with a summary screen that shows how many questions you did not answer and how many you marked. You then have the option of revisiting all of the unanswered questions and "marked" questions.

4. Sylvan Computer Screen Layout

Question 10 of 120	YOUR NAME	Time remaining: 02:51

The sky is _____

○   A.   blue

○   B.   brown

○   C.   green

○   D.   silver

Directions: Select the best answer

←— <u>P</u>revious   <u>N</u>ext —→   <u>M</u>ark   **?** Help

NOTE: A menu offering a number of options is displayed at the bottom of the question screen. The options enable you to view the previous question or the next question, mark a question to be revisited, or request help. You may select an option by pressing the appropriate symbol key or highlighted letter on your keyboard or by clicking on the symbol or letter with your mouse.

1) View the previous question by indicating the letter **P** or the left arrow key.
2) View the next question by indicating the letter **N** or the right arrow key.
3) Mark a question by indicating the letter **M**.
4) Request help by indicating the question mark.

USE GLEIM *CMA/CFM TEST PREP* SOFTWARE. It emulates the SYLVAN testing procedures and environment including computer screen layout, software operation, etc.

TAKING THE CMA/CFM EXAMS

CMA/CFM EXAMINATIONS CHECKLIST

1.   Acquire your study materials. Rely on this book and *CMA/CFM Test Prep* software. It's all you need!

2.   **Apply** for membership in the IMA (see pages 428 and 429) and for admission to the ICMA (pages 430 and 431).

3.   **Register** to take the desired part of the exam using the examination registration form (page 432) and send it with your applications to the ICMA. Take one part at a time. When you register and pay $80 for a part, you have 60 days to take the part. Upon receipt of authorization to take the exam, call SYLVAN to schedule your test.

4.   Plan your preparation process. It's easy. You have 10 study units to complete.

5.   Orderly, controlled preparation builds confidence, reduces anxiety, and produces success!

6.   PASS THE EXAMINATION (study this Introduction)!

LOGISTICAL AND HEALTH CONCERNS

As soon as the ICMA sends you a computer-based test authorization, call and schedule your test at a convenient time and convenient Sylvan testing center. In almost all cases, you should be able to drive to your testing site, take the test, and return home in one day. If the exam is not being given within driving distance of your home, call Sylvan Technology Centers to inquire about accommodations. Stay by yourself at a hotel to be assured of avoiding distractions. The hotel should be soundproof and have a comfortable bed and desk suitable for study. If possible, stay at a hotel with recreational facilities you normally use, e.g., a swimming pool.

Proper exercise, diet, and rest in the weeks before you take your exam are very important. High energy levels, reduced tension, and an improved attitude are among the benefits. A good aerobic fitness program, a nutritious and well-balanced diet, and a regular sleep pattern will promote your long-term emotional and physical well-being as well as contribute significantly to a favorable exam result. Of course, the use of health-undermining substances should be avoided.

EXAM PSYCHOLOGY

Plan ahead and systematically prepare. Then go to the exam and give it your best: neither you nor anyone else can expect more. Having undertaken a systematic preparation program, you will do fine.

Maintain a positive attitude and do not become depressed if you encounter difficulties either before or during the exam. An optimist will usually do better than an equally well-prepared pessimist. Remember, you have reason to be optimistic because you will be competing with many less qualified persons who have not prepared as well as you have.

CALCULATORS

Calculators **are** permitted on the CMA/CFM exams. Only simple six-function calculators are permitted (i.e., addition, subtraction, multiplication, division, square root, percent). You should be thoroughly experienced in the operations of your calculator. Make sure it has fresh batteries just prior to the examination.

1. Consider bringing a backup calculator with you.

2. The calculator must be small, quiet, and battery- or solar-powered so it will not be distracting to other candidates.

3. The calculator may have a memory. However, the memory must be temporary and erase when the memory is cleared or the calculator is turned off.

4. The calculator must not use any type of tape.

5. The calculator must be nonprogrammable.

6. Nonconforming calculators and calculator instruction books are **not** permitted.

7. The CMA/CFM examinations will continue to be designed so that a calculator is not necessary for solving the problems within the estimated time.

EXAMINATION TACTICS

1. Remember to bring your authorization and entry cards and a valid photo ID to the exam site. The photo ID requirement is **strictly** enforced.

2. Arrive at the site a few minutes early to have a margin of safety. Your appointment may be canceled if you are 30 minutes late.

3. Dressing for exam success means emphasizing comfort, not appearance. Be prepared to adjust for changes in temperature, e.g., to remove or put on a sweater.

4. Do not bring notes, this text, other books, etc., into the Sylvan testing center. You will only make yourself nervous and confused by trying to cram the last 5 minutes before the exam. Books are not allowed in the testing room, anyway. You should, however, bring an appropriate calculator.

5. Adequate scratch paper and pencils are provided. You must turn in your scratch paper as you leave the exam site. Any breath mints, gum, etc., should be in your pocket as they may distract other persons taking the test.

6. As soon as you complete the exam, we would like you to e-mail, fax, or write to us with your comments on our books and software. We are particularly interested in which topics need to be added or expanded in our books and software. We are NOT asking about specific CMA/CFM questions; rather we are asking for feedback on our books and software.

RECAP OF PART 2CFM EXAM COVERAGE

ICMA Major Topics and Percent Coverage

A. Use of Financial Statements--10%-20%

B. Advanced Topics in Corporate Financial
    Management--50%-70%

C. Risk Management--10%-15%

D. External Financial Environment--10%-20%

E. Accounting Standard Setting Environment--
    5%-10%

Gleim/Flesher Study Units

1. Financial Statements and Annual Reports
2. Financial Statements: Special Topics
3. Long-Term Capital Financing
4. Financial Markets and Interest Rates
5. Investment Banking and Commercial Banking
6. Comparative Analysis
7. Business Combinations and Restructurings
8. Risk Management
9. External Financial Environment
10. Accounting Standard Setting

GO FOR IT!
IT'S YOURS TO PASS!

STUDY UNIT 1: FINANCIAL STATEMENTS AND ANNUAL REPORTS

19 pages of outline
62 multiple-choice questions

A. Balance Sheet
B. Income Statement
C. Statement of Cash Flows
D. Annual Reports

The first major topic in the CFM content specification outline is "Use of Financial Statements." The subject areas tested are financial statements, annual reports, and special topics in financial statements. The first two subject areas are presented in Study Unit 1. Special financial statement topics are outlined in Study Unit 2.

A. Balance Sheet

1. **Basic Financial Statements.** The balance sheet is a basic financial statement. The others are the statements of income, retained earnings, and cash flows.

   a. Disclosures of **changes in shareholders' equity** and in the number of shares of equity securities are necessary whenever financial position and results of operations are presented.

      1) These disclosures may occur in the basic statements, in the notes thereto, or in separate statements (APB 12, *Omnibus Opinion -- 1967*).

   b. **Purposes.** The basic financial statements and footnotes, including the balance sheet, are vehicles for achieving the objectives of financial reporting. Supplementary information (e.g., on changing prices) and various other means of financial reporting (such as letters to shareholders) are also useful.

      1) The basic financial statements complement each other because they describe different aspects of the same transactions and because more than one statement will be necessary to provide information for a specific economic decision. Moreover, the elements of one statement articulate with those of other statements.

      2) The footnotes are considered part of the basic financial statements. They amplify or explain information recognized in the statements and are an integral part of statements prepared in accordance with GAAP. Footnotes should not be used to correct improper presentations.

2. **Definition.** The balance sheet (statement of financial position) "provides information about an entity's assets, liabilities, and equity and their relationships to each other at a moment in time." It helps users to assess "the entity's liquidity, financial flexibility, profitability, and risk" (SFAC 5).

3. **Conceptual Elements and Classifications**

   a. **Elements.** The balance sheet is a detailed presentation of the basic accounting equation: *Assets = Liabilities + Owners' Equity*. The equation is based on the proprietary theory. The owners' interest in an enterprise (residual equity) is what remains after the economic obligations of the enterprise are deducted from its economic resources.

31

b. **Classifications**. Some variation of the following classifications is used by most enterprises:

Assets	Liabilities
Current assets	Current liabilities
Noncurrent assets	Noncurrent liabilities
Long-term investments and funds	
Property, plant, and equipment	Owners' Equity
Intangible assets	Contributed capital
Other noncurrent assets	Retained earnings
Deferred charges	

1) In the classification scheme, assets are usually presented in descending order of liquidity; for example, inventory (a current asset) is more liquid than property, plant, and equipment.

2) Liabilities are shown in ascending order of time to maturity. Thus, trade payables (a current liability) will appear before bonds payable (a long-term liability).

3) Items in the owners' equity section are presented in descending order of permanence, e.g., common stock before retained earnings.

c. **Presentation formats**. The format of the balance sheet is not standardized, and any method that promotes full disclosure and understandability is acceptable.

1) The account (or horizontal) form presents assets on the left and liabilities and owners' equity on the right.

2) The report (or vertical) form is also commonly used. It differs from the account form only in that liabilities and owners' equity are presented below rather than beside assets.

4. **The Resource Structure**

a. **Current assets**. Current assets consist of "cash and other assets or resources commonly identified as reasonably expected to be realized in cash or sold or consumed during the normal operating cycle of the business" (ARB 43, Ch. 3A).

1) The **operating cycle** is the average time between the acquisition of resources and the final receipt of cash from their sale as the culmination of the entity's revenue-generating activities. If the operating cycle is less than a year, 1 year is the basis for defining current and noncurrent assets.

2) Current assets include cash and cash equivalents, inventories, receivables, trading securities, certain available-for-sale and held-to-maturity securities, and prepaid expenses.

b. **Noncurrent assets**. Assets not qualifying as current are classified as noncurrent.

1) **Long-term investments and funds**. These assets include a variety of nonoperating investments and funds intended to be held beyond the longer of 1 year or the operating cycle. The following assets are typically included:

a) Advances or investments in securities made to control or influence another entity and available-for-sale and held-to-maturity securities not classified as current

b) Restricted funds, for example, funds earmarked to retire long-term debt, satisfy pension obligations, or pay for the acquisition or construction of noncurrent assets

c) Cash surrender value of life insurance policies

d) Capital assets not used in current operations, such as idle facilities or land held for a future plant site or for speculative purposes

2) **Property, plant, and equipment (PP&E).** These assets are tangible items used in operations. They are recorded at cost and are shown net of accumulated depreciation if depreciable. They include

a) Land and depletable natural resources, e.g., oil and gas reserves

b) Buildings, machinery, equipment, furniture, fixtures, leasehold improvements, land improvements, leased assets held under capital leases, and other depreciable assets

3) **Intangible assets.** Intangibles are long-term assets ordinarily used in operations. Intangible assets lack physical substance, and there is usually great uncertainty about their future benefits. They may be acquired externally or developed internally, and may be identifiable or unidentifiable. Intangibles are recorded at cost and shown net of accumulated amortization.

a) Examples are patents, copyrights, trademarks, trade names, franchises, organization costs, and purchased goodwill.

b) The value of an intangible asset must be established in an arm's-length transaction; thus, research and development costs and internally generated goodwill are not capitalized.

c) Accountants arbitrarily amortize intangible assets because valuation is difficult.

4) **Other noncurrent assets.** This category includes noncurrent assets not readily classifiable elsewhere. Accordingly, there is little uniformity of treatment. Among the items typically shown as other assets are

a) Long-term receivables arising from unusual transactions, e.g., loans to officers or employees and sales of capital assets

b) Bond issue costs

c) Machinery rearrangement costs (also classifiable as PP&E)

d) Organization costs

e) Long-term prepayments

f) Deferred tax assets arising from interperiod tax allocation

5) **Deferred charges.** Some balance sheets contain a category for deferred charges (long-term prepayments). Many of these items, for example, bond issue costs, organization costs, and rearrangement costs, which all involve long-term prepayments, are frequently classified as other assets.

5. **The Financing Structure**

    a.   **Current liabilities.** Current liabilities are "obligations whose liquidation is reasonably expected to require the use of existing resources properly classifiable as current assets, or the creation of other current liabilities" (ARB 43, Ch. 3A).

        1)   This classification includes the following:

            a)   Payables for items entering into the operating cycle, for example, those incurred to obtain materials and supplies to be used in producing goods or services for sale

            b)   Payables arising from operations directly related to the operating cycle, such as accrued wages, salaries, rentals, royalties, and taxes

            c)   Collections made in advance of delivering goods or performing services, e.g., ticket sales revenue or magazine subscription revenue

            d)   Other obligations expected to be liquidated in the ordinary course of business during the longer of 1 year or the operating cycle

                i)   These include short-term notes given to acquire capital assets, payments required under sinking-fund provisions, payments on the current portion of serial bonds, and agency obligations incurred by the collection of assets on behalf of third parties.

            e)   Estimated amounts expected to be required within a relatively short time to pay known obligations even though

                i)   The amount can only be approximated, e.g., accrual of bonus payments, or

                ii)   The specific payee has not been designated, for example, in the case of warranties for repair of products already sold.

            f)   Obligations that, by their terms, are due on demand within the longer of 1 year or the operating cycle. Liquidation need not be expected.

            g)   Long-term obligations callable at the balance sheet date because of the debtor's violation of the debt agreement or long-term obligations that will become callable if the violation is not cured within a specified grace period

        2)   Current liabilities require the use of current assets or the creation of other current liabilities and therefore do not include

            a)   Short-term obligations intended to be refinanced on a long-term basis when the ability to consummate the refinancing has been demonstrated

                i)   This ability is demonstrated by a post-balance-sheet-date issuance of long-term debt or by entering into a financing agreement that meets certain criteria.

            b)   Debts to be paid from funds accumulated in accounts classified as noncurrent assets

                i)   Hence, a liability for bonds payable in the next period will not be classified as current if payment is to be from a noncurrent fund.

b. **Noncurrent liabilities**. Liabilities not qualifying as current are noncurrent.

1) The noncurrent portions of the following are shown in this section of the balance sheet:

a) Long-term notes and bonds payable

i) Any unamortized premium (an addition to the face value) or unamortized discount (a deduction) should be separately disclosed in the presentation of bonds payable.

b) Liabilities under capital leases
c) Pension obligations
d) Deferred tax liability arising from interperiod tax allocation
e) Obligations under product or service warranty agreements
f) Advances for long-term commitments to provide goods or services
g) Advances from affiliated companies
h) Deferred revenue

c. **Owners' equity**. Owners' equity is the residual after total liabilities are deducted from total assets. Hence, any transaction affecting total assets and total liabilities differently also affects owners' equity.

1) The owners' equity section of a corporate balance sheet is divided into capital contributed (paid-in or invested) by owners, retained earnings (corporate income reinvested or retained in the enterprise), and accumulated other comprehensive income (all comprehensive income items not included in net income). Treasury stock recorded at cost is a deduction from total shareholders' equity, not an asset. Treasury stock recorded at par directly reduces common stock.

2) See page 83 for a discussion of owners' equity.

6. Stop and review! You have completed the outline for this subunit. Study multiple-choice questions 1 through 10 beginning on page 50.

B. Income Statement

1. The results of operations are reported in the income statement (statement of earnings) on the accrual basis using an approach oriented to historical transactions.

a. The traditional income statement reports revenues from and expenses of the entity's major activities and gains and losses from other activities incurred over a period of time. The basic equation is

Revenues − Expenses + Gains − Losses = Income or Loss

1) Revenue and expense (nominal) accounts are temporary holding accounts, which are periodically closed to permanent (real) accounts. The accountant need not close each revenue and expense transaction directly to capital.

2) Income or loss is closed to the capital accounts in the balance sheet at the end of the period.

3) Revenue is a part of continuing operations; therefore, discontinued operations and the cumulative effect of changes in accounting principle are listed separately.

2.   **Transactions Included in Income**

    a.   **APB 9**, *Reporting the Results of Operations*, prescribes the **all-inclusive approach** with some modifications. Thus, all transactions affecting the net change in proprietorship equity during the period are included except transactions with owners and the rare transaction treated as a prior-period adjustment.

        1)   The net income reported in this way over the life of the entity reflects the sum of the periodic net incomes, including the nonrecurring items that are an appropriate part of the earnings history.

            a)   An additional advantage of the all-inclusive approach is that manipulation is less likely; that is, the income statement will be less subject to variation caused by differences in judgment.

            b)   The utility of the statement as a predictor of future income is not impaired if full disclosure of unusual, irregular, or nonrecurring items is made and an appropriate format is used.

    b.   The current operating performance concept emphasizes the ordinary, normal, recurring operations of the entity during the current period. Inclusion of extraordinary items or prior-period adjustments is believed to impair the significance of net income.

3.   **Income Statement Format**

    a.   **APB 30**, *Reporting the Results of Operations*, requires the following items to be reported separately and in the indicated order on the face of the income statement:

        1)   Pretax income from continuing operations

        2)   The provision for income taxes on income from continuing operations

        3)   Income from continuing operations

        4)   Discontinued operations

            a)   The income or loss from operations of the discontinued segment up to the measurement date and the gain or loss on disposal should both be shown net of tax. The gain or loss on disposal includes estimated operating income or loss of the segment from the measurement date to the disposal date, any direct disposal costs incurred during the phase-out period, and the estimated gain or loss on the actual disposal.

                i)   Taxes applicable to these components should be disclosed in the notes or on the face of the statement.

            b)   The gain or loss on disposal is estimated on the measurement date, which is the date on which management commits itself to a plan to dispose of a segment either by sale or abandonment. An estimated loss is recognized and treated as realized in the period that includes the measurement date. An estimated gain is not recognized until it is actually realized, which is usually the disposal date.

        5)   Income before extraordinary items and the cumulative effect of accounting changes (if any)

6) Extraordinary items

   a) These are material items that are both unusual in nature and infrequent in the environment in which the entity operates. They also include items designated as extraordinary by a pronouncement, e.g., debt extinguishments. This component is also presented net of tax (the tax is shown on the face of the statement or in a footnote).

   b) Individual items should be shown on the face of the statement, but footnote disclosure is acceptable.

   c) If an item is unusual or infrequent but not both, it is reported, not net of tax, as a separate component of income from continuing operations.

   d) APB 30 specifies certain items that are not to be treated as extraordinary gains and losses. These include write-downs of receivables and inventories, translation of foreign currency, disposal of a business segment, sale of productive assets, effects of strikes, and accruals on long-term contracts.

7) Cumulative effect of a change in accounting principle

   a) This amount is shown net of tax (with disclosure of the related tax on the face of the statement or in a footnote).

8) Net income

9) EPS data are not given in the example below. However, SFAS 128 requires that basic and diluted EPS for each period presented be reported for each of the following, if they exist. Items a) and e) are reported on the face of the income statement. The others are reported there or in the notes. Whether the amounts are pretax or net of tax should be stated.

   a) Income from continuing operations
   b) Discontinued operations
   c) Extraordinary items
   d) Cumulative effect of accounting changes
   e) Net income

10) EXAMPLE:

Amy Corp.
Income Statement
For the Year Ended 12/31/97

Income from continuing operations before income tax		$400,000
Income taxes		(100,000)
Income from continuing operations		$300,000
Discontinued operations		
Income from Bird Foods, minus applicable tax of $10,000	$30,000	
Loss on disposal of Bird Foods, net of tax benefit of $3,000	(4,000)	26,000
Income before extraordinary items and the effects of		
cumulative accounting changes		$326,000
Extraordinary items -- loss from hurricane in North Dakota		
plant minus applicable tax of $9,000		(45,000)
Cumulative effect of change in depreciation method,		
minus applicable tax of $14,000		(90,000)
Net income		$191,000

b.   Presentation of income from continuing operations

1)   The **single-step income statement** provides one grouping for revenue items and one for expense items. The single step is the one subtraction necessary to arrive at net income from continuing operations.

Revenues	
Net sales	$XXX
Other revenues	XXX
Gains	XXX
Total revenues	$ XXX
Expenses	
Cost of goods sold	$XXX
Selling and administrative expenses	XXX
Interest expense	XXX
Losses	XXX
Income tax expense	XXX
Total expenses	$(XXX)
Net income from continuing operations	$ XXX

2)   The **multiple-step income statement** matches operating revenues and expenses in a section separate from nonoperating items. This format enhances disclosure by presenting intermediary totals rather than one net income figure.

Net sales	$XXX
Cost of goods sold	(XXX)
Gross profit	$XXX
Selling and administrative expenses	(XXX)
Operating profit	$XXX
Other revenues and gains	XXX
	$XXX
Other expenses and losses	(XXX)
Pretax income from continuing operations	$XXX
Income taxes	(XXX)
Net income from continuing operations	$XXX

c.   **Cost of goods sold** equals cost of goods manufactured (or purchases for a retailer) adjusted for the change in finished goods inventory.

1)   **Cost of goods manufactured** is equivalent to a retailer's purchases. It equals all manufacturing costs incurred during the period, plus beginning work-in-process, minus ending work-in-process.

d.   Other expenses

1)   **General and administrative expenses** are incurred for the direction of the enterprise as a whole and are not related wholly to a specific function, e.g., selling or manufacturing. They include accounting, legal, and other fees for professional services; officers' salaries; insurance; wages of office staff; miscellaneous supplies; and office occupancy costs.

      2)   **Selling expenses** are those incurred in selling or marketing. Examples include sales representatives' salaries, rent for sales department, commissions, and traveling expense; advertising; selling department salaries and expenses; samples; and credit and collection costs. Shipping costs are also often classified as selling costs.

      3)   **Interest expense** is recognized based on the passage of time. In the case of bonds, notes, and capital leases, the effective interest method is used.

4.   Stop and review! You have completed the outline for this subunit. Study multiple-choice questions 11 through 24 beginning on page 53.

C. Statement of Cash Flows

1.   **SFAS 95**, *Statement of Cash Flows*, requires a statement of cash flows as part of a full set of financial statements of all business entities (both publicly and privately held) and not-for-profit organizations.

    a.   If a business enterprise or not-for-profit organization reports financial position and results of operations, it must present a statement of cash flows for any period for which results of operations are presented.

      1)   However, defined benefit pension plans, certain other employee benefit plans, and certain highly liquid investment companies are exempt.

    b.   SFAS 95 states, "Financial statements shall not report an amount of cash flow per share." The per share amount may improperly imply that the cash flow is an alternative to net income as a performance measure.

2.   The **primary purpose** of a statement of cash flows is to provide relevant information about the cash receipts and payments of an entity during a period. A secondary purpose is to provide information about investing and financing activities.

    a.   If used with information in the other financial statements, the statement of cash flows should help investors, creditors, donors, and others to assess

      1)   The entity's ability to generate positive future net cash flows

      2)   The entity's ability to meet its obligations and pay dividends

      3)   The entity's needs for external financing

      4)   The reasons for differences between income and associated cash receipts and payments

      5)   The cash and noncash aspects of the entity's investing and financing activities

        a)   Information about transactions that do not directly affect cash flow for the period must be disclosed. These transactions are excluded from the body of the statement to avoid undue complexity and detraction from the objective of providing information about cash flows.

          i)   Examples of **noncash investing and financing activities** to be reported in related disclosures but not in the statement include converting debt to equity, obtaining assets by assuming liabilities or entering into a capital lease, obtaining a building or investment asset by receiving a gift, and exchanging a noncash asset or liability for another.

3. The changes in cash and in cash equivalents during the period are to be explained in a statement of cash flows.

    a. If an entity invests its cash in excess of immediate needs in short-term, highly liquid investments (cash equivalents), it should use the descriptive term "cash and cash equivalents." Otherwise, the term "cash" is acceptable. Terms such as "funds" or "quick assets" may not be used.

        1) **Cash equivalents** are readily convertible to known amounts of cash and are so near their maturity that they present insignificant risk of changes in value because of changes in interest rates. Thus, an exchange of cash for cash equivalents has no effect on the statement of cash flows.

        2) Usually, only investments with original maturities of 3 months or less qualify as cash equivalents. Money market funds, commercial paper, and treasury bills are examples.

4. A statement of cash flows reports the cash effects of operations, investing transactions, and financing transactions during the period.

    a. **Operating activities** include all transactions and other events not classified as investing and financing activities. In general, the cash effects of transactions and other events that enter into the determination of income are to be classified as operating activities.

        1) Cash flows from operating activities include cash receipts from interest on loans and dividends on equity securities as well as cash payments to employees and suppliers; to governments for taxes, duties, and fees; and to lenders for interest.

        2) **SFAS 102** classifies as operating items cash flows from certain securities and other assets acquired for resale and carried at market value in a trading account (e.g., by banks, brokers, and dealers in securities), or from loans acquired for resale and carried at lower of cost or market.

        3) Moreover, **SFAS 115** states that cash flows from purchases, sales, and maturities of trading securities are cash flows from operating activities.

    b. **Investing activities** include making and collecting loans and acquiring and disposing of debt or equity instruments and property, plant, and equipment and other productive assets, that is, assets held for or used in the production of goods or services (other than the materials held in inventory).

        1) Investing activities exclude transactions in cash equivalents and in certain loans or other debt or equity instruments acquired specifically for resale.

        2) Cash flows from purchases, sales, and maturities of available-for-sale and held-to-maturity securities are cash flows from investing activities and are reported gross for each classification of security in the cash flows statement (SFAS 115).

    c. **Financing activities** include the issuance of stock, the payment of dividends, treasury stock transactions, the issuance of debt, and the repayment or other settlement of debt obligations. It also includes receiving restricted resources that by donor stipulation must be used for long-term purposes.

    d. **Hedging transactions.** Cash flows from a futures, forward, option, or swap contract accounted for as a hedge of an identifiable transaction or event may be classified in the same category as the flows from the hedged item, provided that this policy is disclosed (SFAS 104).

5. **Netting**. In general, cash inflows and outflows should be reported separately at gross amounts in a statement of cash flows. In certain instances, however, the net amount of related cash receipts and payments may provide sufficient information for certain classes of cash flows.

   a. If the turnover of an item is quick, amounts are large, and the maturity is short, or if the entity is essentially holding or disbursing cash for customers, net reporting is proper.

      1) Examples are demand deposits of a bank and customer accounts payable of a broker-dealer.

      2) SFAS 104 permits banks, thrifts, and credit unions to report net cash receipts and payments for deposits, time deposits, and loans.

6. SFAS 95 also requires translation of **foreign currency cash flows**.

   a. A weighted-average exchange rate may be used if the result is substantially the same as would be obtained by using the rates in effect when the flows occurred.

   b. The effect of exchange rate fluctuations must be separately reported as part of the reconciliation of cash and cash equivalents.

7. The statement of cash flows may report operating activities in the form of either an indirect or a direct presentation, although the direct method is encouraged.

   a. The **direct presentation** reports major classes of gross operating cash receipts and payments and their sum (net operating cash flow). At a minimum, the following classes are included in a direct presentation:

      1) Cash collected from customers, including lessees, licensees, and the like

      2) Interest and dividends received (excluding those donor-restricted for long-term purposes)

      3) Other operating cash receipts, if any

      4) Cash paid to employees and other suppliers of goods or services, including suppliers of insurance, advertising and the like

      5) Interest paid

      6) Income taxes paid

      7) Other operating cash payments, if any

   b. The **indirect presentation** reconciles net income of a business enterprise or the change in net assets of a not-for-profit organization to net operating cash flow. It removes from net income or the change in net assets the effects of

      1) All past deferrals of operating cash receipts and payments

         a) Examples are changes in inventory, deferred income, and prepaid expenses.

      2) All accruals of expected future operating cash receipts and payments

         a) Examples are changes in receivables and payables.

      3) Items whose cash effects are investing or financing cash flows

         a) Examples are bad debt expense; depreciation; goodwill amortization; and gains or losses on sales of property, plant, and equipment, on discontinued operations, or on debt extinguishment.

c.   The same net operating cash flow will be reported under both methods. Moreover, the reconciliation of net income or the change in net assets to net operating cash flow must be disclosed regardless of the presentation chosen. The reconciliation may be reported in the statement of cash flows or in related disclosures.

d.   EXAMPLE: Indirect presentation

Dice Corp's balance sheet accounts as of December 31, 1996 and 1995 are presented in the next column. Information relating to 1996 activities is presented below.

Information Relating to 1996 Activities
- Net income for 1996 was $690,000.
- Cash dividends of $240,000 were declared and paid in 1996.
- Equipment costing $400,000 and having a carrying amount of $150,000 was sold on January 1, 1996 for $150,000 in cash.
- A long-term investment was sold in 1996 for $135,000 in cash.
- 10,000 shares of common stock were issued in 1996 for $22 a share.
- Short-term investments consist of Treasury bills maturing on 6/30/97. They are not cash equivalents because their maturities are not 3 months or less.
- The provision for 1996 income taxes was $210,000.
- The accounts receivable balances at the beginning and end of 1996 were net of allowances for bad debts of $50,000 and $60,000, respectively. Dice wrote off $40,000 of bad debts during 1996. The only transactions affecting accounts receivable and the allowance were credit sales, collections, write-offs, and recognition of bad debt expense.
- During 1996, Dice constructed a plant asset. The accumulated expenditures during the year included $11,000 of capitalized interest.

- Dice accounts for its interest in Thrice Corp. under the equity method. Its equity in Thrice's 1996 earnings was $25,000. At the end of 1996, Dice received a $10,000 cash dividend from Thrice.

| | December 31, | |
Assets	1996	1995
Cash	$ 195,000	$ 100,000
Short-term investments	300,000	0
Accounts receivable (net)	480,000	510,000
Inventory	680,000	600,000
Prepaid expenses	15,000	20,000
Long-term investments	215,000	300,000
Plant assets	1,700,000	1,000,000
Accumulated depreciation	(450,000)	(450,000)
Goodwill	90,000	100,000
Total assets	$3,225,000	$2,180,000

Limited and Shareholders' Equity		
Accounts payable	$ 825,000	$ 720,000
Interest payable	15,000	10,000
Income tax payable	20,000	30,000
Short-term debt	325,000	0
Deferred taxes	250,000	300,000
Common stock, $10 par	800,000	700,000
Additional paid-in capital	370,000	250,000
Retained earnings	620,000	170,000
Total assets and stockholders' equity	$3,225,000	$2,180,000

1)   The following computations are required to determine **net cash provided by operations** ($905,000 as shown in the reconciliation on page 44):

a)   **Depreciation**. In 1996, Dice must have recognized $250,000 of depreciation [$450,000 accumulated depreciation at 12/31/96 — ($450,000 accumulated depreciation at 12/31/95 — $250,000 accumulated depreciation on equipment sold on 1/1/95)]. The depreciation and the $10,000 ($100,000 at 12/31/95 — $90,000 at 12/31/96) amortization of goodwill should be added to net income because both are included in the determination of net income but neither had a cash effect.

b)   **Cost of goods sold**. The adjustment from cost of goods sold (an accrual accounting amount included in the determination of net income) to cash paid to suppliers requires two steps: from cost of goods sold to purchases and from purchases to cash paid to suppliers. The $80,000 ($680,000 — $600,000) increase in inventory is a deduction from net income because it indicates that purchases were $80,000 greater than the cost of goods sold amount used to compute net income.

c) **Accounts payable**. The $105,000 ($825,000 – $720,000) increase in accounts payable is an addition to net income because it indicates that cash disbursements to suppliers were $105,000 less than purchases. Thus, the net effect of the changes in inventory and accounts payable is that cash paid to suppliers was $25,000 less than cost of goods sold.

d) **Accounts receivable**. The net accounts receivable balance declined by $30,000 ($510,000 – $480,000), implying that cash collections exceeded net income. Given that sales, collections, write-offs, and recognition of bad debt expense were the only relevant transactions, $30,000 should be added to net income. Use of the change in net accounts receivable as a reconciliation adjustment is a short-cut method. It yields the same net adjustment to net income as separately including the effects of the change in gross accounts receivable [($510,000 + $50,000 bad debt allowance) – ($480,000 + $60,000 bad debt allowance) = an addition of $20,000], bad debt expense (a noncash item resulting in an addition of $50,000), and bad debt write-offs (a deduction of $40,000 to reflect that write-offs did not result in collections).

e) **Prepaid expenses**. The $5,000 decrease in prepaid expenses signifies that noncash expenses were recognized and should be added back to net income.

f) **Dividends received**. Earnings of an affiliate accounted for under the equity method are debited to the investment account and credited to net income. A cash dividend from the affiliate is debited to cash and credited to the investment account. Thus, an adjustment reducing net income by $15,000 ($25,000 earnings – $10,000 cash dividend) for undistributed earnings is necessary.

g) **Long-term investments**. A $100,000 ($300,000 + $25,000 equity in affiliate's earnings – $10,000 cash dividend – $215,000) decrease in the long-term investments account occurred when these investments were sold for $135,000. The resulting $35,000 gain was included in the determination of net income. The cash effect is properly classified as an investing activity, and the $35,000 should be subtracted from net income to remove it from the operating section.

h) **Interest payable**. Interest payable increased by $5,000, which represents a noncash expense and a reconciling addition to net income. The interest capitalized is ignored for reconciliation purposes because it is not reported as interest expense in the income statement or as interest paid in the statement of cash flows or in related disclosures. The $11,000 of capitalized interest is included in the capitalized cost of the plant asset constructed for Dice's own use.

i) **Income tax payable**. Income tax payable decreased by $10,000, giving rise to a reconciling deduction from net income because tax expense was less than cash paid for taxes.

j) **Deferred taxes**. Deferred taxes decreased by $50,000. This reconciling deduction from net interest resulted when temporary differences reversed and cash payments for taxes exceeded tax expense.

Reconciliation of Net Income to Net Operating Cash Flow		
Net income for 1996	$690,000	
Depreciation	250,000	a)
Amortization	10,000	a)
Inventory	(80,000)	b)
Accounts payable	105,000	c)
Accounts receivable (net)	30,000	d)
Prepaid expenses	5,000	e)
Undistributed earnings of an affiliate	(15,000)	f)
Gain on sale of investments	(35,000)	g)
Interest payable	5,000	h)
Income tax payable	(10,000)	i)
Deferred taxes	(50,000)	j)
Net operating cash flow	$905,000	

2) **Net investing cash flow**

  a) The $300,000 increase in short-term investments indicates that a purchase occurred.

  b) The balance sheet further indicates that plant assets increased by $700,000 ($1,700,000 – $1,000,000). Moreover, plant assets (equipment) costing $400,000 were sold. Thus, the cost of constructing the plant asset must have equaled $1,100,000 [$1,700,000 ending plant assets balance – ($1,000,000 beginning balance – $400,000 cost of equipment sold)].

  c) The cash flows from investing activities include the cash effects of the sale of equipment and the long-term investments, the purchases of short-term investments, and the construction of a plant asset. The equipment was sold for $150,000 and the long-term investments for $135,000. Thus, the net cash used in investing activities was $1,115,000.

Purchases:		
Short-term investments	$ (300,000)	a)
Plant assets	(1,100,000)	b)
Sales:		
Equipment	150,000	c)
Long-term investments	135,000	c)
Net investing cash flow	$(1,115,000)	

3) **Net financing cash flow**

  a) Dice Corp.'s 1996 financing activities included the issuance of short-term debt ($325,000 – $0 = $325,000), the issuance of common stock and the recording of additional paid-in capital [($800,000 – $700,000) + ($370,000 – $250,000) = $220,000], and the payment of cash dividends ($240,000). The net cash provided by these financing activities was $305,000.

Short-term debt	$325,000	a)
Common stock	220,000	a)
Cash dividends	(240,000)	a)
Net financing cash flow	$305,000	

4) **Net change in cash.** According to Dice Corp.'s balance sheets, the net change in cash was an increase of $95,000 ($195,000 – $100,000).

    a) This amount reconciles with the net cash provided by (used in) operating, investing, and financing activities ($905,000 – $1,115,000 + $305,000 = $95,000).

5) **Noncash financing and investing activities.** Dice Corp. had no such transactions in 1996 to be reported in supplemental disclosures.

6) **Supplemental cash flow disclosures.** If Dice Corp. uses the indirect method to present its statement of cash flows, the interest paid (excluding amounts capitalized) and income taxes paid must be reported in related disclosures.

    a) Interest paid cannot be calculated here because interest expense is not given in the example.

    b) Income taxes paid were $270,000 ($210,000 provision for income taxes + $50,000 decrease in deferred taxes + $10,000 decrease in taxes payable).

Dice Corp.
Statement of Cash Flows -- Indirect Method
for the Year Ended December 31, 1996
Increase (Decrease) in Cash and Cash Equivalents

Operating cash flows:		
Net income for 1996	$ 690,000	
Depreciation	250,000	
Amortization	10,000	
Inventory	(80,000)	
Accounts payable	105,000	
Accounts receivable (net)	30,000	
Prepaid expenses	5,000	
Undistributed earnings of an affiliate	(15,000)	
Gain on sale of investments	(35,000)	
Interest payable	5,000	
Income tax payable	(10,000)	
Deferred taxes	(50,000)	
Net cash provided by operating activities		$ 905,000
Investing cash flows:		
Proceeds from sale of equipment	$ 150,000	
Proceeds from sale of long-term investments	135,000	
Payments for short-term investments	(300,000)	
Payments for plant assets	(1,100,000)	
Net cash used in investing activities		(1,115,000)
Financing cash flows:		
Proceeds from short-term debt	$ 325,000	
Proceeds from issuing common stock	220,000	
Dividends paid	(240,000)	
Net cash provided by financing activities		305,000
Net increase		$ 95,000
Beginning balance		100,000
Ending balance		$ 195,000

e.   Direct presentation. The difference between the direct and indirect method lies in the way in which the net cash provided by operations is determined. Compare the direct method format presented below with the indirect method format on page 45. Calculations for deriving the amounts of the major classes of gross cash flows have been omitted.

Operating cash flows:		
Cash collected from customers	$ 7,790,000	
Cash paid to employees and suppliers	(6,520,000)	
Dividend from affiliate	10,000	
Interest received	30,000	
Interest paid	(135,000)	
Income taxes paid	(270,000)	
Net cash provided by operating activities		$ 905,000

1)   **Cash collected from customers** may be determined by adjusting sales for the changes in customer receivables. This calculation requires information similar to that used in an indirect presentation to reconcile net income to net operating cash flow: total operating receivables (which are usually separate from those for interest and dividends), bad debt write-offs, and any other noncash entries in customer accounts.

2)   **Cash paid to employees and suppliers** of goods and services may be determined by adjusting cost of goods sold and expenses (excluding interest, income tax, and depreciation) for the changes in inventory, prepaid expenses, and operating payables. This calculation is also similar to the process used in reconciling net income to net operating cash flow. It requires that operating payables and expenses be separated from interest and income tax payable.

3)   Dividends received, not the amount of equity-based earnings recognized in net income, is included.

4)   Interest income is adjusted for changes in interest receivable.

5)   Interest expense is adjusted for changes in interest payable. Interest capitalized is not considered in determining interest paid because it is included in payments for plant assets, not in interest expense.

6)   Income taxes paid equaled tax expense adjusted for the changes in deferred taxes and in taxes payable.

8.   Stop and review! You have completed the outline for this subunit. Study multiple-choice questions 25 through 50 beginning on page 58.

D. Annual Reports

1. The SEC has authority to regulate external financial reporting by publicly traded companies. Nevertheless, its traditional role has been to promote disclosure rather than to exercise its power to establish accounting standards. Thus, it usually allows the accounting profession (through the FASB) to promulgate GAAP.

   a. To promote disclosure, the SEC has adopted a system that integrates the information required to be presented in annual reports to shareholders and in SEC filings (Form 10-K is the annual report to the SEC).

2. Certain information must be included in both Form 10-K (due 90 days after the company's fiscal year-end) and the annual report to the shareholders.

   a. Information about the market for the company's common stock, such as where it is principally traded, high and low sales prices for each quarter of the last two years, frequency and amount of dividends for the last two years, any restrictions on dividends, and number of shares

   b. Selected financial data summarized for the past 5 years, with an emphasis on financial trends, including net sales or operating revenues, income from continuing operations, total assets, long-term obligations, redeemable preferred stock, and cash dividends per share

   c. **Management's discussion and analysis** (MD&A) of financial condition and results of operations

      1) This discussion must address liquidity, capital resources, results of operations, and the effects of inflation and changing prices.

      2) Forward-looking information (a forecast) is encouraged but not required.

         a) The SEC's safe harbor rule protects a company that issues an erroneous forecast if it is prepared on a reasonable basis and in good faith.

      3) The MD&A need not be audited.

      4) SEC Regulation S-K provides guidelines for MD&A disclosures.

   d. Financial statements and supplementary data

      1) Standardized consolidated financial statements are required. They must be audited and include

         a) Balance sheets for the two most recent fiscal year-ends

         b) Statements of income, cash flows, and changes in shareholders' equity for the three most recent fiscal years

      2) The accountant certifying the financial statements must be independent of the management of the filing company. The accountant is not required to be a CPA, but (s)he must be registered with a state.

   e. Changes in accountants and disagreements about accounting and financial disclosures

3. Other matters are required to be included in Form 10-K but not in the annual report. However, companies often include these items in their annual reports.

    a. A history and description of the business encompassing important recent developments, such as reorganizations, bankruptcies, and major dispositions or acquisitions of assets; information on industry segments and foreign operations; and principal products and services

    b. Locations and descriptions of physical properties

    c. Pending litigation, e.g., principal parties, allegations, and relief sought

    d. Matters submitted to shareholders for approval

    e. Information about officers and directors, for example, transactions with the company and executive compensation

    f. Ownership of the company's securities

    g. Description of certain other business relationships, such as those with related parties

    h. Exhibits, supporting schedules, and other reports

4. Management has the responsibility for adoption of sound accounting policies and for establishing and maintaining internal controls that will record, process, summarize, and report transactions, events, and conditions consistent with the assertions in the financial statements. The fairness of the representations made therein is the responsibility of management alone because the transactions and the related assets, liabilities, and equity reflected are within management's direct knowledge and control.

5. The financial statements of a publicly traded company are accompanied by the report of the independent external auditors. Their audit is conducted in accordance with generally accepted auditing standards and is intended to provide assurance to creditors, investors, and other users of financial statements.

    a. The auditors' report is issued in accordance with the following generally accepted auditing standards of reporting:

        1) *The report shall state whether the financial statements are presented in accordance with GAAP.*

        2) *The report shall identify circumstances in which GAAP have not been consistently observed in the current period in relation to the preceding period.*

        3) *Informative disclosures in the financial statements are to be regarded as reasonably adequate unless otherwise stated in the report.*

        4) *The report shall either contain an expression of opinion regarding the financial statements, taken as a whole, or an assertion to the effect that an opinion cannot be expressed. When an overall opinion cannot be expressed, the reasons therefor should be stated. In all cases in which an auditor's name is associated with financial statements, the report should contain a clear-cut indication of the character of the auditor's work, if any, and the degree of responsibility the auditor is taking.*

b. The following types of reports may be issued:

1) **Unqualified opinion.** An unqualified opinion states that the financial statements present fairly, in all material respects, the financial position, results of operations, and cash flows of the entity in conformity with GAAP. This is the most common type of opinion expressed.

2) **Explanatory language added to the auditor's standard report.** Certain circumstances, although not affecting the auditor's unqualified opinion, may require that the auditor add an explanatory paragraph (or other explanatory language) to the report.

3) **Qualified opinion.** A qualified opinion states that, **except for** the effects of the matter(s) to which the qualification relates, the financial statements present fairly, in all material respects, the financial position, results of operations, and cash flows of the entity in conformity with GAAP.

4) **Adverse opinion.** An adverse opinion states that the financial statements do not present fairly the financial position, results of operations, or cash flows of the entity in conformity with GAAP.

5) **Disclaimer of opinion.** A disclaimer of opinion states that the auditor does not express an opinion on the financial statements. It is appropriate when the scope of the audit is not sufficient to permit formation of an opinion or when the auditor is not independent.

c. Below is the auditor's standard report expressing an unqualified opinion.

Standard Audit Report

Independent Auditor's Report

To: <-------------- Addressed to the Board of Directors and/or Shareholders

We have audited the accompanying balance sheets of X Company as of December 31, 19x2 and 19x1, and the related statements of income, retained earnings, and cash flows for the years then ended. These financial statements are the responsibility of the Company's management. Our responsibility is to express an opinion on these financial statements based on our audits.

We conducted our audits in accordance with generally accepted auditing standards. Those standards require that we plan and perform the audit to obtain reasonable assurance about whether the financial statements are free of material misstatement. An audit includes examining, on a test basis, evidence supporting the amounts and disclosures in the financial statements. An audit also includes assessing the accounting principles used and significant estimates made by management, as well as evaluating the overall financial statement presentation. We believe that our audits provide a reasonable basis for our opinion.

In our opinion, the financial statements referred to above present fairly, in all material respects, the financial position of X Company as of [at] December 31, 19x2 and 19x1, and the results of its operations and its cash flows for the years then ended in conformity with generally accepted accounting principles.

Signature <-------------- May be signed, typed, or printed

---

6. Stop and review! You have completed the outline for this subunit. Study multiple-choice questions 51 through 62 beginning on page 67.

MULTIPLE-CHOICE QUESTIONS

A. Balance Sheet

1. The basic financial statements include a

   A. Balance sheet, income statement, statement of retained earnings, and statement of changes in retained earnings.

   B. Statement of financial position, income statement, statement of retained earnings, and statement of changes in retained earnings.

   C. Balance sheet, statement of financial position, income statement, and statement of changes in retained earnings.

   D. Statement of financial position, income statement, statement of cash flows, and statement of retained earnings.

The correct answer is (D). *(CMA 685 4-29)*
REQUIRED: The statements included in the basic financial statements.
DISCUSSION: Under GAAP, the basic required statements are the statement of financial position (balance sheet), income statement, statement of cash flows, and a retained earnings statement or statement of changes in shareholders' equity. A statement of cash flows is now a required part of a full set of financial statements of all business entities (both publicly held and privately held) (SFAS 95). The statement of cash flows has replaced the statement of changes in financial position. Furthermore, SFAS 130 requires that comprehensive income be reported in a financial statement displayed with the same prominence as other financial statements. However, the FASB does not require a particular format for this presentation.
Answers (A), (B), and (C) are incorrect because the basic statements are the statement of financial position, income statement, statement of cash flows, and statement of retained earnings.

2. What are the disclosure requirements with respect to changes in capital accounts other than retained earnings and changes in other owners' equity data?

   A. When the income statement and balance sheet are presented, all changes in the capital accounts and changes in the number of shares of equity securities must be disclosed.

   B. When the balance sheet is presented, all changes in the capital accounts must be disclosed.

   C. When the income statement is presented, all changes in the capital accounts and changes in the number of shares of equity securities must be disclosed.

   D. Changes in the number of shares of equity securities must be disclosed when a balance sheet is presented, but there is no specific disclosure requirement with respect to the capital accounts other than retained earnings.

The correct answer is (A). *(Publisher)*
REQUIRED: The disclosure requirements with respect to changes in capital accounts other than retained earnings and changes in other owners' equity data.
DISCUSSION: APB 12, *Omnibus Opinion-1967*, requires disclosure both of changes in the separate accounts appearing in shareholders' equity (in addition to retained earnings) and of changes in the number of shares of equity securities when both the balance sheet and the income statement are presented. This disclosure may be in separate statements, the basic financial statements, or the footnotes.
Answers (B) and (C) are incorrect because the requirement applies only when both the balance sheet and the income statement are presented. Answer (D) is incorrect because there is a specific disclosure requirement with respect to the changes in the capital accounts.

3. The primary purpose of the statement of financial position is to reflect

   A. The fair value of the firm's assets at some moment in time.

   B. The status of the firm's assets in case of forced liquidation of the firm.

   C. The firm's potential for growth in stock values in the stock market.

   D. Items of value, debts, and net worth.

The correct answer is (D). *(CMA 680 4-15)*
REQUIRED: The primary purpose of the statement of financial position.
DISCUSSION: The balance sheet presents three major financial accounting elements: assets (items of value), liabilities (debts), and owners' equity (net worth). According to SFAC 6, *Elements of Financial Statements*, assets are probable future economic benefits resulting from past transactions or events. Liabilities are probable future sacrifices of economic benefits arising from present obligations as a result of past transactions or events. Equity is the residual interest in the assets after deduction of liabilities.
Answer (A) is incorrect because the measurement attributes of assets include but are not limited to fair value. Answer (B) is incorrect because financial statements reflect the going concern assumption. Hence, they usually do not report forced liquidation values. Answer (C) is incorrect because the future value of a company's stock is more dependent upon future operations and investors' expectations than on the data found in the balance sheet.

4. A statement of financial position allows investors to assess all of the following except

    A.   How efficiently enterprise assets are used.

    B.   The liquidity and financial flexibility of the enterprise.

    C.   The capital structure of the enterprise.

    D.   The net realizable value of enterprise assets.

The correct answer is (D). *(CFM Sample Q. 4)*
    REQUIRED: The attribute not assessable using a statement of financial position.
    DISCUSSION: Assets are usually valued at original historical cost in a statement of financial position, although some exceptions exist. For example, some short-term receivables are reported at their net realizable value. Thus, the statement of financial position cannot be relied upon to assess NRV.
    Answers (A) and (B) are incorrect because efficiency of asset use, liquidity, and financial flexibility are assessed by calculating liquidity, leverage, and asset management ratios. These ratios require balance sheet data. Answer (C) is incorrect because the capital structure of the enterprise is reported in the equity section of the statement of financial position.

5. Footnotes to financial statements are beneficial in meeting the disclosure requirements of financial reporting. The footnotes should not be used to

    A.   Describe significant accounting policies.

    B.   Describe depreciation methods employed by the company.

    C.   Describe principles and methods peculiar to the industry in which the company operates, when these principles and methods are predominantly followed in that industry.

    D.   Correct an improper presentation in the financial statements.

The correct answer is (D). *(CMA 676 3-29)*
    REQUIRED: The improper use of footnotes in financial statements.
    DISCUSSION: Financial statement footnotes should not be used to correct improper presentations. The financial statements should be presented correctly on their own. Footnotes should be used to explain the methods used to prepare the financial statements and the amounts shown.
    Answers (A), (B), and (C) are incorrect because each describes an appropriate and required disclosure that should appear in the footnotes to the financial statements (APB 22, *Disclosure of Accounting Policies*).

6. The accounting equation (assets – liabilities = owners' equity) reflects the

    A.   Entity point of view.

    B.   Fund theory.

    C.   Proprietary point of view.

    D.   Enterprise theory.

The correct answer is (C). *(CMA 684 3-13)*
    REQUIRED: The concept on which the basic accounting equation is based.
    DISCUSSION: The equation is based on the proprietary theory. The owners' interest in an enterprise (residual equity) is what remains after the economic obligations of the enterprise are deducted from its economic resources.
    Answer (A) is incorrect because the entity concept limits accounting information to that related to a specific entity (possibly not the same as the legal entity). Answer (B) is incorrect because fund theory stresses that assets equal obligations (owners' equity and liabilities are sources of assets). Answer (D) is incorrect because the enterprise concept stresses ownership of the assets; that is, the emphasis is on the credit side of the balance sheet.

7. When classifying assets as current and noncurrent for reporting purposes,

   A. The amounts at which current assets are carried and reported must reflect realizable cash values.

   B. Prepayments for items such as insurance or rent are included in an "other assets" group rather than as current assets as they will ultimately be expensed.

   C. The time period by which current assets are distinguished from noncurrent assets is determined by the seasonal nature of the business.

   D. Assets are classified as current if they are reasonably expected to be realized in cash or consumed during the normal operating cycle.

The correct answer is (D). *(CMA 693 2-10)*
   REQUIRED: The true statement about the classification of current assets.
   DISCUSSION: Under ARB 43, current assets are cash and other assets or resources expected to be realized in cash, sold, or consumed during the longer of 1 year or the normal operating cycle of the business.
   Answer (A) is incorrect because current assets are measured using different attributes, for example, lower of cost or market for inventory and net realizable value for accounts receivable. Answer (B) is incorrect because prepayments may qualify as current assets. They often will be consumed during the operating cycle. Answer (C) is incorrect because the classification criterion is based on the normal operating cycle regardless of the seasonality of the business.

8. Abernathy Corporation uses a calendar year for financial and tax reporting purposes and has $100 million of mortgage bonds due on January 15, 1996. By January 10, 1996, Abernathy intends to refinance this debt with new long-term mortgage bonds and has entered into a financing agreement that clearly demonstrates its ability to consummate the refinancing. This debt is to be

   A. Classified as a current liability on the statement of financial position at December 31, 1995.

   B. Classified as a long-term liability on the statement of financial position at December 31, 1995.

   C. Retired as of December 31, 1995.

   D. Considered off-balance-sheet debt.

The correct answer is (B). *(CMA 1295 2-8)*
   REQUIRED: The balance sheet treatment of maturing long-term debt that is to be refinanced on a long-term basis.
   DISCUSSION: SFAS 6 states that short-term obligations expected to be refinanced should be reported as current liabilities unless the firm both plans to refinance and has the ability to refinance the debt on a long-term basis. The ability to refinance on a long-term basis is evidenced by a post-balance-sheet date issuance of long-term debt or a financing arrangement that will clearly permit long-term refinancing.
   Answer (A) is incorrect because the company intends to refinance the debt on a long-term basis. Answer (C) is incorrect because the debt has not been retired. Answer (D) is incorrect because the debt is on the balance sheet.

9. Lister Company intends to refinance a portion of its short-term debt in 1996 and is negotiating a long-term financing agreement with a local bank. This agreement would be noncancelable and would extend for a period of 2 years. The amount of short-term debt that Lister Company can exclude from its statement of financial position at December 31, 1995

   A. May exceed the amount available for refinancing under the agreement.

   B. Depends on the demonstrated ability to consummate the refinancing.

   C. Is reduced by the proportionate change in the working capital ratio.

   D. Is zero unless the refinancing has occurred by year-end.

The correct answer is (B). *(CMA 1287 3-30)*
   REQUIRED: The amount of short-term debt excluded from the current section of the balance sheet.
   DISCUSSION: If an enterprise intends to refinance short-term obligations on a long-term basis and demonstrates an ability to consummate the refinancing, the obligations should be excluded from current liabilities and classified as noncurrent (SFAS 6, *Classification of Short-Term Obligations Expected to Be Refinanced*). The ability to consummate the refinancing may be demonstrated by a post-balance-sheet-date issuance of a long-term obligation or equity securities, or by entering into a financing agreement that meets certain criteria. These criteria are that the agreement does not expire within 1 year, it is noncancelable by the lender, no violation of the agreement exists at the balance sheet date, and the lender is financially capable of honoring the agreement.
   Answer (A) is incorrect because the amount excluded cannot exceed the amount available for refinancing. Answer (C) is incorrect because SFAS 6 has no provision for adjustments or reductions. Answer (D) is incorrect because the refinancing need not have occurred if the firm intends and demonstrates an ability to consummate such refinancing.

10. When treasury stock is accounted for at cost, the cost is reported on the balance sheet as a(n)

A. Asset.

B. Reduction of retained earnings.

C. Reduction of additional paid-in-capital.

D. Unallocated reduction of shareholders' equity.

The correct answer is (D). *(CMA 695 2-18)*

REQUIRED: The reporting of treasury stock.

DISCUSSION: Treasury stock is a corporation's own stock that has been reacquired but not retired. The entry to record the acquisition of treasury stock accounted for at cost is to debit a contra shareholders' equity account and to credit cash. In the balance sheet, treasury stock recorded at cost is subtracted from the total of the capital stock balances, additional paid-in capital, and retained earnings. It is not allocated. If treasury stock is recorded at par, it is a direct reduction of common stock, not total shareholders' equity.

Answer (A) is incorrect because treasury stock is not an asset. A corporation cannot own itself. Answers (B) and (C) are incorrect because treasury stock accounted for at cost is subtracted from the total of the other shareholders' equity accounts.

B. Income Statement

11. APB 9, *Reporting the Results of Operations*, concludes that the all-inclusive income statement concept

A. Is synonymous with the current operating concept, and that both are acceptable per GAAP.

B. Is ordinarily more appropriate than the current operating concept.

C. Is not appropriate. The current operating concept is appropriate under GAAP.

D. Produces an interactive income statement that avoids the problems associated with the changing value of currencies.

The correct answer is (B). *(Publisher)*

REQUIRED: The true statement about the all-inclusive income statement concept.

DISCUSSION: In the calculation of net income, the all-inclusive concept of income includes all income transactions that either increase or decrease owners' equity during the current period. The current operating concept only includes ordinary, normal, recurring operations in the net income of the current period. Other items are direct adjustments to retained earnings. APB 9 follows the all-inclusive concept except for the rare transaction treated as a prior-period adjustment.

Answers (A) and (C) are incorrect because the current operating concept is not consistent with GAAP. Answer (D) is incorrect because an "interactive income statement" does not exist in financial accounting.

12. An income statement for a business prepared under the current operating performance concept would include only the recurring earnings from its normal operations and

A. No other items.

B. Any extraordinary items.

C. Any prior-period adjustments.

D. Any gains or losses from extinguishment of debt.

The correct answer is (A). *(CMA 684 3-15)*

REQUIRED: The items included in a current operating performance income statement.

DISCUSSION: The current operating performance concept emphasizes the ordinary, normal, recurring operations of the entity during the current period. Inclusion of extraordinary items or prior-period adjustments is believed to impair the significance of net income.

Answers (B) and (C) are incorrect because extraordinary items and prior-period adjustments are excluded under the current operating performance concept. Answer (D) is incorrect because gains and losses from extinguishment of debt are extraordinary.

13. Select the best order for the following items appearing in income statements:

1. Cumulative effect of change in accounting principle
2. Extraordinary items
3. Income from continuing operations
4. Discontinued operations
5. Prior-period adjustments
6. Taxes on income from continuing operations
7. Dividends
8. Net income
9. Revenues
10. Expenses
11. Income from continuing operations before income tax

   A. 9 - 10 - 8 - 7 - 6 - 2 - 4

   B. 8 - 6 - 7 - 1 - 2 - 5

   C. 9 - 10 - 8 - 6 - 3 - 2 - 1 - 4

   D. 9 - 10 - 11 - 6 - 3 - 4 - 2 - 1 - 8

The correct answer is (D). *(Publisher)*
   REQUIRED: The order of items in income statements.
   DISCUSSION: The order of income statement items is

9. Revenues
10. Expenses
11. Income from continuing operations before income tax
6. Taxes on income from continuing operations
3. Income from continuing operations
4. Discontinued operations
2. Extraordinary items
1. Cumulative effect of change in accounting principle
8. Net income

Prior-period adjustments (5) and dividends (7) appear only in retained earnings statements.
   Answers (A), (B), and (C) are incorrect because net income is the final amount presented, and dividends and prior-period adjustments are not included in the income statement. Moreover, certain items are in the wrong order and some are missing.

14. A company decided to sell a line of its business. The assets were sold for $100,000 and had a net book value of $70,000. The applicable tax rate was 20%. The result of this transaction will appear on the

   A. Balance sheet as a prior-period adjustment.

   B. Income statement as an extraordinary item.

   C. Income statement as discontinued operations.

   D. Income statement as an accounting change.

The correct answer is (C). *(CIA 592 IV-36)*
   REQUIRED: The reporting of a sale of a line of business.
   DISCUSSION: The results of operations of a segment that has been or will be discontinued, together with any gain or loss on disposal, should be reported separately as a component of income before extraordinary items and the cumulative effect of accounting changes. Income from discontinued operations and the gain or loss on disposal should each be disclosed net of tax.
   Answer (A) is incorrect because gain or loss from discontinued operations appears on the income statement. Answer (B) is incorrect because discontinued operations is a separate caption in the income statement just before extraordinary items. Answer (D) is incorrect because disposal of a segment is not a change in accounting principle.

15. The gain or loss from disposal of a segment

   A. Includes the operating gain or loss realized by the segment from the beginning of the fiscal year to the disposal date.

   B. Is reported as an addition to or subtraction from the beginning balance of retained earnings on the statement of retained earnings.

   C. Is reported as an extraordinary item on the income statement.

   D. Is reported as a component of net income and distinguished from the operating gain or loss realized by the segment prior to the measurement date.

The correct answer is (D). *(CMA 693 2-22)*
   REQUIRED: The true statement about the gain or loss from disposal of a segment.
   DISCUSSION: Discontinued operations should be presented as two subcategories. The first is operating income or loss of the segment prior to the measurement date. The second is the gain or loss on disposal. The gain or loss on disposal includes estimated operating income or loss of the segment from the measurement date to the disposal date, any direct disposal costs incurred during the phase-out period, and the estimated gain or loss on the actual disposal.
   Answer (A) is incorrect because the operating gain or loss for the partial period is not combined with the gain or loss on disposal. Answer (B) is incorrect because gain or loss on disposal is reported on the income statement, not the retained earnings statement. Answer (C) is incorrect because gain or loss on disposal is reported in a discontinued operations section prior to extraordinary items.

16. When reporting the discontinuance of a business segment, APB 30, *Reporting the Results of Operations*, specifies that

A. The results of the segment operations during the phase-out period be reported as part of the gain or loss from continuing operations.

B. The gain or loss on discontinued operations be reported net of tax as a separate item before extraordinary items.

C. The costs directly associated with discontinuance be included as an expense of continuing operations.

D. All gains or losses expected from discontinuance be reported at the measurement date even though the disposal date is in a subsequent period.

The correct answer is (B). *(CMA 687 3-5)*
REQUIRED: The true statement about discontinued operations reporting requirements.
DISCUSSION: The results of operations of a segment that has been or will be discontinued, together with any gain or loss on disposal, should be reported separately as a component of income before extraordinary items and the cumulative effect of accounting changes. Income from discontinued operations and the gain or loss on disposal should each be disclosed net of tax.
Answer (A) is incorrect because operating results during the phase-out period are part of the gain (loss) on disposal. Answer (C) is incorrect because the direct costs of discontinuance are included in the gain (loss) on the actual disposal. Answer (D) is incorrect because losses are to be reported at the measurement date even if the disposal date is in a subsequent period. Gains are not to be recognized until realized.

17. A loss that is material, unusual in nature, and infrequent in occurrence should be reported as

A. Part of continuing operations.

B. Part of discontinued operations.

C. An extraordinary item.

D. A prior-period item.

The correct answer is (C). *(CIA 1193 IV-32)*
REQUIRED: The proper reporting of a loss that is material, unusual in nature, and infrequent in occurrence.
DISCUSSION: APB 30 defines an extraordinary item as one which occurs infrequently and is unusual in nature in the environment in which the entity operates. It must also be material to merit separate classification.
Answer (A) is incorrect because the loss should be treated as extraordinary. It is both infrequent and unusual. Answer (B) is incorrect because no operations have been discontinued. Answer (D) is incorrect because errors are accounted for as prior-period adjustments. Furthermore, this item is presumably current.

18. Which one of the following material events would be classified as an extraordinary item on an income statement?

A. A loss due to the effects of a strike against a major supplier.

B. A gain or loss on the disposal of a portion of the business.

C. A gain or loss from the extinguishment of debt.

D. A gain or loss from the translation of foreign currency due to a major devaluation.

The correct answer is (C). *(CMA 694 2-29)*
REQUIRED: The event classified as an extraordinary item on the income statement.
DISCUSSION: APB 30 gives examples of certain transactions that are not to be considered extraordinary items. These include write-downs of receivables and inventories, translation of foreign exchange, disposal of a business segment, disposal of productive assets, the effects of strikes, and the adjustments of accruals on long-term contracts. A gain or loss on the early extinguishment of debt is to be shown as an extraordinary item under the provisions of SFAS 4.
Answers (A), (B), and (D) are incorrect because APB 30 specifically excludes a loss due to the effects of a strike against a major supplier, a gain or loss on the disposal of a portion of the business, and a gain or loss from the translation of foreign currency due to a major devaluation from the definition of extraordinary items.

19. APB 30, *Reporting the Results of Operations*, recommends which of the following policies regarding extraordinary items?

   A.   Earnings per share data should be presented in a separate schedule.

   B.   Extraordinary items should always be presented as an aggregate amount.

   C.   Income taxes applicable to extraordinary items should be presented in a separate schedule.

   D.   Earnings per share data should be presented on the face of the income statement.

The correct answer is (D). *(Publisher)*
   REQUIRED: The policy recommended by APB 30 regarding extraordinary items.
   DISCUSSION: Paragraph 9 of APB 30 requires that EPS data for income from continuing operations and for net income, computed under APB 15, *Earnings Per Share*, be presented on the face of the income statement.
   Answer (A) is incorrect because EPS data should be presented on the face of the income statements. EPS data for the results of discontinued operations and for gain or loss from disposal of a segment may be presented in a related note if not on the face of the income statement. Answer (B) is incorrect because extraordinary items should be presented individually rather than in the aggregate, and on the face of the income statement, if practicable; otherwise, disclosure in related footnotes is acceptable. Answer (C) is incorrect because extraordinary item income tax data should be presented on the face of the income statement or in a related note.

20. When reporting extraordinary items,

   A.   Each item (net of tax) is presented on the face of the income statement separately as a component of net income for the period.

   B.   Each item is presented exclusive of any related income tax.

   C.   Each item is presented as an unusual item within income from continuing operations.

   D.   All extraordinary gains or losses that occur in a period are summarized as total gains and total losses, then offset to present the net extraordinary gain or loss.

The correct answer is (A). *(CMA 693 2-24)*
   REQUIRED: The true statement about the reporting of extraordinary items.
   DISCUSSION: Extraordinary items should be presented net of tax after income from operations. APB 30 states, "Descriptive captions and the amounts for individual extraordinary events or transactions should be presented, preferably on the face of the income statement, if practicable; otherwise, disclosure in related notes is acceptable."
   Answer (B) is incorrect because extraordinary items are to be reported net of the related tax effect. Answer (C) is incorrect because extraordinary items are not reported in the continuing operations section of the income statement. Answer (D) is incorrect because each extraordinary item is to be reported separately.

21. Which one of the following items is included in the determination of income from continuing operations?

   A.   Discontinued operations.

   B.   Extraordinary loss.

   C.   Cumulative effect of a change in an accounting principle.

   D.   Unusual loss from a write-down of inventory.

The correct answer is (D). *(CMA 688 4-18)*
   REQUIRED: The item included in the computation of income from continuing operations.
   DISCUSSION: APB 30 specifies certain items that are not to be treated as extraordinary gains and losses. Rather, they are included in the determination of income from continuing operations. These include write-downs of receivables and inventories, translation of foreign currency, disposal of a business segment, sale of productive assets, effects of strikes, and accruals on long-term contracts. A write-down of inventory is therefore included in the computation of income from continuing operations.
   Answers (A), (B), and (C) are incorrect because discontinued operations, extraordinary loss, and cumulative effect of a change in an accounting principle are reported separately from income from continuing operations.

22. The major distinction between the multiple-step and single-step income statement formats is the separation of

A. Operating and nonoperating data.

B. Income tax expense and administrative expenses.

C. Cost of goods sold expense and administrative expenses.

D. The effect on income taxes due to extraordinary items and the effect on income taxes due to income before extraordinary items.

The correct answer is (A). *(CIA 590 IV-32)*

REQUIRED: The major distinction between the multiple-step and single-step income statement formats.

DISCUSSION: Within the income from continuing operations classification, the single-step income statement provides one grouping for revenue items and one for expense items. The single-step is the one subtraction necessary to arrive at income from continuing operations prior to the effect of income taxes. In contrast, the multiple-step income statement matches operating revenues and expenses separately from nonoperating items. This format emphasizes subtotals such as gross margin, operating income, and nonoperating income within presentation of income from continuing operations.

Answers (B), (C), and (D) are incorrect because the major distinction is the separation of operating and nonoperating data.

23. In a multiple-step income statement for a retail company, all of the following would be included in the operating section except

A. Sales.

B. Cost of goods sold.

C. Dividend revenue.

D. Administrative and selling expenses.

The correct answer is (C). *(CMA 690 3-5)*

REQUIRED: The item excluded from the operating section of a multiple-step income statement of a retailer.

DISCUSSION: The operating section of a retailer's income statement includes all revenues and costs necessary for the operation of the retail establishment, e.g., sales, cost of goods sold, administrative expenses, and selling expenses. Dividend revenue, however, is classified under other revenues. In a statement of cash flows, cash dividends received are considered an operating cash flow.

Answers (A), (B), and (D) are incorrect because sales, cost of goods sold, and administrative and selling expenses are all part of the normal operations of a retailer.

24. During its recently completed fiscal year, a company incurred the following selling and general and administrative expenses:

Insurance	$50,000
Wages of office staff	150,000
Advertising	300,000
Commissions	25,000
Shipping costs	20,000
Office rental	80,000
Collection costs	10,000
Audit and legal fees	60,000

If 25% of the office space is used by the sales department, the total of general and administrative expenses is

A. $375,000

B. $320,000

C. $300,000

D. $260,000

The correct answer is (B). *(Publisher)*

REQUIRED: The total of general and administrative expenses.

DISCUSSION: General and administrative expenses are incurred for the direction of the enterprise as a whole and are not related wholly to a specific function, e.g., selling or manufacturing. They include accounting, legal, and other fees for professional services; officers' salaries; insurance; wages of office staff; miscellaneous supplies; and office occupancy costs. Selling expenses are those incurred in selling or marketing. Examples include sales representatives' salaries, rent for sales department, commissions, and traveling expense; advertising; selling department salaries and expenses; samples; and credit and collection costs. Shipping costs are also often classified as selling costs. Thus, the total of general and administrative expenses is $320,000 [$50,000 insurance + $150,000 wages of office staff + (75% x $80,000 office rental) + $60,000 audit and legal fees].

Answer (A) is incorrect because $375,000 equals total selling expenses. Answer (C) is incorrect because $300,000 equals the advertising costs. Answer (D) is incorrect because $260,000 omits the audit and legal fees.

C. Statement of Cash Flows

25. A statement of cash flows is to be presented in general purpose external financial statements by which of the following?

A. Publicly held business enterprises only.

B. Privately held business enterprises only.

C. All business enterprises.

D. All business enterprises and not-for-profit organizations.

The correct answer is (D). *(Publisher)*
REQUIRED: The entities required to present a statement of cash flows.
DISCUSSION: SFAS 95 as amended by SFAS 117 requires a statement of cash flows as part of a full set of financial statements of all business entities (both publicly held and privately held) and not-for-profit organizations. Defined benefit pension plans, certain other employee benefit plans, and certain highly liquid investment companies, however, are exempted from this requirement by SFAS 102.
Answers (A), (B), and (C) are incorrect because all business entities and not-for-profit organizations are required to present a statement of cash flows.

26. A corporation issues a balance sheet and income statement for the current year and comparative income statements for each of the 2 previous years. Under SFAS 95, a statement of cash flows

A. Should be issued for the current year only.

B. Should be issued for the current and the previous year only.

C. Should be issued for all 3 years.

D. May be issued at the company's option for any or all of the 3 years.

The correct answer is (C). *(Publisher)*
REQUIRED: The circumstances in which a statement of cash flows should be issued.
DISCUSSION: When a business enterprise provides a set of financial statements that reports both financial position and results of operations, it must also present a statement of cash flows for each period for which the results of operations are provided.
Answers (A) and (B) are incorrect because a statement of cash flows must be provided for all 3 years. Answer (D) is incorrect because the statement of cash flows is not optional in these circumstances.

27. The management of ABC Corporation is analyzing the financial statements of XYZ Corporation because ABC is strongly considering purchasing a block of XYZ common stock that would give ABC significant influence over XYZ. Which financial statement should ABC primarily use to assess the amounts, timing, and uncertainty of future cash flows of XYZ Company?

A. Income statement.

B. Statement of retained earnings.

C. Statement of cash flows.

D. Balance sheet.

The correct answer is (C). *(CIA 1192 IV-30)*
REQUIRED: The financial statement used to assess the amounts, timing, and uncertainty of future cash flows.
DISCUSSION: The primary purpose of a statement of cash flows is to provide information about the cash receipts and cash payments of a business enterprise during a period. This information helps investors, creditors, and other users to assess (1) the enterprise's ability to generate net cash inflows; (2) its ability to meet its obligations, and pay dividends; (3) its needs for external financing; (4) the reasons for the differences between net income and net cash flow; and (5) the effects of cash and noncash financing and investing activities (SFAS 95).
Answer (A) is incorrect because the statement of income is prepared on an accrual basis and is not meant to report cash flows. Answer (B) is incorrect because the statement of retained earnings merely shows the reasons for changes in retained earnings during the reporting period. Answer (D) is incorrect because the balance sheet reports on financial position at a moment in time. It does not provide information about cash flows for the period.

28. A statement of cash flows is intended to help users of financial statements

    A. Evaluate a firm's liquidity, solvency, and financial flexibility.

    B. Evaluate a firm's economic resources and obligations.

    C. Determine a firm's components of income from operations.

    D. Determine whether insiders have sold or purchased the firm's stock.

The correct answer is (A). *(CMA 1295 2-5)*
REQUIRED: The reason companies are required to prepare a statement of cash flows.
DISCUSSION: The primary purpose of a statement of cash flows is to provide information about the cash receipts and payments of an entity during a period. If used with information in the other financial statements, the statement of cash flows should help users to assess the entity's ability to generate positive future net cash flows (liquidity), its ability to meet obligations (solvency) and pay dividends, the need for external financing, the reasons for differences between income and cash receipts and payments, and the cash and noncash aspects of the investing and financing activities.
    Answer (B) is incorrect because the statement of cash flows deals with only one resource--cash. Answer (C) is incorrect because the income statement shows the components of income from operations. Answer (D) is incorrect because the identity of stock buyers and sellers is not shown.

29. Which of the following items is specifically included in the body of a statement of cash flows?

    A. Operating and nonoperating cash flow information.

    B. Conversion of debt to equity.

    C. Acquiring an asset through a capital lease.

    D. Purchasing a building by giving a mortgage to the seller.

The correct answer is (A). *(CMA 1288 4-19)*
REQUIRED: The information specifically included within the body of a statement of cash flows.
DISCUSSION: SFAS 95 excludes all noncash transactions from the body of the statement of cash flows to avoid undue complexity and detraction from the objective of providing information about cash flows. Information about all noncash financing and investing activities affecting recognized assets and liabilities shall be reported in related disclosures.
    Answers (B), (C), and (D) are incorrect because SFAS 95 specifically excludes noncash transactions from the body of the statement of cash flows.

30. A financial statement includes all of the following items: net income, depreciation, operating activities, and financing activities. What financial statement is this?

    A. Balance sheet.

    B. Income statement.

    C. Statement of cash flows.

    D. Statement of shareholders' equity.

The correct answer is (C). *(CIA 592 IV-35)*
REQUIRED: The financial statement that includes net income, depreciation, operating activities, and financing activities.
DISCUSSION: A statement of cash flows is a required financial statement. Its primary purpose is to provide information about cash receipts and payments by reporting the cash effects of an enterprise's operating, investing, and financing activities. Related disclosures report the effects of noncash investing and financing activities. Because the statement or a separate schedule reconciles net income and net operating cash flow, depreciation, a noncash expense, is included in the presentation.
    Answer (A) is incorrect because the balance sheet does not include periodic net income or depreciation expense. Answer (B) is incorrect because the income statement does not have captions for operating and financing activities. Answer (D) is incorrect because shareholders' equity does not include captions for operating and investing activities, depreciation, and net income.

31. Select the combination below that explains the impact of credit card interest incurred and paid during the period on (1) owners' equity on the balance sheet, and (2) the statement of cash flows.

	(1) Effect on Owners' Equity on Balance Sheet	(2) Reflected on Statement of Cash Flows as a(n)
A.	Decrease	Financing outflow
B.	Decrease	Operating outflow
C.	No effect	Financing outflow
D.	No effect	Operating outflow

The correct answer is (B). *(CIA 1193 IV-33)*
REQUIRED: The effect of interest expense on the balance sheet and cash flow statement.
DISCUSSION: Credit card interest incurred is classified as interest expense on the income statement, which in turn reduces owners' equity on the balance sheet by reducing retained earnings. Cash payments to lenders and other creditors for interest, e.g., credit card interest payments, are to be classified on the statement of cash flows as an outflow of cash from operating activities.
Answers (A), (C), and (D) are incorrect because credit card interest charges reduce owners' equity, and interest payments are classified as an operating outflow on the statement of cash flows.

32. SFAS 95, *Statements of Cash Flows*, classifies cash receipts and cash payments as arising from operating, investing, and financing activities. All of the following should be classified as investing activities except

A. Cash outflows to purchase manufacturing equipment.
B. Cash inflows from the sale of bonds of other entities.
C. Cash outflows to lenders for interest.
D. Cash inflows from the sale of a manufacturing plant.

The correct answer is (C). *(CMA 1293 2-29)*
REQUIRED: The cash flow not from an investing activity.
DISCUSSION: Investing activities include the lending of money and the collecting of those loans; the acquisition, sale, or other disposal of debt or equity instruments; and the acquisition, sale, or other disposition of assets (excluding inventory) that are held for or used in the production of goods or services. Investing activities do not include acquiring and disposing of certain loans or other debt or equity instruments that are acquired specifically for resale. Cash outflows to lenders for interest are cash from an operating, not an investing, activity.
Answers (A), (B), and (D) are incorrect because the purchase of equipment, the sale of bonds issued by another entity, and the sale of a plant are investing activities.

33. In the statement of cash flows, the payment of common share dividends appears in the <List A> activities section as a <List B> of cash.

	List A	List B
A.	Operating	Source
B.	Financing	Use
C.	Investing	Use
D.	Investing	Source

The correct answer is (B). *(CIA 1195 IV-34)*
REQUIRED: The treatment of cash dividends in a statement of cash flows.
DISCUSSION: Financing activities include, among other things, obtaining resources from owners and providing them with a return on, and a return of, their investment. Consequently, the payment of cash dividends to providers of common equity financing is a use of cash that appears in the financing section of the statement of cash flows.
Answers (A), (C), and (D) are incorrect because payment of cash dividends is a use of cash for a financing activity.

34. SFAS 95, *Statement of Cash Flows*, classifies business transactions into operating, investing, and financing activities. Which one of the following transactions should be classified as a financing activity?

A. Purchase of equipment.
B. Purchase of treasury stock.
C. Sale of trademarks.
D. Income tax refund.

The correct answer is (B). *(CMA 695 2-21)*
REQUIRED: The financing activity.
DISCUSSION: SFAS 95 defines financing activities to include obtaining resources from owners and providing them with a return on, and a return of, their investment. Cash inflows from financing activities include proceeds from issuing equity instruments. Cash outflows include outlays to reacquire the enterprise's equity instruments. Thus, purchases and sales of treasury stock are financing activities.
Answer (A) is incorrect because purchasing equipment is an investing activity. Answer (C) is incorrect because the sale of trademarks is an investing activity. Answer (D) is incorrect because an income tax refund is an operating activity.

35. Which of the following related cash transactions should be disclosed as gross amounts of cash receipts and cash payments rather than as net amounts?

A. The purchase and sale of fixed assets.

B. Changes in cash and cash equivalents.

C. The purchase and sale of federal funds.

D. The receipts and payments from demand deposits.

The correct answer is (A). *(Publisher)*

REQUIRED: The related receipts and payments that should be classified as gross amounts.

DISCUSSION: In general, cash inflows and cash outflows from operating, investing, and financing activities should be reported separately at gross amounts in a statement of cash flows. In certain instances, however, the net amount of related cash receipts and cash payments may provide sufficient information about particular classes of cash flows. For example, SFAS 104 permits banks, saving institutions, and credit unions to report net amounts for (1) the placement and withdrawal of deposits with other financial institutions, (2) the acceptance and repayment of time deposits, and (3) the making of loans to customers and the collection of principal.

Answers (B), (C), and (D) are incorrect because changes in cash and cash equivalents, the purchase and sale of federal funds, and the receipts and payments from demand deposits are classes of related cash flows that may be presented as net amounts.

36. The following information was taken from the accounting records of Oak Corporation for the year ended December 31, 1996:

Proceeds from issuance of preferred stock	$4,000,000
Dividends paid on preferred stock	400,000
Bonds payable converted to common stock	2,000,000
Payment for purchase of machinery	500,000
Proceeds from sale of plant building	1,200,000
2% stock dividend on common stock	300,000
Gain on sale of plant building	200,000

The net cash flows from investing and financing activities that should be presented on Oak's statement of cash flows for the year December 31, 1996, are, respectively

A. $700,000 and $3,600,000

B. $700,000 and $3,900,000

C. $900,000 and $3,900,000

D. $900,000 and $3,600,000

The correct answer is (A). *(CMA 1294 2-21)*

REQUIRED: The respective net cash flows from investing and financing activities.

DISCUSSION: Investing activities include the lending of money and the collecting of those loans, and the acquisition, sale, or other disposal of securities that are not cash equivalents and of productive assets that are expected to generate revenue over a long period of time. Financing activities include the issuance of stock, the payment of dividends, treasury stock transactions, the issuance of debt, the receipt of donor-restricted resources to be used for long-term purposes, and the repayment or other settlement of debt obligations. Investing activities include the purchase of machinery and the sale of a building. The net inflow from these activities is $700,000 ($1,200,000 − $500,000). Financing activities include the issuance of preferred stock and the payment of dividends. The net inflow is $3,600,000 ($4,000,000 − $400,000). The conversion of bonds into common stock and the stock dividend do not affect cash.

Answer (B) is incorrect because the stock dividend is a noncash transaction. Answers (C) and (D) are incorrect because the gain on the sale of the building is double counted in determining the net cash flow from investing activities.

Questions 37 through 39 are based on the following information. Royce Company had the following transactions during the fiscal year ended December 31, 1996:

- Accounts receivable decreased from $115,000 on December 31, 1995 to $100,000 on December 31, 1996.
- Royce's board of directors declared dividends on December 31, 1996 of $.05 per share on the 2.8 million shares outstanding, payable to shareholders of record on January 31, 1997. The company did not declare or pay dividends for fiscal year 1995.

- Sold a truck with a net book value of $7,000 for $5,000 cash, reporting a loss of $2,000.
- Paid interest to bondholders of $780,000.
- The cash balance was $106,000 on December 31, 1995 and $284,000 on December 31, 1996.

37. Royce Company uses the direct method to prepare its statement of cash flows at December 31, 1996. The interest paid to bondholders is reported in the

A. Financing section, as a use or outflow of cash.

B. Operating section, as a use or outflow of cash.

C. Investing section, as a use or outflow of cash.

D. Debt section, as a use or outflow of cash.

The correct answer is (B). *(CMA 1295 2-2)*
REQUIRED: The proper reporting of interest paid.
DISCUSSION: Payment of interest on debt is considered an operating activity, although repayment of debt principal is a financing activity.
Answer (A) is incorrect because interest paid on bonds is an operating cash flow. Answer (C) is incorrect because investing activities include the lending of money and the acquisition, sale, or other disposal of securities that are not cash equivalents and the acquisition, sale, or other disposal of long-lived productive assets. Answer (D) is incorrect because SFAS 95 does not provide for a debt section.

38. Royce Company uses the indirect method to prepare its 1996 statement of cash flows. It reports a(n)

A. Source or inflow of funds of $5,000 from the sale of the truck in the financing section.

B. Use or outflow of funds of $140,000 in the financing section, representing dividends.

C. Deduction of $15,000 in the operating section, representing the decrease in year-end accounts receivable.

D. Addition of $2,000 in the operating section for the $2,000 loss on the sale of the truck.

The correct answer is (D). *(CMA 1295 2-3)*
REQUIRED: The correct presentation of an item on a statement of cash flows prepared under the indirect method.
DISCUSSION: The indirect method determines net operating cash flow by adjusting net income. Under the indirect method, the $5,000 cash inflow from the sale of the truck is shown in the investing section. A $2,000 loss was recognized and properly deducted to determine net income. This loss, however, did not require the use of cash and should be added to net income in the operating section.
Answer (A) is incorrect because, under the provisions of SFAS 95, the $5,000 inflow would be shown in the investing section. Answer (B) is incorrect because no outflow of cash dividends occurred in 1996. Answer (C) is incorrect because the decrease in receivables should be added to net income.

39. The total of cash provided (used) by operating activities plus cash provided (used) by investing activities plus cash provided (used) by financing activities is

A. Cash provided of $284,000.

B. Cash provided of $178,000.

C. Cash used of $582,000.

D. Equal to net income reported for fiscal year ended December 31, 1996.

The correct answer is (B). *(CMA 1295 2-4)*
REQUIRED: The net total of cash provided and used.
DISCUSSION: The total of cash provided and/or used by the three activities (operating, investing, and financing) should equal the increase or decrease in cash for the year. During 1996, the cash balance increased from $106,000 to $284,000. Thus, the sources of cash must have exceeded the uses by $178,000.
Answer (A) is incorrect because $284,000 is the ending cash balance, not the change in the cash balance; it ignores the beginning balance. Answer (C) is incorrect because the cash balance increased during the year. Answer (D) is incorrect because net income must be adjusted for noncash expenses and other accruals and deferrals.

40. With respect to the content and form of the statement of cash flows,

A. The pronouncements covering the cash flow statement encourage the use of the indirect method.

B. The indirect method adjusts ending retained earnings to reconcile it to net cash flows from operations.

C. The direct method of reporting cash flows from operating activities includes disclosing the major classes of gross cash receipts and gross cash payments.

D. The reconciliation of the net income to net operating cash flow need not be presented when using the direct method.

The correct answer is (C). *(CMA 693 2-13)*
REQUIRED: The true statement about the content and form of the statement of cash flows.
DISCUSSION: SFAS 95 encourages use of the direct method of reporting major classes of operating cash receipts and payments, but the indirect method may be used. The minimum disclosures of operating cash flows under the direct method are cash collected from customers, interest and dividends received, other operating cash receipts, cash paid to employees and other suppliers of goods or services, interest paid, income taxes paid, and other operating cash payments.
Answer (A) is incorrect because SFAS 95 encourages use of the direct method. Answer (B) is incorrect because the indirect method reconciles net income with the net cash flow from operations. Answer (D) is incorrect because the reconciliation is required regardless of the method used.

41. The statement of cash flows may be presented in either a direct or an indirect (reconciliation) format. In which of these formats would cash collected from customers be presented as a gross amount?

	Direct	Indirect
A.	No	No
B.	No	Yes
C.	Yes	Yes
D.	Yes	No

The correct answer is (D). *(R. O'Keefe)*
REQUIRED: The format in which cash collected from customers would be presented as a gross amount.
DISCUSSION: The statement of cash flows may report cash flows from operating activities in either an indirect (reconciliation) or a direct format. The direct format reports the major classes of operating cash receipts and cash payments as gross amounts. The indirect presentation reconciles net income to the same amount of net cash flow from operations that would be determined in accordance with the direct method. To arrive at net operating cash flow, the indirect method adjusts net income by removing the effects of (1) all deferrals of past operating cash receipts and payments, (2) all accruals of expected future operating cash receipts and payments, (3) all financing and investing activities, and (4) all noncash operating transactions.
Answers (A), (B), and (C) are incorrect because only the direct method format for the statement of cash flows presents cash collected from customers as a gross amount.

42. SFAS 95, *Statement of Cash Flows*, classifies business transactions into operating, investing, and financing activities. All of the following should be included in the reconciliation of net income to net operating cash flow except a(n)

A. Decrease in inventory.

B. Decrease in prepaid insurance.

C. Purchase of land and building in exchange for a long-term note.

D. Increase in income tax payable.

The correct answer is (C). *(CMA 695 2-20)*
REQUIRED: The item not included in a reconciliation of net income to net operating cash flow.
DISCUSSION: The purchase of land and a building in exchange for a long-term note is a noncash investing activity that does not affect net income. Thus, it is reported in the related disclosures section of the cash flow statement but is not a reconciling item.
Answer (A) is incorrect because a decrease in inventory is a reconciling item. It indicates that cost of goods sold exceeded purchases. Purchases is then adjusted for the change in accounts payable to determine cash paid to suppliers. Answer (B) is incorrect because a decrease in prepaid insurance is a reconciling item. It implies that insurance expense was greater than cash paid to insurers. Answer (D) is incorrect because an increase in income tax payable is a reconciling item. It means that income tax expense exceeded cash paid for income taxes.

43. When using the indirect method to prepare a statement of cash flows, net cash flows from operating activities are determined by adding back or deducting from net income those items that had no effect on cash. Which one of the following items should be deducted from net income when determining net cash flows from operating activities?

A. An increase in accrued liabilities.

B. Amortization of bond premiums.

C. A loss on the sale of plant assets.

D. A decrease in accounts receivable.

The correct answer is (B). *(CMA 1293 2-30)*

REQUIRED: The item deducted in reconciling net income with net operating cash flow.

DISCUSSION: The indirect presentation begins with net income. It then removes from net income the effects of all past deferrals of operating cash receipts and payments, all accruals of expected future operating cash receipts and payments, and net income items not affecting operating cash flows to arrive at the net cash flow from operating activities. For example, the amortization of bond premium by the issuer involves a debit to premium on bonds payable and a credit to interest expense. Hence, the issuer's income is greater because of the amortization (a noncash item). (For the investor, however, the amortization of premium is a noncash reduction of interest income that must be added back to net income in the reconciliation.) On the cash flow statement, the amortization must be subtracted from net income to arrive at the net operating cash flow.

Answer (A) is incorrect because an increase in accrued liabilities is added to net income. It implies that cash paid to suppliers of goods and services was less than the costs included in the determination of net income. Answer (C) is incorrect because the loss is from an investing, not an operating activity. Answer (D) is incorrect because a decrease in accounts receivable is added to net income. It indicates that cash collections from receivables exceeded sales.

44. When using the indirect method to prepare the statement of cash flows, the amortization of goodwill should be presented as a(n)

A. Cash flow from investing activities.

B. Deduction from net income.

C. Addition to net income.

D. Investing and financing activity not affecting cash.

The correct answer is (C). *(CMA 1294 2-18)*

REQUIRED: The treatment of goodwill amortization in a statement of cash flows based on the indirect method.

DISCUSSION: The statement of cash flows may report operating activities in the form of either an indirect or a direct presentation. The indirect presentation removes from net income the effects of past deferrals of past operating cash flows, all accruals of expected future operating cash flows, and net income items not affecting operating cash flows. The result is net operating cash flow. Goodwill amortization is a noncash expense and should be added to net income.

Answer (A) is incorrect because goodwill amortization is not a cash flow. Answer (B) is incorrect because goodwill amortization is added to net income. Answer (D) is incorrect because goodwill amortization must be included in the reconciliation of net income to net operating cash flow.

45. Depreciation expense is added to net income under the indirect method of preparing a statement of cash flows in order to

A. Report all assets at gross book value.

B. Ensure depreciation has been properly reported.

C. Reverse noncash charges deducted from net income.

D. Calculate net book value.

The correct answer is (C). *(CMA 1295 2-1)*

REQUIRED: The reason depreciation expense is added to net income under the indirect method.

DISCUSSION: The indirect method begins with net income and then removes the effects of past deferrals of operating cash receipts and payments, accruals of expected future operating cash receipts and payments, and net income items not affecting operating cash flows (e.g., depreciation).

Answer (A) is incorrect because assets other than cash are not shown on the statement of cash flows. Answer (B) is incorrect because depreciation is recorded on the income statement. On the statement of cash flows, depreciation is added back to net income because it was previously deducted on the income statement. Answer (D) is incorrect because net book value of assets is shown on the balance sheet, not the statement of cash flows.

46. In reconciling net income on an accrual basis to net cash provided by operating activities, what adjustment is needed to net income because of (1) an increase during the period in prepaid expenses and (2) the periodic amortization of premium on bonds payable?

	(1) Increase in Prepaid Expenses	(2) Amortization of Premium on Bonds Payable
A.	Add	Add
B.	Add	Deduct
C.	Deduct	Add
D.	Deduct	Deduct

The correct answer is (D). *(CIA 593 IV-44)*

REQUIRED: The adjustments to reconcile accrual basis net income to cash provided by operating activities.

DISCUSSION: An increase in prepaid expenses indicates that cash outlays for expenses exceeded the related expense incurred; thus, net income exceeded net cash provided by operations and a deduction is needed in the reconciliation. Also, the amortization of premium on bonds payable causes a reduction of interest expense but does not increase cash; therefore, net income exceeds net cash from operating activities, and a deduction is needed in the reconciliation.

Answers (A), (B), and (C) are incorrect because both the increase in prepaid expenses and amortization of premium on bonds payable require a deduction from net income in the reconciliation.

47. In its statement of cash flows issued for the year ending June 30, Prince Company reported a net cash inflow from operating activities of $123,000. The following adjustments were included in the supplementary schedule reconciling cash flow from operating activities with net income:

Depreciation	$38,000
Increase in net accounts receivable	31,000
Decrease in inventory	27,000
Increase in accounts payable	48,000
Increase in interest payable	12,000

Net income is

A. $29,000

B. $41,000

C. $79,000

D. $217,000

The correct answer is (A). *(Publisher)*

REQUIRED: The net income given cash flow from operating activities and reconciling adjustments.

DISCUSSION: To derive net income from net cash inflow from operating activities, various adjustments are necessary. The depreciation of $38,000 should be subtracted because it is a noncash item included in the determination of net income. The increase in net accounts receivable of $31,000 should be added because it signifies that sales revenue was greater than the cash collections from customers. The increase in accounts payable should be subtracted because it indicates that purchases were $48,000 greater than cash disbursements to suppliers. The second step of the transformation from cash paid to suppliers to cost of goods sold is to subtract the decrease in inventory. This change means that cost of goods sold was $27,000 greater than purchases. The $12,000 increase in interest payable should also be subtracted because it indicates that interest expense was greater than the cash paid to the lenders. Thus, the net adjustment to net cash inflow from operating activities is –$94,000 (–$38,000 + $31,000 – $27,000 – $48,000 – $12,000). Net income is $29,000 ($123,000 net cash inflow – $94,000 net adjustment).

Answer (B) is incorrect because the increase in interest payable is not subtracted. Answer (C) is incorrect because depreciation and the increase in interest payable are not subtracted. Answer (D) is incorrect because depreciation, the increase in accounts payable, the decrease in inventory, and the increase in interest payable should be subtracted, and the increase in net accounts receivable should be added.

48. The following data were extracted from the financial statements of a company for the year ended December 31, 1996:

Net income	$70,000
Depreciation expense	14,000
Amortization of intangibles	1,000
Decrease in accounts receivable	2,000
Increase in inventories	9,000
Increase in accounts payable	4,000
Increase in plant assets	47,000
Increase in contributed capital	31,000
Decrease in short-term notes payable	55,000

There were no disposals of plant assets during the year. Based on the above, a statement of cash flows will report a net increase in cash of

A. $11,000

B. $17,000

C. $54,000

D. $69,000

The correct answer is (A). *(CIA 1188 IV-33)*
REQUIRED: The net increase in cash as reported on the statement of cash flows.
DISCUSSION: Depreciation and amortization are noncash expenses and are added to net income. A decrease in receivables indicates that cash collections exceed sales on an accrual basis, so it is added to net income. To account for the difference between cost of goods sold (a deduction from income) and cash paid to suppliers, a two-step adjustment of net income is necessary. The difference between cost of goods sold and purchases is the change in inventory. The difference between purchases and the amount paid to suppliers is the change in accounts payable. Accordingly, the conversion of cost of goods sold to cash paid to suppliers requires deducting the inventory increase and adding the accounts payable increase. An increase in plant assets indicates an acquisition of plant assets, causing a decrease in cash, so it is deducted. An increase in contributed capital represents a cash inflow and is added to net income. A decrease in short-term notes payable is deducted from net income because it reflects a cash outflow. Thus, cash increased by $11,000 ($70,000 NI + $14,000 + $1,000 + $2,000 – $9,000 + $4,000 – $47,000 + $31,000 – $55,000).

Answer (B) is incorrect because $17,000 results from subtracting the amortization and the decrease in receivables and adding the increase in inventories. Answer (C) is incorrect because $54,000 results from adjusting net income for the increase in plant assets and the increase in contributed capital only. Answer (D) is incorrect because $69,000 results from not making the adjustments for receivables, inventories, notes payable, and accounts payable.

49. The net income for Cypress Inc. was $3,000,000 for the year ended December 31, 1996. Additional information is as follows:

Depreciation on fixed assets	$1,500,000
Gain from cash sale of land	200,000
Increase in accounts payable	300,000
Dividends paid on preferred stock	400,000

The net cash provided by operating activities in the statement of cash flows for the year ended December 31, 1996, should be

A. $4,200,000

B. $4,500,000

C. $4,600,000

D. $4,800,000

The correct answer is (C). *(CMA 1294 2-20)*
REQUIRED: The net cash provided by operations.
DISCUSSION: Net operating cash flow may be determined by adjusting net income. Depreciation is an expense not directly affecting cash flows that should be added back to net income. The increase in accounts payable is added to net income because it indicates that an expense has been recorded but not paid. The gain on the sale of land is an inflow from an investing, not an operating, activity and should be subtracted from net income. The dividends paid on preferred stock do not affect net income or net cash flow from operating activities and do not require an adjustment. Thus, net cash flow from operations is $4,600,000 ($3,000,000 + $1,500,000 – $200,000 + $300,000).

Answer (A) is incorrect because $4,200,000 equals net income, plus depreciation, minus the increase in accounts payable. Answer (B) is incorrect because $4,500,000 equals net income, plus depreciation. Answer (D) is incorrect because $4,800,000 equals net income, plus depreciation, plus the increase in accounts payable.

50. In the indirect presentation of cash flows from operating activities, net income of a business enterprise is adjusted for noncash revenues, gains, expenses, and losses to determine the cash flows from operating activities. A reconciliation of net cash flows from operating activities to net income

A. Must be reported in the statement of cash flows.

B. Must be presented separately in a related disclosure.

C. May be either reported in the statement of cash flows or presented separately in a related disclosure.

D. Need not be presented.

The correct answer is (C). *(Publisher)*

REQUIRED: The proper reporting of a reconciliation of net cash flows from operating activities to net income.

DISCUSSION: When an indirect presentation of net cash flows from operating activities is made, a reconciliation with net income must be provided for all noncash revenues, gains, expenses, and losses. This reconciliation may be either reported in the statement of cash flows or provided separately in related disclosures, with the statement of cash flows presenting only the net cash flows from operating activities.

Answer (A) is incorrect because the reconciliation may be presented in a related disclosure. Answer (B) is incorrect because the reconciliation may be reported in the statement of cash flows. Answer (D) is incorrect because a reconciliation must be reported in an indirect presentation of the statement of cash flows.

D. Annual Reports

51. Regarding financial accounting for public companies, the role of the Securities and Exchange Commission (SEC) as currently practiced is to

A. Make rules and regulations regarding filings with the SEC but not to regulate annual or quarterly reports to shareholders.

B. Regulate financial disclosures for corporate, state, and municipal reporting.

C. Make rules and regulations pertaining more to disclosure of financial information than to the establishment of accounting recognition and measurement principles.

D. Develop and promulgate most generally accepted accounting principles.

The correct answer is (C). *(CMA 694 2-16)*

REQUIRED: The role of the SEC as it applies to financial accounting for public companies.

DISCUSSION: The SEC has authority to regulate external financial reporting. Nevertheless, its traditional role has been to promote disclosure rather than to exercise its power to establish accounting recognition and measurement principles. Its objective is to allow the accounting profession (through the FASB) to establish principles and then to ensure that corporations abide by those principles. This approach allows investors to evaluate investments for themselves.

Answer (A) is incorrect because the SEC regulates both quarterly and annual reporting. Answer (B) is incorrect because the SEC has no jurisdiction over state and municipal reporting. Answer (D) is incorrect because the SEC has allowed the accounting profession to develop and promulgate GAAP.

52. Form 10-K is filed with the SEC to update the information a company supplied when filing a registration statement under the Securities Exchange Act of 1934. Form 10-K is a report that is filed

A. Annually within 90 days of the end of a company's fiscal year.

B. Semiannually within 30 days of the end of a company's second and fourth fiscal quarters.

C. Quarterly within 45 days of the end of each quarter.

D. Within 15 days of the occurrence of significant events.

The correct answer is (A). *(CMA 1286 3-20)*

REQUIRED: The true statement about filing Form 10-K.

DISCUSSION: Form 10-K is the annual report to the SEC. It must be filed within 90 days after the corporation's year-end. It must contain audited financial statements and be signed by the principal executive, financial, and accounting officers and by a majority of the board. The content is essentially that required in the Basic Information Package.

Answer (B) is incorrect because Form 10-K is an annual report. Answer (C) is incorrect because Form 10-Q is filed quarterly within 45 days of the end of each quarter except for the fourth quarter. Answer (D) is incorrect because Form 8-K is filed within 15 days of the occurrence of significant events.

53. The SEC requires that Form 10-Q be filed within

A.   30 days after the occurrence of a significant event.

B.   45 days after the end of each of the first three quarters.

C.   15 days after the quarterly financial reports are issued.

D.   45 days after the end of each quarter.

The correct answer is (B). *(CMA 694 2-18)*
   REQUIRED: The time when Form 10-Q must be filed.
   DISCUSSION: Form 10-Q is a quarterly report to the SEC that includes condensed, unaudited, interim financial statements. It must be filed for each of the first three quarters of the year within 45 days after the end of the quarter. Form 10-Q need not be filed after the fourth quarter because Form 10-K is due within 90 days after year-end.
   Answers (A) and (C) are incorrect because a registrant has 45 days after the end of each quarter to file Form 10-Q. Answer (D) is incorrect because Form 10-Q has to be filed for the first three quarters of the year.

54. Many firms include 5 or 10 years of financial data in their annual reports. This information

A.   Is the forecast of future business.

B.   Highlights trends in the financial statements.

C.   Highlights inventory valuation methods used by the firm.

D.   Is required by generally accepted accounting principles.

The correct answer is (B). *(CMA 696 2-25)*
   REQUIRED: The true statement about financial data in annual reports.
   DISCUSSION: The information required by the SEC to be reported in Part II of Form 10-K and in the annual report includes a 5-year summary of selected financial data. If trends are relevant, management's discussion and analysis should emphasize the summary. Favorable and unfavorable trends and significant events and uncertainties should be identified.
   Answer (A) is incorrect because the required data are for prior periods. Answer (C) is incorrect because the required data include net sales or operating revenues, income from continuing operations, total assets, long-term obligations, redeemable preferred stock, and cash dividends per share. Answer (D) is incorrect because the data are required by the SEC.

55. The contents of the section of the annual report entitled "Management's Discussion and Analysis" (MD&A) are

A.   Mandated by pronouncements of the Financial Accounting Standards Board.

B.   Mandated by regulations of the Securities and Exchange Commission.

C.   Reviewed by independent auditors.

D.   Mandated by regulations of the Internal Revenue Service.

The correct answer is (B). *(CMA 1295 2-15)*
   REQUIRED: The true statement about the MD&A section of the annual financial report to the SEC.
   DISCUSSION: The contents of the MD&A section are mandated by regulations of the SEC. The MD&A, standard financial statements, summarized financial data for at least 5 years, and other matters must be included in annual reports to shareholders and in Form 10-K filed with the SEC. Forward-looking information in the form of forecasts is encouraged in the MD&A but not required.
   Answers (A) and (D) are incorrect because the MD&A is required by the SEC. Answer (C) is incorrect because auditors are expected to read (not review or audit) the contents of the MD&A to be certain it contains no material inconsistencies with the financial statements.

56. The section of a firm's annual report entitled "Management's Discussion and Analysis" (MD&A)

A.   Includes the company president's letter.

B.   Covers three financial aspects of a firm's business: liquidity, capital resources, and results of operations.

C.   Is a technical analysis of past results and a defense of those results by management.

D.   Covers marketing and product line issues.

The correct answer is (B). *(CMA 1295 2-14)*
   REQUIRED: The contents of the MD&A section of the annual report.
   DISCUSSION: The MD&A is included in SEC filings. It addresses in a nonquantified manner the prospects of a company. The SEC examines it with care to determine that management has disclosed material information affecting the company's future results. Disclosures about commitments and events that may affect operations or liquidity are mandatory. Thus, the MD&A section pertains to liquidity, capital resources, and results of operations.
   Answer (A) is incorrect because the MD&A may be separate from the president's letter. Answer (C) is incorrect because a technical analysis and a defense are not required in the MD&A; the section is more forward looking. Answer (D) is incorrect because the MD&A does not have to include marketing and product line issues.

57. The Securities and Exchange Commission continues to encourage management to provide forward-looking information to users of financial statements and has a safe harbor rule that

A. Protects a company that may present an erroneous forecast as long as the forecast is prepared on a reasonable basis and in good faith.

B. Allows injured users of the forecasted information to sue the company for damages but protects management from personal liability.

C. Delays disclosure of such forward-looking information until all major uncertainties have been resolved.

D. Bars competition from using the information to gain a competitive advantage.

The correct answer is (A). *(CMA 1295 2-11)*
REQUIRED: The true statement about the SEC's safe harbor rule applicable to forward-looking information.
DISCUSSION: The SEC does not require forecasts but encourages companies to issue projections of future economic performance. To encourage the publication of such information in SEC filings, the safe harbor rule was established to protect a company that prepares a forecast on a reasonable basis and in good faith.
Answer (B) is incorrect because both the company and management are protected if the forecast is made in good faith. Answer (C) is incorrect because the objective is to encourage forecasts, not to delay them. Answer (D) is incorrect because anyone may use the forecast information.

58. The SEC has issued Regulation S-K to govern disclosures in filings with the SEC of nonfinancial statement matters. It concerns descriptions of the company's securities, business, properties, and legal proceedings; information about its directors and officers; management's discussion and analysis of financial condition and results of operations; and

A. The form and content of the required financial statements, including interim statements.

B. Unofficial interpretations and practices regarding securities laws disclosure requirements.

C. Guidelines for voluntary financial projections.

D. The determination of the proper registration statement form to be used in any specific public offering of securities.

The correct answer is (C). *(CMA 1285 3-26)*
REQUIRED: The item included under the disclosure requirements of Regulation S-K.
DISCUSSION: In addition to those items mentioned in the body of the question, Regulation S-K also provides guidelines for the filing of projections of future economic performance (financial projections). The SEC encourages, but does not require, the filing of management's projections as a supplement to the historical financial statements.
Answer (A) is incorrect because financial statement disclosures are specified in Regulation S-X, not S-K. Answer (B) is incorrect because unofficial interpretations and practices, if codified at all, are made public through the issuance of Staff Accounting Bulletins (SABs). Answer (D) is incorrect because the proper form is determined by reading the instructions for each of the particular forms.

59. The responsibility for the proper preparation of a company's financial statements rests with its

A. Management.

B. Audit committee.

C. Internal auditors.

D. External auditors.

The correct answer is (A). *(CMA 1284 3-21)*
REQUIRED: The persons ultimately responsible for the proper preparation of a company's financial statements.
DISCUSSION: Management has the responsibility for adoption of sound accounting policies and for establishing and maintaining internal controls that will record, process, summarize, and report transactions, events, and conditions consistent with the assertions in the financial statements. The fairness of the representations made therein is the responsibility of management alone because the transactions and the related assets, liabilities, and equity reflected are within management's direct knowledge and control.
Answers (B), (C), and (D) are incorrect because management is ultimately responsible for the assertions in the financial statements.

60. An audit of the financial statements of Camden Corporation is being conducted by an external auditor. The external auditor is expected to

A. Express an opinion as to the fairness of Camden's financial statements.

B. Express an opinion as to the attractiveness of Camden for investment purposes.

C. Certify to the correctness of Camden's financial statements.

D. Critique the wisdom and legality of Camden's business decisions.

The correct answer is (A). *(CMA 685 3-20)*
REQUIRED: The responsibility of an external auditor for an audit of financial statements.
DISCUSSION: The fourth standard of reporting requires the auditor to express an opinion regarding the financial statements taken as a whole or to assert that an opinion cannot be expressed. The opinion concerns the fairness with which the statements have been presented in conformity with GAAP.
Answer (B) is incorrect because the external auditor does not interpret the financial statement data for investment purposes. Answer (C) is incorrect because the external audit normally cannot be so thorough as to permit a guarantee of correctness. Answer (D) is incorrect because the independent audit attests to the fair presentation of the data in the financial statements, not an evaluation of management decisions.

61. If the financial statements contain a departure from an official pronouncement of the Financial Accounting Standards Board that has a material effect on the financial statements, the auditor must express a(n)

A. Adverse opinion.

B. Qualified opinion.

C. Disclaimer of opinion.

D. An adverse opinion or a qualified opinion.

The correct answer is (D). *(CMA 692 2-30)*
REQUIRED: The opinion an auditor must express when financial statements contain a material departure from GAAP.
DISCUSSION: A qualified opinion states that the financial statements are fairly presented except for the effects of a certain matter. It is expressed when the statements contain a material, unjustified departure from GAAP, but only if an adverse opinion is not appropriate. An adverse opinion is expressed when the financial statements, taken as a whole, are not presented fairly in accordance with GAAP.
Answers (A) and (B) are incorrect because a departure from GAAP may justify either a qualified or an adverse opinion, depending on the circumstances. Answer (C) is incorrect because a disclaimer states that the auditor does not express an opinion. A disclaimer is not appropriate given a material departure from GAAP.

62. If the financial statements taken as a whole are not presented fairly in conformity with generally accepted accounting principles, the auditor must express a(n)

A. Unqualified opinion.

B. Qualified opinion.

C. Except for opinion.

D. Adverse opinion.

The correct answer is (D). *(CMA 688 3-22)*
REQUIRED: The opinion if the statements as a whole are not presented fairly in conformity with GAAP.
DISCUSSION: An auditor must express an adverse opinion when the financial statements taken as a whole are not presented fairly in conformity with GAAP. "An adverse opinion states that the financial statements do not present fairly the financial position or the results of operations or cash flows in conformity with GAAP" (AU 508).
Answer (A) is incorrect because an unqualified opinion can be expressed only when statements are fairly presented in accordance with GAAP. Answers (B) and (C) are incorrect because a qualified (except for) opinion is expressed when, except for the matter to which the qualification relates, the financial statements are presented fairly, in all material respects, in conformity with GAAP.

STUDY UNIT 2: FINANCIAL STATEMENTS: SPECIAL TOPICS

23 pages of outline
62 multiple-choice questions

A. Segment Reporting
B. Asset Depreciation
C. Secured Loans
D. Deferred Taxes
E. Leases
F. Pensions
G. Bonds

H. Common Stock
I. Preferred Stock
J. Retained Earnings
K. Stock-Based Compensation
L. Stock Rights
M. Convertible Securities
N. Business Combinations

Study Unit 1, Financial Statements and Annual Reports, and this study unit cover the first major topic in the CFM content specification outline, "Use of Financial Statements." The subject matter is generally covered in intermediate financial accounting courses.

A. Segment Reporting

1. **SFAS 131**, *Disclosure about Segments of an Enterprise and Related Information*, applies to the interim financial reports and annual financial statements of public business enterprises.

2. The objective of segment reporting is to provide information about the different types of business activities of the entity and the economic environments in which it operates. This information is reported on an operating segment basis.

3. SFAS 131 defines an **operating segment** as "a component of an enterprise

   a. "That engages in business activities from which it may earn revenues and incur expenses (including revenues and expenses relating to transactions with other components of the same enterprise),

   b. "Whose operating results are regularly reviewed by the enterprise's chief operating decision maker to make decisions about resources to be allocated to the segment and assess its performance, and

   c. "For which discrete financial information is available."

4. **Aggregation Criteria.** Operating segments may be aggregated if doing so is consistent with the objective of SFAS 131; if they have similar economic characteristics; and if they have similar products and services, production processes, classes of customers, distribution methods, and regulatory environments.

5. **Reportable segments** are those that have been identified in accordance with sections 2. through 4. above and also meet any of the following quantitative thresholds:

   a. **Revenue test.** Reported revenue, including sales to external customers and intersegment sales or transfers, is at least 10% of the combined revenue of all reported operating segments.

   b. **Asset test.** Assets are at least 10% of the combined assets of all operating segments.

   c. **Profit (loss) test.** The absolute amount of reported profit or loss is at least 10% of the greater, in absolute amount, of either the combined reported profit of all operating segments that did not report a loss, or the combined reported loss of all segments that did report a loss.

6. Information about operating segments not meeting the quantitative thresholds may be combined to produce a reportable segment only if the operating segments share a majority of the aggregation criteria.

7. If the total external revenue of the operating segments is less than 75% of consolidated revenue, additional operating segments are identified as reportable until the 75% level is reached.

8. Information about nonreportable activities and segments is combined and disclosed in an "all other" category as a reconciling item.

9. As the number of reportable segments increases above 10, the enterprise may decide that it has reached a practical limit.

10. **Disclosures** include the following:

    a. Such general information as the factors used to identify the reportable segments, including the basis of organization, and the types of revenue-generating products and services for each reportable segment

    b. A measure of profit or loss and total assets for each reportable segment and, if the amounts are included in the measure of segment profit or loss reviewed by the chief operating decision maker, such other items as revenues from external customers, revenues from other operating segments, interest revenue, interest expense, depreciation, depletion, amortization, unusual items, equity in the net income of equity-based investees, income tax expense or benefit, extraordinary items, and other significant noncash items

    c. The amount of investment in equity-based investees and total expenditures for additions to most long-lived assets for each reportable segment if they are included in segment assets reviewed by the chief operating decision maker

11. If a majority of a segment's revenues are from interest, and net interest revenue is the primary basis for assessing its performance and the resources allocated to it, net interest revenue may be reported given proper disclosure.

12. **Measurement**. The general principle is that the information reported is measured in the same way as the internal information used to evaluate a segment's performance and to allocate assets to it.

    a. If the chief operating decision maker uses more than one measure of a segment's profit or loss or assets, the reported measures are those most consistent with the consolidated financial statements.

    b. Explanations of the measurements of segment profit or loss and segment assets should be given for each reportable segment.

13. **Reconciliations** should be provided for the total reportable segments' revenues and consolidated revenues, the total of the reportable segments' measures of profit or loss and pretax consolidated operating income (but if the enterprise allocates other items, such as income taxes, the reconciliation may be to income after those items), the total reportable segments' assets and consolidated assets, and the total reportable segments' amounts for every other significant item of information disclosed and the consolidated amount.

    a. Significant reconciling items should be separately identified and described.

14. **Interim period information** is disclosed for each reportable segment in condensed financial statements. Disclosures include external revenues, intersegment revenues, a measure of segment profit or loss, total assets that have materially changed since the last annual report, differences from the last annual report in the basis of segmentation or of segment profit or loss, and a reconciliation of the total reportable segments' profit or loss and consolidated pretax income.

15. **Restatement of previously reported information** is required if changes in internal organization cause the composition of reportable segments to change. However, an enterprise must restate only items of disclosure that it can practicably restate.

    a. In these circumstances, if segment information for earlier periods, including interim periods, is not restated, segment information for the year of the change must be disclosed under the old basis and the new basis of segmentation if practicable.

16. Certain **enterprise-wide disclosures** must be provided only if they are not given in the reportable operating segment information.

    a. **Information about products and services**. Revenues from external customers for each product and service or each group of similar products and services are reported if practicable based on the financial information used to produce the general-purpose financial statements.

    b.   The following information about geographic areas is also reported if practicable: external revenues attributed to the home country, external revenues attributed to all foreign countries, material external revenues attributed to an individual foreign country, the basis for attributing revenues from external customers, and certain information about assets.

    c.   If 10% or more of revenue is derived from sales to any **single customer**, that fact, the amount of revenue from each such customer, and the segment(s) reporting the revenues must be disclosed. Single customers include entities under common control and each federal, state, local, or foreign government.

17.   Stop and review! You have completed the outline for this subunit. Study multiple-choice questions 1 through 4 beginning on page 94.

B. Asset Depreciation

1.   **Definition**. Depreciation systematically and rationally allocates the historical cost of the productive capacity of a tangible capital asset to the periods benefited. It is not a process of valuation. The periodic charge for depreciation is offset by a credit to accumulated depreciation, a contra-asset account.

2.   Depreciation does not provide resources for asset replacement. Except to the extent that it is tax deductible and reduces cash outlays for taxes, it does not affect cash flows.

3.   Depreciation is not always expensed. For example, under the full-cost method required by GAAP, depreciation on a factory building and machinery used in production of inventory would be charged to overhead, which in turn would be applied to work-in-process.

4.   The amount to be depreciated over the asset's useful life equals the historical cost recorded minus the salvage (residual) value.

    a.   The historical cost itself may result from various assumptions and estimates.

    b.   The consumption of the economic benefits represented by an asset's recorded value follows a pattern that is unique to each asset. The most common factors to which that pattern may be related are the passage of time (months or years), units of production (e.g., units of output by a machine), and amount of service (such as hours of operation or miles driven).

    c.   The estimated useful life may be expressed not only in units of time but also in terms of such variables as machine hours or units of output.

5.   **Methods of Allocating the Depreciable Amount**. The method chosen for depreciating an asset should fairly allocate the expense to the periods benefited by the asset's use.

    a.   **Straight-line**. Under this method, depreciation is a constant amount (depreciable amount ÷ estimated useful life) for each period.

        1)   The depreciable amount equals historical cost minus salvage value.

    b.   **Accelerated methods** are time-based techniques that result in decreasing depreciation charges over the life of the asset.

        1)   **Declining balance (DB)**. DB determines periodic depreciation expense by multiplying some percentage (e.g., 200%, 150%, or 125%) of the book value (NOT a depreciable base equal to cost minus salvage value) at the beginning of each period by the straight-line rate.

            a)   The book value decreases by the depreciation recognized, and the result is the use of a constant rate against a declining balance.

            b)   Salvage value is ignored in determining the book value, but the asset is not depreciated below salvage value.

2)   **Sum-of-the-year's digits (SYD).** SYD multiplies a constant depreciable base (cost − salvage) by a declining fraction. It is a declining-rate, declining-charge method.

   a)   The SYD fraction's numerator is the number of years of remaining useful life (n).

   b)   The formula to compute the denominator is $n\dfrac{(n+1)}{2}$.

3)   The Modified Accelerated Cost Recovery System (MACRS) is used for federal income tax purposes. It establishes asset categories, each of which has a class life and recovery period. For 3-, 5-, 7-, and 10-year assets, 200% DB is used. For 15- and 20-year assets, 150% DB is used. Real property is depreciated under the straight-line method over 27.5, 31.5, or 39 years.

c.   **Usage-centered depreciation.** Some methods calculate depreciation as a function of an asset's use rather than the time it has been held.

   1)   **Units-of-output.** Each unit is charged with a constant amount of depreciation equal to cost minus salvage value, divided by the total units expected to be produced.

   2)   **Services-used.** This method calculates a variable periodic depreciation expense based on a fixed charge per unit of activity, e.g., machine hours or miles driven.

d.   **Group and composite depreciation.** The composite method relates to groups of dissimilar assets with varying useful lives, and the group method applies to similar assets.

   1)   Each method calculates a total depreciable cost for all the assets debited to a control account, a weighted-average estimated useful life, and a weighted-average depreciation rate based on cost.

   2)   Gains and losses on retirements are not recognized. The entry is to credit the asset at cost, debit cash for any proceeds received, and debit or credit accumulated depreciation for the difference.

   3)   Periodic depreciation equals the weighted-average rate times the beginning balance of the asset account for the period.

6.   Stop and review! You have completed the outline for this subunit. Study multiple-choice questions 5 through 9 beginning on page 95.

C.   Secured Loans

1.   A secured loan is a loan that is supported by collateral in the event that the debtor defaults.

2.   Collateral for short-term loans is usually provided by financial assets, such as receivables, or inventory. A company that wishes to obtain cash from its receivables before collection has three options: pledging, assignment, and factoring.

   a.   **Pledging.** A pledge (a general assignment) is the use of receivables as collateral (security) for a loan. The borrower agrees to use collections of receivables to repay the loan. Upon default, the lender can sell the receivables to recover the loan proceeds.

b. **Assignment**. An assignment (a specific assignment) is a more formal borrowing arrangement. The assignor (borrower) signs a promissory note and financing agreement, and specific receivables serve as collateral.

   1) Debtors may be notified to make payments to the assignee, but most assignments are not on a notification basis.

      a) The loan is at a specified percentage of the face value of the collateral, and interest and service fees are charged to the assignor.

c. **Factoring**. Factoring (a sale) transfers ownership of accounts receivable to a finance company or bank (the factor), which will charge a fee to cover its costs and provide a return.

   1) Factoring is normally with notification.

   2) One common form of factoring is the **credit card sale**, which transfers ownership of receivables without recourse.

      a) The retailer benefits by prompt receipt of cash and avoidance of bad debts and other costs. In return, the credit card company and the retailer's bank charge various fees.

   3) Factoring may occur with or without recourse.

      a) A sale of receivables with recourse allows the transferee (the factor) to collect any defaulted receivables from the transferor.

      b) A sale of receivables without recourse transfers the risk of default to the transferee.

3. **SFAS 125**, *Accounting for Transfers and Servicing of Financial Assets and Extinguishment of Liabilities*, is effective for relevant transactions occurring after December 31, 1996. It applies a financial-components approach focusing on control because such transfers may entail dividing an interest in financial assets into its components, with some retained by the transferor and some held by the transferee. After a transfer of financial assets, an entity recognizes the assets it controls and the liabilities it has incurred, derecognizes assets when control has been surrendered, and derecognizes liabilities when extinguished. Transfers that are sales are differentiated from secured borrowings.

   a. A transfer in which the transferor surrenders control is a sale to the extent that consideration other than beneficial interests in the assets is received. The transferor surrenders control and the transaction is treated as a sale only if three conditions are met:

      1) The assets have been isolated from the transferor, that is, are beyond its reach and its creditors.

      2) Either each transferee may pledge or exchange the assets, or the transferee is an entity that meets certain criteria (e.g., certain trusts) and the holders of beneficial interests in that entity may pledge or exchange those interests.

      3) The transferor does not maintain effective control over the transferred assets through certain repurchase or redemption agreements.

   b. After a transfer of financial assets, the transferor carries any retained interests in its balance sheet. It allocates the prior carrying amount between the assets sold and the retained interests based on their fair values at the transfer date.

c.   If the conditions for a sale are met, the transferor derecognizes the assets sold, recognizes assets obtained and liabilities incurred as proceeds of the sale (measured at fair value if practicable), and recognizes any gain or loss in earnings.

d.   If the sale criteria are not met, the parties account for the transfer as a secured borrowing with a pledge of collateral. In certain circumstances in which the secured party controls the pledged assets, debtors must reclassify the assets, and secured parties must recognize the assets and their obligation to return them.

4.   Security for inventory financing is commonly in the form of a blanket inventory lien, a trust receipt, or a field warehousing arrangement.

a.   A **blanket lien** against all inventory of the debtor nevertheless permits sale of the inventory. Thus, the value of the collateral may be reduced.

b.   A **trust receipt** is an instrument in which the debtor acknowledges that the inventory is held in trust for the creditor. Proceeds of sale of the specified goods are remitted promptly to the creditor.

c.   A **field warehousing arrangement** provides for on-site control and supervision of specified goods by a third party.

5.   Stop and review! You have completed the outline for this subunit. Study multiple-choice questions 10 through 12 beginning on page 97.

D.   Deferred Taxes

1.   **SFAS 109**, *Accounting for Income Taxes*, adopts the asset and liability method of interperiod tax allocation. It establishes standards of accounting for income taxes currently payable and for the tax consequences of

a.   Items included in taxable income of a year other than the year in which they are recognized for financial reporting purposes

b.   Other events that create differences between the tax bases of assets and liabilities and their amounts for financial reporting purposes

c.   Operating loss or tax credit carrybacks for refunds of taxes paid in prior years and carryforwards to reduce taxes payable in future years

2.   **Temporary differences (TDs)** include differences between the tax basis of an asset or liability and its reported amount in the financial statements that will result in taxable or deductible amounts in future years when the reported amount of the asset is recovered or the liability is settled. Accelerated tax depreciation and accounting for warranties are examples of items resulting in TDs.

a.   TDs may also result when events have been recognized in the financial statements and will result in future taxable or deductible amounts based on the tax laws, but cannot be identified with a particular asset or liability for financial reporting purposes. An example is an operating loss carryforward.

3.   A **permanent difference** is an event that is recognized either in pretax financial income or in taxable income but never in both. It does not result in a deferred tax asset or liability. Examples are municipal bond interest and the dividends-received deduction.

4. **Other Definitions**

   a. **Income tax expense or benefit** is the sum of the current tax expense or benefit and deferred tax expense or benefit.

   b. **Current tax expense or benefit** is the amount of taxes paid or payable (or refundable) for the year as determined by applying the enacted tax law to the taxable income or excess of deductions over revenues for that year.

   c. **Current tax liability** is equal to taxable income times the applicable tax rate.

   d. **Deferred tax expense or benefit** is the net change during the year in an enterprise's deferred tax liabilities and assets.

   e. A **deferred tax liability** records the deferred tax consequences attributable to taxable TDs. It is measured using the applicable enacted tax rate and provisions of the enacted tax law.

   f. A **deferred tax asset** records the deferred tax consequences attributable to deductible TDs and carryforwards. It is measured using the applicable enacted tax rate and provisions of the enacted tax law.

   g. A **valuation allowance** is a contra account to a deferred tax asset. It should reduce the deferred tax asset to the amount that is more likely than not to be realized.

5. **Determination of Deferred Taxes**. The process below is followed by each taxpaying entity in each tax jurisdiction:

   a. Identify TDs and operating loss and tax credit carryforwards for tax purposes.

   b. Measure the total deferred tax liability for taxable TDs.

   c. Measure the total deferred tax asset for deductible TDs and operating loss carryforwards.

   d. Measure deferred tax assets for each type of tax credit carryforward.

   e. Recognize a valuation allowance if necessary.

6. **Applicable Tax Rates**. A deferred tax liability or asset is measured using the tax rate(s) expected to apply when it is expected to be settled or realized.

   a. The tax rate is, in essence, a flat rate if graduated rates are not significant to the enterprise. Otherwise, an average of the applicable graduated rates is used.

   b. The basic entry to record deferred taxes is

Income tax expense (or benefit)	debit (or credit)
Income tax payable (or refundable)	credit (or debit)
Deferred income tax liability (or asset)	credit (or debit)

7. SFAS 109 requires **intraperiod tax allocation**. Income tax expense (benefit) is allocated to continuing operations, discontinued operations, extraordinary items, and items taken directly to shareholders' equity.

8. Enacted changes in the tax law or rates require an adjustment of a deferred tax liability or asset in the period of the enactment of the tax law or rate. The effect is included in income from continuing operations.

9. **Financial Statement Presentation**. A deferred tax liability or asset should be separated into current and noncurrent components depending on the classification of the related asset or liability.

   a. If the deferred tax liability or asset is not related to an asset or liability for financial reporting, it is classified according to the expected reversal date of the TD.

   b. A valuation allowance is allocated pro rata between current and noncurrent deferred tax assets.

   c. For a given taxpaying entity and within a specific jurisdiction, current deferred tax assets and liabilities are netted. Noncurrent deferred tax assets and liabilities are also offset and shown as a single amount.

10. Stop and review! You have completed the outline for this subunit. Study multiple-choice questions 13 through 18 beginning on page 98.

E. Leases

1. **SFAS 13**, *Accounting for Leases*, is the primary pronouncement applicable to leases. A **lease** is an agreement between a lessor (owner) and a lessee that conveys the right to use specific property for a stated period in exchange for a stated payment. The accounting for leases is based on the substance of the transaction. A lease may be, in effect, a financing agreement in which the lessor finances the purchase. Leases may also be rental agreements.

2. **Lessee Accounting for Capital Leases**. A lease may be classified as either a capital lease or an operating lease by a lessee. A **capital lease** transfers substantially all of the benefits and risks of ownership of the property to the lessee.

   a. A capital lease should be accounted for by the lessee as the acquisition of an asset and the incurrence of an obligation. In subsequent periods, the lessee should depreciate the asset and recognize interest expense on the liability.

   b. The asset will usually be reduced more rapidly than the liability because of the use of an accelerated method of depreciation.

3. A lease must be classified as a capital lease by a lessee if, at its inception, any one of the following four criteria is satisfied:

   a. The lease provides for the transfer of ownership of the leased property.

   b. The lease contains a bargain purchase option.

   c. The lease term is 75% or more of the estimated economic life of the leased property. However, this criterion and the one stated just below are inapplicable if the beginning of the lease term falls within the last 25% of the total estimated economic life.

   d. The present value of the minimum lease payments (excluding executory costs) is at least 90% of the excess of the fair value of the leased property at the inception of the lease over any investment tax credit.

4. The lessee records a capital lease as an asset and an obligation at the present value of the minimum lease payments (not to exceed the fair value of the leased asset).

   a. The discount rate used is the lower of the lessor's implicit interest rate (if known) or the lessee's incremental borrowing rate of interest.

5. Minimum lease payments include the minimum rental payments (excluding executory costs such as insurance, maintenance, and taxes) required during the lease term and the amount of a bargain purchase option.

a.   If no bargain purchase option exists, the minimum lease payments equal the sum of the minimum rental payments, the amount of residual value guaranteed by the lessee, and any nonrenewal penalty imposed. NOTE: From the lessor's standpoint, the minimum lease payments also include the residual value guaranteed by a financially capable third party unrelated to the lessor or lessee.

6. A periodic lease payment has two components: interest expense and the reduction of the lease obligation. Under the effective-interest method, the appropriate interest rate is applied to the carrying value of the lease obligation at the beginning of the interest period to calculate interest expense.

a.   The portion of the minimum lease payment greater than the interest expense reduces the balance sheet liability for the capital lease.

7. **Lessor Accounting for Capital Leases**. Lessors also classify most leases as either an operating or a capital lease. However, lessors must also determine whether a capital lease is a direct financing or sales-type lease.

a.   In a **direct financing lease**, the difference between the gross investment (sum of the lease payments plus unguaranteed residual value) and its cost or carrying amount is recorded as unearned interest revenue. No net profit or loss is recognized.

b.   In a **sales-type lease**, the same amount of unearned interest revenue will be recorded as in a direct financing lease. However, a net profit or loss is also recognized because the cost or carrying amount differs from fair value.

c.   The following are the basic entries:

Direct Financing Lease			Sales-Type Lease		
Lease payments			Cost of goods sold	$XXX	
receivable	$XXX		Asset		$XXX
Asset		$XXX	Lease payments receivable	XXX	
Unearned interest			Sales revenue		XXX
revenue		XXX	Unearned interest revenue		XXX

d.   Although a lease satisfies one of the four capitalization criteria, the lessor may not treat the lease as a capital lease unless collectibility of the remaining payments is reasonably assured and no material uncertainties exist regarding unreimbursable costs to be incurred by the lessor.

8. **Operating leases** do not meet the criteria for capitalization. They are transactions in which lessees rent the right to use lessor assets without acquiring a substantial portion of the rights and risks of ownership of those assets.

a.   Under an operating lease, the lessee records no liability except for rental expense accrued at the end of an accounting period. Thus, an operating lease is a form of off-balance-sheet financing.

b.   Rent is reported as income or expense in accordance with the lease agreement. However, if rentals vary from a straight-line basis, the straight-line basis should be used unless another systematic and rational basis is more representative of the time pattern in which the use benefit from the property is reduced.

9. A **sale-leaseback** involves the sale of property by the owner and a lease of the property back to the seller. In a sale-leaseback transaction, if the lease qualifies as a capital lease, the gain or loss on the sale is normally deferred and amortized by the seller-lessee in proportion to the amortization of the leased asset, that is, at the same rate at which the leased asset is depreciated.

10. Stop and review! You have completed the outline for this subunit. Study multiple-choice questions 19 through 25 beginning on page 100.

F.   Pensions

1.   Pension benefits are periodic payments under a pension plan made to retirees or their beneficiaries. Pension cost is a component of employee compensation. The employer's cost of a defined benefit pension plan is estimated based on the plan benefit formula and relevant future events, such as future compensation levels, pension fund earnings, mortality rates, ages at retirement, and vesting considerations.

2.   **SFAS 87**, *Employers' Accounting for Pensions*, defines accounting for pension expense. Each year, companies with defined benefit plans must recognize pension expense, the funding provided, and any unfunded liability. The pension fund is a separate accounting entity with its own set of books.

3.   The **projected benefit obligation (PBO)** as of a date is equal to the actuarial present value of all benefits attributed by the pension benefit formula to employee services rendered prior to that date. The PBO is measured using assumptions about future as well as past and current salary levels.

   a.   The PBO at the end of a period equals the PBO at the beginning of the period, plus service cost, plus retroactive benefits (prior service cost) granted by a plan amendment during the period, minus benefits paid, plus or minus changes in the PBO resulting from changes in assumptions and from experience different from that assumed.

   b.   The **accumulated benefit obligation (ABO)** is the same as the PBO except that it is based on past and current compensation levels only.

4.   The **net periodic pension cost (NPPC)** is the minimum cost that must be recognized. It consists of six elements.

   a.   **Service cost** is the present value of the future benefits earned by the employees in the current period. It is unaffected by the funded status of the plan.

   b.   **Interest cost** equals the beginning PBO times the current discount rate.

   c.   The actual **return on plan assets** is the difference between the fair value of the plan assets at the beginning and end of the accounting period adjusted for contributions and payments during the period.

   d.   **Amortization of actuarial gains and losses**. Gains and losses arise from changes in the PBO or plan assets that result from experience different from that expected and from changes in assumptions.

      1)   The cumulative unrecognized net gain or loss at the beginning of the year is subject to required amortization only to the extent it exceeds 10% of the greater of the PBO or the market-related value of plan assets.

      2)   The minimum required amortization equals the excess described above divided by the average remaining service period of active employees expected to receive benefits.

   e.   **Amortization of prior service cost**. If a plan is amended to grant additional benefits for past service, the cost of retroactive benefits is the increase in the PBO at the date of the amendment. It should be amortized by assigning an equal amount to each future period of service of each employee active at the date of the amendment who is expected to receive benefits under the plan.

   f.   **Amortization of any unrecognized net obligation or net asset arising when SFAS 87 is first applied**. The transition amount is the difference between the PBO and an amount equal to the fair value of the plan assets, plus any recognized accrued liability, or minus any prepaid pension cost. Straight-line amortization is applied over the average remaining service period of participating employees (if less than 15 years, a 15-year period may be elected).

5. A recognized pension liability (unfunded accrued pension cost recorded as a credit to the accrued/prepaid pension cost account) arises when funding is less than the NPPC. Prepaid pension cost (a debit to accrued/prepaid pension cost) results from funding the plan in excess of the NPPC.

   a. The total net liability reported in the balance sheet equals the unfunded amount of the ABO (ABO − fair value of plan assets).

   b. An **additional minimum pension liability** must be recognized equal to the unfunded ABO, plus prepaid pension cost, or minus accrued pension cost.

   c. Recognition of an additional liability has no effect on earnings. An intangible asset is debited to the extent that unrecognized prior service cost exists. If that amount is not adequate, a separate component of equity is debited for the remainder.

6. The expenses and liabilities reported for a defined benefit plan are greatly affected by the estimates used. For example, optimistic actuarial assumptions about mortality rates, ages at retirement, etc., reduce the PBO, the ABO, and the NPPC. Moreover, if the discount rate used to calculate the PBO and the ABO is too high, the PBO, ABO, and NPPC will be understated. Similarly, increasing the assumed rate of return on plan assets decreases NPPC and the amount of any underfunding. The PBO and the NPPC also may be understated if the estimated future compensation levels are too low.

   a. A financial analysis of pension information should consider that the liability reported is based on the lower ABO, not the PBO. It should also consider the proportion of vested benefits. Furthermore, future NPPC will be increased by currently unrecognized losses and prior service cost.

7. A company may wish to terminate an overfunded defined benefit pension plan. Under **SFAS 88**, *Employers' Accounting for Settlements and Curtailments of Defined Benefit Pension Plans and for Termination Benefits*, the company may report the full gain immediately.

   a. However, the company must comply with the provisions of the Employee Retirement Income Security Act of 1974 (ERISA), and the Pension Benefit Guaranty Corporation (PBGC) must approve the cancellation.

      1) ERISA is the federal law regulating pension plans. It establishes requirements for funding, eligibility, vesting, disclosure, and plan termination insurance.

      2) ERISA created the PBGC, a federal agency that serves as a pension insurance fund. It collects insurance premiums from employers that vary depending on the amount of unfunded vested benefits. If an underfunded plan is terminated, the PBGC can impose a lien of up to 30% of the employer's net worth. This lien has the same status as a tax lien.

8. The foregoing outline concerned defined benefit plans. This type of plan creates the risk that the pension fund's assets will not suffice to pay the defined benefits.

   a. Accordingly, some companies have terminated their overfunded defined benefit plans and switched to defined contribution plans. These plans transfer the risks of pension fund performance to employees because the employer's liability is limited to the contribution specified. The accounting problems are simpler than for defined benefit plans because pension expenses and liabilities need not be estimated.

9. Stop and review! You have completed the outline for this subunit. Study multiple-choice questions 26 through 30 beginning on page 103.

G.   Bonds

1.   Bonds are the most common type of long-term debt securities. To account for bonds issued at a discount or a premium, **APB 21**, *Interest on Receivables and Payables*, requires that the interest method of amortization be used (unless the results of another method are not materially different). Under the interest method, interest expense changes every period, but the interest rate is constant.

   a.   Bonds are sold at the sum of the present values of the maturity value and the interest payments (if interest-bearing). The difference between the face value and the selling price of bonds is either a discount or a premium.

      1)   APB 21 requires that a bond discount or premium appear as a direct deduction from, or addition to, the face amount of the bond payable.

   b.   When bonds are issued between interest payment dates, the price also includes accrued interest.

   c.   Interest expense is equal to the carrying value of the bond at the beginning of the period times the yield (market) interest rate.

   d.   Interest paid is constant. It equals the face value of the bond times the stated rate.

   e.   The difference between interest expense and interest paid is the discount or premium amortization.

   f.   The periodic reduction of the discount (premium) will cause the net carrying value of the bonds to be higher (lower) than the net carrying value at the previous period-end. At the bonds' maturity date, the discount or premium will be fully amortized to zero, and the net carrying value will be equal to the face value of the bonds.

2.   Issue costs should be reported on the balance sheet as deferred charges to be amortized over the life of the bonds. They should not be commingled with the premium or discount.

   a.   Issue costs of bringing a bond to market include printing costs, legal fees, accountants' fees, underwriters' commissions, registration fees, and promotion costs.

   b.   Although the interest method is theoretically superior, issue costs are customarily amortized using the straight-line method.

3.   Accounting for bond investments parallels that for bonds payable except that a separate premium or discount account is rarely used. Thus, if the purchaser has the positive intent and ability to hold the bonds to maturity, they should be classified as held-to-maturity securities and accounted for at amortized cost using the effective interest method.

   a.   If the purchaser does not have both the positive intent and the ability to hold the bonds to maturity, the bonds should be classified as trading securities if they are held for sale in the near term. Otherwise, they are classified as available-for-sale securities. Trading and available-for-sale securities are accounted for at fair value, and unrealized holding gains and losses are recognized in earnings or in a separate component of shareholders' equity, respectively.

4.   Stop and review! You have completed the outline for this subunit. Study multiple-choice questions 31 through 34 beginning on page 106.

H. Common Stock

1. The common shareholders are the owners of the corporation. Their rights as owners, although reasonably uniform, depend on the laws of the state in which the firm is incorporated. Equity ownership involves risk because holders of stock are not guaranteed a return and are last in priority in the event of liquidation. Shareholders' equity provides the cushion for creditors if any losses occur as a result of liquidation.

2. Shareholders' equity consists of contributed capital, retained earnings, and accumulated other comprehensive income.

   a. An important limitation is legal capital, which in many states is the par or stated value of preferred and common stock. Par or stated value is a designated amount per share established in the corporate charter. Legal capital cannot be distributed to shareholders as dividends.

3. **Contributed capital** represents amounts invested by owners in exchange for stock.

   a. The stated capital (capital stock) shows the par, stated value, or amount received of all shares authorized, issued, and outstanding. Amounts for common and preferred stock are listed separately.

   b. Additional paid-in capital consists of the sources of contributed capital in excess of legal capital. They include

      1) Amounts in excess of par or stated value received for the company's stock

      2) A debit item for receipts that are less than par or stated value, for example, discount on common stock

      3) Amounts attributable to treasury stock transactions

      4) Transfers from retained earnings upon the issuance of stock dividends

4. **Retained earnings** is the amount that is to be reinvested in the corporation. Accordingly, it is increased by net income and decreased by net losses, dividends, and certain treasury stock transactions.

5. **SFAS 130**, *Reporting Comprehensive Income* (effective for years beginning after December 15, 1997, divides comprehensive income into net income and other comprehensive income. The latter is classified separately into foreign currency items, minimum pension liability adjustments, and unrealized gains and losses on certain investments. In an exposure draft, the FASB has proposed similar treatment for the change in fair value of derivatives designated as hedges of cash flow exposures.

   a. SFAS 130 requires comprehensive income to be displayed in a financial statement given the same prominence as other statements, but no specific format is specified. The total of other comprehensive income for a period is transferred to a component of equity separate from retained earnings and additional paid-in capital. The accumulated balance for each classification in that component must be disclosed in the balance sheet, a statement of changes in equity, or the notes.

6. **Other Shareholders' Equity Accounts**

   a. Treasury stock is the entity's own stock reacquired for various purposes, e.g., mergers, stock options, or stock dividends.

      1) It is most commonly accounted for at cost, that is, as a temporary lump-sum reduction of (debit to) shareholders' equity. Under the cost method, treasury stock is shown as a contra item after retained earnings.

7. **Issuance of Stock**. Upon issuance of stock, cash is debited and common stock is credited for the par or stated value. The difference between the cash received and the par value is credited to additional paid-in capital.

    a. A discount is unlikely, but would be debited to stock discount.

    b. When stock is subscribed, the corporation recognizes an obligation to issue stock, and the subscriber undertakes to pay for the shares subscribed. If collection of the price is reasonably assured, the corporation should debit subscriptions receivable, credit common stock subscribed, and credit additional paid-in capital for any excess of the stock price over the par value.

        1) The SEC requires public companies to treat subscriptions receivable as a contra equity account, not an asset, unless the amount has been collected before issuance of the financial statements. The reason is that many states prohibit suit to collect an unpaid balance.

        2) When the subscription price is paid and the common stock is issued, the corporation should debit cash, debit the common stock subscribed account, credit subscriptions receivable, and credit the common stock account.

        3) If a subscriber defaults, the subscription entry must be reversed. State laws and corporate policies vary with regard to defaults. The possibilities range from complete refund to complete forfeiture.

            a) To the extent that payment has been forfeited, additional paid-in capital from stock subscription default is credited for the amount forfeited.

8. The charter (articles of incorporation) filed with the secretary of state of the state of incorporation indicates the classes of stock that may be issued and their authorized amounts in terms of shares or total dollar value.

9. Stock may be issued in exchange for cash, services, or property. The transaction should be recorded at the more clearly determinable of the fair values of the stock or the property or services received.

10. **Donated Assets**. In general, **SFAS 116**, *Accounting for Contributions Received and Contributions Made*, requires that contributions received be recognized as revenues or gains in the period of receipt. They should be measured at fair value.

    a. However, SFAS 116 does not apply to tax exemptions, abatement, or incentives, or to transfers of assets from a government to a business enterprise. Hence, a credit to donated capital may be appropriate in these cases.

    b. If a company's stock is donated by a shareholder and the transaction is accounted for by the cost method, the entry is to debit treasury stock and credit a gain.

11. Issuance of stock may be subject to a **preemptive right** of shareholders. It is each shareholder's right to maintain proportionate ownership in the corporation if additional shares are offered for sale.

12. Stock may be issued upon the conversion of convertible securities.

13. The proceeds of the combined issuance of different classes of securities should be allocated based on the relative fair values of the securities.

    a. If the fair value of one of the classes of securities is not known, the other securities should be recorded at their fair values, with the remainder of the proceeds credited to the securities for which the fair value is not determinable.

14. **Retirement**. When stock is retired, cash (or treasury stock) is credited. The stock account is debited for the par or stated value.

    a. Additional paid-in capital is debited to the extent it arose from the original stock issuance. Any remainder is debited to retained earnings or credited to additional paid-in capital from stock retirement.

    b. No gain or loss is reported on transactions in an enterprise's own stock. However, the transfer of nonmonetary assets in exchange for stock requires recognition of any holding gain or loss on the nonmonetary assets.

15. When **cash dividends** are declared, a liability to the shareholders is created because the dividends must be paid once they are declared. At the declaration date, retained earnings must be debited and a liability credited, resulting in a decrease in retained earnings.

    a. When the cash dividends are paid, dividends payable is debited and cash credited. Thus, at the payment date, retained earnings is not affected.

    b. Unlike stock dividends, cash dividends cannot be rescinded.

16. **Property Dividends**. **APB 29**, *Accounting for Nonmonetary Transactions*, ordinarily requires that a nonreciprocal transfer of nonmonetary assets to owners be recorded at the fair value of the asset transferred on the declaration date.

    a. For example, if the property has appreciated, it should first be written up to fair value and a gain recognized. The dividend should then be recognized as a debit to retained earnings and a credit to dividend payable.

        1) The distribution of the property dividend is recognized by a debit to property dividend payable and a credit to the asset account.

17. **Liquidating dividends** are repayments of capital. They are distributions in excess of retained earnings. Because the effect of a liquidating dividend is to decrease contributed capital, additional paid-in capital is debited to the extent available before the other contributed capital accounts are charged.

    a. Thus, declaration of a dividend, a portion of which is liquidating, may decrease both additional paid-in capital and retained earnings.

18. **Stock Dividends**. The purpose of a stock dividend is to provide evidence to the shareholders of their interest in accumulated earnings without distribution of cash or other property. Stock dividends are a reclassification of shareholders' equity.

    a. A small stock dividend (one in which the number of shares issued is fewer than 20 to 25% of those outstanding) is recorded as a debit to retained earnings for the fair value of the stock issued and a credit to the capital stock accounts.

    b. A large stock dividend (one in which the number of shares issued is greater than 20 to 25% of those outstanding) is a split-up effected in the form of a stock dividend. It requires a debit to retained earnings at least equal to the legal requirement in the state of incorporation (usually the par or stated value) and credits to the capital stock accounts.

    c. The recipient of a stock dividend should not recognize income. After receipt of the dividend, the shareholder has the same proportionate interest in the corporation and the same total book value as before the declaration of the stock dividend.

    d. Stock dividends often require the issuance of fractional share rights.

19. **Stock splits** are issuances of stock that do not affect the aggregate par value of shares issued and outstanding. Stock splits have no effect on total shareholders' equity.

   a. No accounting entry is made for stock splits, and no transfer from retained earnings to paid-in capital occurs. Rather, a memorandum change of the par value is made.

20. Stop and review! You have completed the outline for this subunit. Study multiple-choice questions 35 through 38 beginning on page 107.

I.   Preferred Stock

1. Preferred stock is a form of equity that has some features of debt. Thus, it usually does not confer voting rights, thereby permitting control to be held by the common shareholders. Preferred stock is more flexible than debt because it has no maturity date or sinking fund schedule, but, like debt, it allows earnings of the firm beyond a stated rate or amount to be reserved for the common shareholders.

2. Typical provisions of preferred stock issues include

   a. **Priority** in assets and earnings. If the firm goes bankrupt, the preferred shareholders have priority over common shareholders.

   b. **Cumulative dividends**. All past preferred dividends must be paid before any common dividends can be paid.

   c. **Convertibility**. Preferred stock issues may be convertible into common stock at the option of the shareholder.

   d. **Participation**. Preferred stock may participate with common stock in excess earnings. For example, 8% participating preferred stock might pay a dividend each year greater than 8% when the corporation is extremely profitable. But nonparticipating preferred stock will receive no more than is stated on the face of the stock.

   e. **Callability**. Preferred stock may be subject to mandatory redemption at the option of the issuer at a specified price.

3. The accounting for preferred stock is similar to that for common stock.

4. Holding an investment in preferred stock, rather than bonds, provides a corporation with a major tax advantage. At least 70% of the dividends received from preferred stock is tax deductible, whereas all bond interest received is taxable. The **dividends-received deduction** also applies to common stock held by a corporation.

5. Stop and review! You have completed the outline for this subunit. Study multiple-choice questions 39 through 41 beginning on page 108.

J.   Retained Earnings

1. Retained earnings is the accumulated net income or loss of the company after various adjustments. It is reported in a basic financial statement. The income statement and the statement of retained earnings (presented separately or combined) are designed to broadly reflect the results of operations.

2. The statement of retained earnings consists of beginning retained earnings adjusted for any prior-period adjustments (net of tax), net income (loss), dividends paid or declared, and certain other rare items, e.g., quasi-reorganizations. The final figure is ending retained earnings.

    a.   **Prior-period adjustments** constitute the only major exception to the all-inclusive income statement concept. Prior-period adjustments consist solely of corrections of errors in prior-period statements.

        1)   If **comparative financial statements** are presented, all prior periods affected by a prior-period adjustment are restated.

    b.   A **quasi-reorganization** is a method for eliminating a deficit in retained earnings through reductions in other capital accounts. It serves the same purpose as a legal reorganization. Elimination of the deficit permits a company to pay dividends.

    c.   The retained earnings balance is sometimes divided into appropriated and unappropriated amounts. **Appropriations** may arise from legal requirements, contractual agreements, or management decisions. They reduce the amount available for dividends. However, losses are not charged directly against appropriated or unappropriated retained earnings.

  3.   Stop and review! You have completed the outline for this subunit. Study multiple-choice questions 42 through 44 on page 110.

K. Stock-Based Compensation

  1.   According to **APB 25**, *Accounting for Stock Issued to Employees*, a **compensatory stock option plan** involves the issuance of stock in whole or in part for employee services rendered.

    a.   The compensation cost should be recognized as an expense when the employee performs services. It is ordinarily measured by the quoted market price at the measurement date minus the amount, if any, the employee must pay. (If the option price equals or exceeds the market price at the measurement date, there is no compensation expense.)

        1)   If the grant precedes the services, the debit is to deferred compensation expense (a contra equity account). This amount is amortized as services are rendered and expenses are recognized. The credit is to stock options outstanding (an equity account).

            a)   When the services are rendered, deferred compensation expense is credited and compensation expense is debited.

            b)   Upon exercise, the entry is to debit cash and options outstanding and to credit common stock and additional paid-in capital.

            c)   If stock options are not exercised, the balance in stock options outstanding is transferred to a paid-in capital account.

        2)   The measurement date is the first date on which the number of shares to which an employee is entitled and the option or purchase price, if any, are known. This date is usually the **grant date**.

            a)   When the measurement date is later than the grant date, compensation expense in periods prior to the measurement date is based on the stock's quoted market price at the end of each period.

                i)   The measurement date may be later than the grant date because a stock option plan has variable terms; e.g., the amount of stock or the price may depend upon future events.

2. **SFAS 123**, *Accounting for Stock-Based Compensation*, is an alternative to APB 25. It applies to stock purchase plans, stock options, restricted stock, and stock appreciation rights.

   a. Fair-value-based accounting for stock compensation plans is not required. An entity may continue to apply APB 25.

      1) Nevertheless, the fair-value-based method is preferable for purposes of justifying a change in accounting principle. However, initial adoption of an accounting principle for a new transaction is not a change in principle.

   b. The fair-value-based method measures compensation cost at the grant date based on the value of the award. Recognition is over the service period.

      1) APB 25 measures compensation cost based on intrinsic value (quoted market price – amount to be paid).

         a) Many stock option plans have no intrinsic value at grant date, and consequently no compensation cost is recognized under APB 25.

   c. The fair value of stock options is determined using an option-pricing model. The stock price at the grant date, the exercise price, the expected life of the option, the volatility of the stock and its expected dividends, and the risk-free interest rate over the expected life of the option are elements of the model.

      1) Nonpublic entities may exclude the volatility factor, which results in measurement at minimum value.

      2) The fair value of an option is not adjusted for changes in the model.

   d. An employee stock purchase plan that allows purchase at a discount is not compensatory if the discount is small (5% or less meets the condition automatically), substantially all full-time employees may participate, and the plan has no option features. An example of an option feature is a provision that allows an employee to purchase shares at a fixed discount from the lesser of the market price at grant date or date of purchase.

   e. **Stock appreciation rights (SARs)** permit employees to receive cash equal to the excess of the market price of the company's stock over a specified amount.

      1) Under **FASB Interpretation 28**, *Accounting for Stock Appreciation Rights and Other Variable Stock Option or Award Plans*, compensation equals the excess of the quoted market value over the value specified.

      2) The charge to expense is accrued over the service period. If the SARs are for past services and are exercisable immediately, there is no service period.

      3) Accrued compensation is adjusted (but not below zero) in subsequent periods up to the measurement date for changes in the quoted market value, and the adjustment is reflected in income in the period of the change.

      4) SFAS 123 adopts a fair-value-based method of accounting for stock appreciation rights. Nevertheless, it permits the continued application of APB 25 and FASB Interpretation 28.

3. An **employee stock ownership plan (ESOP)** is defined in ERISA as a stock bonus plan, or a combination stock bonus and money purchase pension plan, designed to invest primarily in the employer's stock.

   a. Leveraged ESOPs are allowed to borrow, either from the sponsor (with or without an outside loan) or directly from an outside lender, to acquire employer securities, with the shares usually serving as collateral.

1) These shares are held in a suspense account until the debt is repaid, ordinarily from employer contributions and dividends. As the debt is repaid, the shares are released and allocated to individual accounts. Any outside loan is usually guaranteed by the employer-sponsor.

b. The employer records a debit to unearned ESOP shares (a contra equity account) when shares are issued or treasury shares are sold to the ESOP. Even if the ESOP buys on the market, the employer debits unearned shares and credits cash or debt, depending on whether the ESOP is internally or externally leveraged.

1) When ESOP shares are committed to be released, unearned shares is credited at cost and, depending on the purpose of the release, compensation cost, dividends payable, or compensation liability is debited for the fair value of the shares. The difference between cost and fair value is ordinarily an adjustment of additional paid-in capital.

2) Dividends on unallocated shares reduce liabilities or serve as compensation to participants. Dividends on allocated shares are debited to retained earnings.

3) Redemptions of ESOP shares are treasury stock purchases.

4) If the ESOP has a direct outside loan, the sponsor reports a liability. It also accrues interest cost. Furthermore, it reports cash payments to the ESOP to be used for debt service as reductions of the debt and accrued interest. If the ESOP has an indirect loan (a loan from the sponsor who in turn has an outside loan), essentially the same accounting is followed. If an employer loan is made to the ESOP without an outside loan, the employer does not record the ESOP's note payable, the employer's note receivable, interest cost, or interest income.

c. If the ESOP is not leveraged, shares must be allocated at fiscal year-end. Employer compensation cost is reported equal to the cash or shares (at fair value) contributed or committed to be contributed as provided for in the plan. Dividends are debited to retained earnings.

4. Stop and review! You have completed the outline for this subunit. Study multiple-choice questions 45 through 48 beginning on page 111.

L. Stock Rights

1. Stock rights confer an option to purchase shares. **Stock warrants** are evidence of ownership of such rights. They specify the terms for exercise of the rights, such as the number of rights per warrant, the number of rights necessary to purchase a share, the exercise period, and the option price.

a. When rights are issued for no consideration, such as in a dividend distribution, only a memorandum entry is made by the issuer.

1) If the rights are exercised and stock is issued, the issuing company will reflect the proceeds received as an increase in common stock at par value, with any remainder credited to additional paid-in capital. However, if the rights previously issued without consideration are allowed to lapse, contributed capital is unaffected.

2) From the time the rights offering is announced to the issue date, the stock trades rights-on. After the issue date, it trades ex-rights, and the rights have a separate price.

2. Transaction costs of the redemption of stock rights reduce shareholders' equity.

3.   The recipient of stock rights must allocate the carrying value of the shares owned between those shares and the rights based on their relative fair values.

4.   Stock rights are equity securities under SFAS 115 and should be accounted for by the recipient at fair value as available-for-sale or trading securities. Thus, unrealized holding gains or losses on stock rights are recognized at the balance sheet date. For example, if the carrying value of the rights is less than fair value at year-end, an unrealized holding gain will be recognized.

5.   Debt securities may be issued with **detachable stock warrants**, which are warrants that may be detached from the securities, enabling the securities to still be held while the warrants are exercised. However, if the securities must be surrendered to exercise the warrants, the securities are substantially equivalent to convertible debt.

   a.   Under **APB 14**, *Convertible Debt and Debt Issued with Stock Purchase Warrants*, no portion of the proceeds from the issuance should be accounted for as attributable to the conversion feature or the warrants if the securities must be surrendered.

6.   APB 14 requires the proceeds from debt securities issued with detachable warrants to be allocated between the debt securities and the warrants based on their relative fair values at the time of issuance.

   a.   The portion allocated to the warrants should be accounted for as paid-in capital.

   b.   When the fair value of the warrants but not the bonds is known, paid-in capital from stock warrants should be credited (increased) for the fair value of the warrants, with the remainder credited to the bonds.

7.   When debt securities with detachable stock warrants are purchased, the price should be allocated between the warrants and the securities based upon their relative fair values at issuance.

   a.   The amount debited to investment in stock warrants relative to the total amount paid increases the discount or decreases the premium on the investment.

8.   Stop and review! You have completed the outline for this subunit. Study multiple-choice questions 49 through 51 beginning on page 112.

M. Convertible Securities

1.   The debt and equity aspects of convertible debt are inseparable. The entire proceeds should be accounted for as debt until conversion, but the bond issue price is affected by the conversion feature.

2.   The conversion may be accounted for using the book-value or market-value method.

   a.   Under the **book-value method** for recognizing the conversion of outstanding bonds payable to common stock, the stock issued is recorded at the carrying value of the bonds (credit common stock and additional paid-in capital, debit the payable) with no recognition of gain or loss.

   b.   Under the **market-value method**, the stock is recorded at the market value of the stock (or of the bonds). A gain or loss is recognized equal to the difference between the market value recorded and the carrying value of the bonds payable.

3.   The conversion of debt into common stock is ordinarily based upon the book value of the debt at the time of issuance.

   a.   Because the book value is based on all related accounts, unamortized bond premium or discount, unamortized issue costs, and conversion costs are adjustments of the net carrying value at the time of conversion.

          1)   Consequently, these items should be reflected as adjustments of the additional paid-in capital account.

    4.   According to **SFAS 84**, *Induced Conversions of Convertible Debt*, an issuer of a convertible security may attempt to induce prompt conversion of its convertible debt to equity securities by offering additional securities or other consideration as a sweetener.

        a.   The additional consideration used to induce conversion should be reported as an ordinary expense. The amount equals the fair value of the securities or other consideration transferred in excess of the fair value of the securities that would have been issued under the original conversion privilege.

    5.   The treatment of gains or losses from early extinguishment of convertible debt is the same as for the retirement of ordinary debt; i.e., it is an extraordinary item.

    6.   Convertible preferred stock, unlike convertible debt, is treated as equity unless redemption is required. It is accounted for at book value in the same manner as convertible debt.

    7.   Stop and review! You have completed the outline for this subunit. Study multiple-choice questions 52 through 54 on page 113.

N. Business Combinations

    1.   Under **APB 16**, *Business Combinations*, the **purchase method** is used to account for a business combination that does not satisfy the conditions for a pooling of interests.

        a.   The purchase method treats the combination as an acquisition.

        b.   The acquirer records the identifiable assets obtained and liabilities assumed at their fair values.

        c.   Income of the acquiring company includes its share of the earnings of the acquired company after acquisition (cash flows are also consolidated after acquisition).

        d.   **Goodwill** is the excess of the purchase price of a group of assets or an investee over the sum of the assigned costs (fair values) of the net identifiable assets (sum of the identifiable tangible and identifiable intangible assets, minus liabilities assumed).

            1)   Goodwill is required to be amortized over its useful life, not to exceed 40 years.

            2)   If the fair value of the net identifiable assets is greater than the price, the excess (negative goodwill) should be allocated to reduce proportionately the values assigned to noncurrent assets (except long-term investments in marketable securities) in determining their fair values.

                a)   If the allocation reduces noncurrent assets to zero, the remainder of the excess over cost is classified as a deferred credit to be amortized systematically over the period benefitted (not more than 40 years).

        e.   The **equity method** is used by an investor that can exert significant influence over the investee. A rebuttable presumption of significant influence exists when the investor owns at least 20% of the investee's outstanding voting common stock.

            1)   The investor debits its share of investee income to the investment account. Dividends received from the investee are a credit to this account.

                a)   Amortization of any excess of cost over book value purchased is required.

            2)   Under the **cost method**, investee income is not recognized until realized in the form of dividends.

f.   When a stock investment includes more than 50% but less than 100% of the outstanding stock of a company, a minority interest exists.

  1)   The method of computation of that minority interest is identical under the pooling of interests and the purchase methods.

g.   Three types of costs may be incurred in effecting a purchase combination.

  1)   Direct costs of acquisition, such as legal, accounting, consulting, and finder's fees, are included in the cost of the company acquired.

  2)   The costs of registration and issuance of equity securities reduce the fair value of the securities, ordinarily as a debit to additional paid-in capital.

  3)   Indirect and general expenses are deducted as incurred in determining net income. Examples are time spent by combining company executives negotiating the combination and other normal business expenses.

2.   The **pooling of interests** method of accounting is intended to present, as a single interest, two or more common shareholder interests that were previously independent and to combine the rights and risks represented by those interests. The shareholders neither withdraw nor invest assets but, in effect, exchange voting common stock in a ratio that determines their respective interests in the combined entity.

a.   Assets and liabilities are recorded by the combined entity at carrying (book) value.

  1)   Because no acquisition is deemed to have occurred, no goodwill is recognized.

b.   In a pooling of interests, the surviving corporation will issue stock to one or more combining companies. After the pooling, the balance in the capital stock account should equal the par or stated value of the stock outstanding as a result of the pooling.

  1)   The total consolidated contributed capital should equal the sum of the contributed capital amounts of the combining entities. Accordingly, capital stock will be credited for the par or stated value of the shares issued, with a balancing credit to additional paid-in capital.

    a)   However, if the par or stated value of the shares issued in the combination is greater than the contributed capital of the subsidiary, additional paid-in capital must be debited. Because additional paid-in capital may not be reduced below zero, a debit to retained earnings will be necessary if additional paid-in capital is insufficient.

c.   The retained earnings of the consolidated entity should equal the sum of the retained earnings of the combining entities, except for the effects of the foregoing adjustment and elimination of any intercompany transactions.

d.   Operations of the combined entities must be reported for all periods presented as if the pooling had occurred prior to the earliest statement presented.

  1)   The effects of intercompany transactions on current assets, current liabilities, revenue, cost of sales, and beginning retained earnings should be eliminated to the extent possible.

    a)   The effects on EPS of nonrecurring intercompany transactions involving long-term assets and liabilities need not be eliminated.

e.   All costs incurred to effect a business combination accounted for as a pooling of interests should be treated as expenses of the combined entity.

3. **SFAS 94**, *Consolidation of All Majority-Owned Subsidiaries*, requires **consolidation** of all companies in which a parent has a controlling financial interest through direct or indirect ownership of a majority voting interest.

   a. Consolidation is not required if control is likely to be temporary or if control does not rest with the majority owner, for example, if the subsidiary is in bankruptcy or legal reorganization or is subject to foreign exchange restrictions or other government-imposed restrictions that preclude exercise of control.

   b. Consolidation is an accounting process for a business combination when the combined companies remain legally separate. Consolidated statements present the results of operations, financial position, and cash flows of a parent and its subsidiaries as if they constituted a single economic entity.

   c. ARB 51 gives the following general description of consolidation procedures:

      1) Intercompany balances and transactions, such as open account balances (receivables and payables), the parent's investment in the subsidiary, sales and purchases, interest, holdings of securities, dividends, etc., should be eliminated in full even if a minority interest exists.

         a) Retained earnings of a purchased subsidiary at the date of acquisition is excluded from consolidated retained earnings in the entry eliminating the parent's investment account and the subsidiary's shareholder equity accounts.

         b) Shares of the parent held by a subsidiary should not be treated as outstanding in the consolidated balance sheet. They are eliminated.

      2) Intercompany profits and losses are completely eliminated.

      3) The amount of the minority interest recognized at the date of the combination equals a proportionate share of the subsidiary's book value. Subsequently, the minority interest is adjusted for its share of the subsidiary's income and dividends.

      4) In the income statement, the minority interest's adjusted share of the subsidiary's income is usually treated as a deduction in arriving at consolidated income.

      5) The parent's net income equals the consolidated net income because the parent should account for the investment using the equity method.

      6) In the consolidated balance sheet, the shareholders' equity section should reflect the parent's shareholders' equity section. The placement of the minority interest is in dispute, although SFAC 6 indicates a preference for treating it as equity.

4. Stop and review! You have completed the outline for this subunit. Study multiple-choice questions 55 through 62 beginning on page 114.

MULTIPLE-CHOICE QUESTIONS

A. Segment Reporting

1. SFAS 131, *Disclosures about Segments of an Enterprise and Related Information*, requires reporting of information about

    A.   Industry segments.

    B.   Operating segments.

    C.   For-profit and not-for-profit organizations.

    D.   Public and nonpublic enterprises.

The correct answer is (B). *(Publisher)*
REQUIRED: The reporting required by SFAS 131.
DISCUSSION: The objective of segment reporting is to provide information about the different types of business activities of the entity and the economic environments in which it operates. This information is reported on an operating segment basis. SFAS 131 defines an operating segment as "a component of an enterprise that engages in business activities from which it may earn revenues and incur expenses (including revenues and expenses relating to transactions with other components of the same enterprise), whose operating results are regularly reviewed by the enterprise's chief operating decision maker to make decisions about resources to be allocated to the segment and assess its performance, and for which discrete financial information is available." A reportable segment is one that satisfies the foregoing definition and also meets one of three quantitative thresholds.

Answer (A) is incorrect because SFAS 131 superseded SFAS 14, which required line-of-business information classified by industry segment. Instead, SFAS 131 defines segments based on the entity's internal organization. Answers (C) and (D) are incorrect because SFAS 131 applies to public business enterprises.

2. Company M has identified four operating segments. Which of the following segments meet(s) the quantitative threshold for reported profit or loss?

Segment	Reported Profit (Loss)
S	$ 90,000
T	(100,000)
U	910,000
V	(420,000)

    A.   Segment U only.

    B.   Segments U and V.

    C.   Segments T, U, and V.

    D.   Segments S, T, U, and V.

The correct answer is (C). *(Publisher)*
REQUIRED: The segment(s) meeting the quantitative threshold for reported profit or loss.
DISCUSSION: Under SFAS 131, information must be reported separately about an operating segment that reaches one of three quantitative thresholds. Under the profit or loss test, if the absolute amount of the reported profit or loss equals at least 10% of the greater, in absolute amount, of (1) the combined profit of all segments not reporting a loss, or (2) the combined loss of all segments reporting a loss, the segment meets the threshold.

Segments T, U, and V are reportable segments. As shown below, the sum of the reported profits of S and U ($1,000,000) is greater than the sum of the losses of T and V ($520,000). Consequently, the test criterion is $100,000 (10% x $1,000,000).

Segment	Reported Profit	Reported Loss
S	$ 90,000	$ 0
T	0	100,000
U	910,000	0
V	0	420,000
	$1,000,000	$520,000

Answers (A), (B), and (D) are incorrect because Segments T, U, and V each meet the profit or loss test, but Segment S does not.

3. In accordance with SFAS 131, *Disclosures about Segments of an Enterprise and Related Information*, what ordinarily must be reported for each reportable segment?

- A. Segment cash flow.

- B. Interest revenue net of interest expense.

- C. A measure of profit or loss.

- D. External revenues from export sales if they are 10% or more of consolidated sales.

The correct answer is (C). *(Publisher)*

REQUIRED: The item ordinarily reported for each reportable segment.

DISCUSSION: For each reportable segment, an enterprise must report a measure of profit or loss, certain items included in the determination of that profit or loss, total segment assets, and certain related items. Segment cash flow need not be reported.

Answer (A) is incorrect because segment cash flow need not be reported. Answer (B) is incorrect because interest revenue and expense are reported separately unless a majority of revenues derive from interest and the chief operating decision maker relies primarily on net interest revenue for assessing segment performance and allocating resources. Answer (D) is incorrect because, if practicable, geographic information is reported for external revenues attributed to the home country and to all foreign countries in total. If external revenues attributed to a foreign country are material, they are disclosed separately.

4. For each of the following groups of customers, purchases amounted to 10% or more of the revenue of a publicly held company. For which of these groups must the company disclose information about major customers?

- A. Federal governmental agencies, 6%; state governmental agencies, 4%.

- B. French governmental agencies, 6%; German governmental agencies, 4%.

- C. Parent company, 6%; subsidiary of parent company, 4%.

- D. Federal governmental agencies, 6%; foreign governmental agencies, 4%.

The correct answer is (C). *(Publisher)*

REQUIRED: The set of circumstances requiring disclosure about major customers.

DISCUSSION: For purposes of SFAS 131, a group of customers under common control must be regarded as a single customer in determining whether 10% or more of the revenue of an enterprise is derived from sales to any single customer. A parent and a subsidiary are under common control, and they should be regarded as a single customer. Major customer disclosure is required in situation (C) because total combined revenue is 10% (6% + 4%).

Answers (A), (B), and (D) are incorrect because each governmental unit is to be treated as a separate customer in applying the 10% revenue test.

B. Asset Depreciation

5. Depreciation of a plant asset is the process of

- A. Asset valuation for statement of financial position purposes.

- B. Allocating the cost of the asset to the periods of use.

- C. Accumulating a fund for the replacement of the asset.

- D. Asset valuation based on current replacement cost data.

The correct answer is (B). *(CMA 689 4-6)*

REQUIRED: The purpose of depreciation of fixed assets.

DISCUSSION: In accounting, depreciation is the systematic and rational allocation of the cost of the productive capacity of a fixed asset to the accounting periods the asset benefits. The asset's historical cost minus expected salvage value is the basis for the allocation.

Answers (A) and (D) are incorrect because depreciation is a process of cost allocation, not valuation. Answer (C) is incorrect because depreciation allocates cost; it does not provide for replacement.

Questions 6 through 8 are based on the following information. Patterson Company has the following information on one of its vehicles purchased on January 1, 1993:

Vehicle cost	$50,000
Useful life, years, estimated	5
Useful life, miles, estimated	100,000
Salvage value, estimated	$10,000
Actual miles driven, 1993	30,000
1994	20,000
1995	15,000
1996	25,000
1997	12,000

No estimates were changed during the life of the asset.

6. The 1995 depreciation expense for the vehicle using the sum-of-the-years'-digits (SYD) method was

A. $6,000

B. $8,000

C. $10,000

D. $13,333

The correct answer is (B). *(CMA 695 2-4)*

REQUIRED: The 1995 depreciation expense under the SYD method.

DISCUSSION: Under the SYD method, the amount to be depreciated is $40,000 ($50,000 original cost – $10,000 salvage). The portion expensed each year is based on a fraction, the denominator of which is the summation of the years of life of the asset being depreciated. For an asset with a 5-year life, the denominator is 15 (5 + 4 + 3 + 2 + 1). The numerator equals the years remaining. For 1995, the fraction is 3 ÷15, and depreciation expense is $8,000 [$40,000 × (3 ÷ 15)].

Answer (A) is incorrect because $6,000 is based on the units-of-production method. Answer (C) is incorrect because $10,000 omits the vehicle's salvage value from the calculation. Answer (D) is incorrect because $13,333 is the depreciation expense for 1993.

7. The fiscal 1994 year-end accumulated depreciation balance, using the double-declining-balance method was

A. $12,000

B. $16,000

C. $25,600

D. $32,000

The correct answer is (D). *(CMA 695 2-5)*

REQUIRED: The accumulated depreciation at year-end 1994 using the DDB method.

DISCUSSION: For an asset with a 5-year life, the straight-line rate is 20%. Under DDB, the applicable percentage is 40%. This rate is applied to the book value of the asset, which for the first year is the original cost. Thus, first-year DDB depreciation is $20,000 (40% × $50,000), second-year depreciation is $12,000 [40% × ($50,000 – $20,000)], and total depreciation for 1993 and 1994 is $32,000.

Answer (A) is incorrect because $12,000 is the depreciation expense for 1994. Answer (B) is incorrect because $16,000 is the depreciation expense for 1993 if salvage value is deducted from original cost. Answer (C) is incorrect because $25,600 is the accumulated depreciation balance under DDB if salvage value is deducted from original cost.

8. In the years after mid-service point of a depreciable asset, which of the following depreciation methods will result in the highest depreciation expense?

A. Sum-of-the-year's-digits.

B. Declining-balance.

C. Double-declining-balance.

D. Straight-line.

The correct answer is (D). *(CIA 1195 IV-11)*

REQUIRED: The method resulting in the highest depreciation after the midpoint of the service life.

DISCUSSION: Accelerated depreciation methods, such as sum-of-the-years'-digits, declining-balance, and double-declining-balance, charge higher depreciation costs in the early years of the asset's life and lower depreciation costs in the later years. These decreasing charge methods will therefore charge lower depreciation costs in the later years of the asset's life than the straight-line method, which charges the same amount to depreciation expense each year.

Answers (A), (B), and (C) are incorrect because the SYD, declining-balance, and double-declining balance methods accelerate recognition of depreciation.

9. Using the units-of-production method, what was the 1997 depreciation expense?

A. $4,000

B. $4,800

C. $5,000

D. $6,000

The correct answer is (A). *(CMA 695 2-6)*
REQUIRED: The depreciation expense for 1997 under the units-of-production method.
DISCUSSION: Under the units-of-production method, periodic depreciation is based on the proportion of expected total production that occurred. For the years 1993 through 1996, the total depreciation was $36,000 {(($50,000 – $10,000) × [(30,000 + 20,000 + 15,000 + 25,000) ÷ 100,000]}. Hence, the remaining depreciable base was $4,000 ($50,000 cost – $10,000 salvage – $36,000). Given that the 12,000 miles driven in 1997 exceeded the remaining estimated production of 10,000 miles (100,000 – 30,000 – 20,000 – 15,000 – 25,000), only the $4,000 of the remaining depreciable base should be recognized in 1997.
Answer (B) is incorrect because $4,800 is based on a 1997 rate of 12% (12,000 miles ÷ 100,000 miles of estimated usage). It ignores the effects of depreciation expense deducted in prior years. Answer (C) is incorrect because $5,000 assumes that depreciation is based on original cost without regard to salvage value. Answer (D) is incorrect because $6,000 is based on a 12% rate and ignores salvage value.

C. Secured Loans

10. When a transfer of financial assets qualifies for recognition as a sale, the transferor should recognize

A.   Initially all assets and liabilities obtained at the book value of the assets surrendered.

B.   Gain or loss in full in earnings.

C.   Gain or loss on the straight-line basis as the assets are realized.

D.   Gain or loss in accordance with the interest method as the assets are realized.

The correct answer is (B). *(Publisher)*
REQUIRED: The accounting for a sale of financial assets.
DISCUSSION: If the conditions for a sale are met, the transferor derecognizes the assets sold, recognizes assets obtained and liabilities incurred as proceeds of the sale (measured at fair value if practicable), and recognizes any gain or loss in earnings (SFAS 125, *Accounting for Transfers and Servicing of Financial Assets and Extinguishment of Liabilities*).
Answer (A) is incorrect because measurement is at fair value if practicable. Answers (C) and (D) are incorrect because the gain or loss should be recognized in full at the time of the sale.

11. A transfer of financial assets should be reported as a sale if certain conditions are met. Which of the following is one of the conditions?

A.   Transferees may pledge or exchange the assets.

B.   The assets are within the reach of the transferor's creditors.

C.   The transferor has an option to repurchase the assets.

D.   The transferor receives beneficial interests in the assets as consideration.

The correct answer is (A). *(Publisher)*
REQUIRED: The condition for treating a transfer of financial assets as a sale.
DISCUSSION: The transferor surrenders control and the transaction is treated as a sale only if three conditions are met: (1) The assets have been isolated from the transferor, that is, are beyond its reach and its creditors; (2) either each transferee may pledge or exchange the assets, or the transferee is an entity that meets certain criteria (e.g., certain trusts) and the holders of beneficial interests in that entity may pledge or exchange those interests; and (3) the transferor does not maintain effective control over the transferred assets through certain repurchase or redemption agreements (SFAS 125).
Answer (B) is incorrect because the assets should be isolated from the transferor and its creditors. Answer (C) is incorrect because the transferor should not have effective control through repurchase or redemption agreements. Answer (D) is incorrect because the transfer is a sale only to the extent the transferor receives consideration other than beneficial interests.

12. Factoring in which the transferee is allowed to collect any defaulted receivables from the transferor is known as

A. Factoring with recourse

B. Factoring without recourse.

C. A specific assignment.

D. A credit card sale.

The correct answer is (A). *(Publisher)*

REQUIRED: The type of factoring in which the risk of default remains with the transferor.

DISCUSSION: Factoring with recourse permits the transferee (the factor) to collect any defaulted receivables from the transferor. In other words, the risk of default is not transferred to the factor.

Answer (B) is incorrect because factoring without recourse transfers the risk of default to the transferee. Answer (C) is incorrect because a specific assignment is not considered factoring, but rather an assignment. Answer (D) is incorrect because a credit card sale transfers ownership of receivables without recourse.

D. Deferred Taxes

13. On December 31, 1997, Health Company reported a $150,000 warranty expense in its income statement. The expense was based on actual warranty costs of $30,000 in 1997 and expected warranty costs of $35,000 in 1998, $40,000 in 1999, and $45,000 in 2000. Health Company elected early application of SFAS 109 in 1997. At December 31, 1997, deferred taxes should be based on a

A. $120,000 deductible temporary difference.

B. $150,000 deductible temporary difference.

C. $120,000 taxable temporary difference.

D. $150,000 taxable temporary difference.

The correct answer is (A). *(Publisher)*

REQUIRED: The taxable (deductible) temporary difference resulting from a warranty expense.

DISCUSSION: At year-end 1997, Health Company should report a $120,000 warranty liability in its balance sheet. The warranty liability is equal to the $150,000 warranty expense minus the $30,000 warranty cost actually incurred in 1997. Because warranty costs are not deductible until actually incurred, the tax basis of the warranty liability is $0. The result is a $120,000 temporary difference ($120,000 book basis – $0 tax basis). When the liability is settled through the actual incurrence of warranty costs, the amounts will be deductible. Thus, the temporary difference should be classified as a deductible temporary difference.

Answer (B) is incorrect because $150,000 equals the warranty expense, not the payable. Answer (C) is incorrect because warranty costs will result in a deductible amount. Answer (D) is incorrect because the warranty costs will result in a deductible amount and the $30,000 actual warranty costs are currently deductible.

14. Barth and Garth, Inc. depreciate equipment over 15 years for financial purposes and over 7 years for tax purposes as prescribed by MACRS. As a result of this temporary difference, the deferred income taxes will be reported in its first year of use as a

A. Noncurrent asset.

B. Noncurrent liability.

C. Current liability.

D. Current asset.

The correct answer is (B). *(Publisher)*

REQUIRED: The classification of deferred taxes arising from the excess of tax over book depreciation.

DISCUSSION: When a deferred tax liability or asset is related to an asset or a liability, its classification as current or noncurrent is based on the classification of the related item for financial reporting purposes. Because tax depreciation for the first year is greater than book depreciation, the tax basis of this noncurrent asset differs from (is less than) its book basis. The result is a taxable temporary difference. The related deferred tax liability is classified as noncurrent because the related asset is noncurrent.

Answer (A) is incorrect because a temporary difference related to depreciable equipment results in a liability. Answers (C) and (D) are incorrect because depreciable equipment is classified as a noncurrent asset.

15. Based on its current operating levels, Glucose Corporation estimates that its annual level of taxable income in the foreseeable future will be $200,000 annually. Enacted tax rates for the tax jurisdiction in which Glucose operates are 15% for the first $50,000 of taxable income, 25% for the next $50,000 of taxable income, and 35% for taxable income in excess of $100,000. Which tax rate should Glucose use to measure a deferred tax liability or asset in accordance with SFAS 109, *Accounting for Income Taxes*?

A. 15%

B. 25%

C. 27.5%

D. 35%

The correct answer is (C). *(Publisher)*
REQUIRED: The tax rate applicable to the measurement of a deferred tax liability or asset.
DISCUSSION: In measuring a deferred tax liability or asset, the objective is to use the enacted tax rate(s) expected to apply to taxable income in the periods in which the deferred tax liability or asset is expected to be settled or realized. If graduated tax rates are a significant factor for an enterprise, the applicable tax rate is the average graduated tax rate applicable to the amount of estimated future annual taxable income. As indicated, the applicable tax rate is 27.5%.

Taxable Income		Tax Rate		
$ 50,000	x	15%	=	$ 7,500
50,000	x	25%	=	12,500
100,000	x	35%	=	35,000
$200,000				$55,000

$$\$55,000 \div \$200,000 = 27.5\%$$

Answer (A) is incorrect because 15% is the tax rate for the first $50,000 of income. Answer (B) is incorrect because 25% is the tax rate for income over $50,000 but less than $100,000. Answer (D) is incorrect because 35% is the tax rate for income over $100,000.

16. Using the approach known as intraperiod tax allocation, income tax expense (or benefit) should be allocated to all of the following except

A. Continuing operations.

B. Gain (or loss) on sale of land.

C. Discontinued operations.

D. Extraordinary items and prior-period adjustments.

The correct answer is (B). *(CMA 695 2-27)*
REQUIRED: The item to which income tax expense or benefit is not allocated.
DISCUSSION: SFAS 109 requires intraperiod allocation of income tax expense or benefit among continuing operations, discontinued operations, extraordinary items, and items charged directly to shareholders equity, such as a prior-period adjustment. Tax expense or benefit need not be allocated to a gain or loss on sale of land because it is most likely included in the determination of income from continuing operations or in discontinued operations.
Answers (A), (C), and (D) are incorrect because continuing operations, discontinued operations, extraordinary items, and prior-period adjustments are items to which intraperiod allocations of income tax expense or benefit should be made.

17. Temporary and permanent differences between taxable income and pre-tax financial income differ in that

A. Temporary differences do not give rise to future taxable or deductible amounts.

B. Only permanent differences have deferred tax consequences.

C. Only temporary differences have deferred tax consequences.

D. Temporary differences include items that enter into pre-tax financial income but never into taxable income.

The correct answer is (C). *(CIA 594 IV-73)*
REQUIRED: The difference between temporary and permanent differences.
DISCUSSION: Temporary differences include differences between the tax bases of assets or liabilities and their reported amounts in the financial statements that will result in taxable or deductible amounts in future years when the reported amounts of the assets are recovered or the liabilities are settled. A permanent difference is an event that is recognized either in pretax financial income or in taxable income but never in the other. Accordingly, only temporary differences have deferred tax consequences (SFAS 109).
Answer (A) is incorrect because temporary differences result in taxable or deductible amounts in future years. Answer (B) is incorrect because permanent differences only affect the period in which they occur. Only temporary differences have deferred tax consequences. Answer (D) is incorrect because permanent differences include items that enter into pre-tax financial income but never into taxable income.

18. In preparing its December 31, 1997 financial statements, Irene Company must determine the proper accounting treatment of a $180,000 loss carryforward available to offset future taxable income. There are no temporary differences. The applicable current and future income tax rate is 30%. Available evidence is not conclusive as to the future existence of sufficient taxable income to provide for the future realization of the tax benefit of the $180,000 loss carryforward. However, based on the available evidence, Irene believes that it is more likely than not that future taxable income will be available to provide for the future realization of $100,000 of this loss carryforward. In its 1997 statement of financial condition, Irene should recognize what amounts?

	Deferred Tax Asset	Valuation Allowance
A.	$0	$0
B.	$30,000	$0
C.	$54,000	$24,000
D.	$54,000	$30,000

The correct answer is (C). *(Publisher)*
REQUIRED: The amounts to be recognized as a deferred tax asset and related valuation allowance.
DISCUSSION: The applicable tax rate should be used to measure a deferred tax asset for an operating loss carryforward that is available to offset future taxable income. Irene should therefore recognize a $54,000 ($180,000 x 30%) deferred tax asset. A valuation allowance should be recognized to reduce the deferred tax asset if, based on the weight of the available evidence, it is more likely than not (the likelihood is more than 50%) that some portion or all of a deferred tax asset will not be realized. The valuation allowance should be equal to an amount necessary to reduce the deferred tax asset to the amount that is more likely than not to be realized. Based on the available evidence, Irene believes that it is more likely than not that the tax benefit of $100,000 of the operating loss will be realized. Thus, the company should recognize a $24,000 valuation allowance to reduce the $54,000 deferred tax asset to $30,000 ($100,000 x 30%), the amount of the deferred tax asset that is more likely than not to be realized.
Answer (A) is incorrect because a deferred tax asset equal to $54,000 should be recognized and a valuation allowance should be recognized equal to $24,000 to reduce the deferred tax asset to $30,000. Answer (B) is incorrect because a deferred tax asset of $30,000 results from netting the valuation allowance against the deferred tax asset. Answer (D) is incorrect because $30,000 is the deferred tax asset, not the valuation allowance, after the two are netted.

E. Leases

19. Leases should be classified by the lessee as either operating leases or capital leases. Which of the following statements best characterizes operating leases?

A. The rights and risks of ownership are transferred from the lessor to the lessee.

B. The lessee records leased property as an asset and the present value of the lease payments as a liability.

C. Operating leases transfer ownership to the lessee, contain a bargain purchase option, are for more than 75% of the leased asset's useful life, or have lease payments with a present value in excess of 90% of the value of the leased asset.

D. The lessor records lease revenue, asset depreciation, maintenance, etc., and the lessee records lease payments as rental expense.

The correct answer is (D). *(Publisher)*
REQUIRED: The true statement about operating leases.
DISCUSSION: Operating leases are transactions whereby lessees rent the right to use lessor assets without acquiring a substantial portion of the rights and risks of ownership of those assets.
Answer (A) is incorrect because, when the rights and risks of ownership are transferred from the lessor to the lessee, the transaction is a capital lease. Answer (B) is incorrect because it describes the proper accounting for a lessee's capital lease. Answer (C) is incorrect because satisfaction of any one of these four criteria requires the lease to be treated as a capital lease.

20. What is the difference between a direct financing lease and a sales-type lease?

A. Lessees usually depreciate direct financing leases over the term of the lease and sales-type leases over the useful life of the leased asset.

B. The difference between the sum of all lease payments and the cost of the leased asset to the lessor is interest income for direct financing leases, and is part interest and part sales income for sales-type leases.

C. The lease payments receivable on the books of a lessor are recorded at their present value for sales-type leases and at their gross value for direct financing leases.

D. The lessor records the present value of the residual value of the leased asset for direct financing leases, but records the undiscounted (gross) residual value for sales-type leases.

The correct answer is (B). *(Publisher)*
REQUIRED: The difference between direct financing leases and sales-type leases.
DISCUSSION: Both direct financing and sales-type leases are accounted for by the lessee as capital leases. The difference between the two arises only for lessor accounting. In a direct financing lease, the difference between the gross investment and its cost or carrying amount is recorded as unearned interest revenue. No gross profit is recognized. In a sales-type lease, the same amount of unearned interest revenue will be recorded. However, a gross profit equal to the difference between the cost (plus initial direct costs – the present value of the unguaranteed residual value) and the sales price (present value of the minimum lease payments) is also recognized. The difference between a direct financing and a sales-type lease is that the cost used in accounting for a direct-financing lease is ordinarily the fair value. But the cost for a sales-type lease differs from the fair value.

Answer (A) is incorrect because lessees use the same depreciation methods for both kinds of leases. Answer (C) is incorrect because the receivable for the lease payments is recorded at gross on the books of the lessor for both the sales-type and direct financing leases. Answer (D) is incorrect because the undiscounted (gross) residual value is recorded by the lessor for both direct financing and sales-type leases. It is included as part of the gross investment, i.e., in lease payments receivable.

21. Initial direct costs incurred by the lessor under a sales-type lease should be

A. Deferred and allocated over the economic life of the leased property.

B. Expensed in the period incurred.

C. Deferred and allocated over the term of the lease in proportion to the recognition of rental income.

D. Added to the gross investment in the lease and amortized over the term of the lease as a yield adjustment.

The correct answer is (B). *(CMA 690 3-2)*
REQUIRED: The accounting for initial direct costs in a sales-type lease.
DISCUSSION: SFAS 91, *Accounting for Nonrefundable Fees and Costs Associated with Originating or Acquiring Loans and Initial Direct Costs of Leases*, defines initial direct costs as having two components: (1) the lessor's external costs to originate a lease incurred in dealings with independent third parties and (2) the internal costs directly related to specified activities performed by the lessor for that lease. According to SFAS 13, in a sales-type lease, the cost, or carrying amount if different, plus any initial direct costs, minus the present value of any unguaranteed residual value, is charged against income in the same period that the present value of the minimum lease payments is credited to sales. The result is the recognition of a net profit or loss on the sales-type lease.

Answer (A) is incorrect because initial direct costs are considered an expense in the period of sale. Answers (C) and (D) are incorrect because they describe the proper treatment of initial direct costs in an operating lease and a direct financing lease, respectively.

22. On August 1, Jones Corporation leased property to Smith Company for a 5-year period. The annual $20,000 lease payment is payable at the end of each year. The expected residual value at the end of the lease term is $10,000. Jones Company's implicit interest rate is 12%. The cost of the property to Jones was $50,000, which is the fair value at the lease date. The present value of an ordinary annuity of 1 for five periods is 3.605. The present value of 1 at the end of five periods is .567. At the inception of the lease, the recorded gross investment is

A. $110,000

B. $100,000

C. $72,100

D. $90,000

The correct answer is (A). *(J.O. Hall)*
REQUIRED: The amount to be recorded as gross investment at the inception of the lease.
DISCUSSION: For a direct financing or a sales-type lease, the lessor should record the gross investment in the lease at the undiscounted sum of the minimum lease payments (the total of the periodic payments and any guaranteed residual value, net of executory costs) and any unguaranteed residual value. Accordingly, the gross investment is the same regardless of whether any residual value is guaranteed. The five periodic payments of $20,000 equal $100,000. The expected residual value, including both guaranteed and unguaranteed portions, equals $10,000. Thus, the gross investment in this lease should be $110,000 ($100,000 + $10,000).
Answer (B) is incorrect because it fails to include the residual value in the gross investment. Answer (C) is incorrect because the annual lease payments should be recorded at their undiscounted value. Answer (D) is incorrect because the residual value is added to, not subtracted from, the undiscounted lease payments.

23. Careful reading of an annual report will reveal that off-balance-sheet debt includes

A. Amounts due in future years under operating leases.

B. Transfers of accounts receivable without recourse.

C. Current portion of long-term debt.

D. Amounts due in future years under capital leases.

The correct answer is (A). *(CMA 1295 2-6)*
REQUIRED: The off-balance-sheet debt.
DISCUSSION: Off-balance-sheet debt includes any type of liability that the company is responsible for but that does not appear on the balance sheet. The most common example is the amount due in future years on operating leases. Under SFAS 13, operating leases are not capitalized; instead, only the periodic payments of rent are reported when actually paid. Capital leases (those similar to a purchase) must be capitalized and reported as liabilities.
Answer (B) is incorrect because transfers of accounts receivable without recourse do not create a liability for the company. This transaction is simply a transfer of receivables for cash. Answer (C) is incorrect because the current portion of long-term debt is shown on the balance sheet as a current liability. Answer (D) is incorrect because amounts due in future years under capital leases are required to be capitalized under SFAS 13.

Questions 24 and 25 are based on the following information. On January 1, 1994, Plantation Restaurant is planning to enter as the lessee into the two lease agreements described in the opposite column. Each lease is noncancellable, and Plantation does not receive title to either leased property during or at the end of the lease term. All payments required under these agreements are due on January 1 each year.

Lessor	Hadaway, Inc.	Cutter Electronics
Type of property	Oven	Computer
Yearly rental	$15,000	$4,000
Lease term	10 years	3 years
Economic life	15 years	5 years
Purchase option	None	$3,000
Renewal option	None	None
Fair market value at inception of lease	$125,000	$10,200
Unguaranteed residual value	None	$2,000
Lessee's incremental borrowing rate	10%	10%
Executory costs paid by	Lessee	Lessor
Annual executory costs	$800	$500
Present value factor at 10% (of an annuity due)	6.76	2.74

24. Plantation Restaurant should treat the lease agreement with Hadaway, Inc. as a(n)

A. Capital lease with an initial asset value of $101,400.

B. Operating lease, charging $14,200 in rental expense and $800 in executory costs to annual operations.

C. Operating lease, charging the present value of the yearly rental expense to annual operations.

D. Operating lease, charging $15,000 in rental expense and $800 in executory costs to annual operations.

The correct answer is (D). *(CMA 1293 2-27)*

REQUIRED: The true statement about the Hadaway, Inc. lease.

DISCUSSION: The Hadaway lease is an operating lease with a $15,000 annual rental expense with annual executory costs of $800 to be paid by the lessee. An operating lease does not transfer the rights and risks of ownership to the lessee. The Hadaway lease is nothing more than a rental arrangement. SFAS 13 specifies that if any one of the following criteria is met, the lease is a capital lease: the lease transfers title to the lessee, the lease has a bargain purchase option, the lease term is 75% or more of the useful life of the leased asset, or the present value of the minimum lease payments is 90% or more of the asset's fair value. The Hadaway lease meets none of these four criteria.

Answer (A) is incorrect because the Hadaway lease does not meet any of the criteria of a capital lease. Answer (B) is incorrect because rental expense is $15,000. Answer (C) is incorrect because the actual cash outlay for rent, $15,000, is charged to expense.

25. Plantation Restaurant should treat the lease agreement with Cutter Electronics as a(n)

A. Capital lease with an initial asset value of $10,960.

B. Capital lease with an initial asset value of $10,200.

C. Operating lease, charging $3,500 in rental expense and $500 in executory costs to annual operations.

D. Capital lease with an initial asset value of $9,590.

The correct answer is (D). *(CMA 1293 2-28)*

REQUIRED: The true statement about the Cutter Electronics lease.

DISCUSSION: A capital lease is one in which many of the rights of ownership are transferred to the lessee. For accounting purposes, the lessee treats a capital lease as similar to the purchase of an asset. SFAS 13 specifies that if the present value of the minimum lease payments (excluding executory costs) is 90% or more of the asset's fair value, the lease should be accounted for as a capital lease. Given that the executory costs associated with the lease are to be paid by the lessor, a portion of the lease rental price is for those costs, not for the asset. Executory costs include insurance, maintenance, and similar expenses. Consequently, the annual minimum lease payment equals the annual payment minus the executory costs, or $3,500 ($4,000 yearly rental – $500). The present value of the minimum lease payments is therefore $9,590 (2.74 x $3,500), which is greater than 90% of the fair value of the asset. Thus, the lease should be capitalized. The appropriate amount of the initial asset value is the present value of the minimum lease payments calculated above.

Answer (A) is incorrect because the initial asset value cannot exceed the fair value of the leased asset. Moreover, $10,960 includes the present value of the executory costs. Answer (B) is incorrect because $10,200 is the fair value of the leased asset. Answer (C) is incorrect because the Cutter lease meets the criteria of a capital lease.

F. Pensions

26. If, in a business combination structured as a purchase, the acquired company sponsors a defined benefit pension plan, the acquiring company should

A. Recognize any previously existing unrecognized net gain or loss.

B. Assign part of the purchase price to the unrecognized prior service cost as an intangible asset.

C. Assign part of the purchase price to the excess of plan assets over the projected benefit obligation.

D. Recognize a previously existing unrecognized transition net asset or obligation of the plan.

The correct answer is (C). *(Publisher)*

REQUIRED: The acquiring company's accounting when the acquired company sponsors a pension plan.

DISCUSSION: In a business combination structured as a purchase, the acquiring company should recognize a pension liability if the PBO of the acquired company is in excess of that company's plan assets. Likewise, a pension asset should be recognized if plan assets exceed the PBO.

Answers (A), (B), and (D) are incorrect because, in a business combination accounted for as a purchase, unrecognized net gains and losses, prior service cost, and the transition net asset or obligation of the acquired company's defined benefit plan are eliminated by the assignment of part of the purchase price to a liability (excess of PBO over plan assets) or an asset (excess of plan assets over the PBO).

27. The following information relates to the 1990 activity of the defined benefit pension plan of Twain Publishers, Ltd., a company whose stock is publicly traded:

Service cost	$120,000
Return on plan assets	30,000
Interest cost on pension benefit obligation	40,000
Amortization of actuarial loss	10,000
Amortization of prior service cost	5,000
Amortization of transition obligation	15,000

Twain's 1990 pension cost is

A. $120,000

B. $140,000

C. $150,000

D. $160,000

The correct answer is (D). *(A. Oddo)*

REQUIRED: The net periodic pension cost (NPPC) for the year.

DISCUSSION: Components of NPPC are service cost, interest cost, the expected return on plan assets, and amortization of any (1) unrecognized prior service cost, (2) net transition asset or obligation, or (3) unrecognized net gain (loss). Service cost, interest cost, and the amortization of actuarial loss, prior service cost, and a net transition obligation increase the net periodic pension cost. The expected return on plan assets decreases NPPC. As indicated below, NPPC for 1990 is $160,000.

Service cost	$120,000
Return on plan assets	(30,000)
Interest cost	40,000
Amortization of actuarial loss	10,000
Amortization of prior service cost	5,000
Amortization of transition obligation	15,000
Net periodic pension cost	$160,000

Answer (A) is incorrect because $120,000 only includes the service cost component. Answer (B) is incorrect because $140,000 excludes the amortization of prior service cost and the transition obligation. Answer (C) is incorrect because $150,000 excludes the amortization of the actuarial loss.

28. At end of the year, Penny Company's projected benefit obligation (PBO) was determined to be $1,500,000, which was $200,000 higher than had been expected. The market-related value of the defined benefit plan's assets was equal to its fair value of $1,250,000. No other gains and losses have occurred. If the average remaining service life is 20 years, the minimum required amortization of the unrecognized net gain (loss) in the next year will be

A. $20,000

B. $3,750

C. $2,500

D. $0

The correct answer is (C). *(Publisher)*

REQUIRED: The minimum required amortization of unrecognized net gain (loss) next year.

DISCUSSION: At a minimum, amortization of the cumulative unrecognized net gain or loss (excluding asset gains and losses not yet reflected in market-related value) must be included as a component of NPPC for a year if, as of the beginning of the year, that unrecognized gain or loss exceeds 10% of the greater of the PBO or the market-related value (MRV) of plan assets. At year-end, Penny's PBO was $200,000 greater than estimated (a $200,000 liability loss). Since no other gain or loss has occurred, the unrecognized net loss to be amortized beginning next year is $200,000. The corridor amount is $150,000 (10% of the greater of $1,500,000 PBO or $1,250,000 MRV of plan assets). The amount outside the corridor is $50,000 ($200,000 – $150,000), and the amount to be amortized is thus $2,500 ($50,000 ÷ 20 years of average remaining service life).

Answer (A) is incorrect because $20,000 is the result of using the full $200,000 liability loss without regard to the corridor amount and assumes an amortization period of ten years instead of twenty. Answer (B) is incorrect because $3,750 is the result of using $125,000 (10% x $1,250,000 plan assets) as the corridor amount instead of $150,000. Answer (D) is incorrect because $50,000 of the liability loss must be amortized over the average remaining service life beginning the year following the loss.

29. At the start of its current fiscal year, Emper Co. amended its defined benefit pension plan, resulting in an increase of $600,000 in the PBO. As of the date of the amendment, Emper had 50 employees. Ten employees are expected to leave at the end of each of the next 5 years (including the current year). The minimum amortization of prior service cost in the first year is

A. $80,000

B. $120,000

C. $160,000

D. $200,000

The correct answer is (D). *(Publisher)*

REQUIRED: The minimum amortization of prior service cost.

DISCUSSION: Prior service cost is amortized by assigning an equal amount to each future period of service of each employee active at the date of the plan amendment who is expected to receive benefits under the plan. If all or almost all of a plan's participants are inactive, the prior service cost is amortized based on the remaining life expectancy of the participants. An alternative amortization approach, such as a straight-line method, that recognizes the cost of retroactive amendments more quickly is also permitted if used consistently. For Emper, total service years rendered during the 5-year period is 150 (50 + 40 + 30 + 20 + 10). The amortization fraction for the first year is thus 50/150, and the minimum amortization is $200,000 ($600,000 x 50/150).

Answer (A) is incorrect because 50, not 20, must be used as the numerator of the amortization fraction. Answer (B) is incorrect because the use of straight-line amortization over 5 years does not recognize the cost of retroactive amendments more quickly, so the method described above must be used. Answer (C) is incorrect because 50, not 40, must be used as the numerator of the amortization fraction for the first year.

30. Deerfield Corporation has the following information available regarding its pension plan:

	May 31, 1996	May 31, 1997
Accumulated benefit obligation (ABO)	$180,000	$280,000
Projected benefit obligation (PBO)	200,000	320,000
Fair value of plan assets	162,000	180,000
Unrecognized prior service cost	68,000	52,000
Prepaid pension cost	30,000	--
Accrued pension cost	--	88,000

In accordance with the requirements of SFAS 87, *Employer's Accounting for Pension Plans*, Deerfield's minimum liability at May 31, 1996 and 1997, respectively, was

A. $38,000 and $140,000.

B. $98,000 and $0.

C. $48,000 and $12,000.

D. $18,000 and $100,000.

The correct answer is (D). *(CMA 694 2-20)*

REQUIRED: The minimum pension liability at the beginning and end of a period.

DISCUSSION: SFAS 87 requires the recording of a liability if the ABO is underfunded. Thus, if the ABO is greater than the fair value of plan assets, a net liability must be recognized. At May 31, 1996, the $180,000 ABO is $18,000 greater than the $162,000 fair value of plan assets. At May 31, 1997, a liability of $100,000 exists because the $280,000 ABO is $100,000 greater than the $180,000 fair value of plan assets.

Answer (A) is incorrect because $38,000 and $140,000 equal the excess of the PBO over the fair value of plan assets at May 31, 1996 and 1997, respectively. Answer (B) is incorrect because $98,000 is the sum of unrecognized prior service cost and prepaid pension cost, and $0 is the difference between the PBO at May 31, 1997 and the sum of the fair value of the plan assets, the unrecognized prior service cost, and the accrued pension cost. Answer (C) is incorrect because $48,000 is the amount of the entry at May 31, 1996 to record the additional liability needed to reflect the required minimum liability. It equals the excess of the ABO over the fair value of plan assets, plus the prepaid pension cost. The entry is to debit an intangible asset and to credit the additional liability for $48,000. At May 31, 1997, $12,000 equals the amount of the entry to record the additional liability ($280,000 ABO – $180,000 fair value of plan assets – $88,000 accrued pension cost).

G. Bonds

Questions 31 through 33 are based on the following information. On July 1, 1994, Garrett Corporation issued $500,000 of 8% face value bonds that are due June 30, 1999. Interest on the bonds is payable semiannually on December 31 and June 30, and the bonds were sold to yield 10%. As required by APB Opinion No. 21, *Interest on Receivables and Payables*, Garrett uses the effective interest method for recording bonds, and pertinent present value tables are presented as follows.

Number of Periods	Present Value of $1			
	4%	5%	8%	10%
5	.822	.784	.681	.621
10	.675	.614	.463	.386

Number of Periods	Present Value of an Ordinary Annuity of $1			
	4%	5%	8%	10%
5	4.452	4.329	3.993	3.791
10	8.111	7.722	6.710	6.144

31. As proceeds from this bond issuance, Garrett Corporation should record

- A. $365,700
- B. $420,360
- C. $461,440
- D. $478,580

The correct answer is (C). *(CMA 1294 2-12)*

REQUIRED: The proceeds from the bonds.

DISCUSSION: These bonds will sell at a discount because the contract rate of 8% is less than the 10% market rate. The issue price equals the present value of the future cash flows (principal and interest) discounted at a 10% annual rate. Because the bonds pay interest for 10 semiannual periods, the appropriate present value factors are those for 10 periods at a discount rate of 5% (10% ÷ 2). The proceeds equal the present value of the $500,000 principal plus the present value of the annuity represented by the stream of interest payments. Thus, the amount recorded should be $461,440 [($500,000 x .614) + (8% x 1/2 x $500,000 x 7.722)].

Answer (A) is incorrect because $365,700 is based on an 8% rate for 10 periods. Answer (B) is incorrect because $420,360 is based on an 8% rate for five periods. Answer (D) is incorrect because $478,580 is based on a 5% rate for five periods.

32. The interest expense that Garrett Corporation will incur on these bonds at December 31, 1994, is

- A. $23,072.00
- B. $18,457.60
- C. $25,000.00
- D. $20,000.00

The correct answer is (A). *(CMA 1294 2-13)*

REQUIRED: The interest expense at December 31, 1994.

DISCUSSION: The bonds were issued on July 1, 1994 for $461,440 [($500,000 principal x .614 present value factor for 10 semiannual periods at 5%) + (8% contract rate x 1/2 x $500,000 principal x 7.722 present value of an annuity factor for 10 semiannual periods at 5%)]. Under the effective interest method, interest expense at the end of the first semiannual period equals $23,072 (5% semiannual market rate x $461,440 carrying value at 12/31/94).

Answer (B) is incorrect because $18,457.60 equals 5% of a carrying value of $369,152. Answer (C) is incorrect because $25,000.00 equals 5% of $500,000. Answer (D) is incorrect because $20,000.00 equals 4% of $500,000.

33. The amount of discount that Garrett Corporation should amortize at December 31, 1994, is

- A. $7,712.00
- B. $3,856.00
- C. $1,542.00
- D. $3,072.00

The correct answer is (D). *(CMA 1294 2-14)*

REQUIRED: The discount amortized at December 31, 1994.

DISCUSSION: The bonds were issued on July 1, 1994 for $461,440 [($500,000 principal x .614 present value factor for 10 semiannual periods at 5%) + (8% contract rate x 1/2 x $500,000 principal x 7.722 present value of an annuity factor for 10 semiannual periods at 5%)]. Under the effective interest method, interest expense at the end of the first semiannual period equals $23,072 (5% semiannual market rate x $461,440 carrying value at 12/31/94). Because nominal interest is $20,000 (8% x 1/2 x $500,000), the discount amortization is $3,072 ($23,072 − $20,000).

Answer (A) is incorrect because $7,712.00 equals the discount amortization on the straight-line basis for 12 months. Answer (B) is incorrect because $3,856.00 equals the discount amortization on the straight-line basis for 6 months. Answer (C) is incorrect because $1,542.00 equals the difference between actual interest paid at the contract rate and 5% of a carrying value of $369,152.

34. If the market rate of interest is <List A> the coupon rate when bonds are issued, then the bonds will sell in the market at a price <List B> the face value and the issuing firm will record a <List C> on bonds payable.

	List A	List B	List C
A.	Equal to	Equal to	Premium
B.	Greater than	Greater than	Premium
C.	Greater than	Less than	Discount
D.	Less than	Greater than	Discount

The correct answer is (C). *(CIA 1195 IV-21)*

REQUIRED: The relationship of the market rate, the coupon rate, and the recording of a discount or premium.

DISCUSSION: If the market rate exceeds the coupon rate, the price of the bonds must decline to a level that equates the yield on the bonds with the market rate of interest. Accordingly, the bonds will be recorded by a debit to cash for the proceeds, a debit to discount on bonds payable, and a credit to bonds payable at face value.

Answer (A) is incorrect because, if the market rate equals the coupon rate, the bonds will not sell at a premium or discount. Answer (B) is incorrect because if the market rate exceeds the coupon rate, the bond issue will sell at a discount. Answer (D) is incorrect because, if the market rate is less than the coupon rate, the bonds will sell at a price in excess of the face value. The issuing company will record a premium.

H. Common Stock

35. On December 1, Charles Company's board of directors declared a cash dividend of $1.00 per share on the 50,000 shares of common stock outstanding. The company also has 5,000 shares of treasury stock. Shareholders of record on December 15 are eligible for the dividend, which is to be paid on January 1. On December 1, the company should

- A. Make no accounting entry.
- B. Debit retained earnings for $50,000.
- C. Debit retained earnings for $55,000.
- D. Debit retained earnings for $50,000 and paid-in capital for $5,000.

The correct answer is (B). *(CMA 1292 2-7)*

REQUIRED: The proper journal entry on the declaration date of a dividend.

DISCUSSION: Dividends are recorded on their declaration date by a debit to retained earnings and a credit to dividends payable. The dividend is the amount payable to all shares outstanding. Treasury stock is not eligible for dividends because it is not outstanding. Thus, the December 1 entry is to debit retained earnings and credit dividends payable for $50,000 (50,000 x $1).

Answer (A) is incorrect because a liability should be recorded. Answer (C) is incorrect because the treasury stock is not eligible for a dividend. Answer (D) is incorrect because paid-in capital is not affected by the declaration of a dividend.

36. Corporations purchase their outstanding stock for all of the following reasons except to

A. Meet employee stock compensation contracts.

B. Increase earnings per share by reducing the number of shares outstanding.

C. Make a market in the stock.

D. Improve short-term cash flow.

The correct answer is (D). *(CMA 695 2-17)*

REQUIRED: The item not a reason for a company to buy treasury stock.

DISCUSSION: The acquisition of treasury stock does not improve a company's short-term cash flow. Cash must be expended to purchase the shares.

Answers (A), (B), and (C) are incorrect because a corporation purchases its own stock to facilitate possible acquisitions, to allow stockholders to receive capital gains rather than dividends, to comply with employee stock compensation contracts, to avoid a hostile takeover, to increase EPS and book value, to support the market for the stock, to eliminate dissident shareholders, and to reduce the size of the business.

37. Unless specifically restricted, each share of common stock carries all of the following rights except the right to share proportionately in

A. The vote for directors.

B. Corporate assets upon liquidation.

C. Cumulative dividends.

D. New issues of stock of the same class.

The correct answer is (C). *(CMA 695 2-16)*

REQUIRED: The item that is not a right of common stockholders.

DISCUSSION: Common stock does not have the right to accumulate unpaid dividends. This right is often attached to preferred stock.

Answers (A), (B), and (D) are incorrect because common stockholders have the right to share proportionately in dividends (but only after preferred shareholders have been paid), in voting (although different classes of shares may have different privileges), in corporate assets upon liquidation (but only after other claims have been satisfied), and in any new issues of stock of the same class (this latter right is known as the preemptive right).

38. A company declares and pays both a $200,000 cash dividend and a 10% stock dividend. The effect of the <List A> dividend is to <List B>.

	List A	List B
A.	Cash	Increase retained earnings
B.	Cash	Decrease retained earnings and increase stockholders' equity
C.	Stock	Decrease retained earnings
D.	Stock	Decrease retained earnings and decrease stockholders' equity

The correct answer is (C). *(CIA 1195 IV-10)*

REQUIRED: The effect of a dividend.

DISCUSSION: A small stock dividend (less than 20-25% of the common shares outstanding) results in a transfer from retained earnings to paid-in capital equal to the fair value of the stock.

Answer (A) is incorrect because cash dividends reduce retained earnings. Answer (B) is incorrect because cash dividends decrease both retained earnings and stockholders' equity. Answer (D) is incorrect because stock dividends have no net effect on stockholders' equity.

I. Preferred Stock

39. The following excerpt was taken from a company's financial statements: "... 10% convertible participating ... $10,000,000." What is most likely being referred to?

A. Bonds.

B. Common stock.

C. Stock options.

D. Preferred stock.

The correct answer is (D). *(CIA 592 IV-39)*

REQUIRED: The securities most likely referred to as convertible participating.

DISCUSSION: Preferred stockholders have priority over common stockholders in the assets and earnings of the enterprise. If preferred dividends are cumulative, any past preferred dividends must be paid before any common dividends. Preferred stock may also be convertible into common stock, and it may be participating. For example, 10% fully participating preferred stock will receive additional distributions at the same rates as other stockholders if dividends paid to all stockholders exceed 10%.

Answer (A) is incorrect because bonds normally have a coupon yield stated in percentage and may be convertible but are not participating. Answer (B) is incorrect because common stock is not described as convertible or participating on the financial statements. Answer (C) is incorrect because common stock options are not participating and do not have a stated yield rate.

40. In comparing an investment in preferred stock to an investment in bonds, one substantial advantage to a corporation investing in preferred stock is the

- A. Taxable interest received.
- B. Voting power acquired.
- C. Set maturity date.
- D. Dividends-received deduction.

The correct answer is (D). *(Publisher)*
   REQUIRED: The major advantage associated with an investment in preferred stock rather than in bonds.
   DISCUSSION: By investing in preferred stock instead of bonds, a corporation receives a significant tax advantage in the form of the dividends-received deduction. Under the dividends-received deduction, at least 70% of dividends received from preferred stock is deductible for tax purposes. With bonds, any interest received is fully taxable. Furthermore, the dividends-received deduction also applies when a corporation holds an investment in common stock.
   Answer (A) is incorrect because interest is not paid on preferred stock. Taxability of interest is a disadvantage of bonds. Answer (B) is incorrect because an investment in preferred stock usually does not confer voting rights. Answer (C) is incorrect because an investment in preferred stock does not include a maturity date.

41. At December 31, 1996, a corporation has the following account balances:

Common stock ($10 par, 50,000 shares issued)	$500,000
8% preferred stock ($50 par, 10,000 shares issued)	500,000
Paid-in capital in excess of par on common stock	640,000
Paid-in capital in excess of par on preferred stock	20,000
Retained earnings	600,000

The preferred stock is cumulative, nonparticipating, and has a call price of $55 per share. The journal entry to record the redemption of all preferred stock on January 2, 1997 pursuant to the call provision is

- A.
Preferred stock	$500,000	
Paid-in capital in excess of par: preferred	20,000	
Discount on preferred stock	30,000	
Cash		$550,000

- B.
Preferred stock	$500,000	
Paid-in capital in excess of par: preferred	20,000	
Loss on redemption of preferred stock	30,000	
Cash		$550,000

- C.
Preferred stock	$500,000	
Loss on redemption of preferred stock	50,000	
Retained earnings	300,000	
Cash		$550,000
Paid-in capital in excess of par: preferred		300,000

- D.
Preferred stock	$500,000	
Paid-in capital in excess of par: preferred	20,000	
Retained earnings	30,000	
Cash		$550,000

The correct answer is (D). *(CIA 1188 IV-36)*
   REQUIRED: The journal entry to record the redemption of preferred stock pursuant to the call provision.
   DISCUSSION: The exercise of the call provision resulted in the redemption of the 10,000 shares of preferred stock issued and outstanding at the call price of $550,000 (10,000 shares x $55 call price per share). To eliminate the carrying value of the preferred stock and recognize the cash paid in this transaction, the required journal entry is to debit preferred stock for $500,000, debit paid-in capital in excess of par on preferred stock for $20,000, and credit cash for $550,000. The difference of $30,000 ($550,000 cash – $520,000 carrying value of the preferred stock) is charged to retained earnings. No loss is reported because GAAP do not permit the recognition of a gain or loss on transactions involving a company's own stock.
   Answers (A), (B), and (C) are incorrect because the $30,000 excess of cash paid over the carrying value of the redeemed stock should be debited to retained earnings. Answer (C) is incorrect because paid-in capital in excess of par: preferred should be debited for $20,000.

J. Retained Earnings

42. In applying the quasi-reorganization to a consolidated entity,

A. The quasi-reorganization may only be applied to the parent company.

B. All losses should be written off against paid-in capital prior to charging retained earnings.

C. Paid-in capital cannot arise as a result of the transaction.

D. All consolidated retained earnings should be eliminated if any part of a loss is to be charged to paid-in capital.

The correct answer is (D). *(Publisher)*
REQUIRED: The correct statement about applying a quasi-reorganization to a consolidated entity.
DISCUSSION: Consistent with the treatment of an individual enterprise, all consolidated retained earnings should be eliminated in a quasi-reorganization of a consolidated entity by a charge to paid-in capital.
Answer (A) is incorrect because the procedure may be applied to the parent and/or some or all subsidiaries. Answer (B) is incorrect because losses are first written off to retained earnings. The retained earnings deficit is then written off to paid-in capital. Answer (C) is incorrect because, if the legal capital is reduced by more than the deficit, paid-in capital from quasi-reorganization arises.

43. Items reported as prior-period adjustments

A. Do not include the effect of a mistake in the application of accounting principles as this is accounted for as a change in accounting principle rather than as a prior-period adjustment.

B. Do not affect the presentation of prior-period comparative financial statements.

C. Do not require further disclosure in the body of the financial statements.

D. Are reflected as adjustments of the opening balance of the retained earnings of the earliest period presented.

The correct answer is (D). *(CMA 693 2-9)*
REQUIRED: The true statement about items reported as prior period adjustments.
DISCUSSION: Prior-period adjustments are made for the correction of errors. According to SFAS 16, *Prior Period Adjustments*, the effects of errors on prior-period financial statements are reported as adjustments to beginning retained earnings for the earliest period presented in the retained earnings statement. Such errors do not affect the income statement for the current period.
Answer (A) is incorrect because accounting errors of any type are corrected by a prior-period adjustment. Answer (B) is incorrect because a prior-period adjustment will affect the presentation of prior-period comparative financial statements. Answer (C) is incorrect because prior-period adjustments should be fully disclosed in the notes or elsewhere in the financial statements.

44. An appropriation of retained earnings by the board of directors of a corporation for future plant expansion will result in

A. The establishment of a fund to help finance future plant expansion.

B. The setting aside of cash to be used for future plant expansions.

C. A decrease in cash on the balance sheet with an equal increase in the investments and funds section of the balance sheet.

D. The disclosure that management does not intend to distribute, in the form of dividends, assets equal to the amount of the appropriation.

The correct answer is (D). *(CMA 694 2-30)*
REQUIRED: The effect of an appropriation of retained earnings.
DISCUSSION: An appropriation of retained earnings simply transfers a portion of the retained earnings balance into a separate retained earnings account. The sole purpose of such an event is to disclose that earnings retained in the business are to be used for special purposes and will not be available for dividends. The same result could be obtained as effectively by a footnote. No funds are set aside by an appropriation of retained earnings.
Answer (A) is incorrect because no fund is established by the appropriation of retained earnings. Answers (B) and (C) are incorrect because no cash is involved in an appropriation of retained earnings.

K. Stock-Based Compensation

45. According to APB 25, *Accounting for Stock Issued to Employees*, noncompensatory stock option plans have all of the following characteristics except

A. Participation by substantially all full-time employees who meet limited employment qualifications.

B. Equal offers of stock to all eligible employees.

C. A limited amount of time permitted to exercise the option.

D. A provision related to the achievement of certain performance criteria.

The correct answer is (D). *(CMA 692 2-9)*
REQUIRED: The item that is not a characteristic of a noncompensatory stock option plan.
DISCUSSION: Issuance of stock to employees pursuant to a noncompensatory plan does not result in an expense. A noncompensatory plan is defined as one in which substantially all full-time employees participate, the stock available to each employee is equal or is based on salary, the option exercise period is reasonable, and the discount from market is not greater than reasonable in an offer to stockholders or others. Noncompensatory plans do not provide for the achievement of certain performance criteria.
Answer (A) is incorrect because participation by all full-time employees is a characteristic of noncompensatory plans. Answer (B) is incorrect because noncompensatory plans should make offers of stock equally to all employees or be based on salary levels. Answer (C) is incorrect because a limited exercise period is a characteristic of noncompensatory plans.

46. According to APB 25, *Accounting for Stock Issued to Employees*, a stock option plan may or may not be intended to compensate employees for their work. The compensation expense for compensatory stock option plans should be recognized in the periods the

A. Employees become eligible to exercise the options.

B. Employees perform services.

C. Stock is issued.

D. Options are granted.

The correct answer is (B). *(CMA 692 2-8)*
REQUIRED: The true statement about recognition of compensation expense for compensatory stock option plans.
DISCUSSION: A compensatory stock option plan involves the issuance of stock in whole or in part for employee services. Accordingly, a paid-in capital account such as stock options outstanding should be credited. The compensation cost should be recognized as an expense of one or more periods in which the employee performed services. If the measurement date precedes the rendering of services, a debit is made to deferred compensation expense, a contra stockholders' equity account that will be amortized as employee services are rendered and expenses are recognized.
Answer (A) is incorrect because recognition in the periods the employees become eligible to exercise the options violates the matching concept. Answer (C) is incorrect because recognition when the stock is issued might result in an expense being recorded years after the benefits of the employee's service had accrued. Answer (D) is incorrect because recognition in the periods the options are granted might result in recording the expense prior to services being performed.

47. In determining the fair value of a stock option, which factor is not considered an element in an option-pricing model for a nonpublic entity?

A. The exercise price.

B. The expected life of the option.

C. The volatility of the stock.

D. The risk-free interest rate over the expected life of the option.

The correct answer is (C). *(Publisher)*
REQUIRED: The element of the option-pricing model that may be excluded in determining the fair value of a stock option in a nonpublic entity.
DISCUSSION: The volatility factor may be excluded from the option-pricing model for nonpublic entities, resulting in measurement at minimum value.
Answer (A) is incorrect because the exercise price is still included regardless if the entity is public or nonpublic. Answer (B) is incorrect because the expected life of the option is still a viable element in the model for nonpublic entities. Answer (D) is incorrect because the risk-free interest rate is an important component for both public and nonpublic entities attempting to value stock options.

48. SFAS 123, *Accounting for Stock-Based Compensation*, applies to stock-based compensation arrangements involving employees and others. With regard to accounting for employee compensation, it

A.   Requires a fair-value-based method.

B.   Requires an intrinsic-value-based method.

C.   Measures compensation cost as the difference between the quoted market price and the exercise price at the grant date.

D.   Permits entities to continue measuring compensation cost using intrinsic values.

The correct answer is (D). *(Publisher)*
REQUIRED: The true statement about SFAS 123.
DISCUSSION: SFAS 123, *Accounting for Stock-Based Compensation*, is an alternative to APB 25. It applies to stock purchase plans, stock options, restricted stock, and stock appreciation rights. Fair-value-based accounting for stock compensation plans is not required. An entity may continue to apply APB 25. Nevertheless, the fair-value-based method is preferable for purposes of justifying a change in accounting principle. However, initial adoption of an accounting principle for a new transaction is not a change in principle. Thus, an entity that is already measuring stock-based employee compensation cost using the intrinsic value method stated in APB 25 need not change its accounting.
Answer (A) is incorrect because an entity that already uses the intrinsic value method need not change to the fair-value-based method described in SFAS 123. Answers (B) and (C) are incorrect because SFAS 123 encourages use of a fair-value-based method. The differences between quoted market price and the exercise price at the grant date is the intrinsic value.

L. Stock Rights

49. When bonds with detachable stock warrants are purchased, the price should be allocated between the warrants and the bonds based upon their relative fair values at issuance. The amount debited to investment in stock warrants relative to the total amount paid

A.   Increases the premium on the investment in bonds.

B.   Increases the discount on investment in bonds.

C.   Increases either any premium on the bonds or any discount on the bonds.

D.   Has no effect on the investment of bond premium or discount as the warrants are purchased separately.

The correct answer is (B). *(Publisher)*
REQUIRED: The effect on the carrying value of bonds of debiting investment in stock warrants.
DISCUSSION: The portion of the price allocated to the detachable stock warrants decreases the allocation to investment in bonds. Thus, amounts debited to investment in stock warrants increase the discount or decrease the premium recorded for the investment in bonds.
Answers (A), (C), and (D) are incorrect because the allocation to detachable stock warrants decreases the premium or increases any discount.

50. Early in its fiscal year Starr Co. purchased 1,000 shares of Pack Co. common stock for $54,000. In the same transaction, Starr acquired 2,000 detachable stock warrants. Two of the warrants are required to purchase one additional share of Pack Co. common stock. The market price of the stock without the warrants was $49 per share. The market price of the warrants was $3.50 per warrant. Starr sold 50% of the warrants several weeks later. If the proceeds received by Starr equaled $4,000, it recognized a realized gain of

A. $3,000

B. $625

C. $500

D. $0

The correct answer is (B). *(Publisher)*
REQUIRED: The gain on sale of detachable warrants.
DISCUSSION: The recipient of stock rights must allocate the carrying value of the shares owned between those shares and the rights based on their relative fair values. Thus, the amounts to be allocated to the common stock and warrants are $47,250 ({[($49 x 1,000) ÷ [($49 x 1,000) + ($3.50 x 2,000)]} x $54,000) and $6,750 ($54,000 – $47,250), respectively. The realized gain is therefore $625 [$4,000 – ($6,750 x 50%)].
Answer (A) is incorrect because $3,000 is the excess of the fair value of 2,000 rights over the sale price of 1,000 rights. Answer (C) is incorrect because $500 equals the excess of the sale price of 1,000 rights over their fair value. Answer (D) is incorrect because Starr should recognize a realized gain for the excess of the price over the carrying amount.

51. When stock rights are issued without consideration and are allowed to lapse, the following occurs on the books of the issuing company:

A. Common stock at par value is increased.

B. Additional paid-in capital is credited.

C. Investment in stock warrants is debited.

D. None of the answers are correct.

The correct answer is (D). *(Publisher)*
REQUIRED: The effect on the issuing company when stock rights without consideration are allowed to lapse.
DISCUSSION: When rights are issued without consideration, such as in a dividend distribution, only a memorandum entry is made by the issuer. If the rights are exercised and stock is issued, the effect on the books of the issuing company is an increase in common stock at par value with any remainder credited to additional paid-in capital. However, if the rights are allowed to lapse, contributed capital is unaffected.
Answers (A), (B), and (C) are incorrect because when rights previously issued without consideration are allowed to lapse, there is no effect on contributed capital.

M. Convertible Securities

52. Current authoritative literature recommends that proceeds from the issuance of convertible debt be

A. Allocated to debt only.

B. Allocated to debt and to paid-in capital on the basis of the relative fair values at time of issuance.

C. Allocated to paid-in capital only.

D. Allocated to debt and to paid-in capital on the basis of the evaluation of the convertible feature.

The correct answer is (A). *(Publisher)*
REQUIRED: The accounting for the proceeds from the issuance of convertible debt.
DISCUSSION: The debt and equity aspects of convertible debt are inseparable. The entire proceeds should be accounted for as debt until conversion, but the bond issue price is affected by the conversion feature.
Answers (B), (C), and (D) are incorrect because the proceeds are allocated to debt only.

53. What is the preferred method of handling unamortized discount, unamortized issue costs, and the costs of implementing a conversion of debt into common stock?

A. Expense them in the period bonds are converted.

B. Amortize them over the remaining life of the issue retired.

C. Amortize them over a period not to exceed 40 years.

D. Charge them to paid-in capital in excess of the par value of the stock issued.

The correct answer is (D). *(Publisher)*
REQUIRED: The preferred handling of unamortized discount, unamortized issue costs, and the costs of converting debt into common stock.
DISCUSSION: The conversion of debt into common stock is ordinarily based upon the book value of the debt at the time of issuance. Because the book value is based on all related accounts, the debit balances of unamortized bond discount, unamortized issue costs, and conversion costs should be considered reductions in the net carrying value at the time of conversion. Consequently, these items should be reflected as reductions in the paid-in capital in excess of par account.
Answers (A), (B), and (C) are incorrect because these amounts are not expensed. In effect, each reduces the amount at which the stock is issued.

54. According to SFAS 84, *Induced Conversions of Convertible Debt*, an issuer of a convertible security may attempt to induce prompt conversion of its convertible debt to equity securities by offering additional securities or other consideration. How should this additional consideration be reported?

A. As an extraordinary item.

B. As an ordinary expense.

C. As an adjustment of the additional paid-capital account.

D. None of the answers are correct.

The correct answer is (B). *(Publisher)*
REQUIRED: The proper treatment of additional consideration offered by an issuer of a convertible security to induce conversion.
DISCUSSION: The additional consideration should be properly reported as an ordinary expense. The appropriate amount is the fair value of the consideration transferred in excess of the fair value of the securities that would have been issued under the original conversion privilege.
Answers (A), (C), and (D) are incorrect because the additional consideration should be reported as an ordinary expense.

N. Business Combinations

55. Under accounting for consolidations, the pooling method is characterized by all of the following attributes except that the

A. Assets and liabilities of the acquired company are recorded at book value for consolidation reporting purposes.

B. Business combination expenses for acquiring a company under the pooling method are capitalized.

C. Newly created goodwill, rather than goodwill that was already on the books of the subsidiary, is not recognized.

D. Retained earnings of the acquired company are carried forward to the consolidated financial statements.

The correct answer is (B). *(CMA 695 2-8)*
REQUIRED: The attribute not a characteristic of the pooling method.
DISCUSSION: Costs incurred to effect a business combination accounted for as a pooling of interests are expenses of the combined corporation, not additions to assets or direct reductions of stockholders' equity. Consequently, they are deducted in determining the net income of the combined company for the period in which they are incurred (APB 16).
Answers (A) and (D) are incorrect because pooling of interests accounting assumes a combining of ownership interests, not a purchase, and no basis exists for revaluing assets. No readjustment of asset and liability balances occurs except to conform the accounting principles of the pooled companies. Accordingly, the retained earnings of the acquired company are also carried forward to the consolidated financial statements. Answer (C) is incorrect because no goodwill is recorded in a pooling unless it was already on the books of a combining company. Goodwill is recognized only if a purchase has occurred to establish an objective valuation.

56. Under accounting for consolidations, the purchase method is characterized by all of the following attributes except that the

A. Assets and liabilities are recorded at fair value or the purchase price of the acquired company, whichever is less.

B. Excess of the purchase price over the fair value of identifiable assets and liabilities is recorded as goodwill.

C. Goodwill of the acquired company is always carried forward to the balance sheet of the consolidated entity.

D. Fair value of the shares issued by the acquiring company is added to the paid-in capital of the consolidated entity.

The correct answer is (C). *(CMA 695 2-7)*
REQUIRED: The item not a characteristic of the purchase method.
DISCUSSION: When a business combination is accounted for as a purchase, the cost is allocated to the specifically identifiable assets acquired and liabilities assumed based on their fair values. If the cost exceeds the sum of the amounts assigned to the net identifiable assets, the excess is recorded as goodwill, an intangible that is not specifically identifiable. Thus, the acquiring company will seldom record goodwill equal to the amount on the acquired company's balance sheet. Indeed, goodwill may not be recorded because the fair value of the identifiable net assets exceeds the cost.
Answer (A) is incorrect because purchase accounting requires the identifiable net assets to be recorded at fair value or the purchase price of the acquired company, whichever is less. Answer (B) is incorrect because goodwill is the excess of the price over the fair value of the identifiable net assets. Answer (D) is incorrect because the stock issued by the parent is recorded at its fair value, just as in any purchase transaction.

57. The purpose of consolidated financial statements is to present the financial position and the results of operations of a parent company and its subsidiaries as if the group were a single company. To accomplish this goal, the majority-owned subsidiaries must be

A. Consolidated.

B. Consolidated, unless control is temporary.

C. Consolidated, unless the subsidiary engages in nonhomogeneous operations.

D. Consolidated, unless the minority interest in the subsidiary is very large.

The correct answer is (B). *(CMA 693 2-30)*
REQUIRED: The true statement about majority-owned subsidiaries in a consolidation.
DISCUSSION: SFAS 94 specifies that all majority-owned subsidiaries are to be consolidated unless control is temporary or is not held by the majority owner. Previously, some foreign subsidiaries and subsidiaries with nonhomogeneous operations were not always consolidated. Those exceptions were eliminated by SFAS 94.
Answer (A) is incorrect because consolidation is not required if control is temporary. Answer (C) is incorrect because nonhomogeneous operations must be consolidated under SFAS 94. Answer (D) is incorrect because the degree of minority interest is not a factor, unless it has control.

Questions 58 and 59 are based on the following information. On January 1, 1986, Boggs, Inc. paid $700,000 for 100,000 shares of Mattly Corporation representing 30% of Mattly's outstanding common stock. The following computation was made by Boggs.

Purchase price	$700,000
30% equity in book value of Mattly's net assets	500,000
Excess cost over book value	$200,000

The excess cost over book value was attributed to goodwill and will be amortized over 20 years. Mattly reported net income for the year ended December 31, 1986, of $300,000. Mattly Corporation paid cash dividends of $100,000 on July 1, 1986.

58. If Boggs, Inc. exercised significant influence over Mattly Corporation and properly accounted for the long-term investment under the equity method, the amount of net investment revenue Boggs should report from its investment in Mattly would be

- A. $30,000
- B. $60,000
- C. $80,000
- D. $90,000

The correct answer is (C). *(CMA 687 3-11)*

REQUIRED: The net investment revenue reported using the equity method.

DISCUSSION: Under the equity method, Boggs should recognize 30% of Mattly's reported income of $300,000, or $90,000. However, the annual goodwill amortization ($200,000 ÷ 20 years = $10,000) reduces that amount. Thus, net investment income is $80,000 ($90,000 – $10,000). Dividends received from an investee must be recorded in the books of the investor as a decrease in the carrying value of the investment and an increase in assets (cash).

Answer (A) is incorrect because $30,000 is the net investment revenue reported using the cost method. Answer (B) is incorrect because $60,000 equals 30% of the investee's net income minus 30% of the dividends paid. Answer (D) is incorrect because $90,000 equals 30% of the investee's net income.

59. If Boggs, Inc. did not exercise significant influence over Mattly Corporation and properly accounted for the long-term investment under the cost method, the amount of net investment revenue Boggs should report from its investment in Mattly would be

- A. $20,000
- B. $30,000
- C. $60,000
- D. $80,000

The correct answer is (B). *(CMA 687 3-12)*

REQUIRED: The net investment revenue reported using cost method.

DISCUSSION: Under the cost method, the investor records as revenue only the amount actually received as dividends. Boggs receives 30% of the $100,000 total dividend and records $30,000 of investment revenue. The cost method involves no write-off of goodwill.

Answer (A) is incorrect because $20,000 results from subtracting $10,000 of goodwill. Answer (C) is incorrect because $60,000 equals 30% of the investee's net income minus 30% of the dividends paid. Answer (D) is incorrect because $80,000 is the net investment revenue reported using the equity method.

60. APB 16 states the principles to be followed in allocating the cost of an acquired company when using the purchase method for a business combination. If the current fair value of the net assets acquired exceeds the total cost, the difference should be

A. Added directly to shareholders' equity at the date of acquisition.

B. Treated as goodwill to be amortized over the period benefitted, not to exceed 40 years.

C. Allocated on a pro rata basis to the assets acquired.

D. Applied pro rata to reduce, but not below zero, the amounts initially assigned to noncurrent assets other than long-term investments in marketable securities.

The correct answer is (D). *(CMA 1291 2-8)*
REQUIRED: The proper treatment of the excess of the current fair value of net assets acquired over their total cost.
DISCUSSION: APB 16 requires that the excess (negative goodwill) be allocated proportionately based on their fair values to all noncurrent assets except long-term investments in marketable securities. Any excess remaining after noncurrent assets are adjusted to zero should be classified as a deferred credit to be amortized over a period not exceeding 40 years.
Answer (A) is incorrect because negative goodwill is not added to shareholders' equity. Answer (B) is incorrect because the difference is not goodwill, which is the excess of cost over the fair value of the identifiable net assets, but negative goodwill. Answer (C) is incorrect because allocations are made only to noncurrent assets.

61. In the process of preparing consolidated financial statements, which one of the following items does not need to be eliminated?

A. Intercompany profit in beginning inventory.

B. Intercompany profit on intercompany sale of a fixed asset.

C. Intercompany dividends receivable/payable.

D. Intercompany profit on inventory sold to a nonaffiliated company.

The correct answer is (D). *(CMA 688 4-24)*
REQUIRED: The item that is not eliminated in the preparation of consolidated financial statements.
DISCUSSION: Intercompany profits must be eliminated whenever the assets sold are still within the consolidated group. For example, if the parent sells equipment to a subsidiary at a profit, the intercompany profit must be eliminated before the consolidated statements are prepared or the assets will not be recorded (on the consolidated balance sheet) at historical cost to the group. If the subsidiary subsequently sells the assets to someone outside the group, the original intercompany profit will be realized (through sale to the outsider) and no longer has to be eliminated.
Answers (A) and (B) are incorrect because intercompany profits in inventory, or any other assets still within the group, must be eliminated. Answer (C) is incorrect because intercompany dividends receivable/payable must be eliminated. Otherwise, the consolidated company would report an asset receivable from itself.

62. On September 1, 1992, for $4,000,000 cash and $2,000,000 notes payable, Norbend Corporation acquired the net assets of Crisholm Company, which had a fair value of $5,496,000 on that date. Norbend's management is of the opinion that the goodwill generated has an indefinite life and should be amortized over the longest allowable period. During the December 31, 1994 year-end audit after all adjusting entries have been made, the goodwill is determined to be worthless. The amount of the write-off as of December 31, 1994, should be

A. $504,000

B. $478,800

C. $466,200

D. $474,600

The correct answer is (D). *(CMA 695 2-13)*
REQUIRED: The goodwill write-off.
DISCUSSION: APB 17 requires that goodwill be amortized over a period of 40 years or less. Given that the company paid $6,000,000 for net identifiable assets with a fair value of $5,496,000, goodwill was $504,000. Annual amortization was $12,600 ($504,000 ÷ 40). For the year of purchase, the amortization period was only 4 months; thus, 1992 amortization was $4,200 [$12,600 × (4 ÷ 12)]. Amortization was $12,600 per year for 1993 and 1994, bringing the total amortization to $29,400 [$4,200 + (2 × $12,600)]. Hence, the book value to be written off is $474,600 ($504,000 − $29,400).
Answer (A) is incorrect because $504,000 does not reflect amortization in previous years. Answer (B) is incorrect because $4,200 would have been amortized in 1992. Answer (C) is incorrect because 1992 amortization would have been only $4,200, not the full year's $12,600.

STUDY UNIT 3: LONG-TERM CAPITAL FINANCING

18 pages of outline
66 multiple-choice questions

A. Sources of Long-Term Financing
B. Optimal Capitalization
C. Dividend Policy

This study unit is the first of five relating to the second major topic in the content specification outline, "Advanced Topics in Corporate Financial Management." The five units are

Study Unit 3: Long-Term Capital Financing
Study Unit 4: Financial Markets and Interest Rates
Study Unit 5: Investment Banking and Commercial Banking
Study Unit 6: Comparative Analysis
Study Unit 7: Business Combinations and Restructurings

The principal subject areas covered in this study unit are the instruments that provide long-term financing, elements of an optimal capital structure and the cost of capital, and dividend policy.

A. Sources of Long-Term Financing

1. A firm may have long-term funding requirements that it cannot, or does not want to, meet using retained earnings. It must therefore issue equity or debt securities. Certain hybrid forms are also used for long-term financing, e.g., convertible securities.

2. The principal considerations when reviewing financing choices are cost, risk, and the lender's (the investor's) view of the financing device.

3. **Common Stock.** The common shareholders are the owners of the corporation, and their rights as owners, although reasonably uniform, depend on the laws of the state in which the firm is incorporated. Equity ownership involves risk because holders of common stock are not guaranteed a return and are last in priority in a liquidation. Equity provides the cushion for creditors if any losses occur on liquidation.

   a. Advantages of common stock to the issuer

      1) Dividends are not fixed. They are paid from profits when available.

      2) There is no fixed maturity date for repayment of the capital.

      3) The sale of common stock increases the creditworthiness of the firm by providing more equity.

      4) Common stock is frequently more attractive to investors than debt because it grows in value with the success of the firm.

         a) The higher the common stock value, the more advantageous equity financing is over debt financing.

   b. Disadvantages of common stock to the issuer

      1) Control (voting rights) is usually diluted as more common stock is sold.

      2) New common stock sales dilute earnings available to existing shareholders because of the greater number of shares outstanding.

      3) Underwriting costs are typically higher for common stock issues.

      4) Too much equity may raise the average cost of capital of the firm above its optimal level.

      5) Common stock cash dividends are not deductible as an expense and are after-tax cash deductions to the firm.

    c.   Common shareholders ordinarily have **preemptive rights**.

        1)   Preemptive rights give common shareholders the right to purchase any additional stock issuances in proportion to their current ownership.

        2)   If state law or the corporate charter does not provide preemptive rights, the firm may nevertheless sell to the common shareholders in a **rights** offering. Each shareholder is issued a certificate or warrant that is an option to buy a certain number of shares at a fixed price within a given time.

            a)   Until the rights are actually issued, the stock trades **rights-on**; that is, the stock and the rights are not separable. After the rights are received, the stock trades **ex-rights** because the rights can be sold separately. The price of a stock right sold rights-on is

$$\frac{P - S}{N + 1}$$

If: P = value of a share rights-on
     S = subscription price of a share
     N = number of rights needed to buy a share

    d.   **Stock warrants** (certificates evidencing options to buy stock at a given price within a certain period) may be issued to employees as compensation, or they may be issued with bonds or preferred stock.

    e.   A stock's **par value** represents legal capital. It is an arbitrary value assigned to stock before the stock is issued. It also represents the maximum liability of a shareholder.

4.   **Preferred stock** is a hybrid of debt and equity. It has a fixed charge and increases leverage, but payment of dividends is not a legal obligation.

    a.   Advantages of preferred stock to the issuer

        1)   It is a form of equity and therefore builds the creditworthiness of the firm.

        2)   Control is still held by common shareholders.

        3)   Superior earnings of the firm are usually still reserved for the common shareholders.

    b.   Disadvantages of preferred stock to the issuer

        1)   Preferred stock cash dividends paid are not tax deductible. The result is a substantially greater cost relative to bonds.

        2)   In periods of economic difficulty, accumulated (past) dividends may create major managerial and financial problems for the firm.

    c.   Typical provisions of preferred stock issues

        1)   **Par value.** Par value is the liquidation value, and a percentage of par equals the preferred dividend.

        2)   **Priority** in assets and earnings. If the firm goes bankrupt, the preferred shareholders have priority over common shareholders.

        3)   **Accumulation of dividends.** If preferred dividends in arrears are cumulative, they must be paid before any common dividends can be paid.

4) **Convertibility**. Preferred stock issues may be convertible into common stock at the option of the shareholder.

5) **Participation**. Preferred stock may participate with common in excess earnings of the company. For example, 8% participating preferred stock might pay a dividend each year greater than 8% when the corporation is extremely profitable. But nonparticipating preferred stock will receive no more than is stated on the face of the stock.

6) **Redeemability**. Some preferred stock may be redeemed at a given time or at the option of the holder or otherwise at a time not controlled by the issuer. This feature makes preferred stock more nearly akin to debt, particularly in the case of **transient preferred stock**, which must be redeemed within a short time (e.g., 5 to 10 years). The SEC requires a separate presentation of redeemable preferred, nonredeemable preferred, and common stock.

7) **Voting rights**. These may be conferred if preferred dividends are in arrears for a stated period.

8) **Callability**. The issuer may have the right to repurchase the stock. For example, the stock may be noncallable for a stated period after which it may be called if the issuer pays a call premium (an amount exceeding par value).

9) **Maturity**. Preferred stock may have a sinking fund that allows for the purchase of a given annual percentage of the outstanding shares.

d. Holding preferred stock rather than bonds provides corporations a tax advantage. At least 70% of the dividends received from preferred stock may be tax deductible, whereas all bond interest received is taxable.

1) The **dividends-received deduction** also applies to common stock.

2) Because of the tax advantage, nonconvertible preferred stock is held almost entirely by corporations. Individuals can earn higher yields at lower risk by purchasing bonds.

5. **Bonds** are long-term debt instruments. They are similar to term loans except that they are usually offered to the public and sold to many investors.

a. Advantages of bonds to the issuer

1) Basic control of the firm is not shared with the debtholder.

2) Cost of debt is limited. Bondholders usually do not participate in the superior earnings of the firm.

3) Ordinarily, the expected yield of bonds is lower than the cost of stock.

4) Interest paid on debt is tax deductible.

5) Debt may add substantial flexibility in the financial structure of the corporation through the insertion of call provisions in the bond indenture.

a) A bond indenture is a written agreement between the borrower and a trust company appointed by the borrower. A trust company ensures that the terms of the indenture are followed, manages a sinking fund, and represents the bondholders in the case of default.

b. Disadvantages of bonds to the issuer

1) Debt has a fixed charge. If the earnings of the firm fluctuate, the risk of insolvency is increased by the fixed interest obligation.

2) Debt adds risk to a firm. Shareholders will consequently demand higher capitalization rates on equity earnings, which may result in a decline in the market price of stock.

3) Debt usually has a maturity date.

4) Debt is a long-term commitment, a factor that can affect risk profiles. Debt originally appearing to be profitable may become a burden and drive the firm into bankruptcy.

5) Certain managerial prerogatives are usually surrendered in the contractual relationship defined in the bond indenture.

a) For example, specific ratios may have to remain above a certain level during the term of the loan.

6) The amount of debt financing available to the individual firm is limited. Generally accepted standards of the investment community will usually dictate a certain debt-equity ratio for a firm. Beyond this limit, the cost of debt may rise rapidly, or debt financing may not be available.

c. The **bond indenture** is the contractual arrangement between the issuer and the bondholders. It contains restrictive covenants intended to prevent the issuer from taking actions contrary to the interests of the bondholders. A trustee, often a bank, is appointed to ensure compliance.

1) **Call provisions** give the corporation the right to redeem bonds. If interest rates decline, the company can call high-interest bonds and replace them with low-interest bonds.

2) Bonds are **putable** or redeemable if the holder has the right to exchange them for cash. This option is usually activated only if the issuer takes a stated action, for example, greatly increasing its debt or being acquired by another entity.

3) **Sinking fund** requirements provide for the firm to retire a certain portion of its bonds each year or to set aside money for repayment in the future. Such terms increase the probability of repayment for bondholders but require the use of capital by the firm.

4) The issuer may be required to maintain its financial ratios, e.g., times-interest-earned, at specified levels.

5) Dividends may be limited if earnings do not meet specified requirements.

6) The amount of new bonds issued may be restricted to a percentage of bondable property (fixed assets).

d. Types of bonds

1) A **mortgage bond** is a pledge of certain assets for a loan. It is usually secured by real property as a condition of the loan.

2) A **debenture** is a long-term bond not secured by specific property. It is a general obligation of the borrower. Only companies with the best credit ratings can issue debentures because holders will be general creditors. They will have a status inferior to that of secured parties and creditors with priorities in bankruptcy.

3) **Subordinated debentures** possess a feature undesirable to investors. They are subordinated (inferior) to the claims of other general creditors, secured parties, and persons with priorities in bankruptcy. The bond indenture specifies the claims (senior debt) to which these bonds are subordinate. They are usually issued only when the company has some debt instrument outstanding that prohibits the issuance of additional regular bonds. Subordinated debentures normally have a higher yield than secured bonds.

4) An **income bond** pays interest only if the issuing company has earnings. Such bonds are riskier than other bonds.

5) **Serial bonds** have staggered maturities. These bonds permit investors to choose the maturity dates that meet their needs.

6) **Registered bonds** are issued in the name of the owner. Interest payments are sent directly to the owner. When the owner sells registered bonds, the bond certificates must be surrendered and new certificates issued.

   a) They differ from **coupon (bearer) bonds**, which can be freely transferred and have a detachable coupon for each interest payment.

7) **Participating bonds** participate in excess earnings of the debtor as defined in the indenture.

8) **Indexed bonds** (purchasing power bonds) pay interest that is indexed to a measure of general purchasing power, such as the Consumer Price Index.

9) **Zero-coupon bonds** pay no interest but sell at a deep discount from face value.

   a) The need to reinvest the periodic payments from normal bonds makes their final return uncertain because future reinvestment rates are uncertain. But investors know the exact return on a zero-coupon bond. Investors might therefore be willing to pay a premium for them, which in turn might lead firms to issue them.

   b) The lack of interest payments means the firm faces no additional insolvency risk from the issue until it matures.

10) **Junk bonds** are very high-risk, high-yield securities issued to finance leveraged buyouts and mergers. They are also issued by troubled companies. They exploit the large tax deductions for interest paid by entities with high debt ratios.

11) **International bonds** exist in two forms: foreign bonds and Eurobonds. **Foreign bonds** are denominated in the currency of the nation in which they are sold. **Eurobonds** are denominated in a currency other than that of the nation where they are sold.

   a) Foreign bonds issued in the United States and denominated in dollars must be registered with the SEC, but such extensive disclosure is not required in most European nations. Thus, an American company may elect to issue Eurobonds denominated in dollars in a foreign nation because of the convenience of not having to comply with registration requirements.

6. Stock rights and convertibility are among the common financing arrangements used to increase investor interest in corporate securities. The objective is a lower interest rate on bonds or a higher selling price for stocks.

    a. **Stock rights** evidenced by **warrants** are options that are distributed with debt or preferred stock. They permit a holder to share in a company's prosperity through a future purchase of stock at a special low price. They should be distinguished from put and call options.

        1) A **put option** is a right traded in the stock market to sell stock at a given price within a specified period.

        2) A **call option** is a right to purchase stock at a given price within a specified period.

        3) Neither a put nor a call is issued by the company whose stock is the subject of the option.

    b. **Convertibility**. Bonds or preferred stock may be exchangeable (by the investor) into common stock under certain conditions.

    c. Both the issuance of rights and a conversion feature offer a corporation a means of delayed equity financing when market prices are unfavorable. When the market price rises above the conversion price, holders will presumably exercise the rights or convert the securities.

7. **Employee stock ownership plans (ESOPs)** are established by a corporation under federal income tax laws. Under such a plan, an employee stock ownership trust (ESOT) acquires qualifying employer securities, which may be outstanding shares, treasury shares, or newly issued shares. It holds the stock in the name of the company's employees. Ordinarily, the trust obtains the cash to buy the stock by borrowing from a bank, and the corporation cosigns the note. Each year, the corporation makes payments to the ESOT as deductible contributions to a qualified retirement plan. Furthermore, the employees themselves may make deposits to the ESOT.

    a. This arrangement permits the corporation to receive the proceeds of a bank loan by selling securities to the ESOT. The corporation in effect repays the bank loan through deductible contributions (with pretax dollars) to the ESOT. Thus, use of a leveraged ESOP allows the corporation to obtain a deduction for the principal as well as the interest on the loan.

    b. Another advantage of an ESOP is that employees should be motivated to perform better because they have a financial interest in the success of the company (although, if the market price of the stock declines, morale may be harmed).

    c. Some small business owners have found that an ESOP is an effective way to transfer ownership (to employees) when no other buyer can be found.

8. **American Depository Receipts (ADRs)** are ownership rights in foreign corporations.

    a. Foreign stocks are deposited with a large U.S. bank, which in turn issues ADRs representing ownership in the foreign shares. The ADR shares then trade on a U.S. stock exchange, whereas the company's original shares trade on a foreign stock market.

    b. ADRs permit foreign companies to increase their development of a U.S. shareholder base.

    c. Foreign companies want to participate in the U.S. equity market for a number of reasons, including a desire to increase liquidity of stocks and to raise equity capital without putting pressure on the stock price in the home market.

9. **Dividend Reinvestment Plans (DRPs)**. Any dividends due to shareholders are automatically reinvested in shares of the same corporation's common stock. Broker's fees on such purchases of stock are either zero (the costs absorbed by the corporation) or only a few cents per shareholder because only one purchase is made and the total fee is divided among all shareholders participating.

   a. Dividends may be reinvested in stock bought by a trustee (typically a large bank) on the open market.

   b. DRPs may also be used as a source of financing through the sale of newly issued stock to the trustee. The corporation benefits because it can issue stock at the current market value without incurring underwriting and issue costs.

10. **Intermediate-term financing** refers to debt issues having approximate maturities of greater than 1 but less than 10 years. The principal types of intermediate-term financing are term loans and lease financing. Major lenders under term agreements are commercial banks, life insurance companies, and, to some extent, pension funds.

    a. **Term loans**. One possible feature of term loans is tying the interest payable on the loan to a variable rate. This **floating rate**, usually stated as some percentage over the prime, may result in extremely high borrowing costs.

       1) This risk must be traded off against

          a) The need of the firm to obtain the loan
          b) The flexibility inherent in term borrowing
          c) The ability of the firm to borrow in the capital market
          d) Other available types of debt financing
          e) The amount of privacy desired

       2) Term loans are private contracts between private firms, whereas long-term debt securities usually involve the SEC and massive disclosure.

       3) Variable or floating rate loans are advantageous to lenders because they permit better matching of interest costs and revenues. The market values of these loans also tend to be more stable than those for fixed rate loans.

          a) The disadvantages include a heightened risk of default, losses of expected revenues if interest rates decline or if market rates rise above the ceiling specified in the agreement, and the difficulty of working with a more complex product.

       4) Borrowers may benefit from the lower initial costs of these loans but must accept increased interest rate risk, the difficulty of forecasting cash flow, a possible loss of creditworthiness if interest rates are expected to rise, and the burden of more complex financing arrangements.

       5) If the interest rate is variable but the monthly loan payment is fixed, an increase in the rate means that the interest component of the payment and the total interest for the loan term will be greater.

          a) The term of the loan will also be extended, and the principal balance will increase because amortization is diminished. Indeed, negative amortization may occur if the interest rate increase is great enough.

          b) Floating or variable rate loans have an impact on monetary policy because they render analyses more complex. These loans give the Federal Reserve less control over the money supply and credit. The economy is now more sensitive to interest rate fluctuations, and political pressure to avoid rate increases will become greater.

    b. **Lease financing** must be analyzed by comparing the cost of owning to the cost of leasing. Leasing has become a major means of financing because it offers a variety of tax and other benefits. If leases are not accounted for as installment purchases, they provide off-balance-sheet financing. Thus, under an operating lease, the lessee need not record an asset or a liability, and rent expense rather than interest is recognized. For more on leasing, see Study Unit 2. The three principal forms of leases are discussed below:

1) A **sale-leaseback** is a financing method. A firm seeking financing sells an asset to an investor (creditor) and leases the asset back, usually on a noncancelable lease. The lease payments consist of principal and interest paid by the lessee to the lessor.

2) **Operating leases** usually provide for financing and maintenance services.

3) **Capital leases (or financial leases)**, which do not provide for maintenance services, are noncancelable and fully amortize the cost of the leased asset over the term of the basic lease contract; i.e., they are installment purchases.

11. **Maturity matching** (equalizing the life of an asset acquired with the debt instrument used to finance it) is an important factor in choosing the source of funds. Financing long-term assets with long-term debt allows the company to generate sufficient cash flows from the assets to satisfy obligations as they mature.

12. Stop and review! You have completed the outline for this subunit. Study multiple-choice questions 1 through 23 beginning on page 135.

B. Optimal Capitalization

1. The **financial structure** of a firm encompasses the right-hand side of the balance sheet, which describes how the firm's assets are financed. Capital structure is the permanent financing of the firm and is represented primarily by

   a. Long-term debt

      1) Most firms renew (roll over) their long-term obligations. Thus, long-term debt is often effectively permanent.

   b. Preferred stock
   c. Common shareholders' equity

      1) Common stock
      2) Additional paid-in capital
      3) Retained earnings

2. The following factors influence financial structure:

   a. Growth rate and stability of future sales
   b. Competitive structures in the industry
   c. Asset makeup of the individual firm
   d. Attitude toward risk of owners and management
   e. Control position of owners and management
   f. Lenders' attitudes toward the industry and a particular firm
   g. Tax considerations

3. **Leverage** is the relative amount of the fixed cost of capital, principally debt, in a firm's capital structure. Leverage, by definition, creates financial risk, which relates directly to the question of the cost of capital. The more leverage, the higher the financial risk, and the higher the cost of debt capital.

   a. Earnings per share will ordinarily be higher if debt is used to raise capital instead of equity, provided that the firm is not over-leveraged. The reason is that the cost of debt is lower than the cost of equity because interest is tax deductible. However, the prospect of higher EPS is accompanied by greater risk to the firm resulting from required interest costs, creditors' liens on the firm's assets, and the possibility of a proportionately lower EPS if sales volume fails to meet projections.

b. **The degree of financial leverage (DFL)** is the percentage change in earnings available to common shareholders that is associated with a given percentage change in net operating income. The second formula below can be derived from the first (the derivation is not given).

c. $DFL = \dfrac{\% \ \Delta \ in \ net \ income}{\% \ \Delta \ in \ net \ operating \ income} = \dfrac{EBIT}{EBIT - I}$

   1) Net income means earnings available to common shareholders.

   2) Operating income equals earnings before interest and taxes (EBIT).

   3) I equals interest expense. If the company has preferred stock, the second formula is further modified as follows (if P = preferred dividends and T is the tax rate):

   $$\dfrac{EBIT}{EBIT - I - [P \div (1 - T)]}$$

   4) The greater the DFL, the riskier the firm.

d. If the return on assets exceeds the cost of debt, additional leverage is favorable.

e. Operating leverage concerns the extent to which fixed costs are used in the production process. A company with a high percentage of fixed costs is more risky than a firm in the same industry that relies more on variable costs to produce.

   1) **The degree of operating leverage (DOL)** is the percentage change in net operating income associated with a given percentage change in sales. The second formula below can be derived from the first (the derivation is not given).

   2) $DOL =$

   $$\dfrac{\% \ \Delta \ in \ net \ operating \ income}{\% \ \Delta \ in \ sales} = \dfrac{Contribution \ Margin}{Contribution \ Margin - Fixed \ Costs}$$

   a) EXAMPLE: If operating income increases 20% with a 10% increase in sales, DOL is 2.0.

f. **The degree of total leverage (DTL)** combines the DFL and the DOL. It equals the degree of financial leverage times the degree of operating leverage. Thus, it also equals the percentage change in net income that is associated with a given percentage change in sales.

   1) $DTL = DFL \times DOL = \dfrac{\% \ \Delta \ in \ net \ income}{\% \ \Delta \ in \ sales}$

   a) EXAMPLE: If net income increases 15% with a 5% increase in sales, DTL is 3.0.

   2) Firms with a high degree of operating leverage do not usually employ a high degree of financial leverage and vice versa. One of the most important considerations in the use of financial leverage is operating leverage.

   a) EXAMPLE: A firm has a highly automated production process. Because of automation, the degree of operating leverage is 2. If the firm wants a degree of total leverage not exceeding 3, it must restrict its use of debt so that the degree of financial leverage is not more than 1.5. If the firm had committed to a production process that was less automated and had a lower DOL, more debt could be employed, and the firm could have a higher degree of financial leverage.

4. **Cost of Capital.** Managers must know the cost of capital in making investment (long-term funding) decisions because investments with a return higher than the cost of capital will increase the value of the firm (shareholders' wealth). The theory underlying the cost of capital applies to new, long-term funding because long-term funds finance long-term investments. Short-term funds are used to meet working capital and other temporary needs. Cost of capital is of less concern for short-term funding.

    a. The cost of capital is a weighted average of the various debt and equity components. The **weighted-average cost of capital** weights the percentage cost of each component by the percentage of that component in the financial structure.

        1) The **cost of debt** equals the interest rate times one minus the marginal tax rate because interest is a tax deduction. Hence, an increase in the tax rate decreases the cost of debt.

        2) The **cost of retained earnings** is an opportunity cost. It is the rate that investors can earn elsewhere on investments of comparable risk. The cost of internally generated funds is an imputed cost.

        3) The **cost of new external common equity** is higher than the cost of retained earnings because of stock flotation costs.

            a) Providers of equity capital are exposed to more risk than are lenders because the firm is not obligated to pay them a return. Also, in case of liquidation, creditors are paid before equity investors. Thus, equity financing is more expensive than debt because equity investors require a higher return to compensate for the greater risk assumed.

        4) The **cost of preferred stock** equals the preferred dividend divided by the net issuance price. No tax adjustment is necessary because preferred dividends paid are not deductible.

    b. Standard financial theory states that an **optimal capital structure** exists.

        1) The optimal capital structure minimizes the weighted average cost of capital and thereby maximizes the value of the firm's stock.

            a) The optimal capital structure does not maximize EPS. Greater leverage maximizes EPS but also increases risk. Thus, the highest stock price is not reached by maximizing EPS.

        2) The optimal capital structure usually involves some debt, but not 100% debt.

        3) The relevant relationships are depicted below.

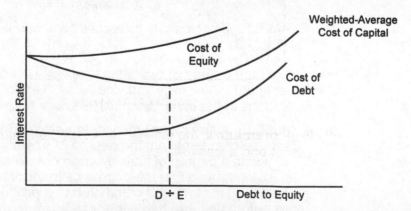

D ÷ E represents the lowest weighted-average cost of capital and is therefore the firm's optimal capital structure.

4) Ordinarily, firms cannot identify this optimal point precisely. Thus, they should attempt to find an optimal range for the capital structure.

c. The required rate of return on equity capital (R) can be estimated as follows.

1) The **Capital Asset Pricing Model** (CAPM) adds the risk-free rate (determined by government securities) to the product of the beta coefficient (a measure of the firm's risk) and the difference between the market return and the risk-free rate. Below is the basic equilibrium equation for the CAPM.

$$R = R_F + \beta(R_M - R_F)$$

a) The **market risk premium** $(R_M - R_F)$ is the amount above the risk-free rate required to induce average investors to enter the market.

b) The **beta coefficient (β)** of an individual stock is the correlation between the volatility (price variation) of the stock market and the volatility of the price of the individual stock.

i) EXAMPLE: If an individual stock rises 10% and the stock market 10%, the beta coefficient is 1.0. If the stock rises 15% and the market only 10%, beta is 1.5.

c) EXAMPLE: Assuming a beta of 1.20, a market rate of return of approximately 17%, and an expected risk-free rate of 12%, the required rate of return on equity capital is .12 + 1.20 (.17 − .12), or 18%.

d) The graph of this equation (with interest rates plotted on the vertical axis and betas on the horizontal axis) is the **Security Market Line**. The slope of the SML equals the market risk premium, and the y-intercept is the risk-free rate.

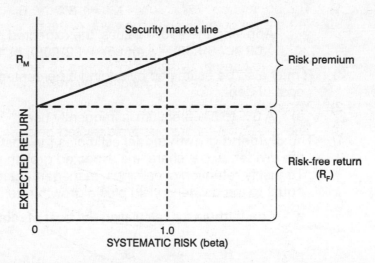

e) **Risk premium** is the difference in expected rates of return on a risky asset and a less risky asset.

2) **Arbitrage pricing theory (APT)** is based on the assumption that an asset's return is based on multiple systematic risk factors. In contrast, the CAPM is a model that uses just one systematic risk factor to explain the asset's return. That factor is the expected return on the market portfolio, i.e., the market-valued weighted average return for all securities available in the market.

a) The difference between actual and expected returns on an asset is attributable to systematic and unsystematic risks. **Unsystematic risk** (also called company-specific risk or diversifiable risk) is specific to a particular asset and can be eliminated by sufficient diversification. However, **systematic risk** (also called market risk or nondiversifiable risk) affects many assets and is undiversifiable. Thus, investors must be paid a risk premium to compensate them for systematic (market) risk.

b) Accordingly, APT provides for a separate beta and a separate risk premium for each systematic risk factor identified in the model. Examples of the many potential systematic risk factors are the gross domestic product (GDP), inflation, and real interest rates. The APT for a three-factor model may be formulated as follows:

$$R = R_F + \beta_1 k_1 + \beta_2 k_2 + \beta_3 k_3$$

If: R = expected rate of return
R_F = risk-free rate
$\beta_{1,2,3}$ = individual factor beta coefficients
$k_{1,2,3}$ = individual factor risk premiums

c) EXAMPLE: Assume R_F = 9% and
K_1 = 2% B_1 = .6
K_2 = 5% B_2 = .4
K_3 = 8% B_3 = .2

Applying the above values, the expected rate of return is .09 + (.6)(.02) + (.4)(.05) + (.2)(.08), or 13.8%.

3) R may also be estimated by adding a percentage to the firm's long-term cost of debt.

a) A 3% to 5% premium is frequently used.

4) The **dividend growth model** estimates the cost of retained earnings using the dividends per share, the expected growth rate, and the market price. To justify retention of earnings, management must expect a return at least equal to the dividend yield plus a growth rate.

a) The formula for calculating the cost of retained earnings is

$$R = \frac{D_1}{P_0} + G$$

If: P_0 = current price

D_1 = next dividend

R = required rate of return

G = growth rate in dividends per share (but the model assumes that the dividend payout ratio, retention rate, and therefore the EPS growth rate are constant).

    i) EXAMPLE: If a company's dividend is expected to be $4 while the market price is $50 and the dividend is expected to grow at a constant rate of 6%, the required rate of return would be $4 ÷ $50 + .06, or 14%.

  b) To determine the cost of new common stock (external equity), the model is altered to incorporate the flotation cost. As the flotation cost rises, R increases accordingly.

$$R = \frac{D_1}{P_0\,(1 - Flotation\ cost)} + G$$

  c) The dividend growth model is also used for stock price evaluation. The formula can be restated in terms of P_0 as follows:

$$P_0 = \frac{D_1}{R - G}$$

  d) The stock price is affected by the dividend payout ratio because some investors may want capital gains, but others may prefer current income. Thus, investors will choose stocks that give the proper mix of capital gains and dividends.

 d. The **marginal cost of capital**. The cost of capital to the firm for the next dollar of new capital increases because lower-cost capital sources are used first.

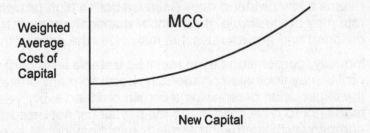

 e. The **marginal efficiency of investment**. The return on additional dollars of capital investment decreases because the most profitable investments are made initially.

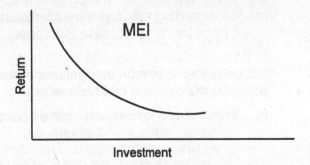

f.   Combining the MCC and MEI schedules (graphs) produces the equilibrium investment level for the firm (Q*) at a particular interest rate (i) and the capital budget.

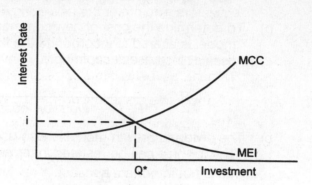

5.   Stop and review! You have completed the outline for this subunit. Study multiple-choice questions 24 through 53 beginning on page 143.

C. Dividend Policy

1.   Dividend policy determines what portion of a corporation's net income is distributed to shareholders and what portion is retained for reinvestment.

a.   A high dividend rate means a slower rate of growth, but a high growth rate usually means a low dividend rate. Because both a high growth rate and a high dividend rate may be desirable, the financial manager attempts to determine the balance of dividend and growth rates that maximizes the price of the firm's shares.

b.   Normally, corporations try to maintain a stable level of dividends, even though profits may fluctuate considerably, because many shareholders buy stock with the expectation of receiving a certain dividend every year. Hence, management tends not to raise dividends if the payout cannot be sustained. For example, a company with fluctuating earnings might pay out $1 every year whether earnings per share are $10 (10% payout rate) or $1 (100% payout rate).

1)   The tendency toward stability is the basis for the **information content or signaling hypothesis**: a change in dividend policy is a signal to the market regarding management's forecast of future earnings. The firm's stock price tends to increase (decrease) if dividends are unexpectedly high (low).

2)   Another possible reason for changes in stock prices after changes in dividend policy is the **clientele effect**.

a)   Some shareholders, e.g., retired people, desire immediate income, whereas other shareholders, e.g., those in the highest tax bracket, may prefer a low payout. The latter may not need income and therefore favor capital gains, which may be taxed at a lower rate, are deferred until shares are sold, and may be avoided altogether by the beneficiaries if the shareholder dies.

b) In accordance with the clientele effect, a firm attracts investors that prefer its dividend policy. Changes in that policy are therefore likely to cause investor switching with its attendant inefficiencies (brokers' fees, capital gains taxes, and, possibly, an insufficient number of investors who prefer the new policy).

c. No theoretical agreement exists concerning the optimal dividend policy.

1) Some theorists argue that capital gains are riskier than dividends and that a high dividend payout will maximize the stock price.

2) A second position is that a low dividend payout is preferable for tax reasons.

3) Still another position is that dividend policy is irrelevant to the firm's valuation. According to this view, the value of the firm is determined solely by its earning capacity and its risk. Whether earnings are paid out or retained is not important because most investors reinvest their dividends in the same or similar companies. Moreover, risk is a function of the firm's future cash flows, not its dividend payout.

2. Other factors influence a company's dividend policy.

a. **Legal restrictions.** Dividends ordinarily cannot be paid out of paid-in capital. A corporation must have a credit balance in its retained earnings account.

b. **Rate of growth.** A company with a faster growth rate will have a greater need to finance that growth with retained earnings. Thus, growth companies usually have lower dividend payout ratios. Shareholders hope for large future capital gains.

c. **Cash position.** Regardless of a firm's earnings record, cash must be available before a dividend can be paid. No dividend can be declared if all of a firm's earnings are tied up in receivables and inventories.

d. **Restrictions in debt agreements.** Bond indentures and other debt agreements often place restrictions on the amount of dividends that a company can declare.

e. **Accumulated earnings tax.** An accumulated earnings tax is assessed on a corporation if it has accumulated retained earnings beyond its reasonably expected needs. Thus, tax law indirectly penalizes shareholders who postpone paying taxes because of low dividend payouts.

f. **Residual theory of dividends.** The amount (residual) of earnings paid as dividends depends on the available investment opportunities and the debt-equity ratio at which the cost of capital is minimized. The rational investor should prefer reinvestment of retained earnings when the return exceeds what the investor could earn on investments of equal risk. However, the firm may prefer to pay dividends when investment opportunities are poor and the use of internal equity financing would move the firm away from its ideal capital structure.

3. **Important Dates concerning the Declaration of Dividends**

a. **Date of declaration** is the date the directors meet and formally vote to declare a dividend. On this date, the dividend becomes a liability of the corporation.

b. **Date of record** is the date as of which the corporation determines the shareholders who will receive the declared dividend. Essentially, the corporation closes its shareholder records on this date. Only those shareholders who own the stock on the date of record will receive the dividend. It typically falls from 2 to 6 weeks after the declaration date.

c.   **Date of payment** is the date on which the dividend is actually paid (when the checks are sent to the investors). The payment date is usually from 2 to 4 weeks after the date of record.

d.   **Ex-dividend date** is a date established by the stock exchanges, such as 4 days before the date of record. Unlike the other dates mentioned above, it is not established by the corporate board of directors. The period between the ex-dividend date and the date of record gives the stock exchange members time to process any transactions so that new shareholders will receive the dividends to which they are entitled. An investor who buys a share of stock before the ex-dividend date will receive the dividend that has been previously declared. An investor who buys the stock after the ex-dividend date (but before the date of record or payment date) will not receive the declared dividend. Instead, the individual who sold the stock will receive the dividend because (s)he owned it on the ex-dividend date.

1)   Usually, a stock price will drop on the ex-dividend date by the amount of the dividend because the new investor will not receive it.

4.   **Stock dividends and stock splits** involve issuance of additional shares to existing shareholders. Shareholders receive no actual increase in the value of their holdings. The previous holdings are simply divided into more pieces (additional shares).

a.   A **stock dividend** is an issuance of stock and entails the transfer of a sum from the retained earnings account to a paid-in capital account.

1)   Casual investors may believe they are receiving something of value when in essence their previous holdings are merely being divided into more pieces.

2)   Stock dividends are often used by growing companies that wish to retain earnings in the business while placating shareholders.

b.   A **stock split** does not involve any accounting entries. Instead, the existing shares are divided into more pieces so that the market price per share will be reduced.

1)   EXAMPLE: If a corporation has 1 million shares outstanding, each of which sells for $90, a 2-for-1 stock split will result in 2 million shares outstanding, each of which sells for about $45.

2)   **Reverse stock splits** reduce the shares outstanding and increase the price per share.

c.   Advantages of issuing stock splits and dividends

1)   Because more shares will be outstanding, the price per share will be lower, and more small investors may purchase the company's stock. Thus, because demand for the stock is greater, the price may increase. However, EPS and book value per share will be lower.

a)   EXAMPLE: In the example above, the additional investors interested in the company at the lower price may drive the price up to $46 or $47, or slightly higher than the theoretical price of $45. Hence, current shareholders may benefit from the split (or dividend) after all.

2)   A dividend or split can be a publicity gesture. Because shareholders may believe they are receiving value (and perhaps indirectly they are), they will have a better opinion of their company.

3)   If more shares are outstanding, the number of shareholders, who are usually good customers for their own company's products, will be larger.

5. **Treasury stock** is stock that a corporation has issued and reacquired. It is usually purchased on the open market at the current market price. The effect is to distribute retained earnings to shareholders. Regular repurchases are therefore a substitute for cash dividends.

   a. Treasury stock is not an asset because a corporation cannot own itself.

   b. Treasury stock is reported as a reduction of shareholders' equity (a contra-equity account). Such stock is considered issued but not outstanding.

   c. A corporation repurchases its stock to

      1) Meet employee stock option and bonus plan requirements

      2) Buy out a shareholder when the stock cannot be sold on the open market or when the sale would adversely affect the market price

      3) Support the market for the company's stock

      4) Reduce the size of the business

      5) Acquire stock needed to undertake a merger

      6) Decrease the number of shares outstanding in hopes of increasing EPS

         a) The purchase of treasury stock may be the best investment opportunity available to the company, especially when management believes that the company's stock is undervalued.

      7) Increase the book value per share of the remaining shares outstanding

         a) The market value must be less than the book value.

      8) Hold the shares until the market rises, at which time the stock will be resold

         a) Management treats the treasury stock as an investment in the belief that the stock is undervalued.

      9) Provide a quick and simple means of adjusting a firm's capital structure

         a) A repurchase of shares using debt financing is an even more dramatic way of quickly changing the relationship between debt and equity.

   d. Dividends are not paid on treasury stock.

   e. Treasury stock does not have voting rights.

   f. The purchase of treasury stock is sometimes criticized as being a selective dividend to shareholders who sell their stock.

      1) Like a dividend, purchase of treasury stock decreases shareholders' equity.

      2) Such dividends are usually not taxed as dividends but rather as capital gains. The advantage is that the capital gains rate may be less than the marginal tax rate of the shareholder.

   g. Disadvantages of buying treasury stock include

      1) A higher debt-equity ratio and increased financial leverage, which may increase the difficulty of obtaining loans

      2) An increase in the company's susceptibility to acquisition by another corporation because fewer shares are outstanding. Alternatively, a treasury stock purchase can thwart a hostile takeover. If the price is above market, this practice is known as "paying greenmail."

      3) Liquidity problems because cash is being paid out to shareholders

h.   To prohibit a corporation from using all of its capital (including borrowed capital) to buy treasury stock and then liquidating once all stock has been acquired, most states stipulate that legal capital (paid-in capital) cannot be reduced by treasury stock purchases.

1)   A company can buy treasury stock only to the extent it has retained earnings.

i.   In addition to buying treasury stock on the open market, a corporation planning a large purchase may make a tender offer for a certain number of shares. The tender offer may specify a particular price, or it may be effected by a Dutch auction.

1)   A tender offer asks shareholders to offer their shares for sale.

2)   Some shareholders may prefer a tender offer to dividends. At their option, they can tender shares and receive cash at favorable tax rates. In contrast, dividends must be accepted and taxes thereon must be paid.

3)   In a Dutch auction involving a solicitation to buy stock, each seller specifies the number of shares (s)he wishes to sell and a minimum price. Given the number of shares tendered and the prices offered by the selling shareholders, the lowest price that enables the buyer to acquire the requisite total of shares is set as the purchase price.

a)   One variation is for the tender offer to specify a range of acceptable prices.

6.   Stop and review! You have completed the outline for this subunit. Study multiple-choice questions 54 through 66 beginning on page 154.

MULTIPLE-CHOICE QUESTIONS

A. Sources of Long-Term Financing

1. The equity section of Smith Corporation's statement of financial position is presented below.

Preferred stock, $100 par	$12,000,000
Common stock, $5 par	10,000,000
Paid-in capital in excess of par	18,000,000
Retained earnings	9,000,000
Net worth	$49,000,000

The common shareholders of Smith Corporation have preemptive rights. If Smith Corporation issues 400,000 additional shares of common stock at $6 per share, a current holder of 20,000 shares of Smith Corporation's common stock must be given the option to buy

A. 1,000 additional shares.

B. 3,774 additional shares.

C. 4,000 additional shares.

D. 3,333 additional shares.

2. If the market price of a stock is $50 per share, the subscription price is $40 per share, and three rights are necessary to buy an additional share of stock, the theoretical market value of one right used to buy the stock prior to the ex-rights date is

A. $2.00

B. $2.50

C. $10.00

D. $40.00

The correct answer is (C). *(CMA 695 1-13)*
REQUIRED: The new shares that a shareholder may buy given preemptive rights.
DISCUSSION: Common shareholders usually have preemptive rights, which means they have the right to purchase any new issues of stock in proportion to their current ownership percentages. The purpose of a preemptive right is to allow shareholders to maintain their current percentages of ownership. Given that Smith had 2,000,000 shares outstanding ($10,000,000 ÷ $5 par), an investor with 20,000 shares has a 1% ownership. Hence, this investor must be allowed to purchase 4,000 (1% × 400,000 shares) of the additional shares.
Answer (A) is incorrect because the investor would be allowed to purchase 1% of any new issues. Answers (B) and (D) are incorrect because preferred shareholders do not share in preemptive rights.

The correct answer is (B). *(CMA 693 1-9)*
REQUIRED: The theoretical value of one right prior to the ex-rights date.
DISCUSSION: The formula for determining the value of one stock right when the price of the stock is rights-on is

$$R = \frac{P - S}{N + 1}$$

if R is the market value of one right when the stock is selling rights-on, P is the market value of one share of stock with rights-on, N is the number of rights necessary to purchase one share of stock, and S is the subscription price per share. Thus, the theoretical value is $2.50 per right [($50 − $40) ÷ (3 + 1)]. To check the answer, assume that an investor purchases three rights at $2.50 each (a total of $7.50) and uses them to buy a share of stock for $40. The total investment is $47.50. Similarly, a person holding a $50 share of stock before the rights are issued will have a basis of $47.50 after selling the right for $2.50. Hence, the value of the stock ex-rights is $47.50, and the value of the right is $2.50.
Answer (A) is incorrect because the right is worth $2.50. Answer (C) is incorrect because $10 is the difference between the price of the stock with rights ($50) and the exercise price ($40). Answer (D) is incorrect because $40 is the exercise price of the new issue.

3. The market value of a share of stock is $50, and the market value of one right prior to the ex-rights date is $2.00 after the offering is announced but while the stock is still selling rights-on. The offer to the shareholder is that it will take three rights to buy an additional share of stock at a subscription price of $40 per share. If the theoretical value of the stock when it goes ex-rights is $47.50, the shareholder

A. Does not receive any additional benefit from a rights offering.

B. Receives an additional benefit from a rights offering.

C. Merely receives a return of capital.

D. Should redeem the right and purchase the stock before the ex-rights date.

The correct answer is (A). *(CMA 693 1-10)*
REQUIRED: The true statement about the effect on the value of stock when it goes ex-rights.
DISCUSSION: The theoretical value is $2.50 (see the preceding question). However, if the stock declines to $47.50 when the right is worth only $2, the original investor is worse off then before the rights issuance; i.e., the investor would have only $49.50 worth of investments. Hence, the original shareholder receives no benefit from the issuance of the rights.
Answer (B) is incorrect because the shareholder would be worse off after the rights offering ($49.50) than before ($50). Answer (C) is incorrect because the shareholder only receives a certificate granting the right to make an additional investment. Answer (D) is incorrect because an investor cannot redeem a right before the ex-rights date, i.e., while the stock is still rights-on.

4. The par value of a common stock represents

A. The estimated market value of the stock when it was issued.

B. The liability ceiling of a shareholder when a company undergoes bankruptcy proceedings.

C. The total value of the stock that must be entered in the issuing corporation's records.

D. The amount that must be recorded on the issuing corporation's record as paid-in capital.

The correct answer is (B). *(CMA 693 1-18)*
REQUIRED: The amount represented by the par value of common stock.
DISCUSSION: Par value represents a stock's legal capital. It is an arbitrary value assigned to stock before it is issued. Par value represents a shareholder's liability ceiling because, as long as the par value has been paid in to the corporation, the shareholders obtain the benefits of limited liability.
Answer (A) is incorrect because par value is rarely the same as market value. Normally, market value will be equal to or greater than par value, but there is no relationship between the two. Answer (C) is incorrect because all assets received for stock must be entered into a corporation's records. The amount received is very rarely the par value. Answer (D) is incorrect because all assets received for stock represent paid-in capital. Thus, paid-in capital may exceed par value.

5. Preferred and common stock differ in that

A. Failure to pay dividends on common stock will not force the firm into bankruptcy while failure to pay dividends on preferred stock will force the firm into bankruptcy.

B. Common stock dividends are a fixed amount while preferred stock dividends are not.

C. Preferred stock has a higher priority than common stock with regard to earnings and assets in the event of bankruptcy.

D. Preferred stock dividends are deductible as an expense for tax purposes while common stock dividends are not.

The correct answer is (C). *(CIA 595 IV-48)*
REQUIRED: The difference between preferred and common stock.
DISCUSSION: In the event of bankruptcy, the claims of preferred shareholders must be satisfied before common shareholders receive anything. The interests of common shareholders are secondary to those of all other claimants.
Answer (A) is incorrect because failure to pay dividends will not force the firm into bankruptcy, whether the dividends are for common or preferred stock. Only failure to pay interest will force the firm into bankruptcy. Answer (B) is incorrect because preferred dividends are fixed. Answer (D) is incorrect because neither common nor preferred dividends are tax deductible.

6. Which of the following is usually not a feature of cumulative preferred stock?

A. Has priority over common stock with regard to earnings.

B. Has priority over common stock with regard to assets.

C. Has voting rights.

D. Has the right to receive dividends in arrears before common stock dividends can be paid.

The correct answer is (C). *(CIA 1195 IV-47)*

REQUIRED: The item not usually a feature of cumulative preferred stock.

DISCUSSION: Preferred stock does not usually have voting rights. Preferred shareholders are usually given the right to vote for directors only if the company has not paid the preferred dividend for a specified period of time, such as ten quarters. Such a provision is an incentive for management to pay preferred dividends.

Answer (A) is incorrect because preferred stock has priority over common stock with regard to earnings, so dividends must be paid on preferred stock before they can be paid on common stock. Answer (B) is incorrect because preferred stock has priority over common stock with regard to assets. In the event of liquidation, for example, because of bankruptcy, the claims of preferred shareholders must be satisfied in full before the common shareholders receive anything. Answer (D) is incorrect because cumulative preferred stock has the right to receive any dividends not paid in prior periods before common stock dividends are paid.

7. Brady Corporation has 6,000 shares of 5% cumulative, $100 par value preferred stock outstanding and 200,000 shares of common stock outstanding. Brady's board of directors last declared dividends for the year ended May 31, 1993, and there were no dividends in arrears. For the year ended May 31, 1995, Brady had net income of $1,750,000. The board of directors is declaring a dividend for common shareholders equivalent to 20% of net income. The total amount of dividends to be paid by Brady at May 31, 1995, is

A. $350,000

B. $380,000

C. $206,000

D. $410,000

The correct answer is (D). *(CMA 695 1-11)*

REQUIRED: The total amount of dividends to be paid given cumulative preferred stock.

DISCUSSION: If a company has cumulative preferred stock, all preferred dividends for the current and any unpaid prior years must be paid before any dividends can be paid on common stock. The total preferred dividends that must be paid equal $60,000 (2 years x 5% x $100 par x 6,000 shares), and the common dividend is $350,000 ($1,750,000 x 20%), for a total of $410,000.

Answer (A) is incorrect because $350,000 is the common stock dividend. Answer (B) is incorrect because $380,000 omits the $30,000 of cumulative dividends for 1994. Answer (C) is incorrect because $206,000 is based on a flat rate of $1 per share of stock.

8. Which one of the following statements correctly compares bond financing alternatives?

A. A bond with a call provision typically has a lower yield to maturity than a similar bond without a call provision.

B. A convertible bond must be converted to common stock prior to its maturity.

C. A call provision is usually considered detrimental to the investor.

D. A sinking fund prohibits the firm from redeeming a bond issue prior to its final maturity.

The correct answer is (C). *(CMA 695 1-2)*

REQUIRED: The true statement comparing bond financing alternatives.

DISCUSSION: A callable bond can be recalled by the issuer prior to maturity. A call provision is detrimental to the investor because the issuer can recall the bond when market interest rates decline. It is usually exercised only when a company wishes to refinance high-interest debt.

Answer (A) is incorrect because callable bonds sometimes pay a slightly higher rate of interest. Investors may demand a greater return because of the uncertainty over the true maturity date. Answer (B) is incorrect because conversion is at the option of the investor. Answer (D) is incorrect because a sinking fund provision requires an issuer to retire a certain portion of its bonds each year or set aside money for repayment in the future. Such a provision increases the probability of repayment for bondholders but does not prohibit early redemption.

9. A bond backed by fixed assets is a(n)

A. Income bond.

B. Subordinated debenture.

C. Debenture.

D. Mortgage bond.

The correct answer is (D). *(CIA 1191 IV-53)*

REQUIRED: The kind of bond backed by fixed assets.

DISCUSSION: A mortgage bond is secured with specific fixed assets, usually real property. Thus, under the rights enumerated in the bond indenture, creditors will be able to receive payments from liquidation of the property in case of default. In a bankruptcy proceeding, these amounts are paid before any transfers are made to other creditors, including those preferences. Hence, mortgage bonds are less risky than the others listed.

Answer (A) is incorrect because an income bond is one that pays interest only if it is earned. Answers (B) and (C) are incorrect because debentures are unsecured forms of long-term debt.

10. Debentures are

A. Income bonds that require interest payments only when earnings permit.

B. Subordinated debt and rank behind convertible bonds.

C. Bonds secured by the full faith and credit of the issuing firm.

D. Mortgage bonds secured by a lien on specific assets of the firm.

The correct answer is (C). *(CMA 692 1-7)*

REQUIRED: The true statement about debentures.

DISCUSSION: Debentures are unsecured bonds. Although no assets are mortgaged as security for the bonds, debentures are secured by the full faith and credit of the issuing firm. Debentures are a general obligation of the borrower. Only companies with the best credit ratings can issue debentures because only the company's credit rating and reputation secure the bonds.

Answer (A) is incorrect because debentures must pay interest regardless of earnings levels. Answer (B) is incorrect because debentures are not subordinated except to the extent of assets mortgaged against other bond issues. Debentures are a general obligation of the borrower and rank equally with convertible bonds. Answer (D) is incorrect because debentures are not secured by mortgages on specific assets.

11. Assume a company has gone bankrupt and will be liquidated. After liquidating the assets and covering tax liabilities, administration fees, and wage expenses, the following claims remain:

Notes payable	$10,000,000
Unsecured bank loans	4,000,000
Subordinated debentures	6,000,000

There is only $10,000,000 available to pay these claims. How much will be allocated to subordinated debentures?

A. $0

B. $3,000,000

C. $4,000,000

D. $6,000,000

The correct answer is (A). *(CIA 593 IV-54)*

REQUIRED: The amount allocated to subordinated debentures.

DISCUSSION: Subordinated debt has claims only on those assets remaining after unsubordinated debt has been paid in full. Because the unsubordinated debt equals $14,000,000 and only $10,000,000 of assets are available, the allocation to subordinated debt should be zero.

Answer (B) is incorrect because $3,000,000 assumes 50% of each class of claims is paid. Answer (C) is incorrect because $4,000,000 is the amount owed on the unsecured bank loans. Answer (D) is incorrect because $6,000,000 is the amount of the subordinated debt.

12. Which one of the following characteristics distinguishes income bonds from other bonds?

A. The bondholder is guaranteed an income over the life of the security.

B. By promising a return to the bondholder, an income bond is junior to preferred and common stock.

C. Income bonds are junior to subordinated debt but senior to preferred and common stock.

D. Income bonds pay interest only if the issuing company has earned the interest.

The correct answer is (D). *(CMA 693 1-17)*

REQUIRED: The characteristic of income bonds.

DISCUSSION: An income bond is one that pays interest only if the issuing company has earned the interest, although the principal must still be paid on the due date. Such bonds are riskier than normal bonds.

Answer (A) is incorrect because bondholders will receive an income only if the issuing company earns sufficient income to pay the interest. Answer (B) is incorrect because all bonds have priority over preferred and common stock. Answer (C) is incorrect because subordinated debt is junior to nonsubordinated debt.

13. Serial bonds are attractive to investors because

A. All bonds in the issue mature on the same date.

B. The yield to maturity is the same for all bonds in the issue.

C. Investors can choose the maturity that suits their financial needs.

D. The coupon rate on these bonds is adjusted to the maturity date.

The correct answer is (C). *(CMA 689 1-2)*

REQUIRED: The reason serial bonds are attractive to investors.

DISCUSSION: Serial bonds have staggered maturities; that is, they mature over a period (series) of years. Thus, investors can choose the maturity date that meets their investment needs. For example, an investor who will have a child starting college in 16 years can choose bonds that mature in 16 years.

Answer (A) is incorrect because serial bonds mature on different dates. Answer (B) is incorrect because bonds maturing on different dates may have different yields, or they may be the same. Usually, the earlier maturities carry slightly lower yields than the later maturities. Answer (D) is incorrect because the coupon rate is the same for all bonds; only the selling price and yield differ.

14. Bondholders are assured of protection against inflation if they hold

A. Income bonds.

B. Convertible bonds.

C. Mortgage bonds.

D. Indexed bonds.

The correct answer is (D). *(CIA 595 IV-39)*

REQUIRED: The bonds that provide protection against inflation.

DISCUSSION: The interest payments on indexed or purchasing power bonds are based on an inflation index, such as the consumer price index. Thus, interest paid to bondholders rises automatically when the inflation rate rises.

Answer (A) is incorrect because income bonds pay interest to the holder only if the interest is earned. The interest paid is not inflation adjusted. Answer (B) is incorrect because convertible bonds can be redeemed for the common stock of the issuer at the option of the holder. Interest payments are not inflation adjusted. Answer (C) is incorrect because mortgage bonds are secured by fixed assets of the issuer. Thus, they provide greater security to bondholders, but the interest payments are not inflation adjusted.

15. Zero-coupon bonds issued by corporations

A. Are initially sold at par value (a zero discount).

B. Are initially sold for a price above par value.

C. Are tax free.

D. Require no cash outlay from the issuer until the bonds mature.

The correct answer is (D). *(CIA 1192 IV-56)*

REQUIRED: The true statement about zero-coupon bonds issued by corporations.

DISCUSSION: Zero-coupon bonds pay no interest but sell at a deep discount from their face value. A relatively new type of bond, these instruments are very useful to both investors and investees. The need to reinvest the interest on normal coupon bonds renders the final return uncertain because future reinvestment rates are uncertain. With zero-coupon bonds, the investor knows exactly the return (s)he will earn. Investors might therefore be willing to pay a premium for them, which in turn might lead firms to issue them. No interest payments means the firm faces no additional insolvency risk from the issue until it matures.

Answers (A) and (B) are incorrect because these bonds are sold at a discount. Answer (C) is incorrect because these bonds are subject to taxes.

16. Junk bonds are

A. Securities rated at less than investment grade.

B. Worthless securities.

C. Securities that are highly risky but offer only low yields.

D. Related only to issues of "fallen angel" companies whose securities have been downgraded.

The correct answer is (A). *(CMA 693 1-16)*

REQUIRED: The definition of junk bonds.

DISCUSSION: Junk bonds are high risk and therefore high-yield securities that are normally issued when the debt ratio is very high. Thus, the bondholders have as much risk as the holders of equity securities. Such bonds are not highly rated by credit evaluation companies. Junk bonds have become accepted because of the tax deductibility of the interest paid.

Answer (B) is incorrect because junk bonds are not yet worthless; they simply bear high interest rates and high risk. Answer (C) is incorrect because junk bonds typically offer high yields. Answer (D) is incorrect because junk bonds are not ones that have been downgraded; they were never high grade.

17. The best reason corporations issue Eurobonds rather than domestic bonds is that

A. These bonds are denominated in the currency of the country in which they are issued.

B. These bonds are normally a less expensive form of financing because of the absence of government regulation.

C. Foreign buyers more readily accept the issues of both large and small U.S. corporations than do domestic investors.

D. Eurobonds carry no foreign exchange risk.

The correct answer is (B). *(CMA 1288 1-7)*

REQUIRED: The best reason for issuing Eurobonds instead of domestic bonds.

DISCUSSION: International bonds are of two types: foreign bonds and Eurobonds. Foreign bonds are denominated in the currency of the nation in which they are sold. Eurobonds are denominated in a currency other than that of the nation where they are sold.

Foreign bonds issued in the United States and denominated in dollars must be registered with the SEC, but such extensive disclosure is not required in most European nations. Thus, an American company may elect to issue Eurobonds denominated in dollars in a foreign nation because of the convenience of not having to comply with governmental registration requirements.

Answer (A) is incorrect because Eurobonds are not denominated in the currency of the nation in which they are sold. The difference is a possible disadvantage because of exchange rate risk. Answer (C) is incorrect because foreign nationals are often hesitant about buying bonds issued by small companies with which they are not familiar. Answer (D) is incorrect because Eurobonds carry foreign exchange risk. The foreign lender may suffer a loss if the dollar declines relative to its domestic currency.

18. Which of the following brings in additional capital to the firm?

A. Two-for-one stock split.

B. Conversion of convertible bonds to common stock.

C. Exercise of warrants.

D. Exercise of option purchased through option exchange.

The correct answer is (C). *(CIA 1191 IV-59)*
REQUIRED: The stockholders' equity transaction that brings in additional capital.
DISCUSSION: Warrants are options that permit the holder to buy stock for a stated price. Their exercise results in inflows and the issuance of stock.
Answer (A) is incorrect because a stock split is merely an accounting action that increases (or occasionally decreases) the number of shares outstanding. It does not generate additional capital. Answer (B) is incorrect because conversion of convertible bonds to common stock simply replaces debt with outstanding common stock. Answer (D) is incorrect because options purchased and exercised through option exchanges are transactions between individual investors not affecting the firm whose stock is involved.

19. Compared to another bond with the same risk and maturity but without a conversion feature, a convertible bond has a

A. Higher face value.

B. Lower face value.

C. Higher coupon rate.

D. Lower coupon rate.

The correct answer is (D). *(CIA 595 IV-40)*
REQUIRED: The true statement about a convertible bond.
DISCUSSION: Convertible bonds are convertible at the holder's option into shares of the issuer's common stock at a specified price. They have a lower coupon rate than nonconvertible bonds because they offer investors a chance for capital gains.
Answers (A) and (B) are incorrect because the face value is not a distinguishing feature of convertible bonds. Answer (C) is incorrect because convertible bonds have lower, not higher, coupon rates.

20. Convertible bonds and bonds issued with warrants differ in that

A. Convertible bonds have lower coupon rates than straight bonds, but bonds issued with warrants have higher coupon rates than straight bonds.

B. Convertible bonds have higher coupon rates than straight bonds, but bonds issued with warrants have lower coupon rates than straight bonds.

C. Convertible bonds remain outstanding after the bondholder exercises the right to become a common shareholder, but bonds that are issued with warrants do not.

D. Bonds that are issued with warrants remain outstanding after the bondholder exercises the right to become a common shareholder, but convertible bonds do not.

The correct answer is (D). *(CIA 1195 IV-46)*
REQUIRED: The difference between convertible bonds and bonds issued with warrants.
DISCUSSION: Warrants represent options to purchase equity securities and should be separately accounted for. Because warrants are usually detachable, the bonds remain outstanding if the warrants are exercised. In contrast, convertible bonds must be surrendered when the conversion privilege is exercised. The equity feature of convertible bonds is not separately accounted for.
Answers (A) and (B) are incorrect because bonds issued with warrants and convertible bonds have lower coupon rates than conventional bonds. Answer (C) is incorrect because convertible bonds do not remain outstanding.

21. Which one of the following is a disadvantage of the use of convertible bonds as a form of financing?

    A. Less restrictive covenants in bond indentures would usually be more acceptable to investors in convertible bonds than to investors in nonconvertible bonds.

    B. Convertible bonds defer equity financing until the stock price is higher.

    C. Convertible bonds carry a lower interest rate at issuance than if the bond were not convertible.

    D. The investor may choose not to convert the convertible bonds.

The correct answer is (D). *(CMA 1291 1-12)*

REQUIRED: The disadvantage of convertible bonds as a form of financing.

DISCUSSION: A conversion feature permits bondholders to convert their bonds into common stock at some future time if the stock price rises. This provision is sometimes incorporated into a bond contract to entice investors to lend money to the issuer at a lower interest rate. Another purpose of issuing convertible bonds is to obtain equity financing at a time when market prices are unfavorable. Issuing convertible bonds is tantamount to selling the stock at a higher price, assuming that bondholders eventually exercise their option to convert. The disadvantage to the corporation is that stock prices may never reach the conversion price, and bondholders will not convert their bonds into stock. The corporation will then have to make interest and principal payments.

Answers (A), (B), and (C) are incorrect because the advantages of convertible bonds are that covenants in the bond indentures are often less restrictive, they defer equity financing until the stock price is higher, and they carry a lower interest rate at issuance.

22. A major use of warrants in financing is to

    A. Lower the cost of debt.

    B. Avoid dilution of earnings per share.

    C. Maintain managerial control.

    D. Permit the buy-back of bonds before maturity.

The correct answer is (A). *(CMA 1291 1-6)*

REQUIRED: The major use of warrants in financing.

DISCUSSION: Warrants are long-term options that give holders the right to buy common stock in the future at a specific price. If the market price goes up, the holders of warrants will exercise their rights to buy stock at the special price. If the market price does not exceed the exercise price, the warrants will lapse. Issuers of debt sometimes attach stock purchase warrants to debt instruments as an inducement to investors. The investor then has the security of fixed-return debt plus the possibility for large gains if stock prices increase significantly. If warrants are attached, debt can sell at an interest rate slightly lower than the market rate.

Answer (B) is incorrect because outstanding warrants dilute earnings per share. They are included in the denominator of the EPS calculation even if they have not been exercised. Answer (C) is incorrect because warrants can, if exercised, result in a dilution of management's holdings. Answer (D) is incorrect because a call provision in a bond indenture, not the use of warrants, permits the buy-back of bonds.

23. A major difference between operating and financial leases is that

    A. Operating leases usually do not provide for maintenance but financial leases do.

    B. Operating lease contracts are written for a period that exceeds the economic life of the leased equipment.

    C. Operating leases frequently contain a cancellation clause, whereas financial leases are not cancelable.

    D. The lessee finances the assets leased for an operating lease.

The correct answer is (C). *(CIA 590 IV-53)*

REQUIRED: The major difference between operating and financial leases.

DISCUSSION: Operating leases provide both financing and maintenance services to the lessee. An operating or service lease is usually for a term less than the economic life of the asset, and the lease payments are for an amount less than the full cost. Moreover, a cancellation clause in the agreement usually permits the lessee to return the asset before expiration of the term, for example, because of technological change. A financial lease is tantamount to a sale financed by the lessor. The payments are equal to the full cost of the asset, cancellation is not permitted, and maintenance is ordinarily not provided.

Answer (A) is incorrect because operating leases usually provide for maintenance but financial leases do not. Answer (B) is incorrect because operating lease contracts are written for a period less than the economic life. Answer (D) is incorrect because the lessor finances the assets leased for an operating lease.

B. Optimal Capitalization

24. A firm must select from among several methods of financing arrangements when meeting its capital requirements. To acquire additional growth capital while attempting to maximize earnings per share, a firm should normally

  A. Attempt to increase both debt and equity in equal proportions, which preserves a stable capital structure and maintains investor confidence.

  B. Select debt over equity initially, even though increased debt is accompanied by interest costs and a degree of risk.

  C. Select equity over debt initially, which minimizes risk and avoids interest costs.

  D. Discontinue dividends and use current cash flow, which avoids the cost and risk of increased debt and the dilution of EPS through increased equity.

The correct answer is (B). *(CIA 1191 IV-58)*
  REQUIRED: The financing arrangement that should be selected to acquire additional growth capital while attempting to maximize earnings per share.
  DISCUSSION: Earnings per share will ordinarily be higher if debt is used to raise capital instead of equity, provided that the firm is not over-leveraged. The reason is that the cost of debt is lower than the cost of equity because interest is tax deductible. However, the prospect of higher EPS is accompanied by greater risk to the firm resulting from required interest costs, creditors' liens on the firm's assets, and the possibility of a proportionately lower EPS if sales volume fails to meet projections.
  Answer (A) is incorrect because EPS is not a function of investor confidence and is not maximized by concurrent proportional increases in both debt and equity. EPS are usually higher if debt is used instead of equity to raise capital, at least initially. Answer (C) is incorrect because equity capital is initially more costly than debt. Answer (D) is incorrect because using only current cash flow to raise capital is usually too conservative an approach for a growth-oriented firm. Management is expected to be willing to take acceptable risks to be competitive and attain an acceptable rate of growth.

25. A higher degree of operating leverage compared with the industry average implies that the firm

  A. Has higher variable costs.

  B. Has profits that are more sensitive to changes in sales volume.

  C. Is more profitable.

  D. Is less risky.

The correct answer is (B). *(CMA 695 1-1)*
  REQUIRED: The effect of a higher degree of operating leverage (DOL).
  DISCUSSION: Operating leverage is a measure of the degree to which fixed costs are used in the production process. A company with a higher percentage of fixed costs (higher operating leverage) has greater risk than one in the same industry that relies more heavily on variable costs. The DOL equals the percentage change in net operating income divided by the percentage change in sales. Thus, profits become more sensitive to changes in sales volume as the DOL increases.
  Answer (A) is incorrect because a firm with higher operating leverage has higher fixed costs and lower variable costs. Answer (C) is incorrect because a firm with higher leverage will be relatively more profitable than a firm with lower leverage when sales are high. The opposite is true when sales are low. Answer (D) is incorrect because a firm with higher leverage is more risky. Its reliance on fixed costs is greater.

26. The degree of operating leverage for Carlisle Company is

A. 2.4

B. 1.78

C. 2.13

D. 1.2

The correct answer is (B). *(CMA 692 1-8)*

REQUIRED: The degree of operating leverage.

DISCUSSION: Operating leverage is the percentage change in operating income resulting from a percentage change in sales. It measures how a change in volume affects profits. An alternative formula for operating leverage divides contribution margin by the contribution margin minus fixed costs. Companies with larger investments and greater fixed costs ordinarily have higher contribution margins and more operating leverage. The degree of operating leverage measures the extent to which fixed assets are used in the production process. A company with a high percentage of fixed costs is more risky than a firm in the same industry that relies more on variable costs to produce. Based on a contribution margin of $.16 per unit ($1 – $.84 variable cost), the degree of operating leverage is

$$(400,000 \times \$.16) \div [(400,000 \times \$.16) - \$28,000] = 1.78.$$

Answer (A) is incorrect because 2.4 is obtained by overstating the contribution margin or the fixed costs. Answer (C) is incorrect because 2.13 includes a nonoperating expense (interest) as a fixed cost. Answer (D) is incorrect because 1.2 is obtained by understating the $64,000 contribution margin or understating the $28,000 of fixed costs.

27. The degree of financial leverage for Carlisle Company is

A. 2.4

B. 1.78

C. 1.35

D. 1.2

The correct answer is (C). *(CMA 692 1-9)*

REQUIRED: The degree of financial leverage.

DISCUSSION: The degree of financial leverage is the percentage change in earnings available to common share-holders that is associated with a given percentage change in net operating income. Operating income equals earnings before interest and taxes. The more financial leverage employed, the greater the degree of financial leverage and the riskier the firm. An alternative formula for financial leverage divides EBIT by EBIT minus interest and preferred dividends (before tax effect). Earnings before interest and taxes equal $36,000 [$400,000 sales – ($.84 x 400,000 units) VC – $28,000 FC]. Using the second formula, the calculation is as follows:

$$\frac{\$36,000}{\$36,000 - \$6,000 - (\$2,000 \div .6)} = \frac{\$36,000}{\$26,667} = 1.35$$

Answer (A) is incorrect because 2.4 is obtained by overstating the contribution margin or the fixed costs. Answer (B) is incorrect because 1.78 is the degree of operating leverage, not financial leverage. Answer (D) is incorrect because 1.2 is obtained by understating the $64,000 of contribution margin or understating the $28,000 of fixed costs.

28. If Carlisle Company did not have preferred stock, the degree of total leverage would

A. Decrease in proportion to a decrease in financial leverage.

B. Increase in proportion to an increase in financial leverage.

C. Remain the same.

D. Decrease but not be proportional to the decrease in financial leverage.

The correct answer is (A). *(CMA 692 1-10)*

REQUIRED: The true statement about the degree of total leverage if the company did not have preferred stock.

DISCUSSION: The degree of total leverage is equal to the degree of operating leverage times the degree of financial leverage. Thus, a decrease in either of these ratios results in a decrease in total leverage. If the company had no preferred stock, the DFL and the DTL would be lower because the pretax income necessary to pay the preferred dividends $[P \div (1 - t)]$ is subtracted from the denominator of the DFL.

Answer (B) is incorrect because the DTL would decrease, not increase. Answer (C) is incorrect because the elimination of preferred stock would change the equation. Answer (D) is incorrect because the decrease would be proportional.

29. The theory underlying the cost of capital is primarily concerned with the cost of

A. Long-term funds and old funds.

B. Short-term funds and new funds.

C. Long-term funds and new funds.

D. Any combination of old or new, short-term or long-term funds.

The correct answer is (C). *(CMA 692 1-13)*

REQUIRED: The true statement about the theory underlying the cost of capital.

DISCUSSION: The theory underlying the cost of capital is based primarily on the cost of long-term funds and the acquisition of new funds. The reason is that long-term funds are used to finance long-term investments. For an investment alternative to be viable, the return on the investment must be greater than the cost of the funds used. The objective in short-term borrowing is different. Short-term loans are used for working capital, not to finance long-term investments.

Answer (A) is incorrect because the concern is with the cost of new funds; the cost of old funds is a sunk cost and of no relevance for decision-making purposes. Answer (B) is incorrect because the cost of short-term funds is not usually a concern for investment purposes. Answer (D) is incorrect because there is less concern with the cost of old funds or short-term funds.

30. The overall cost of capital is the

A. Rate of return on assets that covers the costs associated with the funds employed.

B. Average rate of return a firm earns on its assets.

C. Minimum rate a firm must earn on high-risk projects.

D. Cost of the firm's equity capital at which the market value of the firm will remain unchanged.

The correct answer is (A). *(CMA 692 1-11)*

REQUIRED: The definition of overall cost of capital.

DISCUSSION: The overall cost of capital is the rate of return on a firm's assets that exactly covers the costs associated with the funds employed. It is the weighted average of the various debt and equity components.

Answer (B) is incorrect because the cost of capital is based on what a company pays for its capital, not the return earned on the capital employed. Answer (C) is incorrect because the overall cost of capital is the minimum rate a firm must earn on all investments to cover capital costs. Answer (D) is incorrect because the overall cost of capital is based on both debt and equity components.

31. Which one of the following factors might cause a firm to increase the debt in its financial structure?

    A. An increase in the corporate income tax rate.

    B. Increased economic uncertainty.

    C. An increase in the federal funds rate.

    D. An increase in the price-earnings ratio.

The correct answer is (A). *(CMA 1294 1-29)*

    REQUIRED: The factor that might encourage a firm to increase the debt in its financial structure.

    DISCUSSION: An increase in the corporate income tax rate might encourage a company to borrow because interest on debt is tax deductible, whereas dividends are not. Accordingly, an increase in the tax rate means that the after-tax cost of debt capital will decrease.

    Answer (B) is incorrect because increased uncertainty encourages equity financing. Dividends do not have to be paid in bad years, but interest on debt is a fixed charge. Answer (C) is incorrect because an increase in interest rates discourages debt financing. Answer (D) is incorrect because an increase in the price-earnings ratio means that the return to shareholders (equity investors) is declining; therefore, equity capital is a more attractive financing alternative.

32. In general, it is more expensive for a company to finance with equity capital than with debt capital because

    A. Long-term bonds have a maturity date and must therefore be repaid in the future.

    B. Investors are exposed to greater risk with equity capital.

    C. Equity capital is in greater demand than debt capital.

    D. Dividends fluctuate to a greater extent than interest rates.

The correct answer is (B). *(CMA 690 1-15)*

    REQUIRED: The reason equity financing is more expensive than debt financing.

    DISCUSSION: Providers of equity capital are exposed to more risk than are lenders because the firm is not obligated to pay them a return. Also, in case of liquidation, creditors are paid before equity investors. Thus, equity financing is more expensive than debt because equity investors require a higher return to compensate for the greater risk assumed.

    Answer (A) is incorrect because the obligation to repay at a specific maturity date reduces the risk to investors and thus the required return. Answer (C) is incorrect because greater demand lowers cost to the issuer. Answer (D) is incorrect because dividends are based on managerial discretion and may rarely change; interest rates, however, fluctuate daily based upon market conditions.

33. When calculating the cost of capital, the cost assigned to retained earnings should be

    A. Zero.

    B. Lower than the cost of external common equity.

    C. Equal to the cost of external common equity.

    D. Higher than the cost of external common equity.

The correct answer is (B). *(CIA 1195 IV-43)*

    REQUIRED: The cost assigned to retained earnings when calculating cost of capital.

    DISCUSSION: Newly issued or external common equity is more costly than retained earnings. The company incurs issuance costs when raising new, outside funds.

    Answer (A) is incorrect because the cost of retained earnings is the rate of return stockholders require on equity capital the firm obtains by retaining earnings. The opportunity cost of retained funds will be positive. Answers (C) and (D) are incorrect because retained earnings will always be less costly than external equity financing. Earnings retention does not require the payment of issuance costs.

34. A preferred stock is sold for $101 per share, has a face value of $100 per share, underwriting fees of $5 per share, and annual dividends of $10 per share. If the tax rate is 40%, the cost of funds (capital) for the preferred stock is

A. 6.2%

B. 10.0%

C. 10.4%

D. 5.2%

The correct answer is (C). *(CMA 692 1-14)*

REQUIRED: The cost of capital for a preferred stock issue.

DISCUSSION: Because the dividends on preferred stock are not deductible for tax purposes, the effect of income taxes is ignored. Thus, the relevant calculation is to divide the $10 annual dividend by the quantity of funds received at the time the stock is issued. In this case, the funds received equal $96 ($101 selling price – $5 underwriting fee). Thus, the cost of capital is 10.4% ($10 ÷ $96).

Answer (A) is incorrect because 6.2% assumes that the dividends are deductible. Answer (B) is incorrect because 10% bases the calculation on par value instead of funds received. Answer (D) is incorrect because 5.2% assumes that the underwriter's fee is the dividend.

35. Osgood Products has announced that it plans to finance future investments so that the firm will achieve an optimal capital structure. Which one of the following corporate objectives is consistent with this announcement?

A. Maximize earnings per share.

B. Minimize the cost of debt.

C. Maximize the net worth of the firm.

D. Minimize the cost of equity.

The correct answer is (C). *(CMA 690 1-10)*

REQUIRED: The corporate objective consistent with optimizing capital structure.

DISCUSSION: Financial structure is the composition of the financing sources of the assets of a firm. Traditionally, the financial structure consists of current liabilities, long-term debt, retained earnings, and stock. There are many variations of debt and equity, e.g., preferred stock, convertible debt, etc. Thus, financial structure includes all of the accounts on the credit side of the balance sheet. The capital structure consists of the firm's long-term financing: shareholder's equity, preferred stock, and long-term debt. The objective of a corporation is a capital structure that minimizes the cost of capital and thus maximizes the value of the firm. For most firms, the optimum structure includes a combination of debt and equity. Debt is cheaper than equity, but excessive use of debt increases the firm's risk and drives up the weighted-average cost of capital.

Answer (A) is incorrect because the maximization of EPS may not always suggest the best capital structure. High earnings in the short run may be the result of assuming high levels of risk, which, in turn, can result in low stock prices. Answer (B) is incorrect because the minimization of debt cost may not be optimal; as long as the firm can earn more on debt capital than it pays in interest, debt financing may be pursued. Answer (D) is incorrect because minimizing the cost of equity may signify overly conservative management.

36. A firm's target or optimal capital structure is consistent with which one of the following?

A. Maximum earnings per share.

B. Minimum cost of debt.

C. Minimum cost of equity.

D. Minimum weighted-average cost of capital.

The correct answer is (D). *(CMA 1295 1-16)*

REQUIRED: The true statement about a firm's target or optimal capital structure.

DISCUSSION: Ideally, a firm will have a capital structure that minimizes its weighted-average cost of capital. This cost of capital maximizes the firm's value because it maximizes stock value by balancing the costs of debt and equity capital and their associated risk levels.

Answer (A) is incorrect because EPS is maximized at a higher debt ratio and risk level than allowed for in the optimal capital structure. Maximizing EPS does not maximize the firm's stock price. Answers (B) and (C) are incorrect because the cost of equity capital and the cost of debt capital must also be considered in estimating optimal structure.

37. In referring to the graph of a firm's cost of capital, if **e** is the current position, which one of the following statements best explains the saucer or U-shaped curve?

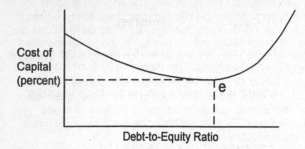

Debt-to-Equity Ratio

A. The composition of debt and equity does not affect the firm's cost of capital.

B. The cost of capital is almost always favorably influenced by increases in financial leverage.

C. The financial markets will penalize firms that borrow even in moderate amounts.

D. Use of at least some debt financing will enhance the value of the firm.

The correct answer is (D). *(CMA 1288 1-5)*
REQUIRED: The best explanation of the U-shaped curve in a cost-of-capital graph.
DISCUSSION: The U-shaped curve indicates that the cost of capital is quite high when the debt-to-equity ratio is quite low. As debt increases, the cost of capital declines as long as the cost of debt is less than that of equity. Eventually, the decline in the cost of capital levels off because the cost of debt ultimately rises as more debt is used. Additional increases in debt (relative to equity) will then increase the cost of capital. The implication is that some debt is present in the optimal capital structure because the cost of capital initially declines when debt is added. However, a point is reached at which debt becomes excessive and the cost of capital begins to rise.
Answer (A) is incorrect because the composition of the capital structure affects the cost of capital since the components have different costs. Answer (B) is incorrect because the cost of debt does not remain constant as financial leverage increases. Eventually, that cost also increases. Answer (C) is incorrect because the initial decline in the U-shaped graph indicates that the financial markets reward moderate levels of debt.

38. An investor uses the capital asset pricing model (CAPM) to evaluate the risk-return relationship on a portfolio of stocks held as an investment. Which of the following would not be used to estimate the portfolio's expected rate of return?

A. Expected risk premium on the portfolio of stocks.

B. Interest rate for the safest possible investment.

C. Expected rate of return on the market portfolio.

D. Standard deviation of the market returns.

The correct answer is (A). *(CIA 1193 IV-47)*
REQUIRED: The item not used to estimate the portfolio's expected rate of return.
DISCUSSION: The expected rate of return of a portfolio is the weighted average of the expected returns of the individual assets in the portfolio.
Answer (B) is incorrect because the interest rate for the safest possible investment is directly used in the capital asset pricing model. Answer (C) is incorrect because the expected rate of return on the market portfolio is the one systematic risk factor in the model. Answer (D) is incorrect because the standard deviation of the market returns is used to compute the beta coefficients for each security held in the investment portfolio and the beta coefficient for the market portfolio.

Questions 39 through 42 are based on the following information. Rogers Inc. operates a chain of restaurants located in the Southeast. The first restaurant was opened in 1981, and the company has steadily grown to its present size of 48 restaurants. The board of directors recently approved a large-scale remodeling of the restaurant, and the company is now considering two financing alternatives.

* The first alternative would consist of
  - Bonds that would have a 9% coupon rate and would net $19.2 million after flotation costs
  - Preferred stock with a stated rate of 6% that would yield $4.8 million after a 4% flotation cost
  - Common stock that would yield $24 million after a 5% flotation cost

* The second alternative would consist of a public offering of bonds that would have an 11% coupon rate and would net $48 million after flotation costs.

Rogers' present capital structure, which is considered optimal, consists of 40% long-term debt, 10% preferred stock, and 50% common stock. The current market value of the common stock is $30 per share, and the common stock dividend during the past 12 months was $3 per share. Investors are expecting the growth rate of dividends to equal the historical rate of 6%. Rogers is subject to an effective income tax rate of 40%.

39. The after-tax cost of the common stock proposed in Rogers' first financing alternative would be

A. 16.00%

B. 16.53%

C. 16.60%

D. 17.16%

The correct answer is (D). *(CFM Sample Q. 7)*
    REQUIRED: The after-tax cost of proposed common stock issuance.
    DISCUSSION:

$$R = \frac{D_1}{P_o(1-Flotation)} + G = \frac{\$3.18}{\$30.00(.95)} + .06 = 17.16\%$$

    Answer (A) is incorrect because 16% ignores the increase in dividends and flotation costs. Answer (B) is incorrect because 16.53% ignores the next dividend increasing to $3.18. Answer (C) is incorrect because 16.6% ignores the flotation costs.

40. Assuming the after-tax cost of common stock is 15%, the after-tax weighted marginal cost of capital for Rogers' first financing alternative consisting of bonds, preferred stock, and common stock would be

A. 7.285%

B. 8.725%

C. 10.285%

D. 11.700%

The correct answer is (C). *(CFM Sample Q. 8)*
    REQUIRED: The weighted marginal cost of the first financing alternative.
    DISCUSSION:

	Weight				
Bonds	40% x 9% x (1–.4)			=	2.16%
Preferred stock	10% x $.3/4.8			=	.625
Common stock	50% x	15%		=	7.50
					10.285%

Flotation costs are ignored for the bonds because $20 million must be repaid at maturity date, which is not the case for preferred stock.
    Answers (A), (B), and (D) are incorrect because they do not appear to be the result of a common error.

41. The after-tax weighted marginal cost of capital for Rogers' second financing alternative consisting solely of bonds would be

A. 5.13%

B. 5.40%

C. 6.27%

D. 6.60%

The correct answer is (D). *(CFM Sample Q. 9)*
    REQUIRED: The weighted marginal cost of the second financing alternative.
    DISCUSSION: Multiply (1 – effective tax rate) times the effective interest rate of 11%, which is 6.60% [11% x (1 – .4)].
    Answer (A) is incorrect because 5.13% is 5.40% reduced by the 5% stock flotation costs. Answer (B) is incorrect because 5.40% is 60% of 9%. Answer (C) is incorrect because 6.25% is 6.60% reduced by the 5% stock flotation costs.

42. The interest rate on the bonds is greater for the second alternative consisting of pure debt than it is for the first alternative consisting of both debt and equity because

A. The diversity of the combination alternative creates greater risk for the investor.

B. The pure debt alternative would flood the market and be more difficult to sell.

C. The pure debt alternative carries the risk of increasing the probability of default.

D. The combination alternative carries the risk of increasing dividend payments.

The correct answer is (C). *(CFM Sample Q. 10)*
    REQUIRED: The reason increases in debt financing relative to equity financing increase the interest rate.
    DISCUSSION: As a larger proportion of an entity's capital is provided by debt, the debt becomes riskier and more expensive, i.e., requires a higher interest rate.
    Answer (A) is incorrect because the diversity decreases, not increases, risk. Answer (B) is incorrect because $50 million is minuscule in the debt markets. Answer (D) is incorrect because the combination alternative maintains the same debt/equity mixture, which would not warrant a rate increase in the cost of debt or equity.

Questions 43 and 44 are based on the following information.

Martin Corporation
Statement of Financial Position
December 31, 1994
(Dollars in millions)

Assets
Current assets	$ 75
Plant and equipment	250
Total assets	$325

Liabilities and shareholders' equity
Current liabilities	$ 46
Long-term debt (12%)	64
Common equity:	
Common stock, $1 par	10
Additional paid-in capital	100
Retained earnings	105
Total liabilities and shareholders' equity	$325

Additional Data

- The long-term debt was originally issued at par ($1,000 per bond) and is currently trading at $1,250 per bond.

- Martin Corporation can now issue debt at 150 basis points over U.S. Treasury bonds.

- The current risk-free rate (U.S. Treasury bonds) is 7%.

- Martin's common stock is currently selling at $32 per share.

- The expected market return is currently 15%.

- The beta value for Martin is 1.25.

- Martin's effective corporate income tax rate is 40%.

43. Martin Corporation's current net cost of debt is

A. 5.5%

B. 7.0%

C. 5.1%

D. 8.5%

The correct answer is (C). *(CMA 695 1-7)*
REQUIRED: The current net cost of debt financing.
DISCUSSION: The current rate for Treasury bonds is 7%. If the company can issue debt at 150 basis points (1.5%) over U.S. Treasury bonds, the market rate of interest for Martin is 8.5%. Given a 40% tax rate, the net cost of debt is 60% of the rate actually paid, or 5.1% (60% × 8.5%).
Answer (A) is incorrect because 5.5% is the Treasury rate minus 150 bonus points. Answer (B) is incorrect because 7.0% is the Treasury rate. Answer (D) is incorrect because 8.5% ignores the income tax effect.

44. Using the Capital Asset Pricing Model (CAPM), Martin Corporation's current cost of common equity is

A. 8.75%

B. 10.00%

C. 15.00%

D. 17.00%

The correct answer is (D). *(CMA 695 1-8)*
REQUIRED: The current cost of common equity capital using the CAPM.
DISCUSSION: The CAPM adds the risk-free rate (determined by government securities) to the product of the beta coefficient (a measure of the firm's risk) and the difference between the market return and the risk-free rate. Thus, the current cost of equity using the CAPM is 17% [7% + 1.25 (15% − 7%)].
Answer (A) is incorrect because 8.75% equals the product of beta and the risk-free rate. Answer (B) is incorrect because 10.00% fails to add the risk-free rate to the risk premium. Answer (C) is incorrect because 15.00% is the expected market return.

Questions 45 through 47 are based on the following information. DQZ Telecom is considering a project for the coming year that will cost $50,000,000. DQZ plans to use the following combination of debt and equity to finance the investment:

- Issue $15,000,000 of 20-year bonds at a price of 101, with a coupon rate of 8%, and flotation costs of 2% of par.

- Use $35,000,000 of funds generated from earnings.

- The equity market is expected to earn 12%. U.S. Treasury bonds are currently yielding 5%. The beta coefficient for DQZ is estimated to be .60. DQZ is subject to an effective corporate income tax rate of 40%.

---

45. The before-tax cost of DQZ's planned debt financing, net of flotation costs, in the first year is

A. 8.08%

B. 10.00%

C. 7.92%

D. 8.00%

The correct answer is (A). *(CMA 1294 1-25)*
REQUIRED: The before-tax cost of the planned debt financing, net of flotation costs.
DISCUSSION: Proceeds are $14,850,000 [(1.01 x $15,000,000) - (.02 x $15,000,000)]. The annual interest is $1,200,000 (.08 coupon rate x $15,000,000). Thus, the company is paying $1,200,000 annually for the use of $14,850,000, a rate of 8.08% ($1,200,000 ÷ $14,850,000).
Answer (B) is incorrect because 10.00% is the sum of the coupon rate and the flotation rate. Answer (C) is incorrect because 7.92% ignores the 2% flotation costs. Answer (D) is incorrect because 8.00% is the coupon rate.

46. Assume that the after-tax cost of debt is 7% and the cost of equity is 12%. Determine the weighted-average cost of capital.

A. 10.50%

B. 8.50%

C. 9.50%

D. 6.30%

The correct answer is (A). *(CMA 1294 1-26)*
REQUIRED: The weighted-average cost of capital given the costs of debt and equity.
DISCUSSION: The 7% debt cost and the 12% equity cost should be weighted by the proportions of the total investment represented by each source of capital. The total project costs $50 million, of which debt is $15 million, or 30% of the total. Equity capital is the other 70%. Consequently, the weighted-average cost of capital is 10.5% [(7%)(30%) + (12%)(70%)].
Answer (B) is incorrect because 8.50% reverses the weights. Answer (C) is incorrect because 9.50% assumes debt and equity are equally weighted. Answer (D) is incorrect because the weighted-average cost cannot be less than any of its components.

47. The Capital Asset Pricing Model (CAPM) computes the expected return on a security by adding the risk-free rate of return to the incremental yield of the expected market return, which is adjusted by the company's beta. Compute DQZ's expected rate of return.

A. 9.20%

B. 12.20%

C. 7.20%

D. 12.00%

The correct answer is (A). *(CMA 1294 1-27)*
REQUIRED: The expected rate of return using the Capital Asset Pricing Model (CAPM).
DISCUSSION: The market return (R_M), given as 12%, minus the risk-free rate (R_F), given as 5%, is the market risk premium. It is the rate at which investors must be compensated to induce them to invest in the market. The beta coefficient (β) of an individual stock, given as 60%, is the correlation between volatility (price variation) of the stock market and the volatility of the price of the individual stock. Consequently, the expected rate of return is 9.20% [$R_F + \beta(R_M - R_F) = .05 + .6(.12 - .05)$].
Answer (B) is incorrect because 12.20% equals the risk-free rate plus 60% of the market rate. Answer (C) is incorrect because 7.20% results from multiplying both the market rate premium and the risk-free rate by 60%. Answer (D) is incorrect because 12.00% is the market rate.

48. The difference between the required rate of return on a given risky investment and that on a riskless investment with the same expected return is the

A. Risk premium.

B. Coefficient of variation.

C. Standard deviation.

D. Beta coefficient.

The correct answer is (A). *(CIA 1192 IV-48)*

REQUIRED: The difference between the required rate of return on a given risky investment and that on a riskless investment with the same expected return.

DISCUSSION: The required rate of return on equity capital in the capital asset pricing model is the risk-free rate (determined by government securities) plus the product of the market risk premium times the beta coefficient (beta measures the firm's risk). The market risk premium is the amount above the risk-free rate that will induce investment in the market. The beta coefficient of an individual stock is the correlation between the volatility (price variation) of the stock market and that of the price of the individual stock.

Answer (B) is incorrect because the coefficient of variation is the standard deviation of an investment's returns divided by the mean return. Answer (C) is incorrect because the standard deviation is a measure of the variability of an investment's returns. Answer (D) is incorrect because the beta coefficient measures the sensitivity of the investment's returns to market volatility.

49. According to the capital asset pricing model (CAPM), the relevant risk of a security is its

A. Company-specific risk.

B. Diversifiable risk.

C. Systematic risk.

D. Total risk.

The correct answer is (C). *(CIA 1194 IV-53)*

REQUIRED: The relevant risk of a security according to the capital asset pricing model.

DISCUSSION: The relevant risk of a security is its contribution to the portfolio's risk. It is the risk that cannot be eliminated through diversification and is synonymous with market risk and systematic risk. The relevant risk results from factors, such as inflation, recession, and high interest rates, that affect all stocks.

Answer (A) is incorrect because company-specific risk can be eliminated through portfolio diversification. Answer (B) is incorrect because diversifiable risk can be eliminated through portfolio diversification. Answer (D) is incorrect because only the systematic component of total risk is relevant to security valuation.

50. Which of the following is directly applied in determining the value of a stock when using the dividend growth model?

A. The firm's capital structure.

B. The firm's cash flows.

C. The firm's liquidity.

D. The investor's required rate of return on the firm's stock.

The correct answer is (D). *(CIA 1190 IV-53)*

REQUIRED: The factor directly applied in determining the value of a stock using the dividend growth model.

DISCUSSION: The dividend growth model is used to calculate the cost of equity. The simplified formula is

$$R = \frac{D_1}{P_0} + G$$

R is the required rate of return, D_1 is the next dividend, P_0 is the stock's price, and G is the growth rate in earnings per share. The equation is also used to determine the stock price.

$$P_0 = \frac{D_1}{R - G}$$

Answers (A), (B), and (C) are incorrect because the model uses the growth rate in dividends and the investor's required rate of return.

51. Assume that nominal interest rates just increased substantially but that the expected future dividends for a company over the long run were not affected. As a result of the increase in nominal interest rates, the company's stock price should

A. Increase.

B. Decrease.

C. Stay constant.

D. Change, but in no obvious direction.

The correct answer is (B). *(CIA 593 IV-49)*

REQUIRED: The effect on a company's stock price of an increase in nominal interest rates.

DISCUSSION: The dividend growth model is used to calculate the price of stock.

$$P_0 = \frac{D_1}{R - G}$$

If: P_0 = current price

D_1 = next dividend

R = required rate of return

G = EPS growth rate

Assuming that D_1 and G remain constant, an increase in R resulting from an increase in the nominal interest rate will cause P_0 to decrease.

Answers (A), (C), and (D) are incorrect because a higher interest rate raises the required return of investors, which results in a lower stock price.

52. By using the dividend growth model, estimate the cost of equity capital for a firm with a stock price of $30.00, an estimated dividend at the end of the first year of $3.00 per share, and an expected growth rate of 10%.

A. 21.1%

B. 11.0%

C. 10.0%

D. 20.0%

The correct answer is (D). *(CMA 1294 1-28)*

REQUIRED: The cost of equity capital calculated using the dividend growth model.

DISCUSSION: The dividend growth model determines the cost of equity by adding the expected growth rate to the quotient of the next dividend and the current market price. Thus, the cost of equity capital is 20% [10% + ($3 ÷ $30)]. This model assumes that the payout ratio, the retention rate, and the earnings per share growth rate are all constant.

Answer (A) is incorrect because the growth rate (10%) is added to the dividend yield (10%). Answer (B) is incorrect because 11.0% equals the growth rate (10%) plus 10% of the current dividend yield (10%). Answer (C) is incorrect because 10.0% is the growth rate.

53. A firm seeking to optimize its capital budget has calculated its marginal cost of capital and projected rates of return on several potential projects. The optimal capital budget is determined by

A. Calculating the point at which marginal cost of capital meets the projected rate of return, assuming that the most profitable projects are accepted first.

B. Calculating the point at which average marginal cost meets average projected rate of return, assuming the largest projects are accepted first.

C. Accepting all potential projects with projected rates of return exceeding the lowest marginal cost of capital.

D. Accepting all potential projects with projected rates of return lower than the highest marginal cost of capital.

The correct answer is (A). *(CIA 1191 IV-57)*

REQUIRED: The determinant of the optimal capital budget.

DISCUSSION: In economics, a basic principle is that a firm should increase output until marginal cost equals marginal revenue. Similarly, the optimal capital budget is determined by calculating the point at which marginal cost of capital (which increases as capital requirements increase) and the marginal efficiency of investment (which decreases if the most profitable projects are accepted first) intersect.

Answer (B) is incorrect because the intersection of average marginal cost with average projected rates of return when the largest (not most profitable) projects are accepted first offers no meaningful capital budgeting conclusion. Answer (C) is incorrect because optimal capital budgeting assumes that the most profitable projects will be accepted first and that the marginal cost of capital increases as capital requirements increase. Thus, it is possible for the optimal capital budget to exclude profitable projects as lower cost capital goes first to projects with higher rates of return. Answer (D) is incorrect because accepting projects with rates of return lower than the cost of capital is not economically rational business.

C. Dividend Policy

54. In practice, dividends

A. Usually exhibit greater stability than earnings.

B. Fluctuate more widely than earnings.

C. Tend to be a lower percentage of earnings for mature firms.

D. Are usually set as a fixed percentage of earnings.

The correct answer is (A). *(CMA 695 1-9)*

REQUIRED: The true statement about dividends and their relation to earnings.

DISCUSSION: Dividend policy determines the portion of net income distributed to stockholders. Corporations normally try to maintain a stable level of dividends, even though profits may fluctuate considerably, because many stockholders buy stock with the expectation of receiving a certain dividend every year. Thus, management tends not to raise dividends if the payout cannot be sustained. The desire for stability has led theorists to propound the information content or signaling hypothesis: a change in dividend policy is a signal to the market regarding management's forecast of future earnings. This stability often results in a stock that sells at a higher market price because stockholders perceive less risk in receiving their dividends.

Answer (B) is incorrect because most companies try to maintain stable dividends. Answer (C) is incorrect because mature firms have less need of earnings to reinvest for expansion; thus, they tend to pay a higher percentage of earnings as dividends. Answer (D) is incorrect because dividend payout ratios normally fluctuate with earnings to maintain stable dividends.

55. Treating dividends as an active policy strategy assumes that

A. Dividends provide information to the market.

B. Dividends are irrelevant.

C. Dividend payments should be made to common shareholders first.

D. Dividends are costly, and the firm should retain earnings and issue stock dividends.

The correct answer is (A). *(CMA 1291 1-11)*

REQUIRED: The assumption made when dividends are treated as an active policy strategy.

DISCUSSION: Stock prices often move in the same direction as dividends. Moreover, companies dislike cutting dividends. They tend not to raise dividends unless anticipated future earnings will be sufficient to sustain the higher payout. Thus, some theorists have proposed the information content or signaling hypothesis. According to this view, a change in dividend policy is a signal to the market regarding management's forecast of future earnings. Consequently, the relation of stock price changes to changes in dividends reflects not an investor preference for dividends over capital gains but rather the effect of the information conveyed.

Answer (B) is incorrect because an active dividend policy suggests management assumes that dividends are relevant to investors. Answer (C) is incorrect because preferred shareholders always receive their dividends ahead of common shareholders. Answer (D) is incorrect because an active dividend policy recognizes that investors want dividends.

56. If the capital gains were taxed at a lower rate than regular dividend income, then the <List A> the dividend payout percentage of a company, the <List B>, everything else equal.

	List A	List B
A.	Higher	Higher would be its stock price
B.	Higher	Lower would be its book value of equity
C.	Lower	Lower would be its cost of equity
D.	Lower	Lower would be its stock price

The correct answer is (C). *(CIA 1195 IV-51)*

REQUIRED: The effect of a lower capital gains tax rate.

DISCUSSION: Lower dividend payout ratios will be favored by investors if dividends are taxed at a higher rate than capital gains. The cost of equity for the company will be lower under the lower dividend payout policy because more retained earnings will be available for reinvestment.

Answer (A) is incorrect because a higher dividend payout ratio is associated with a lower stock price when the tax environment favors capital gains over dividends. The reason is that the after-tax return to investors is lower for dividend payments than for capital gains (share price appreciation). Answer (B) is incorrect because there is no relationship between the book value of equity and the relative taxation of dividends and capital gains. Answer (D) is incorrect because a lower dividend payout ratio is associated with a higher, not a lower, stock price when the tax environment favors dividends over capital gains.

57. A company following a residual dividend payout policy will pay higher dividends when, everything else equal, it has

A. Less attractive investment opportunities.

B. Lower earnings available for reinvestment.

C. A lower targeted debt-to-equity ratio.

D. A lower opportunity cost of retained earnings.

The correct answer is (A). *(CIA 1195 IV-49)*

REQUIRED: The circumstances in which a residual dividend payout policy results in higher dividends.

DISCUSSION: Under the residual theory of dividends, the firm prefers to pay dividends when investment opportunities are poor and internal financing would move the firm away from its ideal capital structure. Thus, a company with less attractive investment opportunities will have a lower optimal capital budget. Under a residual dividend policy, a lower optimal capital budget will result in a higher dividend payout ratio, other factors being constant.

Answer (B) is incorrect because, when lower earnings are available for reinvestment, any level of capital expenditures will require, other factors being constant, a greater proportion of available internal funds. The dividend payout ratio will then be lower, not higher, under a residual payout policy. Answer (C) is incorrect because the lower the debt-to-equity ratio, the higher the proportion of new investments financed with equity. Under a residual dividend payout policy, the result will be a lower, not a higher, dividend payout as more internally available funds are retained for reinvestment. Answer (D) is incorrect because the lower the opportunity cost of funds, the lower the discount rate used to evaluate capital projects and the more attractive the investment opportunities. Under a residual payout policy, more internally generated funds will be required to finance the optimal capital budget, and the dividend payout will be lower, not higher.

58. Residco Inc. expects net income of $800,000 for the next fiscal year. Its targeted and current capital structure is 40% debt and 60% common equity. The director of capital budgeting has determined that the optimal capital spending for next year is $1.2 million. If Residco follows a strict residual dividend policy, what is the expected dividend payout ratio for next year?

A. 90.0%

B. 66.7%

C. 40.0%

D. 10.0%

The correct answer is (D). *(CMA 695 1-14)*
REQUIRED: The expected dividend payout ratio assuming a strict residual dividend policy.
DISCUSSION: Under the residual theory of dividends, the residual of earnings paid as dividends depends on the available investments and the debt-equity ratio at which cost of capital is minimized. The rational investor should prefer reinvestment of retained earnings when the return exceeds what the investor could earn on investments of equal risk. However, the firm may prefer to pay dividends when investment returns are poor and the internal equity financing would move the firm away from its ideal capital structure. If Residco wants to maintain its current structure, 60% of investments should be financed from equity. Hence, it needs $720,000 (60% × $1,200,000) of equity funds, leaving $80,000 of net income ($800,000 NI – $720,000) available for dividends. The dividend payout ratio is therefore 10% ($80,000 ÷ $800,000 NI).
Answer (A) is incorrect because 90% is the reinvestment ratio. Answer (B) is incorrect because 66.7% is the ratio between earnings and investment. Answer (C) is incorrect because 40% is the ratio of debt in the ideal capital structure.

59. The date when the right to a dividend expires is called the

A. Declaration date.

B. Ex-dividend date.

C. Holder-of-record date.

D. Payment date.

The correct answer is (B). *(CIA 590 IV-48)*
REQUIRED: The date when the right to a dividend expires.
DISCUSSION: The ex-dividend date is 4 days before the date of record. Unlike the other relevant dates, it is not established by the corporate board of directors but by the stock exchanges. The period between the ex-dividend date and the date of record gives the stock exchange members time to process any transactions in time for the new shareholders to receive the dividend to which they are entitled. An investor who buys a share of stock before the ex-dividend date will receive the dividend that has been previously declared. An investor who buys after the ex-dividend date (but before the date of record or payment date) will not receive the declared dividend.
Answer (A) is incorrect because, on the declaration date, the directors formally vote to declare a dividend. Answer (C) is incorrect because, on the date of record, the corporation determines which shareholders will receive the declared dividend. Answer (D) is incorrect because, on the date of payment, the dividend is actually paid.

60. The policy decision that by itself is least likely to affect the value of the firm is the

A. Investment in a project with a large net present value.

B. Sale of a risky division that will now increase the credit rating of the entire company.

C. Distribution of stock dividends to shareholders.

D. Use of a more highly leveraged capital structure that resulted in a lower cost of capital.

The correct answer is (C). *(CIA 593 IV-46)*
REQUIRED: The policy decision that is least likely to affect the value of the firm.
DISCUSSION: A stock dividend does not significantly affect the value of the firm. It simply divides ownership interests into smaller pieces without changing any shareholder's proportionate share of ownership.
Answer (A) is incorrect because a positive NPV project should increase the value of the firm. Answer (B) is incorrect because the higher credit rating should reduce the cost of capital and therefore increase the value of the firm. Answer (D) is incorrect because the lower cost of capital should reduce the required rate of return and increase the value of the firm.

61. Which of the following types of dividends do not reduce the shareholders' equity in the corporation?

    A. Cash dividends.

    B. Property dividends.

    C. Liquidating dividends.

    D. Stock dividends.

The correct answer is (D). *(CIA 595 IV-30)*

    REQUIRED: The dividends that do not reduce shareholders' equity.

    DISCUSSION: The issuance of a small stock dividend results in a debit to retained earnings and a credit to capital stock for the fair value of the stock. A large stock dividend requires capitalization of retained earnings equal to the amount established by the issuer's state of incorporation (usually par value). Consequently, a stock dividend has no net effect on shareholders' equity.

    Answers (A), (B), and (C) are incorrect because cash, property, and liquidating dividends reduce shareholders' equity. They involve an immediate or promised future nonreciprocal distribution of assets.

Questions 62 and 63 are based on the following information. A company has 1,000 shares of $10 par value common stock and $5,000 of retained earnings. Two proposals are under consideration. The first is a stock split giving each stockholder two new shares for each share formerly held. The second is to declare and distribute a 50% stock dividend.

---

62. The stock split proposal will <List A> earnings per share by <List B> than will the stock dividend proposal.

	List A	List B
A.	Increase	More
B.	Increase	Less
C.	Decrease	More
D.	Decrease	Less

The correct answer is (C). *(CIA 1194 IV-50)*

    REQUIRED: The effect of a stock split and a stock dividend on earnings per share.

    DISCUSSION: The stock split will double the number of shares outstanding to 2,000. The 50% stock dividend will increase the number of outstanding shares to 1,500. The higher number of shares in the stock split will result in a lower earnings per share than will result from the stock dividend.

    Answers (A), (B), and (D) are incorrect because the stock split results in a greater number of shares outstanding and a lower EPS than results from the stock dividend.

---

63. Under the stock <List A>, the par value per outstanding share will <List B>.

	List A	List B
A.	Dividend	Increase
B.	Split	Increase
C.	Dividend	Decrease
D.	Split	Decrease

The correct answer is (D). *(CIA 1194 IV-51)*

    REQUIRED: The effect of a stock split and a stock dividend on par value.

    DISCUSSION: A stock split results in a lower par value per share because the total number of shares increases but the total par value of outstanding stock does not change.

    Answers (A) and (C) are incorrect because par value per share does not change following a stock dividend. Answer (B) is incorrect because par value per share decreases following a stock split.

64. When a company desires to increase the market value per share of common stock, the company will

    A. Sell treasury stock.

    B. Implement a reverse stock split.

    C. Sell preferred stock.

    D. Split the stock.

The correct answer is (B). *(CMA 693 1-7)*

    REQUIRED: The transaction that increases the market value per share of common stock.

    DISCUSSION: A reverse stock split decreases the number of shares outstanding, thereby increasing the market price per share. A reverse stock split may be desirable when a stock is selling at such a low price that management is concerned that investors will avoid the stock because it has an undesirable image.

    Answer (A) is incorrect because a sale of treasury stock increases the supply of shares and could lead to a decline in market price. Answer (C) is incorrect because a sale of preferred stock will take dollars out of investors' hands, thereby reducing funds available to invest in common stock. Therefore, market price per share of common stock will not increase. Answer (D) is incorrect because a stock split increases the shares issued and outstanding. The market price per share is likely to decline as a result.

65. A stock dividend

    A. Increases the debt-to-equity ratio of a firm.

    B. Decreases future earnings per share.

    C. Decreases the size of the firm.

    D. Increases shareholders' wealth.

The correct answer is (B). *(CMA 689 1-7)*

    REQUIRED: The true statement about a stock dividend.

    DISCUSSION: A stock dividend is a transfer of equity from retained earnings to paid-in capital. The debit is to retained earnings and the credits are to common stock and additional paid-in capital. More shares are outstanding following the stock dividend, but every shareholder maintains the same percentage of ownership. In effect, a stock dividend divides the pie (the corporation) into more pieces, but the pie is still the same size. Hence, a corporation will have a lower EPS and a lower book value per share following a stock dividend, but every shareholder will be just as well off as previously.

    Answers (A), (C), and (D) are incorrect because a stock dividend has no effect except on the composition of the shareholders' equity section of the balance sheet.

66. The purchase of treasury stock with a firm's surplus cash

    A. Increases a firm's assets.

    B. Increases a firm's financial leverage.

    C. Increases a firm's interest coverage ratio.

    D. Dilutes a firm's earnings per share.

The correct answer is (B). *(CMA 1291 1-5)*

    REQUIRED: The true statement about a purchase of treasury stock.

    DISCUSSION: A purchase of treasury stock involves a decrease in assets (usually cash) and a corresponding decrease in shareholders' equity. Thus, equity is reduced and the debt-to-equity ratio and financial leverage increase.

    Answer (A) is incorrect because assets decrease when treasury stock is purchased. Answer (C) is incorrect because a firm's interest coverage ratio is unaffected. Earnings, interest expense, and taxes will all be the same regardless of the transaction. Answer (D) is incorrect because the purchase of treasury stock is antidilutive; the same earnings will be spread over fewer shares. Some firms purchase treasury stock for this reason.

STUDY UNIT 4: FINANCIAL MARKETS AND INTEREST RATES

10 pages of outline
58 multiple-choice questions

A. *Financial Markets*
B. *Interest Rates*

This study unit is the second of five relating to "Advanced Topics in Corporate Financial Management." The first subunit is "Financial Markets," which includes discussion on the exchanges, the over-the-counter markets, the foreign markets, and the efficient markets hypothesis. The second subunit is "Interest Rates," which includes discussion on the components of interest rates, the effects of governmental action, international issues, and the term structure of interest rates.

A. Financial Markets

1. Financial markets facilitate the creation and transfer of financial assets and obligations. They bring together entities that have funds to invest with entities that have financing needs. The resulting transactions create assets for the former and obligations for the latter.

   a. Transfers of funds may be direct or may be through intermediate entities such as banks. The use of intermediate entities and financial markets improves allocative efficiency because of their special expertise. The result is the availability of relatively rapid and low-cost transfers of capital, an essential feature of a modern economy.

2. Financial markets are not particular places but rather the totality of supply and demand for securities. Securities include a very wide variety of instruments. Some of the most basic are stocks, corporate bonds, mortgages, consumer loans, leases, commercial paper, certificates of deposit, and governmental securities of many kinds. Moreover, new kinds of securities are continually being developed.

3. Financial markets may be classified as either money markets or capital markets.

   a. **Money markets** trade debt securities with maturities of less than 1 year. These are dealer-driven markets because most transactions involve dealers who buy and sell instruments at their own risk. The dealer is a principal in most transactions, unlike a stockbroker who acts as an agent. Money markets exist in New York, London, and Tokyo. Money market securities are generally short-term and marketable. They usually have low default risk. Money market securities include

      1) Government Treasury bills
      2) Government Treasury notes and bonds
      3) Federal agency securities
      4) Short-term tax-exempt securities
      5) Commercial paper
      6) Certificates of deposit
      7) Repurchase agreements
      8) Eurodollar CDs
      9) Bankers' acceptances

   b. **Capital markets** trade long-term debt and equity securities. The New York Stock Exchange is an example of a capital market.

4.   Financial markets may also be categorized as either primary or secondary.

   a.   **Primary markets** are the markets in which corporations and governmental units raise new capital by making initial offerings of their securities. The issuer receives the proceeds of sale in a primary market.

   b.   **Secondary markets** provide for trading of previously issued securities among investors. Examples of secondary markets include auction markets and dealer markets.

      1)   Auction markets like the New York Stock Exchange, the American Stock Exchange, and regional exchanges conduct trading at particular physical sites. Furthermore, share prices are communicated immediately to the public.

         a)   Companies that wish to have their shares traded on an exchange must apply for listing and meet certain requirements. For example, the New York Stock Exchange has established requirements relating to the amount and value of shares outstanding, the number of shareholders, earning power, and tangible assets.

            i)   Listing is beneficial because it adds to a firm's prestige and increases the liquidity of a firm's securities. However, increased SEC disclosure requirements and the greater risk of an unfriendly takeover are possible disadvantages.

         b)   Matching of buy and sell orders communicated to brokerages with seats on the exchange is the essence of exchange trading. To facilitate this process, members known as **specialists** undertake to make a market in particular stocks. These firms are obliged to buy and sell those stocks.

            i)   Accordingly, a specialist maintains an inventory of stocks and sets **bid** and **asked prices** (prices at which the specialist will buy or sell, respectively) to keep the inventory in balance.

            ii)   The profit margin for the specialist is the **spread**, or the excess of the asked over the bid price.

      2)   The **over-the-counter (OTC) market** is a dealer market. It consists of numerous brokers and dealers who are linked by telecommunications equipment that enables them to trade throughout the country. The OTC market conducts transactions in securities not traded on the stock exchanges.

         a)   The OTC market handles transactions involving

            i)   Bonds of U.S. companies

            ii)   Bonds of federal, state, and local governments

            iii)   Open-end investment company shares of mutual funds

            iv)   New securities issues

            v)   Most secondary stock distributions, whether or not they are listed on an exchange

         b)   The governing authority for the OTC market is the National Association of Securities Dealers (NASD). Its computerized trading system is the NASD Automated Quotation (NASDAQ) system, which supplies price quotes and volume amounts during the trading day.

      c) The majority of stocks are traded in the OTC market, but the dollar volume of trading on the exchanges is greater because they list the largest companies.

      d) Brokers and dealers of OTC securities may also maintain inventories of securities to match buy and sell orders efficiently.

5. **Financial intermediaries** are specialized firms that help create and exchange the instruments of financial markets. Financial intermediaries increase the efficiency of financial markets through better allocation of financial resources. The financial intermediary obtains funds from savers, issues its own securities, and uses the money to purchase a business's securities. Thus, financial intermediaries create new forms of capital. For example, a savings and loan association purchases a mortgage with its funds from savers and issues a savings account or a certificate of deposit.

    a. Financial intermediaries include

        1) Commercial banks
        2) Life insurance companies
        3) Private pension funds
        4) Savings and loan associations
        5) State and local pension funds
        6) Mutual funds
        7) Finance companies
        8) Casualty insurance companies
        9) Money market funds
        10) Mutual savings banks
        11) Credit unions
        12) Investment bankers

6. **Margin trading** involves the buying of securities on the credit extended from a seller. The purchaser pays the margin requirement of the security price and borrows the remaining amount from the seller. The seller holds the security as collateral. The Federal Reserve establishes the margin requirements for securities. The Federal Reserve raises the margin requirements to slow stock market activity and reduces the margin requirements to stimulate the market.

7. **Short selling** involves an investor who borrows shares of a stock from a broker and then sells them at the current market price. The short seller speculates that the price of the securities will decrease before (s)he must make a purchase of the securities and repay the broker. If the price in fact declines, the short seller profits. If it rises, the short seller loses.

    a. A short sale cannot be made for a price lower than that of the last previously recorded sale.

8. Securities markets perform the following economic functions:

    a. A marketplace in which efficient and inexpensive investment transactions take place

    b. Continuous handling of transactions

    c. Stable security prices because of frequent but smaller price changes

    d. Facilitation of the issuance and purchase of new securities

9. The **efficient markets hypothesis (EMH)** states that current stock prices immediately and fully reflect all relevant information. Hence, the market is continuously adjusting to new information and acting to correct pricing errors. In other words, securities prices are always in equilibrium. The reason is that securities are subject to intense analysis by many thousands of highly trained individuals. These analysts work for well-capitalized institutions with the resources to take very rapid action when new information is available.

    a. The EMH states that it is impossible to obtain abnormal returns consistently with either fundamental or technical analysis.

        1) **Fundamental analysis** is the evaluation of a security's future price movement based upon sales, internal developments, industry trends, the general economy, and expected changes in each factor.

        2) **Technical analysis** is the evaluation of a security's future price based on the sales price and number of shares traded in a series of recent transactions.

    b. Under the EMH, the expected return of each security is equal to the return required by the marginal investor given the risk of the security. Moreover, the price equals its fair value as perceived by investors.

    c. The EMH has three forms (versions).

        1) **Strong form.** All public and private information is instantaneously reflected in securities' prices. Thus, insider trading is assumed not to result in abnormal returns.

        2) **Semistrong form.** All publicly available data are reflected in security prices, but private or insider data are not immediately reflected. Accordingly, insider trading can result in abnormal returns.

        3) **Weak form.** Current securities prices reflect all recent past price movement data, so technical analysis will not provide a basis for abnormal returns in securities trading.

    d. Empirical data have refuted the strong form of the efficient markets hypothesis but not the weak and semistrong forms.

    e. The market efficiently incorporates public information into securities prices. However, when making investment decisions, investors should be aware of economic information about the firm's markets and the strength of the products of the firm.

    f. Because the possibility exists that all information is not reflected in security prices, there is an opportunity for arbitrage.

10. Foreign financial markets provide U.S. citizens the opportunity to acquire securities issued in foreign countries, including those issued by foreign governments as well as corporations. These portfolio investments are distinct from direct investment in physical assets located abroad.

    a. The **Eurodollar** market is created by large interest-bearing time deposits of U.S. dollars in banks located in foreign countries. The rates paid tend to be higher than those in the U.S. because U.S. banking regulations, e.g., FDIC insurance premiums and fractional reserves, do not apply. Other currencies (Eurocurrencies), such as the yen and mark, may also be used for the same purposes.

1) Eurodollars are an international medium of exchange. They are also borrowed for a variety of reasons, e.g., to pay for U.S. exports or to invest in U.S. securities.

b. International bonds are sold outside the borrower's home country. **Foreign bonds** are denominated in the currency of the country where they are sold. For example, if a Japanese company sells dollar-denominated bonds in the U.S., they are called foreign bonds even though they are treated in all respects as if they had been issued by a domestic entity.

1) **Eurobonds** are denominated in a currency different from that of the country where they are sold. For example, dollar-denominated bonds issued in France by a U.S. company are Eurobonds. Transaction costs for Eurobonds are lower because they are subject to less stringent disclosure and other requirements. Furthermore, they are issued in bearer form, an advantage for investors who desire secrecy. They are also not subject to income tax withholding in some countries.

c. **Foreign exchange markets** facilitate the purchase and sale of convertible currencies, that is, currencies that the issuing countries permit to be traded and will redeem at market rates. These markets are networks of brokers and banks in major international financial centers. Most transactions are conducted via telecommunications media. However, not all currencies are convertible, creating problems for international trade.

1) The current international monetary system is characterized by **floating exchange rates** subject to some management by central banks. To the extent they are allowed to float, rates in the foreign exchange markets are not fixed by governments but are determined by supply and demand. When rates are allowed to float, entities with transactions denominated in foreign currencies are subject to the risk of unfavorable exchange rate movements (exchange rate risk). Hedging is a means of managing this risk. See Study Unit 8 for a discussion of hedging.

a) In a managed float, central banks buy and sell currencies at their discretion to avoid erratic short-term fluctuations in the foreign exchange markets, especially those caused by speculators. A managed float stabilizes the level at which a particular currency sells in the open market.

b) **Spot rates** are the rates at which currencies can be exchanged immediately.

c) **Forward rates** are the rates at which currencies can be exchanged in, for example, 30, 90, or 180 days. If the foreign currency is expected to appreciate against the dollar, it will sell at a premium. If the foreign currency is expected to decline against the dollar, it will sell at a discount.

2)   Floating exchange rates may fluctuate differently in the long, medium, and short term.

    a)   According to the **purchasing-power parity** theorem, in the long run, real prices should be the same worldwide (net of government taxes or trade barriers and transportation costs) for a given good. Exchange rates will adjust until purchasing-power parity is achieved. In other words, relative price levels determine exchange rates. In the real world, exchange rates do not perfectly reflect purchasing power parity, but relative price levels are clearly important determinants of those rates.

    b)   Medium-term exchange rates are dictated by the economic activity in a country. When the U.S. is in a recession, spending on imports (as well as domestic goods) will decrease. This reduced spending shifts the supply curve for dollars to the left, causing the equilibrium value of the dollar to increase (assuming the demand for dollars is constant); that is, at any given exchange rate, the supply to foreigners is lower.

        i)   If more goods are exported because of an increased preference for U.S. goods, the demand curve for dollars shifts to the right, causing upward pressure on the value of the dollar.

    c)   Short-term exchange rates are dictated by interest rates. Big corporations and banks invest their large reserves of cash where the real interest rate is highest. A rise in the real interest rate in a country will lead to an appreciation of the currency because it will be demanded for investment at the higher real interest rate, thereby shifting the demand curve outward.

        i)   The reverse holds true for a decline in real interest rates because that currency will be sold as investors move their money out of the country.

        ii)   However, the interplay of interest rates and inflation must also be considered. Inflation of a currency relative to a second currency causes the first currency to depreciate relative to the second. Moreover, nominal interest rates increase when inflation rates are expected to increase. The effect on exchange rates of inflation reflected in nominal interest rates is expressed by the **interest-rate parity theorem**. The ratio of the current forward and spot exchange rates (expressed in units of foreign currency per dollar) equals the ratio of one plus the current nominal foreign rate to one plus the current nominal domestic rate.

$$\frac{Forward\ exchange\ rate}{Spot\ exchange\ rate} = \frac{1 + Foreign\ interest\ rate}{1 + Domestic\ interest\ rate}$$

For example, if the current nominal foreign interest rate increases, the forward rate in terms of units of the foreign currency per dollar will increase. Hence, that currency will trade at a discount in the forward market.

11.   Stop and review! You have completed the outline for this subunit. Study multiple-choice questions 1 through 31 beginning on page 169.

B. Interest Rates

1.   Interest is the cost of debt, that is, the price paid by a borrower to the lender for the temporary use of funds.

2.   A variety of factors determine interest rates.

   a.   The real risk-free rate is the basic component of interest. It assumes no inflation and no default risk. This rate is a function of basic economic conditions, such as savers' willingness to forgo consumption and the returns available to borrowers on their investments. Thus, the supply of lendable funds and the demand therefor determine the price of money, much as the supply and demand for a good determines its price. The real risk-free rate may be thought of as the interest rate on a short-term U.S. Treasury security in an inflation-free world. It is difficult to measure the real risk-free rate precisely, but in the United States experts believe it has fluctuated between 1 and 4%.

   b.   Expected purchasing power fluctuations over the life of the loan result in the inclusion of an inflation premium in the quoted (or nominal) interest rate.

   c.   The risk that a borrower will default on a loan, which includes failing to pay the interest or the principal, also affects the market interest rate on a security. The higher the risk of default, the higher the default premium included in the interest rate.

   d.   The interest rate will also be higher for less liquid investments. The relative difficulty with which a financial asset can be converted to cash at fair value determines the liquidity premium.

   e.   Long-term debt securities are especially subject to interest rate price risk. Thus, if a debt security pays a fixed interest rate and market rates increase, the security's value will decrease. To compensate for this risk, interest on a long-term debt security must be increased. This is called the maturity risk premium.

      1)   Short-term debt securities are subject to reinvestment rate risk. Interest income will decline if market rates are lower when securities mature. This risk is lower for longer-term securities because only their interest payments need to be reinvested.

   f.   The Federal Reserve Board increases the money supply to combat recession and decreases it to prevent inflation. Antirecessionary policies entail lowering interest rates, but the expectation of greater inflation may ultimately increase interest rates. Anti-inflationary policies raise short-term rates. However, the expectation of lower inflation may then result in lower long-term rates.

   g.   If the federal government has a deficit, it must be covered by borrowing. Borrowing money increases the demand for funds, which tends to raise interest rates. The larger the federal deficit, the higher the level of interest rates.

   h.   The nation's trade deficit also increases interest rates because it is primarily financed by borrowing.

    i.   Interest rates in other nations must be considered. Foreign creditors demand interest rates that are comparable to those in other countries. If the Federal Reserve attempts to lower U.S. interest rates to stimulate the economy, bondholders will sell, bond prices will decline, and bond yields will rise. Consequently, antirecessionary policies may be hindered.

        1)   Furthermore, companies that make foreign investments or otherwise engage in foreign trade need to consider the interplay of relative inflation rates, currency exchange rates, and interest rates. Thus, one currency appreciates or depreciates in relation to another currency at about the same percentage as its inflation rate is lower or higher, respectively, than that of the other currency.

        2)   As mentioned previously, inflation is also a major component of interest rates. Therefore, countries with higher inflation also tend to have higher interest rates. Hence, a company may wish to borrow in a country with low inflation and low interest rates. However, the interest and principal payments will be fixed in units of the foreign currency. If the currency of the lender's country appreciates relative to that of the borrower's country, as may be expected given the lower inflation rate, the gain from the lower interest rate may be more than offset by the exchange rate loss.

3.   Interest rates affect the prices of stocks and bonds. Thus, higher rates result in lower prices for existing bonds and higher yields. The effect is to make bonds more attractive. As capital flows out of the stock market into the bond market, stock prices decline. The negative effect of higher rates on economic activity also tends to decrease stock prices because of the reduction in corporate profits. The opposite effects occur when interest rates fall.

4.   The **term structure of interest rates** is the relationship between yield to maturity and time to maturity. It is important to corporate treasurers, who must decide whether to borrow by issuing short- or long-term debt, and to investors, who must decide whether to buy short- or long-term bonds. Therefore, it is important to understand how the long- and short-term rates are related and what causes shifts in their positions. The term structure is graphically depicted by a yield curve.

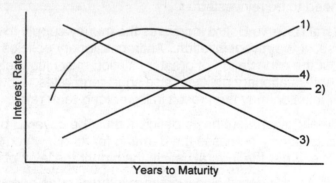

    a.   The graph above illustrates four common yield curves. In most years, long-term rates have been higher than short-term rates, so the yield curve is usually upward sloping.

        1)   Upward sloping
        2)   Flat
        3)   Downward sloping
        4)   Humped

b.   When plotting a yield curve, several factors are held constant:

1)   Default risk of instruments
2)   Taxability of the instruments
3)   Callability of the instruments
4)   Sinking fund provisions

c.   The following are the major theories explaining the slopes of the foregoing yield curves:

1)   The **liquidity preference theory** is based on the concept of **interest rate risk**, which is the risk of loss associated with a change in bond prices caused by a change in interest rates. For a given change in rates, the price change will be greater the longer the term of the security. All other things being equal, short-term securities (and a lower interest rate) may be preferred by investors to long-term securities because their greater liquidity protects against a loss resulting from a change in interest rates. Thus, investors accept lower yields on short-term securities leading to low short-term rates. In contrast, borrowers of funds prefer to borrow long-term (and pay a higher interest rate) to match the maturities of investments with the maturities of assets. Also, long-term borrowing avoids the expense of turning the debt over frequently. Thus, borrowers are willing to pay a higher rate for long-term funds leading to low short-term rates. The preferences of the lenders and the borrowers cause short-term rates to be lower than long-term rates. This theory implies that, under normal conditions, a positive maturity risk premium exists. This premium increases with years to maturity, which causes an upward-sloping yield curve.

2)   **Expectations theory** is based on the belief that a long-term interest rate is an average of future expected short-term interest rates. Future inflation is incorporated into this relationship. For this reason, the yield curve will slope upward if future rates are expected to rise, slope downward if interest rates are anticipated to fall, and remain flat if investors think the rate is stable. Under the pure expectations theory, the maturity risk premium, the default risk premium, and the liquidity premium are all zero.

a)   EXAMPLE: The following are the computed yields to maturity of 1-year, 2-year, and 3-year bonds:

Years to Maturity	Yield to Maturity
1	5%
2	8%
3	10%

i)   Given this yield curve structure, the market's expectations for future interest rates can be estimated by calculating the geometric ratios of the yields to maturity.

$$\text{Year 2: } \frac{(1.08)^2}{(1.05)} - 1 = 0.1109 = 11\%$$

$$\text{Year 3: } \frac{(1.10)^3}{(1.08)^2} - 1 = 0.1411 = 14\%$$

ii)   This example shows clearly how long-term rates are created by a series of expected short-term rates.

3) The **market segmentation theory** assumes that each borrower and lender has a preferred maturity. For example, a bank may prefer short-term investments because its deposit liabilities require security of principal, whereas an insurer may prefer to purchase long-term debt to be certain of a given level of income. Given strong maturity preferences, the slope of the yield curve under the market segmentation theory depends on the supply of funds and the demand therefor in the long-term and short-term markets. Thus, the yield curve could be either flat, upward sloping, or downward sloping. An upward-sloping yield curve occurs when there is a large supply of short-term funds relative to demand but a shortage of long-term funds. A downward-sloping curve indicates strong demand for funds in the short-term market compared to the long-term market. A flat curve indicates a balance between the short-term and long-term markets.

d. A downward-sloping term structure implies that the market expects short-run inflation to be higher than long-run inflation.

e. An upward-sloping term structure implies that the market expects long-run inflation to be higher than short-run inflation.

f. Tests of these three theories indicate that each has some validity. Therefore, the shape of the yield curve at any time is affected by liquidity preferences, by expectations about inflation and interest rates, and by supply and demand in long- and short-term markets.

5. Stop and review! You have completed the outline for this subunit. Study multiple-choice questions 32 through 58 beginning on page 178.

MULTIPLE-CHOICE QUESTIONS

A. Financial Markets

1. Which of the following economic functions is provided by the securities markets?

   A. A marketplace in which inefficient and expensive investment transactions take place.

   B. Unstable security prices because of frequent price changes.

   C. A small number of transactions.

   D. Facilitation of the issuance and purchase of new securities.

The correct answer is (D). *(Publisher)*

REQUIRED: The economic function provided by the securities market.

DISCUSSION: Securities markets facilitate investment by providing a marketplace for investors to conduct inexpensive transactions efficiently. Thus, investors are assured that they will have a place to buy and sell securities. Securities markets can handle continuous transactions that are based on the values and judgments of investors. Securities markets increase liquidity of securities by providing a marketplace. Thus, prices are relatively stable due to smaller price changes. Securities markets also facilitate the issuance and purchase of new securities.

Answer (A) is incorrect because securities markets are a marketplace in which efficient and inexpensive transactions take place. Answer (B) is incorrect because security prices are more stable due to smaller price changes. Answer (C) is incorrect because securities markets continuously handle a large number of transactions.

2. Which of the following is not true about financial markets?

   A. Financial markets are the total supply and demand for securities.

   B. Financial markets facilitate borrowing and lending of financial assets and obligations.

   C. In perfectly competitive markets, financial intermediaries act as price setters to clear the market.

   D. Financial markets change over time, causing people to adjust their pattern of consumption.

The correct answer is (C). *(Publisher)*

REQUIRED: The false statement about financial markets.

DISCUSSION: Financial markets bring entities that have funds to invest together with entities that have financing needs. They facilitate the transfer of assets and obligations. Due to this activity, financial markets cause people to adjust their consumption patterns. Financial intermediaries increase the efficiency of financial markets through better allocation of financial resources, not by clearing the market.

Answers (A), (B), and (D) are incorrect because they are true statements about financial markets.

3. The financial markets that trade debt securities with maturities of less than 1 year and are dealer-driven are

   A. Primary markets.

   B. Capital markets.

   C. Secondary markets.

   D. Money markets.

The correct answer is (D). *(Publisher)*

REQUIRED: The financial markets that trade debt securities with maturities of less than 1 year and are dealer-driven.

DISCUSSION: Money markets trade debt securities with maturities of less than 1 year. These markets are dealer-driven because dealers are the principals who buy and sell instruments at their own risk. Money markets are marketable and short-term with low default risk. They can be found in New York, London, and Tokyo.

Answer (A) is incorrect because primary markets raise capital for initial issues of securities. Answer (B) is incorrect because capital markets trade long-term debt and equity securities. Answer (C) is incorrect because secondary markets provide for trading previously issued securities.

4. Which of the following financial instruments can be traded in international money markets?

A. Mortgages.

B. Preferred stocks.

C. Government treasury bills.

D. Government treasury bonds.

The correct answer is (C). *(CIA 1195 IV-65)*

REQUIRED: The instruments traded in international money markets.

DISCUSSION: Funds are borrowed or lent for short periods (less than one year) in money markets. Examples of instruments traded in money markets are U.S. Treasury bills, bankers' acceptances, commercial paper, negotiable certificates of deposit, money market mutual funds, Eurodollar market time deposits, and consumer credit loans. Capital markets trade stocks and long-term debt.

Answers (A), (B), and (D) are incorrect because mortgages, preferred stocks, and treasury bonds are long-term, capital market securities.

5. In capital markets, the primary market is concerned with the provision of new funds for capital investments through

A. New issues of bond and stock securities.

B. Exchanges of existing bond and stock securities.

C. The sale of forward or future commodities contracts.

D. New issues of bond and stock securities and exchanges of existing bond and stock securities.

The correct answer is (A). *(CMA 693 1-4)*

REQUIRED: The purpose of the primary market.

DISCUSSION: The primary market is the market for new stocks and bonds. In this market, wherein investment money flows directly to the issuer, securities are initially sold by investment bankers who purchase them from issuers and sell them through an underwriting group. Later transactions occur on securities exchanges or other markets.

Answer (B) is incorrect because existing securities are traded on a secondary market (e.g., securities exchanges). Answer (C) is incorrect because the futures market is where commodities contracts are sold, not the capital market. Answer (D) is incorrect because exchanges of existing securities do not occur in the primary market.

6. If a multinational firm were to raise equity capital on the London Stock Exchange, this would be referred to as a

A. Money market transaction.

B. Primary market transaction.

C. Secondary market transaction.

D. Mortgage market transaction.

The correct answer is (B). *(CIA 1194 IV-68)*

REQUIRED: The type of transaction in which a firm raises equity capital.

DISCUSSION: The primary market is one in which a firm raises additional long-term debt or equity capital. It is a market in which newly created securities are bought and sold for the first time.

Answer (A) is incorrect because money market transactions involve debt securities with maturities of less than one year. Answer (C) is incorrect because secondary market transactions involve the trading of already outstanding securities by investors. Answer (D) is incorrect because mortgage market transactions relate to loans on residential, commercial, industrial, and farm real estate.

7. The over-the-counter (OTC) market is

A. An auction market where trading takes place at a particular physical site like the New York Stock Exchange.

B. A dealer market where brokers and dealers are linked by telecommunications equipment to trade securities.

C. An auction market that trades the majority of stocks.

D. A dealer market that trades securities on the stock exchanges due to the high dollar volume of trading.

The correct answer is (B). *(Publisher)*

REQUIRED: The definition of the OTC market.

DISCUSSION: The OTC market is a dealer market, in which brokers and dealers are linked by telecommunications equipment. Securities not traded on the stock exchanges are traded in the OTC market. The dollar volume of trading is much greater on the stock exchanges than the OTC market because the largest companies are usually listed on the stock exchanges. However, the majority of all stocks are traded in the OTC market.

Answer (A) is incorrect because the OTC market is a dealer market that is connected by telecommunications equipment. Answer (C) is incorrect because the OTC market is a dealer market that trades the majority of stocks. Answer (D) is incorrect because the OTC market does not trade securities traded on the stock exchanges.

8. The market for outstanding, listed common stock is called the

A. Primary market.

B. New issue market.

C. Over-the-counter market.

D. Secondary market.

The correct answer is (D). *(CIA 595 IV-47)*

REQUIRED: The market for outstanding, listed common stock.

DISCUSSION: Previously issued (outstanding) stocks of publicly owned companies are traded among investors in the secondary market. The original issuer receives no additional capital as a result of such trades.

Answers (A) and (B) are incorrect because firms raise capital by issuing new securities in the primary market. The initial public offering market is a frequently used term for the market in which previously privately owned firms issue new securities to the public. Answer (C) is incorrect because the over-the-counter market is the network of dealers that provides for trading in unlisted securities.

9. Which of the following is a financial intermediary?

A. Mutual funds.

B. Money markets.

C. The New York Stock Exchange.

D. The over-the-counter market.

The correct answer is (A). *(Publisher)*

REQUIRED: The example of a financial intermediary.

DISCUSSION: Financial intermediaries increase the efficiency of financial markets. A financial intermediary is a specialized firm that obtains funds from savers, issues its own securities, and uses the money to purchase a business's securities. Therefore, they create new forms of capital. Mutual funds are corporations that use funds from savers to invest in stocks, long-term bonds, or short-term debt.

Answer (B) is incorrect because money markets are the supply and demand of debt securities with maturities of less than 1 year. Answer (C) is incorrect because the New York Stock Exchange is a capital market that trades long-term debt and equity securities. Answer (D) is incorrect because the over-the-counter market is a secondary capital market that trades securities not traded on the stock exchanges.

10. The term "margin trading" is the

A. Selling of securities to repay a loan from a broker.

B. Borrowing of the margin requirement to buy securities.

C. Buying of a security by paying the margin requirement and borrowing the remaining amount from the seller.

D. Selling of a security that is not owned by the seller and making a marginal profit.

The correct answer is (C). *(Publisher)*

REQUIRED: The definition of "margin trading."

DISCUSSION: Margin trading is accomplished by buying securities on credit extended from the seller. The purchaser pays the margin requirement that is set by the Federal Reserve and borrows the remaining money from the seller. The seller holds the security as collateral.

Answers (A) and (D) are incorrect because margin trading involves the buying of securities by paying the margin requirement of the price and borrowing the remaining amount. Answer (B) is incorrect because the purchaser must pay the margin requirement to buy securities.

11. The term "short selling" is the

A. Selling of a security that was purchased by borrowing money from a broker.

B. Selling of a security that is not owned by the seller.

C. Selling of all the shares you own in a company in anticipation that the price will decline dramatically.

D. Betting that a stock will increase by a certain amount within a given period of time.

The correct answer is (B). *(CMA 1294 1-16)*

REQUIRED: The definition of "short selling."

DISCUSSION: Short selling is accomplished by borrowing securities from a broker and selling those securities. At a later time, the loan is repaid by buying securities on the open market and returning them to the broker. The seller speculates that the stock's market price will decline.

Answer (A) is incorrect because margin trading involves buying securities by borrowing money from a broker. Answer (C) is incorrect because the investor does not own the shares sold in a short sale. Answer (D) is incorrect because the short seller is betting that the stock will decrease in price.

12. Financial market efficiency implies that

A. All securities are perfect substitutes, and that the net present value of any securities investment is zero.

B. A firm's share price may not be a good estimate of future cash flows because price adjustment to new information is slow.

C. It is possible to systematically gain or lose abnormal profits from trading on the basis of available public information.

D. Because of the speculative nature of securities markets, share prices may not be the best benchmark for corporate financial choices.

The correct answer is (A). *(CFM Sample Q. 1)*

REQUIRED: The correct statement about financial market efficiency.

DISCUSSION: The efficient markets hypothesis (EMH) states that current stock prices immediately and fully reflect all relevant information. Hence, the market is continuously adjusting to new information and acting to correct pricing errors. In other words, securities prices are always in equilibrium.

Answer (B) is incorrect because price adjustments are instantaneous under the EMH. Answer (C) is incorrect because securities prices are always in equilibrium under the EMH, i.e., no abnormal profit with public information. Answer (D) is incorrect because the EMH states that securities prices are, rather than are not, the best benchmark of corporate financial decisions.

13. The strong form of the efficient markets hypothesis (EMH) states that current market prices of securities reflect

A. All publicly available information.

B. All information whether it is public or private.

C. No relevant information.

D. Only information found in past price movements.

The correct answer is (B). *(Publisher)*

REQUIRED: The information reflected in current market prices of securities under the strong form of the EMH.

DISCUSSION: The EMH states that stock prices reflect all relevant information, so the market is continuously adjusting to new information. Stock prices are in equilibrium, so investors cannot earn abnormal returns. The strong form of the EMH states that all public and private information is instantaneously reflected in current market prices of securities. Thus, investors cannot earn abnormal returns.

Answer (A) is incorrect because the semistrong form of EMH states that only publicly available information is reflected in current market prices. Answer (C) is incorrect because the EMH states that current market prices at least reflect past price movements. Answer (D) is incorrect because the weak form of the EMH states that only past price movements are reflected in current market prices.

14. The semistrong form of the efficient markets hypothesis (EMH) states that current market prices of securities reflect

A. No pertinent information.

B. All pertinent information.

C. Only information contained in past price movements.

D. Only publicly available information.

The correct answer is (D). *(CIA 1194 IV-54)*

REQUIRED: The information reflected in current market prices under the semistrong form of the EMH.

DISCUSSION: According to the EMH, stock prices are in equilibrium and investors cannot obtain abnormal returns, that is, returns in excess of the riskiness of their investments. The semistrong form of the EMH postulates that current market prices reflect all publicly available information. However, investors with inside information can still earn an abnormal return.

Answer (A) is incorrect because the EMH states that current prices reflect at least the information contained in past price movements. Answer (B) is incorrect because the strong form of the EMH states that current market prices reflect all pertinent information, including insider information. Answer (C) is incorrect because the weak form of the EMH states that current market prices reflect only information contained in past price movements.

15. The weak form of the efficient markets hypothesis (EMH) states that current market prices of securities reflect

- A. All past price movements.
- B. All public information.
- C. All public and private information.
- D. No relevant information.

The correct answer is (A). *(Publisher)*

REQUIRED: The information reflected in current market prices of securities under the weak form of the EMH.

DISCUSSION: The EMH states that stock prices fully reflect all relevant information, including public and private information. The securities prices are in equilibrium because they are always adjusting to new information. The weak form of the EMH states that only past price movements are reflected in current securities prices, so technical analysis will not provide a basis for earning abnormal returns.

Answer (B) is incorrect because the semistrong form of the EMH states that only public information is reflected in securities prices. Answer (C) is incorrect because the strong form of the EMH states that all information, including public and private, is reflected in securities prices. Answer (D) is incorrect because the EMH states that relevant information is reflected in securities prices from at least the past price movements.

16. Interest rates received by depositors on Eurodollar deposits tend to be higher than domestic U.S. rates on equivalent instruments because

- A. Borrowers pay higher rates than domestic U.S. rates on equivalent instruments.
- B. The deposits involve different currencies.
- C. Eurodollar deposits are for smaller amounts.
- D. The Eurodollar market is outside the direct control of the U.S. monetary authorities and has lower costs.

The correct answer is (D). *(CIA 595 IV-59)*

REQUIRED: The reason that interest rates on Eurodollar deposits exceed U.S. rates.

DISCUSSION: Eurodollars are U.S. dollars deposited in banks outside the U.S. Because it is outside the direct control of the U.S. monetary authorities, the Eurodollar market has lower costs. For example, U.S. reserve requirements and FDIC premium payments do not apply in this market. A lower cost market can offer depositors higher interest rates.

Answer (A) is incorrect because Eurodollar borrowers tend to pay lower, not higher, rates. Borrowers and depositors can both receive more favorable rates because, with its lower costs, the Eurodollar market can offer smaller spreads between borrowing and lending rates. Answer (B) is incorrect because U.S. dollars are on deposit in both cases. Answer (C) is incorrect because Eurodollar deposits tend to be for larger, not smaller, amounts. Furthermore, smaller deposits tend to earn lower, not higher, rates than larger deposits.

17. Which of the following is a characteristic of Eurobonds?

- A. Are always denominated in Eurodollars.
- B. Are always sold in some country other than the one in whose currency the bond is denominated.
- C. Are sold outside the country of the borrower but are denominated in the currency of the country in which the issue is sold.
- D. Are generally issued as registered bonds.

The correct answer is (B). *(CIA 1195 IV-66)*

REQUIRED: The characteristic of Eurobonds.

DISCUSSION: Eurobonds are, by definition, always sold in some country other than the one in whose currency the bond issue is denominated. Their advantage is that they are customarily less stringently regulated than most other bonds. Hence, transaction costs are lower.

Answer (A) is incorrect because Eurobonds are not always denominated in Eurodollars, which are U.S. dollars deposited outside the U.S. Answer (C) is incorrect because foreign bonds are denominated in the currency of the country in which they are sold. Answer (D) is incorrect because Eurobonds are usually issued not as registered bonds but as bearer bonds, so names and nationalities of the investors are not recorded.

18. The best reason corporations issue Eurobonds rather than domestic bonds is that

   A. These bonds are denominated in the currency of the country in which they are issued.

   B. These bonds are normally a less expensive form of financing because of the absence of government regulation.

   C. Foreign buyers more readily accept the issues of both large and small U.S. corporations than do domestic investors.

   D. Eurobonds carry no foreign exchange risk.

The correct answer is (B). *(CMA 1288 1-7)*
   REQUIRED: The best reason for issuing Eurobonds instead of domestic bonds.
   DISCUSSION: International bonds are of two types: foreign bonds and Eurobonds. Foreign bonds are denominated in the currency of the nation in which they are sold. Eurobonds are denominated in a currency other than that of the nation where they are sold.
   Foreign bonds issued in the United States and denominated in dollars must be registered with the SEC, but such extensive disclosure is not required in most European nations. Thus, an American company may elect to issue Eurobonds denominated in dollars in a foreign nation because of the convenience of not having to comply with governmental registration requirements.
   Answer (A) is incorrect because Eurobonds are not denominated in the currency of the nation in which they are sold. The difference is a possible disadvantage because of exchange rate risk. Nevertheless, many foreign bonds are denominated in U.S. dollars. Answer (C) is incorrect because foreign nationals are often hesitant about buying bonds issued by small companies with which they are not familiar. Answer (D) is incorrect because Eurobonds carry foreign exchange risk. The foreign lender may suffer a loss if the dollar declines relative to its domestic currency.

19. A short-term speculative rise in the worldwide value of domestic currency could be moderated by a central bank decision to

   A. Sell domestic currency in the foreign exchange market.

   B. Buy domestic currency in the foreign exchange market.

   C. Sell foreign currency in the foreign exchange market.

   D. Increase domestic interest rates.

The correct answer is (A). *(CIA 592 IV-70)*
   REQUIRED: The central bank decision that could moderate a short-term speculative rise in the worldwide value of domestic currency.
   DISCUSSION: In the short run, a central bank's sale of the currency increases the supply and reduces the price of the currency. In the long run, given the current system of managed floating exchange rates, changes in rates should reflect changes in economic conditions. In other words, exchange rates should float. But central banks are expected to manage the float by buying and selling currencies to counteract the disruptive effects on rates of such temporary factors as speculation.
   Answer (B) is incorrect because buying domestic currency in the foreign exchange market would raise the worldwide value of the domestic currency. Answer (C) is incorrect because selling foreign currency would raise the worldwide value of the domestic currency with respect to that foreign currency. Answer (D) is incorrect because a central bank decision to increase domestic interest rates would make the domestic currency attractive to foreign investors and raise the value of the domestic currency.

20. In foreign exchange markets, the phrase "managed float" refers to the

   A. Tendency for most currencies to depreciate in value.

   B. Tendency for most currencies to appreciate in value.

   C. Discretionary buying and selling of currencies by central banks.

   D. Necessity of maintaining a highly liquid asset, such as gold, to conduct international trade.

The correct answer is (C). *(CMA 688 1-25)*
   REQUIRED: The meaning of the phrase "managed float."
   DISCUSSION: Exchange rates "float" when they are set by supply and demand, not by agreement among countries. In a managed float, central banks buy and sell currencies at their discretion to avoid erratic fluctuations in the foreign exchange market. The objective of such transactions is to "manage" the level at which a particular currency sells in the open market. For instance, if there is an oversupply of a country's currency on the foreign exchange market, the central bank will purchase that currency to support the market.
   Answers (A) and (B) are incorrect because currencies do not have an inherent tendency to depreciate or appreciate. Answer (D) is incorrect because currencies no longer have to be supported by gold.

21. The risk of loss because of fluctuations in the relative value of foreign currencies is called

    A. Expropriation risk.

    B. Sovereign risk.

    C. Multinational beta.

    D. Exchange rate risk.

The correct answer is (D). *(CIA 1191 IV-60)*
    REQUIRED: The risk of loss because of fluctuations in the relative value of foreign currencies.
    DISCUSSION: When amounts to be paid or received are denominated in a foreign currency, exchange rate fluctuations may result in exchange gains or losses. For example, if a U.S. firm has a receivable fixed in terms of units of a foreign currency, a decline in the value of that currency relative to the U.S. dollar results in a foreign exchange loss.
    Answer (A) is incorrect because sovereign or expropriation risk is the risk that the sovereign country in which the assets backing an investment are located will seize the assets without adequate compensation. Answer (B) is incorrect because sovereign or expropriation risk is the risk that the sovereign country in which the assets backing an investment are located will seize the assets without adequate compensation. Answer (C) is incorrect because the beta value in the capital asset pricing model for a multinational firm is the systematic risk of a given multinational firm relative to that of the market as a whole.

22. Currently, foreign exchange rates

    A. Are fixed by government policy and adjusted periodically.

    B. Float without any intervention by the central banks of foreign countries.

    C. Remain fairly stable decreasing the exchange rate risk.

    D. Include spot rates at which currencies can be exchanged immediately.

The correct answer is (D). *(Publisher)*
    REQUIRED: The correct statement about foreign exchange rates.
    DISCUSSION: The current international monetary system uses floating exchange rates. They are not fixed by governments but are determined by supply and demand. Central banks can intervene in the foreign exchange market to stabilize exchange rate fluctuations. Spot rates are the rates at which currencies can be exchanged immediately in the foreign exchange market.
    Answer (A) is incorrect because current foreign exchange rates are floating rates. Answer (B) is incorrect because the central banks can intervene to stabilize foreign exchange rates. Answer (C) is incorrect because foreign exchange rates fluctuate constantly causing the exchange rate risk to rise.

23. Which one of the following did not contribute to the high value of the U.S. dollar during the 1980s?

    A. Relatively high, real interest rates.

    B. A large demand for U.S. dollars.

    C. U.S. demand for foreign goods.

    D. A stable U.S. government and currency.

The correct answer is (C). *(CMA 1293 1-26)*
    REQUIRED: The event that did not contribute to the high value of the U.S. dollar during the 1980s.
    DISCUSSION: Many factors influence the value of a country's currency on the international market. These factors include interest rate differentials, inflation differentials, balance of trade, balance of payments, and stability of governments. However, a demand by Americans for more foreign goods would drive down the price of the dollar because of the resulting increased demand for foreign currencies.
    Answer (A) is incorrect because, in the 1980s, high real interest rates made investments in the U.S. more attractive. Thus, demand for U.S. dollars increased. Answer (B) is incorrect because a large demand for dollars drives up the price of dollars relative to other currencies. Answer (D) is incorrect because the stability of the U.S. government and its currency made the dollar a secure store of value in the eyes of many foreigners; these foreigners therefore acquired dollars to hold as a safeguard against inflation in their own countries.

24. The purchasing-power parity exchange rate

    A.   Is always equal to the market exchange rate.

    B.   Results in an undervalued currency of countries that are net importers.

    C.   Results in an undervalued currency of countries that are net exporters.

    D.   Holds constant the relative price levels in two countries when measured in a common currency.

The correct answer is (D). *(CMA 1285 1-33)*
    REQUIRED: The definition of purchasing-power parity exchange rate.
    DISCUSSION: The purchasing-power parity theorem states that, in the long run, the real price of a good in country A will equal the price of the same good in country B when the prices are expressed in a common currency and converted at the current exchange rate (adjustments for tariffs, taxes, or transportation costs may need to be made).
    Answer (A) is incorrect because the purchasing-power parity exchange rate is a long-run measure, but the market rate may reflect short-term or medium-term conditions. Answers (B) and (C) are incorrect because purchasing-power parity does not affect the valuation of currency.

25. If the U.S. dollar declines in value relative to the currencies of many of its trading partners, the likely result is that

    A.   Foreign currencies will depreciate against the dollar.

    B.   The U.S. trade deficit will worsen.

    C.   U.S. exports will tend to increase.

    D.   U.S. imports will tend to increase.

The correct answer is (C). *(CMA 1287 1-30)*
    REQUIRED: The true statement if the U.S. dollar declines in value.
    DISCUSSION: The decline in the value of the dollar reduces the prices of U.S. goods to foreigners and thus should increase exports. Also, foreign goods will be higher priced (in dollars) and imports from foreign countries should decrease, thus helping the U.S. balance of trade.
    Answer (A) is incorrect because the dollar has depreciated against foreign currencies. Answer (B) is incorrect because the U.S. trade deficit should improve. Answer (D) is incorrect because U.S. imports will decline. Foreign goods will be higher priced than before.

26. A U.S. company and a German company purchased the same stock on the German stock exchange and held the stock for 1 year. The value of the German mark weakened against the dollar over this period. Comparing the returns of the two companies, the United States company's return will be

    A.   Lower.

    B.   Higher.

    C.   The same.

    D.   Indeterminate from the information provided.

The correct answer is (A). *(CIA 1190 IV-58)*
    REQUIRED: The effect of the exchange rate movement.
    DISCUSSION: The returns on the stock are presumably paid in marks. Hence, the change in the value of the mark relative to the dollar does not affect the German company's return. However, the weakening of the mark reduces the number of dollars it will buy, and the U.S. company's return in dollars is correspondingly reduced.
    Answer (B) is incorrect because the return to the U.S. company is adversely affected by the exchange rate movement. Answers (C) and (D) are incorrect because the return to the U.S. company was directly affected by the exchange rate movement, but the return to the German company was not.

27. Assuming exchange rates are allowed to fluctuate freely, which one of the following factors would likely cause a nation's currency to appreciate on the foreign exchange market?

    A.   A relatively rapid rate of growth in income that stimulates imports.

    B.   A high rate of inflation relative to other countries.

    C.   A slower rate of growth in income than in other countries, which causes imports to lag behind exports.

    D.   Domestic real interest rates that are lower than real interest rates abroad.

The correct answer is (C). *(CMA 695 1-24)*
    REQUIRED: The factor causing a currency to appreciate given freely fluctuating exchange rates.
    DISCUSSION: Assuming that exchange rates are allowed to fluctuate freely, a nation's currency will appreciate if the demand for it is constant or increasing while supply is decreasing. For example, if the nation decreases its imports relative to exports, less of its currency will be used to buy foreign currencies for import transactions and more of its currency will be demanded for export transactions. Thus, the supply of the nation's currency available in foreign exchange markets decreases. If the demand for the currency increases or does not change, the result is an increase in (appreciation of) the value of the currency.
    Answer (A) is incorrect because an increase in imports drives down the value of the nation's currency. Answer (B) is incorrect because a high rate of inflation devalues a nation's currency. Answers (D) is incorrect because lower interest rates relative to those in other countries discourage foreign investment, decrease demand for the nation's currency, and reduce its value.

28. Two countries have flexible exchange rate systems and an active trading relationship. If incomes <List A> in country 1, everything else equal, then the currency of country 1 will tend to <List B> relative to the currency of country 2.

	List A	List B
A.	Rise	Remain constant
B.	Fall	Depreciate
C.	Rise	Depreciate
D.	Remain constant	Appreciate

The correct answer is (C). *(CIA 1195 IV-67)*
   REQUIRED: The effect of a change in incomes in one nation on its currency.
   DISCUSSION: If incomes in country 1 rise, consumers in country 1 will increase their imports from country 2. The resulting increase in the supply of currency 1 will result in a tendency for it to depreciate relative to the currency of country 2.
   Answer (A) is incorrect because, if incomes in country 1 rise, the result will be a tendency for it to devalue relative to the currency of country 2. Answer (B) is incorrect because, if incomes in country 1 fall, consumers in country 1 will reduce their imports. The resulting decrease in the supply of currency 1 will result in a tendency for it to appreciate relative to the currency of country 2. Answer (D) is incorrect because, if incomes in country 1 remain constant, the currency of country 1 will not tend to appreciate or depreciate relative to the currency of country 2.

29. Which of the following changes would create pressure for the Japanese yen to appreciate relative to the U.S. dollar?

A. An increase in incomes in Japan.

B. A change in U.S. tastes in favor of Japanese goods.

C. A decrease in U.S. incomes.

D. A change in Japanese tastes in favor of U.S. goods.

The correct answer is (B). *(CIA 1194 IV-66)*
   REQUIRED: The changes that would cause the yen to appreciate relative to the dollar.
   DISCUSSION: Increased demand for Japanese goods in the U.S. would increase the demand for yen. Accordingly, the demand curve for yen would shift to the right. U.S. purchasers would be willing to pay more for any given quantity of yen.
   Answer (A) is incorrect because an increase in incomes in Japan would result in increased consumption of imports and increased demand for dollars. The result would be downward pressure on the yen. Answer (C) is incorrect because a decrease in U.S. incomes would reduce the demand for imports, which would decrease demand for foreign currencies. Answer (D) is incorrect because an increased demand for U.S. goods in Japan would increase the supply of yen, thereby creating pressure for the yen to depreciate.

30. The interest-rate parity theorem states that

A. Nominal interest rates decrease when inflation rates increase.

B. The exchange rate is equal to the market exchange rate.

C. A rise in the real interest rate will lead to a depreciation of currency.

D. As nominal foreign interest rates increase, the forward exchange rate in units of the foreign currency per dollar increases.

The correct answer is (D). *(Publisher)*
   REQUIRED: The definition of the interest-rate parity theorem.
   DISCUSSION: The interest-rate parity theorem explains the effect on exchange rates of inflation reflected in nominal interest rates. The ratio of the current forward and spot exchange rates (expressed in units of foreign currency per dollar) equals the ratio of one plus the current nominal foreign rate to one plus the current nominal domestic rate. If the current nominal foreign interest rate increases, the forward rate in units of the foreign currency per dollar will increase. Thus, the foreign currency will trade at a discount in the forward market.
   Answer (A) is incorrect because nominal interest rates increase when inflation rates are expected to increase. Answer (B) is incorrect because the interest-rate parity theorem shows the effect on exchange rates of inflation reflected in nominal interest rates. Answer (C) is incorrect because a rise in the real interest rate will lead to an appreciation of the currency and is not part of the interest-rate parity theorem.

31. If the central bank of a country raises interest rates sharply, the country's currency will likely

    A. Increase in relative value.

    B. Remain unchanged in value.

    C. Decrease in relative value.

    D. Decrease sharply in value at first and then return to its initial value.

The correct answer is (A). *(CMA 694 1-4)*
    REQUIRED: The effect on a country's currency if its central bank raises interest rates sharply.
    DISCUSSION: Foreign exchange rates fluctuate depending upon the demand for each country's currency. If a country raises its interest rates, its currency will appreciate. The demand for investment at the higher interest rates will shift the demand curve for the currency to the right. The reverse holds true for a decrease in interest rates.
    Answers (B), (C), and (D) are incorrect because the currency should increase in relative value when interest rates in the country rise sharply. More investors will want to earn the higher rates of interest.

B. Interest Rates

32. The real risk-free rate

    A. Includes a default premium.

    B. Assumes that inflation is expected.

    C. Includes a liquidity premium.

    D. Is the basic component of interest.

The correct answer is (D). *(Publisher)*
    REQUIRED: The definition of the real risk-free rate.
    DISCUSSION: The real risk-free rate is the basic component of interest. It is the interest rate that would exist on a riskless security if no inflation were expected. The real risk-free rate equates the supply and demand of lendable funds.
    Answer (A) is incorrect because the real risk-free rate assumes that there is no default risk, so a default premium is not included. Answer (B) is incorrect because the real risk-free rate assumes that there is no inflation. Answer (C) is incorrect because the real risk-free rate exists on a riskless security, so there is no liquidity risk and no need for a liquidity premium.

33. The interest rate that would exist on a riskless security if no inflation were expected is

    A. The nominal rate.

    B. The prime rate.

    C. The real risk-free rate.

    D. The quoted risk-free rate.

The correct answer is (C). *(Publisher)*
    REQUIRED: The interest rate that would exist on a riskless security if no inflation were expected.
    DISCUSSION: The real risk-free rate is the interest rate that would exist on a riskless security in an inflation-free world. It may be thought of as the interest rate that would exist on a short-term U.S. Treasury security without inflation. The rate changes over time due to changes in supply and demand of funds.
    Answer (A) is incorrect because the nominal rate includes inflation and risk premiums. Answer (B) is incorrect because the prime rate is the rate banks charge to large corporations. Answer (D) is incorrect because the quoted risk-free rate includes an inflation premium.

34. From which of the following would an investor be able to obtain abnormal returns?

    A. The risk-free rate for borrowing is above the rate for lending.

    B. The risk-free rate for borrowing is below the rate for lending.

    C. The risk-free rate for borrowing is equal to the rate for lending.

    D. The risk-free rate for borrowing is below the default risk.

The correct answer is (B). *(Publisher)*
    REQUIRED: The situation in which an investor could obtain abnormal returns.
    DISCUSSION: An investor is able to earn abnormal returns when the risk-free borrowing rate is below the rate of lending. The investor can borrow at a lower rate and lend at a higher rate. The difference is the investor's return.
    Answer (A) is incorrect because the investor would lose, not make money, borrowing at a higher rate than the lending rate. Answer (C) is incorrect because the investor would not make an abnormal return because the borrowing rate is equal to the lending rate. Answer (D) is incorrect because an investor earns abnormal returns when the borrowing rate is below the lending rate, not the default risk.

35. The risk that a borrower will not pay the interest or the principal on a loan is added to the market interest rate and is called the

    A. Liquidity premium.

    B. Default risk premium.

    C. Inflation premium.

    D. Maturity risk premium.

The correct answer is (B). *(Publisher)*

REQUIRED: The premium that is added to the market interest rate for the risk of a borrower not paying the principal or the interest on a loan.

DISCUSSION: The default risk premium is added to the market interest rate for the risk that a borrower will not pay the principal or the interest on a loan, which is a default. The greater the risk of default, the higher the interest rate. Treasury securities have no default risk, so they have the lowest interest rates of taxable securities. Bonds with high ratings have lower default risk, so they have lower interest rates.

Answer (A) is incorrect because liquidity premium reflects the relative difficulty with which a financial asset can be converted to cash at fair value. Answer (C) is incorrect because inflation premium refers to upward adjustment of interest to cover expected inflation. Answer (D) is incorrect because maturity risk premium refers to interest-rate risk.

36. A maturity risk premium is included in interest rates because of

    A. Reinvestment rate risk.

    B. Default risk.

    C. Interest rate price risk.

    D. Inflation expectations.

The correct answer is (C). *(Publisher)*

REQUIRED: The reason a maturity risk premium is included in interest rates.

DISCUSSION: All long-term debt securities are subject to interest rate price risk, which is the risk that investors might have capital losses due to changing interest rates. If a debt security pays a fixed interest rate and market rates increase, the security's value will decrease. To compensate for this risk, a maturity risk premium is included in interest rates.

Answer (A) is incorrect because reinvestment rate risk is the risk that when funds are reinvested interest rates will be lower and will lead to a lower income. Answer (B) is incorrect because a default risk premium is added to interest rates for the risk of default. Answer (D) is incorrect because an inflation premium is added to interest rates for expectations about inflation.

37. The Federal Reserve Board stimulates the economy to combat a recession by

    A. Decreasing the money supply to lower short-term interest rates.

    B. Increasing the money supply to lower short-term interest rates.

    C. Increasing the money supply to lower the expectations for higher inflation.

    D. Decreasing the money supply to raise expectations for higher inflation.

The correct answer is (B). *(Publisher)*

REQUIRED: The policy the Federal Reserve Board uses to stimulate the economy and combat a recession.

DISCUSSION: The Federal Reserve Board affects the economic activity and rate of inflation by controlling the money supply. To combat a recession, the money supply is increased, causing interest rates to fall. However, a larger money supply may cause an increase in the expected rate of inflation, which could raise interest rates.

Answers (A) and (D) are incorrect because the Federal Reserve Board decreases the money supply to increase interest rates and prevent inflation. Answer (C) is incorrect because an increase in the money supply raises the expectation of inflation.

38. The Federal Reserve Board decreases the money supply to prevent inflation, which causes

- A. Short-term interest rates to fall.
- B. The expected rate of inflation to increase.
- C. Long-term rates to rise.
- D. Short-term interest rates to rise.

The correct answer is (D). *(Publisher)*
REQUIRED: The effect when the Federal Reserve Board decreases the money supply to tighten credit.
DISCUSSION: The Federal Reserve Board controls the money supply to affect economic activity and the rate of inflation. To prevent inflation, the Federal Reserve Board decreases the money supply. The initial effect of this action causes short-term interest rates to rise. The rise in interest rates leads to a decrease in the expectations for inflation. Thus, long-term rates may fall. The Federal Reserve Board primarily deals in the short-term market.
Answer (A) is incorrect because short-term interest rates fall when the money supply is increased, not decreased. Answer (B) is incorrect because an increase, not a decrease, in the money supply causes an increase in the expected rate of inflation. Answer (C) is incorrect because inflation fighting by the Fed usually results in a decrease in long-term rates.

39. The inflation premium built into interest rates

- A. Is the rate of expected inflation in the future.
- B. Is the rate of inflation experienced in the past.
- C. Equals the real risk-free rate of interest.
- D. Is zero.

The correct answer is (A). *(Publisher)*
REQUIRED: The definition of the inflation premium built into interest rates.
DISCUSSION: Investors are aware that inflation causes loss of money in real terms. Therefore, they include an inflation premium in interest rates. The inflation premium built into interest rates is equal to the expected inflation rate in the future, not the rate experienced in the past. Expectations about inflation relate to inflation rates in the past but are not perfect.
Answers (B), (C), and (D) are incorrect because the inflation premium is the expected inflation rate in the future.

40. What is likely to be the most direct and immediate effect of governmental borrowing to finance the federal budget deficit?

- A. The demand for funds increases interest rates.
- B. The demand for funds decreases interest rates.
- C. The nation's trade deficit increases.
- D. The inflation rate increases.

The correct answer is (A). *(Publisher)*
REQUIRED: The effect when the government borrows funds to finance the federal budget deficit.
DISCUSSION: When the federal government has a budget deficit, it must borrow funds. If the government decides to borrow funds, the interest rate rises due to the increased demand for funds.
Answer (B) is incorrect because the demand for funds increases interest rates. Answer (C) is incorrect because the effect on the trade deficit is likely to be indirect. Many factors other than interest rates affect the trade deficit. Answer (D) is incorrect because the demand for funds causes interest rates (but not necessarily inflation) to rise.

41. A trade deficit in the United States

- A. Increases the inflation rate.
- B. Causes more borrowing and increases interest rates.
- C. Allows the Federal Reserve to lower interest rates and combat a recession.
- D. Occurs when the United States sells more than it buys.

The correct answer is (B). *(Publisher)*
REQUIRED: The true statement about a trade deficit.
DISCUSSION: The United States is running a trade deficit. The deficit is primarily financed by borrowing, which increases the demand for funds, causing higher interest rates. Foreigners are willing to finance the rest of the U.S. debt only if interest rates are competitive. Thus, the Federal Reserve is hindered from combatting a recession by lowering interest rates because, if interest rates are lowered, foreigners will sell U.S. bonds, decreasing their prices and causing higher interest rates.
Answer (A) is incorrect because the trade deficit increases interest rates, not the inflation rate. Answer (C) is incorrect because a trade deficit increases, not decreases, interest rates. Answer (D) is incorrect because a trade deficit occurs when the U.S. buys more than it sells, not the opposite.

42. The term structure of interest rates is the relationship of

- A. Interest rates over different structures of bonds.
- B. Interest rates over different structures of securities.
- C. Interest rates over time.
- D. The maturity dates of an issuance of bonds.

The correct answer is (C). *(Publisher)*

   REQUIRED: The relationship found in the term structure.

   DISCUSSION: The term structure of interest rates is the relationship of interest rates and years to maturity. Corporate treasurers use the term structure to decide whether to borrow short-term debt or long-term debt. Investors use the term structure to decide whether to buy short-term or long-term bonds.

   Answers (A) and (B) are incorrect because term structure is the relationship of interest rates over time, not different structures of securities. Answer (D) is incorrect because maturity dates refer to the time element, but the interest rate element is missing.

43. A curve on a graph with the rate of return on the vertical axis and time on the horizontal axis depicts

- A. The internal rate of return on an investment.
- B. A yield curve showing the term structure of interest rates.
- C. The present value of future returns, discounted at the marginal cost of capital, minus the present value of the cost.
- D. A series of payments of a fixed amount for a specified number of years.

The correct answer is (B). *(CIA 589 IV-48)*

   REQUIRED: The representation of a curve on a graph with a rate of return on the vertical axis and time on the horizontal axis.

   DISCUSSION: The term structure of interest rates is the relationship between long- and short-term interest rates, that is, between yield to maturity and time to maturity. It is graphically depicted by a yield curve with a rate of return on the vertical axis and time to maturity on the horizontal axis. If short-term rates are higher than long-term rates, the curve will be downward sloping. If the reverse is true, the curve will be upward sloping.

   Answer (A) is incorrect because the internal rate of return is the interest rate at which the present value of the expected future net cash inflows is equal to the cost of the investment. Answer (C) is incorrect because it states the definition of net present value. Answer (D) is incorrect because this series is an annuity.

44. The term structure of interest rates is depicted by a yield curve. What variables are plotted on the horizontal axis and on the vertical axis?

- A. Interest rate and inflation rate, respectively.
- B. Years to maturity and interest rate, respectively.
- C. Real risk-free rate and inflation rate, respectively.
- D. Years to maturity and real risk-free rate, respectively.

The correct answer is (B). *(Publisher)*

   REQUIRED: The relationship on a yield curve.

   DISCUSSION: The term structure of interest rates is the relationship between long- and short-term interest rates. The term structure is graphically depicted by a yield curve. The interest rate is plotted on the vertical axis, and the years to maturity is plotted on the horizontal axis. The yield curve may change in both slope and position over time.

   Answers (A), (C), and (D) are incorrect because the yield curve plots the interest rate on the vertical axis and years to maturity on the horizontal axis.

45.

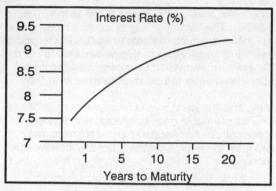

The yield curve shown above implies that the

A. Credit risk premium of corporate bonds has increased.

B. Credit risk premium of municipal bonds has increased.

C. Long-term interest rates have a higher annualized yield than short-term rates.

D. Short-term interest rates have a higher annualized yield than long-term rates.

The correct answer is (C). *(CIA 593 IV-48)*

REQUIRED: The implication of the yield curve.

DISCUSSION: The term structure of interest rates is the relationship between yield to maturity and time to maturity. This relationship is depicted by a yield curve. Assuming the long-term interest rate is an average of expected future short-term rates, the curve will be upward sloping when future short-term interest rates are expected to rise. Furthermore, the normal expectation is for long-term investments to pay higher rates because of their higher risk. Thus, long-term interest rates have a higher annualized yield than short-term rates.

Answers (A) and (B) are incorrect because the yield curve does not reflect the credit risk premium of bonds. Answer (D) is incorrect because long-term interest rates should be higher than short-term rates.

46. A downward-sloping yield curve depicting the term structure of interest rates implies that

A. Interest rates have declined over recent years.

B. Interest rates have increased over recent years.

C. Prevailing short-term interest rates are lower than prevailing long-term interest rates.

D. Prevailing short-term interest rates are higher than prevailing long-term interest rates.

The correct answer is (D). *(CIA 1192 IV-47)*

REQUIRED: The implication of a downward-sloping yield curve.

DISCUSSION: The term structure of interest rates is the relationship between long- and short-term interest rates, that is, between yield to maturity and time to maturity. It is graphically depicted by a yield curve with a rate of return on the vertical axis and time to maturity on the horizontal axis. If short-term rates are higher than long-term rates, the curve will be downward sloping. If the reverse is true, the curve will be upward sloping.

Answers (A) and (B) are incorrect because the yield curve does not reflect past interest rate trends. Answer (C) is incorrect because the downward-sloping yield curve implies that prevailing short-term interest rates are higher than prevailing long-term interest rates.

47. The yield curve depicting the term structure of interest rates

A. Holds the default risk constant.

B. Is usually downward sloping.

C. Never changes the slope.

D. Shows the relationship between inflation and years to maturity.

The correct answer is (A). *(Publisher)*

REQUIRED: The characteristic of a yield curve.

DISCUSSION: The yield curve graphically depicts the relationship between interest rates and years to maturity. When plotting a yield curve, several factors are held constant. These include default risk, taxability, callability, and sinking fund provisions. Over time, the yield curve changes in slope and position.

Answer (B) is incorrect because, historically, most long-term rates have been above short-term rates, so the yield curve usually has been upward sloping. Answer (C) is incorrect because the yield curve changes over time in position and slope. Answer (D) is incorrect because yield curves show the relationship between long- and short-term interest rates.

48. Increases in interest rates affect bonds and stocks

    A. Causing the bond prices to increase and the yields to decrease, while causing stock prices to decline.

    B. Causing the stock prices to decline and the bond prices to decline.

    C. Because the higher rate has a positive economic effect.

    D. Causing bond and stock sales to decrease.

The correct answer is (B). *(Publisher)*
    REQUIRED: The effect of increases in the interest rate on bonds and stocks.
    DISCUSSION: Higher interest rates result in lower prices for bonds and higher yields, thus making bonds more attractive to investors. As investors remove capital from the stock market to invest in bonds, stock prices decline. The higher rates also have a negative effect on economic activity, further reducing stock prices.
    Answer (A) is incorrect because higher interest rates cause the prices of bonds to fall and the yields to increase. Answer (C) is incorrect because higher interest rates have a negative effect on economic activity. Answer (D) is incorrect because bonds look better to investors because of lower prices and higher yields.

49. Short-term interest rates are

    A. Usually lower than long-term rates.

    B. Usually higher than long-term rates.

    C. Lower than long-term rates during periods of high inflation only.

    D. Not significantly related to long-term rates.

The correct answer is (A). *(CMA 691 1-5)*
    REQUIRED: The true statement about short-term interest rates.
    DISCUSSION: Historically, one facet of the term structure of interest rates (the relationship of yield and time to maturity) is that short-term interest rates have ordinarily been lower than long-term rates. One reason is that less risk is involved in the short run. Moreover, future expectations concerning interest rates affect the term structure. Most economists believe that a long-term interest rate is an average of future expected short-term interest rates. For this reason, the yield curve will slope upward if future rates are expected to rise, downward if interest rates are anticipated to fall, and remain flat if investors think the rate is stable. Future inflation is incorporated into this relationship. Another consideration is liquidity preference: investors in an uncertain world will accept lower rates on short-term investments because of their greater liquidity, whereas business debtors often prefer to pay higher rates on long-term debt to avoid the hazards of short-term maturities.
    Answer (B) is incorrect because short-term rates are usually lower than long-term rates. Answer (C) is incorrect because short-term rates are more likely to be greater than long-term rates if current levels of inflation are high. Answer (D) is incorrect because long-term rates may be viewed as short-term rates adjusted by a risk factor.

50. Which of the following scenarios would encourage a company to use short-term loans to retire its 10-year bonds that have 5 years until maturity?

    A. The company expects interest rates to increase over the next 5 years.

    B. Interest rates have increased over the last 5 years.

    C. Interest rates have declined over the last 5 years.

    D. The company is experiencing cash flow problems.

The correct answer is (C). *(CIA 593 IV-56)*
    REQUIRED: The scenario that would encourage a company to use short-term debt to retire long-term debt.
    DISCUSSION: If interest rates have declined, refunding with short-term debt may be appropriate. The bonds pay a higher interest rate than the new short-term debt. Assuming that rates continue to fall, the short-term debt can itself be refunded with debt having a still lower interest charge. The obvious risk is that interest rates may rise, thereby compelling the company to choose between paying off the debt or refunding it at higher rates.
    Answer (A) is incorrect because the company will not benefit from short-term loans if interest rates rise. Answer (B) is incorrect because the company should maintain the existing debt if prevailing interest rates are higher. Answer (D) is incorrect because the company increases the cash flow problem by shifting to short-term loans.

51. The liquidity preference theory explains that

A. A negative maturity risk premium exists and causes the yield curve to be downward sloping.

B. Long-term rates are lower than short-term rates because of lenders' and borrowers' preferences.

C. Investors require higher interest rates to buy long-term bonds due to the risk of loss.

D. Investors prefer 2-year bonds because they are less risky than 1-year bonds.

The correct answer is (C). *(Publisher)*
REQUIRED: The explanation of the liquidity preference theory.
DISCUSSION: The liquidity preference theory explains that long-term bonds have higher yields than short-term bonds due to preferences of investors and borrowers. Investors prefer short-term securities because they are more liquid and there is less chance of a change in interest rates. They will accept lower yields, causing lower short-term rates. Borrowers, however, prefer long-term debt because of the chance of repaying short-term debt with higher interest rates. They will pay higher rates for long-term debt than short-term debt, causing lower short-term rates. Therefore, investors must be influenced to buy long-term bonds with higher rates because of the riskiness of a loss.
Answer (A) is incorrect because a positive maturity risk premium exists and causes an upward-sloping yield curve. Answer (B) is incorrect because long-term rates are greater than short-term rates due to investors' and borrowers' preferences. Answer (D) is incorrect because investors prefer short-term securities because of liquidity and a lower chance of changes in interest rates.

52. According to the liquidity preference theory, investors

A. Prefer long-term securities.

B. Accept higher yields on securities.

C. Because of their preference, cause high short-term rates.

D. Prefer short-term securities.

The correct answer is (D). *(Publisher)*
REQUIRED: The preference of investors, according to the liquidity preference theory.
DISCUSSION: The liquidity preference theory is based on interest rate risk, which is the risk of loss with a change in bond prices from a change in interest rates. Investors prefer short-term securities because they are more liquid and reduce the chance of a loss from interest rate changes. Borrowers prefer long-term debt because they are less exposed to the risk of having to repay the debt. Therefore, investors will accept lower yields on short-term securities, and borrowers will pay a higher rate on long-term securities. These preferences cause short-term rates to be lower than long-term rates.
Answer (A) is incorrect because investors prefer short-term securities. Answer (B) is incorrect because investors accept lower yields on short-term securities because there is a lower chance of loss. Answer (C) is incorrect because investors cause short-term rates to be lower than long-term rates.

53. According to the liquidity preference theory, borrowers

A. Prefer long-term debt.

B. Are willing to pay a higher rate for short-term securities.

C. And lenders cause long-term rates to be lower than short-term rates.

D. Because of their preferences, cause higher short-term rates.

The correct answer is (A). *(Publisher)*
REQUIRED: The borrowers' preferences under the liquidity preference theory.
DISCUSSION: The liquidity preference theory is based on the concept of interest rate risk. Borrowers prefer long-term debt to avoid the risk of having to repay the debt under adverse conditions. Thus, they are willing to pay a higher rate for long-term funds. Investors prefer short-term securities because of the higher liquidity and lower chance of a loss from changes in interest rates. Together, these preferences cause lower short-term rates than long-term rates.
Answer (B) is incorrect because, according to the liquidity preference theory, borrowers are willing to pay higher rates for long-term debt. Answers (C) and (D) are incorrect because, according to the liquidity preference theory, borrower and lender preferences operate to cause short-term rates to be lower than long-term rates.

54. If the liquidity preference theory is correct, then

A. The long-term interest rate is less than the investor's expectations of the following year's short-term interest rate.

B. The long-term rate is greater than the short-term interest rate.

C. The long-term interest rate is equal to the investor's expectations of the following year's short-term interest rate.

D. The long-term rate is equal to the risk-free rate.

The correct answer is (B). *(Publisher)*
REQUIRED: The correct statement according to the liquidity preference theory.
DISCUSSION: According to the liquidity preference theory, investors prefer short-term securities because of the risk of loss with a change in bond prices due to fluctuations in interest rates. Also, these securities have a greater liquidity. Thus, investors will accept lower yields on short-term securities because of the expectations of higher interest rates. Borrowers, on the other hand, prefer long-term securities because of expectations for the risk of loss in the short term due to high interest rates. Thus, borrowers will pay a higher rate for long-term funds. These preferences usually cause short-term rates to be lower than long-term rates.
Answers (A) and (C) are incorrect because investors expect higher short-term rates in the following years than in the long term. Answer (D) is incorrect because the long-term rate includes inflation and interest-rate risk premiums.

55. The expectations theory states that the long-term rate over the second period is

A. The average of the future expected short-term interest rates for the first and second periods.

B. Equal to the short-term rate for the first period.

C. Always greater than the short-term rate for the first period.

D. Always greater than the long-term rate for the third period.

The correct answer is (A). *(Publisher)*
REQUIRED: The long-term rate over the second period under the expectations theory.
DISCUSSION: The expectations theory states that a long-term interest rate is an average of future short-term interest rates. It also incorporates expectations about inflation. The yield curve will slope upward if future rates are expected to rise, slope downward if future rates are expected to fall, and remain flat if the rate is expected to be stable.
Answer (B) is incorrect because, according to the expectations theory, long-term rates are an average of future expected short-term interest rates. Answers (C) and (D) are incorrect because long-term rates are lower when interest rates are expected to decrease.

56. According to the expectations theory of the term structure of interest rates, if inflation is expected to increase, the yield curve is

A. Humped, with an upward slope that peaks and then turns downward.

B. Downward sloping.

C. Upward sloping.

D. Flat.

The correct answer is (C). *(CIA 1191 IV-51)*
REQUIRED: The effect on the yield curve of an increase in inflation according to the expectations theory of the term structure of interest rates.
DISCUSSION: Most economists believe that a long-term interest rate is an average of future expected short-term interest rates. For this reason, the yield curve (plotted with the interest rate on the vertical axis and years to maturity on the horizontal axis) will slope upward (downward) if interest rates are expected to rise (fall). Future inflation is reflected in interest rates, so an expected increase in inflation will result in an expected increase in interest rates and an upward-sloping yield curve.
Answer (A) is incorrect because a humped yield curve is not applicable when using expectations theory. Answer (B) is incorrect because a downward-sloping yield curve would occur if inflation were expected to decline. Answer (D) is incorrect because a flat yield curve indicates inflation is expected to remain constant.

57. According to the expectations theory, if the yield curve on the New York money market is upward sloping while that on the Tokyo money market is downward sloping, then inflation in

A. The United States is expected to decrease.

B. The United States is expected to remain constant.

C. Japan is expected to decrease.

D. Japan is expected to remain constant.

The correct answer is (C). *(CIA 595 IV-58)*

REQUIRED: The predicted effect on inflation based on the expectations theory.

DISCUSSION: The term structure of interest rates is the relationship between yield to maturity and time to maturity. It is reflected in a yield curve. According to the expectations theory, a long-term interest rate is an average of expected short-term future rates. An upward- (downward-) sloping yield curve indicates that future rates are expected to rise (fall). Moreover, future inflation is incorporated in this relationship; that is, interest rates rise and fall with inflation. Thus, if the Japanese yield curve is downward sloping, inflation is expected to fall. Investors are requiring lower yields on longer term securities because they require less compensation for expected losses in purchasing power over longer terms.

Answer (A) is incorrect because an upward-sloping yield curve indicates that inflation is expected to increase. Answers (B) and (D) are incorrect because a flat yield curve is consistent with constant expected inflation.

58. According to the market segmentation theory, a person buying a house wants

A. To lend in the short-term market.

B. To buy long-term securities.

C. A long-term loan.

D. A short-term loan.

The correct answer is (C). *(Publisher)*

REQUIRED: The preference of a buyer of a house, according to the market segmentation theory.

DISCUSSION: The market segmentation theory assumes that each borrower and lender has a preferred maturity. A person buying a house prefers a long-term loan because (s)he is buying a long-term asset. The market segmentation theory can have any type of yield curve because it depends upon the supply and demand in the long-term and short-term markets.

Answers (A) and (B) are incorrect because a person buying a house wants to borrow, not lend or invest, funds. Answer (D) is incorrect because a buyer of a long-term asset like a house prefers a long-term loan according to the market segmentation theory.

STUDY UNIT 5: INVESTMENT BANKING AND COMMERCIAL BANKING

12 pages of outline
50 multiple-choice questions

A. Investment Banking
B. Initial Public Offerings
C. Private Placements
D. Other Exemptions from SEC Registration
E. Commercial Banking

This study unit is the third of five covering "Advanced Topics in Corporate Financial Management." It includes the investment and commercial banking subject areas.

A. **Investment Banking**. Investment bankers serve as intermediaries between businesses and the providers of capital. Moreover, they not only help to sell new securities but also assist in business combinations, act as brokers in secondary markets, and trade for their own accounts.

1. In their traditional role in the sale of new securities, investment bankers help determine the method of issuing the securities and the price to be charged, distribute the securities, provide expert advice, and perform a certification function.

   a. An issuer of new securities ordinarily selects an investment banker in a **negotiated deal**. Only a few large issuers seek **competitive bids**. The reason for the predominance of negotiated deals is that the costs of learning about the issuer and setting an issue price and fees are usually prohibitive unless the investment banker has a high probability of closing the deal.

   b. A choice must be made as to whether to have the securities underwritten or sold through the best efforts of the investment banker.

      1) **Best efforts** sales of securities provide no guarantee that the securities will be sold or that enough cash will be raised. The investment banker receives commissions and is obligated to use its best efforts to sell the securities.

      2) An **underwritten deal** or a **firm commitment** provides a guarantee. The investment banker agrees to purchase the entire issue and resell it.

   c. Investment bankers contribute to the efficiency with which securities are sold. An investment banker has a professional staff, a network of dealers, and a regular clientele.

   d. The certification function of an investment banker derives from its **reputation capital**. The expertise, integrity, and experience of the investment banker help to offset the **information asymmetry** between the management of the issuing firm and potential buyers of the securities. Thus, buyers rely on the investment banker's reputation for pricing the issue fairly.

2. A prospective issuer and an investment banker conduct **preunderwriting conferences** to discuss such basic questions as the amount to be raised, the type of securities to issue, and the nature of their agreement. After the parties agree that a flotation will occur, the investment banker conducts an investigation of the issuer. Thus, a firm of public accountants is engaged to audit the issuer and to assist in preparing the registration statement to be filed with the SEC. Attorneys are hired as advisers concerning the legal issues, and other experts are consulted as necessary.

    a.   The investment banker that serves as the managing underwriter will also analyze the issuer's financial condition and prospects.

    b.   The result of this phase is an agreement establishing all of the terms of the arrangement, including the amount of capital to be raised, the type of securities, and the basis for determining the offering price.

3. The next step is the filing of a registration statement with the SEC. This process may be necessary whether the issue is an initial public offering (see the next subunit) or a **seasoned issue** (one made by a company whose securities are already publicly traded).

4. Determining the offering price of the securities is crucial. For a seasoned issue, the offering price may be pegged to the price of the existing securities, such as the market price of stock or the yield on bonds. For example, an issue of common stock may be priced at a certain percentage below the closing price on the last day of the registration period.

    a.   The **spread** is the difference between the price paid by the investment banker (underwriter) and the price paid by investors. It provides a profit and covers the costs of underwriting.

    b.   However, if the closing price falls below a certain price (the **upset price**), the agreement is voided.

    c.   The issuer and the investment banker obviously have divergent interests regarding price. The investment banker wants to set a price as low as possible to facilitate sale, whereas the issuer desires as high a price as possible to raise the maximum amount of funds. For seasoned issues, recent market prices may provide clear guidelines, but the problem may be acute for an initial public offering.

5. A single investment banker ordinarily does not underwrite an entire issue of securities unless the amount is relatively small. To share the risk of overpricing the issue or of a market decline during the offering period, the investment banker (the **lead or managing underwriter**) forms an **underwriting syndicate** with other firms. The members of the syndicate share in the underwriting commission, but their risk is limited to the percentage of their participation.

    a.   The formation of a syndicate also improves marketing efficiency by combining the efforts of the firms' selling organizations.

    b.   For a large offering, a **selling group** is also formed. It consists of the members of the syndicate and other dealers who take small shares of the issue (**participations**) from the original underwriters. Accordingly, the syndicate members are in effect wholesalers of the securities, and the additional members of the selling group are retailers.

        1)   The members of the selling group agree to subscribe to the new issue at the public offering price minus the **concession** they receive as a commission. They also agree not to sell below the public offering price.

    c.   While the public offering is in force, but not for more than approximately 30 days, the lead underwriter customarily attempts to maintain a stable price for the securities by placing orders to buy in the market. One incidental effect of this operation is that the certificate numbers of repurchased securities are examined to determine whether members of the selling group have violated their agreement not to sell below the public offering price.

6.   **Flotation costs**, or the costs of issuing new securities, are relatively lower for large than small issues. These costs include the following:

    a.   The underwriting spread is the difference between the price paid by purchasers and the net amount received by the issuer.

    b.   The issuer incurs expenses for filing fees, taxes, accountants' fees, and attorneys' fees. These costs are essentially fixed.

    c.   The issuer incurs indirect costs because of management time devoted to the issue.

    d.   Announcement of a new issue of seasoned securities usually results in a price decline. One theory is that the announcement is a negative signal to the market. Management may not want to issue new stock when it is undervalued. Moreover, existing owners do not want to share the company's growth with additional owners.

    e.   The **Green Shoe option** allows underwriters to buy additional shares to compensate for oversubscriptions. A cost is involved because the option will be exercised only when the offer price is lower than the market price.

    f.   An offer of unseasoned securities (an initial public offering) tends to be significantly underpriced compared with the price in the after market.

7.   Flotation costs tend to be greater for common stock than for preferred stock and for stocks than for bonds.

8.   Stop and review! You have completed the outline for this subunit. Study multiple-choice questions 1 through 10 beginning on page 199.

B.   **Initial Public Offerings (IPOs).** A firm's first issuance of securities to the public is an initial public offering. The process by which a closely held corporation issues new securities to the public is called **going public**. When a firm goes public, it issues its stock on a **new issue** or **initial public offering market**.

1.   Advantages of going public include

    a.   The ability to raise additional funds
    b.   The establishment of the firm's value in the market
    c.   An increase in the liquidity of the firm's stock

2.   Disadvantages of going public include

    a.   Costs of the reporting requirements of the SEC and other agencies

    b.   Access to the company's operating data by competing firms

    c.   Access to net worth information of major shareholders

    d.   Limitations on self-dealing by corporate insiders, such as officers and major shareholders

    e.   Pressure from outside shareholders for earnings growth

      f.   Stock prices that do not accurately reflect the true net worth of the company

      g.   Loss of control by management as ownership is diversified

      h.   Need for improved management control as operations expand

      i.   Increased shareholder servicing costs

3.   To have its stock listed (have it traded on a stock exchange), the firm must apply to a stock exchange, pay a fee, and fulfill the exchange's requirements for membership.

      a.   Included in the requirements for membership is disclosure of the firm's financial data.

4.   Once the decision to make an initial public offering has been made, the questions are similar to those for seasoned issues: the amount to be raised, the type of securities to sell, and the method of sale. For example, the following matters should be considered in selecting the type of securities to issue:

      a.   Should fixed charges be avoided? The issuance of debt would create fixed charges.

      b.   Is a maturity date on the security preferable, or is permanent capital more attractive?

      c.   Does the firm want a cushion to protect itself from losses to the firm's creditors?

      d.   How quickly and easily does the firm want to raise the capital?

      e.   Is the firm concerned about losing control of the company?

      f.   How does the cost of underwriting differ among the types of securities?

5.   The company's next step is to prepare and file an SEC registration statement and prospectus.

      a.   The Securities Act of 1933 prohibits the offer or sale through the use of the mails or any means of interstate commerce of any security unless a registration statement for that security is in effect or an exemption from registration is applicable. Thus, any offer or sale of a security to the public requires registration unless a specific exemption applies.

            1)   A **registration statement** is a complete disclosure to the SEC of all material information with respect to the issuance of the specific securities.

            2)   The purpose of registration is to provide adequate and accurate disclosure of financial and other pertinent information with which potential investors may evaluate the merits of the securities. Registration calls for

                a)   A description of the registrant's business and property, the significant provisions of the security to be offered for sale, and its relationship to the registrant's other securities

                b)   Information about management

                c)   The most recent audited financial statements

                d)   Disclosure of the principal purposes for which the offering's proceeds will be used

            3)   The SEC does not make any judgment on the financial health of an investment or guarantee the accuracy of the information contained in the registration statement.

                a)   Registration does not insure investors against loss.

4) In response to the Emerging Company Marketplace initiative of the American Stock Exchange (Amex), the SEC has proposed rules to simplify the process for small businesses to register securities.

    a) Simpler financial reporting forms are being devised.

    b) The rules would facilitate active auction-type trading of stock of emerging companies on a branch of the Amex. This could provide greater access to capital than the over-the-counter markets.

b. The registration process has three distinct periods.

    1) During the **prefiling period**, the issuer may engage in preliminary negotiations and agreements with underwriters. Offers to buy or sell securities are prohibited during this period.

    2) The **waiting period** begins when the registration statement is filed. During this time, selling a security is still illegal; however, making an oral offer to buy or sell a security is not.

        a) Information may be published during the waiting period in **tombstone ads**. These ads must state that they are not offers and must identify

            i) The name and the business of the issuer

            ii) The amount of securities being offered and the price if known

            iii) The approximate date when the offering will be made

            iv) The party by whom the orders will be executed and from whom a prospectus may be obtained

        b) Dealers may make offers to buy from underwriters subject to later acceptance.

        c) There are no restrictions on oral offers made during the waiting period. Moreover, a **preliminary prospectus** may be distributed. It contains information similar to that in a registration statement.

            i) The outside front cover page of the preliminary prospectus must bear, in red ink and printed in large type, the title "preliminary prospectus," the date of issuance, and a required legend.

            ii) The legend states, among other things, that a registration statement has been filed, it has not yet become effective, the securities may not be sold and offers to buy may not be accepted prior to the time the registration statement becomes effective, and the prospectus shall not constitute an offer to sell or the solicitation of an offer to buy.

            iii) A preliminary prospectus is called a **red-herring prospectus**.

        d) The SEC uses the 20-day waiting period to review the registration statement. If the registration statement does not substantially comply with the statutory requirements, the SEC will issue detailed comments as to how the statement can be brought into conformity. Any amendments to the registration statement have the effect of starting the 20-day waiting period anew.

        3)   The **post-effective period** begins once a registration statement becomes effective. The underlying securities may then be sold.

             a)   The SEC may issue a **bedbug letter** during the 20-day waiting period. In a bedbug letter, the SEC states that the registration statement is poorly prepared or fails to disclose information adequately.

             b)   An issuer who receives a bedbug letter must either redraft the registration statement or cancel the public offering.

             c)   If the registration is not rewritten, the SEC will issue a stop order preventing registration.

             d)   A registration becomes effective 20 days (the waiting period) after it is filed, unless the SEC accelerates the effective date or issues a bedbug letter.

   c.   A **prospectus** must be furnished to any interested investor. Its purpose is to supply sufficient facts to make an informed investment decision.

        1)   The prospectus contains material information (financial and otherwise) with respect to the offering and the issuer.

        2)   An issuer can amend a prospectus by filing 10 copies of the modified document with the SEC.

        3)   The Securities Act of 1933 requires that any prospectus still in use more than 9 months after its effective date be updated so that the information contained in the prospectus is not more than 16 months old.

             a)   Developments after the effective date that render the existing prospectus misleading impose an obligation to update the prospectus without regard to the 9-month period.

        4)   A disclaimer must be printed on the outside front cover of the prospectus in boldface type. It states that the securities have not been approved or disapproved by the SEC and that the SEC has not passed upon the accuracy or adequacy of the prospectus. It also states that any representation to the contrary is a criminal offense.

   d.   The entire allotment of securities ordinarily is made available for purchase on the effective date of the registration statement. An exception is a shelf registration.

        1)   In a **shelf registration** under the SEC's Rule 415, a master registration statement is filed for securities that the company reasonably expects to sell within 2 years. However, they are put "on the shelf" until the most opportune time for offering is determined.

             a)   Shelf registrations allow issuers to respond rapidly in volatile markets and to reduce flotation costs.

        2)   A shelf registration is available only to large, well-established issuers.

        3)   The information in the master registration statement must be updated with a short-form statement just prior to a new issue.

   e.   The final price of the stock will be set at the close of the day on which the SEC clears the issuance of the stock.

   f.   Investment bankers must pay for underwritten stock by the fourth day after the offering's commencement. Investors must pay by the tenth day.

6. A public issue of securities may be sold through a cash offer or a rights offer.

   a. A **cash offer** follows the procedures previously described.

   b. A **rights offer** gives existing shareholders an option to purchase **new shares** before they are offered to the public. If the corporate charter provides for a preemptive right, a rights offer is mandatory.

      1) The rights or options are evidenced by warrants that state the terms of the arrangement, including subscription price, the number of rights required to purchase one share, and the expiration date. Shareholders may exercise the rights, sell them, or allow them to expire.

      2) Under a **standby underwriting** arrangement, an underwriter may agree to buy undersubscribed shares. However, granting other shareholders an **oversubscription privilege** reduces the probability of needing to resort to the underwriter.

   c. A cash offer is made to any interested party, whereas a rights offer is made to current security holders. Debt is normally sold by cash offer, but equity securities may be sold by either means.

   d. An IPO necessarily involves a cash offer because, if existing security holders desired to purchase the new issue, no public offer would be made.

   e. A seasoned equity issue may be sold in a cash offer or a rights offer.

7. Stop and review! You have completed the outline for this subunit. Study multiple-choice questions 11 through 29 beginning on page 202.

C. **Private Placements**. A private placement is exempt from registration with the SEC. It involves the sale of securities to a very few parties, such as institutional investors. A private placement of stocks or bonds is allowed, but bond placements are more common.

   1. A typical private placement is made by selling the securities directly to a financial institution.

      a. Advantages of private placement include lower flotation costs and the ease with which the issue may be sold.

      b. A significant disadvantage of private placement is that the securities are not registered with the SEC and cannot be sold without registration except to another large, sophisticated buyer.

         1) The SEC permits an entity with a portfolio of at least $100,000,000 to purchase and sell private placement securities.

   2. Direct business loans with maturities of 15 years or less are called term loans. If they have longer maturities, they are considered private placements.

      a. Private placements are likely to have more restrictive covenants than public issues and are usually easier to renegotiate in case of default. Moreover, private placements typically have higher interest rates.

3.   The SEC promulgated Regulation D to govern private placements. Rules 504, 505, and 506 under Regulation D describe the exemptions from registration.

    a.   Three procedural rules must usually be complied with to qualify for a Regulation D exemption.

        1)   No general advertising or soliciting is permitted.

        2)   The issuer must exercise reasonable care to ensure that purchasers are not underwriters and that such purchasers are buying strictly for their own investment.

        3)   The SEC must be notified within 15 days of the first offering.

    b.   The rules provide exemption only for the transactions in which securities are offered or sold by the issuer, not for the securities themselves.

        1)   The securities are restricted securities. Resale must be after registration or under some exemption.

        2)   Immediate rollover of the securities is precluded.

    c.   **Rule 504**. Qualified issuers may sell up to $1,000,000 of securities during a 12-month period to any number of purchasers without registration or specific financial information being provided, if other applicable conditions are met.

        1)   No more than $500,000 of the securities may be offered or sold without registration under state law.

        2)   Sales to directors, officers, and employees are not included in the $1,000,000 limitation.

        3)   The restrictions on advertising and resale do not apply if the offering is made only in states with laws requiring registration of the securities and disclosure to investors prior to sale.

            a)   Compliance with these laws is required.

        4)   Unaccredited and accredited investors may purchase the securities.

        5)   The issuer must advise each purchaser that the securities have not been registered and therefore cannot be sold unless they are subsequently registered or an exemption from registration is available.

    d.   **Rule 505** provides exemption from registration to all issuers other than investment companies for sales of securities up to $5,000,000 in any 12-month period.

        1)   The aggregate offering price must not exceed $7,500,000.

        2)   An unlimited number of **accredited investors** may purchase the issue. They include

            a)   Banks, insurance companies, registered investment companies, business development companies, and certain employee benefit plans within the meaning of Title I of the Employee Retirement Income Security Act with total assets in excess of $5,000,000

            b)   Private placement development companies

       c)   Charitable organizations with assets in excess of $5,000,000

       d)   Directors, executive officers, and general partners of the issuer who purchase at least $150,000 of securities being offered as long as the total purchase price does not exceed 20% of the purchaser's net worth

       e)   Any person who had an income over $200,000 in each of the last 2 years and who reasonably expects such an income in the current year

       f)   Any person with a net worth of at least $1,000,000

   3)   The issuer must reasonably believe that no more than 35 investors/offerees are nonaccredited.

       a)   If the offering is to any nonaccredited investors, prior to the sale all investors, whether or not accredited, must be furnished with material information about the issuer, its business, and the securities being offered.

  e.   **Rule 506** provides a safe harbor for limited offers and sales without regard to dollar amount. The requirements are as follows:

   1)   The amount that may be raised is unlimited.

   2)   The offering may be purchased by an unlimited number of accredited investors.

   3)   The issuer must reasonably believe that no more than 35 investors/offerees are nonaccredited.

       a)   If the offering involves any nonaccredited investor, prior to the sale all investors, whether accredited or not, must be furnished with material information about the issuer, its business, and the securities being offered.

       b)   Each nonaccredited investor (either alone or with his/her purchaser representative) must demonstrate to the issuer the knowledge and experience in financial and business matters needed to evaluate the merits and risks of the prospective investment. (This requirement is ordinarily met by using a purchaser questionnaire.)

   4)   The issuer usually requires the purchaser to sign an investment letter stating that (s)he is buying for investment only and not for resale.

       a)   For this reason, shares issued pursuant to Rule 506 are commonly referred to as lettered stock.

4.   Stop and review! You have completed the outline for this subunit. Study multiple-choice questions 30 through 37 beginning on page 208.

D.   Other Exemptions from SEC Registration

1.   The following securities are exempt from SEC registration:

    a.   Securities of domestic governments used for a governmental purpose

    b.   Securities of not-for-profit organizations

    c.   Securities of domestic banks and savings and loan associations

    d.   Securities of issuers regulated by the Interstate Commerce Commission

    e.   Securities issued by a receiver or trustee in bankruptcy with prior court approval

    f.   Insurance policies and annuity contracts issued by state-regulated insurance companies

    g.   Securities issued with respect to a corporate reorganization

    h.   Securities issued solely for exchange with the issuer's existing security holders if no commission is paid

        1)   Thus, stock dividends and stock splits are usually exempt.

        2)   Also, securities issued in mergers and other reorganizations are exempt if no cash is involved and the securities are given solely for other securities.

    i.   **Short-term commercial paper.** The Securities Act of 1933 exempts from registration any note, draft, or banker's acceptance, issued to acquire working capital, that has a maturity of not more than 9 months when issued.

        1)   The exemption is not available if the proceeds are to be used for permanent purposes, such as acquisition of a manufacturing plant, or if the paper is of a type not ordinarily purchased by the general public.

2.   **Intrastate Offerings.** Any security of an issue offered and sold only to persons residing within a single state is exempt if the issuer is a resident or a corporation doing business in that state.

    a.   The intrastate offering exemption is intended to apply to local issues representing local financing by local persons.

    b.   This exemption does not apply if any offeree, who need not be a purchaser, is not a resident of the state in which the issuer is a resident.

    c.   The courts and the SEC interpret the intrastate offering exemption strictly.

    d.   The SEC's **Rule 147** provides a safe harbor for qualifying for the exemption. It requires that

        1)   The issuer be incorporated or organized in the state

        2)   All of the offerees and purchasers be residents of the state

        3)   The issuer derive at least 80% of its gross revenue from the state

        4)   At least 80% of the issuer's assets be located within the state

        5)   At least 80% of the net proceeds from the issuance be used in the state

        6)   During the 12-month sale period and for 9 months thereafter, the securities not be resold to nonresidents

        7)   Safeguards against interstate distributions be established, such as

            a)   Placing a legend on the certificate stating that the securities are unregistered securities and resales are limited to residents only

              b)   Obtaining a written statement of residence from each purchaser

    e.   State law may require state registration prior to the intrastate offering.

3.   **Regulation A** permits an issuer to offer up to $5,000,000 of securities in any 12-month period without the normal registration process.

    a.   The SEC integrates offerings; e.g., three offerings of $2,000,000 each would not qualify for exemption under Regulation A if issued within one 12-month period. Each would qualify if issued over 3 years.

        1)   Otherwise exempt offerings are integrated if they constitute a unitary plan of financing, they concern the same class of securities, they serve the same general purpose, and they are priced similarly.

        2)   The integration rules also apply to securities issued under Regulation D.

        3)   The SEC has adopted a rule under which an offering is not integrated unless it is made within 6 months before or after another offering.

        4)   EXAMPLE: Cap Corp. issues $4,500,000 in cumulative 6% preferred stock on March 1, 1997. A Regulation A exemption is unavailable for any further issue of more than $500,000 until September 1, 1997.

    b.   Regulation A filings are less detailed, time consuming, and costly than full registration statements.

        1)   A formal registration statement and prospectus are not required.

        2)   An offering circular (a short-form registration statement) must be filed with the SEC's regional office.

        3)   The offering circular must be provided to offerees and purchasers of the underlying securities.

    c.   In addition to being available to issuer companies, Regulation A is available on a limited basis (up to $1,500,000) to shareholders who desire to make resales of their securities but cannot find another exemption from registration.

4.   Stop and review! You have completed the outline for this subunit. Study multiple-choice questions 38 through 43 beginning on page 210.

E.   Commercial Banking. Commercial banks have traditionally offered savings (time deposit) and checking (demand deposit) accounts and served as lenders for a variety of purposes. Thus, they have been instrumental in the Federal Reserve's efforts to manage the money supply. However, other financial institutions have emerged that perform such functions. Furthermore, commercial banks have expanded their operations to include stock brokerage, insurance, and other services.

1.   Under the **Glass-Steagall Act**, commercial banks are not permitted to provide investment banking services. This limitation puts U.S. institutions at a competitive disadvantage in global markets. Accordingly, commercial banks are seeking the repeal of the Glass-Steagall Act.

2.   Commercial bank lending is very significant to firms needing sources of short-term and intermediate-term financing. It is second only to trade credit as a source of financing.

    a.   Characteristics of commercial bank loans

        1)   The majority of lending by commercial banks is on a short-term basis. Many short-term loans are written for a term of 90 days.

        2)   The loan is obtained by signing a promissory note. Repayment is made in a lump sum at the maturity date, or installments are paid throughout the loan's life.

3) A **line of credit** may be extended to a borrowing firm. An amount is credited to the borrower's checking account for business use. At the maturity date, the checking account is charged the amount constituting repayment, usually principal and interest.

   a) A revolving credit agreement (committed line of credit) imposes a legal obligation on the bank, but the borrower pays a commitment fee.

4) Commercial banks typically require compensating balances in checking accounts equal to some percentage of the loan. The result is an increase in the effective interest rate.

5) The interest rate at which the bank will lend to a firm will depend on the firm's financial strength. The interest rate may be anywhere from the **prime interest rate** to 2 or 3 points above it.

6) The cost of a bank loan may be determined in several ways. **Simple interest** is based on the borrowed amount and is paid at the end of the loan term. **Discounted interest** is based on the borrowed amount but is paid in advance. The add-on interest rate for an installment loan equals the interest divided by the average balance.

   a) Simple interest rate for a 1-year loan: $\dfrac{Interest}{Borrowed\ amount}$

   b) Discounted interest rate for a 1-year loan:

   $$\dfrac{Interest}{Borrowed\ amount\ -\ Interest}$$

   c) Add-on installment interest rate for a 1-year loan:

   $$\dfrac{Interest}{Average\ borrowed\ amount}$$

b. When choosing a commercial lender, a borrower should consider the following:

   1) The bank's policy toward risk

   2) The additional services and counseling the bank provides to customers

   3) The degree of support a bank will provide in times of financial distress. Will the bank pressure a firm to repay its loans on time or negotiate extensions?

   4) The degree of loan specialization provided by a bank. For example, a bank may specialize in loans to companies in a given line of business.

   5) The size of the bank and its lending capacity. Thus, given that a bank cannot lend more than 15% of its capital to one customer, a large company ordinarily will choose a large bank.

   6) The financial strength of the bank

3. Stop and review! You have completed the outline for this subunit. Study multiple-choice questions 44 through 50 beginning on page 212.

MULTIPLE-CHOICE QUESTIONS

A. Investment Banking

1. An issuer of new securities selects an investment banker by either

- A. A negotiated deal or competitive bids.
- B. Best efforts or a firm commitment.
- C. A general cash offer or a rights offer.
- D. A competitive bid or a firm commitment.

The correct answer is (A). *(Publisher)*
REQUIRED: The methods an issuer of new securities uses when selecting an investment banker.
DISCUSSION: An issuer of new securities ordinarily selects an investment banker in a negotiated deal because of the costs incurred in learning about the issuer and setting an issue price. The probability of closing a deal is high in a negotiated deal, so the banker is willing to incur such costs. On the other hand, the likelihood of closing the deal is smaller in a competitive bid system, so the banker is less willing to take the risk.
Answer (B) is incorrect because these are methods of issuing securities through an underwriter. Answer (C) is incorrect because these are the types of offers through which a public issue of securities is sold. Answer (D) is incorrect because an issuer selects an investment banker by means of a negotiated deal or a competitive bid.

2. Which of the following services do investment bankers not perform for securities issuers?

- A. Consultation about types of securities to issue and the procedure for issuing them.
- B. Pricing and selling of the new issue.
- C. Market stabilization services.
- D. Providing a line of credit to the issuer prior to issuance of the securities.

The correct answer is (D). *(Publisher)*
REQUIRED: The service not provided by investment bankers to securities issuers.
DISCUSSION: Commercial bankers, not investment bankers, provide lines of credit to their clients. The traditional role of investment bankers includes determining the method of issuing the securities and the price to be charged, distributing the securities, providing expert advice, and performing a certification function. Additionally, during the public offering, the lead underwriter attempts to maintain a stable price for the securities by placing orders to buy in the market. The placement of orders occurs for approximately 30 days and provides market stabilization.
Answers (A), (B), and (C) are incorrect because all are services provided by investment bankers to securities issuers.

3. Which of the following is a group of investment bankers that collectively underwrite a securities issue?

- A. Amalgamate.
- B. Conglomerate.
- C. Green Shoe.
- D. Syndicate.

The correct answer is (D). *(Publisher)*
REQUIRED: The name of the group of investment bankers that collectively underwrite a securities issue.
DISCUSSION: An underwriting syndicate is a group of investment bankers that combine to limit their risk by the percentage of their participation. The formation of a syndicate also improves marketing efficiency by combining the efforts of the firms' selling organization.
Answer (A) is incorrect because an amalgamate is used to describe a uniting of different elements rather than those possessing similar characteristics. Answer (B) is incorrect because a conglomerate is made up of parts from various sources and of various kinds. Answer (C) is incorrect because a Green Shoe option allows underwriters to buy additional shares to compensate for oversubscriptions.

4. All of the following are examples of services normally offered by investment bankers except

    A. Securities sales.

    B. Consultation on the offering price.

    C. Underwriting.

    D. Checking accounts to corporations.

The correct answer is (D). *(Publisher)*
    REQUIRED: The service not offered by investment bankers.
    DISCUSSION: Investment bankers provide assistance with selling securities, determining an offering price, and underwriting securities in a firm commitment. They do not usually offer checking accounts to corporations but instead serve as intermediaries between businesses and providers of capital.
    Answers (A), (B), and (C) are incorrect because all are examples of services normally offered by investment bankers.

5. In what way do investment bankers make money under best efforts offerings?

    A. By receiving the difference between the purchasing price and the offering price.

    B. By receiving a commission.

    C. By receiving a discount of the difference between the purchasing price and the offering price.

    D. By purchasing unsold securities for their own account.

The correct answer is (B). *(Publisher)*
    REQUIRED: The form of compensation an investment banker receives under best efforts offerings.
    DISCUSSION: Best efforts sales of securities provide no guarantee that the securities will be sold or that enough cash will be raised. In this type of offering, the investment banker receives commissions and is obligated to use its best efforts to sell the securities.
    Answer (A) is incorrect because the difference between the purchasing price and the offering price (the spread or discount) is the compensation received by the investment banker under a firm commitment. Answer (C) is incorrect because the difference between the purchasing price and the offering price is the discount, which is used to compensate the underwriter in a firm commitment. Answer (D) is incorrect because the investment bankers do not guarantee sale of securities under the best efforts method.

6. An underwriter may purchase more shares at the offering price from an issuer under what kind of provision?

    A. Aftermarket provision.

    B. Green Shoe provision.

    C. Privileged subscription provision.

    D. Red-herring provision.

The correct answer is (B). *(Publisher)*
    REQUIRED: The provision that allows underwriters to purchase more shares at the offering price from an issuer.
    DISCUSSION: A Green Shoe provision permits underwriters to buy additional shares to compensate for oversubscriptions. Although the provision is a benefit to the underwriting syndicate, it is a cost to the issuer because the option to buy will be exercised only when the offer price is lower than the market price.
    Answer (A) is incorrect because aftermarket provision is a nonsense term. The aftermarket is simply the market for the shares after their initial issuance. Answer (C) is incorrect because a privileged subscription provision reflects the preemptive right of current security owners to purchase a proportionate share of the new issue. Answer (D) is incorrect because red herring is the term given to the preliminary prospectus because of the red, bold lettering on the cover.

7. An underwriter buys securities for less than the offering price and bears the risk of not selling the entire issue under which of the following methods?

   A. Best efforts.

   B. Firm commitment.

   C. General cash offer.

   D. Competitive bid.

The correct answer is (B). *(Publisher)*

   REQUIRED: The method of issuing securities whereby the underwriter bears the risk of not selling the entire issue.

   DISCUSSION: Under the firm commitment method, the investment banker underwrites the securities. On a practical level, the underwriter purchases the entire issue at less than the offering price and bears the risk of not being able to sell it. Because this method involves significant risk, the underwriter often forms an underwriting syndicate with other firms to minimize the risk.

   Answer (A) is incorrect because, under best efforts, the investment banker does not bear the risk of not selling the entire issue because (s)he is under no obligation to sell the securities. Answer (C) is incorrect because a general cash offer occurs when stock is sold to interested investors and usually involves an investment banker only when the stock is sold to the public. Answer (D) is incorrect because a competitive bid is a method for selecting an investment banker.

8. All of the following are costs associated with issuing new securities except

   A. Price or underwriter's discount.

   B. Underpricing.

   C. Indirect expenses.

   D. Premiums on securities issued.

The correct answer is (D). *(Publisher)*

   REQUIRED: The various costs associated with issuing new securities.

   DISCUSSION: A premium on securities issued is part of the proceeds received by the issuer, not a cost of issuance. The costs of issuing new securities can be attributed to the spread or discount, direct expenses, indirect expenses, price declines associated with an issue of seasoned securities, a Green Shoe option, and underpricing in connection with initial public offerings. The spread or discount is the difference between the price paid by purchasers and the net amount received by the issuer. Direct expenses include such items as filing fees, taxes, accountants' fees, and attorneys' fees. Indirect costs are incurred because of management time devoted to the issue. With a new issue of seasoned securities, the announcement usually results in a price decline possibly because it is perceived as a negative signal. A Green Shoe option allows underwriters to buy additional shares to compensate for oversubscriptions. Lastly, in an initial public offering, the offer tends to be underpriced.

   Answers (A), (B), and (C) are incorrect because they are all costs associated with issuing new securities.

9. Why would a corporation prefer NOT to have its securities issued by an underwriter?

   A. Underwriters bear some risk of loss on the securities sale.

   B. Underwriters provide cash proceeds to the issuer sooner through best efforts sales.

   C. Underwriting provides some assurance of the quality of the issue to potential investors.

   D. A registration with the SEC is not required.

The correct answer is (D). *(Publisher)*

   REQUIRED: The reason for not having a corporation's securities issue underwritten.

   DISCUSSION: Use of an underwriter has no bearing on whether SEC registration is required. When an investment banker underwrites a securities issue, (s)he agrees to purchase the shares for less than the offering price and bears the risk of not being able to resell them. Under this type of deal, a firm commitment is entered into between the issuing company and the investment banker. Cash proceeds are obtained sooner because the underwriter buys the entire issue. Furthermore, the underwriter provides assurance of the level of quality of the issue, which attracts potential investors.

   Answers (A), (B), and (C) are incorrect because all are benefits achieved by having a securities issue underwritten.

10. A subsequent public securities issue of a company is called a(n)

- A. Initial public offering.
- B. Seasoned equity issue.
- C. Unseasoned equity issue.
- D. Private placement.

The correct answer is (B). *(Publisher)*

REQUIRED: The term for a subsequent public securities issue.

DISCUSSION: A seasoned issue is one made by a company whose securities are already publicly traded. In a seasoned issue of common stock, a cash offer or a rights offer may be used.

Answer (A) is incorrect because an initial public offering is an unseasoned issue. It is a firm's first public issuance of securities. Answer (C) is incorrect because an unseasoned equity issue applies to a company issuing shares publicly for the first time. Answer (D) is incorrect because a private placement involves the sale of securities to a very few parties, such as institutional investors.

B. Initial Public Offerings

11. When issuing securities to the public, management must first

- A. File an SEC registration form.
- B. Distribute copies of the preliminary prospectus.
- C. Distribute copies of the final prospectus.
- D. Obtain board of director approval.

The correct answer is (D). *(Publisher)*

REQUIRED: The first step management must take when issuing securities to the public.

DISCUSSION: Prior to issuing securities to the public, management must first obtain approval from the board of directors. This step is performed during the preunderwriting conferences, in which the prospective issuer and the investment banker discuss the amount to be raised, the type of securities to issue, and the nature of the agreement.

Answer (A) is incorrect because management files an SEC registration form after the preunderwriting conferences have transpired. Answer (B) is incorrect because the preliminary prospectus is distributed during the waiting period that commences when the registration statement is filed. Answer (C) is incorrect because the final prospectus is distributed after the registration statement becomes effective.

12. When a firm is going public, its first public securities issue is called a(n)

- A. Rights issue.
- B. General cash offer.
- C. Initial public offering.
- D. Seasoned issue.

The correct answer is (C). *(Publisher)*

REQUIRED: The firm's first issuance of securities.

DISCUSSION: An initial public offering (IPO), also referred to as an unseasoned new issue, is the firm's first issuance of securities to the public. Essentially, all IPOs are cash offers because the shares are being sold to the public since the existing shareholders do not want to buy them.

Answer (A) is incorrect because a rights issue, or rather a rights offer, gives existing shareholders an option to purchase new shares before they are offered to the public. Answer (B) is incorrect because the appropriate title for the firm's first issuance of securities is IPO, not general cash offer, even though the IPO is a cash offer. Answer (D) is incorrect because a seasoned issue refers to an issue by a firm whose securities are already publicly traded.

13. A privately owned business might decide to issue stock to the public ("go public") in order to

- A. Reduce its cost of filing reports with the regulatory authorities.
- B. Assure that its net worth cannot be estimated by the public.
- C. Increase the owners' control of the firm.
- D. Establish a value for the firm.

The correct answer is (D). *(CIA 1190 IV-56)*

REQUIRED: The reason a privately owned business might decide to issue stock to the public.

DISCUSSION: Selling shares to the public is a means of establishing the stock price and thus the value of the firm. One advantage is that it provides an accurate appraisal for estate tax purposes when a shareholder dies. Another is that stock options granted to employees can be more readily valued, and employees prefer to own options or shares that are publicly traded.

Answer (A) is incorrect because going public raises (not reduces) the cost of reporting. Answer (B) is incorrect because going public raises (not reduces) the degree of disclosure of information to the public. Answer (C) is incorrect because going public reduces (not increases) control.

14. Disadvantages of going public include all of the following except

- A. Access to the company's operating data by competing firms.
- B. Pressure from outside shareholders for earnings growth.
- C. Need for improved management control.
- D. Decreased shareholder servicing costs.

The correct answer is (D). *(Publisher)*

REQUIRED: The exception to the disadvantages of going public.

DISCUSSION: When a company goes public, it is subject to reporting requirements that do not apply to privately held entities. Because reports filed with the SEC are in the public domain, competitors will have greater access to information about the company. Moreover, pressure from outside shareholders for earnings growth increases due to the increase in the number of shareholders who want returns on their investment. Additional funds enable operations to expand, but increased management control is needed to monitor the expansion. As the number of shareholders increases, the costs to meet their informational needs increase rather than decrease.

Answers (A), (B), and (C) are incorrect because they are all disadvantages of going public.

15. To list a stock, a firm must do all of the following except

- A. Apply to a stock exchange.
- B. File a registration statement.
- C. Fulfill the exchange's requirements for membership.
- D. Pay a fee.

The correct answer is (B). *(Publisher)*

REQUIRED: The step not required of a firm listing stock on an exchange.

DISCUSSION: To trade a stock on an exchange, a firm must pay a fee, apply to an exchange, and fulfill that exchange's requirements. Included in the requirements of a stock exchange is disclosure of the firm's financial data. Filing a registration statement is an SEC, not a stock exchange, requirement.

Answers (A), (C), and (D) are incorrect because they are all required in order to list a stock on a stock exchange.

16. An advantage of issuing new securities to the public is

- A. Stock prices accurately reflect the true net worth of the company.
- B. Pressure is applied from outside shareholders for earnings growth.
- C. The liquidity of the firm's stock increases.
- D. Self-dealing by corporate insiders is limited.

The correct answer is (C). *(Publisher)*

REQUIRED: The advantage of issuing new securities to the public.

DISCUSSION: A firm's first issuance of securities to the public increases the liquidity of the firm's stock. Other advantages of going public include the ability of the firm to raise additional funds and the establishment of the firm's value in the market.

Answer (A) is incorrect because stock prices do not accurately reflect the true net worth of the company, which is a disadvantage of going public. Answers (B) and (D) are incorrect because both are disadvantages rather than advantages of going public.

17. Which of the following questions should a firm NOT consider in determining the type of securities to issue?

    A. Can the firm afford issuance costs?

    B. Should fixed charges be avoided?

    C. Is the firm concerned about losing control of the company?

    D. How quickly does the firm wish to raise the necessary capital?

The correct answer is (A). *(Publisher)*

REQUIRED: The question a firm should NOT consider in deciding the type of securities to issue.

DISCUSSION: Issuance (flotation) costs are ordinarily netted against the issuance proceeds. Because they are unavoidable, the decision to issue securities is a decision to incur issuance costs. Thus, the determination of the type of securities to issue concerns, in part, the amount of issuance costs, not whether to incur them. Additional concerns include such matters as the amount of fixed charges, maturity dates, cushions to protect the firm from losses to creditors, immediacy of the need for capital, and loss of control.

Answers (B), (C), and (D) are incorrect because they are all questions that should be considered by the firm before issuing a certain type of security.

18. Which of the following is the correct order of events necessary to issue securities?

    A. Filing of a registration statement, prefiling period, waiting period, and post-effective period.

    B. Prefiling period, filing of a registration statement, waiting period, and post-effective period.

    C. Post-effective period, prefiling period, period in which registration statement is filed, waiting period.

    D. Period in which registration statement is filed, post-effective filing period, waiting period, prefiling period.

The correct answer is (B). *(Publisher)*

REQUIRED: The order of events concerning the issuance of securities.

DISCUSSION: During the period before the registration statement is filed, the firm may negotiate with potential investors, but it may not sell securities. This period is the prefiling period. Once the registration statement is filed, the company may not sell securities until the SEC has approved the offering. The waiting period is the time beginning when the registration statement is filed and ending before the sale of the securities. During this time, the company may make oral offers to sell, and investors may make oral agreements to buy. The securities, however, may not be sold until the post-effective period.

Answer (A) is incorrect because the prefiling period is before the registration statement is filed. Answer (C) is incorrect because the post-effective period is the last, not the first, period. Answer (D) is incorrect because the waiting period is after the registration statement is filed and before the post-effective period.

19. A complete disclosure to the SEC of all material information with respect to the issuance of the specific securities is a

    A. Red-herring prospectus.

    B. Prospectus.

    C. Registration statement.

    D. Preliminary prospectus.

The correct answer is (C). *(Publisher)*

REQUIRED: The document that discloses to the SEC all material information regarding a specific securities issuance.

DISCUSSION: The Securities Act of 1933 does not allow the sale or offer of a security to the public unless the firm has filed a registration statement. A registration statement is a complete disclosure to the SEC of all material information with respect to the issuance of the specific securities. Its purpose is to provide adequate and accurate disclosure of financial and other pertinent information so that potential investors may evaluate the security fairly.

Answers (A), (B) and (D) are incorrect because a preliminary prospectus (red-herring prospectus) and a prospectus are sent to prospective investors, not the SEC.

20. A preliminary prospectus of a potential issuing company issued during the SEC waiting period contains

A. The same information as a final prospectus except for proof of SEC approval.

B. The same information as a final prospectus except that it states it is a red-herring.

C. Financial information that is limited and red writing expressing that it is preliminary.

D. Similar information to the final prospectus but without the approval of the SEC and the price of the security.

The correct answer is (D). *(Publisher)*
REQUIRED: The components of a preliminary prospectus of a potential issuing company.
DISCUSSION: The preliminary prospectus contains much of the same information as that in the final prospectus. However, because the preliminary prospectus is distributed during the waiting period, it must state that the pending registration statement has not yet become effective. It also differs from the final prospectus because the price of the security is not included.
Answer (A) is incorrect because the information is similar, but not identical, and the price is not included in the preliminary prospectus. Answer (B) is incorrect because the preliminary prospectus lacks the approval of the SEC and does not include the price of the security. Answer (C) is incorrect because the information on the preliminary and the final prospectus is similar, and the SEC approval and price of the security are not components on the preliminary prospectus.

21. The post-effective period begins when the

A. Registration statement becomes effective.

B. Registration statements are filed.

C. Red-herring prospectus is issued.

D. Company decides to go public.

The correct answer is (A). *(Publisher)*
REQUIRED: The time the post-effective period begins.
DISCUSSION: The post-effective period is the period during which the underlying securities may be sold. It begins when the registration statement becomes effective. The registration statement is effective 20 days after it is filed unless a bedbug letter is issued by the SEC or the SEC accelerates the effective date.
Answers (B), (C), and (D) are incorrect because the post-effective period begins when the registration statement becomes effective.

22. A bedbug letter is a letter sent by the

A. IRS stating that the registration statement is poorly prepared.

B. SEC stating that the registration is effective.

C. SEC stating that the registration statement is poorly prepared or fails to disclose information adequately.

D. SEC stating that the registration has been accelerated.

The correct answer is (C). *(Publisher)*
REQUIRED: The definition of a bedbug letter.
DISCUSSION: Registration is effective 20 days after a statement is filed unless the SEC sends a bedbug letter or accelerates the effective date. A bedbug letter tells the firm that its registration statement was poorly prepared or failed to disclose information adequately. The issuer may either redraft the registration statement or cancel the public offering upon receipt of a bedbug letter.
Answer (A) is incorrect because the SEC, not the IRS, issues a bedbug letter. Answer (B) is incorrect because a bedbug letter tells the firm that the registration statement is not effective. Answer (D) is incorrect because a bedbug letter does not accelerate the effective date.

23. A potential investor may obtain information about a firm making a new securities issue from which of the following publications?

    A.   Registration statement sent by its broker.

    B.   Prospectus.

    C.   Letter of comment.

    D.   Regulation A filing.

The correct answer is (B). *(Publisher)*

REQUIRED: The publication from which a potential investor may obtain information about a firm making a new securities issue.

DISCUSSION: A prospectus is distributed to interested investors to provide sufficient facts so they can make informed investment decisions. It contains significant information (financial and otherwise) regarding the offering and the issuer.

Answer (A) is incorrect because the registration statement is sent to the SEC for approval. The prospectus contains most of the information in the registration statement but is designed for interested investors. Answer (C) is incorrect because the letter of comment (bedbug letter) is sent by the SEC to the potential issuing company suggesting changes to the submitted registration statement. Answer (D) is incorrect because Regulation A governs certain issues of less than $5,000,000. A Regulation A filing is submitted to the SEC, not to interested investors.

24. How may a prospectus be modified?

    A.   It cannot be modified.

    B.   By filing 10 copies of the modified document with the SEC.

    C.   By sending a new prospectus to any investor who requests one.

    D.   By printing a new prospectus.

The correct answer is (B). *(Publisher)*

REQUIRED: The modification of a prospectus.

DISCUSSION: A prospectus may be modified by filing 10 copies of the modified document with the SEC. A prospectus that is still in use more than 9 months after its effective date should be updated so that the information contained in it is not more than 16 months old.

Answer (A) is incorrect because a prospectus can be corrected and updated if necessary. Answer (C) is incorrect because a prospectus is modified upon receipt of a bedbug letter from the SEC or the firm's initiative, not an investor's request. Answer (D) is incorrect because a modified prospectus has a 20-day waiting period before becoming effective.

25. Advertisements announcing the availability of new corporate securities issues are known as

    A.   Prospectus ads.

    B.   Red-herring ads.

    C.   Shelf ads.

    D.   Tombstone ads.

The correct answer is (D). *(Publisher)*

REQUIRED: The advertisement that presents the availability of new corporate securities issues.

DISCUSSION: Tombstone ads may be used during and after the waiting period. They include the name and the business of the issuer, the amount of securities being offered, the price of the securities (if known), the approximate date when the offering will be made, and the party executing the orders from whom a prospectus may be obtained.

Answers (A), (B), and (C) are incorrect because a prospectus, a red-herring, and a shelf registration are not advertisements.

26. Why do companies use the shelf registration method to sell securities?

A. Preregistered securities can be brought to market more quickly.

B. The SEC registration process for new securities is not affected.

C. Investment bankers require it.

D. Small companies prefer it.

The correct answer is (A). *(Publisher)*

REQUIRED: The primary reason for using the shelf registration method to sell securities.

DISCUSSION: The SEC's Rule 415 explains that the shelf registration method involves the filing of a master registration statement for securities that the company reasonably expects to sell within 2 years. The company can place such securities "on the shelf" until the most appropriate time for the offering is determined. Because the securities are preregistered, they can be issued quickly in response to volatile markets and thereby reduce flotation costs associated with issuance. The shelf registration method is available only to large, well-established issuers.

Answer (B) is incorrect because the SEC registration process is modified under the shelf registration method. Answer (C) is incorrect because the firm, not the investment banker, determines the registration method. Answer (D) is incorrect because only large companies use shelf registration.

27. Which of the following is **Incorrect** about a rights offer?

A. A rights offer gives shareholders an option to purchase new shares after they are offered to the public at a discounted price.

B. A rights offer gives shareholders an option to purchase new shares before they are offered to the public.

C. If the corporate charter provides for a preemptive right, a rights offer is mandatory.

D. The options are evidenced by warrants.

The correct answer is (A). *(Publisher)*

REQUIRED: The incorrect statement regarding a rights offer.

DISCUSSION: A rights offer is given to existing shareholders as an option to purchase new shares before they are offered to the public, not after they are offered to the public at a discount.

Answer (B) is incorrect because the shareholders are entitled to purchase new shares before they are offered to the public if there is a rights offer. Answer (C) is incorrect because a preemptive right makes a rights offer mandatory. Answer (D) is incorrect because rights or options are evidenced by warrants that state the terms of the arrangement.

28. An underwriter may agree to buy undersubscribed shares under what arrangement?

A. Oversubscription underwriting.

B. Undersubscription underwriting.

C. Standby underwriting.

D. Oversubscription privilege.

The correct answer is (C). *(Publisher)*

REQUIRED: The arrangement under which an underwriter may agree to buy undersubscribed shares.

DISCUSSION: A standby underwriting agreement is the obligation of an underwriter to buy undersubscribed shares. However, the likelihood that the issuer will invoke this agreement may be reduced by granting shareholders an oversubscription privilege, i.e., the right to purchase additional shares, if they become available.

Answers (A) and (B) are incorrect because oversubscription underwriting and undersubscription underwriting are nonsense terms. Answer (D) is incorrect because oversubscription privilege reduces the probability of needing to resort to the underwriter.

29. A rights offer cannot be made to which of the following parties?

A. Nonshareholders.

B. Current security holders.

C. Current common shareholders.

D. Current preferred shareholders.

The correct answer is (A). *(Publisher)*

REQUIRED: The parties to which a rights offer cannot be made.

DISCUSSION: A rights offer is made to current security holders, whereas a cash offer is made to all interested parties. Thus, a rights offer may be made to both common and preferred shareholders, but not to nonshareholders.

Answers (B), (C) and (D) are incorrect because a rights offer is made to existing shareholders.

C. Private Placements

30. A sale of securities to a very few parties that is exempt from registration with the SEC is known as a

- A. Cash offer.
- B. Rights offer.
- C. Private placement.
- D. Shelf registration.

The correct answer is (C). *(Publisher)*

REQUIRED: The sale of securities to a small number of investors that is exempt from registration with the SEC.

DISCUSSION: A private placement is exempt from registration with the SEC. It is typically a sale of securities to a very few parties, such as institutional investors. Private placements are usually accomplished by selling directly to a financial institution and result in lower flotation costs.

Answers (A) and (B) are incorrect because an issue in the form of a cash offer or a rights offer may or may not be exempt. Answer (D) is incorrect because a shelf registration occurs when a master registration statement is filed for securities that the company reasonably expects to sell publicly within 2 years.

31. Which of the following statements is true concerning private placement?

- A. A private placement must be registered with the SEC.
- B. A private placement of stocks is more common than one involving bonds.
- C. Typically a private placement involves selling securities directly to a financial institution.
- D. Bonds are the only type of securities which may be sold by a private placement.

The correct answer is (C). *(Publisher)*

REQUIRED: The true statement concerning private placement sales.

DISCUSSION: A private placement involves a sale of securities, both stocks and bonds, to a few investors. The investors are usually financial institutions. Bond placements are more common, but private placement of stocks or bonds is allowed.

Answer (A) is incorrect because a private placement is not required to be registered with the SEC. Answer (B) is incorrect because the private placement of bonds is more common than that of stocks. Answer (D) is incorrect because both stocks and bonds may be privately placed.

32. Which of the following would not be considered to be a private placement?

- A. A direct business loan with a maturity of 10 years.
- B. A stock sold to only two large financial institutions.
- C. A stock sold to three investors only.
- D. A bond sold to a financial institution.

The correct answer is (A). *(Publisher)*

REQUIRED: The transaction that is NOT a private placement.

DISCUSSION: A private placement involves a sale of securities, both stocks and bonds, to a few investors. The investors are usually financial institutions. A direct business loan with maturity of more than 15 years is considered to be a private placement. A direct business loan with maturity of less than 15 years is considered to be a term loan.

Answers (B), (C), and (D) are incorrect because they are all considered private placements.

33. Which of the following rules does not have to be complied with to qualify for a Regulation D exemption?

- A. The SEC must be notified within 15 days of the first offering.
- B. A registration statement must be submitted to the SEC.
- C. The issuer must exercise reasonable care to ensure that purchasers are not underwriters.
- D. No general advertising or soliciting is permitted.

The correct answer is (B). *(Publisher)*

REQUIRED: The rule not required to qualify for a Regulation D exemption.

DISCUSSION: Regulation D governs private placements. To qualify for a Regulation D exemption, three procedural rules must be met. First, no general advertising or soliciting is permitted. Second, the issuer must exercise reasonable care to ensure that purchasers are not underwriters and that such purchasers are buying strictly for their own investment. Third, the SEC must be notified within 15 days of the first offering. No registration statement is filed when a private placement follows these rules and meets the criteria under Rule 504, Rule 505, or Rule 506.

Answers (A), (C), and (D) are incorrect because they each represent the three procedural rules required for a Regulation D exemption.

34. Under Rule 504, qualified issuers may sell up to a certain amount of securities during a 12-month period to any number of purchasers without registration or the provision of specific financial information. This amount is

A. $500,000

B. $1,000,000

C. $1,500,000

D. $2,000,000

The correct answer is (B). *(Publisher)*

REQUIRED: The maximum amount of securities that can be sold in a 12-month period under Rule 504.

DISCUSSION: Qualified issuers may sell up to $1,000,000 of securities during a 12-month period to any number of purchasers without registration or specific financial information being provided, as long as they follow other applicable conditions of the rule.

Answers (A), (C), and (D) are incorrect because $1,000,000 is the limit.

35. Under Rule 504, qualified issuers may sell up to a certain amount of securities during a 12-month period to any number of purchasers without registration or the provision of specific financial information. Sales to which of the following parties are included in the limitation under Rule 504?

A. Directors.

B. Shareholders.

C. Employees.

D. Officers.

The correct answer is (B). *(Publisher)*

REQUIRED: The parties whose purchases of securities under Rule 504 are included in the Rule 504 limitation.

DISCUSSION: Qualified issuers may sell up to $1,000,000 of securities during a 12-month period to any number of purchasers without registration or the provision of specific financial information as long as they follow other applicable conditions of the rule. Sales to directors, officers, and employees are not included in the limitation.

Answers (A), (C), and (D) are incorrect because sales to directors, employees, and officers are not included in the $1,000,000 limitation.

36. Accredited investors who may not purchase an issue under Rule 505 include

A. Insurance companies.

B. Business development companies.

C. Banks.

D. All charitable organizations.

The correct answer is (D). *(Publisher)*

REQUIRED: The investors who may NOT purchase an issue under Rule 505.

DISCUSSION: Rule 505 allows issuers of securities, other than investment companies, to issue up to $5,000,000 in any 12-month period without registering the securities. An unlimited number of accredited investors may purchase the issue including banks, insurance companies, registered investment companies, business development companies, and charitable organizations with assets in excess of $5,000,000.

Answers (A), (B), and (C) are incorrect because all three are allowed to purchase an issue under Rule 505.

37. Stock issued pursuant to Rule 506 is

A. Lettered stock.

B. Numbered stock.

C. 506 stock.

D. Nonaccredited stock.

The correct answer is (A). *(Publisher)*

REQUIRED: The stock issued pursuant to Rule 506.

DISCUSSION: Rule 506 provides a safe harbor for limited offers and sales without regard to dollar amount. An issuer must reasonably believe that no more than 35 investors/offerees are nonaccredited. A purchaser usually must sign an investment letter stating that (s)he is purchasing for investment purposes only and not for resale. The requirement to sign an investment letter is the reason shares issued pursuant to Rule 506 are commonly referred to as lettered stock.

Answers (B), (C) and (D) are incorrect because they are all nonsense titles.

D. Other Exemptions from SEC Registration

38. Securities issued by which of the following are NOT exempt from SEC registration?

    A.   Nonprofit organizations.

    B.   Domestic governments if the securities are not used for a governmental purpose.

    C.   Issuers regulated by the Interstate Commerce Commission.

    D.   Domestic banks.

The correct answer is (B). *(Publisher)*
    REQUIRED: The securities not exempt from SEC registration.
    DISCUSSION: Certain issuances of securities are exempt from SEC registration, including securities issued by a domestic government, but they must be used for a governmental purpose.
    Answers (A), (C), and (D) are incorrect because nonprofit organizations, issuers regulated by the ICC, and domestic banks may all issue securities without registering them with the SEC.

39. Security issues may be exempt from normal SEC registration under Regulation A if

    A.   The issue is for less than $5,000,000.

    B.   Insiders sell no more than $5,000,000 of stock.

    C.   Insiders sell no more than 1,500,000 shares.

    D.   All of the answers are correct.

The correct answer is (A). *(Publisher)*
    REQUIRED: The type of security issues that may be exempt from SEC registration under Regulation A.
    DISCUSSION: Regulation A permits an issuer to offer up to $5,000,000 of securities in any 12-month period without registering them. On a practical level, a Regulation A filing is less detailed, time consuming, and costly than a full registration statement. For example, the formal registration statement and prospectus are not required.
    Answers (B), (C), and (D) are incorrect because the Regulation A exemption applies only to a company that issues up to $5,000,000 of securities in any 12-month period.

40. Securities exempt from SEC registration include those issued solely for exchange with the issuer's existing security holders if no commission is paid. Examples of these types of securities do NOT include

    A.   Stock dividends.

    B.   Stock warrants enabling purchase of additional shares of stock.

    C.   Stock splits.

    D.   Securities issued in a merger in which no cash is involved and other securities are received.

The correct answer is (B). *(Publisher)*
    REQUIRED: The securities issued solely for exchange with the issuer's existing security holders in transactions in which no commission is paid.
    DISCUSSION: Securities issued solely for exchange with the issuer's existing security holders in transactions in which no commission is paid are exempt from registration with the SEC. Stock dividends and stock splits are usually exempt. Furthermore, securities issued in mergers and other reorganizations are exempt if no cash is involved and the securities are given solely for other securities. Stock warrants are offers to purchase additional stock and are not exempt.
    Answers (A), (C), and (D) are incorrect because all are securities issued for exchange with the issuer's existing security holders in transactions in which no commission is paid.

41. Jennifer Corp. issues a note on January 1, 1997 with a face value of $1,000,000 dollars due on August 1, 1997. The proceeds are used to purchase a 36-story building. The note is NOT exempt from registration with the SEC because

- A. It matures in more than 6 months.

- B. It is paper not ordinarily purchased by the general public.

- C. The proceeds are not used for a permanent purpose.

- D. The proceeds are used for a permanent purpose.

The correct answer is (D). *(Publisher)*
    REQUIRED: The reason short-term commercial paper is not exempt from SEC registration.
    DISCUSSION: Short-term commercial paper, such as a note, draft, or banker's acceptance, issued for working capital is exempt from SEC registration if certain conditions are met. The paper must mature within 9 months, the proceeds cannot be used for permanent purposes, and the paper must be of a type ordinarily purchased by the general public. The proceeds are used for a permanent purpose, a new building, so the securities are not exempt from SEC registration.
    Answer (A) is incorrect because the note must mature within 9 months, not 6 months. In this case, the note issued by Jennifer Corp. matures in 8 months which meets the maturity condition for exemption. Answer (B) is incorrect because the note is a type of commercial paper ordinarily purchased by the general public. Therefore, the type of paper requirement is met to qualify for exemption. Answer (C) is incorrect because the proceeds are used for a permanent purpose, a new building, so the securities are not exempt from SEC registration.

42. Securities offered and sold only to persons residing within a single state are exempt from SEC registration if the issuer is a resident or a corporation doing business in that state. The SEC's Rule 147 provides a safe harbor for qualifying for the exemption. Which of the following conditions must be met?

- A. The issuer must derive at least 95% of its gross revenue from the state where the securities are issued.

- B. The securities cannot be resold during the 12-month sale period and for 9 months thereafter.

- C. All of the purchasers, but not the offerees, must be residents of the state.

- D. All of the net proceeds from the issuance must be used in the state.

The correct answer is (B). *(Publisher)*
    REQUIRED: The condition that must be met for an intrastate offering to be exempt from SEC registration.
    DISCUSSION: The courts and the SEC interpret the intrastate offering exemption strictly. Rule 147 provides a safe harbor for qualifying for the exemption. It requires that the issuer be incorporated or organized in the state, all of the offerees and purchasers be residents of the state, the issue derive at least 80% of its gross revenue from the state, at least 80% of the issuer's assets be located within the state, at least 80% of the net proceeds from the issuance be used in the state, the securities not be resold to nonresidents during the 12-month sale period or for 9 months thereafter, and safeguards against interstate distributions be established.
    Answer (A) is incorrect because the issuer must derive 80%, not 95%, of its gross revenue from the state. Answer (C) is incorrect because all of the purchasers and the offerees must be residents of the state. Answer (D) is incorrect because at least 80% of the net proceeds from the issuance must be used in the state.

43. Menge Corp. issues $3,000,000 in cumulative 5% preferred stock on January 15, 1997, $1,250,000 in cumulative 6% preferred stock on May 10, 1997, and $1,000,000 in cumulative 4% preferred stock on October 31, 1997. Which of the following is a reason that the 1997 issues do NOT qualify for exemption under Regulation A?

- A. The three issues are within a 12-month period.

- B. The SEC integrates registrations issued within a 12-month period.

- C. The three issues are for preferred stock.

- D. The offerings are integrated because one is made within 6 months before or after another offering.

The correct answer is (C). *(Publisher)*
    REQUIRED: The reason NOT affecting exemption from SEC registration under Regulation A.
    DISCUSSION: Regulation A permits an issuer to offer up to $5,000,000 of securities in any 12-month period without registering them. The exemption does not apply if several small offerings exceed $5,000,000 over a 12-month period. The offerings are integrated if they occur within 6 months before or after one another. The offerings by Menge are integrated because they occur within 6 months before or after one another. The total amount offered exceeds $5,000,000, so they must be registered with the SEC. Whether the offerings are for preferred stock, common stock, or other securities is not relevant.
    Answers (A), (B), and (D) are incorrect because they are all reasons that the offerings do not meet the requirements of the Regulation A exemption.

E. Commercial Banking

44. A compensating balance

A. Compensates a financial institution for services rendered by providing it with deposits of funds.

B. Is used to compensate for possible losses on a marketable securities portfolio.

C. Is a level of inventory held to compensate for variations in usage rate and lead time.

D. Is an amount paid by financial institutions to compensate large depositors.

The correct answer is (A). *(CMA 688 1-13)*
    REQUIRED: The true statement about compensating balances.
    DISCUSSION: Banks sometimes require a borrower to keep a certain percentage of the face amount of a loan in a non-interest-bearing checking account. This requirement raises the effective rate of interest paid by the borrower. This greater rate compensates a bank for services provided and results in greater profitability for the financial institution.
    Answer (B) is incorrect because, in financial accounting, a valuation allowance is used to reflect losses on marketable securities. Answer (C) is incorrect because a safety stock of inventory is held to avoid inventory stockouts. Answer (D) is incorrect because large depositors may receive favorable treatment, but compensating balances are funds maintained by loan recipients for the benefit of the lender.

45. The prime rate is the

A. Size of the commitment fee on a commercial bank loan.

B. Effective cost of a commercial bank loan.

C. Rate charged on business loans to borrowers with high credit ratings.

D. Rate at which a bank borrows from the Federal Reserve central bank.

The correct answer is (C). *(CMA 688 1-18)*
    REQUIRED: The definition of the prime rate.
    DISCUSSION: The prime interest rate is the rate charged by commercial banks to their best (the largest and financially strongest) business customers. It is traditionally the lowest rate charged by banks. However, in recent years, banks have been making loans at still lower rates in response to competition from the commercial paper market.
    Answer (A) is incorrect because the prime rate is entirely separate from the commitment fee on a bank loan. Answer (B) is incorrect because the effective rate on most companies' bank loans is higher than the prime rate. Answer (D) is incorrect because the discount rate is the rate at which a bank borrows from the Federal Reserve.

46. Which one of the following financial instruments generally provides the largest source of short-term credit for small firms?

A. Installment loans.

B. Commercial paper.

C. Trade credit.

D. Mortgage bonds.

The correct answer is (C). *(CMA 1295 1-9)*
    REQUIRED: The largest source of short-term credit for small firms.
    DISCUSSION: Trade credit is a spontaneous source of financing because it arises automatically as part of a purchase transaction. Because of its ease in use, trade credit is the largest source of short-term financing for many firms both large and small.
    Answer (A) is incorrect because installment loans are usually a longer-term source of financing and are more difficult to acquire than trade credit. Answer (B) is incorrect because commercial paper is normally used only by large companies with high credit ratings. Answer (D) is incorrect because mortgage bonds are a long-term source of financing.

47. Elan Corporation is considering borrowing $100,000 from a bank for 1 year at a stated interest rate of 9%. What is the effective interest rate to Elan if this borrowing is in the form of a discounted note?

A. 8.10%

B. 9.00%

C. 9.81%

D. 9.89%

The correct answer is (D). *(CMA 1295 1-11)*

REQUIRED: The effective interest rate when a loan is in the form of a discounted note.

DISCUSSION: Applying the 9% interest rate to a $100,000 loan results in interest expense of $9,000. If the loan is processed in the form of a discounted note, the interest will be deducted from the proceeds of the loan. Thus, the $9,000 of interest will be deducted from the $100,000 note, resulting in loan proceeds of $91,000. The borrower is paying $9,000 for a loan of $91,000, resulting in an effective interest rate of 9.89%.

Answer (A) is incorrect because the lesser amount of funds available on a discounted note means the effective rate will be higher than the contract rate. Answer (B) is incorrect because 9% is the nominal rate (discount rate). Answer (C) is incorrect because 9.81% equals the nominal rate multiplied by 9%.

48. A minimum checking account balance that a firm must maintain with a commercial bank is a

A. Transactions balance.

B. Compensating balance.

C. Precautionary balance.

D. Speculative balance.

The correct answer is (B). *(CIA 1190 IV-49)*

REQUIRED: The term for the minimum checking account balance a firm must maintain at a commercial bank.

DISCUSSION: A minimum checking account balance that a firm must maintain with a commercial bank is a compensating balance. A bank may require a borrower to keep a certain percentage of the face value of a loan in the firm's account. This requirement raises the real rate of interest to the borrower.

Answer (A) is incorrect because the cash balance necessary for a firm to conduct day-to-day business is a transactions balance. Answer (C) is incorrect because a cash balance held in reserve for random, unforeseen fluctuations in cash inflows and outflows is a precautionary balance. Answer (D) is incorrect because a cash balance that is held to enable the firm to take advantage of any bargain purchases that might arise is a speculative balance.

49. A manufacturing firm wants to obtain a short-term loan and has approached several lending institutions. All of the potential lenders are offering the same nominal interest rate, but the terms of the loans vary. Which of the following combinations of loan terms will be most attractive for the borrowing firm?

A. Simple interest, no compensating balance.

B. Discount interest, no compensating balance.

C. Simple interest, 20% compensating balance required.

D. Discount interest, 20% compensating balance required.

The correct answer is (A). *(CIA 594 IV-51)*

REQUIRED: The loan terms most attractive to the borrower.

DISCUSSION: The most desirable set of terms are those that result in the lowest cost of borrowing. Discount interest results in a higher effective borrowing cost than simple interest because the bank deducts interest in advance so the borrower receives less than the face value of the loan. A compensating balance results in a higher effective borrowing cost because the compensating balance is an amount of cash that the firm is unable to use. The cheapest terms, given that all options have the same nominal interest rate, will be simple interest with no compensating balance.

Answers (B), (C), and (D) are incorrect because discount interest and a compensating balance are disadvantageous to the borrower.

50. Discounted interest is based on the borrowed amount but is paid in advance. The formula for calculating the discounted interest rate for a 1-year loan is

A. $$\frac{Interest}{Borrowed\ amount}$$

B. $$\frac{Interest}{Average\ borrowed\ amount}$$

C. $$\frac{Interest}{Borrowed\ amount\ -\ Interest}$$

D.   None of the answers are correct.

The correct answer is (C). *(Publisher)*
REQUIRED: The formula for the discounted rate for a 1-year loan.
DISCUSSION: The discounted interest rate is based on the amount borrowed but is paid in advance. It is calculated using the following formula:

$$\frac{Interest}{Borrowed\ amount\ -\ Interest}$$

Answer (A) is incorrect because it is the formula for the simple interest rate for a 1-year loan. Answer (B) is incorrect because it is the formula for the add-on installment interest for a 1-year loan. Answer (D) is incorrect because the correct formula for the discounted interest rate is interest divided by the borrowed amount less interest.

STUDY UNIT 6: FINANCIAL STATEMENT ANALYSIS

17 pages of outline
60 multiple-choice questions

A. Ratio Analysis
B. Limitations of Ratio Analysis
C. Comparative Analysis
D. Effects of Changing Price Levels

This study unit is the fourth of five covering "Advanced Topics in Corporate Financial Management."

The essence of financial statement analysis is the calculation of financial ratios. These ratios establish relationships among financial statement accounts at a moment in time or for a given accounting period. Once calculated, the firm's ratios can be compared with its historical data and with its projections for the future. Moreover, ratios can also be evaluated by comparison with those for other firms or with industry averages. However, users of such information must be aware of the limitations of ratio analysis, for example, those arising from differences in the nature of the firms being compared, changes in accounting principles, and the effects of changing price levels. Ratios must also be evaluated in terms of broad economic and strategic factors and from the unique perspectives of particular users.

A. Ratio Analysis

1. Ratio analysis addresses such issues as the firm's liquidity, use of leverage, asset management, cost control, profitability, growth, and valuation.

2. Ratio analysis permits determination of standards and trends.

   a. Normal or average ratios can be computed for broad industrial categories.

   b. Ratios for individual firms can be compared with those of competitors, especially industry leaders.

   c. Changes in ratios over time provide insight about the future (trend analysis).

3. **Liquidity ratios** measure the relationship of a firm's liquid assets to current liabilities. Thus, such ratios provide information about the short-term viability of the business, i.e., the firm's ability to pay its current obligations and to continue operations.

   a. The **current ratio** (working capital ratio) equals current assets divided by current liabilities and is the most common measure of near-term solvency.

      1) $\dfrac{Current\ assets}{Current\ liabilities}$

      2) **Current assets** include cash, net accounts receivable, trading securities, other marketable securities classified as current, inventories, and prepaid items.

         a) **Current liabilities** include accounts payable, notes payable, current maturities of long-term debt, unearned revenues, taxes payable, wages payable, and other accruals.

      3) A low ratio indicates a possible solvency problem. An overly high ratio indicates that management may not be investing idle assets productively.

      4) The general principle is that the current ratio should be proportional to the operating cycle. Thus, a shorter cycle may justify a lower ratio.

5) The quality of accounts receivable and merchandise inventory should be considered before evaluating the current ratio. Accordingly, a low receivables turnover (net credit sales ÷ average accounts receivable) and a low inventory turnover (cost of sales ÷ average inventory) indicate a need for a higher current ratio.

6) Use of LIFO understates the current ratio.

b. A conservative version of the **acid test or quick ratio** divides the quick assets (cash, net receivables, and marketable securities) by current liabilities.

1) $$\frac{Cash \; + \; Net \; receivables \; + \; Marketable \; securities}{Current \; liabilities}$$

2) This ratio measures the firm's ability to pay its short-term debts from its most liquid assets and avoids the problem of inventory valuation.

3) A less conservative variation divides the difference between current assets and inventory by current liabilities.

4) A more conservative variation is the cash ratio [(cash equivalents + marketable securities) ÷ current liabilities].

c. **Working capital** is the excess of current assets over current liabilities.

1) *Current assets – Current liabilities*

2) Working capital is a less useful measure than the current and quick ratios because it is the absolute difference between current assets and liabilities and therefore does not facilitate comparisons.

d. The **defensive interval** equals the sum of cash equivalents, net receivables, and marketable securities, divided by the expected daily operating cash outflows.

1) $$\frac{Cash \; equivalents \; + \; Net \; receivables \; + \; Marketable \; securities}{Daily \; operating \; cash \; outflow}$$

e. The **investment financing** equals cash flow (increase in retained earnings + depreciation) divided by the current investment requirements.

1) $$\frac{Increase \; in \; retained \; earnings \; + \; Depreciation}{Current \; investment}$$

f. The ratio of **operating cash flow to the sum of the current maturities of long-term debt and current notes payable** is another liquidity ratio.

1) $$\frac{Operating \; cash \; flow}{Current \; maturities \; of \; long\text{-}term \; debt \; + \; Current \; notes \; payable}$$

4. **Leverage ratios** measure the firm's use of debt to finance assets and operations. Leverage (**trading on the equity**) is advantageous when earnings from borrowed funds exceed borrowing costs. However, risk increases as interest rates increase and returns decrease. Accordingly, as leverage increases, the risk that the firm may not be able to meet its maturing obligations and the risk borne by creditors increase. Nevertheless, interest is tax deductible, so leverage increases the firm's return when it is profitable. Furthermore, debt financing permits the owners to retain control.

a. The **leverage factor** equals total assets divided by shareholders' equity.

1) $$\frac{Total \; assets}{Shareholders' \; equity}$$

2) The leverage factor is a component of the return-on-equity calculation. It measures the extent to which debt financing enhances equity financing.

a) $\dfrac{Net\ income}{Net\ sales} \times \dfrac{Net\ sales}{Total\ assets} \times \dfrac{Total\ assets}{Shareholders'\ equity} = \dfrac{Net\ income}{Shareholders'\ equity}$

3) The higher the ratio, the greater the leverage and the greater the risk.

b. The **interest-bearing debt ratio** equals interest-bearing debt divided by the total capital (shareholders' equity + interest-bearing debt).

1) $\dfrac{Interest\text{-}bearing\ debt}{Shareholders'\ equity\ +\ Interest\text{-}bearing\ debt}$

2) The total assets of the firm equal shareholders' equity, plus interest-bearing debt (notes payable, bonds, etc.), plus noninterest-bearing debt (accounts payable, wages and taxes payable, etc.). This ratio measures the extent to which the assets having explicit costs (total capital) are financed by interest-bearing debt. It may be calculated using either the book or fair value of equity.

c. The **debt ratio** equals total liabilities divided by total assets.

1) $\dfrac{Total\ liabilities}{Total\ assets}$

2) The debt ratio measures the percentage of funds provided by creditors. It determines long-term debt-payment ability and the degree to which creditors are protected from the firm's insolvency. Hence, creditors prefer this ratio to be low as a cushion against losses.

3) The conservative approach to calculation of this ratio is to include short-term liabilities contingencies, deferred taxes, the minority interest, and redeemable preferred stock in the numerator.

d. The **debt-equity ratio** equals total debt divided by total shareholders' equity.

1) $\dfrac{Total\ liabilities}{Shareholders'\ equity}$

2) It compares the resources provided by creditors with resources provided by shareholders.

3) Like the debt ratio, the debt-equity ratio determines long-term debt-payment ability, and the conservative approach is to include all liabilities and near liabilities in the numerator.

e. The **debt to tangible net worth ratio** equals total liabilities divided by the excess of shareholders' equity over intangible assets.

1) $\dfrac{Total\ liabilities}{Shareholders'\ equity\ -\ Intangible\ assets}$

2) This ratio is a more conservative measure of long-term debt-payment ability than the debt ratio or the debt-equity ratio. The denominator is smaller because such assets as goodwill, patents, and copyrights are excluded.

f.   The **times-interest-earned ratio** (interest coverage ratio) equals earnings before interest and taxes (EBIT), divided by interest.

   1) $$\frac{EBIT}{Interest\ expense}$$

   2)   This ratio is an income statement approach to evaluating debt-payment ability. It indicates the margin of safety for payment of fixed interest charges, so a consistently high ratio is desirable.

   3)   Interest is tax deductible. Hence, interest and tax must be added to net income to determine the amount available to pay interest.

   4)   The most accurate calculation of the numerator includes only earnings expected to recur. Consequently, unusual or infrequent items, extraordinary items, discontinued operations, and the effects of accounting changes should be excluded. Undistributed equity earnings should also be excluded because they are not available to cover interest. However, the minority income exclusion should be added back. Interest expense of a consolidated entity is included in consolidated income, so the income of that entity should be included.

   5)   The denominator should include capitalized interest.

g.   The **fixed charge coverage ratio** extends the times-interest-earned ratio to include the interest portion associated with long-term lease obligations.

   1) $$\frac{EBIT\ +\ Interest\ portion\ of\ operating\ leases}{Interest\ +\ Interest\ portion\ of\ operating\ leases}$$

   2)   Other items, e.g., the entire amount of annual lease payments instead of the interest component, preferred dividends, pension payments, or depreciation may be included. Furthermore, the adjustments made to the times-interest-earned ratio may also be made.

h.   The **operating cash flow to total debt ratio** equals the net cash provided by operations divided by total debt.

   1) $$\frac{Operating\ cash\ flow}{Total\ debt}$$

   2)   A high ratio is desirable. Moreover, the most conservative approach is to include all debt items in the denominator.

5.   **Asset management ratios** measure the firm's use of assets to generate revenue and income. Thus, they also relate to liquidity.

a.   The **inventory turnover ratio** equals cost of sales divided by average inventory.

   1) $$\frac{Cost\ of\ sales}{Average\ inventory}$$

   2)   If the average of the beginning and ending inventory is not representative because of cyclical factors, a monthly or quarterly average is preferable.

   3)   A high turnover implies that the firm does not hold excessive stocks of inventories that are unproductive and that lessen the firm's profitability.

   4)   A high turnover also implies that the inventory is truly marketable and does not contain obsolete goods.

     5)   The ratio of a firm that uses LIFO may not be comparable with that of a firm with a higher inventory valuation.

  b.   The **number of days of inventory** (days' sales in average inventory) equals the number of days in the year divided by the inventory turnover ratio.

     1)

$$\frac{365,\ 360,\ or\ 300}{Inventory\ turnover\ ratio}$$

     2)   This ratio measures the average number of days that inventory is held before sale. Thus, it reflects the efficiency of inventory management.

     3)   It may also be computed as average inventory divided by average daily cost of sales.

     4)   Still another possibility is to calculate the days' sales in ending inventory. This ratio equals ending inventory divided by the average daily cost of sales.

  c.   The **receivables turnover ratio** equals net credit sales divided by average accounts receivable. (However, net sales is often used because credit sales data may be unavailable.)

     1)

$$\frac{Net\ credit\ sales}{Average\ accounts\ receivable}$$

     2)   This ratio measures the efficiency of accounts receivable collection.

     3)   A high turnover is preferable.

     4)   As in the case of inventory, cyclical factors may cause the average of the beginning and ending balances to be unrepresentative. In that event, a monthly or quarterly average should be used.

  d.   The **number of days of receivables** (days' sales in average receivables or the average collection period) equals the number of days in the period divided by the receivables turnover ratio.

     1)

$$\frac{365,\ 360,\ or\ 300}{Receivables\ turnover\ ratio}$$

     2)   This ratio is the average number of days to collect a receivable.

     3)   It may also be computed as average accounts receivable divided by average daily sales.

        a)   Average daily sales are net credit sales divided by the number of days in the period.

        b)   Another possibility is to calculate days' sales in ending receivables. This ratio equals ending receivables divided by the average daily sales.

     4)   The number of days of receivables should be compared with the company's credit terms to determine whether the average customer is paying within the credit period.

     5)   The **operating cycle** of an enterprise may be estimated by adding days' sales in average inventory to days' sales in average receivables.

e.   The **fixed assets turnover ratio** equals net sales divided by average net fixed assets.

   1) $$\frac{Net\ sales}{Average\ net\ fixed\ assets}$$

   2)   This ratio measures the level of use of property, plant, and equipment.

   a)   It is largely affected by the capital intensiveness of the company and its industry, by the age of the assets, and by the depreciation method used.

   3)   A high turnover is preferable to a low turnover.

f.   The **total assets turnover ratio** equals net sales divided by average total assets.

   1) $$\frac{Net\ sales}{Average\ total\ assets}$$

   2)   This ratio measures the level of capital investment relative to sales volume.

   3)   For all turnover ratios, high turnover is preferable because it implies effective use of assets to generate sales.

   4)   Certain assets, for example, investments, do not relate to net sales. Their inclusion decreases the ratio.

g.   The **total capital turnover ratio** equals net sales divided by total capital.

   1) $$\frac{Net\ sales}{Total\ capital}$$

   2)   Total capital is defined as total assets having explicit costs (shareholders' equity + interest-bearing debt).

h.   The **investment rate** is the percentage change in total capital.

   1) $$\frac{Total\ capital\ (Year\ X + 1) - Total\ capital\ (Year\ X)}{Total\ capital\ (Year\ X)}$$

   2)   A high rate is a predictor of increased future sales if the investment program is effective.

6.   **Cost management ratios** measure how well a firm controls its costs. However, they may be difficult for an external analyst to determine because firms conceal their detailed cost data from competitors.

a.   The **gross margin** equals sales minus cost of sales, divided by sales.

   1) $$\frac{Net\ sales - Cost\ of\ sales}{Net\ sales}$$

   2)   A high gross margin implies effective cost control.

   3)   This ratio measures how much can be spent for marketing, R&D, and administrative costs while still reaching targeted net income.

b.   The **labor cost ratio** equals labor cost divided by sales.

   1) $$\frac{Labor\ cost}{Net\ sales}$$

2) Labor cost is an important determinant of profitability.

3) In evaluating a business combination, labor cost and the employment growth rate should be considered in connection with any changes in profitability. In other words, will the presumed reductions in the workforce and in labor cost resulting from the combination produce increased profits?

c. The **employment growth rate** from period to period (the percentage change in the number employed) is a measure of operational growth. It should be compared with the investment rate to determine whether capital is being substituted for labor.

d. The **pension expense per employee** is another determinant of a firm's ability to control its labor costs. Postretirement benefits other than pensions (especially medical care) should also be considered. An important question is the extent to which the ultimate liability from pensions and other benefits is reflected in the financial statements.

e. Other useful ratios may be calculated for the relationship of marketing, administrative, or R&D costs to sales. For example, relatively high R&D expenditures may indicate future growth in sales, and a low level of administrative costs indicates successful cost control efforts.

7. **Profitability ratios** measure earnings relative to some base, for example, productive assets, sales, or capital. Increased profits benefit shareholders not only because they make additional funds available for dividend payments but also because they may result in appreciation of the firm's stock price. Profits also provide a cushion for debt coverage. Hence, profitability ratios are used by investors, creditors, and others to evaluate management's stewardship of the firm's assets.

a. The **profit margin on sales** equals net income divided by sales.

1) $$\frac{Net\ income\ after\ interest\ and\ taxes}{Net\ sales}$$

2) The numerator may also be stated in terms of the net income available to common shareholders.

3) Another form of the ratio excludes nonrecurring items from the numerator, e.g., unusual or infrequent items, discontinued operations, extraordinary items, and effects of accounting changes. The result is sometimes called the **net profit margin**. This adjustment may be made for any ratio that includes net income.

a) Still other numerator refinements are to exclude equity-based earnings and items in the other income and other expense categories.

b. The ratio of **net operating income to sales** may be defined as earnings before interest and taxes (EBIT) divided by sales.

1) $$\frac{EBIT}{Net\ sales}$$

2) Use of EBIT emphasizes operating results and more nearly approximates cash flows than other income measures.

c. The **return on total assets** (also called return on investment or ROI) may be defined as net income divided by average total assets.

1) $$\frac{Net\ income\ after\ interest\ and\ taxes}{Average\ total\ assets}$$

2) Once again the numerator may be defined in various ways. One possibility is net income available to common shareholders. Another is found in the **basic earning power ratio**, which divides EBIT by average total assets. This ratio enhances comparability of firms with different capital structures and tax planning strategies.

3) The denominator may be defined to include only operating assets. Thus, investments, intangibles, and the other asset category would be excluded.

d. The **Du Pont equation** relates the return on total assets, the total asset turnover, and the profit margin on sales.

1) $$\frac{Net\ income\ after\ interest\ and\ taxes}{Average\ total\ assets} = \frac{Net\ sales}{Average\ total\ assets} \times \frac{Net\ income\ after\ interest\ and\ taxes}{Net\ sales}$$

2) This formula emphasizes that ROI may be explained in terms of the efficiency of asset management and the profit margin.

3) The effects of modifying the Du Pont equation to reflect net operating income (EBIT) and operating assets should be understood.

4) Multiplying the return on assets by the equity multiplier (also called the leverage factor) gives the return on common equity. The equity multiplier equals total assets divided by common equity.

e. The ratio of **net operating income to total capital** is a variation of the return on total assets that excludes noninterest-bearing debt from total assets.

1) $$\frac{EBIT}{Shareholders'\ equity\ +\ Interest\text{-}bearing\ debt}$$

2) Total capital is defined in the same way as in the section on asset management.

3) A variation is the **marginal profitability rate** (change in EBIT ÷ change in total capital).

f. The **return on common equity** equals the net income available to common shareholders divided by their average equity.

1) $$\frac{Net\ income\ after\ interest\ and\ taxes\ -\ Preferred\ dividends}{Average\ common\ shareholders'\ equity}$$

2) The average common shareholders' equity includes total equity minus the preferred shareholders' capital and any minority interest.

3) This ratio and the next one measure the return on the book value of equity.

4) A variation of the return on common equity is the **marginal return on common equity** (change in net income ÷ change in common equity).

g. The **return on total equity** equals net income minus dividends on redeemable preferred stock, divided by average total equity.

1) $$\frac{Net\ income\ after\ interest\ and\ taxes\ -\ Dividends\ on\ redeemable\ preferred\ stock}{Average\ total\ equity}$$

        2)   Redeemable preferred stock is usually considered to be equivalent to debt. Indeed, the SEC requires it to be reported separately from other equity.

    h.   **Equity multiplier** is Total assets ÷ common equity.

8.   **Growth ratios** measure the changes in the economic status of a firm over a period of years. Firms compare their growth in sales, operating income, net income, EPS, and dividends per share with the results of competitors and the economy as a whole.

    a.   The most accurate analysis adjusts nominal growth rates for price level changes to determine real growth rates.

    b.   **Basic earnings per share (BEPS)** equals income available to common shareholders divided by the weighted-average number of common shares outstanding.

        1) $$\frac{Income\ available\ to\ common\ shareholders}{Average\ outstanding\ shares}$$

        2)   Income available to common shareholders reflects an adjustment for preferred dividends declared and cumulative preferred dividends.

        3)   In some cases, **diluted earnings per share (DEPS)** is also required by SFAS 128. The calculation of DEPS necessitates adjustments to the numerator and denominator of the BEPS fraction.

            a)   The denominator is increased by the number of dilutive potential common shares that might have been issued. The control number used to determine whether those potential shares are dilutive is income from continuing operations.

            b)   In accordance with the if-converted method, the numerator is adjusted for the hypothetical dilutive effects of the conversion of convertible securities, e.g., by adding back convertible preferred dividends or after-tax interest associated with convertible debt.

            c)   Dilutive call options and warrants written by the entity are reflected in DEPS by using the treasury stock method. The reverse treasury stock method is used for dilutive written put options. However, purchased puts and calls are not included because their exercise would be antidilutive.

            d)   Contingent shares are included in the calculation of DEPS if all necessary conditions have been satisfied by period-end. If not, the contingent shares included equal the number issuable if the end of the current period were the end of the contingency period.

    c.   **Cash flow per share** equals net cash provided by operations minus preferred dividends, divided by common shares outstanding.

        1) $$\frac{Cash\ provided\ by\ operations - Preferred\ dividends}{Common\ shares\ outstanding}$$

        2)   This ratio is a better indicator of short-term capacity to make capital outlays and dividend payments than EPS. However, it is not a substitute for EPS as a measure of profitability. Hence, the FASB has stated that cash flow per share is not to be reported in the financial statements.

        3)   The denominator is the same as that used in the EPS calculation.

d.   The **dividend payout ratio** equals dividends per common share divided by EPS.

    1) $$\frac{Dividends\ per\ common\ share}{EPS}$$

    2)   The most conservative version of this ratio uses a fully diluted EPS amount that excludes nonrecurring items. Firms develop dividend policies based on recurring earnings because they usually prefer a stable pattern of dividends.

    3)   The appropriate ratio depends on the firm's unique circumstances, including shareholder preferences regarding dividend income and capital gains. The general principle, however, is that growth companies have a low payout.

    4)   A related ratio is the **dividend yield**. It equals dividends per share of common stock divided by the market price per share of common stock.

e.   The ratio of **operating cash flow to cash dividends** measures the ability to pay dividends from current operating sources. A high ratio is obviously desirable.

    1) $$\frac{Net\ cash\ provided\ by\ operations}{Cash\ dividends}$$

    2)   This ratio gives a better approximation of the ability to pay dividends than the **percentage of earnings retained** [(net income – all dividends) ÷ net income]. The reason is that the latter is accrual based.

9.   **Valuation ratios** are broad performance measures. They reflect the basic principle that management's ultimate goal is to maximize shareholder value reflected in the price of the firm's stock.

a.   **Book value per share** equals the amount of net assets available to the share-holders of a given type of stock divided by the number of those shares outstanding.

    1) $$\frac{Shareholders'\ equity}{Shares\ outstanding}$$

    2)   When a company has preferred as well as common stock outstanding, the computation of book value per common share must consider potential claims by preferred shareholders, such as whether the preferred stock is cumulative and in arrears or participating. It must also consider whether the call price (or possibly the liquidation value) exceeds the carrying amount of the preferred stock.

    3)   Book value per share is ordinarily based on historical cost expressed in nominal dollars. Accordingly, it may be misleading because book values ordinarily differ materially from fair values.

b.   The book value per share is used to calculate the **market-to-book ratio**.

    1) $$\frac{Market\ price\ per\ share}{Book\ value\ per\ share}$$

    2)   Well-managed firms should sell at high multiples of their book value, which reflects historical cost.

   c. The **price-earnings (P-E) ratio** equals the market price per share of common stock divided by EPS.

     1) $\dfrac{Market\ price}{EPS}$

     2) Most analysts prefer to use fully diluted EPS.

     3) Growth companies are likely to have high P-E ratios. A high ratio may also indicate that the firm is relatively low risk or that its choice of accounting methods results in a conservative EPS.

   d. The **q-ratio** equals the market value of all securities (not just equity) divided by the replacement cost (not book value) of all assets.

     1) $\dfrac{Market\ value\ of\ all\ securities}{Replacement\ cost\ of\ assets}$

     2) The q-ratio reflects the market's valuation of new investment. Because a firm with a ratio exceeding one is earning returns greater than the amount invested, it should attract new resources and competition.

   e. The **return to shareholders** equals what shareholders actually earn over a specified period of years, e.g., 5 or 8 years. It equals the sum of dividend yield and capital gains over the measurement period.

     1) *Dividend yield + Capital gains*

     2) The return to shareholders facilitates comparisons among a wide variety of financial instruments.

10. Stop and review! You have completed the outline for this subunit. Study multiple-choice questions 1 through 50 beginning on page 232.

B. Limitations of Ratio Analysis

1. Although ratio analysis provides useful information pertaining to the efficiency of operations and the stability of financial condition, it has inherent limitations.

   a. Development of ratios for comparison with industry averages is more useful for firms that operate within a particular industry than for conglomerates (firms that operate in a variety of industries).

   b. The effects of inflation misstate a firm's balance sheet and income statement because of the effects on fixed assets and depreciation, inventory costs, long-term debt, and profitability. For example, fixed assets and depreciation will be understated, and inventory also will be understated if LIFO is used. Moreover, the interest rate increases that accompany inflation will decrease the value of outstanding long-term debt. Many assets are recorded at historical cost, so their true value may not be reflected on the balance sheet.

   c. Ratio analysis may be affected by seasonal factors. For example, inventory and receivables may vary widely, and year-end balances may not reflect the averages for the period.

   d. A firm's management has an incentive to **window dress** financial statements to improve results.

e.   Comparability of financial statement amounts and the ratios derived from them is impaired if different firms choose different accounting policies. Also, changes in a firm's own accounting policies may create some distortion in the comparison of the results over a period of years.

f.   Generalizations about which ratios are strong indicators of a firm's financial position may change from industry to industry, firm to firm, and division to division.

g.   Ratios are constructed from accounting data, much of which is subject to estimation.

h.   Current performance and trends may be misinterpreted if sufficient years of historical analysis are not considered.

i.   Ratio analysis may be distorted by failing to use an average or weighted average.

j.   Misleading conclusions may result if improper comparisons are selected.

k.   Whether a certain level of a ratio is favorable depends on the underlying circumstances. For example, a high quick ratio indicates high liquidity, but it may also imply that excessive cash is being held.

l.   Different ratios may yield opposite conclusions about a firm's financial health. Thus, the net effects of a set of ratios should be analyzed.

m.   Industry averages may include data from capital-intensive and labor-intensive firms. They may also include data from firms with greatly divergent policies regarding leverage.

n.   Some industry averages may be based on small samples.

o.   Different sources of information may compute ratios differently.

p.   Some data may be presented either before or after taxes.

q.   Comparability among firms may be impaired if they have different fiscal years.

r.   The geographical locations of firms may affect comparability because of differences in labor markets, price levels, governmental regulation, taxation, and other factors.

s.   Size differentials among firms affect comparability because of differences in access to and cost of capital, economies of scale, and width of markets.

2.   Stop and review! You have completed the outline for this subunit. Study multiple-choice question 51 on page 247.

C. Comparative Analysis

1. Comparative analysis involves both horizontal and vertical analysis. Horizontal (trend) analysis compares analytical data over a period of time. Vertical analysis makes comparisons among a single year's data.

    a. Comparison with competitors and industry averages.

        1) Comparing a company's performance with respect to its industry may identify the company's strengths and weaknesses. Horizontal analysis of the industry may identify industrywide trends and practices.

        2) Common-size financial statements are used to compare firms of different sizes.

            a) Items on common-size financial statements are expressed as percentages of corresponding base-year figures. The base amount is assiged the value of 100%.

                i) The **horizontal** form of common-size (percentage) analysis is useful for evaluating trends. The amounts for subsequent years are stated in percentages of a base-year amount.

                ii) **Vertical** common-size (percentage) analysis presents figures for a single year expressed as percentages of a base amount on the balance sheet (e.g., total assets) and on the income statement (e.g., sales).

    b. Many sources of standards for evaluating a firm's ratios are available, including the financial statements of individual firms. Researching many of the sources of comparative ratios is facilitated by the Standard Industrial Classification (SIC), a categorization of firms by industry that was developed for use in generating governmental financial statistics. However, a user of information organized based on the SIC should be aware that not every firm clearly fits one of the categories.

        1) The following are some of the major sources of financial data:

            a) *The Department of Commerce Financial Report* is a quarterly publication for manufacturing, mining, and trading firms. It provides financial statement data reported in industry dollars. It also includes a variety of ratios and industrywide common-size vertical financial statements.

            b) *Robert Morris Associates Annual Statement Studies* is published by an organization of bank loan and credit officers. The data relate to many thousands of firms in more than 350 industries. Included are common-size statements, certain ratios, and 5-year comparative historical information.

            c) Dun & Bradstreet publishes *Industry Norms and Key Business Ratios*, which covers over 1 million firms in over 800 lines of business.

            d) *Value Line Investment Service* provides financial data and rates the stocks of over 1,700 firms.

            e) Standard & Poor's, Moody's Investors' Service, and various brokerages compile industry studies.

2. Stop and review! You have completed the outline for this subunit. Study multiple-choice questions 52 through 54 beginning on page 247.

D. Effects of Changing Price Levels

1. **Inflation** is an increase and **deflation** is a decrease in the general price level. The more common occurrence is inflation.

    a. The general price level is inversely related to the purchasing power of money.
    b. Measuring inflation

        1) **The consumer price index (CPI)** measures inflation by a monthly pricing of a specified set of goods and services purchased by a typical urban consumer.

        2) The **Gross Domestic Product (GDP) deflator** includes all goods and services produced in the U.S. at the prices at which they were included in the GDP account. It includes investments, government purchases, and exports as well as consumer goods and services.

        3) The **Producer Price Index** measures the prices of specified commodities at the time of their first commercial sale.

        4) Other price indexes are also calculated, for example, the import price index and the export price index.

    c. Impact of inflation on financial management

        1) Interest rates include an inflation premium. Higher rates of inflation lead to higher interest rates. In turn, higher interest rates discourage investment because required rates of return are greater.

        2) Inflation also increases resource prices, including the costs of fixed assets, inventory, and payments to employees. Thus, inflation increases the demand for capital. However, the government usually follows a restrictive monetary policy to reduce inflation. The resulting competition for a lower amount of loanable funds increases interest rates still more.

        3) If inflation is not neutral, that is, if some prices and costs rise more rapidly than others, some entities may gain and some may lose. For example, if wages rise more rapidly than a firm's prices, revenues and income will be reduced.

        4) If the tax structure is not indexed for inflation, taxpayers may be pushed into higher brackets even though real income has not increased. Moreover, the real value of the tax shield, such as depreciation, is reduced.

        5) Profits are distorted by inflation because of inadequate valuation of inventories and fixed assets. Higher nominal profits may result in higher taxes and lower cash flows. Thus, a firm must be careful to establish dividend and investment policies based on real rather than nominal income.

        6) The accuracy of predictions required for business planning is reduced during periods of rapid inflation. Expected long-term revenues and costs are difficult to forecast in the best of circumstances, but inflation not only increases the need for accurate predictions but also makes them more difficult.

    d. Redistributive effects of inflation

        1) Inflation is an arbitrary redistribution of income that does not reflect the operations of the free market or the government's attempt to alter income distribution.

    2) Inflation hurts creditors, fixed-income groups, and savers.

        a) But inflation benefits debtors because they pay back their debts in less valuable units of money.

2. **Accounting for Changing Prices**. SFAS 89, *Financial Reporting and Changing Prices*, is the relevant pronouncement.

    a. Basic financial statements presented in accordance with GAAP are primarily based on the effects of historical transactions measured in terms of historical cost.

        1) These financial statements assume that the unit of measure does not fluctuate in value significantly.

            a) Although this assumption has the virtues of simplicity and objectivity, it produces financial statements that do not reflect price changes.

        2) SFAS 89 encourages but does not require firms to provide supplementary **current cost** and **constant purchasing power** disclosures.

            a) A 5-year summary reported in constant dollars is recommended. It should provide many disclosures, including current cost operating income and income per common share from continuing operations on a current cost basis; purchasing power gain or loss on net monetary items; net sales and other operating revenues; change in the current cost or lower recoverable amount of inventory and property, plant, and equipment; cash dividends declared per common share and its market price at year-end; and current cost of net assets at year-end.

            b) The 5-year summary should be stated in average-for-the-year units of constant purchasing power, in end-of-the-year units of constant purchasing power, or in dollars having a purchasing power equal to that of the dollars of the base period used by the Bureau of Labor Statistics in calculating the Consumer Price Index for All Urban Consumers.

            c) Current cost is often approximated by reference to current prices or by applying a specific price index.

        3) Inventory is measured at current cost or lower recoverable amount. The current cost is the cost of purchasing the goods or the current cost of the resources needed to produce the goods.

            a) The recoverable amount is the current worth of the net amount of cash expected to be recoverable from the use or sale of an asset.

            b) If the recoverable amount of a group of assets is materially and permanently lower than current cost, the recoverable amount is used to measure the assets and the expenses associated with them.

        4) Property, plant, and equipment (PP&E) is measured at the current cost (lower recoverable amount) of the remaining service potential. The current cost is the cost of acquiring the same service potential.

        5) Net assets on a current cost basis equals net assets in the primary statements adjusted for the difference between historical cost and the current cost (lower recoverable amount) of inventory and PP&E.

6) Cost of goods sold is measured at current cost (lower recoverable amount) at the date of sale or when resources are committed to a contract.

    a) The practical approach multiplies units sold times average current cost (lower recoverable amount) based on beginning and end-of-period values [(current cost at beginning of the year + current cost at year-end) ÷ 2].

    b) According to SFAS 89, if "turnover is rapid and material amounts of depreciation are not allocated to inventory, cost of goods sold measured on a LIFO basis may provide an acceptable approximation of cost of goods sold, measured at current cost, provided that the effect of any LIFO inventory liquidations (that is, decreases in earlier years' LIFO layers) is excluded."

    c) However, the FIFO basis more closely approximates the current cost of ending inventory purchases that are the last to be sold.

7) Depreciation, depletion, and amortization expense for PP&E is measured on the basis of average current cost of the assets' service potential or lower recoverable amount during the period.

8) Other revenues, expenses (including income tax), gains, and losses are measured at the same amounts as in the primary statements.

9) Historical cost/constant purchasing power amounts may be used in lieu of current cost amounts if the substitution would not result in a significantly different number for income from continuing operations.

10) The change (holding gain or loss) in the current cost (lower recoverable amount) of inventory and PP&E is the difference between the measures of the assets at their entry dates and their exit dates.

    a) A holding gain or loss is realized through use, sale, or commitment.

    b) An unrealized holding gain or loss is recognized on assets held at the end of the period.

    c) For the current year, the change in current cost amounts is reported before and after eliminating the effects of general inflation.

b. **Constant purchasing power accounting.** The historical cost/constant purchasing power method retains the historical cost principle but restates the unit of measure to reflect changes in its general purchasing power.

1) Hence, this method adjusts for general price level changes but not for changes in specific prices.

2) Historical financial statements are restated by adjusting each nonmonetary account with the TO/FROM ratio. TO is the current price level/index. FROM is the price level/index when the asset or other nonmonetary item was acquired.

    a) The TO/FROM ratio for sales is the price level at the end of the year divided by the average price level for the year. The ratio for depreciation is the price level at the end of the year divided by the price level when the asset was purchased.

        i) The net purchasing power gain or loss on net monetary items is included in the income statement.

c. **Monetary vs. nonmonetary items**

   1) A monetary asset is either cash or a claim to receive cash, the amount of which is fixed or determinable without regard to future prices of specific goods or services. Examples are net long-term receivables and demand bank deposits.

   2) A monetary liability is an obligation to pay cash, the amount of which is fixed or determinable without regard to future prices of specific goods and services.

   3) All other items are nonmonetary. Nonmonetary assets change in relationship to future prices of specific goods and services. Examples are patents and trademarks and accumulated depreciation of equipment.

d. Purchasing power gains and losses on net monetary items (NMI) are determined by restating in units of constant purchasing power the opening and closing balances of, and transactions in, monetary assets and liabilities.

e. EXAMPLE:

	Amount in Nominal Dollars	
	December 31, 1995	December 31, 1996
Net monetary assets	$800,000	$943,000

	Index Number
Consumer Price Index at December 31, 1995	100
Consumer Price Index at December 31, 1996	115
Average Consumer Price Index for 1996	110

   1) If gain or loss is to be computed in end-of-year dollars, use a TO/FROM ratio to adjust beginning-of-year NMI and the change in the NMI during the year to end-of-year amounts. Compare the adjusted total amount with actual end-of-year NMI to determine the gain or loss.

Beginning NMI	$800,000 × 115/100 =	$ 920,000
Change during the year	143,000 × 115/110 =	149,500
End-of-year NMI if no gain or loss		$1,069,500
Actual end-of-year NMI		943,000
		$ 126,500 loss

   2) If gain or loss is to be computed in average-for-the-year dollars, the beginning NMI, the change during the year, and the end-of-year NMI should be adjusted to average amounts with TO/FROM ratios.

EXAMPLE:	Nominal Dollars	Adjustment Fraction	Constant Dollars
	$ 800,000	110 ÷ 100	$ 880,000
	+143,000	110 ÷ 110	+143,000
	−943,000	110 ÷ 115	−902,000
	Purchasing power loss		$ 121,000

   3) During inflationary periods, if balances remain constant, monetary assets will suffer purchasing power losses. Monetary liabilities will enjoy purchasing power gains.

3. Stop and review! You have completed the outline for this subunit. Study multiple-choice questions 55 through 60 beginning on page 248.

MULTIPLE-CHOICE QUESTIONS

A. Ratio Analysis

1. What type of ratio is earnings per share?

    A. Profitability ratio.

    B. Activity ratio.

    C. Liquidity ratio.

    D. Leverage ratio.

The correct answer is (A). *(Publisher)*
    REQUIRED: The proper classification of the earnings per share ratio.
    DISCUSSION: Earnings per share is a profitability ratio. It measures the level of profitability of the firm on a per share basis.
    Answer (B) is incorrect because activity ratios measure management's efficiency in using specific resources. Answer (C) is incorrect because liquidity ratios indicate the ability of a company to meet short-term obligations. Answer (D) is incorrect because leverage or equity ratios concern the relationship of debt to equity and measure the impact of the debt on profitability and risk.

2. Given an acid test ratio of 2.0, current assets of $5,000, and inventory of $2,000, the value of current liabilities is

    A. $1,500

    B. $2,500

    C. $3,500

    D. $6,000

The correct answer is (A). *(CIA 590 IV-47)*
    REQUIRED: The value of current liabilities given the acid test ratio, current assets, and inventory.
    DISCUSSION: The acid test or quick ratio equals the ratio of the quick assets (cash, net accounts receivable, and trading securities) divided by current liabilities. Current assets equal the quick assets plus inventory and prepaid expenses. This question assumes that the entity has no prepaid expenses. Given current assets of $5,000, inventory of $2,000, and no prepaid expenses, the quick assets must be $3,000. Because the acid test ratio is 2.0, the quick assets are double the current liabilities. Current liabilities therefore are equal to $1,500 ($3,000 quick assets ÷ 2.0).
    Answer (B) is incorrect because $2,500 results from dividing the current assets by 2.0. Current assets includes inventory, which should not be included in the calculation of the acid test ratio. Answer (C) is incorrect because $3,500 results from adding inventory to current assets rather than subtracting it. Answer (D) is incorrect because $6,000 results from multiplying the quick assets by 2 instead of dividing by 2.

3. Which one of the following inventory cost flow assumptions will result in a higher inventory turnover ratio in an inflationary economy?

    A. FIFO.

    B. LIFO.

    C. Weighted average.

    D. Specific identification.

The correct answer is (B). *(CMA 688 4-16)*
    REQUIRED: The cost flow assumption that will result in a higher inventory turnover ratio in an inflationary economy.
    DISCUSSION: The inventory turnover ratio equals the cost of goods sold divided by the average inventory. LIFO assumes that the last goods purchased are the first goods sold and that the oldest goods purchased remain in inventory. The result is a higher cost of goods sold and a lower average inventory than under other inventory cost flow assumptions if prices are rising. Because cost of goods sold (the numerator) will be higher and average inventory (the denominator) will be lower than under other inventory cost flow assumptions, LIFO produces the highest inventory turnover ratio.
    Answers (A), (C), and (D) are incorrect because when prices are rising LIFO results in a higher cost of goods sold and a lower average inventory than under other inventory cost flow assumptions.

4. Using the data presented below, calculate the cost of sales for the Beta Corporation for 1996.

Current ratio	3.5
Acid test ratio	3.0
Current liabilities 12/31/96	$600,000
Inventory 12/31/95	$500,000
Inventory turnover	8.0

- A. $1,600,000
- B. $2,400,000
- C. $3,200,000
- D. $6,400,000

The correct answer is (C). *(CMA 688 4-12)*

REQUIRED: The cost of sales given various ratios, ending liabilities, and beginning inventory.

DISCUSSION: Inventory turnover equals cost of sales divided by average inventory. The turnover ratio and the beginning inventory are known. If ending inventory can be determined, average inventory and cost of sales can also be calculated. The relationship among the current ratio, acid test ratio, and current liabilities facilitates this calculation. The current ratio is the ratio of current assets to current liabilities. Thus, Beta's current assets are 3.5 times its current liabilities. Given that current liabilities at year-end are $600,000, current assets at year-end must be $2,100,000 (3.5 x $600,000). The acid test ratio is equal to the ratio of the sum of cash, net accounts receivable, and short-term marketable securities to current liabilities. Accordingly, Beta's quick assets are 3.0 times its current liabilities. If current liabilities at year-end are $600,000, the quick assets are $1,800,000 (3.0 x $600,000). The difference between current assets and quick assets is equal to inventory (assuming no prepaid expenses are included in current assets). Because current assets at year-end are $2,100,000 and quick assets are $1,800,000, ending inventory must be $300,000. Average inventory is equal to $400,000 [($500,000 beginning inventory + $300,000 ending inventory) ÷ 2]. An inventory turnover (cost of sales ÷ average inventory) of 8.0 indicates that cost of sales is 8.0 times average inventory. Cost of sales is therefore equal to $3,200,000 (8.0 x $400,000).

Answers (A), (B), and (D) are incorrect because cost of sales equals average inventory times inventory turnover.

5. Return on investment may be calculated by multiplying total asset turnover by

- A. Average collection period.
- B. Profit margin.
- C. Debt ratio.
- D. Fixed-charge coverage.

The correct answer is (B). *(CIA 586 IV-24)*

REQUIRED: The method of calculating return on investment.

DISCUSSION: Return on investment is equal to profit divided by the average total assets. Asset turnover is equal to net sales divided by average total assets. Profit margin is equal to the profit divided by net sales. Thus, multiplying the asset turnover by the profit margin results in the cancellation of net sales from both ratios, leaving a ratio composed of profit in the numerator and average total assets in the denominator, which equals return on investment.

Answers (A), (C), and (D) are incorrect because return on investment cannot be determined using these ratios.

6. Return on investment (ROI) is a term often used to express income earned on capital invested in a business unit. A company's ROI is increased if

- A. Sales increase by the same dollar amount as expenses and total assets.
- B. Sales remain the same and expenses are reduced by the same dollar amount that total assets increase.
- C. Sales decrease by the same dollar amount that expenses increase.
- D. Net profit margin on sales increases by the same percentage as total assets.

The correct answer is (B). *(CMA 684 4-9)*

REQUIRED: The change that would increase a company's ROI.

DISCUSSION: If equal amounts are added to the numerator and denominator of a fraction that is less than one, the ratio will increase. Assuming that the ROI (net income ÷ total assets) is less than one, keeping sales constant while reducing expenses and increasing total assets by equal amounts will increase the ROI because the increase in net income equals the increase in total assets.

Answer (A) is incorrect because increasing sales and expenses by the same amount does not change net income (sales – expenses). Increasing the denominator without increasing the numerator reduces the ratio. Answer (C) is incorrect because decreasing the numerator without changing the denominator reduces the ratio. Answer (D) is incorrect because equal percentage changes in its elements neither increase nor decrease the ratio.

7. Assume that a company's debt ratio is currently 50%. It plans to purchase fixed assets either by using borrowed funds for the purchase or by entering into an operating lease. The company's debt ratio as measured by the balance sheet will

A. Increase whether the assets are purchased or leased.

B. Increase if the assets are purchased, and remain unchanged if the assets are leased.

C. Increase if the assets are purchased, and decrease if the assets are leased.

D. Remain unchanged whether the assets are purchased or leased.

The correct answer is (B). *(CIA 1190 IV-55)*
REQUIRED: The effect on the debt ratio of the acquisition of fixed assets.
DISCUSSION: Under an operating lease, the lessee records neither a lease asset nor a lease liability on the balance sheet. The ratio of debt to total assets is therefore unchanged if this method of financing is used. In contrast, borrowing results in equal increases of both debt and total assets. The debt ratio is equal to the amount of debt divided by total assets. Given that the ratio of debt to total assets is currently 50% (less than 1.0), increasing both the debt (numerator) and the total assets (denominator) by an equal amount will increase the ratio.
Answers (A), (C), and (D) are incorrect because the ratio will increase if the funds are borrowed and remain unchanged if financed through an operating lease.

8. A drop in the market price of a firm's common stock will immediately affect its

A. Return on equity.

B. Dividend payout ratio.

C. Debt to net worth ratio.

D. Dividend yield.

The correct answer is (D). *(CMA 685 4-16)*
REQUIRED: The effect of a drop in the market price of a firm's common stock.
DISCUSSION: Dividend yield equals dividends per common share divided by the market price per common share. Hence, a drop in the market price of the stock will affect this ratio.
Answers (A), (B), and (C) are incorrect because these ratios are based on book values in their calculation rather than the market price of the common stock.

Questions 9, 10, and 11 are based on the following information.

Lisa, Inc.
Statement of Financial Position
December 31, 1996
(in thousands)

Assets	1996	1995
Current assets		
Cash	$ 30	$ 25
Trading securities	20	15
Accounts receivable (net)	45	30
Inventories (at lower of cost or market)	60	50
Prepaid items	15	20
Total current assets	170	140
Long-term investments		
Securities (at cost)	25	20
Property, plant, & equipment		
Land (at cost)	75	75
Building (net)	80	90
Equipment (net)	95	100
Intangible assets		
Patents (net)	35	17
Goodwill (net)	20	13
Total long-term assets	330	315
Total assets	$500	$455

Liabilities & shareholders' equity	1996	1995
Current liabilities		
Notes payable	$ 23	$ 12
Accounts payable	47	28
Accrued interest	15	15
Total current liabilities	85	55
Long-term debt		
Notes payable 10% due 12/31/2003	10	10
Bonds payable 12% due 12/31/2002	15	15
Total long-term debt	25	25
Total liabilities	110	80
Shareholders' equity		
Preferred - 5% cumulative, $100 par, nonparticipating, authorized, issued and outstanding, 1,000 shares	100	100
Common - $10 par 20,000 shares authorized, 15,000 issued and outstanding shares	150	150
Additional paid-in capital - common	75	75
Retained earnings	65	50
Total shareholders' equity	390	375
Total liabilities & equity	$500	$455

9. Lisa Inc.'s acid test (quick) ratio at December 31, 1996 was

    A.   .6 : 1.0

    B.   1.1 : 1.0

    C.   1.8 : 1.0

    D.   2.0 : 1.0

The correct answer is (B). *(CMA 693 2-1)*
    REQUIRED: The acid-test (quick) ratio.
    DISCUSSION: The acid-test, or quick, ratio is calculated by dividing total quick assets by current liabilities. Quick assets are those that can be quickly converted into cash. Besides cash, they include trading securities and accounts receivable. Lisa's quick assets total $95,000 ($30,000 + $20,000 + $45,000). Dividing $95,000 by $85,000 of current liabilities results in a ratio of 1.1.
    Answer (A) is incorrect because .6 ignores receivables as a component of the numerator. Answer (C) is incorrect because 1.8 erroneously includes inventories in the numerator. Answer (D) is incorrect because 2.0 is obtained by dividing total current assets by total current liabilities.

10. Assume net credit sales and cost of good sold for 1996 were $300,000 and $220,000 respectively. Lisa Inc.'s accounts receivable turnover for 1996 was

    A.   4.9 times.

    B.   5.9 times.

    C.   6.7 times.

    D.   8.0 times.

The correct answer is (D). *(CMA 693 2-2)*
    REQUIRED: The accounts receivable turnover.
    DISCUSSION: The accounts receivable turnover is computed by dividing the net credit sales by average accounts receivable. The average is $37,500 [($45,000 + $30,000) ÷ 2]. Hence, the turnover is 8.0 ($300,000 ÷ $37,500).
    Answer (A) is incorrect because 4.9 can be obtained only by using year-end receivables in the denominator and cost of goods sold in the numerator. Answer (B) is incorrect because 5.9 equals cost of goods sold divided by average receivables. Answer (C) is incorrect because 6.7 is based on ending receivables.

11. Assuming that Lisa, Inc.'s net income for 1996 was $35,000, and there were no preferred stock dividends in arrears, Lisa's return on common equity for 1996 was

    A.   7.8%

    B.   10.6%

    C.   10.9%

    D.   12.4%

The correct answer is (B). *(CMA 693 2-6)*
    REQUIRED: The 1996 return on common equity assuming no preferred stock dividends are in arrears.
    DISCUSSION: The preferred stock dividend requirement is 5%, or $5,000 (5% x $100,000). Deducting the $5,000 of preferred dividends from the $35,000 of net income leaves $30,000 for the common shareholders. The firm began the year with common equity of $275,000 and ended with $290,000. Thus, the average common equity during the year was $282,500. The return on common equity was 10.6% ($30,000 ÷ $282,500).
    Answer (A) is incorrect because 7.8% results from $100,000 of preferred stock included in the denominator. Answer (C) is incorrect because 10.9% is based on the beginning shareholders' equity of $275,000. Answer (D) is incorrect because 12.4% is based on total net income of $35,000.

Questions 12 through 16 are based on the following information. The data presented in the next column show actual figures for selected accounts of McKeon Company for the fiscal year ended May 31, 1995, and selected budget figures for the 1996 fiscal year. McKeon's controller is in the process of reviewing the 1996 budget and calculating some key ratios based on the budget. McKeon Company monitors yield or return ratios using the average financial position of the company. (Round all calculations to three decimal places if necessary.)

	5/31/96	5/31/95
Current assets	$210,000	$180,000
Noncurrent assets	275,000	255,000
Current liabilities	78,000	85,000
Long-term debt	75,000	30,000
Common stock ($30 par value)	300,000	300,000
Retained earnings	32,000	20,000

1996 Operations

Sales*	$350,000
Cost of goods sold	160,000
Interest expense	3,000
Income taxes (40% rate)	48,000
Dividends declared and paid in 1996	60,000
Administrative expense	67,000

*All sales are credit sales.

| | Current Assets ||
	5/31/96	5/31/95
Cash	$ 20,000	$10,000
Accounts receivable	100,000	70,000
Inventory	70,000	80,000
Other	20,000	20,000

12. McKeon Company's debt-to-total-asset ratio for 1996 is

A. 0.352

B. 0.315

C. 0.264

D. 0.237

The correct answer is (B). *(CMA 688 4-2)*
REQUIRED: The debt to total asset ratio.
DISCUSSION: The debt-to-total-asset ratio is equal to the total debt at year-end divided by total assets at year-end. Total debt at year-end is $153,000 ($78,000 current liabilities + $75,000 long-term debt). Total assets equal $485,000 ($210,000 current assets + $275,000 noncurrent assets). Thus, the debt-to-total-asset ratio is .315 ($153,000 ÷ $485,000).
Answers (A), (C), and (D) are incorrect because the debt-to-total-asset ratio equals total debt at year-end divided by total assets at year-end.

13. The 1996 accounts receivable turnover for McKeon Company is

A. 1.882

B. 3.500

C. 5.000

D. 4.118

The correct answer is (D). *(CMA 688 4-3)*
REQUIRED: The accounts receivable turnover.
DISCUSSION: The accounts receivable turnover is equal to the total credit sales divided by the average balance in accounts receivable. The average accounts receivable is equal to $85,000 [($70,000 beginning balance + $100,000 ending balance) ÷ 2]. The accounts receivable turnover is therefore equal to 4.118 ($350,000 credit sales ÷ $85,000 average receivables).
Answers (A), (B), and (C) are incorrect because the accounts receivable turnover ratio equals total credit sales divided by average accounts receivable.

14. Using a 365-day year, McKeon's inventory turnover is

A. 171 days.

B. 160 days.

C. 183 days.

D. 78 days.

The correct answer is (A). *(CMA 688 4-4)*
REQUIRED: The inventory turnover in terms of days.
DISCUSSION: Inventory turnover in terms of days is determined by dividing 365 by the inventory turnover ratio. The inventory turnover ratio is equal to the $160,000 cost of goods sold divided by the $75,000 average balance in inventory [($80,000 beginning balance + $70,000 ending balance) ÷ 2]. Hence, the inventory turnover ratio is 2.133 times per year. Dividing 365 by 2.133 results in an inventory turnover of 171 days.
Answers (B), (C), and (D) are incorrect because inventory turnover in terms of days is determined by dividing 365 days by the inventory turnover ratio. The inventory turnover ratio equals the cost of goods sold divided by average inventory.

15. McKeon Company's total asset turnover for 1996 is

A. 0.805

B. 0.761

C. 0.722

D. 0.348

The correct answer is (B). *(CMA 688 4-5)*

REQUIRED: The total asset turnover.

DISCUSSION: Total asset turnover is equal to $350,000 sales divided by average total assets. The amount of average total assets is equal to the average of beginning total assets of $435,000 ($180,000 current assets + $255,000 noncurrent assets) and ending total assets of $485,000 ($210,000 current assets + $275,000 noncurrent assets). The total asset turnover is therefore equal to .761 ($350,000 ÷ $460,000).

Answers (A), (C), and (D) are incorrect because total asset turnover equals sales divided by average total assets.

16. The 1996 return on assets for McKeon Company is

A. 0.261

B. 0.148

C. 0.157

D. 0.166

The correct answer is (C). *(CMA 688 4-6)*

REQUIRED: The return on assets.

DISCUSSION: Return on assets is equal to net income divided by average total assets. As indicated below, net income is equal to $72,000. As determined in the previous question, average total assets is equal to $460,000. Hence, return on assets is 15.7% ($72,000 ÷ $460,000).

Sales	$350,000
Cost of goods sold	(160,000)
Interest expense	(3,000)
Taxes	(48,000)
Administrative expense	(67,000)
Net income	$ 72,000

Answers (A), (B), and (D) are incorrect because return on assets equals net income divided by average total assets.

17. Book value per common share represents the amount of shareholders' equity assigned to each outstanding share of common stock. Which one of the following statements about book value per common share is correct?

A. Market price per common share usually approximates book value per common share.

B. Book value per common share can be misleading because it is based on historical cost.

C. A market price per common share that is greater than book value per common share is an indication of an overvalued stock.

D. Book value per common share is the amount that would be paid to shareholders if the company were sold to another company.

The correct answer is (B). *(CMA 685 4-14)*

REQUIRED: The true statement about book value per common share.

DISCUSSION: Book value is based on the financial statements, which are stated in terms of historical cost and nominal dollars. The figure can be misleading because fair values may differ substantially from book figures.

Answer (A) is incorrect because market price may be more or less than book value. Answer (C) is incorrect because fair value may be more accurate than the carrying values if the historical cost figures are out of date. Answer (D) is incorrect because the amount another company would pay would be based on fair values, not book values.

18. Which one of the following statements about the price-earnings (P-E) ratio is correct?

A. A company with high growth opportunities ordinarily has a high P-E ratio.

B. A P-E ratio has more meaning when a firm has losses than when it has profits.

C. A P-E ratio has more meaning when a firm has abnormally low profits in relation to its asset base.

D. A P-E ratio expresses the relationship between a firm's market price and its net sales.

The correct answer is (A). *(CMA 685 4-13)*

REQUIRED: The true statement about the P-E ratio.

DISCUSSION: A company with high growth opportunities typically has a high P-E ratio because investors are willing to pay a price for the stock higher than that justified by current earnings. In effect, they are trading current earnings for potential future earnings.

Answer (B) is incorrect because a P-E ratio cannot be computed when a firm has losses. Answer (C) is incorrect because a firm with abnormally low profits could have an extremely high, and thus meaningless, P-E ratio. Answer (D) is incorrect because the P-E ratio expresses the relationship between market price and a firm's EPS.

Questions 19 through 25 are based on the following information. Depoole Company is a manufacturer of industrial products and employs a calendar year for financial reporting purposes. These questions present several of Depoole's transactions during the year. Assume that total quick assets exceeded total current liabilities both before and after each transaction described. Further assume that Depoole has positive profits during the year and a credit balance throughout the year in its retained earnings account.

19. Payment of a trade account payable of $64,500 would

   A.   Increase the current ratio but the quick ratio would not be affected.

   B.   Increase the quick ratio but the current ratio would not be affected.

   C.   Increase both the current and quick ratios.

   D.   Decrease both the current and quick ratios.

The correct answer is (C). *(CMA 1280 4-1)*
   REQUIRED: The effect of paying a trade account payable on the current and quick ratios.
   DISCUSSION: Given that the quick assets exceed current liabilities, both the current and quick ratios exceed one because the numerator of the current ratio includes other current assets in addition to the quick assets of cash, net accounts receivable, and short-term marketable securities. An equal reduction in the numerator and the denominator, such as a payment of a trade payable, will cause each ratio to increase.
   Answers (A), (B), and (D) are incorrect because both the current ratio and the quick ratio would increase.

20. The purchase of raw materials for $85,000 on open account would

   A.   Increase the current ratio.

   B.   Decrease the current ratio.

   C.   Increase net working capital.

   D.   Decrease net working capital.

The correct answer is (B). *(CMA 1280 4-2)*
   REQUIRED: The effect of a credit purchase of raw materials on the current ratio and/or working capital.
   DISCUSSION: The purchase increases both the numerator and denominator of the current ratio by adding inventory to the numerator and payables to the denominator. Because the ratio before the purchase was greater than one, the ratio is decreased.
   Answer (A) is incorrect because the current ratio is decreased. Answers (C) and (D) are incorrect because the purchase of raw materials on account has no effect on working capital (current assets and current liabilities change by the same amount).

21. The collection of a current accounts receivable of $29,000 would

   A.   Increase the current ratio.

   B.   Decrease the current ratio and the quick ratio.

   C.   Increase the quick ratio.

   D.   Not affect the current or quick ratios.

The correct answer is (D). *(CMA 1280 4-3)*
   REQUIRED: The effect of collection of a current account receivable on the current and/or quick ratios.
   DISCUSSION: Collecting current accounts receivable has no effect on either the current ratio or the quick ratio because current assets, quick assets, and current liabilities are unchanged by the collection.
   Answers (A), (B), and (C) are incorrect because collecting current accounts receivable does not change current assets, quick assets or current liabilities which means the current and quick ratios are not changed.

22. Obsolete inventory of $125,000 was written off during the year. This transaction

   A.   Decreased the quick ratio.

   B.   Increased the quick ratio.

   C.   Increased net working capital.

   D.   Decreased the current ratio.

The correct answer is (D). *(CMA 1280 4-4)*
   REQUIRED: The effect of writing off obsolete inventory.
   DISCUSSION: Writing off obsolete inventory reduced current assets, but not quick assets (cash, receivables, and marketable securities). Thus, the current ratio was reduced and the quick ratio was unaffected.
   Answers (A) and (B) are incorrect because the quick ratio was not affected. Answer (C) is incorrect because working capital was decreased.

23. The issuance of new shares in a five-for-one split of common stock

    A. Decreases the book value per share of common stock.

    B. Increases the book value per share of common stock.

    C. Increases total shareholders' equity.

    D. Decreases total shareholders' equity.

The correct answer is (A). *(CMA 1280 4-5)*
    REQUIRED: The effect of a five-for-one split of common stock.
    DISCUSSION: Given that five times as many shares of stock are outstanding, the book value per share of common stock is one-fifth of the former value after the split.
    Answer (B) is incorrect because the book value per share is decreased. Answers (C) and (D) are incorrect because the stock split does not change the amount of shareholders' equity.

24. The issuance of serial bonds in exchange for an office building, with the first installment of the bonds due late this year,

    A. Decreases net working capital.

    B. Decreases the current ratio.

    C. Decreases the quick ratio.

    D. Affects all of the answers as indicated.

The correct answer is (D). *(CMA 1280 4-6)*
    REQUIRED: The effect of issuing serial bonds with the first installment due late this year.
    DISCUSSION: The first installment is a current liability, thus the amount of current liabilities increases with no corresponding increase in current assets. The effect is to decrease working capital, the current ratio, and the quick ratio.
    Answer (A) is incorrect because the bond issuance would also decrease the current ratio and the quick ratio. Answer (B) is incorrect because the bond issuance would also decrease net working capital and the quick ratio. Answer (C) is incorrect because the bond issuance would also decrease net working capital and the quick ratio.

25. The early liquidation of a long-term note with cash affects the

    A. Current ratio to a greater degree than the quick ratio.

    B. Quick ratio to a greater degree than the current ratio.

    C. Current and quick ratio to the same degree.

    D. Current ratio but not the quick ratio.

The correct answer is (B). *(CMA 1280 4-7)*
    REQUIRED: The effect of an early liquidation of a long-term note with cash.
    DISCUSSION: The numerators of the quick and current ratios are decreased when cash is expended. Early payment of a long-term liability has no effect on the denominator (current liabilities). Since the numerator of the quick ratio, which includes cash, net receivables, and marketable securities, is less than the numerator of the current ratio, which includes all current assets, the quick ratio is affected to a greater degree.
    Answers (A), (C), and (D) are incorrect because the quick ratio is affected to a greater degree than the current ratio.

26. If the ratio of total liabilities to shareholders' equity increases, a ratio that must also increase is

    A. Times interest earned.

    B. Total liabilities to total assets.

    C. Return on shareholders' equity.

    D. The current ratio.

The correct answer is (B). *(CMA 685 4-17)*
    REQUIRED: The ratio that will increase if the ratio of total liabilities to shareholders' equity increases.
    DISCUSSION: Because total assets will be the same as the sum of liabilities and shareholders' equity, an increase in the liabilities to equity ratio will simultaneously increase the liabilities to assets ratio.
    Answer (A) is incorrect because no determination can be made of the effect on interest coverage without knowing the amounts of income and interest expense. Answer (C) is incorrect because the return on shareholders' equity may be increased or decreased as a result of an increase in the liabilities to equity ratio. Answer (D) is incorrect because the current ratio equals current assets divided by current liabilities, and additional information is necessary to determine whether it would be affected. For example, an increase in current liabilities from short-term borrowing would increase the liabilities to equity ratio but decrease the current ratio.

27. Baylor Company paid out one-half of its 1995 earnings in dividends. Baylor's earnings increased by 20%, and the amount of its dividends increased by 15% in 1996. Baylor's dividend payout ratio for 1996 was

A. 50%

B. 57.5%

C. 47.9%

D. 78%

The correct answer is (C). *(CMA 685 4-20)*
REQUIRED: The dividend payout ratio.
DISCUSSION: The dividend payout ratio was 50% in 1995. Hence, if 1995 net income was X, the total dividend payout would have been 50%X. If earnings increase by 20%, the 1996 income will be 120%X. If dividends increase by 15%, the total dividends paid out will be 57.5%X (115% x 50%X), and the new dividend payout ratio will be 47.9% (57.5%X ÷ 120%X).
Answer (A) is incorrect because 50% is the 1995 payout ratio. Answer (B) is incorrect because 57.5% is 115% of the 1995 payout ratio. Answer (D) is incorrect because 78% equals 65% of 120%.

28. Watson Corporation computed the following items from its financial records for 1996:

Price-earnings ratio   12
Payout ratio   .6
Asset turnover   .9

The dividend yield on Watson's common stock for 1996 is

A. 5.0%

B. 7.2%

C. 7.5%

D. 10.8%

The correct answer is (A). *(CMA 685 4-21)*
REQUIRED: The dividend yield.
DISCUSSION: Dividend yield is computed by dividing the dividend per share by the market price per share. The payout ratio (.6) is computed by dividing dividends by net income per share (EPS). The P-E ratio (12) is computed by dividing the market price per share by net income per share. Thus, assuming that net income per share (EPS) is $X, the market price must be $12X and the dividends per share $.6X (.6 x $X net income per share). Consequently, the dividend yield is 5.0% ($.6X dividend ÷ $12X market price per share).
Answer (B) is incorrect because 7.2% equals 12% times the payout ratio. Answer (C) is incorrect because 7.5% equals asset turnover divided by the P-E ratio. Answer (D) is incorrect because 10.8% equals 12% times the asset turnover.

29. Windham Company has current assets of $400,000 and current liabilities of $500,000. Windham Company's current ratio would be increased by

A. The purchase of $100,000 of inventory on account.

B. The payment of $100,000 of accounts payable.

C. The collection of $100,000 of accounts receivable.

D. Refinancing a $100,000 long-term loan with short-term debt.

The correct answer is (A). *(CMA 1285 4-23)*
REQUIRED: The transaction that would increase a current ratio of less than 1.0.
DISCUSSION: The current ratio equals current assets divided by current liabilities. An equal increase in both the numerator and denominator of a current ratio less than 1.0 causes the ratio to increase. Windham Company's current ratio is .8 ($400,000 ÷ $500,000). The purchase of $100,000 of inventory on account would increase the current assets to $500,000 and the current liabilities to $600,000, resulting in a new current ratio of .833.
Answers (B) and (D) are incorrect because each transaction decreases the current ratio. Answer (C) is incorrect because the current ratio would be unchanged.

30. When compared to a debt-to-assets ratio, a debt-to-equity ratio would

A. Be about the same as the debt-to-assets ratio.

B. Be higher than the debt-to-assets ratio.

C. Be lower than the debt-to-assets ratio.

D. Have no relationship at all to the debt-to-assets ratio.

The correct answer is (B). *(CMA 687 4-27)*
REQUIRED: The true statement comparing the debt-to-equity and debt-to-assets ratios.
DISCUSSION: Because debt plus equity equals assets, a debt-to-equity ratio would have a lower denominator than a debt-to-assets ratio. Thus, the debt-to-equity ratio would be higher than the debt-to-assets ratio.
Answer (A) is incorrect because the ratios would always be different unless either debt or equity equaled zero. Answer (C) is incorrect because the lower denominator in the debt-to-equity ratio means that it would always be higher than the debt-to-assets ratio. Answer (D) is incorrect because the two ratios are related in that they always move in the same direction.

31. When a balance sheet amount is related to an income statement amount in computing a ratio,

A. The balance sheet amount should be converted to an average for the year.

B. The income statement amount should be converted to an average for the year.

C. Both amounts should be converted to market value.

D. Comparisons with industry ratios are not meaningful.

The correct answer is (A). *(CMA 1287 4-1)*
REQUIRED: The true statement about relating balance sheet to income statement amounts in a ratio.
DISCUSSION: In ratios such as inventory turnover, asset turnover, receivables turnover, and return on assets, the balance sheet figure should be an average for the period. The reason is that the income statement amounts represent activity over a period. Thus, the balance sheet figure should be adjusted to reflect assets available for use throughout the period.
Answer (B) is incorrect because the income statement amount is a single figure for an entire year; there is nothing to average. Answer (C) is incorrect because traditional financial statements and the ratios computed from the data they present are mostly stated in historical cost terms. Answer (D) is incorrect because comparison is the purpose of ratio usage. All ratios are meaningless unless compared to something else, such as an industry average.

32. A measure of long-term debt-paying ability is a company's

A. Length of the operating cycle.

B. Return on assets.

C. Inventory turnover.

D. Times interest earned.

The correct answer is (D). *(CMA 688 4-11)*
REQUIRED: The measure of long-term debt-paying ability.
DISCUSSION: The times-interest-earned ratio is one measure of a firm's ability to pay its debt obligations out of current earnings. This ratio equals earnings before interest and taxes divided by interest expense.
Answer (A) is incorrect because the length of the operating cycle does not affect long-term debt-paying ability. By definition, long-term means longer than the normal operating cycle. Answer (B) is incorrect because return on assets measures only how well management uses the assets that are available. It does not compare the return with debt service costs. Answer (C) is incorrect because inventory turnover is a measure of how well a company is managing one of its assets.

33. A high sales-to-working-capital ratio could indicate

A. Unprofitable use of working capital.

B. Sales are not adequate relative to available working capital.

C. The firm is undercapitalized.

D. The firm is not susceptible to liquidity problems.

The correct answer is (C). *(CMA 688 4-14)*
REQUIRED: The meaning of a high sales-to-working-capital ratio.
DISCUSSION: A high sales-to-working-capital ratio is usually favorable because working capital, by itself, is an unprofitable use of resources. A firm does not earn money by holding cash, inventory, or receivables. A high ratio of sales to working capital may indicate either very high sales or a low supply of working capital. A high ratio could indicate that a firm is undercapitalized and does not have resources to invest in working capital.
Answers (A) and (B) are incorrect because a high ratio means low levels of working capital compared to sales. The firm may be using its current assets effectively. Answer (D) is incorrect because a high ratio may indicate insufficient working capital to support the company's sales level.

34. The days' sales-in-receivables ratio will be understated if the company

A. Uses a natural business year for its accounting period.

B. Uses a calendar year for its accounting period.

C. Uses average receivables in the ratio calculation.

D. Does not use average receivables in the ratio calculation.

The correct answer is (A). *(CMA 688 4-15)*
REQUIRED: The reason the days' sales-in-receivables ratio will be understated.
DISCUSSION: The days' sales-in-receivables ratio equals the days in the year divided by the receivables turnover ratio (sales ÷ average receivables). Days' sales may also be computed based only on ending receivables. In either case, use of the natural business year tends to understate the ratio because receivables will usually be at a low point at the beginning and end of the natural year.
Answer (B) is incorrect because using a calendar year will not necessarily affect the usefulness of the days' sales ratio. Answers (C) and (D) are incorrect because using average receivables would not always understate the ratio.

Questions 35 through 41 are based on the following information. Pubco is a public company that uses a calendar year and has a complex capital structure. In the computation of its basic and diluted earnings per share (BEPS and DEPS, respectively) in accordance with SFAS 128, *Earnings per Share*, Pubco uses income before extraordinary items as the control number. Pubco reported no cumulative effect of accounting changes or discontinued operations, but it had an extraordinary loss (net of tax) of $1,200,000 in the first quarter when its income before the extraordinary item was $1,000,000.

The average market price of Pubco's common stock for the first quarter was $25, the shares outstanding at the beginning of the period equaled 300,000, and 12,000 shares were issued on March 1.

At the beginning of the quarter, Pubco had outstanding $2,000,000 of 5% convertible bonds, with each $1,000 bond convertible into 10 shares of common stock. No bonds were converted.

At the beginning of the quarter, Pubco also had outstanding 120,000 shares of preferred stock paying a quarterly dividend of $.10 per share and convertible to common stock on a one-to-one basis. Holders of 60,000 shares of preferred stock exercised their conversion privilege on February 1.

Throughout the first quarter, warrants to buy 50,000 shares of Pubco's common stock for $28 per share were outstanding but unexercised.

Pubco's tax rate was 30%.

35. The weighted-average number of shares used to calculate BEPS amounts for the first quarter is

A. 444,000

B. 372,000

C. 344,000

D. 300,000

The correct answer is (C). *(Publisher)*

REQUIRED: The weighted-average number of shares used to calculate BEPS amounts for the first quarter.

DISCUSSION: The number of shares outstanding at January 1 was 300,000, 12,000 shares were issued on March 1, and 60,000 shares of preferred stock were converted to 60,000 shares of common stock on February 1. Thus, the weighted-average number of shares used to calculate BEPS amounts for the first quarter is 344,000 $\{300,000 + [12,000 \times (1 \div 3)] + [60,000 \times (2 \div 3)]\}$.

Answer (A) is incorrect because 444,000 is the adjusted weighted-average number of shares used in the DEPS calculation. Answer (B) is incorrect because 372,000 is the total outstanding at March 31. Answer (D) is incorrect because 300,000 equals the shares outstanding at January 1.

36. The control number for determining whether potential common shares are dilutive or antidilutive is

A. $1,000,000

B. $994,000

C. $(206,000)

D. $(1,200,000)

The correct answer is (B). *(Publisher)*

REQUIRED: The control number for determining whether potential common shares are dilutive or antidilutive.

DISCUSSION: If a company reports discontinued operations, extraordinary items, or accounting changes, it uses income from continuing operations (in Pubco's case, income before extraordinary item), adjusted for preferred dividends, as the control number for determining whether potential common shares are dilutive or antidilutive. Hence, the number of potential common shares used in calculating DEPS for income from continuing operations is also used in calculating the other DEPS amounts even if the effect is antidilutive with respect to the corresponding BEPS amounts. However, if the entity has a loss from continuing operations available to common shareholders, no potential common shares are included in the calculation of any DEPS amount (SFAS 128). The control number for Pubco is $994,000 $\{\$1,000,000$ income before extraordinary item – [$.10 per share dividend $\times$ (120,000 preferred shares – 60,000 preferred shares converted)]$\}$.

Answer (A) is incorrect because $1,000,000 is unadjusted income from continuing operations. Answer (C) is incorrect because $(206,000) is the net loss available to common shareholders after subtracting the extraordinary loss. Answer (D) is incorrect because $(1,200,000) is the extraordinary loss.

37. The BEPS amount for the net income or loss available to common shareholders after the extraordinary item is

A. $2.89

B. $(0.46)

C. $(0.60)

D. $(3.49)

The correct answer is (C). *(Publisher)*

REQUIRED: The BEPS amount for the net income or loss available to common shareholders after the extraordinary item.

DISCUSSION: The weighted-average of shares used in the BEPS denominator is 344,000 (see question 35). The numerator equals income before extraordinary item, minus preferred dividends, minus the extraordinary loss. Thus, it equals the control number (see question 36) minus the extraordinary loss, or $(206,000) [$994,000 – $1,200,000]. The BEPS amount for the net income or loss available to common shareholders after the extraordinary item is $(0.60) [$(206,000) ÷ 344,000 shares].

Answer (A) is incorrect because $2.89 is the BEPS amount for income available to common shareholders before the extraordinary item. Answer (B) is incorrect because $(0.46) uses the denominator of the DEPS calculation. Answer (D) is incorrect because $(3.49) is the BEPS amount for the extraordinary loss.

38. The weighted-average number of shares used to calculate DEPS amounts for the first quarter is

A. 444,000

B. 438,000

C. 372,000

D. 344,000

The correct answer is (A). *(Publisher)*

REQUIRED: The weighted-average number of shares used to calculate DEPS amounts for the first quarter.

DISCUSSION: The denominator of DEPS equals the weighted-average number of shares used in the BEPS calculation (344,000 as determined in question 35) plus dilutive potential common shares (assuming the control number is not a loss). The incremental shares from assumed conversion of warrants is zero because they are antidilutive. The $25 market price is less than the $28 exercise price. The assumed conversion of all the preferred shares at the beginning of the quarter results in 80,000 incremental shares {[120,000 shares x (3 ÷ 3)] – [60,000 shares x (2 ÷ 3)]}. The assumed conversion of all the bonds at the beginning of the quarter results in 20,000 incremental shares [($2,000,000 ÷ $1,000 per bond) x 10 common shares per bond]. Consequently, the weighted-average number of shares used to calculate DEPS amounts for the first quarter is 444,000 (344,000 + 0 + 80,000 + 20,000).

Answer (B) is incorrect because 438,000 assumes the hypothetical exercise of all the warrants at the beginning of the period at a price of $28 and the repurchase of shares using the proceeds at a price of $25. Answer (C) is incorrect because 372,000 is the total outstanding at March 31. Answer (D) is incorrect because 344,000 is the denominator of the BEPS fraction.

39. The effect of assumed conversions on the numerator of the DEPS fraction is

A. $31,000

B. $25,000

C. $23,500

D. $17,500

The correct answer is (C). *(Publisher)*

REQUIRED: The effect of assumed conversions on the numerator of the DEPS fraction.

DISCUSSION: If all of the convertible preferred shares are assumed to be converted on January 1, $6,000 of dividends [$.10 x (120,000 – 60,000) preferred shares] will not be paid. Furthermore, if the bonds are assumed to be converted on January 1, interest of $17,500 {[5% x $2,000,000 ÷ 4] x (1.0– .3 tax rate)} will not be paid. Accordingly, the effect of assumed conversions on the numerator of the DEPS fraction is an addition of $23,500 ($6,000 + $17,500) to the income available to common shareholders.

Answer (A) is incorrect because $31,000 disregards the tax shield provided by bond interest. Answer (B) is incorrect because $25,000 equals one quarter's bond interest payment. Answer (D) is incorrect because $17,500 is the effect of the assumed conversion of the bonds alone.

40. The difference between BEPS and DEPS for the extraordinary item is

A. $2.89

B. $2.10

C. $.79

D. $.60

The correct answer is (C). *(Publisher)*
REQUIRED: The difference between BEPS and DEPS for the extraordinary item.
DISCUSSION: BEPS for the extraordinary loss is $(3.49) [$(1,200,000) ÷ 344,000]. DEPS for the extraordinary item is $(2.70) [$(1,200,000) ÷ 444,000 shares].
Answer (A) is incorrect because $2.89 is the difference between DEPS and BEPS for the extraordinary loss. Answer (B) is incorrect because $2.10 is the difference between DEPS for the extraordinary loss and the BEPS for the net loss available to common shareholders after the extraordinary loss. Answer (D) is incorrect because $.60 is the BEPS for the net loss available to common shareholders after the extraordinary loss.

41. The DEPS amount for the net income or loss available to common shareholders after the extraordinary item is

A. $2.29

B. $(0.41)

C. $(0.53)

D. $(2.70)

The correct answer is (B). *(Publisher)*
REQUIRED: The DEPS amount for the net income or loss available to common shareholders.
DISCUSSION: The numerator equals the income available to common shareholders (the control number), plus the effect of the assumed conversions, minus the extraordinary loss. The denominator equals the weighted-average of shares outstanding plus the dilutive potential common shares. Hence, the DEPS amount for the net income or loss available to common shareholders after the extraordinary item is $(.41) [($994,000 + $23,500 − $1,200,000) ÷ 444,000].
Answer (A) is incorrect because $2.29 is the DEPS amount for income before the extraordinary item. Answer (C) is incorrect because $(0.53) is based on the BEPS denominator. Answer (D) is incorrect because $(2.70) is the DEPS for the extraordinary item.

42. Rice, Inc. uses the allowance method to account for uncollectible accounts. An account receivable that was previously determined uncollectible and written off was collected during May. The effect of the collection on Rice's current ratio and total working capital is

	Current Ratio	Working Capital
A.	None	None
B.	Increase	Increase
C.	Decrease	Decrease
D.	None	Increase

The correct answer is (A). *(CMA 690 4-11)*
REQUIRED: The effect on the current ratio and working capital of collecting an account previously written off.
DISCUSSION: The entry to record this transaction is twofold: debit receivables and credit the allowance; debit cash and credit receivables. The result is to increase both an asset (cash) and a contra asset (allowance for bad debts). These appear in the current asset section of the balance sheet. Thus, the collection changes neither the current ratio nor working capital because the effects are offsetting. The credit for the journal entry is made to the allowance account on the assumption that another account will become uncollectible. The company had previously estimated its bad debts and established an appropriate allowance. It then (presumably) wrote off the wrong account. Accordingly, the journal entry reinstates a balance in the allowance account to absorb future uncollectibles.
Answers (B), (C), and (D) are incorrect because neither the current ratio nor working capital is affected.

43. Merit, Inc. uses the direct write-off method to account for uncollectible accounts receivable. If the company subsequently collects an account receivable that was written off in a prior accounting period, the effect of the collection of the account receivable on Merit's current ratio and total working capital would be

	Current Ratio	Working Capital
A.	None	None
B.	Increase	Increase
C.	Increase	None
D.	None	Decrease

The correct answer is (B). *(CMA 690 4-12)*
REQUIRED: The effect on the current ratio and working capital of collecting an account written off in a prior period under the direct write-off method.
DISCUSSION: Because the company uses the direct write-off method, the original entry involved a debit to a bad debt expense account (closed to retained earnings). The subsequent collection required a debit to cash and a credit to bad debt expense or retained earnings. Thus, only one current asset account was involved in the collection entry, and current assets (cash) increased as a result. If current assets increase, and no change occurs in current liabilities, the current ratio and working capital both increase.
Answers (A), (C), and (D) are incorrect because the current ratio and working capital increase.

44. To determine the operating cycle for a retail department store, which one of the following pairs of items is needed?

A. Days' sales in accounts receivable and average merchandise inventory.

B. Cash turnover and net sales.

C. Accounts receivable turnover and inventory turnover.

D. Asset turnover and return on sales.

The correct answer is (C). *(CMA 690 4-13)*

REQUIRED: The pair of items needed to determine the operating cycle for a retailer.

DISCUSSION: The operating cycle is the time needed to turn cash into inventory, inventory into receivables, and receivables back into cash. For a retailer, it is the time from purchase of inventory to collection of cash. Thus, the operating cycle of a retailer is equal to the sum of the number of days' sales in inventory and the number of days' sales in receivables. Inventory turnover equals cost of goods sold divided by average inventory. The days' sales in inventory equals 365 (or another period chosen by the analyst) divided by the inventory turnover. Accounts receivable turnover equals net credit sales divided by average receivables. The days' sales in receivables equals 365 (or other number) divided by the accounts receivable turnover.

Answer (A) is incorrect because cost of sales must be known to calculate days' sales in inventory. Answers (B) and (D) are incorrect because they are insufficient to permit determination of the operating cycle.

45. Accounts receivable turnover will normally decrease as a result of

A. The write-off of an uncollectible account (assume the use of the allowance for doubtful accounts method).

B. A significant sales volume decrease near the end of the accounting period.

C. An increase in cash sales in proportion to credit sales.

D. A change in credit policy to lengthen the period for cash discounts.

The correct answer is (D). *(CMA 690 4-14)*

REQUIRED: The event that will cause the accounts receivable turnover to decrease.

DISCUSSION: The accounts receivable turnover equals net credit sales divided by average receivables. Hence, it will decrease if a company lengthens the credit period or the discount period because the denominator will increase as receivables are held for longer times.

Answer (A) is incorrect because write-offs do not reduce net receivables (gross receivables – the allowance) and will not affect the receivables balance and therefore the turnover ratio if an allowance system is used. Answer (B) is incorrect because a decline in sales near the end of the period signifies fewer credit sales and receivables, and the effect of reducing the numerator and denominator by equal amounts is to increase the ratio if the fraction is greater than 1.0. Answer (C) is incorrect because an increase in cash sales with no diminution of credit sales will not affect receivables.

46. If a company is profitable and is effectively using leverage, which one of the following ratios is likely to be the largest?

A. Return on total assets.

B. Return on operating assets.

C. Return on common equity.

D. Return on total shareholders' equity.

The correct answer is (C). *(CMA 690 4-18)*

REQUIRED: The ratio that is likely to be largest if a profitable company is effectively using leverage.

DISCUSSION: The purpose of leverage is to use creditor capital to earn income for shareholders. If the return on the resources provided by creditors or preferred shareholders exceeds the cost (interest or fixed dividends), leverage is used effectively, and the return to common equity will be higher than the other measures. The reason is that common equity provides a smaller proportion of the investment than in an unleveraged company.

Answers (A), (B), and (D) are incorrect because each will be lower than the return on common equity if the firm is profitable and using leverage effectively.

Questions 47 and 48 are based on the following information. Selected data from Ostrander Corporation's financial statements for the years indicated are presented in thousands.

	1996 Operations
Net sales	$4,175
Cost of goods sold	2,880
Interest expense	50
Income tax	120
Gain on disposal of a segment (net of tax)	210
Net income	385

December 31	1996	1995
Cash	$ 32	$ 28
Trading securities	169	172
Accounts receivable (net)	210	204
Merchandise inventory	440	420
Tangible fixed assets	480	440
Total assets	1,397	1,320
Current liabilities	370	368
Total liabilities	790	750
Common stock outstanding	226	210
Retained earnings	381	360

47. The times interest was earned for Ostrander Corporation for 1996 is

A. .57 times.

B. 7.70 times.

C. 3.50 times.

D. 6.90 times.

The correct answer is (D). *(CMA 691 2-7)*

REQUIRED: The times interest was earned for 1996.

DISCUSSION: The interest coverage ratio is computed by dividing net income from operations before taxes and interest by interest expense. Net income of $385, minus the disposal gain of $210, is added to income taxes of $120 and interest expense of $50 to produce a ratio numerator of $345. Dividing $345 by $50 results in an interest coverage of 6.90 times.

Answer (A) is incorrect because .57 is the debt ratio. Answer (B) is incorrect because 7.70 times is based on net income from operations after taxes and interest. Answer (C) is incorrect because 3.50 times results from not adding interest and taxes to net income after the gain on disposal is subtracted.

48. The total debt-to-equity ratio for Ostrander Corporation in 1996 is

A. 3.49

B. 0.77

C. 2.07

D. 1.30

The correct answer is (D). *(CMA 691 2-8)*

REQUIRED: The total debt-to-equity ratio for 1996.

DISCUSSION: Total shareholders' equity consists of the $226 of capital stock and $381 of retained earnings, or $607. Debt is given as the $790 of total liabilities. Thus, the ratio is 1.30 ($790 ÷ $607).

Answer (A) is incorrect because 3.49 equals total liabilities divided by common stock outstanding. Answer (B) is incorrect because 0.77 equals equity divided by debt. Answer (C) is incorrect because 2.07 equals total liabilities divided by retained earnings.

49. The ratio of sales to working capital is a measure of

A. Collectibility.

B. Financial leverage.

C. Liquidity.

D. Profitability.

The correct answer is (C). *(CMA 692 2-25)*

REQUIRED: The quality measured by the ratio of sales to working capital.

DISCUSSION: Like most ratios involving working capital, the working capital turnover (sales ÷ working capital) is a measure of liquidity, which is the ability to meet obligations as they mature. However, it is also an activity measure, and a high turnover is preferable.

Answer (A) is incorrect because working capital includes cash and inventory, neither of which involves collectibility. Answer (B) is incorrect because financial leverage concerns the relationship between the use of debt capital and equity capital. Answer (D) is incorrect because profitability measures incorporate costs as well as revenues, assets, and liabilities.

50. The following information is provided about the common stock of Evergreen Inc. at the end of the fiscal year:

Number of shares outstanding	1,800,000
Par value per share	$ 10.00
Dividends paid per share (last 12 months)	12.00
Market price per share	108.00
Primary earnings per share	36.00
Fully diluted earnings per share	24.00

The price/earnings ratio for Evergreen's common stock is

A. 3.0 times.

B. 4.5 times.

C. 9.0 times.

D. 10.8 times.

The correct answer is (B). *(CFM Sample Q. 1)*
REQUIRED: The price earnings ratio.
DISCUSSION: The price earnings ratio is

$$\frac{Market\ price}{Fully\ diluted\ EPS} = \frac{\$108}{\$24} = 4.5$$

Answer (A) is incorrect because 3.0 is based on PEPS rather than FDEPS in the denominator. Answer (C) is incorrect because 9.0 is based on dividends rather than FDEPS in the denominator. Answer (D) is incorrect because 10.8 is based on par value rather than FDEPS in the denominator.

B. Limitations of Ratio Analysis

51. Which of the following is not a limitation of ratio analysis affecting comparability among firms?

A. Different accounting policies.

B. Different fiscal years.

C. Different sources of information.

D. All of the above are limitations of ratio analysis.

The correct answer is (D). *(Publisher)*
REQUIRED: The factor that is not a limitation of ratio analysis affecting comparability among firms.
DISCUSSION: Ratio analysis provides useful information regarding the efficiency of operations and the stability of financial condition. Nevertheless, it has several inherent limitations, such as firms using different accounting policies, different fiscal years, and different sources of information. Each of these factors impairs the comparability of financial statement amounts and the ratios derived from them.

Answers (A), (B), and (C) are incorrect because each represents a limitation of ratio analysis.

C. Comparative Analysis

52. In assessing the financial prospects for a firm, financial analysts use various techniques. An example of vertical, common-size analysis is

A. An assessment of the relative stability of a firm's level of vertical integration.

B. A comparison in financial ratio form between two or more firms in the same industry.

C. Advertising expense in 1996 is 2% greater than it was in 1995.

D. Advertising expense in 1996 is 2% of sales.

The correct answer is (D). *(CMA 1295 2-21)*
REQUIRED: The example of vertical, common-size analysis.
DISCUSSION: Vertical, common-size analysis compares the components within a set of financial statements. A base amount is assigned a value of 100%. For example, total assets on a common-size balance sheet and net sales on a common-size income statement are valued at 100%. Common-size statements permit evaluation of the efficiency of various aspects of operations. An analyst who states that advertising expense is 2% of sales is using vertical, common-size analysis.

Answer (A) is incorrect because vertical integration occurs when a corporation owns one or more of its suppliers or customers. Answer (B) is incorrect because vertical, common-size analysis restates financial statements amounts as percentages. Answer (C) is incorrect because a statement that advertising expense is 2% greater than in the previous year results from horizontal analysis.

53. In financial statement analysis, expressing all financial statement items as a percentage of base-year amounts is called

A. Horizontal common-size analysis.

B. Vertical common-size analysis.

C. Trend analysis.

D. Ratio analysis.

The correct answer is (A). *(CMA 688 4-17)*
REQUIRED: The term for expressing all financial statement items as a percentage of base-year amounts.
DISCUSSION: Expressing financial statement items as percentages of corresponding base-year figures is a horizontal form of common-size (percentage) analysis that is useful for evaluating trends. The base amount is assigned the value of 100%, and the amounts for other years are denominated in percentages compared to the base year.
Answer (B) is incorrect because vertical common-size (percentage) analysis presents figures for a single year expressed as percentages of a base amount on the balance sheet (e.g., total assets) and on the income statement (e.g., sales). Answer (C) is incorrect because the term "trend analysis" is most often applied to the quantitative techniques used in forecasting to fit a curve to given data. Answer (D) is incorrect because it is a general term.

54. Under GAAP, comparative financial statements are

A. Required for at least the current and the prior year.

B. Required for at least the current and the prior 2 years.

C. Recommended for at least the current and the prior year.

D. Neither required nor recommended.

The correct answer is (C). *(S. Rubin)*
REQUIRED: The position of GAAP concerning comparative financial statements.
DISCUSSION: ARB 43, Ch. 2A, states that in any 1 year it is ordinarily desirable that financial statements of two or more periods be presented. This position is generally understood to be a recommendation rather than a requirement.
Answers (A) and (B) are incorrect because comparative financial statements are not required. Answer (D) is incorrect because comparative financial statements are recommended.

D. Effects of Changing Price Levels

55. Which of the following items is included in the 5-year summary of selected financial data recommended by SFAS 89, *Financial Reporting and Changing Prices*?

A. Net income.

B. Income from continuing operations on a current cost basis.

C. Purchasing power gain or loss on net nonmonetary items.

D. Cash dividends paid per common share.

The correct answer is (B). *(Publisher)*
REQUIRED: The item included in the 5-year summary of selected financial data.
DISCUSSION: SFAS 89 recommends that an enterprise disclose the following information for each of the 5 most recent years:

a) Net sales and other operating revenues
b) Income from continuing operations on a current cost basis
c) Purchasing power gain or loss on net monetary items
d) Increase or decrease in the current cost or lower recoverable amount of inventory and property, plant, and equipment, net of inflation
e) The aggregate foreign currency translation adjustment on a current cost basis (if applicable)
f) Net assets at year-end on a current cost basis
g) Income per common share from continuing operations on a current cost basis
h) Cash dividends declared per common share
I) Market price per common share at year-end

Answers (A), (C), and (D) are incorrect because SFAS 89 does not recommend that an enterprise disclose net income, purchasing power gain or loss on net nonmonetary items, and cash dividends paid per common share.

56. SFAS 89, *Financial Reporting and Changing Prices*, recommends that the information presented in the 5-year summary of selected financial data be stated in terms of

A. Beginning-of-the-year units of constant purchasing power.

B. Average-for-the-year units of constant purchasing power.

C. Nominal units of money.

D. In dollars equivalent in purchasing power to dollars used in calculating the current period Consumer Price Index for All Urban Consumers.

The correct answer is (B). *(Publisher)*
REQUIRED: The unit of measure used to state the selected financial data included in the 5-year summary.
DISCUSSION: SFAS 89 recommends that the information presented in the 5-year summary be stated in average-for-the-year units of constant purchasing power, in end-of-the-year units of constant purchasing power, or in dollars having a purchasing power equal to that of the dollars of the base period used by the Bureau of Labor Statistics in calculating the Consumer Price Index for All Urban Consumers.
Answers (A), (C), and (D) are incorrect because SFAS 89 does not recommend that information presented in the 5-year summary be stated in beginning-of-the-year units of constant purchasing power, nominal units of money, or in dollars equivalent in purchasing power to dollars used in calculating the current period Consumer Price Index for All Urban Consumers.

57. Cascade Company had sales of $300,000 in 1995 and the price index for its industry is expected to rise from 300 in 1995 to 320 in 1996. The level of sales that Cascade must reach in 1996 in order to achieve a real growth rate of 20% is

A. $360,000

B. $320,000

C. $337,500

D. $384,000

The correct answer is (D). *(CMA 685 4-19)*
REQUIRED: The sales needed to realize a specified real growth rate.
DISCUSSION: Given that the price index increased from 300 to 320, sales must increase from $300,000 to $320,000 to realize a zero real growth rate. If the firm desires a 20% real growth rate, it must increase sales to $384,000 (120% x $320,000).
Answer (A) is incorrect because $360,000 assumes no change in the price index. Answer (B) is incorrect because $320,000 reflects a zero growth rate. Answer (C) is incorrect because $337,500 assumes the price index declined from 320 to 300.

58. SFAS 89 recommends that a 5-year summary of certain selected financial data be presented. If the current year income from continuing operations on a current cost/constant purchasing power basis differs significantly from income from continuing operations in the primary financial statements, an enterprise should also disclose

A. All components of income from continuing operations for the current year on a current cost basis.

B. All components of net income for the current year on a current cost basis.

C. Certain components of income from continuing operations for the current year on a current cost basis.

D. All operating expenses for the current year on a current cost basis.

The correct answer is (C). *(Publisher)*
REQUIRED: The required current cost/constant purchasing power disclosures.
DISCUSSION: When income from continuing operations on a current cost/constant purchasing power basis differs significantly from income from continuing operations reported in the primary financial statements, SFAS 89 recommends that certain components of income from continuing operations for the current year be disclosed on a current cost basis. The information may be presented in a statement format, in a reconciliation format, or in notes to the 5-year summary. Whichever format is used, the presentation should disclose or allow the reader to determine the difference between the amount in the primary statements and the current cost amount of the following: cost of goods sold, depreciation, depletion, and amortization expense.
Answers (A), (B), and (D) are incorrect because SFAS 89 recommends that only certain components of income from continuing operations for the current year be disclosed on a current cost basis.

59. The following data summarize a company's fixed asset acquisitions:

Year	Cost of Acquisitions	Price Index
1981	$1,000	200 ÷ 80
1991	1,000	200 ÷ 150
1996	1,000	200 ÷ 200

The total of these assets in constant purchasing power at the end of 1996 is

A. C$4,833

B. C$2,000

C. C$650

D. C$3,300

The correct answer is (A). *(CIA 583 IV-14)*

REQUIRED: The total fixed assets in constant purchasing power at the end of the current period.

DISCUSSION: In historical cost/constant purchasing power accounting, the historical cost principle is retained but the unit of measure is restated to reflect changes in the general purchasing power of the monetary unit. Thus, each asset should be restated using the price index in effect at the time of acquisition. The 1981 acquisition should be valued at $2,500 [(200 ÷ 80) x $1,000], the 1991 acquisition at $1,333 [(200 ÷ 150) x $1,000], and the 1996 acquisition at $1,000 [(200 ÷ 200) x $1,000]. The total in constant purchasing power is C$4,833 ($2,500 + $1,333 + $1,000).

Answers (B), (C), and (D) are incorrect because the total of the assets in constant purchasing power is C$4,833 as calculated above.

60. A corporation has gathered the following data in order to compute the purchasing power gain or loss to be included in its supplementary information for the year ended December 31, 1996:

	Amount in Nominal Dollars	
	December 31 1995	December 31 1996
Net monetary assets	$800,000	$943,000

	Index Number
Consumer Price Index at December 31, 1995	200
Consumer Price Index at December 31, 1996	230
Average Consumer Price Index for 1996	220

The purchasing power gain or loss on net monetary items (expressed in average-for-the-year dollars for 1996) should be reported at what amount for the year ended December 31, 1996?

A. $121,000 purchasing power loss.

B. $121,000 purchasing power gain.

C. $126,500 purchasing power loss.

D. $126,500 purchasing power gain.

The correct answer is (A). *(CIA 1190 IV-39)*

REQUIRED: The amount to be reported as purchasing power gain or loss on net monetary items.

DISCUSSION: Purchasing power gain or loss expressed in average constant monetary units equals the beginning net monetary position restated to average constant monetary units, plus the actual change in the net monetary position during the year expressed in average constant monetary units, minus the ending net monetary position restated to average constant monetary units. The restatement to average constant monetary units requires multiplying the nominal dollar amount by a fraction with a numerator equal to the average CPI (220) and the denominator equal to the CPI at the date of the recording of the net monetary assets. For December 31, 1995, the denominator is 200. For the $943,000 December 31, 1996 balance, the denominator is 230. For the $143,000 difference between the beginning and ending balances, the denominator is 220, based on the assumption this change occurred evenly throughout the year. As indicated below, a purchasing power loss (inflation is unfavorable to holders of monetary assets) of $121,000 results.

Nominal Dollars	Adjustment Fraction	Constant Dollars
$ 800,000	220 ÷ 200	$ 880,000
+143,000	220 ÷ 220	+143,000
− 943,000	220 ÷ 230	−902,000
Purchasing power loss		$ 121,000

Answers (B) and (D) are incorrect because there is a purchasing power loss. Answers (C) and (D) are incorrect because the purchasing power loss is equal to $121,000.

STUDY UNIT 7: BUSINESS COMBINATIONS AND RESTRUCTURINGS

19 pages of outline
59 multiple-choice questions

A. Types of Combinations
B. Reasons for Combinations
C. Tax Issues
D. Other Regulatory Issues
E. Accounting for Combinations
F. Valuation and Pricing the Combination
G. Opposition to the Combination
H. Other Restructurings
I. Bankruptcy

This is the fifth and final study unit covering the major topic, "Advanced Topics in Corporate Financial Management."

The circumstances of a firm may dictate a policy either of growth or restructuring. Internal expansion is the most usual form of growth, but business combinations provide opportunities for dramatic and rapid change. A combination of two firms is a means of corporate growth with many financial, legal, accounting, and tax implications. It is in effect an investment that is intended to generate a positive net present value for shareholders. Thus, the increase in firm value from the combination should exceed its costs, including any premium paid (cost − market value). Combinations are undertaken for many reasons, and they may be resisted by the management of the targeted firms. However, a firm's best strategy may involve restructuring through divestitures of assets, changes in ownership structure, and other means. In an extreme case, a financially distressed firm may even decide to reorganize or liquidate under the bankruptcy statutes.

A. Types of Combinations

1. A **merger** is a business transaction in which an acquiring firm absorbs a second firm, and the acquiring firm remains in business as a combination of the two merged firms. A merger is legally straightforward; however, approval of the shareholders of each firm is required. A **consolidation** is similar to a merger, but a new company is formed and neither of the merging companies survives. There are four groups of mergers:

    a. A **horizontal merger** occurs when two firms in the same line of business combine.

    b. A **vertical merger** combines a firm with one of its suppliers or customers.

    c. A **congeneric merger** is a combination of firms with related products or services; however, the firms do not produce the same product or have a producer-supplier relationship.

    d. A **conglomerate merger** involves two unrelated firms in different industries.

2. An **acquisition** is the purchase of all of another firm's assets or a controlling interest in its stock.

    a. An acquisition of all of a firm's assets requires a vote of that firm's shareholders. It also entails the costly transfer of legal title, but it avoids the minority interest that may arise if the acquisition is by purchase of stock.

b. An acquisition by stock purchase is advantageous because it can be effected when management and the board of directors are hostile to the combination, and it does not require a formal vote of the firm's shareholders. If the acquiring firm's offer is rejected by the acquiree's management, a tender offer may be made directly to the acquiree's shareholders to obtain a controlling interest.

   1) A **tender offer** is a general invitation by an individual or a corporation to all shareholders of another corporation to tender their shares for a specified price.

      a) In 1968, Congress enacted the Williams Act to extend reporting and disclosure requirements under the Securities and Exchange Act of 1934 to tender offers.

      b) Any person or group that acquires more than 5% of a class of registered securities is required, within 10 days of the tender, to file a statement with the SEC and the issuing company.

      c) The tender offer may be friendly (acceptable to the target corporation's management) or hostile. If it is the latter, the target must also file a statement with the SEC. The target has 10 days in which to respond to the bidder's tender offer. Moreover, a tender offer must be kept open for at least 20 business days.

   2) Direct solicitation of shareholders when management and the board resist the combination has been called a **Saturday night special** or a **hostile takeover**. This solicitation may be by advertisement in the media or, when a shareholder list can be obtained, by a general mailing.

c. An acquisition of stock may eventually result in the merger or consolidation of the two firms.

d. **Takeover** is a broad term often used in the description of business combinations. It signifies a shift of control from one set of shareholders to another and may be **friendly** or **hostile**. A takeover includes not only mergers and acquisitions but also proxy contests and going private.

   1) A **proxy contest** is an attempt by dissident shareholders to gain control of the corporation, or at least to gain influence, by electing directors. A proxy is a power of attorney given by a shareholder that authorizes the holder to exercise the voting rights of the shareholder.

      a) Ten days prior to mailing a proxy statement to shareholders, the issuer must file a copy with the SEC.

      b) SEC rules require the solicitor of proxies to furnish shareholders with all material information concerning the matter subject to vote.

      c) A form by which shareholders may indicate their agreement or disagreement must be provided.

      d) Proxies solicited for the purpose of voting for directors must be accompanied by an annual report.

   2) **Going private** entails the purchase of the publicly owned stock of a corporation by a small group of private investors, usually including senior managers. Accordingly, the stock is delisted (if it is traded on an exchange) because it will no longer be traded. Such a transaction is usually structured as a leveraged buyout.

a) A **leveraged buyout (LBO)** is a financing technique by which a company is purchased using very little equity. The cash-offer price is financed with large amounts of debt. An LBO is often used when a company is sold to management or some other group of employees, but it is also used in hostile takeovers.

    i) The company's assets serve as collateral for a loan to finance the purchase.

- Junk bonds are often issued in an LBO. They are high-risk and therefore high-yield securities that are normally issued when the debt ratio is very high. Thus, the bondholders will have as much risk as the holders of equity securities.

- The tax deductibility of interest paid by the restructured company is an advantage of an LBO. Given a high debt ratio, that is, greater financial leverage, after-tax cash flows increase.

    ii) In addition to greater financial leverage, the firm may benefit from an LBO because of savings in administrative costs from no longer being publicly traded. Furthermore, if the managers become owners, they have greater incentives and greater operational flexibility.

    iii) Characteristics of firms that are candidates for an LBO include

- An established business with proven operating performance

- Stable earnings and cash flows

- Very little outstanding debt

- A quality asset base that can be used as collateral for a new loan

- Stable technology that will not require large expenditures for R&D

    iv) The high degree of risk in LBOs results from the fixed charges for interest on the loan and the lack of cash for expansion.

3) A merger is usually a negotiated arrangement between a single bidder and the acquired firm. Payment is most frequently in stock. Moreover, the bidder is often a cash-rich firm in a mature industry and is seeking growth possibilities. The acquired firm is usually growing and in need of cash.

4) Takeovers effected through tender offers may be friendly or hostile.

a) When the takeover is friendly, the target is usually a successful firm in a growth industry, payment may be in cash or stock, and management of the target often has a high percentage of ownership.

b) When the takeover is hostile, the target is usually in a mature industry and is underperforming, more than one bidder may emerge, management ownership is likely to be low, payment is more likely to be in cash, and the initial bidder is probably a corporate raider.

3. Stop and review! You have completed the outline for this subunit. Study multiple-choice questions 1 through 16 beginning on page 270.

B.   Reasons for Combinations

1.   Inefficient management may be replaced in a merger or acquisition by the management of the acquiring or merging firm, or the competency of existing management may be improved.

2.   **Synergy** exists if the value of the combined firm exceeds the sum of the values of the separate firms. It can be determined by using the risk-adjusted discount rate (usually the cost of equity of the acquired firm) to discount the incremental cash flows (changes in revenues, costs, taxes, and capital needs) of the newly formed entity.

   a.   **Operational synergy** arises because the combined firm may be able to increase its revenues and reduce its costs. For example, the new firm created by a horizontal merger may have a more balanced product line and a stronger distribution system. Furthermore, costs may be decreased because of economies of scale in production, marketing, purchasing, and management.

      1)   Operating economies also arise from vertical integration because of the improved coordination of successive activities in the production process.

   b.   **Financial synergy** may also result from the combination. The cost of capital for both firms may be decreased because the cost of issuing both debt and equity securities are lower for larger firms. Moreover, uncorrelated cash flow streams will provide for increased liquidity and a lower probability of bankruptcy. Still another benefit is the availability of additional internal capital. The acquired company is often able to exploit new investment opportunities because the acquiring company has excess cash flows.

   c.   Greater **market power** because of reduced competition might appear to be a benefit of business combinations, but the evidence does not support this conclusion. Antitrust restrictions, the globalization of markets, and the emergence of new forms of competition work against concentration of market power.

   d.   A combination may provide not only specific new investment opportunities but also a **strategic position** that will allow the combined entity to exploit conditions that may arise in the future. For example, the acquisition of a firm in a different industry may provide a **beachhead** that eventually permits development of a broad product line if circumstances are favorable.

   e.   **Tax benefits** may arise from a combination if the acquired firm has an unusual net operating loss and the acquiring firm is profitable.

      1)   Another advantage is that the combined firm's optimal capital structure may allow for increased use of debt financing, with attendant tax savings from greater interest deductions.

      2)   Furthermore, a combination may be the best use of surplus cash from a tax perspective. Dividends received by individual shareholders are fully taxable, whereas the capital gains from a combination are not taxed until the shares are sold. In addition, amounts remitted from the acquired to the acquiring firm are not taxable.

         a)   An alternative use of surplus cash is a stock repurchase. However, the effect might be to increase the firm's share price above its equilibrium level. The result might be that the repurchase would have an excessive cost. The IRS will disallow this strategy if its sole purpose is to avoid taxes.

        b)   Surplus cash may be invested in short-term fixed-income securities, but the returns from this strategy tend to be low.

        c)   Buying shares in other firms permits the firm to take advantage of the dividends-received deduction, but the IRS may also disallow these benefits if the sole motive is tax avoidance.

3.   **Undervaluation** of the firm to be acquired may result if the market focuses on short-term earnings rather than long-term prospects. Thus, such a firm may be a bargain for the acquirer.

    a.   Another aspect of undervaluation is that a firm's **q ratio** (market value of the firm's securities ÷ replacement cost of its assets) may be less than one. Hence, an acquiring firm that wishes to add capacity or diversify into new product lines may discover that a combination is less expensive than internal expansion.

4.   **Managerial motivation** is an issue because not all business decisions are based purely on economic considerations. Thus, the increased salary, fringe benefits, power, and prestige that often result from managing a larger enterprise may affect a manager's decision to consummate a business combination that is not favorable to the shareholders. Fear of negative personal consequences may also cause a manager to resist a favorable combination, perhaps by entering into another combination that preserves the manager's position by making the firm a less desirable acquisition.

    a.   The inconsistency between a manager's personal goals and the goal of maximizing shareholder wealth has been called the **agency problem**. It arises from the separation between ownership and control of corporations. When the manager does not own all of the firm's shares, (s)he is an agent for the other shareholders, and a possible conflict of interest exists. Managerial actions will then have costs and benefits that are shared by others. Accordingly, a manager may be more inclined to incur certain costs and less inclined to pursue certain benefits.

    b.   Ways of addressing the agency problem include tying managerial compensation to the firm's stock price performance; direct shareholder intervention, especially by large institutional investors such as pension funds and insurance companies; and the threat of a hostile takeover, which often results in the ouster of incumbent management.

        1)   Shareholders often seek more independence for the board of directors and the ability to introduce a wider range of proposals to be voted on at shareholder meetings.

5.   A firm may be a target if its **breakup value** exceeds the cost of its acquisition. Thus, the acquirer may earn a profit by selling the assets piecemeal.

6.   **Diversification** is sometimes claimed to be an advantage of a combination because it stabilizes earnings and reduces the risks to employees and creditors. Thus, the **coinsurance effect** applies. If one of the combining firms fails, creditors can be paid from the assets of the other. However, whether shareholders benefit is unclear. The variability of the firm's returns is subject to systematic and unsystematic risk. The former affects all firms and cannot be diversified.

    a.   Unsystematic risk is unique to the firm and can be diversified in a combination, but shareholders can diversify simply by purchasing shares in a variety of firms. Diversification by individual shareholders is therefore easier and cheaper than by the firm except in the case of closely held firms.

      b.   Another argument supporting the view that diversification by itself does not benefit shareholders is that the decrease in earnings variability increases the value of debt at the expense of equity. Absent synergy, the value of the combined firm is the same as the total of the values of the separate firms. Because the debt increases in value as a result of the decreased risk of default (the coinsurance effect), the value of the equity must therefore decrease if the total value of debt and equity is unchanged.

      c.   Nevertheless, the coinsurance effect can be offset by issuing additional debt after the combination, thereby increasing the firm's unsystematic risk and decreasing the value of debt. Moreover, the greater leverage may increase the firm's value. Another possibility is to reduce debt prior to the combination at the lower, pre-combination price and then to reissue the same amount of debt afterward.

7.   The level of mergers and acquisitions increased dramatically in the 1980s because of changes in the global and U.S. economies, technological advances, political events, interest and exchange rate fluctuations, the emergence of new financial instruments, etc. Some of these factors included

      a.   General undervaluation of stocks in the early 1980s

      b.   High inflation that increased the replacement cost of a firm's assets

      c.   Political acceptance of large mergers, especially in view of greater competition, for example, as a result of the increased strength of large foreign firms, deregulation, the emergence of new financial services, and the development of new technologies

      d.   The decline of the dollar, which facilitated acquisition of U.S. firms by foreign firms

      e.   The belief of oil, gas, and other natural resource companies that reserves could be obtained more cheaply by merger than by exploration

      f.   Reduced marginal corporate and personal tax rates and an increase in the capital gains rate

      g.   Deregulation of numerous industries, e.g., transportation, oil, gas, broadcasting, cable, banking, the S&L industry, and other financial services

      h.   The U.S. government's budget deficits, the nation's trade deficits, high interest rates, and other economic factors

      i.   Defensive combinations by takeover targets

8.   Stop and review! You have completed the outline for this subunit. Study multiple-choice questions 17 through 26 beginning on page 275.

C. Tax Issues

1.   Regardless of whether business combinations are undertaken to achieve tax synergy, they are nevertheless structured to provide the maximum tax advantages. Thus, a combination should preferably be in the form of a tax-free reorganization.

2.   **Tax-Free Reorganizations**. For federal tax purposes, a **qualified** reorganization of one or more corporations is considered a mere change in form of investment rather than a disposition of assets. For this reason, a general rule of nonrecognition of gain or loss applies to qualifying reorganizations. However, gain is recognized to the extent of boot.

      a.   **Boot.** Gain on nonqualifying property (usually, property other than stock or securities in a corporation that is a party to the reorganization) is recognized.

3. **Types of Reorganization**. Nonrecognition treatment applies only if the change in corporate structure fits within the definition of one of the following types.

   a. Type A: Statutory merger or consolidation. Under state law, two corporations merge into one. Stock in the non-surviving corporation is canceled. In exchange, its shareholders receive stock in the surviving corporation.

      1) Merger. The resulting corporation was one of the corporations merged.
      2) Consolidation. Existing corporations are merged into a newly formed one.

   b. Type B: Stock-for-stock. Shareholders acquire stock of a corporation solely for part or all of the voting stock of the acquiring corporation or its parent. No boot is allowed.

      1) The acquiring corporation must control the acquired corporation after the exchange; i.e., it must own at least 80% of the stock (voting and all other).

      2) Type A and B reorganizations use the pooling of interests method of accounting.

   c. Type C: Stock-for-assets. One corporation acquires substantially all the assets of another in exchange for its voting stock (or its parent's). The transferor (seller) corporation must liquidate.

      1) Only 20% of the assets acquired may be exchanged for (paid for with) other than voting stock of the acquiring corporation.

         a) Limited amounts of boot are thus allowable.

      2) "Substantially all assets" means at least 90% of the fair market value of net assets and at least 70% of the fair market value of gross assets.

      3) Type C reorganizations use the purchase method of accounting.

   d. Type D: Division

      1) A corporation transfers all or part of its assets to another in exchange for the other's stock.

      2) The transferor or its shareholders must control the transferee after the exchange.

         a) Control means owning 80% of voting power and 80% of each class of nonvoting stock.

      3) The stock or securities of the controlled corporation must be distributed to shareholders of the corporation that transferred assets to the controlled corporation.

      4) Distribution of the stock need not be pro rata among the shareholders of the corporation that transferred assets to the controlled corporation.

         a) Thus, division of the original corporation may result.

   e. Type E: Recapitalization. The capital structure of the corporation is modified by exchanges of stock and securities between the corporation and its shareholders.

   f. Type F: Reincorporation. Stock and securities are exchanged upon a mere change in the name, form, or place of incorporation.

   g. Type G: Bankruptcy reorganization. Stock, securities, and property are exchanged pursuant to a court supervised bankruptcy proceeding whereby the corporation is restructured.

4. **Other Requirements.** Nonrecognition applies only to the extent each of several statutory and judicial requirements are met.

    a. The reorganization must be pursuant to a plan, a copy of which is filed with the tax return of each participating corporation.

    b. Nonrecognition treatment applies only with respect to distributions in exchange for stock or securities of a corporation that is a party to the reorganization.

    c. The reorganization must have a business purpose other than tax avoidance.

    d. Continuity of interest. Owners of the reorganized enterprise(s) must retain an interest in the continuing enterprise. At least 50% continuity of equity interest by value is a benchmark.

    e. Continuity of business enterprise

        1) The acquiring corporation must continue one of the following:

            a) Operating the historical business of the acquired corporation

            b) Using a significant portion of the acquired corporation's historical business assets

        2) Continuing a significant line of business is sufficient if more than one existed.

5. Tax-free reorganizations allow the acquiring firm to use the target firm's net operating loss (NOL) and tax credit carryovers if the target firm is not maintained as a separate entity. Moreover, the assets of the acquired firm have a carryover basis.

    a. The NOLs of the target firm may offset future income only; i.e., only carryforwards are allowed, but the carryforward period is 15 years.

    b. If the target firm still operates after the reorganization, only the target is allowed to use the NOLs (for the preceding 3 years or the following 15 years) and tax credits.

6. **Taxable reorganizations** result in a step-up (or step-down) in basis of the target firm's assets. However, the target firm's NOLs and tax credits disappear and will never be usable.

    a. Taxable reorganizations require the immediate recognition of gain by the target firm and its shareholders.

        1) The target firm must recognize ordinary income (depreciation recapture) from any gain attributable to excess depreciation deductions. The target firm will also recognize capital gain on the appreciation of any of its capital assets.

        2) The target firm's shareholders must recognize capital gain from the sale of the firm.

7. Stop and review! You have completed the outline for this subunit. Study multiple-choice questions 27 and 28 on page 279.

D. Other Regulatory Issues

1.   Corporate takeover specialists have increasingly turned to tender offers as the preferred strategy because of management's ability to prolong proxy contests. The advantage of a tender offer is that management has less time to organize a defense. However, shareholders may also be at a disadvantage if they lack time to determine the proper value of their holdings.

   a.   Accordingly, the Williams Act was passed in 1968 to protect the interests of shareholders. See subunit A on "Types of Combinations" for its major provisions.

   b.   The states have also enacted legislation to regulate hostile takeovers. Indeed, some early statutes virtually prohibited such activity. In a 1979 case, however, the U.S. Supreme Court declared unconstitutional an Illinois statute as placing an undue burden on interstate commerce.

      1)   In 1987, the U.S. Supreme Court upheld an Indiana statute that effectively slows the takeover process. Any acquirer of control shares (at least 20% of the voting stock) must seek approval of disinterested shareholders (not officers, inside directors, or associates of the acquirer) before the shares can be voted. Furthermore, the acquirer has the right to require that a shareholders' meeting be called within 50 days to determine whether the control shares may be voted. Similar statutes were later enacted by a number of influential states, including Delaware (where most companies are incorporated) and New York.

      2)   New state laws also regulate the use of defensive tactics by management. They limit golden parachutes, poison pills, burdensome debt-financing schemes, etc. See subunit G on "Opposition to the Combination."

2.   **Mergers**. Section 7 of the Clayton Act is the primary authority in the merger and acquisition area. It was originally adopted in 1914 and later amended by the Celler-Kefauver Act of 1950.

   a.   Section 7, as amended, provides that no business engaged in commerce shall acquire any of the stock or assets of another such business if the effect may be to substantially lessen competition, or to produce a monopoly in any segment of commerce in any area of the country.

      1)   However, a firm may purchase stock for investment given no attempt to lessen competition.

      2)   A corporation may form a subsidiary to carry on a part of its business when the effect is not to substantially lessen competition.

   b.   The goal of Section 7 is to maintain competition in the marketplace despite the frequency of corporate mergers.

   c.   In determining whether a merger or an acquisition is illegal under Section 7, courts examine the relevant markets or lines of commerce. The analysis is similar to, although more extensive than, that used for a monopolization case under Section 2 of the Sherman Act; i.e., courts analyze the size of the market share, the number of competitors and their financial strength, etc.

      1)   The relevant markets or lines of commerce are

         a)   Relevant product market
         b)   Relevant geographic market or area of effective competition

2)   In determining whether a merger is illegal, both the product market and the geographic market of **both** businesses are factual issues considered by the court.

3)   Antitrust law focuses on the size of the merged firm in relation to the relevant market and not on the absolute size of the resulting entity.

a)   The Department of Justice publishes guidelines for mergers and acquisitions in its amended *Mergers Guidelines*. These guidelines use a statistical test for determining whether to challenge horizontal mergers known as the Herfindahl-Hirschman Index (HHI).

i)   Under the HHI formula, the postmerger market share of each firm is calculated by summing the squares of the individual market shares of all firms in the market.

ii) The guidelines use three categories of market concentration to analyze horizontal mergers and determine whether the Department of Justice will challenge the merger.

b)   The Department of Justice and the Federal Trade Commission (FTC) will consider other relevant factors when making a determination on whether to challenge a merger; e.g., is there a trend in the particular industry toward concentration?

d.   The **failing company doctrine** provides that a merger that may reduce competition is allowable if the company acquired is failing and there is no other purchaser whose acquisition of the company would reduce competition less.

e.   The Department of Justice and the FTC have indicated that they are primarily concerned with horizontal mergers in highly or moderately concentrated industries.

1)   The Antitrust Improvement Act of 1976 requires corporations with annual sales or assets exceeding $100,000,000 to give advance notice to the Department of Justice and the FTC of any acquisition of a corporation with annual sales or assets of $10,000,000 or more.

3.   Stop and review! You have completed the outline for this subunit. Study multiple-choice questions 29 and 30 beginning on page 279.

E.   Accounting for Combinations

1.   **Purchase Accounting.** Under **APB 16**, *Business Combinations*, the purchase method must be used to account for a business combination that does not involve all of the distinctive conditions that require a pooling of interests.

a.   The purchase method treats the combination as an acquisition of one company by another.

b.   The acquirer records the identifiable assets obtained and liabilities assumed at their fair values.

c.   Income of the acquiring company includes its share of the earnings of the acquired company after acquisition (cash flows are also consolidated after acquisition).

1)   **ARB 51**, *Consolidated Financial Statements*, states that when a subsidiary is purchased during the year, the preferred method of presenting the results of operations is to include the subsidiary's operations in the consolidated

income statement as though it had been acquired at the beginning of the year and to deduct from the total earnings the preacquisition earnings. The minority interest income for the entire year is also deducted.

d. **Goodwill** is the excess of the purchase price of a group of assets or an investee over the sum of the assigned costs (fair values) of the net identifiable assets (sum of the identifiable tangible and identifiable intangible assets, minus liabilities assumed).

    1) Goodwill is required to be amortized over its useful life, not to exceed 40 years.

    2) **Negative goodwill** results when the fair value of the net identifiable assets exceeds the purchase price. The amount of negative goodwill reduces proportionately the values assigned to noncurrent assets (excluding marketable securities) in determining their fair values. If the allocation reduces noncurrent assets to zero, any remainder is amortized over not more than 40 years.

e. When a stock investment includes more than 50% but less than 100% of the outstanding stock of a company, a minority interest exists.

    1) The method of computation of that minority interest is identical under the pooling of interests and the purchase methods.

f. Three types of costs may be incurred in effecting a purchase combination.

    1) Direct costs of acquisition, such as legal, accounting, consulting, and finder's fees, are included in the cost of the company acquired.

    2) The costs of registration and issuance of equity securities reduce the otherwise determinable fair value of the securities, ordinarily as a debit to additional paid-in capital.

    3) Indirect and general expenses are deducted as incurred in determining net income. Examples are time spent by combining company executives negotiating the combination and other normal business expenses involving a combination.

    4) In pooling accounting, all of the above costs are expensed as incurred.

2. **Pooling Accounting.** The pooling of interests method of accounting is intended to present, as a single interest, two or more common shareholder interests that were previously independent and to combine the rights and risks represented by those interests. The shareholders neither withdraw nor invest assets but, in effect, exchange voting common stock in a ratio that determines their respective interests in the combined entity.

a. A business combination that meets 12 specific conditions should be accounted for by the pooling of interests method.

    1) Combining companies

        a) Each combining company is autonomous.

        b) Each company is independent of the other combining companies; that is, an intercorporate investment at the time of initiation and consummation of the pooling may not exceed 10% of the voting common stock of any combining company.

2) Combining interests

   a) A combination is a single transaction or is completed within 1 year of initiation.

   b) An issuance is made solely of common stock for at least 90% of the outstanding voting common stock of the other company.

   c) No change in shareholders' equities is made in contemplation of the combination.

   d) No reacquisition of more than a normal number of shares prior to the combination occurs.

   e) The ratio of ownership among individual shareholders remains the same.

   f) Voting rights of shareholders are not restricted.

   g) No contingent stock issuances, payments, etc., exist after the combination is consummated.

3) Absence of planned transactions

   a) There are no plans to retire any of the common stock issued in the combination.

   b) No special arrangements exist to benefit former shareholders.

   c) There is no intention to dispose of significant assets, except duplicate facilities or excess capacity, for 2 years.

b. Assets and liabilities are recorded by the combined entity at their carrying (book) value, a treatment compatible with historical cost.

   1) If the separate companies recorded assets and liabilities using different methods, the amounts may be adjusted to the same basis of accounting if the change would have been appropriate for the separate company.

      a) This change is retroactive and prior-period statements should be restated, including adjustments to retained earnings.

   2) Because no acquisition is deemed to have occurred, no goodwill is recognized.

c. The surviving corporation will issue stock to one or more combining companies.

   1) After the pooling, the balance in the capital stock account should equal the par or stated value of the stock outstanding as a result of the pooling.

   2) The total consolidated contributed capital should equal the sum of the contributed capital amounts of the combining entities. Accordingly, capital stock will be credited for the par or stated value of the shares issued, with a balancing credit to additional paid-in capital.

      a) However, if the par or stated value of the shares issued in the combination is greater than the contributed capital of the subsidiary, additional paid-in capital must be debited. Because additional paid-in capital may not be reduced below zero, a debit to retained earnings will be necessary if additional paid-in capital is insufficient.

   3) The retained earnings of the consolidated entity should equal the sum of the retained earnings of the combining entities, except for the effects of the foregoing adjustment and elimination of any intercompany transactions.

d. Operations of the combined entities must be reported for all periods presented as if the pooling had occurred prior to the earliest statement presented.

1) Thus, the results of operations for the year of combination include the combined results of operations of the separate companies for the entire year whether or not the combination occurred at the beginning of the year.

2) The effects of intercompany transactions on current assets, current liabilities, revenue, and cost of sales for periods presented and on retained earnings at the beginning of the periods presented should be eliminated to the extent possible.

a) The effects on EPS of nonrecurring intercompany transactions involving long-term assets and liabilities need not be eliminated.

3. **Consolidation.** **SFAS 94**, *Consolidation of All Majority-Owned Subsidiaries*, requires consolidation of all companies in which a parent has a controlling financial interest through direct or indirect ownership of a majority voting interest (over 50% of the outstanding voting shares).

a. However, consolidation is not required if control is likely to be temporary or if control does not rest with the majority owner, for example, because the subsidiary is in bankruptcy or in legal reorganization or is subject to foreign exchange restrictions or other government-imposed restrictions that preclude exercise of control.

b. If the conditions dictating consolidation are met, subsidiaries should be shown on a consolidated basis with the parent company.

4. Stop and review! You have completed the outline for this subunit. Study multiple-choice questions 31 through 34 beginning on page 280.

F. Valuation and Pricing the Combination

1. The most fundamental approach to valuing a business combination is capital budgeting analysis. If the net present value is positive, that is, if the present value of the estimated incremental cash flows from the combination exceeds the present value of the amounts to be paid for the acquired firm, the investment is financially sound for the acquirer. The shareholders of the acquired firm should perform a similar analysis and compare the result with the net present value of remaining an independent entity. Accordingly, the analysis must emphasize

a. Accurate estimates of expected cash flows
b. The effect on the cost of capital and the optimal capital structure of the acquirer
c. How the combination will be financed
d. The price to be paid

1) If the combination is synergistic or otherwise results in the creation of new value, a premium can be paid to the shareholders of the acquired firm while still permitting the shareholders of the acquiring firm to benefit. However, most of the gain in value usually is paid to the acquired firm's shareholders as an inducement to sell.

2.   Crucial aspects of valuation analysis are the estimates of the incremental cash flows from the combination and the required rate of return (cost of capital) for those incremental cash flows. This rate is the discount rate to be used in calculating the net present value.

    a.   Projecting incremental cash flows from the combination becomes relatively more difficult when the firms' operations are to be merged or if the acquired firm's operations are to be changed.

        1)   The cash flow analysis should also consider the transaction costs involved.

    b.   In comparison with the usual capital budgeting analysis, a combination often requires consideration of more complex debt arrangements. The debt acquired will have different rates from that held by the acquiring firm, debt may be issued to finance the combination, and new debt may be issued to finance expansion of the acquired firm. Accordingly, the projected cash flow analysis should incorporate interest. Because the net cash flows will be calculated after subtraction of interest, the valuation will reflect the equity residual, i.e., the value to the shareholders of the acquiring firm.

    c.   The forecast of the incremental cash flows available to the acquiring firm's shareholders should be based on analyses of the sensitivity of the net present value to changes in the crucial variables. It should also consider the range of the probable values of these variables based on their probability distributions. Consequently, a computer simulation may be a useful technique for evaluating the combination, assuming probabilities can be estimated for the components of the projected cash flows.

    d.   If the net incremental cash flows to the acquiring firm's shareholders are to be calculated, the discount rate used should be the cost of equity capital. Moreover, this rate should reflect the risk associated with the use of funds rather than their source. The rate therefore should not be the cost of capital of the acquiring firm but rather the cost of equity of the combined firm after the combination. This calculation requires a new estimate of beta to be used in the Capital Asset Pricing Model.

    e.   Estimating the value of the combination using discounted cash flows should not ignore the market prices of comparable investments. If the market is efficient, market prices should equal the values of those investments.

    f.   The nature of the bid for the acquired firm (cash, stock, debt, or a combination) has important effects on

        1)   The combined firm's capital structure

        2)   The tax position of the acquiring company and the shareholders of the acquired company (See subunit C on "Tax Issues.")

        3)   Whether the acquired firm's shareholders will benefit from postcombination gains by the combined firm

        4)   The extent of governmental regulatory involvement (See subunit D, "Other Regulatory Issues.")

3.   Stop and review! You have completed the outline for this subunit. Study multiple-choice questions 35 and 36 beginning on page 281.

G. Opposition to the Combination

1. **Greenmail** or a targeted repurchase is a defensive tactic used to protect against takeover after a bidder buys a large number of shares on the open market and then makes (or threatens to make) a tender offer. If management and the board are opposed to the takeover (a hostile tender offer), the potential acquirer is offered the opportunity to sell his/her already acquired shares back to the corporation at an amount substantially above market value (i.e., paying greenmail).

    a. In conjunction with greenmail, management may reach a **standstill agreement** in which the bidder agrees not to acquire additional shares.

2. **Staggered election of directors** requires new shareholders to wait several years before being able to place their own people on the board.

    a. Another **antitakeover amendment** to the corporate charter may require a **supermajority** (e.g., 80%) for approval of a combination.

3. **Golden parachutes** are provisions passed by a board of directors requiring large payments to specified executives if their employment is terminated by the acquiring firm following a takeover.

    a. A 1984 change in the tax law created a 20% excise tax on such payments and nondeductibility by the corporation. It was specifically designed to reduce the use of golden parachutes.

    b. Shareholders have often been unhappy with golden parachute payoffs and have filed suit to stop such payments.

4. **Fair price provisions** (shareholder rights plans) have become popular.

    a. Warrants are issued to shareholders that permit purchase of stock at a small percentage (often half) of market price in the event of a takeover attempt.

    b. The plan is intended to protect shareholder interests if the corporation is confronted by a coercive or unfair takeover attempt.

    c. The objective is not to deter takeovers but to ensure that all shareholders are treated equally.

    d. In the event of a friendly tender offer, the outstanding stock rights (warrants) may be repurchased by the corporation for a few cents per share, thus paving the way for the takeover.

    e. In many cases, these rights are not even issued in certificate form to shareholders because they are not immediately exercisable and are not traded separately from the common stock.

5. **Going private** and **LBOs** are defensive tactics that have been previously discussed.

6. **Poison Pill.** A target corporation's charter, bylaws, or contracts may include a wide variety of provisions that reduce the value of the target to potential tender offerors. For example, a valuable contract may terminate by its terms upon a specified form of change of ownership of the target. A poison pill is typically a right to purchase shares, at a reduced price, in the merged firm resulting from a takeover.

7. **Flip-over Rights.** The charter of a target corporation may provide for its shareholders to acquire in exchange for their stock (in the target) a relatively greater interest (e.g., twice the shares of stock of equivalent value) in an acquiring entity.

8. **Flip-in Rights**. Acquisition of more than a specified ownership interest (e.g., 25%) in the target corporation by a raider is a contingency, the occurrence of which triggers additional rights in the stock other than the stock acquired by the raider; e.g., each share becomes entitled to two votes.

9. **Issuing Stock**. The target corporation significantly increases the amount of outstanding stock.

10. **Reverse Tender**. The target corporation may respond with a tender offer to acquire control of the tender offeror.

11. **ESOP**. The trustees of an employee stock ownership plan are usually favorable to current management. Thus, they are likely to vote the shares allocated to the ESOP against a raider, who will probably destabilize the target corporation's current structure.

12. **White Knight Merger**. Target management arranges an alternative tender offer with a different acquirer that will be more favorable to incumbent management and shareholders.

13. **Crown Jewel Transfer**. The target corporation sells or otherwise disposes of one or more assets that made it a desirable target.

14. **Legal Action**. A target corporation may challenge one or more aspects of a tender offer. A resulting delay increases costs to the raider and enables further defensive action.

15. Stop and review! You have completed the outline for this subunit. Study multiple-choice questions 37 and 38 on page 282.

H. Other Restructurings

1. A **spin-off** is the creation of a new separate entity from another entity, with the new entity's shares being distributed on a pro rata basis to existing shareholders of the parent entity.

   a. Existing shareholders will have the same proportion of ownership in the new entity that they had in the parent.

   b. A spin-off is a type of dividend to existing shareholders.

2. A **divestiture** involves the sale of an operating unit of a firm to a third party.

   a. Some writers define the term divestiture to include spin-offs and liquidations.

3. A liquidation of assets of an operating unit occurs when they are sold piecemeal.

4. A **leveraged cash-out** is borrowing heavily to issue a very large dividend which acts as a poison pill.

5. An **equity carve-out** involves the sale of a portion of the firm through an equity offering of shares in the new entity to outsiders.

6. Reasons for spin-offs and divestitures include governmental antitrust litigation, refocusing of a firm's operations, and raising capital for the core business operation.

7. Stop and review! You have completed the outline for this subunit. Study multiple-choice questions 39 through 42 on page 283.

I. **Bankruptcy**

1.   A firm may be insolvent either when its debts exceed its assets (stock-based insolvency) or when cash flows are insufficient to meet maturing obligations (flow-based insolvency). The early signals of financial distress include late payments, plant closings, negative earnings, employee layoffs, falling stock prices, and dividend reductions. A firm may respond to insolvency by combining with another firm, selling assets, reducing costs, issuing new debt or equity securities, or negotiating with creditors to restructure its obligations. However, these private workouts may be unlikely to succeed or may already have failed. Consequently, a formal bankruptcy may be declared either voluntarily by the debtor or involuntarily due to a petition brought by creditors. The two major options are bankruptcy reorganization and liquidation.

2.   In a **liquidation** under Chapter 7 of the Bankruptcy Reform Act of 1978, the following procedures are usually followed:

   a.   A voluntary or an involuntary petition is filed in the federal bankruptcy court.

      1)   An involuntary petition must be joined by three or more creditors with unsecured claims totaling at least $10,000 if the debtor has 12 or more creditors. If there are fewer than 12, one creditor with a claim of at least $10,000 may file.

      2)   A contested involuntary petition will be granted if the debtor is not paying its bills when due or if, within 120 days prior to filing, a custodian took possession of the debtor's property to enforce a lien.

   b.   When the court issues an order for relief, creditors' collection activities must cease immediately. Moreover, the court usually appoints an interim trustee to take control of the debtor's estate.

   c.   At the first creditor's meeting, a permanent trustee may be elected. The trustee notifies creditors, collects the debtor's nonexempt property, distributes that property to creditors, and otherwise administers the bankruptcy estate. Secured creditors are entitled to the proceeds of the sale of specific property pledged for a lien or a mortgage. If the proceeds do not fully satisfy the secured creditors' claims, the balances are treated as claims of general or unsecured creditors. The other assets of the bankruptcy estate are distributed according to the absolute priority rule. A claim with a higher priority is fully satisfied before claims with a lower priority are paid. The following are the classes of priority claims listed in order of rank:

      1)   Claims for administrative expenses and claims for expenses incurred in preserving and collecting the estate

      2)   Claims of tradespeople who extended unsecured credit after an involuntary case has begun but before a trustee is appointed

      3)   Wages due workers if earned within the 90 days preceding the earlier of the filing of the petition or the cessation of business. The amount of wages is limited to $4,000 per person.

4) Claims for unpaid contributions to employee benefit plans that were to have been paid within 180 days prior to filing. However, these claims, plus wages, are not to exceed the $4,000 per employee limit.

5) Unsecured claims for customer deposits, not to exceed a maximum of $1,800 per individual

6) Taxes due to federal, state, and any other governmental agency

7) Unfunded pension plan liabilities. These claims are superior to those of the general creditors for an amount up to 30% of the common and preferred equity; any remaining unfunded pension claims rank with those of the general creditors.

8) Claims of general or unsecured creditors

9) Claims of preferred shareholders, who may receive an amount up to the par value of the issue

10) Claims of common shareholders

   d. Individual debtors may receive a discharge under Chapter 7 from most debts that remain unpaid after distribution of the debtor's estate. A corporation or a partnership does not receive a discharge in bankruptcy.

3. A Chapter 11 **reorganization** allows a distressed business enterprise to restructure its finances. The primary purpose of the restructuring is usually the continuation of the business. Reorganization is a process of negotiation whereby the debtor firm and its creditors develop a plan for the adjustment and discharge of debts. Partnerships, corporations, and any person who may be a debtor under Chapter 7 (except stock and commodity brokers) are eligible debtors under Chapter 11.

   a. Such a plan may provide for a change of management or liquidation.

   b. A case under Chapter 11 is commenced by the filing of a petition that may be either voluntary or involuntary.

      1) The petition may be filed by the debtor or by the creditors.

      2) Insolvency is not a condition precedent to a voluntary Chapter 11 petition.

      3) The debtor has the exclusive right to file a plan during the 120 days after the order for relief is issued by the court, unless a trustee has been appointed, and may file a plan of reorganization at any time.

      4) A plan of reorganization must divide creditors' claims and shareholders' interests into classes, and claims in each class must be treated equally.

         a) The plan must specify which classes of creditors are impaired creditors and how they will be treated. A class is impaired if its rights are altered under the plan.

   c. To become effective, the plan ordinarily must be accepted by a certain percentage (usually, at least two-thirds) of persons whose rights as creditors or owners have been impaired, provide for full payment of administration expenses, and be confirmed (approved and put into operation) by the bankruptcy court.

      1) Confirmation makes the plan binding not only on the debtor but also on creditors, equity security holders, and others.

d.   A bankruptcy court may force an impaired class of creditors to participate in, and the court may confirm, a plan of reorganization that is fair and equitable to the impaired class.

e.   In a Chapter 11 reorganization, the court has limited power to appoint a trustee. Instead, to better accomplish the rehabilitative aspirations of a reorganization, a firm seeking protection under Chapter 11 may be permitted to operate its own business as a debtor-in-possession.

1)   A strong presumption exists that a debtor-in-possession should be permitted to continue to operate the business unless there is evidence of incompetence or mismanagement on the part of the debtor.

2)   A debtor-in-possession has basically all the same rights and duties as a trustee but does not receive special compensation for performing the function.

3)   The judge may appoint a trustee upon a sufficient showing of dishonesty or incompetence of the debtor or management. The duties are identical to those of a trustee in a liquidation.

4)   If the court does not appoint a trustee, the court will appoint an examiner to conduct investigations into any allegations of fraud, misconduct, or mismanagement if appointment of an examiner is requested by a party in interest, appointment is in the interests of creditors or equity security holders, and the debtor's fixed, liquidated, unsecured debts exceed $5,000,000.

f.   As soon as practicable after an order for relief has been granted, a committee of unsecured creditors is appointed by the court.

1)   The committee usually consists of persons who hold the seven largest unsecured claims against the debtor, but the court may order the appointment of additional committees of creditors or of equity security holders to assure adequate representation.

2)   The committee may employ attorneys, accountants, and other professionals to perform services on behalf of the committee or to represent it.

3)   The committee may consult with the debtor-in-possession or the trustee, request appointment of a trustee, independently investigate the debtor's affairs, and participate in formulating the plan of reorganization.

g.   A plan can only be put into effect when it is accepted by each class of impaired creditors.

1)   All persons who are entitled to participate in the plan of reorganization have a period of not less than 5 years from the date of the final decree within which to exchange their old securities in the old business organization for new securities in the new business organization.

4.   Stop and review! You have completed the outline for this subunit. Study multiple-choice questions 43 through 59 beginning on page 284.

MULTIPLE-CHOICE QUESTIONS

A. Types of Combinations

1. A business combination may be legally structured as a merger, a consolidation, or an investment in stock (also known as an acquisition). Which of the following describes a business combination that is legally structured as a merger?

A. The surviving company is one of the two combining companies.

B. The surviving company is neither of the two combining companies.

C. An investor-investee relationship is established.

D. A parent-subsidiary relationship is established.

The correct answer is (A). *(Publisher)*

REQUIRED: The characteristic of a business combination legally structured as a merger.

DISCUSSION: In a business combination legally structured as a merger, the assets and liabilities of one of the combining companies are transferred to the books of the other combining company (the surviving company). The surviving company continues to exist as a separate legal entity. The nonsurviving company ceases to exist as a separate entity. Its stock is canceled, and its books are closed.

Answer (B) is incorrect because it describes a consolidation, in which a new firm is formed to account for the assets and liabilities of the combining companies. Answers (C) and (D) are incorrect because they describe an investment in stock. A parent-subsidiary relationship exists when the investor company holds more than 50% of the outstanding stock of the investee company.

2. A horizontal merger is a merger between

A. Two or more firms from different and unrelated markets.

B. Two or more firms at different stages of the production process.

C. A producer and its supplier.

D. Two or more firms in the same market.

The correct answer is (D). *(CMA 1293 1-6)*

REQUIRED: The example of a horizontal merger.

DISCUSSION: A horizontal merger is one between competitors in the same market. From the viewpoint of the Justice Department, it is the most closely scrutinized type of merger because it has the greatest tendency to reduce competition.

Answer (A) is incorrect because a merger between firms in different and unrelated markets is a conglomerate merger. Answers (B) and (C) are incorrect because a merger between two or more firms at different stages of the production process, or between a producer and a supplier, is a vertical merger.

3. When should a business combination be undertaken?

A. When a positive net present value is generated to the shareholders of an acquiring firm.

B. When the two firms are in the same line of business, but economies of scale cannot be attained by the acquiror.

C. When two firms are in different lines of business, creating diversification.

D. When cash will be paid for the acquired firm's stock.

The correct answer is (A). *(Publisher)*

REQUIRED: The reason for a combination.

DISCUSSION: A business combination is beneficial when the result is a positive NPV. This effect results from synergy, which exists when the value of the combined firm exceeds the sum of the values of the separate firms. It can be determined by using the risk-adjusted rate to discount the change in cash flows of the newly formed entity. If a positive net present value is generated, a combination is indicated.

Answer (B) is incorrect because a combination is indicated if economies of scale can be attained. Answer (C) is incorrect because diversification may or may not result in a positive NPV. Answer (D) is incorrect because some beneficial combinations involve exchanges of stock.

4. Which type of acquisition does not require shareholders to have a formal vote to approve?

    A.   Merger.

    B.   Acquisition of stock.

    C.   Acquisition of all of the firm's assets.

    D.   Consolidation.

The correct answer is (B). *(Publisher)*

REQUIRED: The type of acquisition that does not require a formal vote by shareholders for approval.

DISCUSSION: An acquisition of stock does not require a formal vote of the firm's shareholders. It is advantageous when management and the board of directors are hostile to the combination because an acquisition of all the firm's assets requires a vote of the shareholders. Thus, the management and board of directors may influence the votes of the shareholders. However, in an acquisition of stock, a formal vote by the shareholders is not required, so management and the board of directors cannot influence shareholders. If the acquiring firm's offer is rejected, a tender offer is usually made to the shareholders to obtain a controlling interest.

Answer (A) is incorrect because a merger is a transaction in which an acquiring firm absorbs a second firm, and the acquiring firm is a combination of the two merged companies. A merger is not a type of acquisition. Answer (C) is incorrect because an acquisition of all of the firm's assets requires a vote from the shareholders. Answer (D) is incorrect because a consolidation is similar to a merger, but a new company is formed and neither of the merging companies survives. Thus, consolidation is not a type of acquisition.

5. When firm B merges with firm C to create firm BC, what has occurred?

    A.   A tender offer.

    B.   An acquisition of assets.

    C.   An acquisition of stock.

    D.   A consolidation.

The correct answer is (D). *(Publisher)*

REQUIRED: The occurrence when firm B merges with firm C to create firm BC.

DISCUSSION: A consolidation is a business transaction in which an acquiring firm absorbs a second firm. An entirely new company is formed, and neither of the merging companies survives. Firm B merges with firm C to form an entirely new company called BC, and neither B nor C survives. Therefore, this is a consolidation.

Answer (A) is incorrect because a tender offer is used in an acquisition by a firm to the shareholders of another firm to tender their shares for a specified price. Answers (B) and (C) are incorrect because an acquisition of assets or stock results in the ending of the existence of the acquired firm with the acquiring firm remaining in existence.

6. All of the following are true of mergers except

    A.   Mergers are legally straightforward.

    B.   Approval by shareholder vote of each firm involved in the merger is required.

    C.   The acquiring firm maintains its name and identity in a merger.

    D.   A merger may never result from a public offer to the shareholders of the target firm to buy its shares directly.

The correct answer is (D). *(Publisher)*

REQUIRED: The false statement regarding mergers.

DISCUSSION: A merger is a business combination in which the acquiring firm absorbs a second firm, and the acquiring firm remains in business as a combination of the two merged firms. The acquiring firm usually maintains its name and identity. Mergers are legally straightforward because there is usually a single bidder and payment is made primarily with stock. The shareholders of each firm involved with the merger are required to vote to approve the merger. However, merger of the operations of two firms may ultimately result from an acquisition of stock.

Answers (A), (B), and (C) are incorrect because they are all true statements about mergers.

7. Which of the following is a combination involving the absorption of one firm by another?

- A. Merger.
- B. Consolidation.
- C. Proxy fight.
- D. Acquisition.

The correct answer is (A). *(Publisher)*

REQUIRED: The combination involving the absorption of one firm by another.

DISCUSSION: A merger is a business combination in which an acquiring firm absorbs another firm. The acquiring firm remains in business as a combination of the two merged firms. Thus, the acquiring firm maintains its name and identity. The combination is legally straightforward. However, approval of the merger is required by votes of the shareholders of each firm.

Answer (B) is incorrect because a consolidation merges two companies and forms a new company in which neither of the two merging firms survives. It is similar to a merger, but one firm is not absorbed by another. Answer (C) is incorrect because a proxy fight is an attempt by dissident shareholders to gain control of the corporation by electing directors. Answer (D) is incorrect because an acquisition involves the purchase of all of another firm's assets or a controlling interest in its stock.

8. The merger of General Motors and Ford would be categorized as a

- A. Diversifying merger.
- B. Horizontal merger.
- C. Conglomerate merger.
- D. Vertical merger.

The correct answer is (B). *(Publisher)*

REQUIRED: The categorization of a merger of two firms in the same industry.

DISCUSSION: A horizontal merger occurs when two firms in the same industry combine. General Motors and Ford are both in the automobile industry. A merger of these two companies would be a horizontal merger.

Answer (A) is incorrect because a diversifying merger brings together companies in different industries. Answer (C) is incorrect because a conglomerate merger is a combination of two firms in unrelated industries. Answer (D) is incorrect because a vertical merger is a combination of a firm with one of its suppliers or customers.

9. When choosing a merger over an acquisition of stock to accomplish a business combination, which of the following is irrelevant to the decision?

- A. Dealing directly with shareholders in an acquisition of stock.
- B. Absence of tender by some minority shareholders in a tender offer.
- C. Resistence to an acquisition by the target's management usually causing an increase in the stock price.
- D. Whether the companies are in the same industry.

The correct answer is (D). *(Publisher)*

REQUIRED: The factor which is irrelevant to the decision to transact a merger rather than an acquisition of stock.

DISCUSSION: Many factors influence whether a transaction should be a merger or an acquisition of stock. Whether the companies are in the same industry or not is usually not a factor. In an acquisition of stock, an acquiring firm usually makes a tender offer directly to the shareholders of another firm to obtain a controlling interest. Therefore, the acquiring firm must directly deal with shareholders of the other firm. There is the possibility that some minority shareholders will not tender their shares. Management may be hostile to the combination, which usually causes an increase in the stock price. This increase will require the acquiring firm to pay more money in its tender offer. On the other hand, a merger is much more straightforward legally. It is usually a negotiated arrangement between a single bidder and the acquired firm. However, a merger does require a formal vote of the shareholders of each of the merging firms, whereas an acquisition does not.

Answers (A), (B), and (C) are incorrect because each supports choosing a merger over an acquisition.

10. An attempt to replace management in which a group of shareholders try to solicit votes is a

    A. Tender offer.

    B. Takeover.

    C. Proxy fight.

    D. Leveraged buyout.

The correct answer is (C). *(Publisher)*

REQUIRED: The attempt to replace management in which a group of shareholders try to solicit votes.

DISCUSSION: A proxy fight is an attempt by dissident shareholders to gain control of the corporation, or at least gain influence, by electing directors. A proxy is a power of attorney given by a shareholder that authorizes the holder to exercise the voting rights of the shareholder. The proxy is limited in its duration, usually for a specific occasion like the annual shareholders' meeting. The issuer of a proxy statement must file a copy with the SEC ten days prior to mailing it to shareholders. SEC rules require the solicitor of proxies to give shareholders all material information concerning the issues. A form that indicates the shareholder's agreement or disagreement must be provided. Also, if the purpose is for voting for directors, proxies must be accompanied by an annual report.

Answer (A) is incorrect because a tender offer is a general invitation by an individual or corporation to all shareholders of another corporation to tender (sell) their shares for a specified price. Answer (B) is incorrect because a takeover is an attempt by one corporation to take control over another by purchasing a majority of common stock. Answer (D) is incorrect because a leveraged buyout is a largely debt-financed acquisition of a firm's publicly owned stock.

11. The merger of an oil refinery by a chain of gasoline stations is an example of a

    A. Conglomerate merger.

    B. White knight.

    C. Vertical merger.

    D. Horizontal merger.

The correct answer is (C). *(Publisher)*

REQUIRED: The acquisition of an oil refinery by a chain of gasoline stations.

DISCUSSION: A vertical merger is the combination of a firm with one or more of its suppliers or customers. The acquiring firm remains in business but is a combination of the two merged firms. The chain of gasoline stations is acquiring an oil refinery, which is a supplier. The chain of gasoline stations will keep its name and identity. Therefore, this is a vertical merger.

Answer (A) is incorrect because a conglomerate merger involves the combination of two firms in unrelated industries. Answer (B) is incorrect because a white knight is a firm from which the target firm seeks a competitive offer to avoid being acquired by a less desirable suitor. Answer (D) is incorrect because horizontal mergers combine companies in the same industry.

12. All of the following statements about acquisition of stock through tender offers is true except

    A. Shareholder meetings do not need to be held.

    B. A vote is not required.

    C. The acquiring firm directly deals with the target firm's stockholders.

    D. All of the outstanding stock of the target firm must be tendered.

The correct answer is (D). *(Publisher)*

REQUIRED: The false statement about the acquisition of stock through tender offers.

DISCUSSION: An acquisition of stock by a corporation does not require a formal vote of the target firm's shareholders. Thus, stockholder meetings do not need to be held. A tender offer is usually made in an acquisition of stock. This is a general invitation by an individual or corporation to the other corporation's shareholders to tender their shares for a specified price. The acquiring firm or individual must directly deal with the target firm's shareholders. Minority shareholders are not required to tender their shares. Therefore, not all of the target firm's stock is usually tendered.

Answers (A), (B), and (C) are incorrect because they are all true statements about the acquisition of stock through tender offers.

13. The acquisition of a retail shoe store by a shoe manufacturer is an example of

    A. Vertical integration.

    B. A conglomerate.

    C. Market extension.

    D. Horizontal integration.

The correct answer is (A). *(CMA 1295 1-25)*
    REQUIRED: The type of transaction represented.
    DISCUSSION: The acquisition of a shoe retailer by a shoe manufacturer is an example of vertical integration. Vertical integration is typified by a merger or acquisition involving companies that are in the same industry but at different levels in the supply chain. In other words, one of the companies supplies inputs for the other.
    Answer (B) is incorrect because a conglomerate is a company made up of subsidiaries in unrelated industries. Answer (C) is incorrect because market extension involves expanding into new market areas. Answer (D) is incorrect because horizontal integration involves a merger between competing firms in the same industry.

14. Which of the following is a defensive tactic against a hostile takeover by tender offer?

    A. Leveraged buyout (LBO).

    B. Acquisition.

    C. Conglomerate merger.

    D. Saturday night special.

The correct answer is (A). *(Publisher)*
    REQUIRED: The defensive tactic against a hostile takeover by a tender offer.
    DISCUSSION: A leveraged buyout (LBO) entails the company going private. A small group of investors, usually including senior management purchases the publicly owned stock. The stock is then delisted because it will no longer be traded. Thus, a LBO competes with a hostile tender offer as an alternative.
    Answer (B) is incorrect because an acquisition is the purchase of all of another firm's assets or a controlling interest in its stock. Answer (C) is incorrect because a conglomerate merger is a combination of two unrelated firms in different industries. Answer (D) is incorrect because a Saturday night special is direct solicitation of shareholders through advertisements or general mailing.

15. Which of the following statements about the benefits and costs of mergers is correct?

    A. The shareholders of target firms that are acquired substantially benefit.

    B. The shareholders of acquiring firms substantially benefit in successful takeovers.

    C. The shareholders of target firms not acquired substantially benefit.

    D. Both shareholders of the acquiring firm and the target firm are required to receive positive returns.

The correct answer is (A). *(Publisher)*
    REQUIRED: The correct statement about the benefits and costs of mergers.
    DISCUSSION: Studies have been made to estimate the effect of mergers and takeovers on stock prices of the bidding and target firms. The results suggest that the shareholders of target firms that are acquired receive the greatest benefit. The gains tend to be larger for tender offers than in mergers. This is often due to raising the tender offer because management rejects and uses defensive tactics to oppose offers. Shareholders of the acquiring firms appear to earn little from takeovers because the gains from the merger were not achieved. Also, shareholders of target firms not acquired frequently receive negative returns.
    Answer (B) is incorrect because shareholders of acquiring firms frequently do not benefit in successful takeovers. Answer (C) is incorrect because the shareholders of target firms not acquired may receive negative returns. Answer (D) is incorrect because requirements regarding positive returns in business combinations do not exist.

16. A parent company sold a subsidiary to a group of managers of the subsidiary. The purchasing group invested $1,000,000 and borrowed $49,000,000 against the assets of the subsidiary. This is an example of a

A. Spin-off.

B. Leveraged buyout.

C. Joint venture.

D. Liquidation.

The correct answer is (B). *(CIA 1191 IV-49)*
REQUIRED: The term describing a debt-financed purchase of a subsidiary.
DISCUSSION: A leveraged buyout is a financing technique through which a company is purchased using very little equity capital. All of the company's stock is purchased using mostly borrowed funds. The assets of the acquired company are used as collateral for the loans that financed the purchase.
Answer (A) is incorrect because a spin-off is a divestiture in which the stock of the subsidiary is distributed to the parent company's stockholders. Answer (C) is incorrect because a joint venture is an undertaking in which two or more independent companies combine their resources to accomplish a specific objective. Answer (D) is incorrect because liquidation is the piecemeal sale of a company's assets.

B. Reasons for Combinations

17. Which of the following would cause a reduction in average production costs following a merger?

A. A conglomerate merger.

B. The existence of economies of scale.

C. A vertical merger.

D. Net operating losses of an acquired firm.

The correct answer is (B). *(Publisher)*
REQUIRED: The cause of a reduction in average production costs following a merger.
DISCUSSION: A reason to merge exists if the value of the combined firm exceeds the sum of the values of the separate firms. The combined firm may operate more efficiently. Following a merger, if the average cost of production falls as a result of production level increases, then there are economies of scale.
Answer (A) is incorrect because a conglomerate merger is the combination of firms in unrelated industries. Answer (C) is incorrect because a vertical merger is when a firm combines with a supplier or customer. Answer (D) is incorrect because a net operating loss of an acquired firm disappears in taxable reorganizations.

18. All of the following are potential sources of tax savings in an acquisition except

A. Economies of scale.

B. Net operating losses.

C. Unused debt capacity.

D. Surplus funds of the acquiring firm.

The correct answer is (A). *(Publisher)*
REQUIRED: The item that is not a potential source of tax savings in an acquisition.
DISCUSSION: Net operating losses (NOLS) are a potential source of tax savings because NOLs can be used to offset an acquiring firms' taxable income. The combined firm capital structure may allow for increased use of debt financing, which results in tax savings from greater interest reductions. Surplus funds of an acquiring firm offer a tax savings because amounts remitted from the acquired firm as dividends to the acquiring firm are not taxable. Economies of scale refers to economic savings from joint operation of companies involved in a business combination.
Answers (B), (C), and (D) are incorrect because they are all potential sources of tax savings in an acquisition.

19. A firm is most likely to be a bargain for an acquirer if

    A. Its q ratio is greater than one.

    B. Its q ratio is less than one.

    C. The replacement cost of its assets is less than the value of the firm's securities.

    D. The combination is more expensive than internal expansion.

The correct answer is (B). *(Publisher)*

    REQUIRED: The circumstances in which a firm is most likely to bargain.

    DISCUSSION: Undervaluation of the firm to be acquired may result if the market focuses on short-term earnings rather than long-term prospects. Such a firm may be a bargain for the acquirer. Another aspect of undervaluation is that a firm's q ratio (market value of the firm's securities ÷ replacement cost of its assets) may be less than one. Hence, an acquiring firm that wishes to add capacity or diversify into new product lines may discover that a combination is less expensive than internal expansion.

    Answer (A) is incorrect because if the q ratio of a firm to be acquired exceeds one, the market value of the firm's securities exceed the replacement value of assets. Answer (C) is incorrect because, if replacement cost is less than book value, internal expansion is less expensive. Answer (D) is incorrect because internal expansion may be the better bargain for the acquirer.

20. Which of the following is true if no synergies occur after the merger of two firms?

    A. The shareholders benefit from the reduction in the systematic risk of the combined entity.

    B. The value of the combined firms' debt will be less than the value of the previously separate firms' debt.

    C. Unsystematic risk will be unaffected.

    D. The coinsurance effect results in a gain for the bondholders.

The correct answer is (D). *(Publisher)*

    REQUIRED: The true statement about a merger involving no synergies.

    DISCUSSION: Diversification is sometimes claimed to be an advantage of a combination because it stabilizes earnings and reduces the risks to employees and creditors. Thus, the coinsurance effect applies. If one of the combining firms fails, creditors can be paid from the assets of the other. However, whether shareholders benefit is unclear. One argument supporting the view that diversification by itself does not benefit shareholders is that the decrease in earnings variability increases the value of debt at the expense of equity. Absent synergy, the value of the combined firm is the same as the total of the values of the separate firms. Because the debt increases in value as a result of the decreased risk of default (the coinsurance effect), the value of the equity must therefore decrease if the total value of debt and equity is unchanged.

    Answer (A) is incorrect because systematic risk cannot be diversified. Answer (B) is incorrect because the debt should be more valuable if the risk of default is lower. Answer (C) is incorrect because unsystematic risk is reduced by diversification.

21. The coinsurance effect can be reduced by

	Retirement of Debt before a Combination	Issuance of Debt after a Combination
A.	Yes	Yes
B.	Yes	No
C.	No	Yes
D.	No	No

The correct answer is (A). *(Publisher)*

    REQUIRED: The means, if any, of reducing the coinsurance effect.

    DISCUSSION: The coinsurance effect can be offset by issuing additional debt after the combination, thereby increasing the firm's unsystematic risk and decreasing the value of debt. Moreover, the greater leverage may increase the firm's value. Another possibility is to reduce debt prior to the combination at the lower, pre-combination price and then to reissue the same amount of debt afterward.

    Answer (B) is incorrect because debt should also be issued after the combination. Answer (C) is incorrect because debt should also be retired before the combination. Answer (D) is incorrect because retirement of debt before and issuance of debt after a combination are strategies to reduce the coinsurance effect.

22. Ogden Enterprises is a holding company for several successful retail businesses including bookstores, pharmacies, and gourmet food shops. Ogden has excess cash and long-range plans to acquire businesses outside the retail industry. The company is currently considering the acquisition of G-Tech Inc., a company involved in the research and development of genetically engineered pharmaceuticals. G-Tech was founded four years ago and received its initial financing from a venture capital group. G-Tech recently submitted its first product to the Food and Drug Administration for testing and is readying a second product for submission; however, it will be several years before either of these products can be marketed. The venture capital group would like to sell the company but does not believe a public offering would do well. G-Tech is in need of cash and close monitoring to improve its operational efficiency. G-Tech is most likely to be an attractive investment to Ogden because of

A. Operating synergy, tax considerations, and market power.

B. Financial synergy, strategic realignment, and tax considerations.

C. Differential efficiency, undervaluation, and operating synergy.

D. Strategic realignment, financial synergy, and market power.

The correct answer is (B). *(CFM Sample Q. 6)*
REQUIRED: The reasons the company to be acquired is an attractive investment.
DISCUSSION: Financial synergy may also result from the combination. The cost of capital for both firms may be decreased because the cost of issuing both debt and equity securities are lower for larger firms. Moreover, uncorrelated cash flow streams will provide for increased liquidity and a lower probability of bankruptcy. Still another benefit is the availability of additional internal capital. The acquired company is often able to exploit new investment opportunities because the acquiring company has excess cash flows. Moreover, the strategic position of the combined firm will be improved because G-Tech provides a beachhead in the field of genetically engineered pharmaceuticals. Finally, G-Tech is a development stage enterprise that most likely has a net operating loss carryforward that Ogden, a successful conglomerate, can use to reduce its tax liability.
Answer (A) is incorrect because there are no operating synergies or market power. Answer (C) is incorrect because undervaluation is not an issue. G-Tech is privately held, so its stock cannot be acquired in the open market at a bargain price. Answer (D) is incorrect because there is no market power.

23. After a merger, the difference between the value of the combined entity and the sum of the values of the separate entities is

A. A pooling of interests.

B. Consolidation.

C. Goodwill.

D. Synergy.

The correct answer is (D). *(Publisher)*
REQUIRED: The difference between the value of the combined entity and the sum of the values of the separate entities.
DISCUSSION: Operational synergy arises because the combined firm may be able to increase its revenues and reduce its costs. For example, the new firm created by a horizontal merger may have a more balanced product line and a stronger distribution system. Furthermore, costs may be decreased because of economies of scale in production, marketing, purchasing, and management. Financial synergy may also result from the combination. The cost of capital for both firms may be decreased because the cost of issuing both debt and equity securities are lower for larger firms. Moreover, uncorrelated cash flow streams will provide for increased liquidity and a lower probability of bankruptcy. Still another benefit is the availability of additional internal capital. The acquired company is often able to exploit new investment opportunities because the acquiring company has excess cash flows.
Answer (A) is incorrect because a pooling of interests is a method of accounting. Answer (B) is incorrect because consolidation occurs when a new company is formed after a merger, with neither merging company surviving. Answer (C) is incorrect because goodwill is the excess of the price paid over the fair value of the identifiable net assets in a combination accounted for as a purchase.

24. Which of the following is most likely to be a bad reason for a business combination involving publicly held companies?

    A.   Diversification.

    B.   Greater leverage through the increase of debt capacity.

    C.   Ouster of incumbent management.

    D.   A breakup value in excess of the cost.

The correct answer is (A). *(Publisher)*
    REQUIRED: The bad reason for a combination
    DISCUSSION: Unsystematic risk is unique to the firm and can be diversified in a combination, but shareholders can diversify simply by purchasing shares in a variety of firms. Diversification by individual shareholders is therefore easier and cheaper than by the firm except in the case of closely held firms.
    Answer (B) is incorrect because a combination may permit an increase in the amount of debt in a firm's optimal capital structure. Answer (C) is incorrect because the managers of the acquired firm may be incompetent, or their goals may not be congruent with those of the shareholders. Answer (D) is incorrect because a firm may be a target if its breakup value exceeds the cost of its acquisition. Thus, the acquirer may earn a profit by selling the assets piecemeal.

25. The synergy of a business combination can be determined by

    A.   Calculating the change in revenue minus the charge in cost.

    B.   Calculating the change in revenue minus the change in taxes.

    C.   Using the risk adjusted discount rate to discount the incremental cash flows of the newly formed entity.

    D.   Using the risk adjusted discount rate to discount the change in revenues of the newly formed entity.

The correct answer is (C). *(Publisher)*
    REQUIRED: The determination of synergy.
    DISCUSSION: Synergy equals the value of the combined firm minus the sum of the values of the separate firms. These values can be calculated using the capital budgeting technique of discounted cash flow analysis. The difference between the cash flows of the combined firm and the sum of the cash flows of the separate firms is discounted at the appropriate rate, usually the cost of equity of the acquired firm. The compnents of the incremental cash flows are the incremental revenues, costs, taxes, and capital needs.
    Answers (A), (B), and (D) are incorrect because discounting the incremental cash flows involves consideration of revenues, costs, taxes, and capital needs.

26. Which of the following is not a revenue enhancement advantage of acquiring another firm?

    A.   Improvement of media efforts.

    B.   A strategic advantage in a new product line.

    C.   Enlarging an already existing distribution network.

    D.   Economies of scale.

The correct answer is (D). *(Publisher)*
    REQUIRED: The item not a revenue enhancement advantage of acquiring another firm.
    DISCUSSION: Economies of scale in production, marketing, purchasing, management, etc., arise from decreasing unit cost resulting from higher levels of activity. Thus, economies of scale produce synergy in the form of cost reduction rather than revenue enhancement.
    Answer (A) is incorrect because improved advertising improves revenues, not reduces costs. Answer (B) is incorrect because new product lines improve revenues, not reduce costs. Answer (C) is incorrect because better distribution networks improve revenues, not reduce costs.

C. Tax Issues

27. Pursuant to a plan of reorganization adopted in 1996, Eagle Corporation exchanged property with an adjusted basis of $100,000 for 10,000 of the shares of the Hawkeye Corporation. The shares of Hawkeye had a fair market value of $120,000 on the date of the exchange. Eagle Corporation was liquidated shortly after the exchange with its sole shareholder A receiving the Hawkeye shares. The sole shareholder A had a $110,000 basis in the Eagle shares surrendered. As a result of this exchange, A's recognized gain and her basis in the Hawkeye stock are as follows:

	Recognized Gain	Stock Basis
A.	$0	$100,000
B.	$0	$110,000
C.	$0	$120,000
D.	$20,000	$120,000

The correct answer is (B). *(Publisher)*
REQUIRED: The gain recognized on receipt of stock for property under a plan of reorganization and the basis in the acquired stock.
DISCUSSION: The asset-for-stock exchange entered into by Eagle and Hawkeye Corporations is a Type C reorganization [Sec. 368(a)(1)(C)]. Sec. 354(a) provides that no gain or loss is recognized on a Type C reorganization if a shareholder exchanges stock or securities pursuant to a plan of reorganization solely for stock or securities in another corporation. Thus, A will recognize no gain.
The basis of the stock received by the shareholder is determined under Sec. 358(a) and is the same as the basis of the stock exchanged. The shareholder's basis in the Eagle stock exchanged was $110,000, so her basis in the Hawkeye stock received will also be $110,000.
Answers (A) and (C) are incorrect because the stock basis will be A's basis in Eagle stock. Answer (D) is incorrect because the stock basis will be A's basis in Eagle stock and there is no gain.

28. Tax-free reorganizations may take what form(s)?

	Statutory Merger	Stock-for-Stock	Stock-for-Assets
A.	No	No	No
B.	Yes	No	No
C.	Yes	Yes	No
D.	Yes	Yes	Yes

The correct answer is (D). *(Publisher)*
REQUIRED: The form(s), if any, of a tax-free reorganization.
DISCUSSION: Types A, B, and C reorganizations are tax free. In a statutory merger (Type A), two companies merge into one under state law. Stock in the nonsurvivor is canceled, and its shareholders receive stock in the survivor. In a stock-for-stock reorganization (Type B), shareholders acquire stock of a corporation solely for part or all of the voting stock of the acquiring corporation or its parent. No boot is allowed. In a stock-for-assets reorganization (Type C), one corporation acquires substantially all the assets of another in exchange for its voting stock (or its parent's). The transferor (seller) corporation must liquidate. Only 20% of the assets acquired may be exchanged for (paid for with) other than voting stock of the acquiring corporation. Limited amounts of boot are thus allowable.
Answers (A), (B), and (C) are incorrect because Types A, B, and C reorganizations are tax free.

D. Other Regulatory Issues

29. The advantage of a tender offer in a corporate takeover is that

A. Target shareholders have less time to evaluate the offer.

B. Target management has less time to organize a defense.

C. The failing company doctrine might otherwise prohibit the combination.

D. It is exempt from the Clayton Act.

The correct answer is (B). *(Publisher)*
REQUIRED: The advantage of a tender offer in a corporate takeover.
DISCUSSION: Corporate takeover specialists prefer tender offers because proxy fights can be prolonged by target firm management. With less time to organize a defense, target management is less effective than when they contest proxy fights.
Answer (A) is incorrect because shareholders may not sell (tender) their stock if they have insufficient time to evaluate a tender offer. Answer (C) is incorrect because the failing company doctrine permits mergers that reduce competition if there is no other purchaser available to combine with the failing company. Answer (D) is incorrect because the Clayton Act concerns all business combinations that may reduce competition.

30. The Herfindahl-Hirschman Index (HHI) is used by the Department of Justice to evaluate

    A. Horizontal mergers.

    B. Vertical mergers.

    C. Hostile takeover mergers.

    D. All mergers.

The correct answer is (A). *(Publisher)*
    REQUIRED: The purpose of the HHI.
    DISCUSSION: The HHI is used to determine market shares of all firms in the postcombination market after a horizontal merger. At issue is whether the merger results in excessive market concentration.
    Answer (B) is incorrect because HHI is used for horizontal, not vertical, mergers. Answer (C) is incorrect because HHI is used for horizontal, not all, mergers. Answer (D) is incorrect because HHI is used for horizontal, not hostile, mergers.

E. Accounting for Combinations

31. Business combinations are accomplished either through a direct acquisition of assets and liabilities by a surviving corporation or by stock investments in one or more companies. A parent-subsidiary relationship always arises from a

    A. Tax-free reorganization.

    B. Vertical combination.

    C. Horizontal combination.

    D. Greater than 50% stock investment in another company.

The correct answer is (D). *(Publisher)*
    REQUIRED: The situation creating a parent-subsidiary relationship.
    DISCUSSION: A parent-subsidiary relationship arises from an effective investment in the stock of another enterprise in excess of 50%. The financial statements for the two companies ordinarily should be presented on a consolidated basis. To the extent the corporation is not wholly-owned, a minority interest is presented.
    Answer (A) is incorrect because a tax-free reorganization may or may not be a combination, and it may or may not result in a parent-subsidiary relationship. Answers (B) and (C) are incorrect because vertical and horizontal combinations may also be accomplished by a merger or a consolidation, in which case the combining companies become one. A vertical combination combines a supplier or a customer firm with the acquiring company. A horizontal combination combines two firms in the same line of business.

32. What form of accounting is used when the assets of the acquired firm are added to the assets of the acquiring firm at book value after business combination?

    A. Consolidation.

    B. Aggregation.

    C. Purchase.

    D. Pooling.

The correct answer is (D). *(Publisher)*
    REQUIRED: The form of accounting used when the assets of the acquired firm are added to the assets of the acquiring firm at book value after business combination.
    DISCUSSION: In pooling of interests, assets and liabilities are recorded by the combined entity at their carrying (book) value, a treatment compatible with historical cost. If the separate companies recorded assets and liabilities using different methods, the amounts may be adjusted to the same basis of accounting if the change would have been appropriate for the separate company.
    Answer (A) is incorrect because a consolidation may be accounted for as a purchase wherein assets are recorded at fair values. Answer (B) is incorrect because aggregation is a nonsense term in this context. Answer (C) is incorrect because purchase accounting records fair, not book, values.

33. Which form of accounting for a business combination must result in recognition of goodwill when the amount paid exceeds the fair value of the identifiable net assets?

- A. Consolidation.
- B. Aggregation.
- C. Purchase.
- D. Pooling.

The correct answer is (C). *(Publisher)*
REQUIRED: The form of accounting for a business combination that creates goodwill.
DISCUSSION: The purchase method treats the combination as an acquisition of one company by another. The acquirer records the identifiable assets obtained and liabilities assumed at their fair values. Goodwill is the excess of the purchase price of the assets or an investee over the sum of the assigned costs (fair values) of the net identifiable assets (sum of the identifiable tangible and identifiable intangible assets, minus liabilities assumed).
Answer (A) is incorrect because a consolidation may be accounted for as a pooling, a method that records only book values. Answer (B) is incorrect because aggregation is a nonsense term in this context. Answer (D) is incorrect because, in a pooling, assets and liabilities are recorded at book value, so goodwill is not recognized.

34. Which of the following is a true statement about the accounting treatment of business combinations?

- A. The excess amount paid over the book value of the target's assets is added to retained earnings under the pooling method.
- B. The purchase method results in higher taxes on the transaction.
- C. The purchase method is preferable to the pooling method because it eliminates any minority interest.
- D. Purchase accounting results in a write-up of the assets of the acquired firm when their book value is less than fair value.

The correct answer is (D). *(Publisher)*
REQUIRED: The true statement about accounting for business combinations.
DISCUSSION: In a pooling, assets are recorded at their existing book values. In a purchase, assets are recorded at fair value. Thus, if book value exceeds fair value, the pooling method records the larger amounts on the balance sheet.
Answer (A) is incorrect because a pooling involves an issuance solely of common stock, and retained earnings is ordinarily unaffected. Answer (B) is incorrect because certain tax-free reorganizations are accounted for using the purchase method. Answer (C) is incorrect because when a stock investment includes more than 50% but less than 100% of the outstanding stock of a company, a minority interest exists in the consolidated balance sheet.

F. Valuation and Pricing the Combination

35. A common mistake in valuing the firm to be acquired in a business combination is

- A. Using market values in the valuation.
- B. Including incremental cash flows in the valuation.
- C. Using the acquiring firm's discount rate when valuing the incremental cash flows.
- D. Including all related transaction costs associated with an acquisition.

The correct answer is (C). *(Publisher)*
REQUIRED: The common mistake in valuing the acquired firm.
DISCUSSION: If the net incremental cash flows to the acquiring firm's shareholders are to be valued, the discount rate used should be the cost of equity capital. Moreover, this rate should reflect the risk associated with the use of funds rather than their source. The rate therefore should not be the cost of capital of the acquiring firm but rather the cost of equity of the combined firm after the combination. This calculation requires a new estimate of beta to be used in the Capital Asset Pricing Model.
Answers (A), (B), and (D) are incorrect because market values, incremental cash flows, and transaction costs are essential elements of the valuation.

36. The appropriate discount rate to use in valuing a business combination is the

    A.   Combined firm's cost of debt.

    B.   Acquiring firm's weighted average cost of capital.

    C.   Acquiring firm's cost of equity.

    D.   Combined firm's cost of equity.

The correct answer is (D). *(Publisher)*

    REQUIRED: The appropriate discount rate to use in valuing a business combination.

    DISCUSSION: If the net incremental cash flows to the acquiring firm's shareholders are to be calculated, the discount rate used should be the cost of equity capital. Moreover, this rate should reflect the risk associated with the use of funds rather than their source. The rate therefore should not be the cost of capital of the acquiring firm but rather the cost of equity of the acquired firm after the combination. This calculation requires a new estimate of beta to be used in the Capital Asset Pricing Model.

    Answer (A) is incorrect because the cost of equity not the cost of debt should be the discount rate. Answers (B) and (C) are incorrect because the discount rate should be that of the combined firm, not the acquiring firm.

G. Opposition to the Combination

37. What is a payment to compensate top management after the occurrence of a takeover called?

    A.   Greenmail.

    B.   A golden parachute.

    C.   A poison pill.

    D.   Blackmail.

The correct answer is (B). *(Publisher)*

    REQUIRED: The payment to compensate top management after the occurrence of a takeover.

    DISCUSSION: A golden parachute provides large payments to specified executives if their employment is terminated by the acquiring firm after a takeover. These provisions are passed by the board of directors. Shareholders are unhappy about golden parachute payoffs and have filed suits because they feel that these payoffs enrich management at their expense. In 1984, a change in the tax law created a 20% excise tax on these payoffs and nondeductibility by the corporation. This was designed to reduce golden parachutes.

    Answer (A) is incorrect because greenmail is payments to potential bidders to delay or stop unfriendly takeover attempts. Answer (C) is incorrect because a poison pill is rights granted to the target firm's shareholders contingent on a takeover to dilute the target firm's stock. Answer (D) is incorrect because blackmail is obtaining a desired result by threats such as public exposure of a negative attribute and is usually not relevant to corporate takeover defenses.

38. Which of the following defense maneuvers is the issuance of rights to buy shares at an extremely reduced price upon the occurrence of a takeover?

    A.   Greenmail.

    B.   Flip-over rights.

    C.   A poison pill.

    D.   Crown jewels.

The correct answer is (C). *(Publisher)*

    REQUIRED: The defense maneuver that is the issuance of rights to buy shares at an extremely reduced price upon the occurrence of a takeover.

    DISCUSSION: A poison pill may be included in a target corporation's charter, by-laws, or contracts to reduce the value of the target corporation to potential tender offerors. A poison pill is generally a right for the target firm's shareholders to purchase shares of the merged firm resulting from a takeover. The bidding company loses money on its shares because this right dilutes the value of the target's stock.

    Answer (A) is incorrect because greenmail is when the potential acquiror is offered the opportunity to sell his/her already acquired shares back to the corporation above the market value. Answer (B) is incorrect because flip-over rights provide the target shareholders to acquire in exchange for their stock a relatively greater interest in an acquiring entity. Answer (D) is incorrect because a crown jewel transfer is when the target corporation sells or disposes of one or more assets that made it a desirable target.

H. Other Restructurings

39. A large U.S. company recently set up a new corporation based on the assets from one of its divisions. The stock of the new corporation was titled to the stockholders of the original firm. This change is an example of a

A. Merger.

B. Synergistic merger.

C. Holding company.

D. Divestiture.

The correct answer is (D). *(CIA 1189 IV-57)*

REQUIRED: The term for setting up a new corporation based on the assets from one of the firm's divisions.

DISCUSSION: The transaction described is a spin-off, which is a kind of divestiture. The types of divestiture are sale of a subunit to another company, sale of a subunit to the subunit's management, piecemeal liquidation of the subunit's assets, and a spin-off. This last form of divestiture is characterized by establishing a new and separate entity and transferring its newly issued stock to the shareholders of the original company.

Answer (A) is incorrect because a merger is a combination of companies. Answer (B) is incorrect because a synergistic merger is one in which the value of the combined entity exceeds the sum of the values of the separate entities. Answer (C) is incorrect because a holding company is a firm that owns sufficient stock in another company to control it.

40. A company transferred ownership of one of its divisions to the company's existing shareholders, and the shareholders received new stock representing separate ownership rights in the division. That process is referred to as a

A. Liquidation.

B. Spin-off.

C. Leveraged buyout.

D. Managerial buyout.

The correct answer is (B). *(CIA 1193 IV-56)*

REQUIRED: The type of restructuring.

DISCUSSION: A spin-off is a type of restructuring that is characterized by establishing a new and separate entity and transferring its newly issued stock to the shareholders of the original company.

Answer (A) is incorrect because, in a liquidation, assets are sold piecemeal. Answer (C) is incorrect because, in an LBO, the acquirer borrows heavily from third parties to finance the transaction and uses the acquired company's assets as collateral. Answer (D) is incorrect because, in a managerial buyout, the managers become the owners.

41. A corporation issued a property dividend to its shareholders. The dividend was distributed in the form of 100% of the common stock of a subsidiary. This is known as a

A. Spin-off.

B. Stock split.

C. Scrip dividend.

D. Reverse split.

The correct answer is (A). *(CIA 591 IV-54)*

REQUIRED: The term for a property dividend in the form of 100% of the common stock of a subsidiary.

DISCUSSION: A spin-off creates a new, separate entity. It is accomplished by distributing a property dividend in the form of stock of another corporation to shareholders, who then become shareholders of both corporations.

Answer (B) is incorrect because a stock split is accomplished by a corporation issuing additional shares of its own stock to shareholders. Answer (C) is incorrect because a scrip dividend is one that is payable in the form of notes payable. Answer (D) is incorrect because a reverse split occurs when a corporation reduces the number of its outstanding shares.

42. Clover Inc. recently sold a portion of the firm via an offering of shares in the new entity to public investors. This type of sell-off is classified as a(n)

A. Spin-off.

B. Equity carve-out.

C. Leveraged cash-out.

D. Liquidation.

The correct answer is (B). *(CFM Sample Q. 3)*

REQUIRED: The type of sell-off when a portion of a firm is sold to public investors.

DISCUSSION: An equity carve-out involves the sale of a portion of the firm through an equity offering of shares in the new entity to outsiders.

Answer (A) is incorrect because a spin-off is the creation of a new separate entity from another entity, with the new entity's shares being distributed on a pro rata basis to existing shareholders of the parent entity. Answer (C) is incorrect because a leveraged cash-out is borrowing heavily to issue a very large dividend which acts as a poison pill. Answer (D) is incorrect because, in a liquidation, assets are sold piecemeal.

I. Bankruptcy

43. Chapter 7 of the Federal Bankruptcy Code will grant a debtor a discharge when the debtor

- A. Is a corporation or a partnership.
- B. Is an entity that could successfully reorganize under Chapter 11 of the Federal Bankruptcy Code.
- C. Is an insurance company.
- D. Unjustifiably destroyed information relevant to the bankruptcy proceeding.

The correct answer is (B). *(Publisher)*
REQUIRED: The basis for granting a discharge to a debtor under Chapter 7 of the Bankruptcy Code.
DISCUSSION: A general discharge of most debts is provided a person under Chapter 7. Certain entities are not eligible, including railroads, insurance companies, banks, credit unions, and savings and loan associations. Liquidation and discharge under Chapter 7 are not restricted to cases in which Chapter 11 reorganization would not be successful.
Answer (A) is incorrect because partnerships and corporations do not receive a general discharge under Chapter 7. They are simply liquidated. Answer (C) is incorrect because insurance companies are ineligible to file under Chapter 7. Answer (D) is incorrect because destroying information can result in denial of general discharge. Only if it is justified, e.g., accidental and not to defraud creditors, might it not result in denial of discharge.

44. A plan of reorganization under Chapter 11

- A. May be filed by any party in interest for 120 days after entry of the order for relief.
- B. Must be filed by the trustee and approved by the creditors within 180 days after entry of the order for relief.
- C. Must treat all classes of claims and ownership interests equally.
- D. Must treat all claims or interests in the same class equally.

The correct answer is (D). *(Publisher)*
REQUIRED: The correct statement about a plan of reorganization.
DISCUSSION: A Chapter 11 plan must designate classes of creditors' claims and owners' interests; state the treatment to be given each class; indicate which classes will or will not be impaired; allow for equal treatment of the members within a class unless they agree otherwise; and provide for an adequate method of payment. If the debtor is a corporation, the plan must also protect voting rights, state that no nonvoting stock will be issued, and require that selection of officers and directors be effected in a manner to protect the parties in interest.
Answers (A) and (B) are incorrect because only the debtor may file a plan within 120 days after entry of the order for relief. If the debtor fails to file or if the creditors do not approve of the plan within 180 days of the entry of the order for relief, any party in interest (including the trustee) may file a plan. Answer (C) is incorrect because the plan must be fair and equitable but all classes need not be treated the same. However, no party may receive less than the amount that would have been distributed in a liquidation.

45. Which of the following is indicative of insolvency?

- A. Payments to creditors are late.
- B. The market value of the firm's stock has declined substantially.
- C. Operating cash flows of the firm cannot meet current obligations.
- D. Dividends are not declared because of inadequate retained earnings.

The correct answer is (C). *(Publisher)*
REQUIRED: The indicator of insolvency.
DISCUSSION: A firm is insolvent when its debts exceed its assets (stock-based insolvency) or when its cash flows are inadequate to meet maturing obligations (flow-based insolvency).
Answer (A) is incorrect because late payments are an early signal of potential insolvency. Answer (B) is incorrect because a declining share price is an early signal of potential insolvency. Answer (D) is incorrect because elimination of dividends is an early signal of potential insolvency.

46. A plan of reorganization formulated under Chapter 11 must be submitted to the creditors for acceptance and to the court for confirmation. Which of the following is correct?

A. The effect of confirmation is to make the plan binding on all parties and to grant the debtor a discharge from claims not protected by the plan.

B. A plan cannot be confirmed if any impaired class of claims or interests rejects it.

C. If no class of claims or interests accepts a plan, the court may nevertheless confirm it if the plan is in the best interests of the creditors.

D. A class that is not impaired is presumed to accept, but more than half of the claims in a class by amount must accept if the class is impaired.

The correct answer is (A). *(Publisher)*
REQUIRED: The correct statement about acceptance and confirmation of a plan.
DISCUSSION: Confirmation is the court's approval of the plan after notice and a hearing. Confirmation makes the plan binding on the creditors, equity security holders, and debtor, whether or not they accepted the plan. It also operates as a discharge of unprotected debts, except for those claims previously denied discharge in a Chapter 7 case, and vests the estate property in the debtor. Confirmation is contingent upon the plan's feasibility, the good faith in which it was proposed, and the provision for cash payment of certain allowed claims, such as administration expenses.
Answer (B) is incorrect because an impaired class may be required to accept a plan over its objection if the court finds that the plan is "fair and equitable," for instance, if no junior claim or interest receives anything. Answer (C) is incorrect because at least one class of claims (not ownership interests) must accept. Answer (D) is incorrect because a class of claims accepts if approval is given by more than half the allowed claims, provided they represent at least two-thirds of the claims by amount. A class of interests (shareholders) accepts if approval is given by two-thirds in amount of the allowed interests.

47. Which of the following is not an early signal of potential financial distress?

A. Negative earnings.

B. Employee layoffs.

C. Rapidly falling stock prices.

D. Stagnant cash flows.

The correct answer is (D). *(Publisher)*
REQUIRED: The item not an early signal of financial distress.
DISCUSSION: Mere stagnation of cash flows does not indicate potential insolvency. Flow-based insolvency occurs when cash flows are inadequate, not when they are simply not growing at the desired rate.
Answer (A) is incorrect because negative earnings are an early signal of potential insolvency. Answer (B) is incorrect because layoffs are an early signal of potential insolvency. Answer (C) is incorrect because a declining share price is an early signal of potential insolvency.

48. Insolvency is

A. A low cash balance.

B. Lack of liquidity.

C. Not being able to pay one's debts.

D. Lack of borrowing capacity.

The correct answer is (C). *(Publisher)*
REQUIRED: The definition of insolvency.
DISCUSSION: A firm is insolvent when its debts exceed its assets (stock-based insolvency) or when its cash flows are inadequate to meet maturing obligations (flow-based insolvency).
Answer (A) is incorrect because a low cash balance does not, by itself, indicate insolvency. Answer (B) is incorrect because lack of liquidity does not, by itself, indicate insolvency. Answer (D) is incorrect because a lack of borrowing capacity does not, by itself, indicate insolvency.

49. Which of the following is the most likely option to be chosen by an insolvent firm?

A. Increase R&D and capital expenditures.

B. Purchase a stable firm.

C. File for bankruptcy.

D. Repurchase stock.

The correct answer is (C). *(Publisher)*
REQUIRED: The most likely action of an insolvent firm.
DISCUSSION: An insolvent firm may agree to be acquired by a stronger firm or it may sell important assets, slash costs, issue additional securities, negotiate with creditors to restructure its obligations, or exchange equity for debt. It may also choose a reorganization in bankruptcy. A final option is bankruptcy liquidation.
Answer (A) is incorrect because the firm is more likely to cut costs. Answer (B) is incorrect because an insolvent firm is more likely a takeover target. Answer (D) is incorrect because the firm is more likely to issue additional stock to raise money.

50. A spin-off

    A. Is a type of dividend.

    B. Is a sale of an operating unit to a third party.

    C. Is an equity carve out.

    D. Is a sale to employees.

The correct answer is (A). *(Publisher)*

    REQUIRED: The definition of a spin-off.

    DISCUSSION: A spin-off is the creation of a new separate entity from another entity, with the new entity's shares being distributed on a pro rata basis to existing shareholders of the parent entity. Existing shareholders will have the same proportion of ownership in the new entity that they had in the parent. A spin-off is a typ_ of dividend to existing shareholders.

    Answer (B) is incorrect because a divestiture may be defined as a sale of an operating unit to a third party. Answer (C) is incorrect because an equity carve-out involves the sale of a portion of the firm through an equity offering of shares in the new entity to outsiders. Answer (D) is incorrect because a spin-off is a dividend, not a sale.

51. A firm may benefit from insolvency in all but which of the following ways?

    A. Being forced to focus upon core operations.

    B. Realigning its capital structure.

    C. Entering Chapter 11 bankruptcy proceedings and reorganizing the firm.

    D. Being forced to liquidate the business.

The correct answer is (D). *(Publisher)*

    REQUIRED: The item not a potential benefit of insolvency.

    DISCUSSION: Benefits of insolvency may include restructuring of the firm's assets and capital structure, divestiture of noncore operations, development of new strategies and new forms of organization, and relief from creditors' actions while the firm is in a Chapter 11 reorganization. However, being forced to liquidate is the result that a firm most wants to avoid.

    Answer (A) is incorrect because focusing on core operations is a possible advantage. Answer (B) is incorrect because capital restructuring is a possible advantage. Answer (C) is incorrect because reorganization under the protection of Chapter 11 is a possible advantage.

52. Which of the following, if any, may be commenced by the filing of a voluntary or an involuntary petition in a bankruptcy court?

	Chapter 7 Liquidation	Chapter 11 Reorganization
A.	Yes	Yes
B.	Yes	No
C.	No	Yes
D.	No	No

The correct answer is (A). *(Publisher)*

    REQUIRED: The bankruptcy option(s), if any, that may be invoked by a voluntary or an involuntary petition.

    DISCUSSION: In a Chapter 7 liquidation, or in a Chapter 11 reorganization, a voluntary or an involuntary petition is filed in the federal bankruptcy court. An involuntary petition must be joined by three or more creditors with unsecured claims of at least $10,000 if the debtor has 12 or more creditors. If there are fewer than 12, one creditor with a claim of at least $10,000 may file.

    Answers (B), (C), and (D) are incorrect because both liquidation and reorganization may be commenced by either a voluntary or an involuntary petition.

53. After a petition for bankruptcy liquidation has been filed and the court has issued an order for relief,

    A. The court usually appoints a permanent trustee to take control of the debtor's estate.

    B. Creditors must immediately cease their collection activities.

    C. The bankruptcy judge notifies creditors, collects the debtor's nonexempt property, and distributes that property to the creditors.

    D. A meeting is held by the creditors to vote on a plan of reorganization.

The correct answer is (B). *(Publisher)*

    REQUIRED: The effect of issuing an order for relief.

    DISCUSSION: A debtor files a bankruptcy petition to obtain relief from creditors' collection efforts. Creditors may file to ensure an equitable division of the debtor's estate, an outcome that may not be reached if creditors are allowed to continue their individual collection activities. Thus, the order for relief stays those activities.

    Answer (A) is incorrect because the court usually appoints a temporary trustee, and the creditors usually elect a permanent trustee. Answer (C) is incorrect because the trustee, not the judge, administers the estate. Answer (D) is incorrect because the creditors vote on a plan of reorganization under Chapter 11.

54. The creditors of a firm have filed an involuntary petition seeking a Chapter 7 liquidation of the firm under federal bankruptcy law. The firm contests the petition. What is a basis for the court denying the petition?

   A. A custodian took possession of the debtor's property to enforce a lien 60 days prior to filing.

   B. A custodian took possession of the debtor's property to enforce a lien 120 days prior to filing.

   C. The debtor has 12 creditors and three creditors with unsecured claims totaling $10,000 joined in the petition.

   D. The debtor has 10 creditors and one creditor with a claim of $5,000 filed.

The correct answer is (D). *(Publisher)*
   REQUIRED: The basis for denying an involuntary petition.
   DISCUSSION: An involuntary petition must be joined by three or more creditors with unsecured claims totaling at least $10,000 if the debtor has 12 or more creditors. If there are fewer than 12, one creditor with a claim of at least $10,000 may file.
   Answers (A) and (B) are incorrect because a contested involuntary petition will be granted if the debtor is not paying its bills when due or if, within 120 days prior to filing, a custodian took possession of the debtor's property to enforce a lien. Answer (C) is incorrect because the plaintiff's claims total at least $10,000 and the involuntary petition is joined by three creditors with unsecured claims.

55. The correct priority of claims in a bankruptcy liquidation is

   A. Administrative expenses, wage claims of no more than $4,000, taxes due, claims of general or unsecured creditors, and shareholder claims.

   B. Administrative expenses, wage claims of no more than $4,000, taxes due, shareholder claims and debtholder claims.

   C. All wage claims, administrative expenses, debtholder claims, taxes due and shareholder claims.

   D. All wage claims, administrative expenses, debtholder claims, shareholder claims, and taxes due.

The correct answer is (A). *(Publisher)*
   REQUIRED: The correct priority of claims in a bankruptcy liquidation.
   DISCUSSION: After secured creditors receive the proceeds of the sale of specific collateral, the other assets are distributed according to the following scheme: (1) administrative expenses, (2) claims of gap creditors, (3) wages of no more than $4,000, (4) unpaid contributions to employee benefit plans, (5) customer deposits, (6) taxes, (7) certain unfunded pension plan liabilities, (8) claims of general or unsecured creditors, (9) claims of preferred shareholders, and (10) claims of common shareholders.
   Answers (B) is incorrect because wage claims are limited to $4,000/employee. Answer (C) is incorrect because administrative expenses come first and taxes come before debtholder claims. Answer (D) is incorrect because administrative expenses come first and taxes come before debtholders.

56. A discharge in bankruptcy under Chapter 7 (liquidation) may be obtained by a(n)

	Individual	Corporation	Partnership
A.	Yes	Yes	Yes
B.	No	Yes	Yes
C.	Yes	No	No
D.	No	No	Yes

The correct answer is (C). *(Publisher)*
   REQUIRED: The party(ies) that may receive a discharge.
   DISCUSSION: Individual debtors may receive a discharge under Chapter 7 from most debts that remain unpaid after distribution of the debtor's estate. However, corporations and partnerships are merely liquidated. They are not eligible for a Chapter 7 discharge.
   Answers (A), (B), and (D) are incorrect because individuals but not corporations and partnerships may receive a discharge.

57. Chapter 11 of the bankruptcy law concerns reorganizations. Under Chapter 11,

    A.   Individuals are not eligible debtors.

    B.   A case may be commenced only by a voluntary petition.

    C.   Insolvency is condition precedent to the filing of a petition.

    D.   The primary purpose is usually the continuation of the business.

The correct answer is (D). *(Publisher)*
    REQUIRED: The true statement about bankruptcy reorganization.
    DISCUSSION: A Chapter 11 reorganization allows a distressed business enterprise to restructure its finances. The primary purpose of the restructuring is usually the continuation of the business. Reorganization is a process of negotiation whereby the debtor firm and its creditors develop a plan for the adjustment and discharge of debts.
    Answer (A) is incorrect because partnerships, corporations, and any person who may be a debtor under Chapter 7 (except stock and commodity brokers) are eligible debtors under Chapter 11. Answer (B) is incorrect because a reorganization may be commenced by a voluntary or involuntary petition. Answer (C) is incorrect because the debtor need not be insolvent.

58. Which of the following is a true statement about a plan of reorganization in a Chapter 11 bankruptcy case?

    A.   A debtor may have the exclusive right to file a plan of reorganization for a certain period.

    B.   A plan of reorganization must treat all creditors similarly.

    C.   Only a committee of creditors may file a plan of reorganization.

    D.   The plan of reorganization must be approved by a supermajority of each class of creditors.

The correct answer is (A). *(Publisher)*
    REQUIRED: The true statement about a plan of reorganization.
    DISCUSSION: The debtor has the exclusive right to file a plan during the 120 days after the order for relief is issued by the court, unless a trustee has been appointed, and may file a plan of reorganization at any time.
    Answer (B) is incorrect because a plan of reorganization must divide creditors' claims and shareholders' interests into classes, and claims in each class must be treated equally. Answer (C) is incorrect because the debtor may file a plan at any time. Answer (D) is incorrect because to become effective, the plan ordinarily must be accepted by a certain percentage (usually, at least two-thirds) of persons whose rights as creditors or owners have been impaired, provide for full payment of administration expenses, and be confirmed (approved and put into operation) by the bankruptcy court. Furthermore, a bankruptcy court may force an impaired class of creditors to participate in, and the court may confirm, a plan of reorganization that is fair and equitable to the impaired class.

59. The trusteeship function in a Chapter 11 bankruptcy reorganization is usually performed by the

    A.   Court.

    B.   Debtor-in-possession.

    C.   Committee of creditors.

    D.   Examiner.

The correct answer is (B). *(Publisher)*
    REQUIRED: The party(ies) performing the trusteeship function in a reorganization.
    DISCUSSION: In a Chapter 11 reorganization, the court has limited power to appoint a trustee. Instead, to better accomplish the rehabilitative aspirations of a reorganization, a firm seeking protection under Chapter 11 may be permitted to operate its own business as a debtor-in-possession. A strong presumption exists that a debtor-in-possession should be permitted to continue to operate the business unless there is evidence of incompetence or mismanagement on the part of the debtor. A debtor-in-possession has basically all the same rights and duties as a trustee but does not receive special compensation for performing the function.
    Answer (A) is incorrect because the court may sometimes appoint a trustee but does not serve as trustee. Answer (C) is incorrect because the committee consults with the court, the debtor, and the trustee; investigates the debtor's affairs; and participates in formulating the plan of reorganization. Answer (D) is incorrect because an examiner may be appointed to examine allegations of fraud, misconduct, or mismanagement.

Study Unit 8: RISK MANAGEMENT

19 pages of outline
61 multiple-choice questions

A. Types of Risk
B. Risk Measurement
C. Portfolio Management

D. Options and Futures
E. Corporate Insurance
F. Foreign Operations

This study unit covers "Risk Management," the third major topic in the CFM content specification outline.

A. Types of Risk

1. **Risk** is the possibility of an unfavorable event. **Investment risk** is analyzed in terms of the probability that the actual return will be lower than the expected return. The concepts of probability distributions and expected value are basic to risk management.

   a. The risk of a security may be considered in isolation or from the perspective of its inclusion in a portfolio of assets chosen to minimize the riskiness of the whole.

2. **Specific Types of Risks**

   a. **Interest-rate risk** is the risk of fluctuations in the value of an asset due to changes in interest rates. In general, it is greater the longer the maturity of the asset.

      1) One component of interest-rate risk is **price risk**. Thus, the value of bonds declines when interest rates increase.

      2) A second component of interest-rate risk is **reinvestment-rate risk**. If interest rates decline, lower returns will be available for reinvestment of interest and principal payments received.

   b. **Purchasing-power risk** is the risk that a general rise in the price level will reduce what can be purchased with a fixed sum of money. Accordingly, required returns include an inflation premium.

   c. **Default risk** is the risk that a borrower will be unable to repay debt. Hence, the higher the default risk, the higher the return required by an investor.

   d. **Market risk** is the risk that changes in price will result from changes that affect all firms. Prices of all securities, even the values of portfolios, are correlated to some degree with broad swings in the economy. Market risk is also known as systematic risk or nondiversifiable risk.

   e. **Nonmarket risk** or **company-specific risk** is the risk that is influenced by an individual firm's policies and decisions. Nonmarket risk is diversifiable because it is firm specific. Thus, it is also known as diversifiable or unsystematic risk.

   f. **Portfolio risk** is the risk remaining after allowing for the risk-reducing effects of combining securities into a portfolio.

   g. **Total risk** is the risk of a single asset, whereas market risk is its risk if it is held in a large portfolio of diversified securities.

   h. **Liquidity risk** is the possibility that an asset cannot be sold on short notice for its market value. If an asset must be sold at a deep discount, it is said to have a substantial amount of liquidity risk.

    i.   **Business risk** is the risk of fluctuations in earnings before interest and taxes or in operating income when the firm uses no debt. It is the risk inherent in its operations that excludes **financial risk**, which is the risk to the shareholders from the use of financial leverage. Business risk depends on factors such as demand variability, sales price variability, input price variability, and amount of operating leverage.

    j.   **Exchange-rate risk** is the risk that a foreign currency transaction will be negatively exposed to fluctuations in exchange rates.

3.   Stop and review! You have completed the outline for this subunit. Study multiple-choice questions 1 through 7 beginning on page 308.

B. Risk Measurement

1.   **Probability** provides a method for mathematically expressing doubt or assurance about the occurrence of a chance event. There are two types of probability -- objective and subjective. They differ in how they are calculated.

    a.   **Objective probabilities** are calculated from either logic or actual experience. For example, in rolling a six-sided die one would logically expect the probability for each outcome to be about .167.

    b.   **Subjective probabilities** are estimates, based on judgment and past experience, of the likelihood of future events. Weather forecasts often include the subjective probability of rain. In finance, subjective probability can indicate the degree of confidence a person has that a certain outcome will occur, e.g., the future performance of a stock.

2.   A **probability distribution** is the set of all possible outcomes of a decision, with a probability assigned to each outcome. For example, a simple probability distribution might be defined for the possible returns on a stock investment. A different return could be estimated for each of a limited number of possible states of the economy, and a probability could be determined for each state. Such a probability distribution is **discrete** because the outcomes are limited.

    a.   A **continuous distribution** is one for which the outcomes are theoretically infinite. The normal distribution is the best-known continuous distribution. The **normal distribution** has a symmetrical, bell-shaped curve centered about the mean.

        1)   Normal distributions have the following fixed relationships concerning the area under the curve and the distance from the mean.

Distance in Standard Deviations	Area under the Curve
1.0	68%
1.64	90%
1.96	95%
2.0	95.5%
2.57	99%

        2)   EXAMPLE: The following illustrates a normal distribution with a standard deviation of 10:

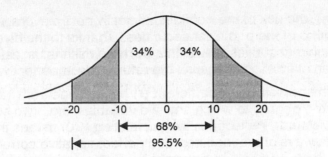

3. The **expected rate of return** on an investment is determined using an expected value calculation. It is an average of the outcomes weighted according to their probabilities. Consequently, the expected rate of return is the mean of the probability distribution of the possible outcomes. If k_i is the return from the ith possible outcome and if p_i is its probability, the expected return ($\hat{k}$) may be expressed as

$$\hat{k} = \sum_{i=1}^{n} k_i \, p_i$$

    a. The greater the standard deviation of the expected return, the riskier the investment. A large standard deviation implies that the range of possible returns is wide; i.e., the probability distribution is broadly dispersed. Conversely, the smaller the standard deviation, the tighter the probability distribution and the lower the risk.

    b. The **standard deviation** gives an exact value for the tightness of the distribution and the riskiness of the investment. The standard deviation (σ) is the square root of the variance. If k_i is the return from the ith outcome, p_i is its probability, and $\hat{k}$ is the expected (mean) return, the variance (σ^2) is

$$\sigma^2 = \sum_{i=1}^{n} (k_i - \hat{k})^2 \, p_i$$

    c. The **coefficient of variation** is useful when the rates of return and standard deviations of two investments differ. It measures the risk per unit of return because it divides the standard deviation (σ) by the expected return ($\hat{k}$).

$$Coefficient\ of\ variation = \frac{\sigma}{\hat{k}}$$

4. Whether the expected return on an investment is sufficient to entice an investor depends on its risk, the risks and returns of alternative investments, and the investor's attitude toward risk.

    a. Most serious investors are risk averse. They have a diminishing marginal utility for wealth. In other words, the utility of additional increments of wealth decreases. The utility of a gain for serious investors is less than the disutility of a loss of the same amount.

    b. Due to this risk aversion, risky securities must have higher expected returns.

5. The foregoing sections apply to investments in individual securities. When a portfolio is held, however, additional considerations apply. Risk and return should be evaluated for the entire portfolio, not for individual assets.

    a. The expected return on a portfolio is the weighted average of the returns on the individual securities.

b. However, the risk of the portfolio is usually not an average of the standard deviations of the particular securities. Thanks to the diversification effect, combining securities results in a portfolio risk that is less than the average of the standard deviations because the returns are imperfectly correlated.

1) The **correlation coefficient (r)** has a range from 1.0 to −1.0. It measures the degree to which any two variables, e.g., two stocks in a portfolio, are related. Perfect positive correlation (1.0) means that the two variables always move together, and perfect negative correlation (−1.0) means that the two variables always move in the opposite direction.

a) Given perfect positive correlation, risk for a two-stock portfolio with equal investments in each stock would be the same as that for the individual assets.

b) Given perfect negative correlation, risk would in theory be eliminated.

2) In practice, securities are usually positively but imperfectly correlated. The normal range for the correlation of two randomly selected stocks is .50 to .70. The result is a reduction in, but not elimination of, risk.

c. The measurement of the standard deviation of a portfolio's returns is based on the same formula as that for a single security (see B.4.b.).

1) Another important measurement used in portfolio analysis is the **covariance**. It measures the volatility of returns together with their correlation with the returns of other securities. For two stocks X and Y, if $\hat{k}$ is the expected return, k_i is a given outcome, and p_i is its probability, the covariance of X and Y is

$$COV(XY) = \sum_{i=1}^{n} (k_{xi} - \hat{k}_x)(k_{yi} - \hat{k}_y)p_i$$

2) The correlation coefficient (r) mentioned earlier is calculated to facilitate comparisons of covariances. It standardizes the covariance by dividing by the product of the standard deviations of the two assets.

$$r_{xy} = \frac{COV_{XY}}{\sigma_X \, \sigma_Y}$$

6. Stop and review! You have completed the outline for this subunit. Study multiple-choice questions 8 through 14 beginning on page 310.

C. Portfolio Management

1. An investor wants to maximize expected return and minimize risk when choosing a portfolio. A feasible portfolio that offers the highest expected return for a given risk or the least risk for a given expected return is an **efficient portfolio**. A portfolio that is selected from the efficient set of portfolios because it is tangent to the investor's highest indifference curve is the **optimal portfolio**.

a. An indifference curve represents combinations of portfolios having equal utility to the investor. Given that risk and returns are plotted on the horizontal and vertical axes, respectively, and that the investor is risk averse, the curve has an increasingly positive slope. As risk increases, the additional required return per unit of additional risk also increases.

1) The steeper the slope of an indifference curve, the more risk averse an investor is.

2) The higher the curve, the greater is the investor's level of utility.

3) In the diagram below, A, B, C, D, and E are indifference curves. A represents the highest level of utility and E the lowest. On a given curve, each point represents the same total utility to a risk-averse investor. For example, points 1, 2, and 3 are different combinations of risk and return that yield the same utility. The investor is indifferent as to which combination is chosen.

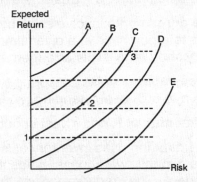

2. Two important decisions are involved in managing a company's portfolio:

   a. The amount of money to invest
   b. The securities in which to invest

3. The investment in securities should be based on expected net cash flows and cash flow uncertainty evaluations.

   a. Arranging a portfolio so that the maturity of funds will coincide with the need for funds will maximize the average return on the portfolio and provide increased flexibility.

      1) Maturity matching ensures that securities will not have to be sold unexpectedly.

   b. If its cash flows are relatively uncertain, a security's marketability and market risk are important factors to be considered. Transaction costs are also a consideration.

      1) Higher yield long-term securities provide less certainty.

   c. When cash flows are relatively certain, the maturity date is a paramount concern.

4. **Financial Instruments.** Financial managers may select from a wide range of financial instruments in which to invest and with which to raise money.

   a. Ranked from the lowest rate of return to the highest, the following is a short list of widely available long-term financial instruments:

      1) U.S. Treasury bonds
      2) First mortgage bonds
      3) Second mortgage bonds
      4) Subordinated debentures
      5) Income bonds
      6) Preferred stock
      7) Convertible preferred stock
      8) Common stock

b. These instruments also are ranked according to the level of security backing them. An unsecured financial instrument is much riskier than an instrument that is secured. Thus, the riskier asset earns a higher rate of return. Mortgage bonds are secured by assets, whereas common stock is completely unsecured. Accordingly, common stock will earn a higher rate of return than mortgage bonds. For more on long-term financing, see Study Unit 3.

c. Short-term financial instruments increase the liquidity of an entity. All of the following short-term instruments may be used to obtain funds or invest them.

   1) **Bankers' acceptances** are drafts drawn on deposits at a bank. The acceptance by the bank is a guarantee of payment at maturity.

   2) **Repurchase agreements** involve sales by a dealer in government securities who agrees to repurchase at a given time for a specific price. Maturities may be very short-term. This arrangement is in essence a secured loan.

   3) **Pledging receivables** involves securing loans with receivables. A bank will often lend up to 80% of outstanding receivables.

   4) **Money-market mutual funds** invest in portfolios of short-term securities.

   5) **Warehouse financing** uses inventory as security for the loan. A third party, for example, a public warehouse, holds the collateral and serves as the creditor's agent. The creditor receives the warehouse receipts evidencing rights in the collateral.

   6) **Agency securities** are issued by government agencies (not the Treasury), such as the Federal Home Loan Banks and other agencies that provide credit to farmers, home buyers, etc. An example is the Federal National Mortgage Association (Fannie Mae), which issues mortgage-backed securities. Agency securities may be long- or short-term.

   7) **Treasury bills** are short-term U.S. government obligations issued by the Treasury at a discount from their face value. A T-bill is highly liquid and nearly free of risk. It is often held as a cash substitute.

   8) **Treasury notes and bonds** are long-term investments, but issues near maturity are effectively short-term securities with high liquidity.

   9) State and local governmental entities issue short-term securities exempt from taxation.

   10) **Chattel mortgages** are loans secured by movable personal property (e.g., equipment or livestock).

   11) **Floating liens** attach to property, such as inventory, the composition of which is constantly changing.

   12) **Commercial paper** consists of unsecured, large denomination promissory notes typically issued for less than 9 months.

5. **Risk Management**

   a. **Portfolio theory** concerns the composition of an investment portfolio that is efficient in balancing the risk with the rate of return of the portfolio.

   b. The expected rate of return of a portfolio is the weighted average of the expected returns of the individual assets in the portfolio.

   c. The variability (risk) of a portfolio's return is determined by the correlation of the returns of individual portfolio assets.

        1) To the extent the returns are not perfectly positively correlated, variability is decreased.

        2) In principle, diversifiable risk should continue to decrease as the number of different securities held increases. However, in practice, the benefits of diversification become extremely small when more than 30 to 40 different securities are held.

   d. **Company-specific (investee-specific) risk** or **unsystematic risk** is associated with a specific company's (investee's) operations: new products, patents, acquisitions, competitors, activities, etc.

        1) This risk can be largely eliminated by proper diversification of investments.

        2) The relevant risk of an individual security held in a portfolio is its contribution to the overall risk of the portfolio.

        3) When much of a security's risk can be eliminated by diversification, its relevant risk is low.

   e. The risk of an individual security that is unaffected by diversification is **market** or **systematic risk** and is measured by the **beta coefficient**.

        1) According to the Capital Asset Pricing Model discussed in Study Unit 3, beta measures the volatility of the returns of a security relative to the returns on the market portfolio (a portfolio of all securities). An average-risk stock has a beta of 1.0 because its returns are perfectly positively correlated with those on the market portfolio. For example, if the market return increases by 20%, the return on the security increases by 20%.

        2) A beta of less than 1.0 means that the security is less volatile than the market; e.g., if the market return increases by 20% and the security's return increases only 10%, the security has a beta of .5.

        3) A beta over 1.0 indicates a volatile security; e.g., if the return increases 30% when the market return increases by 15%, the security has a beta of 2.0.

        4) The word **beta** is derived from the regression equation for regressing the return of an individual security (the dependent variable) to the overall market return. The beta coefficient is the slope of the regression line.

           a) The beta for a security may also be calculated by dividing the covariance of the return on the market and the return on the security by the variance of the return on the market.

        5) Beta is the best measure of the risk of an individual security held in a diversified portfolio because it determines how the security affects the risk of the portfolio.

           a) The beta of a portfolio is the weighted average of the betas of the individual securities. For example, adding high-beta securities to a portfolio tends to increase its risk.

  6. Stop and review! You have completed the outline for this subunit. Study multiple-choice questions 15 through 25 beginning on page 312.

D. Options and Futures

  1. Options and futures are derivative securities. They are not claims on business assets, such as those represented by equity securities. Instead, they are created by the parties who trade in them.

a. An **American option** is a contractual arrangement that gives the owner the right to buy or sell an asset at a fixed price at any moment in time before or on a specified date. A **European option** is exercisable only at the expiration date.

b. Exercising the option is the act of buying or selling the asset underlying the option contract.

c. An option is a right of the owner, not an obligation.

d. The **exercise or striking price** is the price at which the owner can purchase the asset underlying the option contract.

e. An option usually has an expiration date after which it can no longer be exercised.

f. The longer the time before its expiration, the more valuable the option. The reason is the increased time available for the asset's price to rise or fall.

g. A **covered option** is one that is written against stock held in the option writer's portfolio.

h. A **naked option** is one that does not have the backing of stock.

i. A **call option** is the most common type of option. It gives the owner the right to purchase the underlying asset at a fixed price. Thus, it represents a long position because the owner gains from a price increase.

    1) Call options usually involve common stock as the underlying asset; however, any type of asset may underlie an option.

    2) If the value of the asset underlying a call option is less than the exercise price of the option, the option is "out-of-the-money," or not worth exercising. If the value of the asset underlying the option is greater than the exercise price, it is "in-the-money" and can earn the owner a profit.

    3) A call option's expiration value equals the excess of the current price of the asset over the striking price. If the striking price exceeds the current price, the option is worthless.

j. A **put option** gives the owner the right to sell the underlying asset for a fixed price. It represents a short position because the owner benefits from a price decrease.

    1) If the value of the asset underlying a put option is greater than its exercise price, the put option is worthless.

    2) If the value of the asset underlying the put option is less than the exercise price of the put option, the put is "in-the-money."

    3) A put option's expiration value equals either zero or the excess of the striking (exercise) price over the current market price.

k. **Put-call parity**. For European options, given market equilibrium for all relevant prices (no arbitrage possibilities), equal exercise prices for the put and the call, and the same expiration date, the put-call parity theorem states that a fixed relationship applies to the market values of the put and call options on a security. For example, a strategy of selling one call option, buying one share of the stock, and buying one put option should result in a risk-free return. The gain (loss) from the stock and the put should equal the gain (loss) on the call. If V_S is the value of the stock, V_P is the value of the put, V_C is the value of the call, and PV_E is the present value of the exercise price (the time interval is the time to expiration), the formula for put-call parity may be stated as follows:

$$V_S + V_P - V_C = PV_E$$

I. The value of a call option is based on its exercise price, its expiration date, the price of the underlying asset, the variability of that asset, and the risk-free interest rate. The well-known **Black-Scholes Option - Pricing Model** uses these factors.

1) If C is the current value of a call option with time t in years until expiration, S is the current stock price, $N(d_i)$ is the cumulative probability that a deviation less than d_i will occur in a standardized normal distribution [$N(d_i)$ is an area to the left of d_i under the curve for the standard normal distribution], E is the call's exercise price, e is a constant (approximately 2.7183), r is the annualized continuous risk-free rate of return, $\ln(S/E)$ is the natural logarithm of S/E, and σ^2 is the variance of the continuous rate of return on the stock, the Black-Scholes formula is

$$C = SN(d_1) - Ee^{-rt} N(d_2)$$

$$d_1 = \frac{\ln(S/E) + [r + (\sigma^2 \div 2)]t}{\sigma\sqrt{t}}$$

$$d_2 = d_1 - \sigma\sqrt{t}$$

a) In effect, the first term of the equation for C is the expected present value of the final stock price, and the second term is essentially the present value of the exercise price.

2) Of interest is the issuance by the FASB of SFAS 123, *Accounting for Stock-Based Compensation*. Under that pronouncement, public entities that decide to account for employee stock compensation using the fair-value-based method must apply an option-pricing model such as the Black-Scholes.

2. A futures contract is a specific kind of **forward contract**, which is simply an executory contract. The parties to a forward contract agree to the terms of a purchase and sale, but performance, that is, payment by the buyer and delivery by the seller, is deferred. A **futures contract** is a definite agreement that allows a trader to purchase or sell an asset at a fixed price during a specific future month. Futures contracts for agricultural commodities, metals, oil, and financial assets are traded on numerous exchanges.

a. One characteristic of a futures contract is that it may be highly leveraged. The initial **margin** paid may be a very small percentage of the price.

b. A futures contract differs from a forward contract in part because it is traded on an exchange. The result is a liquid market in futures that permits buyers and sellers to net out their positions. For example, a party who has sold a contract can net out his/her position by buying a futures contract.

c. Because futures contracts are for delivery during a given month, not a specific day, they are more flexible arrangements than forward contracts. The seller notifies the exchange clearinghouse when delivery is to be made, and the clearinghouse randomly matches the seller with a buyer who has purchased a contract for the same month.

d. Another distinguishing feature of futures contracts is that their prices are **marked to market** every day at the close of the day. Thus, the market price is posted at the close of business each day. A mark-to-market provision minimizes a futures contract's chance of default because profits and losses on the contracts must be received or paid each day through a clearinghouse.

e.   A futures contract is entered into as either a speculation or a hedge.

1)   A financial manager can protect a company against adverse changes in prices and interest rates by hedging in the futures market. **Hedging** is the process of using offsetting commitments to minimize or avoid the impact of adverse price movements.

a)   Long hedges are futures contracts that are purchased to protect against price increases.

b)   Short hedges are futures contracts that are sold to protect against price declines.

c)   EXAMPLE: In the commodities market, a company might have a contract with a farmer to buy soybeans at a future date. The price is agreed upon as the current price. The company would lose money if the soybean prices declined before the beans were delivered. To avoid any loss (or gain), the company could sell soybeans in the future at today's price. If the price of soybeans does decline before the delivery date, the company will lose money on the beans bought from the farmer, but it will gain money on the beans sold through the futures contract by buying cheap beans in the future to cover the delivery.

i)   Because commodities can be bought and sold on margin, considerable leverage is involved. This high degree of leverage is most beneficial to the speculator who is looking for large returns and is willing to bear the risk to get them. For hedgers, however, the small margin requirement is useful only because the risk can be hedged without tying up a large amount of cash.

f.   **Interest rate futures contracts** involve risk-free bonds such as Treasury bonds, T-bills, Ginnie-Maes, and money-market certificates.

1)   The quantity traded is either $100,000 or $1,000,000, depending on which market is used.

2)   EXAMPLE: If a corporation wants to borrow money in 6 months for a major project, but the lender refuses to commit itself to an interest rate, the interest rate futures market can be used to hedge the risk that interest rates might increase in the interim. The company agrees to sell Treasury bonds in 6 months. If interest rates do increase over the period, the value of the Treasury bonds will decline. The company can buy Treasury bonds in 6 months and use them to cover the delivery that it had promised in the futures contract. Because the price of Treasury bonds has declined over the period, the company will make a profit on their delivery. The interest rates that the company will have to pay on the upcoming loan will be higher, however. It has cost the company money to wait 6 months for the loan. The profit from the futures contract should approximately offset the loss resulting from the higher interest loan. If interest rates had declined, the company would have had the benefit of a lower interest loan but would have lost money on the Treasury bonds. The goal of any such hedging operation is to break even on the change in interest rates.

a)   By hedging, the financial manager need not worry about fluctuations in interest rates but can concentrate instead on the day-to-day operations of the company.

g. **Duration hedging** involves hedging interest-rate risk by matching the duration of assets with the duration of liabilities. **Duration** is the weighted average of the times to interest and principal payments. If duration increases, the volatility of the price of the debt instrument increases.

   1) Duration is lower if the nominal rate on the instrument is higher because more of the return is received earlier. The formula for duration is as follows if C_T is the interest or principal payment, T is the time to the payment, n is the time to maturity, r is the yield to maturity, and V is the value of the instrument:

$$\sum_{T=1}^{n} \left(\frac{C_T \times T}{(1 + r)^T} \right) \div V$$

   2) The goal of duration hedging is not to equate the duration of assets and the duration of liabilities but for the following relationship to apply:

   (Value of assets) × *(Duration of assets)* =
   (Value of liabilities) × *(Duration of liabilities)*

   a) The firm is immunized against interest-rate risk when the total price change for assets equals the total price change for liabilities.

h. **Swaps** are contracts to hedge risk by exchanging cash flows.

   1) In an **interest-rate swap**, one firm exchanges its fixed interest and principal payments for a series of payments based on a floating rate. If a firm has debt with fixed charges, but its revenues fluctuate with interest rates, it may prefer to swap for cash outflows based on a floating rate. The advantage is that revenues and the amounts of debt service will then move in the same direction, and interest-rate risk will be reduced.

   2) A **currency swap** is an exchange of an obligation to pay out cash flows denominated in one currency for an obligation to pay in another. For example, a U.S. firm with revenues in francs has to pay suppliers and workers in dollars, not francs. To minimize exchange-rate risk, it might agree to exchange francs for dollars held by a firm that needs francs. The exchange rate will be an average of the rates expected over the life of the agreement.

3. Stop and review! You have completed the outline for this subunit. Study multiple-choice questions 26 through 34 beginning on page 316.

E. Corporate Insurance

1. **Types of Insurance**. An insurance policy is a contract to shift the risk of financial loss caused by certain specified occurrences from the insured to the insurer in exchange for a payment called a **premium**. Insurance may protect a business from virtually any type of liability. The following list contains many types of insurance commonly encountered by a business person. Life, property, and liability insurance will be discussed later in this subunit.

   a. **Accident and health insurance** (commonly referred to as medical insurance) covers accidental injury or sickness, as well as other specified perils, under explicit conditions. Accident and health insurance is designed to pay at least a portion of an insured's expenses that arise from injury or sickness, disability, and hospitalization.

b. **Disability insurance** provides income to those who become physically or mentally disabled and are unable to perform the tasks of their chosen occupation. While medical insurance covers a person's hospital and medical expenses during illness, disability insurance provides a source of income for a person during the time of the disability.

   1) Disability coverage usually covers only a percentage of a person's former income.

c. **Title insurance** repays the insured for a loss arising from defects in the title to real property.

d. **Business interruption insurance** provides benefits to cover losses due to interruptions in business operations caused by a specified and insured peril.

e. **No-fault insurance** provides coverage to the insured and others protected under the policy regardless of any fault or liability of the parties. This type of insurance plan often applies to automobiles.

f. **Credit insurance** protects both the creditor and the debtor by providing for payment of the debt of the insured in the event of his/her death. Credit insurance is typically used to insure payment of mortgage indebtedness, for both personal- and business-use property.

g. **Workers' compensation insurance** requires employers to compensate workers who are injured while on the job (even if an employee is injured because of an act of another employee).

   1) Workers' compensation laws are not based on negligence or fault by the employer; rather, employers are held strictly liable for injuries that occur in the workplace.

   2) The employers are the purchasers of workers' compensation insurance.

   3) An employer **self-insures** when it does not purchase workers' compensation insurance but instead uses company assets to pay for any claim.

2. **Life insurance** is a contract for the payment of a specified sum to a named beneficiary or to the estate of the insured when the insured dies.

   a. Life insurance protects against the **risk of mortality**, the financial uncertainty associated with dying.

      1) Life insurance transfers the mortality risk to the insurance company.

   b. Life insurance may be obtained by a corporation to insure the life of a corporate employee. The company is entitled to the life insurance proceeds if it is named as the beneficiary.

   c. Life insurance takes the following principal forms:

      1) **Whole life insurance.** Whole life or ordinary life insurance is designed to remain in force for the entire life of the insured and ordinarily requires the payment of premiums until the insured's death.

         a) Whole life is often considered a form of savings or investment because the insured has a right to borrow from the insurer an amount not to exceed the cash surrender value of the policy.

            i) The **cash surrender value** of a policy is the amount the insurance company will pay on a given life insurance policy if the policy is canceled prior to the death of the insured.

b) **Limited-payment whole life** requires the payment of premiums for only a fixed number of years.

c) **Single-premium whole life** allows for prepayment of the entire premium in one lump sum. The policy remains in force until either it is cashed in or proceeds are paid to the beneficiary upon the death of the insured.

2) **Term insurance.** Term life insurance is a contract that furnishes life insurance protection for a fixed term.

a) Under **level term** policies, the benefits payable on the insured's death remain level during the term of the policy.

b) Term insurance does not build up cash surrender value or loan value. Thus, term insurance is the least expensive form of insurance.

   i) Term insurance can usually be renewed for additional periods until the insured reaches age 65.

   ii) The cost of term insurance may increase rapidly with each renewal because the risk of death increases with the increased age of the insured.

3) **Endowment insurance.** An endowment contract pays a stated amount if the insured dies during a specified period of time, or pays the same amount if the insured is living at the end of the period.

a) Endowment policies build up cash value. The cash value gradually increases until, at the end of the endowment period, it equals the face amount of the policy.

b) Endowment policies are written for a variety of periods, such as 20, 25, or 30 years. They are also written to endow at a stated age.

c) Endowment insurance is a form of forced savings protected by life insurance. Insureds who live until their policies mature (endow) complete their savings goals by means of their premium payments. Moreover, the protection aspect of the policy assures them that their savings goal will be completed whether or not they live to complete it themselves.

d) Endowment contracts are very expensive.

4) **Hybrids.** One of the cornerstones of whole life insurance is that coverage both provides protection and represents a kind of forced savings.

a) Insurers were quick to respond to the public's interest in the investment element of life insurance. (Life insurance cash values build up income tax free.) A number of companies offer hybrid financial products that possess basic insurance protection combined with an increased return on tax-free buildup of cash value.

   i) **Variable life** insurance permits the policyholder to participate in the investment expertise of the insuring company.

   NOTE: To the dismay of many purchasers, the policyholder also has the dubious privilege of participating in decreases in value of the investments.

   ii) **Universal life insurance** combines the features of an investment that earns current money market interest rates with a term insurance policy.

d. Life insurance policies become incontestable after a stated period established by law or in the policy. The purpose is to protect the insured against stale defenses by insurers. They are also more freely assignable than other policies.

3. **Property Insurance**. Fire or property insurance protects the owner of, or another person with an insurable interest in, real or personal property against loss resulting from damage to, or destruction of, insured property by certain specified perils.

   a. A **loss** is an unexpected destruction, reduction, or disappearance of economic value.

      1) Insured losses are unintended. They do not include

         a) The wearing out or normal depreciation of property used in a trade or business

         b) Damage that is intentionally inflicted to property by the insured

   b. A **peril** is the cause of a loss. A single peril can cause more than one type of loss. Commonly insured perils include fire, theft, explosion, and illness.

   c. A **hazard** is a condition that increases likelihood of loss due to a particular peril.

      1) EXAMPLE: Fireworks are a hazard because they increase the likelihood of the peril of a fire, which would cause a loss.

   d. Property or fire insurance is distinct from casualty insurance.

      1) **Casualty insurance** typically covers loss due to damage or destruction of personal property by various causes other than fire or the elements.

      2) At one time companies licensed to write fire insurance and other property lines of insurance could not write casualty insurance and vice versa. The law now permits multi-line insurers, enabling a single company to provide any or all lines of property-casualty insurance.

   e. Property insurance may be provided by two principal means.

      1) Under a **specified-perils contract**, the insurer indemnifies only for losses resulting from one or more specified perils.

      2) Under an **all-risk contract**, the insurer indemnifies the insured for loss resulting from any perils except those specifically excluded by the contract.

         a) All-risk contracts are useful when the exact nature of the perils is difficult to predict.

4. **Fire Insurance**. Fire insurance is one of the most common types of property insurance.

   a. Fire insurance is a contract by which the insurer agrees to pay the insured a specified amount for property loss or property damage due to fire.

   b. Most states recognize the standard fire policy, which is a standard contract of insurance prescribed by statute or administrative rule or regulation.

      1) Frequently, fire insurance policies also insure against damage from wind, hail, and other forces of nature, as well as faulty plumbing or smoke damage.

   c. Fire insurance policies are usually limited to cover loss from hostile fires, not friendly fires.

      1) A **friendly fire** is one that is contained where it is intended to be, e.g., a fire in a fireplace, furnace, or stove.

2) A **hostile fire** is any other fire that is unintended or not in its usual place.

5. A **coinsurance clause** is used by many property and casualty insurers to encourage policyholders to insure property, especially commercial property, for an amount that is near to its full replacement cost.

   a. A coinsurance clause typically provides that, if the property is insured for at least a stated percentage (usually 80%) of its actual cash value, any loss will be paid in full up to the face amount of the policy.

   b. The coinsurance requirement is the stated percentage times the fair market value of the insured property at the time of the loss.

   Coinsurance requirement = Stated % x FMV at time of loss

   c. If the amount of insurance coverage is less than the required coinsurance amount, the insurance company pays only a fraction of the repair or replacement cost:

   $$\frac{Amount\ of\ insurance}{Coinsurance\ requirement} \times Loss = Recovery\ amount$$

   d. The coinsurance requirement applies only to partial losses. Total losses result in recovery of the face amount of the policy.

   NOTE: The insurer is liable to pay no more than the face amount of the policy, even if the coinsurance formula applies and yields a recovery amount greater than the face amount of the policy.

6. **Liability Insurance**. Liability insurance provides the insured with money (policy proceeds) to cover losses (injuries) suffered by others for personal injury or property damage if the insured is held liable.

   a. Liability insurance protects against tort liability only, not criminal liability.

      1) Insurers routinely exclude intentional torts from insurance coverage.

   b. **Personal liability**. Personal liability coverage typically protects the policyholder against the financial risk of injuries or damage to the property of others that might occur in the course of the policyholder's personal activities.

      1) The primary purpose of this liability coverage is to insure against the policyholder's negligence.

      2) Personal liability protection is usually part of a homeowner's or renter's insurance policy, but it can be purchased as a separate personal liability policy.

      3) Liability coverage under a homeowner's policy usually applies only to personal activities, not to business or professional activities.

   c. **Business liability**. Businesses may insure against their own negligence by obtaining either comprehensive general liability insurance or specific insurance, e.g., product liability or dramshop coverage (for sellers of alcoholic beverages).

      1) **Products liability** holds a manufacturer or a seller liable if a defective product is placed into the market and causes injury. The liability may be based on negligence, a warranty, or strict liability.

      2) **Strict liability as a basis for products liability**. If negligence cannot be proved and the manufacturer/seller has made no warranty, an injured plaintiff may rely on a theory of strict liability to recover for injuries due to a defective product.

a) Two basic types of defects are covered by strict liability: manufacturing defects and design defects.

   i) No negligence or fraud need be proved.

b) A defective product does not meet reasonable expectations as to safety.

3) Coverage of products liability is usually provided by the **commercial general liability** policy.

a) Coverage under this broad, all-risk policy is for bodily injury or property damage arising from

   i) The insured's product or

   ii) Reliance upon a representation or warranty made regarding such a product.

b) Injury or damage on the insured's premises is not covered.

c) Damage to **impaired property** is also not covered. Impaired property is tangible property that is less useful because it incorporates the product and the product is thought to be defective, deficient, inadequate, or dangerous, or because the insured has breached an agreement.

   i) Such property is deemed to be impaired, however, only if it can be restored by removal or repair of the product or by fulfillment of an agreement.

d) Physical possession of the product must have been relinquished by the insured.

e) Losses resulting from withdrawal of a product from the market because of known or suspected defects are not covered. Thus, a customer's claim for damages resulting from nonavailability of a product as a result of a recall would not be indemnified.

   i) Coverage also may not extend to subsequent product liability claims if a defective product is not recalled following a damage claim.

   ii) A separate recall policy is necessary.

d. **Professional liability.** Most professionals, e.g., doctors, lawyers, accountants, and architects, can obtain malpractice insurance to shift risk of loss due to their negligence to the insurance carrier.

1) Most professional liability policies are written on either a claims made basis or an occurrence basis.

a) On a **claims made basis**, the insurer is responsible only for claims filed during the policy period.

b) On an **occurrence basis**, the insurer is responsible for all events occurring during the policy period regardless of when any claims are filed.

7. Stop and review! You have completed the outline for this subunit. Study multiple-choice questions 35 through 46 beginning on page 318.

F. Foreign Operations

1. For international trade to occur, the currencies involved must be easily converted at some prevailing exchange rate. The **exchange rate** is the price of one country's currency in terms of another country's currency.

   a. Currency appreciates when a specified amount can buy more units of another currency than it previously could.

   b. Currency depreciates when a specified amount can purchase fewer units of another currency than it previously could.

   c. In other words, depreciation in country A's currency is an appreciation of the currency of country B.

2. **Exchange Rate Determination**

   a. Fixed exchange rates are set by some outside force (e.g., the government). One traditional method of establishing rates is to require that currencies be convertible to specified amounts of gold.

      1) An exchange rate set too high creates a deficit balance of payments. This deficit must be financed by drawing down foreign reserves or by borrowing from the central banks of the foreign countries.

         a) A major reason for a country's currency devaluation is to improve its balance of payments.

   b. The United States and other major countries currently operate under a system of **floating exchange rates**; that is, the prices of different currencies attain their own levels with relatively little government intervention.

   c. If foreign currency exchange rates are allowed to float, their fluctuation creates **exchange-rate risk**, which is the risk that the dollar-equivalent value of future cash flows may decrease.

   d. Short-term floating exchange rates are dictated by interest rates.

      1) Big corporations and banks invest their large reserves of cash where the real interest rate is highest.

      2) An increase in the real interest rate will lead to an appreciation of that currency because it will be demanded for investment, thereby shifting the demand curve outward.

      3) The reverse holds true for a decline in real interest rates because that currency will be sold as investors move their money out of the country.

3. **Interaction in Foreign Exchange Markets**

   a. **Foreign currency transactions** result when an entity buys or sells on credit, borrows or lends, is a party to a forward exchange contract, or for other reasons acquires or disposes of assets, or incurs or settles liabilities, denominated in any currency other than the entity's functional currency.

      1) Forward exchange contracts are futures in foreign currencies that are traded on foreign exchange markets. They are foreign currency transactions that are entered into for speculation or to hedge a recognized transaction (an exposed net asset or net liability position), an identifiable commitment, or a foreign equity investment.

   b. A firm's functional currency is the currency of the primary economic environment in which it operates; normally, that environment is the one in which the entity primarily generates and expends cash.

c.   **Foreign currency translation** expresses in the reporting currency amounts denominated or measured in different currencies.

d.   **Transaction gain (loss)** results from a change in exchange rates between the functional currency and the currency in which the transaction is denominated. It is the change (1) in actual functional currency cash flows realized on settlement and (2) in expected functional currency cash flows on unsettled transactions.

e.   An exchange rate may be stated in dollars per foreign currency unit (in direct or American terms) or in foreign currency units per dollar (in indirect or European terms).

1)   In the U.S., indirect quotations are used for all currencies except the British pound. Moreover, foreign currency exchanges worldwide also follow this convention.

2)   A **cross rate** is an exchange rate between two currencies neither of which is the dollar. If a party desires to convert foreign currency A to foreign currency B, the cross rate will equal the exchange rate (in foreign currency units per dollar) for B divided by the exchange rate for A. If one of the currencies is the British pound, the exchange rates are multiplied to determine the units of the second currency per pound.

f.   The **spot rate** is the exchange rate paid for delivery of currency on the spot (today).

g.   The **forward exchange rate** is the future price of the currency.

1)   If the forward rate in terms of foreign currency units per dollar is greater than the spot rate, the dollar is selling at a premium and the foreign currency at a discount. Speculators expect the dollar to appreciate.

2)   If the spot rate is greater than the forward rate, the dollar is selling at a discount and the foreign currency at a premium. Speculators expect the dollar to depreciate.

h.   According to the **interest-rate parity theorem**, the discount or premium reflected in a forward rate is related to the difference between the nominal interest rates paid by foreign and domestic banks (differences in interest rates are largely caused by differences in expected inflation).

1)   When the foreign nominal interest rate is lower than the domestic nominal rate, the forward foreign currency sells at a premium.

a)   If this were not true, investors would borrow at the lower interest rate, invest at the higher rate, and buy a forward contract for the principal and interest.

2)   If the foreign nominal rate exceeds the domestic nominal rate, the forward foreign currency sells at a discount.

i.   A foreign currency will depreciate or appreciate relative to the dollar at a rate equivalent to the amount by which its inflation rate exceeds or is less than the dollar's inflation rate (assuming everything else remains constant).

1)   EXAMPLE: If the inflation rate in the UK is 12% and the inflation rate in the U.S. is 10%, the dollar should appreciate by 2%.

j.   Borrowing in a country with the lowest nominal rate is not always best. The reason is that the advantage of the lower interest rate may be offset by an exchange rate loss if the borrower's currency depreciates relative to the lender's.

1)   The foreign currency exchange rates equalize inflation rates.

      k.   A **foreign currency swap** is a two-party agreement to exchange one type of currency for another at a specific date in the future at a specific exchange rate.

          1)   A company may enter into a swap with another party to assure that it will receive an amount that will offset any gain or loss from another foreign transfer of funds to be returned in the future.

4.   **Avoidance of Risk in Foreign Exchange Markets**. Exchange-rate risk can be avoided in a variety of ways.

    a.   Hedging

          1)   A firm may buy or sell forward exchange contracts to cover liabilities or receivables, respectively, denominated in a foreign currency.

          2)   Any gain or loss on the foreign receivables or payables because of changes in exchange rates is offset by the loss or gain on the forward exchange contract.

    b.   Maintaining a monetary balance between receivables and payables denominated in a foreign currency avoids a net receivable or net liability position in a foreign currency. Monetary items are those with fixed cash flows.

          1)   In general, a firm should attempt to achieve a net monetary debtor position in countries with currencies expected to depreciate. A net monetary creditor position should be achieved in countries with strengthening currencies.

          2)   Large multinational corporations have established multinational netting centers as special departments to attempt to achieve balance between foreign receivables and payables.

               a)   They also enter into forward exchange contracts when necessary to achieve balance.

    c.   A firm may seek to minimize its exchange-rate risk by diversification. If it has transactions in both strong and weak currencies, the effects of changes in rates may be offsetting.

5.   **Political risk** is the risk that a foreign government may act in a way that will reduce the value of the company's investment. Political risk may include

    a.   Expropriation of a company's assets without compensation

          1)   The potential loss from expropriation may be reduced by financing with local capital and obtaining insurance against economic losses from expropriation.

    b.   Increased taxes
    c.   The requirement to pay higher wages than other firms in the country
    d.   Terrorism against the firm or its employees

6.   Political risk may be reduced by

    a.   Entering into a joint venture with a company from the host country

    b.   Making foreign operations dependent on the domestic parent for technology, markets, and supplies

7.   Political risk must always be considered in the analysis of whether to open a business in a foreign country.

8.   Stop and review! You have completed the outline for this subunit. Study multiple-choice questions 47 through 61 beginning on page 322.

MULTIPLE-CHOICE QUESTIONS

A. Types of Risk

1. The risk that securities cannot be sold at a reasonable price on short notice is called

- A. Default risk.
- B. Interest-rate risk.
- C. Purchasing-power risk.
- D. Liquidity risk.

The correct answer is (D). *(CIA 1190 IV-51)*
REQUIRED: The term for the risk that securities cannot be sold at a reasonable price on short notice.
DISCUSSION: An asset is liquid if it can be converted to cash on short notice. Liquidity (marketability) risk is the risk that assets cannot be sold at a reasonable price on short notice. If an asset is not liquid, investors will require a higher return than for a liquid asset. The difference is the liquidity premium.
Answer (A) is incorrect because default risk is the risk that a borrower will not pay the interest or principal on a loan. Answer (B) is incorrect because interest-rate risk is the risk to which investors are exposed because of changing interest rates. Answer (C) is incorrect because purchasing-power risk is the risk that inflation will reduce the purchasing power of a given sum of money.

2. The type of risk that is not diversifiable and even affects the value of a portfolio is

- A. Purchasing-power risk.
- B. Market risk.
- C. Nonmarket risk.
- D. Interest-rate risk.

The correct answer is (B). *(Publisher)*
REQUIRED: The term for the type of risk that is not diversifiable.
DISCUSSION: Prices of all stocks, even the value of portfolios, are correlated to some degree with broad swings in the stock market. Market risk is the risk that changes in a stock's price will result from changes in the stock market as a whole. Market risk is commonly referred to as nondiversifiable risk.
Answer (A) is incorrect because purchasing-power risk is the risk that a general rise in the price level will reduce the quantity of goods that can be purchased with a fixed sum of money. Answer (C) is incorrect because nonmarket risk is the risk that is influenced by an individual firm's policies and decisions. Nonmarket risk is diversifiable because it is specific to each firm. Answer (D) is incorrect because interest-rate risk is the risk that the value of an asset will fluctuate due to changes in the interest rate.

3. Which of the following are components of interest-rate risk?

- A. Purchasing-power risk and default risk.
- B. Price risk and market risk.
- C. Portfolio risk and reinvestment-rate risk.
- D. Price risk and reinvestment-rate risk.

The correct answer is (D). *(Publisher)*
REQUIRED: The components of interest-rate risk.
DISCUSSION: Interest-rate risk is the risk of fluctuations in the value of an asset due to changes in interest rates. One component of interest-rate risk is price risk, which is portrayed as a decline in the value of bonds as interest rates increase. Reinvestment-rate risk is another component of interest-rate risk. If interest rates decline, lower returns will be available for reinvestment of interest and principal payments received.
Answer (A) is incorrect because purchasing-power risk concerns inflation, and default risk concerns nonpayment by the debtor. Answer (B) is incorrect because market risk concerns price changes in the overall securities markets. Answer (C) is incorrect because portfolio risk is the risk remaining in a portfolio after diversifying investments.

4. O & B Company, a U.S. corporation, is in possession of accounts receivable denominated in German deutsche marks. To what type of risk are they exposed?

A. Liquidity risk.

B. Business risk.

C. Exchange-rate risk.

D. Price risk.

The correct answer is (C). *(Publisher)*

REQUIRED: The risk to which a business is exposed when accounts receivable are denominated in a foreign currency.

DISCUSSION: Exchange-rate risk is the risk that a foreign currency transaction will be negatively exposed to fluctuations in exchange rates. Because O & B Company sells goods to German customers and records accounts receivable denominated in deutsche marks, O & B Company is exposed to exchange-rate risk.

Answer (A) is incorrect because liquidity risk is the possibility that an asset cannot be sold on short notice for its market value. Answer (B) is incorrect because business risk is the risk of fluctuations in earnings before interest and taxes or in operating income when the firm uses no debt. Answer (D) is incorrect because price risk is a component of interest-rate risk.

5. Business risk is the risk inherent in a firm's operations that excludes financial risk. It depends on all of the following factors except

A. Amount of financial leverage.

B. Sales price variability.

C. Demand variability.

D. Input price variability.

The correct answer is (A). *(Publisher)*

REQUIRED: The factor not affecting business risk of a firm.

DISCUSSION: Business risk is the risk of fluctuations in earnings before interest and taxes or in operating income when the firm uses no debt. It depends on factors such as demand variability, sales price variability, input price variability, and the amount of operating leverage. Financial leverage affects financial risk and is not a factor affecting business risk.

Answers (B), (C), and (D) are incorrect because they are all factors affecting business risk.

6. Catherine & Co. has extra cash at the end of the year and is analyzing the best way to invest the funds. The company should invest in a project only if

A. The expected return on the project exceeds the return on investments of comparable risk.

B. The return on investments of comparable risk exceeds the expected return on the project.

C. The expected return on the project is equal to the return on investments of comparable risk.

D. The return on investments of comparable risk equals the expected return on the project.

The correct answer is (A). *(Publisher)*

REQUIRED: The rule for deciding whether to invest in a project.

DISCUSSION: Investment risk is analyzed in terms of the probability that the actual return on an investment will be lower than the expected return. Comparing a project's expected return to the return on an asset of similar risk, helps determine whether the project is worth investing in. If the expected return on a project exceeds the return on an asset of comparable risk, then the project should be pursued.

Answers (B), (C), and (D) are incorrect because a project should be pursued only if its expected return exceeds the return on investments of similar risk.

B. Risk Measurement

7. An asset with high risk will have a(n)

A. Low expected return.

B. Lower price than an asset with low risk.

C. Increasing expected return.

D. High standard deviation of returns.

The correct answer is (D). *(Publisher)*

REQUIRED: The characteristic of an asset with high risk.

DISCUSSION: The greater the standard deviation of returns, the greater the risk is for an asset. The expected return can vary anywhere between the large standard deviation of returns, creating the risk that the actual return is significantly low in the range of the standard deviation of returns.

Answer (A) is incorrect because an asset with high risk will have a high expected return to compensate for the additional risk. Answer (B) is incorrect because an asset with high risk will have a higher price than an asset with low risk due to the high expected return. Answer (C) is incorrect because an asset with high risk will have a constant expected return, not an increasing expected return.

8. An ambitious investor has assigned a probability of 30% to the potential increase of ABC stock. This type of probability is

A. Strong.

B. Risky.

C. Objective.

D. Subjective.

The correct answer is (D). *(Publisher)*
REQUIRED: The type of probability typically used when predicting the future performance of a stock.
DISCUSSION: The two types of probabilities--objective and subjective--differ in the way they are calculated. Objective probabilities rely on either logic or actual experience. Subjective probabilities are estimates of the likelihood of future events based on judgment and past experience. Subjective probabilities in finance can indicate the degree of confidence a person has that a certain outcome will occur, e.g., the degree of confidence in the prediction of how a stock will perform.
Answers (A) and (B) are incorrect because the two types of probabilities are objective and subjective, not strong and risky. Answer (C) is incorrect because objective probabilities rely on logic or actual experience, not intuition.

9. The expected rate of return for the stock of Cornhusker Enterprises is 20%, with a standard deviation of 15%. The expected rate of return for the stock of Mustang Associates is 10%, with a standard deviation of 9%. The riskier stock is

A. Cornhusker because its return is higher.

B. Cornhusker because its standard deviation is higher.

C. Mustang because its standard deviation is higher.

D. Mustang because its coefficient of variation is higher.

The correct answer is (D). *(CMA 692 1-6)*
REQUIRED: The riskier stock.
DISCUSSION: The standard deviation is a measure of the degree of compactness of the values in a population. It is a measure of dispersion. The standard deviation is found by taking the square root of the quotient of the sum of the squared deviations from the mean, divided by the number of items in the population. Cornhusker has a mean return of 20% and a standard deviation of 15%. Hence, it is not as risky as Mustang, which has a standard deviation of 9% relative to a mean of only 10%. The coefficient of variation (standard deviation ÷ expected return) is much higher for Mustang (0.9 ÷ .10 = .9) than for Cornhusker (.15 ÷ .20 = .75).
Answer (A) is incorrect because the existence of a higher return is not necessarily indicative of high risk. Answer (B) is incorrect because the higher standard deviation must be viewed relative to the mean of the population. Answer (C) is incorrect because Mustang does not have the higher standard deviation.

Questions 10 through 12 are based on the following information. Techspace has been a successful stock over the past few years despite its riskiness. The state of the economy has a tremendous effect on the expected returns for Techspace as shown below:

Probability	State of the Economy	Techspace Returns
.05	Depression	−45%
.15	Recession	−10%
.20	Minimal Slowdown	5%
.40	Stable	10%
.15	Expansion	30%
.05	Significant Expansion	35%

10. What is the expected rate of return on Techspace stock?

A. 7.5%

B. 15%

C. 35%

D. 25%

The correct answer is (A). *(Publisher)*

REQUIRED: The expected rate of return on a stock given probabilities for different situations and corresponding returns.

DISCUSSION: The expected rate of return on an investment is determined using an expected value calculation. It is an average of the outcomes weighted according to their probabilities. For Techspace, the average is accomplished by multiplying each probability by the corresponding return for each state of the economy and then calculating the sum of the products. Numerically, the calculation is performed as follows: .05(−.45) + .15(−.10) + .2(.05) + .4(.10) + .15(.30) + .05(.35) = .075 = 7.5%.

Answer (B) is incorrect because 15% adds positive products instead of negative products for the first two states. Answer (C) is incorrect because 35% is the sum of the returns (assuming all are positive) minus 1. Answer (D) is incorrect because 25% is the sum of the returns.

11. The variance of Techspace returns is

A. .1735

B. .0301

C. .075

D. .2738

The correct answer is (B). *(Publisher)*

REQUIRED: The variance on a stock given probabilities for different situations and corresponding returns.

DISCUSSION: The variance (σ^2) is calculated using the equation

$$\sigma^2 = \sum_{i=1}^{n} (k_i - \hat{k})^2 p_i$$

If: k_i is the return from the ith outcome, $\hat{k}$ is the expected return, and p_i is the probability of the ith outcome.

$$\hat{k} = \sum_{i=1}^{n} k_i p_i \text{ or } .05(-.45) + .15(-.10) + .2(.05)$$
$$+ .4(.10) + .15(.30) + .05(.35) = .075$$

$$\sigma^2 = .05(-.45 - .075)^2 + .15(-.1 - .075)^2$$
$$+ .2(.05 - .075)^2 + .4(.1 - .075)^2 + .15(.30 - .075)^2$$
$$+ .05(.35 - .075)^2 = .0301$$

Answer (A) is incorrect because .1735 is the standard deviation of Techspace returns. Answer (C) is incorrect because .075 is the expected return. Answer (D) is incorrect because .2738 is the square root of the expected return.

12. The standard deviation of Techspace returns is

A. 7.5%

B. 17.35%

C. 3.01%

D. None of the answers are correct.

The correct answer is (B). *(Publisher)*

REQUIRED: The standard deviation of Techspace returns.

DISCUSSION: The standard deviation (σ) gives an exact value for the tightness of the distribution and the riskiness of the investment. It is calculated by taking the square root of the variance. Given that the variance is .0301, the standard deviation is .1735, or 17.35%.

Answer (A) is incorrect because 7.5% is the expected return. Answer (C) is incorrect because 3.01% is the variance. Answer (D) is incorrect because the standard deviation is 17.35%.

13. The returns on two stocks can be correlated in values except those that are

A. Positive.

B. Negative.

C. Neutral.

D. Skewed.

The correct answer is (D). *(Publisher)*

REQUIRED: The range of correlation between two stocks.

DISCUSSION: The correlation coefficient (r) measures the degree to which any two variables are related. It ranges from −1.0 to 1.0. Perfect positive correlation (1.0) means that the two variables always move together. Perfect negative correlation (−1.0) means that the two variables always move inversely to one another. A neutral correlation, or no correlation, is 0.0. Skewed is a nonsense concept in this context.

Answers (A), (B), and (C) are incorrect because returns on two stocks can be correlated in any value that falls within the range of −1.0 to 1.0.

14. If the covariance of stock A with stock B is −.0076, then what is the covariance of stock B with stock A?

A. +.0076

B. −.0076

C. Greater than .0076.

D. Less than −.0076.

The correct answer is (B). *(Publisher)*

REQUIRED: The covariance of two stocks.

DISCUSSION: The covariance measures the volatility of returns together with their correlation with the returns of other securities. It is calculated with the following equation:

$$COV(XY) = \sum_{i=1}^{n} (k_{xi} - \hat{k}_x)(k_{yi} - \hat{k}_y)p_i$$

The covariance of two stocks is the same regardless of which stock is compared to the other.

Answers (A), (C), and (D) are incorrect because the covariance of stock B with stock A is the same as the covariance of stock A with stock B.

C. Portfolio Management

15. A measure that describes the risk of an investment project relative to other investments in general is the

A. Coefficient of variation.

B. Beta coefficient.

C. Standard deviation.

D. Expected return.

The correct answer is (B). *(CIA 1187 IV-66)*

REQUIRED: The measure of the risk of an investment relative to investments in general.

DISCUSSION: The required rate of return on equity capital in the Capital Asset Pricing Model is the risk-free rate (determined by government securities), plus the product of the market risk premium times the beta coefficient (beta measures the firm's risk). The market risk premium is the amount above the risk-free rate that will induce investment in the market. The beta coefficient of an individual stock is the correlation between the volatility (price variation) of the stock market and that of the price of the individual stock. For example, if an individual stock goes up 15% and the market only 10%, beta is 1.5.

Answer (A) is incorrect because the coefficient of variation compares risk with expected return (standard deviation ÷ expected return). Answer (C) is incorrect because standard deviation measures dispersion (risk) of project returns. Answer (D) is incorrect because expected return does not describe risk.

16. Which of the following classes of securities are listed in order from lowest risk/opportunity for return to highest risk/opportunity for return?

- A. U.S. Treasury bonds; corporate first mortgage bonds; corporate income bonds; preferred stock.
- B. Corporate income bonds; corporate mortgage bonds; convertible preferred stock; subordinated debentures.
- C. Common stock; corporate first mortgage bonds; corporate second mortgage bonds; corporate income bonds.
- D. Preferred stock; common stock; corporate mortgage bonds; corporate debentures.

The correct answer is (A). *(CIA 589 IV-49)*

REQUIRED: The correct listing of classes of securities from lowest to highest risk/opportunity for return.

DISCUSSION: The general principle is that risk and return are directly correlated. U.S. Treasury securities are backed by the full faith and credit of the federal government and are therefore the least risky form of investment. However, their return is correspondingly lower. Corporate first mortgage bonds are less risky than income bonds or stock because they are secured by specific property. In the event of default, the bondholders can have the property sold to satisfy their claims. Holders of first mortgages have rights paramount to those of any other parties, such as holders of second mortgages. Income bonds pay interest only in the event the corporation earns income. Thus, holders of income bonds have less risk than stockholders because meeting the condition makes payment of interest mandatory. Preferred stockholders receive dividends only if they are declared, and the directors usually have complete discretion in this matter. Also, stockholders have claims junior to those of debtholders if the enterprise is liquidated.

Answer (B) is incorrect because the proper listing is mortgage bonds, subordinated debentures, income bonds, and preferred stock. Debentures are unsecured debt instruments. Their holders have enforceable claims against the issuer even if no income is earned or dividends declared. Answer (C) is incorrect because the proper listing is first mortgage bonds, second mortgage bonds, income bonds, and common stock. The second mortgage bonds are secured, albeit junior, claims. Answer (D) is incorrect because the proper listing is mortgage bonds, debentures, preferred stock, and common stock. Holders of common stock cannot receive dividends unless the holders of preferred stock receive the stipulated periodic percentage return, in addition to any averages if the preferred stock is cumulative.

17. From the viewpoint of the investor, which of the following securities provides the least risk?

- A. Mortgage bond.
- B. Subordinated debenture.
- C. Income bond.
- D. Debentures.

The correct answer is (A). *(CIA 1191 IV-50)*

REQUIRED: The least risky security from the viewpoint of the investor.

DISCUSSION: A mortgage bond is secured with specific fixed assets, usually real property. Thus, under the rights enumerated in the bond indenture, creditors will be able to receive payments from liquidation of the property in case of default. In a bankruptcy proceeding, these amounts are paid before any transfers are made to other creditors, including those preferences. Hence, mortgage bonds are less risky than the others listed.

Answer (B) is incorrect because a debenture is long-term debt that is not secured (collateralized) by specific property. Subordinated debentures have a claim on the debtor's assets that may be satisfied only after senior debt has been paid in full. Debentures of either kind are therefore more risky than mortgage bonds. Answer (C) is incorrect because an income bond pays interest only if the debtor earns it. Such bonds are also more risky than secured debt. Answer (D) is incorrect because unsecured debt is riskier than a mortgage bond.

18. The following forms of short-term borrowing are available to a firm:

- Floating lien
- Factoring
- Revolving credit
- Chattel mortgages
- Bankers' acceptances
- Lines of credit
- Commercial paper

The forms of short-term borrowing that are unsecured credit are

    A. Floating lien, revolving credit, chattel mortgage, and commercial paper.

    B. Factoring, chattel mortgage, bankers' acceptances, and line of credit.

    C. Floating lien, chattel mortgage, bankers' acceptances, and line of credit.

    D. Revolving credit, bankers' acceptances, line of credit, and commercial paper.

The correct answer is (D). *(CMA 1286 1-35)*

REQUIRED: The forms of short-term borrowing that are unsecured credit.

DISCUSSION: An unsecured loan is a loan made by a bank based on credit information about the borrower and the ability of the borrower to repay the obligation. The loan is not secured by collateral, but is made on the signature of the borrower. Unsecured credit is not backed by collateral. Revolving credit, bankers' acceptances, lines of credit, and commercial paper are all unsecured means of borrowing.

Answers (A), (B), and (C) are incorrect because a chattel mortgage is a loan secured by personal property (movable property such as equipment or livestock). Also, a floating lien is secured by property, such as inventory, the composition of which may be constantly changing. Factoring is a form of financing in which receivables serve as security.

19. The best example of a marketable security with minimal risk would be

    A. Municipal bonds.

    B. The common stock of a Aaa rated company.

    C. The commercial paper of a Aaa rated company.

    D. Stock options of a Aaa rated company.

The correct answer is (C). *(CMA 688 1-15)*

REQUIRED: The best example of a marketable security with minimal risk.

DISCUSSION: Of the choices given, the commercial paper of a top-rated (most creditworthy) company has the least risk. Commercial paper is preferable to stock or stock options because the latter represent only a residual equity in a corporation. Commercial paper is debt and thus has priority over stockholders' claims. Also, commercial paper is a very short-term investment. The maximum maturity allowed without SEC registration is 270 days. However, it can be sold only to sophisticated investors without registration.

Answer (A) is incorrect because municipal bonds are rarely considered marketable securities in that they constitute long-term debt. Answers (B) and (D) are incorrect because common stock does not have as high a priority in company assets as commercial paper or other debt.

20. Short-term, unsecured promissory notes issued by large firms are known as

    A. Agency securities.

    B. Bankers' acceptances.

    C. Commercial paper.

    D. Repurchase agreements.

The correct answer is (C). *(CMA 689 1-13)*

REQUIRED: The name for a short-term promissory note typically issued by a large firm.

DISCUSSION: Commercial paper is the term for the short-term (typically less than 9 months), unsecured, large denomination (often over $100,000) promissory notes issued by large, creditworthy companies to other companies and institutional investors. In many instances, the maturity date is only a few days after issuance.

Answer (A) is incorrect because an agency security is issued by a corporation or agency created by the U.S. government. Examples are government securities issued by the bodies that finance mortgages, such as the Federal National Mortgage Association (Fannie Mae). Answer (B) is incorrect because bankers' acceptances are drafts drawn on deposits at a bank. The acceptance by the bank guarantees payment at maturity. They are normally used to finance a specific transaction. Answer (D) is incorrect because a repurchase agreement involves a secured loan to a government securities dealer. It allows the buyer to retain interest income although the seller-dealer can repurchase after a specified time.

21. Which security is most often held as a substitute for cash?

- A. Treasury bills.
- B. Common stock.
- C. Gold.
- D. Aaa corporate bonds.

The correct answer is (A). *(CMA 1289 1-14)*
REQUIRED: The security most often held as a substitute for cash.
DISCUSSION: A Treasury bill is a short-term U.S. government obligation that is sold at a discount from its face value. A Treasury bill is highly liquid and nearly risk-free, and it is often held as a substitute for cash.
Answers (B), (C), and (D) are incorrect because each lacks the liquidity necessary to be a cash substitute. They can also be quite risky investments.

22. The marketable securities with the least amount of default risk are

- A. Federal government agency securities.
- B. U.S. Treasury securities.
- C. Repurchase agreements.
- D. Commercial paper.

The correct answer is (B). *(CMA 691 1-11)*
REQUIRED: The marketable securities with the least default risk.
DISCUSSION: The marketable securities with the lowest default risk are those issued by the federal government because they are backed by the full faith and credit of the U.S. Agency securities are issued by agencies and corporations created by the federal government, such as the Federal Housing Administration. They are backed by a secondary promise from the government.
Answer (A) is incorrect because securities issued by a federal agency are first backed by that agency and secondarily by the U.S. government. Answer (C) is incorrect because repurchase agreements could become worthless if the organization agreeing to make the repurchase goes bankrupt. Answer (D) is incorrect because commercial paper is unsecured.

23. All of the following are valid reasons for a business to hold cash and marketable securities except to

- A. Satisfy compensating balance requirements.
- B. Maintain adequate cash needed for transactions.
- C. Meet future needs.
- D. Earn maximum returns on investment assets.

The correct answer is (D). *(CMA 694 1-22)*
REQUIRED: The item that is not a valid reason for a company to hold cash and marketable securities.
DISCUSSION: A company will hold cash and marketable securities to facilitate business transactions because cash is a primary medium of exchange. Cash and near-cash items are also held to meet future needs, to satisfy compensating balance requirements imposed by lenders, and to provide a precautionary balance for security purposes. Cash is usually not held in an attempt to earn maximum returns on investment because cash and marketable securities are not usually the highest-paying investments.
Answers (A), (B), and (C) are all incorrect because cash is held to satisfy compensating balance requirements, to facilitate transactions, and to meet future needs.

24. All of the following are alternative marketable securities suitable for investment except

- A. U.S. Treasury bills.
- B. Eurodollars.
- C. Commercial paper.
- D. Convertible bonds.

The correct answer is (D). *(CMA 694 1-25)*
REQUIRED: The item that is not a marketable security.
DISCUSSION: Marketable securities are near-cash items used primarily for short-term investment. Examples include U.S. Treasury bills, Eurodollars, commercial paper, money-market mutual funds with portfolios of short-term securities, bankers' acceptances, floating-rate preferred stock, and negotiable CDs of U.S. banks. A convertible bond is not a short-term investment because its maturity date is usually more than one year in the future and its price can be influenced substantially by changes in interest rates or by changes in the investee's stock price.
Answers (A), (B), and (C) are incorrect because U.S. Treasury bills, Eurodollars, and commercial paper are short-term marketable securities.

25. A feasible portfolio that offers the highest expected return for a given risk or the least risk for a given expected return is a(n)

- A. Optimal portfolio.
- B. Desirable portfolio.
- C. Efficient portfolio.
- D. Effective portfolio.

The correct answer is (C). *(Publisher)*
REQUIRED: The term for a portfolio that offers the highest expected return for a given risk.
DISCUSSION: A feasible portfolio that offers the highest expected return for a given risk or the least risk for a given expected return is called an efficient portfolio.
Answer (A) is incorrect because an optimal portfolio is a portfolio selected from the efficient set of portfolios because it is tangent to the investor's highest indifference curve. Answer (B) is incorrect because a desirable portfolio is a nonsense term. Answer (D) is incorrect because an effective portfolio is a nonsense term.

D. Options and Futures

26. A company has recently purchased some stock of a competitor as part of a long-term plan to acquire the competitor. However, it is somewhat concerned that the market price of this stock could decrease over the short run. The company could hedge against the possible decline in the stock's market price by

- A. Purchasing a call option on that stock.
- B. Purchasing a put option on that stock.
- C. Selling a put option on that stock.
- D. Obtaining a warrant option on that stock.

The correct answer is (B). *(CIA 590 IV-57)*
REQUIRED: The means of hedging against the possible decline in the stock's market price.
DISCUSSION: A put option is the right to sell stock at a given price within a certain period. If the market price falls, the put option may allow the sale of stock at a price above market, and the profit of the option holder will be the difference between the price stated in the put option and the market price, minus the cost of the option, commissions, and taxes. The company that issues the stock has nothing to do with put (and call) options.
Answer (A) is incorrect because a call option is the right to purchase shares at a given price within a specified period. Answer (C) is incorrect because selling a put option could force the company to purchase additional stock if the option is exercised. Answer (D) is incorrect because a warrant gives the holder a right to purchase stock from the issuer at a given price (it is usually distributed along with debt).

27. When a firm finances each asset with a financial instrument of the same approximate maturity as the life of the asset, it is applying

- A. Working capital management.
- B. Return maximization.
- C. Financial leverage.
- D. A hedging approach.

The correct answer is (D). *(CMA 1291 1-13)*
REQUIRED: The technique used when a firm finances a specific asset with a financial instrument having the same approximate maturity as the life of the asset.
DISCUSSION: Maturity matching, or equalizing the life of an asset and the debt instrument used to finance that asset, is a hedging approach. The basic concept is that the company has the entire life of the asset to recover the amount invested before having to pay the lender.
Answer (A) is incorrect because working capital management is short-term asset management. Answer (B) is incorrect because return maximization is more aggressive than maturity matching. It entails using the lowest cost forms of financing. Answer (C) is incorrect because financial leverage is the relationship between debt and equity financing.

28. If a call option is "out-of-the-money,"

- A. It is not worth exercising.
- B. The value of the underlying asset is less than the exercise price.
- C. The option no longer exists.
- D. Both (A) and (B) are correct.

The correct answer is (D). *(Publisher)*
REQUIRED: The meaning behind a call option being "out-of-money."
DISCUSSION: When the value of the asset underlying a call option is less than the exercise price of the option, the option is "out-of-money," which means it is not worth exercising.
Answer (A) is incorrect because, although the call option is not worth exercising, the value of the underlying asset is also less than the exercise price. Answer (B) is incorrect because, although the value of the underlying asset is less than the exercise price, it is also not worth exercising. Answer (C) is incorrect because the option does exist; it is just not worth exercising.

29. The type of option that does not have the backing of stock is called a(n)

A. Covered option.

B. Unsecured option.

C. Naked option.

D. Put option.

The correct answer is (C). *(Publisher)*

REQUIRED: The type of option that does not have the backing of stock.

DISCUSSION: A naked option is an option that does not have the backing of stock.

Answer (A) is incorrect because a covered option is one that is written against stock held in the option writer's portfolio. Answer (B) is incorrect because an unsecured option is a nonsense term. Answer (D) is incorrect because a put option is an option that gives the owner the right to sell the underlying asset for a fixed price.

30. A contractual arrangement that gives the owner the right to buy or sell an asset at a fixed price at any moment in time before or on a specified date is a(n)

A. European option.

B. Foreign option.

C. Future option.

D. American option.

The correct answer is (D). *(Publisher)*

REQUIRED: The type of option that can be exercised at any time before or on a specified date.

DISCUSSION: An American option is a contractual arrangement that gives the owner the right to buy or sell an asset at a fixed price at any moment in time before or on a specified date.

Answer (A) is incorrect because a European option is exercisable only at the expiration date. Answer (B) is incorrect because a foreign option is a nonsense term. Answer (C) is incorrect because, although an option can be exercised in the future, it is not called a future option.

31. The use of derivatives to either hedge or speculate results in

A. Increased risk regardless of motive.

B. Decreased risk regardless of motive.

C. Offset risk when hedging and increased risk when speculating.

D. Offset risk when speculating and increased risk when hedging.

The correct answer is (C). *(Publisher)*

REQUIRED: The effects of hedging and speculating on risk.

DISCUSSION: Derivatives, including options and futures, are contracts between the parties who contract. Unlike stocks and bonds, they are not claims on business assets. A futures contract is entered into as either a speculation or a hedge. Speculation involves the assumption of risk in the hope of gaining from price movements. Hedging is the process of using offsetting commitments to minimize or avoid the impact of adverse price movements.

Answer (A) is incorrect because hedging decreases risk by using offsetting commitments that avoid the impact of adverse price movements. Answer (B) is incorrect because speculation involves the assumption of risk in the hope of gaining from price movements. Answer (D) is incorrect because speculating increases risk while hedging offsets risk.

32. A forward contract involves

A. A commitment today to purchase a product on a specific future date at a price to be determined some time in the future.

B. A commitment today to purchase a product some time during the current day at its present price.

C. A commitment today to purchase a product on a specific future date at a price determined today.

D. A commitment today to purchase a product only when its price increases above its current exercise price.

The correct answer is (C). *(Publisher)*

REQUIRED: The terms of a forward contract.

DISCUSSION: A forward contract is an executory contract in which the parties involved agree to the terms of a purchase and a sale, but performance is deferred. Accordingly, a forward contract involves a commitment today to purchase a product on a specific future date at a price determined today.

Answer (A) is incorrect because the price of a future contract is determined on the day of commitment, not some time in the future. Answer (B) is incorrect because performance is deferred in a future contract, and the price of the product is not necessarily its present price. The price can be any price determined on the day of commitment. Answer (D) is incorrect because a forward contract is a firm commitment to purchase a product. It is not based on a contingency. Also, a forward contract does not involve an exercise price (exercise price is in an option contract).

33. An automobile company that uses the futures market to set the price of steel to protect a profit against price increases is an example of

- A. A short hedge.
- B. A long hedge.
- C. Selling futures to protect the company from loss.
- D. Selling futures to protect against price declines.

The correct answer is (B). *(Publisher)*

REQUIRED: The example of the use of the futures market to protect a profit.

DISCUSSION: A change in prices can be minimized or avoided by hedging. Hedging is the process of using offsetting commitments to minimize or avoid the impact of adverse price movements. The automobile company desires to stabilize the price of steel so that its cost to the company will not rise and cut into profits. Accordingly, the automobile company uses the futures market to create a long hedge, which is a futures contract that is purchased to protect against price increases.

Answer (A) is incorrect because a short hedge is a futures contract that is sold to protect against price declines. The automobile company wishes to protect itself against price increases. Answer (C) is incorrect because the automobile company needs to purchase futures in order to protect itself from loss, not sell futures. Selling futures protects against price declines. Answer (D) is incorrect because it is the definition of a short hedge, which is used for avoiding price declines. The automobile company wants to protect itself against price increases.

34. If a corporation holds a forward contract for the delivery of U.S. Treasury bonds in 6 months and, during those 6 months, interest rates decline, at the end of the 6 months the value of the forward contract will have

- A. Decreased.
- B. Increased.
- C. Remained constant.
- D. Any of the answers may be correct, depending on the extent of the decline in interest rates.

The correct answer is (B). *(Publisher)*

REQUIRED: The impact of an interest rate decline on the value of a forward contract.

DISCUSSION: Interest rate futures contracts involve risk-free bonds, such as U.S. Treasury bonds. When interest rates decrease over the period of a forward contract, the value of the bonds and the forward contract increase.

Answers (A) and (C) are incorrect because the value of the forward contract will increase when interest rates decrease. Answer (D) is incorrect because any decline in interest rates increases the value of the bonds.

E. Corporate Insurance

35. Insurance may best be defined as

- A. A system for transferring risk through risk avoidance or loss control.
- B. Any contract that conveys an insurable interest.
- C. A form of pure risk called gambling.
- D. A means of combining many loss exposures so that losses are shared by all participants.

The correct answer is (D). *(Publisher)*

REQUIRED: The best definition of insurance.

DISCUSSION: Insurance is a method of spreading losses that arise from risks to which many persons are subject. Loss is an unanticipated diminution in economic value as opposed to normal depreciation. Risk is uncertainty about the occurrence or the amount of loss. For example, buildings are subject to the risk of loss by fire. If the owners all pay small fees (premiums) for insurance coverage, every participant bears part of the loss instead of a few bearing all the loss.

Answer (A) is incorrect because risk avoidance and loss control do not transfer risk of loss. Answer (B) is incorrect because an insurable interest is merely a potential for economic loss if an event occurs. Answer (C) is incorrect because there must be an insurable interest, which is basically potential for loss if an event occurs. Gambling occurs when only a bet is at risk.

36. Which of the following is the best functional definition of insurance?

A. A legal contract by which the insurer, in return for consideration, agrees to pay another person if a stated loss or injury occurs.

B. A legal contract by which an insurance company, in return for premiums, agrees to pay the policyholder if a certain event occurs.

C. A written promise by the insurer to pay the beneficiary if loss occurs from the occurrence of a contingent event.

D. A writing issued by an insurance company, for a consideration, that promises to indemnify a beneficiary for a loss from an existing risk or one which arises later.

The correct answer is (A). *(Publisher)*
REQUIRED: The best functional definition of insurance.
DISCUSSION: An insurance contract (a policy) must satisfy the usual requirements: offer and acceptance, consideration, legality, and capacity of the parties. The insured must have an insurable interest in the subject matter of the contract. Also, the subject matter generally must exist at the time of contracting. In the contract, the insurer makes a promise to pay a stated amount for loss or injury incurred as a result of a contingent event.
Answer (B) is incorrect because the payee may be a stranger to the contract. A person who insures his/her own life names a third party as a beneficiary. Moreover, not every insurer is an insurance company, and the contingent event insured against must involve a risk. Answer (C) is incorrect because there is no general requirement that an insurance contract be written. Answer (D) is incorrect because the contract may often be oral, and, if the risk is not already in existence, the transaction is in essence a wager, not insurance.

37. In which way does the formation of an insurance contract differ from any other contract?

A. The requirement that the insured must have an insurable interest.

B. The insurance contract is not valid unless written.

C. Consideration is not needed for the formation of an insurance contract.

D. In insurance, only the insured can commit a breach.

The correct answer is (A). *(Publisher)*
REQUIRED: The manner in which the formation of an insurance contract differs from other contracts.
DISCUSSION: An insurance contract is very similar to any other contract. However, an additional requirement is that the insured must have an insurable interest.
Answer (B) is incorrect because there is no general requirement that an insurance contract be written. Oral binders are given every day in the insurance business. Answer (C) is incorrect because consideration is needed for the initial formation of an insurance contract. The premium may be paid immediately, or a promise to pay is required. Answer (D) is incorrect because the insurance company can also commit a breach by refusing to pay the proceeds of the policy upon the occurrence of the event.

38. Life insurance

A. Is a contract of indemnity.

B. Usually has short-term policies.

C. Covers only the mortality risk.

D. Generally has no cash value.

The correct answer is (A). *(Publisher)*
REQUIRED: The correct statement about the characteristics of life insurance.
DISCUSSION: Life insurance is usually purchased to protect against the cessation of income needed for support of the family and to shield them from the decedent's debts.
Answer (B) is incorrect because life insurance is customarily long-term, if not for life. Answer (C) is incorrect because, unlike other forms of insurance, life insurance does not attempt to reimburse for the actual amount of a loss since loss of life is not measurable. Life insurance is intended to replace economic benefits lost by a person's death. Answer (D) is incorrect because, except for term policies, life insurance differs from other kinds of coverage in providing cash value.

39. Life insurance is offered in several forms. The kind that offers no investment feature is

A. Whole life.

B. Endowment.

C. Straight life.

D. Term.

The correct answer is (D). *(Publisher)*

REQUIRED: The kind of life insurance not offering an investment feature.

DISCUSSION: Term life insurance provides protection for a specified period. Premiums are level throughout the period. When the term ends, the insured receives no payment. Term insurance may be renewable (possibly at higher premiums) or convertible to another form. It is the cheapest kind of life insurance.

Answer (A) is incorrect because whole life furnishes lifetime insurance protection with a cash surrender value. Answer (B) is incorrect because an endowment policy provides life insurance protection for its duration. A cash payment is made (the policy endows) at the end of the term. Premiums for endowment policies are higher than for whole life insurance. Answer (C) is incorrect because a straight life or ordinary policy is whole life insurance with level premiums payable for life.

40. Jon Berstock is an employee of PR, Inc. During his employment, the corporation's earnings have doubled, largely because of Jon's ability to attract new accounts. PR therefore insured his life for a substantial sum. If Jon dies, will PR be able to collect the insurance proceeds?

A. Yes, because a corporation has an insurable interest in all its employees since it can act only through agents.

B. Yes, because PR has a pecuniary interest in Jon's continued life.

C. No, because PR will continue to exist after Jon's death.

D. No, because Jon was not a stockholder or officer of PR, Inc.

The correct answer is (B). *(Publisher)*

REQUIRED: The correct statement about a corporation's insurance on an employee's life.

DISCUSSION: When one person insures the life of another, the policyholder must have an insurable interest in the insured. That interest is found among persons who have a close family relationship or expect to suffer substantial economic loss from the death. Business entities are thus permitted to insure key people in their organizations whose death might have an adverse effect on profits.

Answer (A) is incorrect because a corporation has an insurable interest only in its key employees, i.e., those whose death would cause loss to the firm. Answer (C) is incorrect because the required loss need not be so great as to cause cessation of business. Answer (D) is incorrect because one need not be an owner or an officer to be insurable as a key person.

41. Which of the following is a characteristic of fire insurance?

A. It is more standardized than life insurance.

B. It is written for a relatively short period but usually includes an incontestability clause.

C. A policy must be valued and contain a pro rata clause.

D. The insurable interest must be an ownership interest in the property itself.

The correct answer is (A). *(Publisher)*

REQUIRED: The characteristic of fire insurance.

DISCUSSION: Fire insurance is the most standardized kind of insurance. Following the lead of New York, almost all states have enacted a standard policy either by legislative or administrative action.

Answer (B) is incorrect because, given that fire insurance is usually written for a 1- to 3-year period, an incontestability clause is not necessary. Such a clause bars insurer defenses after a period specified by law or the policy. Answer (C) is incorrect because a policy may state a definite value of the insured property or simply a maximum amount of coverage that is not conclusive as to valuation when loss occurs. A policy may thus be valued or open (unvalued). A pro rata clause is often included (but not required) which requires the loss to be shared pro rata when there is more than one insurer. Answer (D) is incorrect because the insurable interest merely requires the person, e.g., mortgagee, bailee, etc., to suffer a loss if the event insured against occurs.

42. The typical life insurance policy contains

    A. No exclusion for death during military service.

    B. A clause allowing coverage for death during noncommercial flight.

    C. A prohibition on reinstatement.

    D. A provision for a grace period for premium payment.

The correct answer is (D). *(Publisher)*

    REQUIRED: The correct statement about the provisions of a life insurance policy.

    DISCUSSION: If a premium is not received by the due date, the policyholder has a grace period under state law, usually a month or 31 days, in which to pay. After the grace period, the cash surrender value is not forfeited but can be withdrawn or used to buy a paid-up policy.

    Answers (A) and (B) are incorrect because life insurance policies often do not cover death while the insured is in the military or as a result of a noncommercial air flight. Answer (C) is incorrect because a lapsed policy may often be reinstated by payment of overdue premiums plus interest.

43. A fire insurance policy ordinarily indemnifies for losses arising from

    A. Friendly, but not hostile, fires.

    B. Hostile, but not friendly, fires.

    C. Both hostile and friendly fires.

    D. Smoke produced by friendly or hostile fires.

The correct answer is (B). *(Publisher)*

    REQUIRED: The losses caused by fire that will be indemnified.

    DISCUSSION: Ordinarily, smoke, water, or other damage caused by hostile, but not friendly, fires will be indemnified under a fire insurance policy. Hostile fires are those ignited in places where they are not meant to be. A friendly fire is one that burns where it is intended to burn, such as a fireplace or furnace. For example, if a friendly fire is kept within its usual container, damage caused by smoke from it will not be reimbursed.

    Answers (A), (C), and (D) are incorrect because fire insurance usually indemnifies for loss caused by hostile, but not friendly, fires.

44. Which of the following wrongful acts prevents recovery under a policy of fire insurance?

    A. Arson by the insured's employees or agents.

    B. Arson by third persons unrelated to the insured.

    C. An act by the insured intended to cause the damage.

    D. Gross negligence but not amounting to recklessness and willful misconduct.

The correct answer is (C). *(Publisher)*

    REQUIRED: The wrongful act preventing an insurance recovery.

    DISCUSSION: Arson, fraud, or another intentional act of the insured calculated to cause the damage insured against will preclude recovery. The parties to an insurance contract have an implied duty not to bring about the very event that is the subject matter of the policy.

    Answer (A) is incorrect because agency rules do not apply; i.e., the intentional act of an agent will not be imputed to the insured under the doctrine of *respondeat superior*. Arson by an agent without the actual knowledge or conspiracy of the insured will not preclude recovery. Answer (B) is incorrect because arson is compensable unless intended by the insured. Answer (D) is incorrect because negligence without fraud will not prevent recovery by an insured who has acted in good faith.

45. Which of the following is not a type of insurance policy that provides liability coverage?

    A. Malpractice insurance.

    B. Homeowners insurance.

    C. Automobile insurance.

    D. Fire insurance.

The correct answer is (D). *(Publisher)*

    REQUIRED: The type of insurance policy not providing liability coverage.

    DISCUSSION: Fire insurance generally protects the insured from damage to the insured property as a result of fire. It does not cover the insured for causing a fire on someone else's property.

    Answer (A) is incorrect because malpractice insurance is a special form of liability insurance protecting professionals from lawsuits by third parties for negligence. Answer (B) is incorrect because homeowners insurance generally contains a liability section in the event guests are injured on the premises. Answer (C) is incorrect because a primary purpose of automobile insurance is to protect the owner or driver from liability in the event (s)he is responsible for damage to another person or property.

46. The purpose of a co-insurance clause is to

A. Encourage policyholders to bear a proportionate part of any loss.

B. Encourage insurers to pay the face amount of the policy in the event of a partial loss on the part of the insured.

C. Encourage policyholders to insure commercial property for an amount that is near to its full replacement cost.

D. Encourage policyholders to insure commercial property for an amount that is significantly less than its full replacement cost.

The correct answer is (C). *(Publisher)*
REQUIRED: The purpose of a co-insurance clause.
DISCUSSION: Co-insurance is a method of sharing risk between the insurer and the insured. A co-insurance clause typically provides that, if the policyholder insures his/her property for at least a stated percentage (usually 80%) of its actual cash value, any loss will be paid in full up to the face amount of the policy. Thus, a co-insurance clause is used by many property and casualty insurers to encourage policyholders to insure commercial property for an amount that is near to its full replacement cost.
Answer (A) is incorrect because, if a policyholder does not insure the property for an amount close enough to its full replacement cost, the policyholder must bear a proportionate part of any partial loss. Answer (B) is incorrect because the co-insurance requirement applies only to partial losses. Total losses result in recovery of the face amount of the policy. Answer (D) is incorrect because a co-insurance clause encourages policyholders to insure commercial property for an amount that is near to its full replacement cost.

F. Foreign Operations

47. The premium or discount on a forward exchange contract is calculated using the difference between the

A. Spot rate at the balance sheet date and the spot rate at the date of inception of the forward contract.

B. Spot rate at the balance sheet date and the spot rate last used to measure a gain or loss on that contract for an earlier period.

C. Spot rate at the date of inception of the forward contract and the spot rate last used to measure a gain or loss on that contract for an earlier period.

D. Contracted forward rate and the spot rate at the date of inception of the contract.

The correct answer is (D). *(CMA 1288 3-29)*
REQUIRED: The calculation of the premium or discount on a foreign exchange contract.
DISCUSSION: The difference between the contract rate and the spot rate at the date of a forward exchange contract's inception is a discount or premium on the forward contract. A discount or premium should be accounted for separately from the gain or loss on the contract, and should be included in net income over the life of the contract through amortization of the discount or premium. An exception to this amortization requirement is a hedge of an identifiable foreign currency commitment. In this case, the discount or premium related to the commitment period may be included in the related foreign currency transaction when it is recorded.
Answers (A), (B), and (C) are incorrect because a premium or discount is calculated as the difference between the contracted forward rate and the spot rate at the date of inception of the contract.

48. For which kind of forward foreign exchange contracts are both the receivable and the liability recorded at the forward exchange rate?

A. Speculative forward contract.

B. Hedge of a net investment.

C. Hedge of an identifiable foreign currency commitment.

D. Hedge of an exposed liability position.

The correct answer is (A). *(Publisher)*
REQUIRED: The kind of forward foreign exchange contract for which both the receivable and the liability are recorded at the forward exchange rate.
DISCUSSION: A speculative forward contract is a contract that does not hedge any exposure to foreign currency fluctuations; it creates the exposure. Both the receivable from the broker and the liability to the broker are recorded at the forward exchange rate existing at the date of the contract. The receivable or liability denominated in the foreign currency is adjusted to reflect the forward rate at each ensuing balance sheet date and at the date of settlement, with a corresponding recognition of exchange gain or loss.
Answers (B), (C), and (D) are incorrect because for foreign exchange hedges the receivable or payable denominated in dollars is recorded at the forward exchange rate, and the payable or receivable denominated in foreign exchange units is recorded at the spot rate. The difference is recorded as a discount or premium.

49. A U.S. company and a German company purchased the same stock on the German stock exchange and held the stock for 1 year. The value of the German mark weakened against the dollar over this period. Comparing the returns of the two companies, the United States company's return will be

A. Lower.

B. Higher.

C. The same.

D. Indeterminate from the information provided.

The correct answer is (A). *(CIA 1190 IV-58)*
REQUIRED: The effect of the exchange rate movement.
DISCUSSION: The returns on the stock are presumably paid in marks. Hence, the change in the value of the mark relative to the dollar does not affect the German company's return. However, the weakening of the mark reduces the number of dollars it will buy, and the U.S. company's return in dollars is correspondingly reduced.

Answer (B) is incorrect because the return to the U.S. company is adversely affected by the exchange rate movement. Answers (C) and (D) are incorrect because the return to the U.S. company was directly affected by the exchange rate movement, but the return to the German company was not.

50. An American importer of English clothing has contracted to pay an amount fixed in British pounds three months from now. If the importer worries that the U.S. dollar may depreciate sharply against the British pound in the interim, it would be well advised to

A. Buy pounds in the forward exchange market.

B. Sell pounds in the forward exchange market.

C. Buy dollars in the futures market.

D. Sell dollars in the futures market.

The correct answer is (A). *(CMA 1285 1-34)*
REQUIRED: The action to hedge a liability denominated in a foreign currency.
DISCUSSION: The American importer should buy pounds now. If the dollar depreciates against the pound in the next 90 days, the gain on the forward exchange contract would offset the loss from having to pay more dollars to satisfy the liability.

Answer (B) is incorrect because selling pounds would compound the risk of loss for someone who has incurred a liability. However, it would be an appropriate hedge of a receivable denominated in pounds. Answer (C) is incorrect because the importer needs pounds, not dollars. Answer (D) is incorrect because, although buying pounds might be equivalent to selling dollars for pounds, this is not the best answer. This choice does not state what is received for the dollars.

51. If the annual U.S. inflation rate is expected to be 5% while the Italian lira is expected to depreciate against the U.S. dollar by 10%, an Italian firm importing from its U.S. parent can expect its lira costs for these imports to

A. Decrease by about 10%.

B. Decrease by about 5%.

C. Increase by about 5%.

D. Increase by about 15%.

The correct answer is (D). *(CMA 1286 1-18)*
REQUIRED: The combined effect of inflation and currency depreciation.
DISCUSSION: Assuming the original exchange rate is $1 to 2,000 lira and that U.S. inflation is 5%, the cost in lira to purchase what once cost $1 will now be 2,100 lira (2,000 x 1.05). However, if the lira also depreciates by 10%, the exchange rate will be $1 to 2,200 lira. At this rate, 2,310 lira (2,200 x 1.05) will be required to purchase $1.05. Lira costs will thus increase by just over 15% (310 ÷ 2,000).

Answers (A) and (B) are incorrect because the combined effect of U.S. inflation and the decline in value of the lira would cause the lira costs for U.S. imports to increase. Answer (C) is incorrect because 5% is the difference between the currency depreciation and the inflation rate.

52. An overvalued exchange rate

A. Represents a tax on exports and a subsidy to imports.

B. Represents a subsidy to exports and a tax on imports.

C. Has an effect on capital flows but no effect on trade flows.

D. Has no effect on capital flows but does affect trade flows.

The correct answer is (A). *(CMA 1286 1-19)*
REQUIRED: The effect of an overvalued exchange rate.
DISCUSSION: An overvalued exchange rate is a tax on exports because they will be overvalued in terms of the foreign currency. For example, if the true value of $1 is 5 marks but the exchange rate is $1 to 6 marks, the cost of goods priced in dollars will include a 20% tax for holders of marks. It is also a subsidy to imports because the overly high exchange rate causes the price of foreign goods and services to be undervalued. In the same example, $1 will buy 6 marks' worth of imports instead of 5, a 20% subsidy.

Answer (B) is incorrect because devaluation taxes imports and subsidizes exports. Answers (C) and (D) are incorrect because both will be affected.

53. If the value of the U.S. dollar in foreign exchange markets changes from $1 = 6 marks to $1 = 4 marks,

A. The German mark has depreciated against the dollar.

B. German imported products in the U.S. will become more expensive.

C. The dollar has appreciated against the mark.

D. U.S. tourists in Germany will find their dollars will buy more German products made.

The correct answer is (B). *(CMA 1287 1-28)*

REQUIRED: The effect of a depreciation in the value of the dollar.

DISCUSSION: The dollar has declined in value relative to the mark. If an American had previously wished to purchase a German product that was priced at 12 marks, the dollar price would have been $2. After the decline in value, the dollar cost of the item has increased to $3. Therefore, imports from Germany should decrease and exports increase.

Answers (A) and (C) are incorrect because the mark has appreciated (increased in value) relative to the dollar. Answer (D) is incorrect because dollars will buy fewer German products.

54. If consumers in Japan decide they would like to increase their purchases of consumer products in the United States, in foreign exchange markets there will be a tendency for

A. The supply of dollars to increase.

B. The supply of dollars to decrease.

C. The Japanese yen to appreciate relative to the U.S. dollar.

D. The demand for dollars to increase.

The correct answer is (D). *(CMA 1287 1-29)*

REQUIRED: The effect of Japanese consumers deciding to increase their purchases of U.S. products.

DISCUSSION: The increase in demand for U.S. products will increase the demand for the dollars necessary to pay for those products.

Answers (A) and (B) are incorrect because the demand for dollars, not the supply, will be affected by the decision to purchase additional U.S. products. Answer (C) is incorrect because the dollar should appreciate relative to the yen owing to the increased demand for dollars.

55. Exchange rates are determined by

A. Each industrial country's government.

B. The International Monetary Fund.

C. Supply and demand in the foreign exchange market.

D. Exporters and importers of manufactured goods.

The correct answer is (C). *(CMA 688 1-22)*

REQUIRED: The factor that determines foreign exchange rates.

DISCUSSION: Although currencies can be supported by various means for short periods, the primary determinant of exchange rates is the supply of, and demand for, the various currencies. Under current international agreements, exchange rates are allowed to "float." During periods of extreme fluctuations, however, governments and control banks may intervene to maintain stability in the market.

Answers (A), (B), and (D) are incorrect because they have only temporary influence, if any, on the setting of exchange rates.

56. If risk is purposely undertaken in the foreign exchange market, the investor in foreign exchange then becomes

    A. A speculator.

    B. An arbitrageur.

    C. Involved in hedging.

    D. An exporter.

The correct answer is (A). *(CMA 688 1-23)*
    REQUIRED: The term for an investor who purposely undertakes risk in the foreign exchange market.
    DISCUSSION: An individual who purposely accepts foreign exchange risk is a speculator. Speculators buy and sell foreign exchange in anticipation of favorable changes in rates.
    Answer (B) is incorrect because an arbitrageur is someone who simultaneously buys foreign exchange in one market and sells in another market at a slightly higher price. Thus, the arbitrageur's risk is slight. Answer (C) is incorrect because hedging avoids the risk of foreign exchange trans-actions for those who do not seek to gain from fluctuations in exchange rates. Hedging is the sale or purchase of a foreign currency forward exchange contract to offset a possible exchange rate loss. When a foreign currency forward ex-change contract is intended and is effective as an economic hedge against an exposed net asset or net liability position (e.g., an outstanding receivable or liability denominated in a foreign currency), any exchange gain or loss on the forward contract will offset any exchange gain or loss on the exposed net asset or net liability position. Thus, no exchange gain or loss will result. Answer (D) is incorrect because exporters are likely to engage in hedging to avoid exchange risk.

57. The U.S. dollar has a free-floating exchange rate. If the dollar falls considerably in relation to other currencies over the next 2 years, the

    A. Capital account in the U.S. balance of pay-ments will be neither in a deficit nor in a surplus because of the floating exchange rates.

    B. Fall in the dollar's value will not be expected to have any effect on the U.S. trade balance.

    C. Cheaper dollar will help U.S. importers of foreign goods.

    D. Cheaper dollar will help U.S. exporters of domestically produced goods.

The correct answer is (D). *(CMA 1288 1-15)*
    REQUIRED: The true statement about the fall in the price of the dollar relative to other currencies.
    DISCUSSION: The decline in the value of the dollar relative to other currencies will lower the price of U.S. goods to foreign consumers. Thus, exporters of domestically produced goods will benefit. The low value of the dollar will decrease imports by making foreign goods more expensive.
    Answer (A) is incorrect because the capital account will benefit from the cheaper dollar because foreigners can buy more dollars with fewer yen, marks, etc. Moreover, foreign capital inflow will increase because of the federal government's budget deficits. Answers (B) and (C) are incorrect because the fall in the dollar will have a positive effect on the nation's trade deficit since exports will increase and imports will decrease.

58. Caroline Brown, the product manager for a U.S. computer manufacturer, is being asked to quote prices of desktop computers to be used in Kuwait. The Kuwaiti government wants the price in British pounds, for delivery next year. Brown knows that the general price level in the United States will increase by 3%. Her banker forecasts that the British pound will depreciate about 5% this year with respect to the U.S. dollar. If Brown is able to quote £700 for immediate delivery, the price that should be quoted for delivery to Kuwait next year is about

    A. £735

    B. £721

    C. £757

    D. £745

The correct answer is (C). *(CMA 1288 1-17)*
    REQUIRED: The foreign exchange price to quote for a future delivery of goods.
    DISCUSSION: Two factors are to be considered: (1) the 3% inflation rate and (2) the 5% decline in the pound. Considering the inflation rate first, 3% should be added to the immediate delivery price to arrive at a future price of £721. However, to allow for the foreign currency exchange risk, an additional 5% should be added to the inflation-adjusted price. The bid price should be £757 [£721 + (5% x £721)].
    Answer (A) is incorrect because £735 results from considering only the effect of the 5% decline in the pound. Answer (B) is incorrect because £721 results from considering only the effect of the 3% U.S. inflation rate. Answer (D) is incorrect because the effects of both the 3% U.S. inflation rate and the 5% decline in the pound need to be added to the initial £700.

59. Consider a world consisting of only two countries, Canada and Italy. Inflation in Canada in 1 year was 5%, and in Italy 10%. Which one of the following statements about the Canadian exchange rate (rounded) during that year will be true?

A. Inflation has no effect on the exchange rates.

B. The Canadian dollar will appreciate by 5%.

C. The Canadian dollar will depreciate by 5%.

D. The Canadian dollar will depreciate by 15%.

The correct answer is (B). *(CMA 1288 1-18)*
REQUIRED: The true statement about the exchange rate of a currency given domestic and foreign inflation.
DISCUSSION: Because Italy has experienced the greater inflation, its currency should depreciate in relation to Canada's. For example, if Canada trades 100 units of a product to Italy for a pre-inflation price of $100 (the domestic price in Canada), and Italy pays with 10,000 units of an Italian product that sells domestically for 10,000 pre-inflation lira, the exchange rate without regard to inflation is 100 lira per $1 (10,000 lira/$100). Allowing for the inflation, the 100 units of the Canadian product would sell for $105. The 10,000 units of the Italian product would sell for 11,000 lira. Thus, the new exchange rate will be 104.76 lira per $1 (11,000 lira/$105), and the price of the Canadian dollar will increase by 4.76% (rounded to 5%).
Answer (A) is incorrect because inflation affects exchange rates by diminishing a currency's purchasing power. Answers (C) and (D) are incorrect because the Canadian currency will appreciate relative to Italy's since Canadian inflation was lower.

60. Political risk may be reduced by

A. Entering into a joint venture with another foreign company.

B. Making foreign operations dependent on the domestic parent for technology, markets, and supplies.

C. Refusing to pay higher wages and higher taxes.

D. Financing with capital from a foreign country.

The correct answer is (B). *(Publisher)*
REQUIRED: The way to reduce political risk.
DISCUSSION: Political risk is the risk that a foreign government may act in a way that will reduce the value of the company's investment. Political risk may be reduced by making foreign operations dependent on the domestic parent for technology, markets, and supplies.
Answer (A) is incorrect because political risk may be reduced by entering into a joint venture with a company from the host country rather than from a foreign country. Answer (C) is incorrect because refusing to pay higher wages and higher taxes will only increase political risk. Answer (D) is incorrect because political risk may be reduced by financing with local capital, rather than foreign capital.

61. Bonner Electronics has subsidiaries in several international locations and is concerned about its exposure to foreign exchange risk. In countries where currency values are likely to fall, Bonner should encourage all of the following policies except

A. Granting trade credit whenever possible.

B. Investing excess cash in inventory or other real assets.

C. Purchasing materials and supplies on a trade credit basis.

D. Borrowing local currency funds if an appropriate interest rate can be obtained.

The correct answer is (A). *(CFM Sample Q. 5)*
REQUIRED: The unwise action in countries where foreign currency values are likely to fall.
DISCUSSION: Extension of credit in a foreign currency would result in a loss if the foreign currency became less valuable. In general, a firm should attempt to achieve a net monetary debtor position in countries with currencies expected to depreciate. A net monetary creditor position should be achieved in countries with strengthening currencies.
Answer (B) is incorrect because investing monetary assets into nonmonetary assets is advantageous when the monetary unit is going to lose value. Answers (C) and (D) are incorrect because it is advantageous to become a debtor when the monetary unit is losing value.

STUDY UNIT 9: EXTERNAL FINANCIAL ENVIRONMENT

23 pages of outline
54 multiple-choice questions

A. Shareholder Participation and Meetings
B. Corporate Bylaws and Charters
C. Board of Directors
D. Rating Agencies
E. Effect of Governmental Regulation of Business
F. Federal Reserve Board
G. International Tax Considerations
H. International Business and Law

Study Unit 9, External Financial Environment, covers the next to last major topic of the CFM content specification outline.

A. Shareholder Participation and Meetings

1. Corporations are formed under authority of state statutes. Accordingly, the incorporation statute of a state is one source of shareholder rights. However, some shareholder rights have common law origins, for example, the power to remove directors for cause, the right to inspect corporate records, and the preemptive right. The articles of incorporation may grant specific shareholder rights not detailed in the general language of a statute. Federal law is still another source of shareholder rights, for example, regulation of the issuance and trading of securities.

2. Shareholders own the corporation. However, they have no right to manage the corporation directly. The shareholders' primary participation in corporate policy and management is by meeting annually and electing directors (usually by straight voting) who, in turn, select the management. Management actually controls the company. By their power to remove the directors, shareholders indirectly control the actions of the corporation. Because shareholders are geographically dispersed, management can essentially control a large corporation by owning a small percentage of stock.

3. **Voting Rights.** Unless a class of stock is established with no voting rights (nonvoting stock) or the articles of incorporation provide for more or less than one vote per share, each shareholder is entitled to one vote for each outstanding share owned.

    a. The state incorporation statutes may permit the issuance of one or more classes of nonvoting stock if at least one class of shares possesses voting rights.

    b. Shareholders may exercise their voting rights at either annual or special meetings.

    c. To mitigate the sometimes harsh effect of straight voting on minority shareholders, most states permit or require **cumulative voting**. Cumulative voting enables minority shareholders to obtain representation on the board in proportion to the number of shares they own.

        1) The number of votes a shareholder casts is equal to the number of directors to be elected multiplied by the shareholder's number of shares.

        2) EXAMPLE: Y Corporation is electing five directors to its board. Mary, a shareholder owning 200/1,000 of the voting shares, can elect at least one director under cumulative voting, i.e.,

            a) Five directors to be elected x 200 voting shares = 1,000

            b) Mary casts all 1,000 of her votes for the one director of her choice as opposed to splitting her vote among all five directorships to be filled.

        3) Staggering the terms of directors may prevent the minority shareholders from enjoying the advantages of cumulative voting.

d.   Another alternative to straight voting is **class voting**. A corporation may designate the voting rights of each class. Thus, a corporation may have two or more classes of common shares with different voting rights.

1)   EXAMPLE: XYZ Corporation is a small, closely held corporation with four shareholders, each of whom owns 25 shares. Straight voting would not permit a shareholder to elect him/herself as director. However, given four classes of shares, each with the right to elect one director, a shareholder who owns all the shares of one class can elect him/herself to the board.

e.   Some additional shareholder control devices include shareholder voting agreements, voting trusts, and proxies.

1)   Shareholders are free to agree contractually upon how they will vote their shares.

a)   A voting agreement may be perpetual in existence and kept secret from other shareholders.

2)   A **voting trust** occurs when shareholders transfer legal title to their shares to one or more trustees, who vote for the shares, in exchange for voting trust certificates. The purpose of a voting trust is to ensure that the shareholders' group will control the corporation via the trustees, despite future differences of opinion among the shareholders.

a)   The trustees may vote the shares based on instructions in the trust agreement or may be allowed to use their discretion.

b)   The statutory limit of voting trusts is 10 years, but shareholders can agree to extend it beyond 10 years.

c)   A voting trust indenture (document) must be made public, and copies must be available for inspection at the corporate offices.

3)   Because many shareholders are unable to attend meetings, they sometimes delegate authority to vote their shares by issuing **proxies**.

a)   A proxy authorizes someone else to vote on the shareholder's behalf.

i)   Typically, a valid proxy must be written and is revocable at any time.

ii)   A proxy is effective for no more than 11 months, unless otherwise permitted by statute and specifically included in the writing.

b)   A proxy is different from a voting trust in that the holder of a proxy does not have legal title or possession of the stock as does a voting trustee.

c)   A **general proxy** permits a holder to vote on all corporate proposals other than fundamental corporate changes.

i)   A **limited proxy** permits voting only on specified matters.

d)   A proxy may be revoked expressly, by signing a new proxy, by the shareholder's voting the shares at the meeting, or by the shareholder's death.

i)   An otherwise irrevocable proxy is revocable by a bona fide purchaser of the shares who has no notice of the proxy.

    e)   Proxy solicitation is regulated by the Securities Exchange Act of 1934.

       i)   Disclosure of all pertinent facts is required to facilitate informed choice when management or a dissident minority requests authority to vote on behalf of shareholders.

    f)   The directors make decisions about policy and certain major transactions but delegate day-to-day operational control to officers and other employees. The directors are chosen by, and are accountable to, the shareholders, who exert only indirect control over the corporation. However, the reality in most publicly held companies is that management uses the proxy solicitation process to nominate and secure the election of directors favorable to its policies. Hence, management is usually in effective control of the company.

4.   Shareholders have the right to **inspect** the corporate books and records after presentation of a written request. However, this right is subject to certain conditions. The shareholder must give notice, act in good faith, and have a proper purpose.

5.   **Shareholder Meetings.** Shareholders exercise their rights at annual or special meetings.

   a.   **Annual meetings** are required and must be held at a time fixed in the bylaws.

     1)   Their purpose is to elect new directors and to conduct necessary business.

     2)   Notice of an annual meeting is usually not necessary because the time and place of such events should be stated in the bylaws. If given, notice need not include all the purposes of the meeting unless shareholders will be asked to approve fundamental corporate changes.

     3)   Lack of notice or defective notice voids any action taken at the meeting.

       a)   A shareholder may waive objection to defective notice by attending without objection or by signing a written waiver.

   b.   **Special shareholder meetings** may be called whenever an issue arises that requires shareholder action, such as the approval of a merger.

     1)   Special meetings require a detailed written notice.

     2)   Special meetings may be called by the directors, holders of a specified percentage of the shares entitled to be voted at the meeting, or any other persons authorized in the articles of incorporation.

     3)   Notice may be waived in writing by any shareholder entitled to notice.

   c.   A quorum of the outstanding shares must be represented in person or by proxy to conduct business at a shareholders' meeting.

     1)   A **quorum** is a majority of shares outstanding.

       a)   Most state statutes permit a greater percentage of shares outstanding to be established in the articles (supermajority requirement).

   d.   Resolutions are usually adopted by a simple majority of voting shares.

     1)   To protect minority shareholders, a statute, the articles of incorporation, or the bylaws may require a supermajority with regard to extraordinary matters.

   e.   Shareholders ordinarily may act only at a duly called meeting. However, shareholders may act without a meeting if all shareholders entitled to vote consent in writing to the action.

6.   Stop and review! You have completed the outline for this subunit. Study multiple-choice questions 1 through 7 beginning on page 350.

B. **Corporate Bylaws and Charters.** A corporation is created under a state statute. It usually incorporates in the state where it intends to transact business.

1.   A corporation may be formed in one state but have its principal place of business or conduct its business operations in another state or states.

2.   Although the means of organizing a corporation may vary to some extent, each state usually requires that articles of incorporation (the charter) be filed with the secretary of state or another designated official.

   a.   The persons who sign the articles are **incorporators**.

      1)   Incorporators' services are necessary but perfunctory and short-lived. Their services end with the organizational meeting and the election of the initial board of directors.

      2)   State statutes typically require that incorporators be natural persons.

         a)   Some states insist on three incorporators; however, the modern trend is to require only one.

         b)   The incorporators normally may not be minors.

         c)   A corporation may act as an incorporator.

   b.   The articles of incorporation must include

      1)   The corporation's name

         a)   In many states, the corporate name must contain the word corporation, incorporated, company, limited, or an abbreviation thereof.

         b)   A corporate name may not be the same as, or deceptively similar to, the name of any domestic corporation or any foreign corporation authorized to do business within the state.

      2)   The purpose of the corporation

      3)   The number of shares of stock the corporation is authorized to issue

      4)   The street address of the corporation's principal office

      5)   The name and address of the corporation's registered agent for receiving service of process and other notices

      6)   The name and address of each incorporator

      7)   Names and addresses of the initial directors

      8)   The length of the corporation's life, which is usually perpetual

   c.   Most states provide standardized forms for corporate organization. These forms must be completed and filed, along with the appropriate fee, with the designated state official.

      1)   When the articles have been received and processed, they are considered officially filed and are thus approved by the state.

      2)   A corporation is usually recognized as a legal entity when the articles are filed or when the certificate of incorporation is issued. Some states also require additional filings in designated counties.

    d.   After filing, the following steps are necessary:

        1)   The incorporators elect the directors if they are not named in the articles.

        2)   The incorporators resign.

        3)   The directors meet to complete the organizational structure. At this meeting they

            a)   Adopt **bylaws** for the internal management of the corporation, including how directors are to be elected, whether existing shareholders have the first right to buy new shares, and how the bylaws are to be changed. The shareholders, directors, and officers are bound by the bylaws. Employees are not bound by the bylaws unless they have reason to be familiar with them.

                i)   Bylaws must be consistent with all state laws and the articles.

                ii)   The directors ordinarily have the power to enact, amend, or repeal bylaws, but this authority may be reserved to the shareholders.

            b)   Elect officers, including specifically the president, treasurer, and secretary

            c)   Select the corporate bank and designate persons authorized to draw checks on the account

            d)   Adopt, ratify, or reject preincorporation contracts

            e)   Adopt the form of certificate representing shares of the company's stock and accept or reject stock subscriptions

            f)   Comply with requirements for doing business in other states

            g)   Adopt a corporate seal to be affixed to or impressed upon corporate documents required by law to be under seal

            h)   Consider all other transactions necessary or appropriate for carrying on the business purpose of the corporation

3.   Modern corporate statutes permit the articles to be amended freely.

    a.   The amended articles may contain only those provisions that might lawfully have been included in the original articles of incorporation.

    b.   The board usually adopts a resolution containing the proposed amendment.

    c.   The resolution must then be approved by a majority of the voting shares.

        1)   Some corporate statutes require a two-thirds vote.
        2)   A class of shareholders may be entitled to vote as a group.

    d.   Shareholders may amend the articles by unanimous written consent without prior adoption of a resolution by the board.

    e.   After approval, articles of amendment are filed with the secretary of state.

        1)   They are effective upon issuance of a certificate of amendment.

    f.   The board may adopt certain amendments (e.g., changing the registered agent) without shareholder action, unless the articles provide otherwise.

4.   Stop and review! You have completed the outline for this subunit. Study multiple-choice questions 8 through 12 beginning on page 352.

C.   Board of Directors. The powers of a corporation are exercised by or under the authority of its board of directors. Directors are elected by the shareholders.

1.   Apart from statute, every corporation is governed by a board of directors.

2.   The board makes overall policy and directs the corporate business; the officers implement the board's directives to conduct day-to-day transactions.

3.   The minimum number of directors may be from one to three, depending on state guidelines.

    a.   Some states provide that the number of directors may be equal to the number of shareholders when there are fewer than three.

    b.   Moreover, some states permit a corporation with 50 or fewer shareholders to dispense with directors.

4.   Most publicly held corporations have **inside directors**, who are officers of the corporation and full-time employees, and **outside directors**, who may be unaffiliated except as shareholders.

5.   **Election and Removal of Directors.** One of the most important functions of the shareholders is to elect the board of directors.

    a.   A director usually serves a 1-year term, although the articles or bylaws may provide a longer term.

    b.   Typically, if a director dies or resigns, the board can elect a replacement.

    c.   Power authorizing the board to increase its size without shareholder approval can be reserved in the articles of incorporation or the bylaws.

    d.   Under most statutes, if the board has nine or more directors, either the articles of incorporation or the bylaws may provide for staggering their terms to allow for continuity of membership.

    e.   Normally, each shareholder has one vote per share, and directors are elected by a plurality.

    f.   In certain states, shareholders have the right of **cumulative voting** (see page 327).

    g.   In most states, shareholders may by a majority vote remove, with or without cause, any director or the entire board of directors.

    h.   Many state statutes specifically permit the board to remove a director for cause, such as adjudication of insanity or conviction of a felony.

6.   **Authority of Directors.** The board of directors determines overall corporate policy.

    a.   The board establishes and implements overall corporate policy through

        1)   Financial decisions, e.g., declaration of dividends
        2)   Authorization of major policy decisions, e.g., determination of new product lines
        3)   Selection and removal of officers and setting their compensation

    b.   The board may usually enact, amend, or repeal bylaws.

    c.   The directors are not agents of the corporation because they cannot act individually to bind the corporation. They may bind the corporation only when acting as a board.

    d.   Directors are fiduciaries who must perform their duties in good faith, with due care, and in the best interests of the corporation.

7. **Compensation of Directors**. Directors may fix their compensation unless the articles or bylaws provide otherwise.

8. **Actions by the Board of Directors**

   a. The traditional rule permits the board to act only at a formal meeting. However, statutes now usually permit action by simultaneous telephone conference call, by video conference, or without a meeting if unanimous written consent is obtained. The board need not meet at the corporate offices, in the state of incorporation, or even in the U.S.

   b. Formal meetings are held at fixed intervals established in the bylaws.

   c. Special meetings can be held after proper notice has been given to all directors.

      1) A director's attendance at any meeting is a waiver of such notice, unless the director attends for the express purpose of objecting to the transaction on the ground that the meeting is not lawfully convened.

   d. Actions taken by a board are expressed in formal resolutions adopted by a majority of the board during a meeting at which a quorum is present.

      1) A director is not allowed to vote by proxy. The director must attend the meeting in person to be counted for purposes of attaining a quorum.

      2) If a director wishes to dissent from an action of the board, the normal rule is that the dissent must be officially entered in the minutes.

   e. The board may form committees composed of its members or corporate officers, such as a compensation committee, audit committee, or finance committee.

      1) A committee usually consists of board members who have specific skills or extensive experience in a given area.

      2) The committees present proposals and reports to the board. The board may even delegate authority to act on its behalf to committees.

         a) The committees can exercise powers of the board consistent with the limits of the resolutions by which they were established, but they may not initiate extraordinary transactions.

         b) New York Stock Exchange rules require every listed corporation to have an audit committee consisting of outside directors to review audit reports and the internal controls of the company.

   f. Directors have the right to inspect corporate books and records.

9. **The Duty of Care**. Directors have a fiduciary responsibility. They owe a very high degree of care to the corporation and the shareholders. Thus, they must be diligent and careful in managing the corporation's business, and they should reasonably supervise those to whom they delegate authority.

   a. A director shall discharge his/her duties in good faith, with the care an ordinarily prudent person in a similar position would exercise under similar circumstances, and in a manner believed to be in the best interests of the corporation.

   b. In exercising reasonable care, a director may rely on information, reports, opinions, and statements prepared or presented by officers or employees who the director reasonably believes are competent.

      1) A director may also rely on the specialized knowledge of lawyers, accountants, investment bankers, board committees, etc.

    c.   A director has not exercised the required care if (s)he does not attend meetings, fails to analyze corporate financial statements or review legal opinions pertinent to corporate activities, and does not become conversant with the available information relevant to his/her duties.

    d.   Directors may be personally liable for failure to be informed of matters internal to, or external but relevant to, the corporation. The test used to measure a director's conduct in corporate affairs is an objective test.

10. Directors owe a **duty of loyalty** to the corporation.

    a.   A director must fully disclose any financial interest (s)he may have in any transaction to which both the director and the corporation may be a party.

    b.   However, a transaction is not voidable merely on the grounds of a director's conflict of interest if it is fair to the corporation, has been approved by a majority of informed and disinterested directors, or has been approved by a majority of shares held by informed, disinterested shareholders.

    c.   A contract between a director and the corporation that does not meet these criteria may be rescinded by the corporation.

        1)   Alternatively, the contract may be upheld, and the director may be required to pay damages to the corporation.

        2)   A transaction is fair if reasonable persons in an arm's-length transaction would have bound the corporation to the bargain.

        3)   Unanimous approval of an unfair transaction by disinterested informed shareholders may release an interested director from liability.

    d.   Directors may not usurp corporate business opportunities.

        1)   The corporation has the right of first refusal to act upon any corporate business opportunity that may come to the director's attention if the corporation has a right, a property interest, or an expectancy incidental to its business.

        2)   A corporate opportunity does not exist if action would be beyond the authority of the corporation, it is unable to take advantage of the opportunity, or the opportunity is rejected by a majority vote of disinterested directors.

11. The **business judgment rule** protects directors from liability related to decisions that were less than optimal if they acted in good faith; were not motivated by fraud, conflict of interest, or illegality; and were not guilty of gross negligence in reaching the decisions.

    a.   This rule recognizes that directors cannot guarantee satisfactory results because many factors are beyond their control. When the board complies with the business judgment rule, its action is conclusive.

        1)   The business judgment rule precludes the courts from substituting their business judgment for that of officers or directors, who are presumed best able to make difficult decisions involving the corporation.

        2)   The rule protects and encourages directors who make difficult decisions.

        3)   Courts are reluctant to ignore the business judgment rule. However, an increasing number of suits are being filed alleging that directors have failed to exercise requisite care and that the business judgment rule was not satisfied.

        a)   Some recent decisions concern opposition to tender offers, i.e., offers to shareholders by a third party to buy stock at a favorable price.

           i)   Directors may be liable if they oppose a tender offer before they have carefully studied it or in an effort to preserve their jobs.

    4)   Most states permit corporations to indemnify directors for expenses associated with litigation pursuant to questions of business judgment.

12.   Stop and review! You have completed the outline for this subunit. Study multiple-choice questions 13 through 19 beginning on page 353.

D.   Rating Agencies. A firm must pay to have its debt rated. Standard & Poor's and Moody's are the most frequently used agencies.

1.   Ratings are based upon the probability of default and the protection for investors in case of default.

2.   The ratings are determined from corporate information such as financial statements.

    a.   Important factors involved in the analysis include the ability of the issuer to service its debt with its cash flows, the amount of debt it has already issued, the type of debt issued, and the firm's cash flow stability.

    b.   A rating may change because the rating agencies periodically review outstanding securities. A decrease in the rating may increase the firm's cost of capital or reduce its ability to borrow long-term. One reason is that many institutional investors are not allowed to purchase lower-grade securities.

    c.   A rating agency review of existing securities may be triggered by a variety of factors, e.g., a new issue of debt, an intended merger involving an exchange of bonds for stock, or material changes in the economic circumstances of the firm.

3.   The ratings are significant because higher ratings lower interest costs to issuing firms. Lower ratings incur higher required rates of return.

    a.   The lower the risk of default, the lower the interest rate the market will demand.

4.   Standard & Poor's rates bonds from very high quality to very poor quality.

    a.   AAA and AA are the highest, signifying little chance of default and high quality.

    b.   A- and BBB-rated bonds are of **investment grade**. They have strong interest- and principal-paying capabilities. Bonds with these ratings are the lowest-rated securities that many institutional investors are permitted to hold.

    c.   Debt rated BB and below is speculative; such bonds are junk bonds.

        1)   Junk bonds are high-yield or low-grade bonds.

        2)   These high-risk bonds have received much attention in the last decade because of their use in corporate mergers and restructurings and the increase in junk-bond defaults.

    d.   CCC to D are very poor debt ratings. The likelihood of default is significant, or the debt is already in default (D rating).

    e.   Standard & Poor's adjusts its ratings with the use of a plus-minus system. A plus indicates a stronger rating in a category and a minus a weaker rating.

5.   Moody's rates bonds in a similar manner. Its ratings vary from Aaa for very high quality debt to D for very poor debt.

6.   Stop and review! You have completed the outline for this subunit. Study multiple-choice questions 20 and 21 on page 355.

E.   Effect of Governmental Regulation of Business

1.   **Federal Statutes (Legislation).** In the Commerce Clause of Article 1, the Constitution grants Congress the power to regulate business activity.

   a.   The Commerce Clause has been interpreted broadly to empower Congress to enact laws affecting any business activity that has a substantial effect, either positive or negative, on interstate commerce.

      1)   Federal regulation is permissible even if the object of the regulation never enters the stream of interstate commerce. Congress may regulate any activity that has a mere possibility of affecting interstate commerce.

   b.   A federal statute must be passed by a majority vote of both the House of Representatives and the Senate, and then be signed by the President.

      1)   If the President does not sign, a statute can still be passed by a two-thirds vote of the House and Senate.

   c.   A statute is required for an agency or a commission to be created.

2.   **Agencies and Commissions.** An administrative agency is any public officer, bureau, authority, board, or commission that has the power to make rules and render decisions.

   a.   An agency or commission may regulate a specific industry or one area affecting all industries.

      1)   EXAMPLE (specific industries): The Federal Communications Commission (FCC) regulates use of the airwaves by broadcasters, the Federal Aviation Administration (FAA) regulates the field of aviation, and the Interstate Commerce Commission (ICC) regulates other interstate carriers.

      2)   EXAMPLE (all industries): The Occupational Safety and Health Administration (OSHA) regulates labor safety, and the Federal Trade Commission (FTC) regulates unfair business practices and competition.

   b.   Agencies and commissions may have the functions of investigation, enforcement, rule making, and adjudication, but they do not have the power to impose criminal sanctions.

   c.   They must act within the authority granted by the enabling statutes.

3.   **Administrative Agency Rules and Regulations**

   a.   An agency may only promulgate rules and regulations that do not go beyond the scope of the delegated authority of its enabling statutes.

   b.   They may be promulgated under a general grant of authority to an agency to regulate an industry. For example, the Federal Energy Regulatory Commission (FERC) makes rules for rate setting under its authority to regulate public utilities.

   c.   They may be promulgated under a specific grant of authority to an agency to make detailed rules carrying out objectives of a statute. For example, the Internal Revenue Service (IRS) makes rules to carry out specific statutes, but it is not given the general authority to make rules for the collection of revenue.

4.   **Courts** interpret statutes, regulations, and the actions of agencies when a dispute develops and one or both parties wish a judicial determination.

5.   Some rules and regulations, agencies, and legislation have **sunset provisions** that require periodic review and reenactment or they terminate.

6.   Regulation may be economic or social.

    a.   Economic regulation usually concerns price and service to the public and is ordinarily industry specific.

    b.   Social regulation has broader objectives and more pervasive effects. It addresses quality of life issues that are difficult for market forces to remedy, such as workplace and product safety, pollution, and fair employment practices, and it applies to most industries. Social regulation has been criticized on the grounds that it is costly, contributes to overregulation, may inhibit innovation, increases inflation, and may place a disproportionate burden on small companies, thereby having an anticompetitive effect. Another criticism is that regulators are perceived to have little concern for the relation of marginal benefits and costs.

7.   **Securities Law**. The primary purpose of federal securities regulation is to prevent fraudulent practices during the issuance and trading of securities.

    a.   The purpose of the **Securities Act of 1933** is to provide complete and fair **disclosure** to potential investors.

        1)   The act applies only to initial issuance of securities.

        2)   The *Howey* test defines a security as evidence of a debt or property interest arising in a transaction in which a person invests in a common enterprise reasonably expecting profits derived from others' efforts.

        3)   Disclosure is accomplished through an integrated system based on filing a registration statement with the Securities and Exchange Commission (SEC).

            a)   Potential investors must receive a prospectus, the contents of which are highly regulated. It is first filed with the SEC as part of the registration.

        4)   Certain securities and transactions are exempt. For example,

            a)   A private placement may be offered only to knowledgeable and sophisticated investors and to no more than 35 purchasers.

            b)   Intrastate issues may be offered and sold only to persons within one state.

            c)   A Regulation A offering of up to $5,000,000 of securities in a 12-month period is subject to less detailed and costly requirements.

    b.   The **Securities Exchange Act of 1934** is intended to regulate trading of securities after initial issuance, provide adequate information to investors, and prevent insiders from unfairly using nonpublic information.

        1)   Securities exchanges, brokers and dealers, securities traded on exchanges, and high-volume securities traded over the counter must be registered.

        2)   Issuers must file frequent reports.

        3)   Insiders (officers, directors, and 10%-or-more shareholders) must turn over to the corporation any profits earned on purchases and sales that fall within 6 months of each other. They are also prohibited from buying or selling stock based on inside information not available to the public.

            a)   Insider trading is buying or selling securities of an entity by individuals with access to nonpublic material information, and these individuals have a fiduciary obligation to shareholders or potential shareholders.

b) Penalties include up to triple profits gains or losses avoided with bounty payments of up to 10% of triple penalties to informants.

4) Antifraud provisions make it unlawful to use any manipulative or deceptive practices in the purchase or sale of securities.

a) It is unlawful to make a false statement of a material fact or to omit a material fact that is necessary for a statement not to be misleading.

5) The SEC was created to enforce securities laws and regulate the issuance and trading of securities.

6) The **Foreign Corrupt Practices Act (FCPA)** amended the Securities Exchange Act of 1934. The FCPA is designed to prevent secret payments of corporate funds for purposes that Congress has determined to be contrary to public policy (bribes to foreign officials, foreign political parties, or foreign public office candidates).

a) A domestic concern, including any person acting on its behalf, whether or not doing business overseas and whether or not registered with the SEC, may not offer or authorize corrupt payments to any foreign official, foreign political party or official thereof, or a candidate for political office in a foreign country for the purpose of obtaining or retaining business.

b) The FCPA imposes record keeping and internal control requirements on firms subject to the Securities Exchange Act.

c. **Blue-sky laws** are state laws designed to prevent fraudulent or misleading security issues.

8. **Employment Regulation**

a. The **Norris-LaGuardia Act of 1932** removed the power of federal courts to issue injunctions against unions without a showing of fraud or violence. This act made it illegal for employers to prohibit employees from joining a union.

b. The **National Labor Relations Act (NLRA) of 1935** (the Wagner Act) granted employees the right to associate with, join, or form labor unions; bargain collectively with employers; and engage in concerted activities for collective bargaining (in effect, exempting unions from antitrust laws).

1) Employers are required to bargain in good faith with unions.

2) The **National Labor Relations Board (NLRB)** administers the act. It oversees elections to certify or decertify unions and investigates unfair labor practices.

c. The **Labor-Management Relations Act (Taft-Hartley Act) of 1947** placed restraints on unions that resulted in a more even balance of power between labor and management.

1) Unions are required to bargain in good faith.

2) The Federal Mediation and Conciliation Service was created to assist in mediation of disputes.

3) The President was given authority to seek an injunction against a lockout or strike for 80 days (**cooling-off period**) in a national emergency.

4)   The **closed shop** was outlawed.

    a)   A closed shop required union membership as a condition of employment.

    b)   The **union shop** is still allowed in many states. In a union shop, an employee must join the union upon or after employment. However, individual states may enact right-to-work laws that allow employees to work at any job without union membership.

d.   The **Fair Labor Standards Act (Wage and Hour Law) of 1938** provides for minimum wages and overtime and regulated child labor.

    1)   The **Equal Pay Act of 1963** prohibits sex discrimination regarding compensation. Its scope is greater than that of the FLSA because it reaches state and local governmental employees and executive, administrative, and professional personnel.

e.   The **Labor Management Reporting and Disclosure Act (Landrum-Griffin Act) of 1959** was intended to promote democracy in unions and to require reporting and disclosure by unions and union officials.

    1)   It established a bill of rights for union members and required union officials to abide by financial reporting and disclosure requirements.

f.   Title VII of the **Civil Rights Act of 1964** prohibits discrimination in employment on the basis of race, color, religion, sex, or national origin. However, employers do have the right to use nondiscriminatory selection procedures in hiring, e.g., preemployment tests directly related to job requirements.

    1)   The **Equal Employment Opportunity Commission (EEOC)** enforces Title VII. It issues binding regulations and may initiate its own investigations, but most EEOC actions result from complaints filed by individuals. The EEOC has set goals and timetables for employers to bring female and minority workforces up to the appropriate percentages as they relate to the available labor pool. The means of achieving these goals, such as affirmative action programs, are often highly controversial.

        a)   Illegal discrimination occurs when a plaintiff is a victim of disparate treatment, when an employer has engaged in a pervasive pattern or practice of discrimination, when the employer's adoption of a neutral rule not necessary to the business has an adverse impact on a protected class, and when the adoption of a neutral rule perpetuates past discrimination.

            i)   Some violations must be proved, at least in part, by statistical evidence.

            ii)   An affirmative action order provides preferences to members of the class that previously suffered from discrimination. Affirmative action is sometimes criticized because employment preferences are often viewed as reverse discrimination. Moreover, it may not result in the hiring, retention, and promotion of the most productive workers.

g.   The **Age Discrimination in Employment Act of 1967** protects individuals at least 40 years of age from arbitrary age discrimination. Job applicants and employees are to be evaluated on the basis of ability, not age.

h. The **Occupational Safety and Health Act of 1970** created the **Occupational Safety and Health Administration (OSHA)** to protect the health and safety of all workers by developing safety standards, preventing injuries, and promoting job safety.

    1) All businesses that affect interstate commerce must adhere to OSHA regulations unless specifically exempted (governmental entities and businesses regulated under other statutes are exempt).

    2) Entities subject to the act must provide a workplace free of known hazards. OSHA encourages labor-management committees to formulate safety and health programs.

    3) OSHA may inspect workplaces, but employers may insist that it obtain a search warrant. OSHA may impose civil penalties and seek injunctions, and intentional violations may result in criminal sanctions.

i. **Employee Retirement Income Security Act (ERISA) of 1974**

    1) ERISA prohibits discrimination in favor of highly paid and key employees, provides uniform rules for eligibility and vesting, and requires extensive reporting to and approval by the IRS.

    2) Under provisions of ERISA, an employer must fully fund the annual cost of any retirement program.

    3) Employers are not required to offer pension programs, but if such a program is offered, it is fully regulated by ERISA.

j. The **Americans with Disabilities Act (ADA) of 1991** bans employment discrimination against people with disabilities, provides tax incentives for compliance costs, and addresses access rights regarding public lodging, restaurants, transportation, telecommunications, and retail stores.

    1) Organizations with 25 or more employees must make reasonable accommodations for qualified workers and job applicants with disabilities.

    2) Employers are prohibited from inquiring into a job applicant's disability with questions concerning medical history, prior workers' compensation or health insurance claims, work absenteeism due to illness, past treatment for alcoholism, drug abuse, or mental illness.

k. The **Family and Medical Leave Act (FMLA) of 1993**, which mandates unpaid leave for child care and other family and personal needs, applies to companies with 50 or more employees. Eligible employees must have worked for the employer for an average of 25 hours a week for one year.

    1) Either parent may receive up to 12 weeks of unpaid leave after the birth or adoption of a child. Leave may also be taken to care for a sick spouse, child, or parent, or when an employee is too sick to work.

    2) Employers must provide health benefits during the leave period and give returning workers the same or an equivalent job in terms of pay, responsibilities, and other working conditions.

9.   **Antitrust**

   a.   Competition controls private economic power, increases output, and lowers prices. It promotes

      1)   Efficient allocation of resources (resulting in lower prices)
      2)   Greater choice by consumers
      3)   Greater business opportunities
      4)   Fairness in economic behavior
      5)   Avoidance of concentrated political power resulting from economic power

   b.   Section 1 of the **Sherman Act of 1890** makes illegal every contract, combination, or conspiracy in restraint of trade in interstate or foreign commerce.

      1)   To avoid a literal application of this broad prohibition, the Supreme Court adopted the **rule of reason**, under which only unreasonable restraints are illegal. For example, a covenant not to compete is enforceable as long as it is for a reasonable time and a reasonable area.

      2)   The Supreme Court has also ruled that some restraints are ***per se* violations**. These include price fixing (agreement by sellers to a maximum or minimum price), division of markets by competitors, group boycotts (agreeing not to deal with another), and resale price maintenance (limiting a buyer's resale price).

         a)   Price fixing is the most prosecuted violation under the Sherman Act.

      3)   Section 2 of the Sherman Act prohibits the acts of monopolizing, conspiring to monopolize, and attempting to monopolize.

   c.   The **Clayton Act of 1914**, as amended, prohibits the acquisition of stock or assets of another corporation if the effect may be to lessen competition substantially or tend to create a monopoly in any line of commerce in any part of the country.

      1)   The act also prohibits the following if they lessen competition substantially or tend to create a monopoly:

         a)   Tying or tie-in sales (sales in which a buyer must take other products to buy the first product)

            i)   However, tie-ins are acceptable if they are needed to maintain the goodwill of the tying product, if they facilitate entry into a new market, or if the tying product is of little importance in the market and the buyer is not forced to accept the tied product.

         b)   Exclusive dealing (a requirement by the seller that a buyer not deal with the seller's competitors)

         c)   Price discrimination

            i)   The **Robinson Patman Act of 1936** amended the Clayton Act to strengthen its prohibition against price discrimination in interstate commerce. Sellers may not grant, and buyers may not induce, unfair discounts and other preferences. However, price discrimination may be justified by cost savings or the need to meet competition.

      2)   Interlocking directorates are also prohibited if one company has capital of greater than $1,000,000 and if antitrust law would be violated if the companies ceased to be competitors.

d. The **Federal Trade Commission Act of 1914** prohibits unfair methods of competition and unfair or deceptive acts in commerce, including false or misleading advertisement. It created the Federal Trade Commission (FTC) to enforce this legislation and to determine what constitutes unfair competition or deceptive acts.

   1) The FTC's functions are to investigate possible antitrust violations and to protect consumers.

   2) The FTC also has broad authority to enforce the other antitrust laws in conjunction with the antitrust division of the U.S. Justice Department.

e. Antitrust regulation does not apply to

   1) Intrastate commerce

   2) Labor unions unless a union primarily intends to restrain trade or conspires with nonlabor groups to monopolize

   3) Regulated utilities

   4) Reasonable noncompetition clauses between buyers and sellers of businesses, partners in a partnership, or purchasers of technology or equipment

   5) Patents and copyrights

   6) Agricultural and fishing organizations

   7) Financial institutions

   8) Transport industries

   9) Major league baseball

   10) Companies qualifying for certificates of antitrust immunity issued by the Commerce Department (after concurrence by the Justice Department) under the Export Trading Company Act

10. **Consumer Protection**

a. The **Pure Food and Drug Act of 1906**, as amended by the **Food, Drug, and Cosmetic Act of 1938** and much other legislation, is administered by the Food and Drug Administration (FDA).

   1) The FDA helps to maintain the safety of drugs, food, cosmetics, etc.

   2) The FDA also oversees the requirements of the Federal Hazardous Substances Labeling Act of 1960.

   3) New drugs and food additives must be thoroughly tested before they are marketed. The premarket review is based upon research supplied by the drug companies.

      a) The FDA can extend patent lives of pharmaceutical products to allow for time lost during the premarket FDA review.

b. The **Fair Packaging and Labeling Act of 1967** prohibits deceptive packaging and labeling.

c. The **Fair Credit Reporting Act of 1970** gives consumers the right to obtain the information reported by credit bureaus.

d. The **Consumer Product Safety Act of 1972** is intended to protect the public from unreasonable risk of injury from consumer products. It emphasizes safety standards for new products. The Consumer Product Safety Commission enforces this and other product safety legislation. The CPSC promotes voluntary safety standards, develops and enforces mandatory standards, prohibits unsafe products if safety standards will not be sufficient, recalls hazardous products, furnishes information to consumers, and works with state and local governments which have product liability laws to provide consumer remedies.

e.   The **Equal Credit Opportunity Act of 1974** prohibits discrimination in providing credit.

f.   The **Fair Credit Billing Act of 1975** provides consumers with rights in contesting billing errors, prohibits mailing of unsolicited credit cards, and limits a consumer's liability for unauthorized use of lost or stolen credit cards.

g.   The **Magnuson-Moss Warranty Act of 1975** regulates written warranties on consumer products. It requires disclosures about written warranties and places limitations on disclaimers of written and implied warranties.

h.   The **Fair Debt Collection Practices Act of 1977** prohibits certain abuses of consumers' rights by collection agencies.

i.   The **Truth-in-Lending Act of 1982** requires disclosure of the terms and conditions of consumer credit. For a closed-end credit transaction, e.g., the typical car loan, the total finance charge, annual percentage interest rate, amount financed, late charges, security interest held by the creditor, the number and amounts of payments, due dates, and the total amount of payments must be disclosed. Open-end credit transactions, such as those involving credit cards, also have specific, detailed disclosure requirements.

11. **Environmental Protection**

a.   The **Environmental Protection Agency (EPA)** was created in 1970 to centralize the environmental control functions of the federal government.

b.   The **National Environmental Policy Act of 1970** declares a national environmental policy and promotes consideration of environmental issues by federal agencies. Thus, it requires federal agencies to consider the adverse environmental effects of their actions, proposals, legislation, and regulations.

c.   The **Clean Air Act of 1970**, as amended in 1977 and expanded in 1990, establishes air quality standards for listed pollutants. It divides the country into air quality control regions and determines emission standards for stationary and mobile sources of pollution.

d.   The **Clean Water Act of 1977**, which was revised in 1990, seeks to restore and maintain the physical and biological purity of the waters of the U.S. It establishes national water quality standards and effluent (pollution) standards for each industry. It also provides for a discharge permit program and grants and loans for publicly owned treatment plants. The act has additional provisions related to oil spills and toxic chemicals.

e.   The **Resource Conservation and Recovery Act of 1976** was designed to control hazardous waste from its inception to its disposal. The act imposes management requirements on generators, transporters, and owners of hazardous waste and on operators of treatment, storage, and disposal facilities.

f.   The **Comprehensive Environmental Response, Compensation and Liability Act (CERCLA) of 1980**, also known as the **Superfund**, provides funds for cleanup of pollution caused by past hazardous waste activities.

12. Stop and review! You have completed the outline for this subunit. Study multiple-choice questions 22 through 46 beginning on page 356.

F.   Federal Reserve Board. The Federal Reserve Board (the Fed) controls the money supply independently of the federal government. Any policy designed by the Fed to affect the money supply, and thus the economy, is known as monetary policy. Control of the growth of the money supply by the Fed is viewed as essential to control the availability of credit, spending, and inflation. One reason is that the economic health of the nation requires the money supply to grow at the same rate as the economy.

1.   The Board of Governors of the Fed has seven members appointed by the President and confirmed by the Senate for staggered 14-year terms. Their responsibilities include administering the banking system as well as determining the money supply.

   a.   The Federal Open Market Committee consists of the seven Governors and five of the presidents of the 12 Federal Reserve Banks. The FOMC determines policy regarding market transactions in government bonds.

   b.   The Federal Advisory Council consists of 12 commercial bankers who meet with the Board of Governors to give their opinions on banking policy.

2.   The functions of the Federal Reserve include

   a.   Control of the money supply
   b.   Check collection
   c.   Serving as the fiscal agent of the U.S. government
   d.   Supervision of the entire banking system
   e.   Holding deposits (reserves) for member institutions

      1)   As a result, a federal funds market has developed for the lending of member banks' reserves to other members. Thus, if one bank has excess reserves, it can earn additional interest by lending to another member bank that needs additional reserves.

         a)   Federal funds loans are usually made for 1 day at a time, and the federal funds rate is the rate paid on these overnight loans.

3.   The Fed controls the money supply by using monetary policy tools.

   a.   **Open-market operations**. Purchase and sale of government securities is the primary mechanism of monetary control.

      1)   Fed purchases are expansionary; they increase bank reserves and the money supply. Fed sales are contractional. Paying money into the Federal Reserve takes the money out of circulation, reduces bank reserves, and contracts the money supply.

   b.   **Reserves**. The legal reserve requirement is the percentage of deposits that must be kept on hand.

      1)   Lowering the percentage is expansionary (allowing banks to put more of their excess reserves into circulation through loans). Raising the percentage has the opposite effect.

      2)   This tool is not often used because of its powerful effects.

c. **Changing the discount rate**. This rate is the interest rate at which member banks may borrow from the Fed. Lowering the rate encourages borrowing and increases the money supply, whereas raising the rate discourages borrowing, increases saving, and decreases the money supply.

4. The Fed cannot stabilize interest rates and at the same time control growth in reserves and the money supply because of the inverse relationship between (1) interest rates and bank reserves and (2) interest rates and the money supply. Thus, the Fed has adopted the pragmatic policy of alternately targeting interest rates and the money supply.

   a. EXAMPLE: If the reserve requirement increases and banks have lower free reserves to lend, they will not be able to supply all borrowers who want loans. Interest rates will rise to equalize the supply and demand for loans.

5. Stop and review! You have completed the outline for this subunit. Study multiple-choice questions 47 and 48 on page 364.

G. International Tax Considerations

1. Multinational corporations frequently derive income from several countries. The government of each country in which a corporation does business may enact statutes imposing one or more types of tax on the corporation.

2. **Treaties**. To avoid double taxation, two or more countries may adopt treaties to coordinate or synchronize the effects of their taxing statutes.

   a. Treaties are also used to integrate other governmental goals, e.g., providing incentive for desired investment.

   b. If a U.S. statute and a treaty to which the U.S. is a party conflict, the one enacted or adopted last controls.

   c. A treaty might modify the rules in a country's statutes that designate to which country income is sourced or of which country a firm is a resident.

3. **Multinational Corporations**

   a. Most countries tax only the income sourced to that country.

   b. The U.S. taxes worldwide income (from whatever source derived) of a domestic corporation.

      1) Double taxation is avoided by allowing a credit for income tax paid to foreign countries or by treaty provisions.

   c. In the case of foreign corporations, the U.S. taxes only income sourced to the U.S. Ordinarily, such income is effectively connected with engaging in a trade or business of the U.S. Certain U.S. source income, e.g., gain on the sale of most stock, is not taxed by the U.S.

4. Stop and review! You have completed the outline for this subunit. Study multiple-choice question 49 on page 365.

H.   International Business and Law

1.   **International business law** is a body of law recognized by otherwise independent nations. No sovereign nation is compelled to obey external law. But nations can and do voluntarily agree to be governed by international law to facilitate commerce. Such law governs the actions of individuals and business associations, e.g., corporations, partnerships, and joint ventures.

    a.   **Sources of international law.** International law is drawn from a variety of sources. No single body of law binds all nations, and no system of courts renders decisions binding across all national boundaries. Nevertheless international law does exist.

        1)   Customs between nations develop over time, based on their business and political dealings.

        2)   Treaties are formalized agreements between or among independent nations.

            a)   Conventions are a functional equivalent of treaties. They are agreements signed by two or more countries and sponsored by international organizations.

        3)   Judicial precedent, set by a series of decisions, can be used as guidelines.

        4)   Scholarly writings have contributed greatly to the body of international law.

        5)   International political organizations contribute significantly. An example is the judicial branch of the United Nations known as the International Court of Justice or World Court.

            a)   **The UN Commission on International Trade Law** was formed to develop standard commercial practices and agreements.

            b)   **The UN Conference on Trade and Development** deals with international trade reform and redistribution of income through trade.

        6)   International trade communities are groups of nations that adopt common trade policies and rules. Their purpose is to reduce trade barriers among members and to achieve a measure of regional economic integration.

            a)   The best known and most powerful international trade community is the European Union.

        7)   International trade agreements provide regulatory authority for businesses in international trade. Until recently, the broadest and most important of these agreements was the General Agreement on Tariffs and Trade (GATT). Under GATT, the signatory countries agreed to equal treatment of all member nations, multilateral negotiations to reduce tariffs, and the abolition of import quotas.

            a)   However, GATT has now been replaced by the **World Trade Organization (WTO)**. The WTO, which was established on January 1, 1995, is the product of the Uruguay Round of international trade negotiations. It is a permanent body with a secretariat based in Geneva, Switzerland.

                i)   The WTO Agreement is a permanent set of commitments designed to prohibit trade discrimination among member nations and between imported and domestic products.

ii) The WTO Agreement applies to trade in services and intellectual property as well as goods.

iii) The WTO provides for a multilateral dispute settlement apparatus. If bilateral consultations and mediation efforts fail, a panel is established to examine the case and make recommendations. Ultimately, if a violation is found, trade retaliation by the complainant against an offending country may be approved if that country does not comply with the recommendations.

b) The **North American Free Trade Agreement (NAFTA)** essentially provides for free trade among the U.S., Canada, and Mexico. The pact creates the world's largest free trade zone.

i) The consensus is that Mexico will benefit the most because many U.S. firms are likely to transfer assembly operations to Mexican subsidiaries with lower labor costs.

- To a great extent, NAFTA will correct the gross disparities between the open markets of the U.S. and the relatively closed markets of Mexico.

- U.S. companies should be able to sell more goods to Mexico because Mexicans will have greater disposable income as new industries relocate there.

ii) The greatest concern in the U.S. is that NAFTA will cause the loss of U.S. jobs to Mexico because of its lower labor costs and weaker environmental standards. Supporters of NAFTA believe that the pact will create more jobs in the U.S. than it eliminates because of the increase in exports.

iii) The financial services industry, such as mutual funds, banks, and brokers, should benefit from the NAFTA because it allows U.S. financial firms, for the first time, to have easy access to Mexican investors. Also, with the opening of Mexico's financial markets, more opportunities for U.S. investors will emerge.

iv) American low-tech industries, such as shoe and apparel manufacturers, may be hurt by increased competition from cheaper Mexican products. U.S. citrus and vegetable farmers also fear increased competition from Mexico.

v) High-tech firms in the U.S. may benefit because they face few Mexican competitors.

c) NAFTA ended tariffs on about half of the more than 9,000 products covered by the agreement. Tariffs on another 15% of the goods will end after 5 years, and the rest of the products will be duty-free after 15 years.

i) One of the biggest controversies during the negotiation process concerned the products to be protected with the longest tariff phaseouts. The U.S. won long phaseouts for such items as athletic shoes, household glassware, asparagus, broccoli, peanuts, and orange juice concentrate.

2. **International Monetary System**. The monetary system that prevailed in the post-World War II period was devised in 1944. It was a system of fixed exchange rates based on a modified gold standard. International reserves in this system included foreign currencies and the right to borrow in specified situations. It was intended to stabilize currency exchange rates. The **International Monetary Fund (IMF)** was created and is still active today.

    a. Resources of the IMF consist of a pool of currency from which participating countries can draw during short-term balance of payments difficulties.

    b. The World Bank was created at the same time as the IMF. Its purpose is to provide credit for development purposes to underdeveloped countries.

    c. In the 1970s, the international community moved to a system of managed floating exchange rates. Thus, the current international monetary system does not tie currency values to gold or any other fixed standard.

    d. **Eurodollars** are U.S. dollars held at banks outside of the U.S., either foreign banks or branches of U.S. banks. Eurodollars facilitate the exchange of goods between other nations (often the exchanges use dollars even if the U.S. is not involved in the transaction).

3. **Multinational Corporations**. The host country for a multinational operation reaps the advantages of the investment of capital, technology, and management abilities. Output and efficiency often improve along with exports and the balance of payments. The presence of a multinational corporation may stimulate competition, increase tax revenues, and produce a higher standard of living.

    a. But payment of royalties, dividends, and profits can result in a net capital outflow. Multinational corporations sometimes establish economically unreasonable transfer prices among subsidiaries so that profits will be earned where taxes are lowest or restrictions on the export of profits are least stringent. Moreover, multinational corporations may engage in anticompetitive activities, such as formation of cartels.

4. **International Trade Restrictions**. Even though individuals (as a whole) benefit from free trade, governments often establish policies designed to block the importation of certain products. Governmental devices used to control trade are discussed below and on the next page.

    a. Tariffs are consumption taxes designed to restrict imports, e.g., a tax on German beer. They raise prices and lower consumption of imports.

    b. Import quotas set fixed limits on different products, e.g., French wine.

        1) In the short run, import quotas help a country's balance of payments, and domestic employment will increase, but the prices of the products produced will also increase.

    c. Export subsidies are payments by the government to producers in certain industries in an attempt to increase exports.

        1) Special tax benefits to exporters are an indirect form of export subsidy. The best U.S. examples are Foreign Sales Corporations (FSCs). They are entities that must be located in U.S. possessions or in countries with tax information exchange agreements with the U.S. FSCs receive an exemption of about 15% of qualified export income.

d. Domestic content rules require that at least a portion of any imported product be constructed from parts manufactured in the importing nation.

1) This rule is sometimes used by capital-intensive nations. Parts can be produced using idle capacity available on machinery and then be sent to a labor-intensive country for final assembly.

e. Certain exports may require licenses. For example, sales of technology with military applications are limited by western nations that are members of the Coordinating Committee for Multilateral Export Controls. The related U.S. legislation is the Export Administration Act of 1979.

f. The Export Trading Company Act of 1982 permits competitors to form export trading companies without regard to U.S. antitrust legislation.

g. The economic effect of restrictions on free trade is to shift workers from relatively efficient export industries into less efficient protected industries. Real wage rates will decline as a result, as will total world output.

h. A major reason for trade restrictions is that the costs of competition are direct and concentrated (people lose jobs and firms go out of business), but benefits of unrestricted trade are less noticeable and occur in the future (lower prices, higher wages, more jobs in export industries).

5. Stop and review! You have completed the outline for this subunit. Study multiple-choice questions 50 through 54 beginning on page 365.

MULTIPLE-CHOICE QUESTIONS

A. Shareholder Participation and Meetings

1. Which of the following is the most accurate listing of the sources of shareholder rights?

A. The articles of incorporation, state and federal statutes, and the common law.

B. The articles of incorporation and statutory law only.

C. State and federal statutes and the common law only.

D. The articles of incorporation and state law only.

The correct answer is (A). *(Publisher)*

REQUIRED: The most accurate list of the sources of shareholder rights and duties.

DISCUSSION: Corporations are formed under authority of state statutes. Accordingly, the incorporation statute of a state is one source of shareholder rights. However, some shareholder rights have common law origins, for example, the power to remove directors for cause, the right to inspect corporate records, and the preemptive right. The articles of incorporation may grant specific shareholder rights not detailed in the general language of a statute. Federal law is still another source of shareholder rights, for example, regulation of the issuance and trading of securities.

Answers (B), (C), and (D) are incorrect because the articles of incorporation, state and federal statutes, and the common law are sources of shareholder rights.

2. Which type of voting disallows a freeze-out of minority shareholders?

A. Straight voting.

B. Cumulative voting.

C. Proxy voting.

D. Trustee voting.

The correct answer is (B). *(Publisher)*

REQUIRED: The true statement about minority shareholder voting rights.

DISCUSSION: In straight voting, a majority shareholder has the ability to elect the entire board of directors because each shareholder has a single vote for each share owned for each director to be elected, resulting in a "freeze-out" of minority shareholders. Cumulative voting, on the other hand, enables a shareholder to cast his total number of votes for a director. Thus, minority shareholders can obtain representation on the board of directors.

Answer (A) is incorrect because straight voting allows a freeze-out. Answer (C) is incorrect because proxy voting allows management to gain control of minority shareholder votes. Answer (D) is incorrect because trustee voting refers to transferring voting rights to a trustee to allow a group of owners not to lose control of a corporation.

3. The most accurate statement about managerial control of traditional corporations is that shareholders

A. Are similar to general partners in that they have direct managerial authority.

B. Have no legal power to exercise effective control over management of large corporations.

C. Can exert control over the corporation only by choosing directors.

D. Have little operational control of a corporation.

The correct answer is (D). *(Publisher)*

REQUIRED: The most accurate statement about shareholder control over corporate management.

DISCUSSION: The directors make decisions about policy and certain major transactions but delegate day-to-day operational control to officers and other employees. The directors are chosen by and are accountable to the shareholders, who exert only indirect control over the operations of the corporation. However, in most publicly held companies, management uses the proxy solicitation process to nominate and secure the election of directors favorable to its policies. Hence, management is usually in effective control of the company.

Answer (A) is incorrect because general partners operate the business, but shareholders who are not directors or officers have only an indirect effect on management. Answers (B) and (C) are incorrect because shareholders have the right to exercise indirect control by electing or removing directors; by adoption, amendment, or repeal of bylaws; by amending the corporate charter; or by effecting other fundamental changes.

4. Shareholders representing a majority of the voting shares of Nadier, Inc. have transferred their shares to Thomasina Trusty to hold and vote irrevocably for ten years. Trusty has issued certificates to the shareholders and pays them the dividends received. The agreement

    A. Is an illegal voting trust because it is against public policy.

    B. Is valid if entered into pursuant to a written voting trust agreement.

    C. Need not be filed with the corporation.

    D. May be revoked because it is in essence a proxy.

The correct answer is (B). *(Publisher)*
    REQUIRED: The legal status of a voting trust agreement.
    DISCUSSION: Irrevocable voting trust agreements authorizing a trustee to hold and vote shares for up to 10 years are valid if they are written, filed with the corporation, and available for inspection by shareholders.
    Answer (A) is incorrect because the voting trust is a legal arrangement that has a statutory or case law basis in most states. Answer (C) is incorrect because one of the usual statutory requirements for a valid voting trust is that the agreement be filed with the corporation and be available for inspection. Answer (D) is incorrect because the voting trust differs substantially from a proxy. It is irrevocable for the agreed period.

5. Shareholder voting

    A. Is required to be cumulative in all states.

    B. May usually be accomplished by oral or written proxy.

    C. May usually be by proxy, but the agency thus created is ordinarily limited to a specific issue.

    D. May be by proxy, but a proxy may be revoked if the shareholder signs a later proxy.

The correct answer is (D). *(Publisher)*
    REQUIRED: The true statement about shareholder voting.
    DISCUSSION: A proxy is a written authorization to vote another person's shares. The rule that the last proxy signed by a shareholder revokes prior proxies is a significant issue in proxy battles. A proxy is also revoked when the shareholder actually attends the meeting and votes his/her shares or when (s)he dies.
    Answer (A) is incorrect because cumulative voting is not required in all states. Answer (B) is incorrect because a proxy must usually be written. Answer (C) is incorrect because proxies commonly authorize action regarding all matters presented at the shareholders' meeting.

6. The board of directors of the Garrett Co. wishes to call a special meeting of shareholders to consider a proposed merger.

    A. The directors must give specific notice of the meeting and the issues on the agenda.

    B. The directors are not empowered to call a special meeting.

    C. If notice is not given to shareholders entitled to vote at the record date, action taken will be invalid even if all the shareholders attend and participate in the meeting.

    D. A majority of shareholders entitled to vote must be represented in person at the meeting to constitute a quorum, unless otherwise provided in the articles.

The correct answer is (A). *(Publisher)*
    REQUIRED: The legal requirements for special shareholders' meetings.
    DISCUSSION: Notice is not usually required for regular meetings because the time and place of such meetings are normally specified in the bylaws. The ordinary business of the corporation may be transacted at regular meetings without specific notice being given to shareholders. However, a special meeting requires a timely notice specifying the time, place, and issues on the agenda.
    Answer (B) is incorrect because the directors, holders of a specified percentage of shares, or others may call a special meeting. Answer (C) is incorrect because attendance and participation in the meeting by shareholders who did not receive notice usually constitute a waiver of the right to notice. Answer (D) is incorrect because a majority of the shares entitled to vote must be represented to constitute a quorum, but they may be represented in person or by proxy.

7. Shareholder meetings must be held annually but special meetings may also be convened. If a quorum is present at a meeting, the shareholders may act by voting to approve or disapprove resolutions. Which statement about this process is true?

    A.   Shareholders cannot act without a meeting.

    B.   Notice of meetings must be given and a waiver of the requirement can only be by a signed writing.

    C.   Certain shareholder actions may require more than a simple majority.

    D.   All holders of voting shares at the date of the meeting are entitled to vote.

The correct answer is (C). *(Publisher)*
    REQUIRED: The true statement about shareholder action at meetings.
    DISCUSSION: If a quorum is present (50% of the outstanding shares), resolutions ordinarily may be adopted by a simple majority of the voting shares. To protect minority shareholders, however, the bylaws, articles, or a statute may require more than a simple majority with regard to extraordinary matters.
    Answer (A) is incorrect because most states allow shareholders to act without a meeting if unanimous written consent is given. Answer (B) is incorrect because attendance at the meeting is also an effective waiver. Answer (D) is incorrect because only those owning stock at the record date may vote. The record date is a date prior to the meeting used to determine those eligible to vote.

B. Corporate Bylaws and Charters

8. Corporations are chartered by

    A.   The federal government.

    B.   State governments.

    C.   The Securities and Exchange Commission.

    D.   The board of directors of the respective corporations.

The correct answer is (B). *(CMA 1286 1-23)*
    REQUIRED: The entity that charters corporations.
    DISCUSSION: Corporations do not exist at common law. They are entirely creatures of statutory law. In the U.S., private corporations are chartered by the individual state governments.
    Answers (A) and (C) are incorrect because all private corporations are created under state statutes. No federal incorporation statute exists. Answer (D) is incorrect because a private corporation can only come into being if the state incorporation statute is complied with. The corporation must exist before directors can be elected.

9. The corporate existence is most likely to begin when

    A.   The certificate of incorporation is issued.

    B.   The articles of incorporation are signed by the incorporators.

    C.   Corporate officers are elected at the organizational meeting.

    D.   Corporate directors are elected at the organizational meeting.

The correct answer is (A). *(Publisher)*
    REQUIRED: The time corporate existence begins.
    DISCUSSION: Corporate existence is usually deemed to begin upon the filing of the articles of incorporation or issuance of the certificate of incorporation.
    Answer (B) is incorrect because the date of filing is the earliest corporate existence commences. Answer (C) is incorrect because the corporation should already be in existence at the time of the organizational meeting. Answer (D) is incorrect because the initial directors are usually named in the articles or elected at the organizational meeting after the corporation is formed.

10. The bylaws contain information concerning

    A.   The purpose of the corporation.

    B.   The name and address of the corporation's registered agent for receiving service of process and other notices.

    C.   Procedures for amending bylaws.

    D.   The incorporators.

The correct answer is (C). *(Publisher)*
    REQUIRED: The information contained in the bylaws.
    DISCUSSION: The articles of incorporation must include the corporation's name, the purpose of the corporation, the number of shares of stock the corporation is authorized to issue, the street address of the corporation's principal office, the name and address of the corporation's registered agent for receiving service of process and other notices, the name and address of each incorporator, names and addresses of the initial directors, and the length of the corporation's life. Procedures for amending bylaws are in the bylaws.
    Answers (A), (B), and (D) are incorrect because they are each contained in the articles of incorporation.

11. The bylaws are not required to be adhered to by

- A. Majority shareholders.
- B. Minority shareholders.
- C. Directors.
- D. Managerial employees.

The correct answer is (D). *(Publisher)*

REQUIRED: The correct statement about corporate bylaws.

DISCUSSION: The shareholders, directors, and officers are bound by the bylaws. Employees can be bound by the bylaws only if they have reason to be knowledgeable of them.

Answers (A), (B), and (C) are incorrect because majority shareholders, minority shareholders, and directors are bound by the bylaws.

12. Which of the following statements about amending the articles of incorporation is true?

- A. Once filed, the articles of incorporation may not be amended.
- B. Amendments to the articles of incorporation are filed with the SEC.
- C. Shareholder action is not necessary in order to adopt certain amendments.
- D. The amended articles contain all provisions that may have been included in the original articles of incorporation.

The correct answer is (C). *(Publisher)*

REQUIRED: The true statement about amending the articles of incorporation.

DISCUSSION: The articles of incorporation can be amended fully. The board of directors proposes the amendment, and shareholders approve the proposed amendment. Certain amendments, such as changing the registered agent, do not require shareholder action, unless the articles provide otherwise.

Answer (A) is incorrect because the articles of incorporation may be amended. Answer (B) is incorrect because amendments to the articles of incorporation are filed with the secretary of state of state governments. Answer (D) is incorrect because the amended articles are not required to contain all provisions that may have been included in the original articles.

C. Board of Directors

13. Which of the following statements about the directors of a corporation is true?

- A. In some states, a board of directors may be dispensed with in certain circumstances.
- B. Directors may serve only from one annual meeting to the next.
- C. Directors may be elected by the shareholders only.
- D. The number of directors may not exceed the number of shareholders.

The correct answer is (A). *(Publisher)*

REQUIRED: The true statement about corporate directors.

DISCUSSION: Some states permit a corporation to have only one director. Others require a minimum of three directors but permit the number of directors to equal the number of shareholders if less than three. Another possibility is that a corporation with 50 or fewer shareholders may dispense with directors.

Answer (B) is incorrect because staggered multi-year terms are allowed. Answer (C) is incorrect because the remaining directors may fill vacancies resulting from the death, removal, or resignation of directors until the next shareholders' meeting. They may also fill new positions if permitted by the bylaws or articles. Answer (D) is incorrect because the number of directors may exceed the number of stockholders.

14. A director of a corporation

- A. Must usually be a resident of the state of incorporation.
- B. Is usually removable for cause by the other directors.
- C. Must ordinarily be a shareholder.
- D. Must usually be at least 21 years old.

The correct answer is (B). *(Publisher)*

REQUIRED: The correct statement about a corporate director.

DISCUSSION: Shareholders may remove a director with or without cause at a meeting called for that purpose. Many states permit the board to remove a director for cause, e.g., insanity or conviction of a felony, subject to shareholder review.

Answers (A) and (D) are incorrect because age and residency requirements are imposed by statute in only a few states. An incorporator, not a director, must usually be of age. Answer (C) is incorrect because directors ordinarily need not be shareholders.

15. Iago and Des are the sole directors, officers, and shareholders of the ID Corporation. They regularly hold board meetings by long distance telephone calls. Recently, without a meeting, Des increased compensation of the directors and declared the regular dividend. Iago later filed in the minutes a signed, written consent to the actions taken. The articles and by-laws are silent on these matters.

A. Board meetings must be held in the state of incorporation or where the corporation has its principal business and must be conducted in person.

B. The board may declare dividends but may not fix its own compensation.

C. ID is most likely in violation of state law because it has fewer than three directors.

D. Unanimous written consent of all directors may substitute for a meeting.

The correct answer is (D). *(Publisher)*
    REQUIRED: The correct statement concerning the formalities required of a close corporation.
    DISCUSSION: Traditionally, the board of directors could act only after a formal meeting at which a quorum was present. Under modern statutes, unanimous written consent filed in the minutes is a sufficient basis for action by the board.
    Answer (A) is incorrect because board meetings may be conducted anywhere and are not required to be in person; e.g., the meetings may be held by conference telephone call. Answer (B) is incorrect because the board of directors may routinely declare dividends and may also fix its own compensation unless the articles or bylaws provide otherwise. Answer (C) is incorrect because some modern statutes allow the board to be dispensed with entirely. Others require only one director. Still others permit the number of directors to equal the number of shareholders.

16. Delegation of the powers of the board of directors is usually

A. Prohibited.

B. Allowed with regard to any matter upon which the board may act.

C. Prohibited except when required by an outside agency, for example, a stock exchange that requires members to have audit committees.

D. Allowed except with regard to specified important transactions.

The correct answer is (D). *(Publisher)*
    REQUIRED: The correct statement about delegation of directors' authority.
    DISCUSSION: If the articles or bylaws permit, the directors may by majority vote of the full board delegate authority to specified directors constituting an executive or other committee. The committee may exercise all the powers of the board except with regard to significant or extraordinary transactions, such as declaring dividends, issuing stock, or amending bylaws. The committee must consist only of directors.
    Answer (A) is incorrect because executive, audit, finance, and other committees are normally allowed. Answer (B) is incorrect because certain powers may not be delegated. Answer (C) is incorrect because committees are not established solely to meet requirements such as the New York Stock Exchange's rule requiring members to establish audit committees of outside directors.

17. A director of a corporation is best characterized as

A. An agent.

B. A trustee.

C. A fiduciary.

D. A principal.

The correct answer is (C). *(Publisher)*
    REQUIRED: The best characterization of a corporate director.
    DISCUSSION: Officers and employees as well as directors are fiduciaries with regard to the corporation. They owe a duty of loyalty, good faith, and fair dealing when transacting business with or on behalf of the company. This duty requires full disclosure of any personal interest in transactions with the corporation, avoidance of conflicts of interest and the making of secret profits, and placing the corporate interest ahead of personal gain.
    Answer (A) is incorrect because a director is not an agent. (S)he cannot act alone to bind the corporation. As a group, directors control the corporation in a manner that agents cannot. Answer (B) is incorrect because a trustee holds legal title to property used for the benefit of others. Answer (D) is incorrect because the corporation itself is the principal.

18. A corporate director commits a breach of duty if

    A. (S)he fails to exercise great care and skill.

    B. A contract is awarded by the company to an organization owned by the director.

    C. An interest in property is acquired by the director without prior approval of the board.

    D. The director's action, prompted by confidential information, results in an abuse of corporate opportunity.

The correct answer is (D). *(CIA 580 IV-21)*

    REQUIRED: The breach of duty by a corporate director.

    DISCUSSION: Corporate directors have a fiduciary duty not to usurp business opportunities of the corporation if it has a right, a property interest, or an expectancy incidental to its business.

    Answer (A) is incorrect because, under the business judgment rule, a director must act in good faith; not be motivated by fraud, conflict of interest, or illegality; and not be grossly negligent in reaching decisions. However, (s)he is not held to the highest standard of care and skill. Answer (B) is incorrect because a director is not prohibited from entering into transactions with the corporation as long as full disclosure is made. Answer (C) is incorrect because a director is under no duty to report personal property investments unless they relate to corporate business.

19. A director may be held personally liable for which of the following situations?

    A. Taking advantage of an opportunity arising from his/her corporate capacity for personal satisfaction before the corporation has refused the opportunity.

    B. Unsatisfactory results from a director's decision when the director acted in good faith; was not motivated by fraud, conflict of interest, or illegality; or was not guilty of gross negligence in reaching that decision.

    C. Related party transactions between the director's personal outside interests and the corporation in the ordinary course of business.

    D. Informed decisions.

The correct answer is (A). *(Publisher)*

    REQUIRED: The situation for which a director of a corporation may be held liable.

    DISCUSSION: A director of a corporation has a duty of loyalty to the corporation not to usurp corporate business opportunities. The corporation must first have the right to refuse any corporate business opportunity that comes to the director's attention if the corporation has a right, property interest, or expectancy incidental to its business. The director is not precluded from carrying on business with the corporation. A director may have a related party transaction, but he/she must fully disclose such information.

    Answers (B) and (D) are incorrect because the business judgment rule protects directors from such liabilities. Answer (C) is incorrect because directors may participate in related party transactions, but they must disclose such facts.

D. Rating Agencies

20. Moody's and Standard & Poor's debt ratings depend on

    A. The chances of default.

    B. The size of the company.

    C. The size and the type of issue.

    D. The firm's industry.

The correct answer is (A). *(Publisher)*

    REQUIRED: The basis for debt ratings.

    DISCUSSION: Debt ratings are based on the probability of default and the protection for investors in case of default.

    Answers (B), (C), and (D) are incorrect because the size of the company, the size and the type of issue, and the firm's industry are relevant only insofar as they bear upon the probability of default.

21. If a bond is rated below BBB, it is called

    A. A zero-coupon bond.

    B. An investment grade bond.

    C. A junk bond.

    D. An income bond.

The correct answer is (C). *(Publisher)*

    REQUIRED: The bond rated below BBB.

    DISCUSSION: AAA and AA are Standard & Poor's highest ratings. They signify the highest quality. Bonds rated A and BBB are investment grade. Bonds rated below BBB are speculative high-yield or low-grade bonds (junk bonds).

    Answer (A) is incorrect because a zero-coupon bond pays no interest and is sold at a discount. Answer (B) is incorrect because an investment grade bond is rated A or BBB. Answer (D) is incorrect because an income bond pays interest only if the issuer earns income sufficient to pay the interest.

E. Effect of Government Regulation of Business

22. Federal regulatory agencies do not have power to

A. Impose agency taxes on private industry.

B. Issue rules and regulations.

C. Investigate violations of statutes and rules.

D. Conduct hearings and decide whether violations have occurred.

The correct answer is (A). *(CMA 1291 1-22)*

REQUIRED: The true statement about the powers that federal regulatory agencies do not have.

DISCUSSION: A federal regulatory agency may regulate some aspect of all industries or may regulate a specific industry in accordance with power delegated by Congress in the enabling legislation. Agency functions include executive, adjudicatory, and rule-making activities. Such agencies, however, may not impose taxes.

Answers (B), (C), and (D) are incorrect because federal regulatory agencies have the power to issue rules and regulations, to investigate violations of statutes and rules, and to conduct hearings and decide whether violations have occurred.

23. The basic purpose of the securities laws of the United States is to regulate the issue of investment securities by

A. Providing a regulatory framework in those states that do not have their own securities laws.

B. Requiring disclosure of all relevant facts so that investors can make informed decisions.

C. Prohibiting the issuance of securities that the Securities and Exchange Commission determines are not of investment grade.

D. Channeling investment funds into uses that are economically most important.

The correct answer is (B). *(CMA 1289 1-29)*

REQUIRED: The means of regulating the issue of investment securities.

DISCUSSION: The basic purpose of the federal securities laws is to provide disclosure of adequate information so that investors can evaluate investments. This is accomplished through complex registration and reporting requirements concerning the issuance and subsequent trading of securities. However, the federal government does not assess the merits of these securities.

Answer (A) is incorrect because federal law applies in all states and supplements state blue-sky (securities) laws. Answer (C) is incorrect because the SEC does not determine the merits of securities; it evaluates whether sufficient information is provided. Answer (D) is incorrect because the securities laws are not intended to influence the investment of capital in more socially or economically beneficial ways.

24. The basic purpose of the Securities Exchange Act of 1934 was to

A. Regulate outstanding securities.

B. Regulate new issues of securities.

C. Protect investors from investment losses.

D. Ensure the public that stock market crashes like that of 1929 would not occur again.

The correct answer is (A). *(CMA 693 1-11)*

REQUIRED: The basic purpose of the Securities Exchange Act of 1934.

DISCUSSION: The 1934 act was designed to regulate securities after initial issuances. Other purposes of the 1934 act were to provide adequate information to investors and to prevent insiders from unfairly using their information.

Answer (B) is incorrect because the Securities Act of 1933 was designed to regulate new issues of securities. Answer (C) is incorrect because the objective is not to protect investors from losses, but to provide investors with adequate information upon which to base investment decisions. Answer (D) is incorrect because the objective was to regulate securities and provide investors with adequate information.

25. The Foreign Corrupt Practices Act prohibits

A. Bribes to all foreigners.

B. Small bribes to foreign corporate officers.

C. Bribery only by corporations and their representatives.

D. Bribes to foreign officials to influence official acts.

The correct answer is (D). *(Publisher)*

REQUIRED: The prohibition of the Foreign Corrupt Practices Act.

DISCUSSION: The Foreign Corrupt Practices Act (FCPA) prohibits any U.S. firm from making corrupt political payments for the purpose of obtaining or retaining business. The businesses subject to the FCPA include corporations, partnerships, limited partnerships, business trusts, and unincorporated organizations. Violations of the FCPA are federal felonies.

Answers (A) and (B) are incorrect because the FCPA bars payments to governmental officials, political parties and their officials, candidates for office, and anyone who is known to be likely to pass along such payments to one of the foregoing. Answer (C) is incorrect because all U.S. firms are subject to the anti-bribery provisions.

26. A major result of the Foreign Corrupt Practices Act is that corporations are now required to

A. Keep accurate accounting records and maintain adequate internal controls.

B. Permit authorized agencies access to company records.

C. Prepare financial statements in accordance with U.S. and international accounting standards.

D. Produce information to the SEC on foreign commerce and foreign political party information.

The correct answer is (A). *(Publisher)*

REQUIRED: The major impact of the Foreign Corrupt Practices Act of 1977.

DISCUSSION: The accounting requirements of the FCPA apply to all companies required to register and report under the Securities Exchange Act of 1934. These companies must maintain books, records, and accounts in reasonable detail that accurately and fairly reflect transactions. The FCPA also requires these companies to maintain a system of internal accounting control that provides certain reasonable assurances, including that corporate assets are not used for bribes. If payoffs are made, they must be reflected in the company's records.

Answer (B) is incorrect because authorized agents of the federal government already have access to records of SEC registrants. Answer (C) is incorrect because although some international accounting standards have been promulgated, they are incomplete and have not gained widespread acceptance. Answer (D) is incorrect because there are no requirements for providing periodic reports on foreign commerce or foreign political party affiliations.

27. Which one of the following federal acts requires unions to retain financial records and submit financial reports to federal authorities?

A. Taft-Hartley Act of 1947.

B. Wagner Act of 1935.

C. Securities Exchange Act of 1934.

D. Landrum-Griffin Act of 1959.

The correct answer is (D). *(CMA 1295 1-27)*

REQUIRED: The act requiring unions to retain financial records and submit financial reports to federal authorities.

DISCUSSION: The Landrum-Griffin Act of 1959 (the Labor Management Reporting and Disclosure Act) requires unions to maintain financial records and submit reports to the federal government. The intent of the act was to extend the provisions of the National Labor Relations Act to the internal affairs of unions to make the organizations more democratic and give members more rights.

Answer (A) is incorrect because the Taft-Hartley Act did not address internal affairs such as financial records and reports. Answer (B) is incorrect because the Wagner Act of 1935 gave more power to unions. Answer (C) is incorrect because the Securities Exchange Act of 1934 did not address reports by labor unions.

28. Equal employment opportunity is concerned with, among other issues, the recruitment and selection of employees. A U.S. Supreme Court ruling in 1971 involved the use of pre-employment tests (Griggs v. Duke Power Co.). In that case, which was determined under Title VII of the Civil Rights Act of 1964, the Court ruled that pre-employment tests

A. Given to minorities, regardless of the reason given, violate Title VII.

B. Are legal, as long as there is no intent to discriminate.

C. In any form are illegal.

D. Must be directly related to job requirements.

The correct answer is (D). (CMA 690 1-6)

REQUIRED: The true statement about pre-employment tests.

DISCUSSION: The equal employment opportunity laws are designed to prohibit discrimination in employment. Employers do, however, have the right to use selection procedures in hiring as long as the procedures are not discriminatory. For example, an employer may use professionally developed pre-employment tests that are directly related to job requirements.

Answer (A) is incorrect because appropriate tests can be given to all applicants. Answer (B) is incorrect because the tests are not legal if they are not directly related to job requirements. Answer (C) is incorrect because the tests are legal if related to job requirements. Professionally developed tests that meet EEOC guidelines are most likely to survive scrutiny.

29. A major policy of the Equal Employment Opportunity Commission (EEOC) is

A. To restrict enforcement of the Equal Employment Opportunity Act of 1972 to relatively small companies in order to minimize disruptions.

B. To rank the goal of employee productivity ahead of the goal of equal employment opportunity considerations.

C. To emphasize equality of result over equality of opportunity.

D. To have businesses achieve employment mixes reflecting the local labor pool of protected groups.

The correct answer is (D). (CMA 691 1-21)

REQUIRED: The major policy of the Equal Employment Opportunity Commission (EEOC).

DISCUSSION: The EEOC has set goals and timetables for employers to bring female and minority work forces up to the appropriate percentages as they relate to the available labor pool. The means of achieving these goals, such as affirmative action programs, are often highly controversial.

Answer (A) is incorrect because the EEOC deals mostly with large companies. Answer (B) is incorrect because the EEOC is not concerned with employee productivity. Answer (C) is incorrect because equal opportunity is the main goal.

30. Violations of federal regulations on equal employment opportunity are sometimes inferred from the fact that a firm has a very small percentage of protected groups among its employees. These regulations are sometimes attacked on the grounds that they may be in conflict with the economic concept that

A. The applicant who would be most productive for the job should be hired.

B. The work force employed should be in the same proportion as the demographics of the total population.

C. Equal opportunity strengthens the seniority system.

D. Wages are inversely related to marginal productivity.

The correct answer is (A). (CMA 1291 1-24)

REQUIRED: The grounds upon which equal employment opportunity laws are sometimes criticized.

DISCUSSION: A controversial remedy sometimes adopted in employment discrimination cases is an affirmative action order, which provides preferences to members of the class that previously suffered from discrimination. Affirmative action preferences apply even though the specific persons benefitted are not necessarily those who were victimized by illegal discrimination. Affirmative action programs are sometimes criticized because employment preferences are often viewed as reverse discrimination. Moreover, they may not result in the hiring, retention, and promotion of the most productive workers.

Answer (B) is incorrect because a work force in the same proportion as the demographics of the total population is not in conflict with the equal employment opportunity laws. Answer (C) is incorrect because even a bona fide seniority system may violate Title VII if it is found to perpetuate past discrimination. An affirmative action remedy would necessarily have the effect of weakening such a system. Answer (D) is incorrect because wages should be directly related to marginal productivity.

31. Which one of the following is not a characteristic of the Occupational Safety and Health Administration (OSHA)? OSHA

A. Encourages labor-management committees to formulate safety and health programs.

B. Inspections are primarily focused on health issues, including long-term exposure to such substances as asbestos and cotton dust.

C. Has the authority to levy monetary penalties on non-compliant employers.

D. Inspections are primarily reactionary; that is, take place after major injuries have occurred.

The correct answer is (D). *(CMA 693 1-23)*

REQUIRED: The item that is not a characteristic of OSHA.

DISCUSSION: OSHA is empowered to conduct surprise inspections to determine whether standards are being met. However, an employer may demand that the inspector obtain a search warrant. Thus, no precipitating event must occur prior to an inspection.

Answer (A) is incorrect because OSHA encourages labor-management committees to formulate safety and health programs. Answer (B) is incorrect because inspections are intended to determine whether OSHA standards are being followed. These standards relate to workplace safety and health. Answer (C) is incorrect because OSHA has the authority to levy civil monetary penalties of up to $1,000 per violation and up to $10,000 for a repeat offense.

32. Antitrust laws are intended to

A. Establish set profit percentages for firms in regulated industries.

B. Prohibit firms in the same industry from engaging in joint ventures.

C. Require firms in regulated industries to share any patent rights with other firms in that industry.

D. Ensure a free and competitive market in which consumer demand dictates prices.

The correct answer is (D). *(Publisher)*

REQUIRED: The intent of antitrust laws.

DISCUSSION: Antitrust laws are designed to promote more efficient allocation of resources, greater choice for consumers, greater business opportunities, fairness in economic behavior, and avoidance of concentrated political power resulting from economic power. Competition results in greater output and lower prices than other market structures.

Answer (A) is incorrect because profit percentages are not set by antitrust laws other than to the extent that price discrimination is prohibited. Answer (B) is incorrect because firms may enter into joint ventures. Answer (C) is incorrect because patents are available to all inventors, regardless of size.

33. The impact of successful prosecution for restraint of trade violations of the Sherman Antitrust Act has been less than many proponents hoped for because

A. Only a limited number of criminal prosecutions have ever been filed under Section 1 of the Act.

B. Most companies avoid behaviors that might be construed as antitrust violations because of the likelihood of fines and even jail sentences.

C. The predominant criterion for criminal prosecution is market share; a company's intent is inconsequential.

D. The courts created in the beginning a "rule of reason" that required determining whether competition was lessened by the company's behavior.

The correct answer is (D). *(CMA 693 1-27)*

REQUIRED: The reason for the disappointing impact of prosecutions under the Sherman Act.

DISCUSSION: The Sherman Antitrust Act of 1890 makes illegal every contract, combination, or conspiracy in restraint of trade in interstate or foreign commerce. Successful prosecutions have been few because the courts developed a rule of reason stipulating that only unreasonable restraints of trade are illegal. Thus, courts balance the anti-competitive effects against the pro-competitive effects of a restraint of trade. Unless a restraint is unreasonable by its very nature (a per se violation), the rule of reason applies.

Answer (A) is incorrect because many cases have been filed under the Sherman Act; however, the rule of reason has limited the number of successful prosecutions. Answer (B) is incorrect because numerous companies still engage in anti-competitive conduct. Answer (C) is incorrect because intent is significant; for example, a company that has a monopoly thrust upon it is not in violation.

34. Which one of the following examples of corporate behavior would most clearly represent a violation of the Sherman Act?

   A. A retailer offers quantity discounts to large institutional buyers.

   B. The members of a labor union meet and agree not to work for a specific firm unless the starting wage is at least $10 per hour.

   C. Two firms that are in different, unrelated industries merge.

   D. Two firms in the same industry agree in a telephone conversation to submit identical bids on a government contract.

The correct answer is (D). *(CMA 1295 1-23)*
   REQUIRED: The item that would most clearly represent a violation of the Sherman Act.
   DISCUSSION: The Sherman Act of 1890 makes illegal every contract, combination, or conspiracy in restraint of trade in interstate or foreign commerce. Some types of arrangements, called *per se* violations, are considered unreasonable without inquiry. These violations include price fixing, division of markets, group boycotts, and resale price maintenance. Agreeing to submit identical bids on a government contract is a form of price fixing, a *per se* violation.
   Answer (A) is incorrect because quantity discounts are not prohibited by the Sherman Act. Answer (B) is incorrect because the Sherman Act does not apply to labor unions. Answer (C) is incorrect because the Sherman Act does not prohibit mergers; only those that could lead to restraint of trade are outlawed.

35. The Clayton Act, as amended, prohibits all of the following except

   A. Price discrimination by sellers.

   B. Interlocking directorates in large competing organizations.

   C. Unfair and deceptive business practices, such as misleading advertising.

   D. A merger of companies that substantially lessens competition.

The correct answer is (C). *(CMA 1295 1-24)*
   REQUIRED: The item not prohibited by the Clayton Act.
   DISCUSSION: The Clayton Act of 1914 prohibits (1) mergers that may lessen competition or tend to create a monopoly, (2) sales that prevent the buyer from dealing with the seller's competitors, (3) tie-in sales (requiring a buyer to take other products in order to buy the first product), (4) price discrimination, and (5) interlocking directorates. The Federal Trade Commission Act addresses unfair and deceptive business practices such as false advertising.
   Answers (A), (B), and (D) are incorrect because the Clayton Act prohibits price discrimination by sellers, interlocking directorates in large competing organizations, and a merger of companies that substantially lessens competition.

36. Tie-in sales (e.g., the sale of camera and film together) are legal if

   A. The tie-in is necessary to assure product quality.

   B. The tying product is patented.

   C. Used to facilitate price discrimination.

   D. Used by all firms in an industry.

The correct answer is (A). *(CMA 687 1-15)*
   REQUIRED: The situation in which tie-in sales are legal.
   DISCUSSION: Tie-in sales involve a seller's requirement that the buyer purchase another distinct product to obtain the first. They are usually prohibited under the Clayton Act of 1914 unless a small company is attempting to enter a market or the tie-in is needed to protect the firm's goodwill (e.g., by maintaining a certain quality standard).
   Answers (B), (C), and (D) are incorrect because tie-in sales requirements are usually illegal if the seller has enough market power to restrict competition.

37. Which one of the following transactions would be considered a violation of the Robinson-Patman Act?

    A. The sale of goods of like quality at different prices to two different wholesalers, both of whom are located outside the United States.

    B. The sale of goods of like quality within the United States at different prices based on cost differences related to the method of delivery.

    C. The sale of goods of like quality within the United States at different prices to two different wholesalers; all parties are located within the same state.

    D. The sale of goods of like quality within the United States but across state lines at different prices to two different wholesalers in the same geographic area.

The correct answer is (D). *(CMA 1295 1-22)*

REQUIRED: The transaction that would be in violation of the Robinson-Patman Act of 1936.

DISCUSSION: The Robinson-Patman Act of 1936, an amendment to the Clayton Act, outlaws price discrimination that would lead to restraint of trade. Both buyer and seller can be found guilty of price discrimination under the provisions of the Robinson-Patman Act. Price differentiation between customers is allowed if there is a difference in costs. For instance, quantity discounts are permitted if it can be shown that larger quantities can be shipped with a cost savings. Charging competing wholesalers different prices for similar goods would be a violation of the act.

Answer (A) is incorrect because the act does not apply to export sales. Answer (B) is incorrect because cost differences related to delivery are a justification for charging different prices. Answer (C) is incorrect because the act applies only to sales in interstate commerce.

38. The two major functions of the Federal Trade Commission are

    A. Antitrust actions and the regulation of foreign trade.

    B. Import quality inspections and anti-dumping measures.

    C. Antitrust actions and consumer protection.

    D. Price discrimination and unfair trade practices.

The correct answer is (C). *(CMA 1295 1-30)*

REQUIRED: The two major functions of the Federal Trade Commission (FTC).

DISCUSSION: The FTC Act of 1914 prohibits unfair methods of competition and unfair or deceptive acts in commerce. The basic objectives are to initiate antitrust actions and protect consumers.

Answers (A) and (B) are incorrect because the FTC is not concerned with the regulation of foreign trade. Answer (D) is incorrect because price discrimination and unfair trade practices are merely elements of the overall mission of the FTC.

39. Which one of the following is not exempted from federal antitrust regulation?

    A. Labor unions.

    B. Intrastate commerce.

    C. Telecommunications companies.

    D. Major league baseball.

The correct answer is (C). *(CMA 1295 1-28)*

REQUIRED: The entity that is not exempted from federal antitrust regulation.

DISCUSSION: Several types of entities and contracts are exempt from antitrust regulation. These include firms not operating in interstate commerce, labor unions, regulated public utilities, patents and copyrights, agricultural and fishing organizations, financial institutions, transport industries, professional baseball, and companies qualifying under the Export Trading Company Act. The telecommunications industry is not exempt.

Answers (A), (B), and (D) are incorrect because labor unions, intrastate commerce, and major league baseball are specifically exempted.

40. Truth-in-lending is one form of price standardization that, since the adoption of the Consumer Credit Protection Act on July 1, 1969, has been provided by U.S. government regulations. The purpose of this legislation is to

A. Regulate the amount of interest that may be charged.

B. Allow immediate wage garnishment by creditors.

C. Prohibit the use of usurious interest rates.

D. Disclose the finance charge and the annual percentage rate.

The correct answer is (D). (CMA 690 1-5)

REQUIRED: The purpose of truth-in-lending legislation.

DISCUSSION: The Truth-in-Lending Act applies to creditors that extend consumer credit to individual debtors (not organizations) in amounts of $25,000 or less. For a closed-end credit transaction, e.g., the typical car loan, the total finance charge, annual percentage interest rate, amount financed, late charges, security interest held by the creditor, the number and amounts of payments, due dates, and the total amount of payments must be disclosed. Open-end credit transactions, such as those involving credit cards, also have specific, detailed disclosure requirements.

Answers (A) and (C) are incorrect because the Consumer Credit Protection Act merely requires disclosure. It does not regulate interest rates. Answer (B) is incorrect because the act had nothing to do with wage garnishment.

41. The general approach to regulation by the Consumer Product Safety Commission is to

A. Levy fines against the producers of unsafe products.

B. Set safety standards for various products.

C. Increase the freedom of consumer choice.

D. Depend upon voluntary action by manufacturers to produce safe products.

The correct answer is (B). (CMA 1291 1-25)

REQUIRED: The general approach to regulation by the Consumer Product Safety Commission.

DISCUSSION: The Consumer Product Safety Act created the Consumer Product Safety Commission, which promotes voluntary safety standards, develops and enforces mandatory standards, prohibits unsafe products if safety standards will not be sufficient, recalls hazardous products, furnishes information to consumers, and works with state and local governments. Thus, the emphasis of the Commission's work is the prevention of problems through standard setting, not the punishment of wrongdoers.

Answer (A) is incorrect because the CPSC does not levy fines, although it may bring suit for violations, and a court may levy fines as a result. Answer (C) is incorrect because consumer choice is lessened when the CPSC keeps unsafe products off the market. Answer (D) is incorrect because the requirements of the CPSC are mandatory.

42. The Consumer Product Safety Commission (CPSC) has been called by its critics "the most powerful regulatory agency in Washington." The most likely reason for this concern is that the CPSC

A. Covers all consumer products.

B. May ban the production and sale of a product until it has formulated a standard.

C. Does not permit an industry group to adopt a voluntary standard.

D. May order the recall of products it has determined to be unsafe.

The correct answer is (D). (CMA 690 1-2)

REQUIRED: The reason the CPSC has been called the most powerful regulatory agency.

DISCUSSION: The CPSC promotes voluntary safety standards, develops and enforces mandatory standards, prohibits unsafe products if safety standards will not be sufficient, recalls hazardous products, furnishes information to consumers, and works with state and local governments. Thus, if a product is hazardous and presents an unreasonable risk of injury and safety standards will not adequately protect the public, the CPSC may issue an appropriate order banning the product. If a hazard is deemed to be imminent, it may seek a U.S. District Court's authorization to seize the product or halt its distribution.

Answer (A) is incorrect because the Consumer Product Safety Act of 1972 exempts certain products, e.g., aircraft, motor vehicles, food, drugs, and cosmetics. Answer (B) is incorrect because a ban on a product is appropriate only if specific standards will be ineffective. Answer (C) is incorrect because industry standards are encouraged.

43. The primary reason for social regulation (Clean Air Act, Water Pollution Control Act, Food and Drug Act, etc.) is that

   A. The free market provides minimal safety and environmental protection.

   B. Consumer and environmental groups are politically powerful.

   C. Social benefits from such regulations always exceed the costs.

   D. Social regulation is more desirable.

The correct answer is (A). *(CMA 1293 1-4)*
   REQUIRED: The primary reason for social regulation.
   DISCUSSION: Social regulation concerns quality of life issues, e.g., workplace and product safety, environmental degradation, and fair employment practices. The abuses addressed are those that are difficult for market forces to remedy. For example, consumers may purchase products on the basis of price and quality but without regard to the environmental impact of their production, and unsafe working conditions may be tolerated by individuals who have few opportunities for other employment.
   Answer (B) is incorrect because, although consumer and environmental groups may occasionally exercise some lobbying power, they are typically underfunded and would have little impact on legislatures in the absence of an obvious need for social regulation. Answer (C) is incorrect because there is great difficulty in measuring both the benefits and costs of most social regulation. Answer (D) is incorrect because no regulation is desirable, but some regulation is necessary when market forces are ineffective.

44. Pharmaceutical companies must be in compliance with regulations set forth by the Food and Drug Administration (FDA). The FDA is responsible for all of the following except

   A. Allowing extensions to patent lives of pharmaceutical companies in order to recover time lost during the premarket FDA regulatory review.

   B. Considering benefit-risk trade-offs when evaluating the safety of drugs prior to approval.

   C. Maintaining purity standards and regulations concerning drug composition and potency.

   D. Approving drugs that lack substantial evidence that they will have the effects that are represented in advertisements.

The correct answer is (D). *(CMA 693 1-30)*
   REQUIRED: The item not the responsibility of the Food and Drug Administration (FDA).
   DISCUSSION: The FDA was created by the Federal Food, Drug, and Cosmetics Act of 1938 to help maintain the safety of drugs, food, cosmetics, and medicinal products and devices. It regulates the testing, distribution, and sale of drugs. Upon receiving a new drug application, the FDA conducts hearings and investigates the merits of the drug in a process that may require years. Thus, an application must be supported by substantial evidence that the drug will have the asserted effects.
   Answers (A), (B), and (C) are incorrect because the FDA can extend patent lives to allow for time lost during the regulatory review, considers benefit-risk tradeoffs, and maintains purity standards.

45. Which of the following statements is true with respect to the Clean Water Act (CWA)?

   A. Despite the CWA's prohibitions, it allows persons to discharge pollutants into waters subject to its jurisdiction as long as navigation thereon will not be permanently obstructed.

   B. The CWA subjects all bodies of water located in the United States, whether flowing or not, to its protection.

   C. The notion of protecting waters within the jurisdiction of the United States began with the CWA.

   D. The CWA seeks to restore and maintain the physical and biological integrity of the waters of the United States.

The correct answer is (D). *(Publisher)*
   REQUIRED: The true statement about the CWA.
   DISCUSSION: The CWA (1972) substantially amended the Federal Water Pollution Control Act of 1948. It seeks to restore and maintain the physical and biological integrity of the waters of the United States. Its objectives are to render water suitable for recreation and propagation of fish and other wildlife and to eliminate discharges of pollutants.
   Answer (A) is incorrect because the CWA broadly prohibits any discharges of pollutants into waters subject to the jurisdiction of the United States by any person, except in compliance with the Act. Under the CWA, impairment of navigation is irrelevant. Answer (B) is incorrect because, to be subject to federal jurisdiction and the CWA, the waters in which pollutants are discharged must be so-called "navigable waters," which are defined as waters of the United States (including the territorial waters). This broad definition does not encompass all bodies of water located within the bounds of the United States. Answer (C) is incorrect because the Rivers and Harbors Act of the late 1800s was the first major piece of federal legislation promulgated to protect U.S. waterways. Until the passage of the CWA, the Rivers and Harbors Act was also used to combat pollutive discharges, although its original purpose was to keep waterways clear from obstructions to navigation.

46. The Environmental Protection Agency (EPA) might control pollution by setting effluent standards for maximum discharge or by constructing a sliding-tax charge based on the amount of effluent emitted. One advantage of the sliding-tax charge is that

A. It will totally eliminate pollution.

B. There is greater business incentive to discover new methods of controlling pollution.

C. It increases the necessity for the EPA to fully understand pollution control technology.

D. It increases the degree of direct government intervention in the economy.

The correct answer is (B). *(CMA 1291 1-20)*
REQUIRED: The advantage of the sliding tax charge method of controlling the discharge of effluents.
DISCUSSION: The setting of effluent standards has been criticized as inefficient. Economists prefer a sliding tax based on the amount of effluent emitted. This method is preferable because, as effluent discharge increases, the tax increases, providing an incentive for firms to discover new methods of controlling pollution. Rather than dictating technology, the tax allows firms to seek out the technology that is the most cost effective.
Answer (A) is incorrect because pollution would not be totally eliminated. Some firms might find that a low level of pollution is more cost beneficial than total elimination. Answer (C) is incorrect because the EPA would not be directly involved in technology. Answer (D) is incorrect because the tax would be an indirect method of economic intervention.

F. Federal Reserve Board

47. The discount rate set by the Federal Reserve System is the

A. Required percentage of reserves deposited at the central bank.

B. Rate that commercial banks charge for loans to each other.

C. Rate that commercial banks charge for loans to the general public.

D. Rate that the central bank charges for loans to commercial banks.

The correct answer is (D). *(CMA 694 1-1)*
REQUIRED: The true statement about the Federal Reserve discount rate.
DISCUSSION: The discount rate is the interest rate at which member banks may borrow money from the Fed. A lowering of the discount rate encourages borrowing, which increases the money supply. An increase in the discount rate discourages borrowing and correspondingly increases saving, which decreases the money supply.
Answer (A) is incorrect because the required percentage of reserves deposited at the central bank is the legal reserve requirement. Answer (B) is incorrect because the discount rate is the amount the Fed charges to member banks, not what banks charge each other. Answer (C) is incorrect because the rate that commercial banks charge for loans to the general public is usually scaled upward from the prime rate, which is the rate charged to the most creditworthy customers.

48. If the Federal Reserve Board wanted to implement an expansionary monetary policy, which one of the following actions would the Federal Reserve Board take?

A. Raise the reserve requirement and the discount rate.

B. Purchase additional U.S. government securities and lower the discount rate.

C. Reduce the reserve requirement and raise the discount rate.

D. Raise the discount rate and sell U.S. government securities.

The correct answer is (B). *(CMA 695 1-22)*
REQUIRED: The action by the Federal Reserve to implement an expansionary monetary policy.
DISCUSSION: The Federal Reserve affects monetary policy primarily through the purchase and sale of government securities in open-market operations. A purchase of securities is expansionary because it increases bank reserves and the money supply. However, the sale of government securities by the Federal Reserve contracts the money supply by removing resources from the economy. Lowering the legal reserve requirement (the percentage of deposits that a bank must keep on hand) also expands the money supply by increasing the loanable funds held by banks. Similarly, lowering the discount rate (the rate at which member banks may borrow from the Federal Reserve) encourages borrowing and increases the money supply.
Answers (A), (C), and (D) are incorrect because raising the reserve requirement and the discount rate and selling U.S. government securities reduce the money supply.

G. International Tax Considerations

49. When a U.S. statute and a treaty to which the U.S. is a part conflict, the

- A. Treaty always controls.
- B. Statute always controls.
- C. One adopted most recently controls.
- D. One adopted first controls.

The correct answer is (C). *(Publisher)*
REQUIRED: The treatment of a conflict between a U.S. statute and a U.S. treaty.
DISCUSSION: U.S. statutes and U.S. treaties are the supreme law of the land under the U.S. Constitution. When they conflict with one another, whichever was enacted or adopted most recently will control.
Answers (A), (B), and (D) are incorrect because the treaty or statute enacted or adopted most recently will control when the two conflict.

H. International Business and Law

50. The sources of international law do not include

- A. Treaties.
- B. Common law.
- C. Customs.
- D. Conventions.

The correct answer is (B). *(Publisher)*
REQUIRED: The sources of international law.
DISCUSSION: International law is a broad area. It is the law that nations recognize when dealing with one another. International law consists of treaties, conventions, and customs. A treaty is a formal agreement between nations, which usually must be ratified by their lawmaking bodies, e.g., the U.S. Congress. A convention is another term for a treaty. It is often used to describe an agreement among many nations, e.g., the Geneva Convention on the treatment of prisoners of war. Customs are long-established practices serving as unwritten law. Common law is not a source of international law because it relates to law made within a country founded upon judicial decisions.
Answers (A), (C), and (D) are incorrect because treaties, customs, and conventions are sources of international law.

51. What is the role of gold in the current international monetary system?

- A. Gold is quoted in United States dollars only.
- B. All of the major currencies of the world, except the United States dollar, have a fixed value in terms of gold.
- C. Gold is like any other asset whose value depends upon supply and demand.
- D. Gold is the reserve asset of the International Monetary Fund.

The correct answer is (C). *(CMA 688 1-30)*
REQUIRED: The role of gold in the present international monetary system.
DISCUSSION: Gold has no special role in the modern international monetary system. The current system is based upon managed floating currency exchange rates. Consequently, gold is treated as a commodity, the price of which depends upon supply and demand.
Answer (A) is incorrect because, although most exchanges quote the price of gold in U.S. dollars, the dollar's value is not linked to that of gold. Answer (B) is incorrect because floating exchange rates have existed since the 1970s. Tying currency values to a gold standard, in effect, fixes exchange rates. Answer (D) is incorrect because the only reserves of the IMF are international currencies.

52. Which of the following is a tariff?

- A. Licensing requirements.
- B. Consumption taxes on imported goods.
- C. Unreasonable standards pertaining to product quality and safety.
- D. Domestic content rules.

The correct answer is (B). *(CIA 594 IV-64)*
REQUIRED: The example of a tariff.
DISCUSSION: Tariffs are excise taxes on imported goods imposed either to generate revenue or protect domestic producers. Thus, consumption taxes on imported goods are tariffs.
Answer (A) is incorrect because licensing requirements limit exports, e.g., of militarily sensitive technology. Answer (C) is incorrect because unreasonable standards pertaining to product quality and safety are nontariff trade barriers. Answer (D) is incorrect because domestic content rules require that a portion of an imported good be made in the importing country.

53. Which of the following is a direct effect of imposing a protective tariff on an imported product?

A. Lower domestic prices on the imported item.

B. Lower domestic consumption of the item.

C. Reduced domestic production of the item.

D. Higher sales revenues for foreign producers of the item.

The correct answer is (B). *(CIA 594 IV-65)*

REQUIRED: The direct effect of imposing a protective tariff on an imported product.

DISCUSSION: A protective tariff adds to the purchase price of imported goods. If an imported good's sales price is higher than a comparable, less expensive domestic good, consumers will purchase the domestic good. Thus, the direct effect of imposing a protective tariff on an imported good is lower domestic consumption.

Answer (A) is incorrect because a protective tariff can only increase the domestic price of the imported item. Answer (C) is incorrect because, as the imported item's domestic price increases, demand for domestic goods will increase. Thus, domestic production will increase, not decrease. Answer (D) is incorrect because, as the imported item's domestic price increases, demand for the item decreases. Lower sales revenues will result.

54. Which one of the following groups would be the primary beneficiary of a tariff?

A. Domestic producers of export goods.

B. Domestic producers of goods protected by the tariff.

C. Domestic consumers of goods protected by the tariff.

D. Foreign producers of goods protected by the tariff.

The correct answer is (B). *(CMA 695 1-23)*

REQUIRED: The primary beneficiaries of a tariff.

DISCUSSION: Despite the advantages of free trade, nations often levy tariffs to discourage the importation of certain products. A tariff is a tax on imports intended to protect a domestic producer from foreign competition. For instance, a tariff on imported autos benefits U. S. auto manufacturers because it is an additional cost imposed on U.S. consumers of such products. The disadvantages of the tariff are that it may protect an inefficient domestic producer and increase prices paid by domestic consumers.

Answer (A) is incorrect because domestic producers of export goods are not benefitted. Indeed, they may be harmed by retaliatory tariffs. Answer (C) is incorrect because domestic consumers must pay higher prices for imported goods. Answer (D) is incorrect because the foreign producers will be forced to bear an additional cost.

STUDY UNIT 10: ACCOUNTING STANDARD SETTING

24 pages of outline
54 multiple-choice questions

A. *External Financial Statements; Users and Their Needs*
B. *Development of Accounting Standards*
C. *Conceptual Framework Underlying Financial Accounting*
D. *Limitations of Financial Statement Information*
E. *Application of Public Reporting Standards*
F. *The SEC and Its Reporting Requirements*

This study unit covers "Accounting Standard Setting Environment," the last major topic covered in the CFM content specification outline.

A. External Financial Statements; Users and Their Needs

1. Users of financial statements may directly or indirectly have an economic interest in a specific business. Users with direct interests usually invest in or manage the business, whereas users with indirect interests advise, influence, or represent users with direct interests.

    a. Users with direct interests include

    1) Investors or potential investors
    2) Suppliers and creditors
    3) Employees
    4) Management

    b. Users having indirect interests include

    1) Financial advisers and analysts
    2) Stock markets or exchanges
    3) Regulatory authorities

2. The users of financial statements can also be grouped by their relation to the business.

    a. Internal users use financial statements to make decisions affecting the internal operations of the business. These users include management, employees, and the board of directors.

    1) Internal users gather information so that they may more efficiently plan and control the business and its allocation of resources.

    b. External users of financial statements need to determine whether to create, continue, or terminate a relationship with a firm. Creditors, investors, and the general public use the statements to decide whether doing business with the firm will be beneficial.

3.   The needs of users of financial statements are diverse.

   a.   Investors need information to decide whether to increase, decrease, or obtain an investment in a firm.

   b.   Creditors need information to determine whether to extend credit and under what terms.

   c.   Employees want financial information to negotiate wages and fringe benefits based on the increased productivity and value they provide to a profitable firm.

   d.   Management needs financial statements to assess financial strengths and deficiencies, to evaluate performance results and past decisions, and to plan for future financial goals and steps toward accomplishing them.

   e.   Financial advisers and analysts need financial statements to help investors evaluate particular investments.

   f.   Stock exchanges need financial statements to evaluate whether to accept a firm's stock for listing or whether to suspend the stock's trading.

   g.   Regulatory agencies may need financial statements to evaluate the firm's conformity with regulations and to determine price levels in regulated industries.

4.   Stop and review! You have completed the outline for this subunit. Study multiple-choice questions 1 and 2 on page 391.

B.   Development of Accounting Standards

1.   Prior to the Securities Act of 1933 and the Securities Exchange Act of 1934, little financial reporting was required. The securities acts assigned the power of accounting rule making for publicly held companies to the Securities and Exchange Commission (SEC). They also required most publicly held companies to be audited by independent CPAs. The SEC in turn delegated the rule-making authority to the American Institute of Accountants (later the AICPA), which formed the Committee on Accounting Procedure (CAP) and later the Accounting Principles Board (APB). The APB was terminated after 15 years because the increasing number of financial reporting issues demanded full-time attention. Consequently, the Financial Accounting Standards Board (FASB) was established in the early 1970s.

2.   The FASB has seven salaried members, all having extensive experience in financial accounting, with four required to be CPAs. Each member severs all other business affiliations during his/her term. Two related organizations assist the FASB. The Financial Accounting Foundation selects the board members, appoints an advisory council, raises supporting funds, and reviews the whole plan and operation periodically. The Financial Accounting Standards Advisory Council advises on priorities and proposed standards and evaluates the FASB's performance.

3.   A majority of the FASB decides its agenda. The members determine which subjects require attention and the order of their importance. A separate task force is appointed to consider each subject on the agenda. The task force is responsible for considering all aspects of a problem (in a discussion memorandum) rather than selecting from among the possible solutions.

4.   Due process for the FASB's development of accounting standards includes public hearings on each issue. A 60-day notice of the hearings is given so that anyone wishing to prepare presentations will have sufficient time. A written position or outline must be submitted by those who wish to participate in the hearing.

5.   All proposed statements of the FASB must be exposed to the public (by means of an exposure draft) for 60 days before being made official. Official pronouncements require five or more affirmative votes. All dissenting opinions of board members must be published along with the statement. Each pronouncement includes the opinion of the FASB, background on the research results and the various solutions considered, the effective date, and the date of implementation.

6.   FASB procedures may be summarized as follows:

   a.   A project is placed on the agenda.

   b.   A task force of experts defines specific problems and alternatives.

   c.   The FASB technical staff conducts research and analysis.

   d.   A discussion memorandum is drafted and released.

   e.   A public hearing is held (at least 60 days after the discussion memorandum is released).

   f.   Public response is evaluated.

   g.   The FASB deliberates on various issues and prepares an exposure draft of a proposed Statement of Financial Accounting Standards (SFAS).

   h.   The exposure draft is released.

   i.   There is at least a 30-day waiting period for public comment.

   j.   All letters and comments are evaluated.

   k.   The FASB revises the draft if necessary.

   l.   The entire FASB gives final consideration to the draft.

   m.   The FASB votes on the issuance of the statement.

7.   Subsequently, the FASB may issue formal interpretations of its own statements. Like the original pronouncement, interpretations require at least five affirmative votes. Unlike the AICPA's accounting interpretations, FASB interpretations are developed and voted upon by the Board itself and have the same status as Statements of Financial Accounting Standards. Accounting Research Bulletins (ARBs) issued by the CAP and APB Opinions continue to be authoritative until they are amended or superseded by FASB pronouncements.

8.   **The SEC and Its Relationship with the FASB.** As mentioned earlier, the SEC was granted the power to establish accounting practices and procedures. The SEC originally delegated this authority to the accounting profession. With the creation of the FASB, the SEC issued Accounting Series Release No. 150, which acknowledged that the SEC would continue to look to the private sector (through the FASB) for leadership in establishing and improving accounting principles. However, the release also stated that the SEC would identify areas for which additional information is needed and would determine the appropriate methods of disclosure to meet those needs. The SEC is a strong supporter of the FASB. The Commission provides the FASB with advice when requested and has declared "that financial statements conforming to standards set by the FASB will be presumed to have authoritative support."

9. Groups of users of accounting standards are very influential in the development of accounting principles. Each group may want transactions and events to be accounted for in a particular way. Accordingly, they seek to persuade the FASB during the process of standard setting. Each of the following user groups has an effect on the establishment of accounting principles by the FASB.

    a. **Emerging Issues Task Force (EITF).** In 1984, the FASB created the Emerging Issues Task Force to develop principles of accounting for new and unusual accounting issues. The EITF is composed of 17 members, one of whom is a representative from the FASB. To reach a consensus, at least 15 of the 17 members must agree on how to account for new types of transactions. The purpose of the EITF is to resolve new accounting issues quickly. Essentially, the EITF identifies controversial accounting issues as they arise and determines whether it is necessary for the FASB to become involved in solving them. The EITF works on short-term issues, leaving the FASB with more time to concentrate on long-term issues.

    b. **Accounting Standards Executive Committee (AcSEC).** Following the demise of the APB, the AICPA created the AcSEC to act as its official representative in regard to accounting and reporting issues. Initially, the AcSEC promulgated Statements of Position (SOPs) on questions not addressed by the FASB. However, so many SOPs were issued that the FASB feared the AICPA would become a competing standard-setting body. Accordingly, the AcSEC now focuses on releasing issues papers that identify current accounting issues and present alternative treatments. If the FASB does not choose to address a topic in an issues paper, the AcSEC may still decide to promulgate an SOP. The AcSEC also publishes Practice Bulletins and Audit and Accounting Guides.

    c. **International Accounting Standards Committee (IASC).** The IASC was established to harmonize accounting standards used by member countries. Currently, 13 nations are voting members, and 31 standards have been issued. An affirmative vote by three-fourths of the IASC members is required to pass a standard. However, IASC pronouncements are not binding. Its authority is restricted to the willingness of foreign governments to adopt its standards. The IASC is composed of members from various national professional accounting organizations, such as the AICPA. No members of the IASC are from national standard-setting bodies. Thus, the IASC's members have no direct influence on governmental legislation.

    d. **Cost Accounting Standards Board (CASB).** Probably the least known organization promulgating accounting principles is the Cost Accounting Standards Board. The CASB was created by Congress in 1970 with the objective of establishing cost accounting principles for federal defense contractors and subcontractors. The creation of the CASB was a response to complaints about inconsistent accounting practices of companies that had cost-plus contracts with the government. Many state governments also require adherence to CASB standards in cost-plus contract situations.

        1) The standards established by the CASB are not necessarily acceptable for financial statement reporting purposes. They are required only for price-setting.

        2) Once the CASB standards are approved, they are published twice in the *Federal Register*. The standards become law 60 days after the second publication if Congress does not enact a contrary resolution.

　　　3)　The original CASB had five members, including the Comptroller General of the United States. Although the CASB was only a part-time board, it had a large staff of full-time employees. With its objectives significantly accomplished, the CASB was abolished in 1980, but many standards that were promulgated by the original CASB are still law and must be followed by government contractors.

　　　　　a)　In 1988, Congress reestablished the CASB as an independent body in the Office of Federal Procurement Policy. It has "exclusive authority to make, promulgate, amend, and rescind cost accounting standards and interpretations thereof" for negotiated contracts and subcontracts over $500,000.

　　　　　b)　CASB standards are incorporated into Federal Acquisition Regulations (FARs).

　e.　**Governmental Accounting Standards Board (GASB)**. The Governmental Accounting Standards Board, the newest authoritative body for setting accounting standards, establishes standards for state and local governmental entities with the oversight of the Financial Accounting Foundation. The GASB was formed to address the problem of comparability of governmental financial statements with those of private business. GASB pronouncements have the status of GAAP. As of August 1996, the GASB has issued 30 statements.

　　　1)　Until changed by a GASB pronouncement, all currently effective statements from the National Council on Governmental Accounting and the AICPA remain in force.

　　　2)　The GASB uses Technical Bulletins to clarify, explain, or elaborate an underlying statement or interpretation. Technical Bulletins apply to issues that are too specific to be addressed by a statement.

　f.　**Other groups**. Other groups that have some influence on the development of accounting principles include the American Accounting Association (AAA), Institute of Management Accountants (IMA, formerly the National Association of Accountants or NAA), Financial Executives Institute (FEI), Congress, and the Internal Revenue Service (IRS).

　　　1)　The AAA affects the development of accounting theory through the influence its members exert on future accountants. Many of the AAA's members are accounting professors who shape future principles by their current teaching activity and by promoting and sponsoring accounting research. The AAA has had a pronounced effect on accounting principles, but many years may elapse before those effects become obvious.

　　　2)　The IMA and FEI affect the development of accounting principles through the publication of monthly magazines and various research studies.

　　　3)　The U.S. Congress has affected accounting principles through the Internal Revenue Code. The IRS is one of the most influential groups on accounting practice because an effort to minimize taxable income through accounting procedures is often inconsistent with good financial accounting.

　　　　　a)　The IRS also has the power to influence accounting principles by adopting regulations affecting various practices for tax reporting purposes.

10.　Stop and review! You have completed the outline for this subunit. Study multiple-choice questions 3 through 6 beginning on page 391.

C.   Conceptual Framework Underlying Financial Accounting. The conceptual framework is described in the Statements of Financial Accounting Concepts (SFACs) issued by the FASB. It is a coherent set of interrelated objectives and fundamental concepts promulgated by the FASB.

1.   **Objectives of Financial Reporting by Business Enterprises (SFAC 1)**

   a.   **Scope of financial reporting.** The objectives extend to all means of general purpose external financial reporting by business enterprises (financial reporting). They are a response to the needs of external users who lack the authority to prescribe the information they need.

   1)   Financial statements, including the notes and parenthetical disclosures, are crucial to financial reporting because they communicate accounting information to external parties, but the scope of financial reporting is much broader. It also embraces "other means of communicating information that relates, directly or indirectly, to the information provided by the accounting system."

      a)   Examples are disclosures required by authoritative pronouncements as supplementary information, annual reports, prospectuses, other filings with the SEC, news releases, and letters to shareholders.

   2)   Financial statements are often audited by independent accountants, but the information included in financial reporting is often not subject to outside scrutiny that would enhance its reliability or credibility.

   b.   **Characteristics and limitations of information**

   1)   Most information provided by financial reporting is financial in nature and quantified in nominal units of money, but as the general purchasing power of the unit of measure changes, financial statements expressed in nominal monetary units become less comparable and useful.

   2)   Financial reporting is ordinarily focused on individual entities.

   3)   Information supplied by financial reporting involves estimation, classification, summarization, judgment, and allocation.

   4)   Most forms of financial reporting reflect historical transactions, events, and circumstances (forecasts and projections are examples to the contrary).

   5)   Financial reporting requires the incurrence of costs, and the cost-benefit criterion must be considered in weighing the extent of financial reporting.

   6)   Financial reporting is not the only source of information required by economic decision makers.

   c.   **Objectives -- General considerations**

   1)   Although focused on investment and credit decisions, the objectives are intended to apply to information that is useful to anyone interested in the related enterprise's ability to meet its obligations or reward its investors.

   2)   Financial reporting should provide "evenhanded, neutral, or unbiased information" to facilitate business and economic decisions but not to determine what those decisions should be.

   d.   **Objective -- Information useful in investment and credit decisions**

   1)   Financial reporting should provide information that is useful to current and potential investors and creditors and other users in making rational investment, credit, and other similar decisions.

      2)   The information should be comprehensible to those who have a reasonable understanding of business and economic activities and who are willing to study the information with reasonable diligence.

  e.   **Objective -- Information useful in assessing cash flow prospects**

      1)   Financial reporting should provide information to help current and potential investors and creditors and other users in assessing the amounts, timing, and uncertainty of prospective cash receipts from dividends or interest and the proceeds from the sale, redemption, or maturity of securities or loans.

      2)   Financial reporting should also provide information to help investors, creditors, and others assess the amounts, timing, and uncertainty of prospective net cash inflows to the related enterprise.

      3)   Investing, lending, and similar activities are undertaken to obtain not merely a return of cash expended but also a return proportionate to the risk. Thus, information should be useful in assessing risk.

  f.   **Objective -- Information about enterprise resources, claims to those resources, and changes in them**

      1)   Financial reporting furnishes information that helps to identify the financial strengths and weaknesses of an enterprise, to assess its liquidity and solvency, and to evaluate its performance during a period. However, financial accounting does not directly measure the value of an enterprise, although it may provide information to those who wish to do so.

      2)   According to SFAC 1, "The primary focus of financial reporting is information about an enterprise's performance provided by measures of earnings and its components."

          a)   Although such information concerns the past, investors and creditors commonly use it to evaluate an enterprise's prospects. Information about past performance is most valuable when the going concern assumption is appropriate, that is, when an enterprise is expected to continue in operation for an indefinite time.

          b)   Measures of earnings and its components are of special interest to those concerned with an enterprise's cash flow potential. However, cash-basis financial statements for a short period, such as a year, are less valuable for this purpose than accrual-basis statements.

      3)   Although the primary focus is on earnings, information about cash flows is useful for understanding operations, evaluating financing activities, assessing liquidity and solvency, and interpreting earnings information.

      4)   Financial reporting should provide information about management's stewardship of resources, including their efficient and profitable use.

          a)   However, it does not separate management performance from enterprise performance. The latter is affected by many factors other than management's activities. Thus, financial reporting does not directly provide information about management performance.

      5)   Financial reporting should include management's explanations and interpretations.

2.   SFAC 4, *Objectives of Financial Reporting by Nonbusiness Organizations*, is beyond the scope of this text.

3. **Qualitative Characteristics of Accounting Information (SFAC 2)**

   a. SFAC 2 describes the qualities or characteristics of accounting information required by accounting standards, i.e., the qualities that make accounting information useful for decision making. These qualities apply to information of both business enterprises and not-for-profit organizations.

      1) SFAC 2 presents the hierarchy of accounting qualities in the following table:

A HIERARCHY OF ACCOUNTING QUALITIES

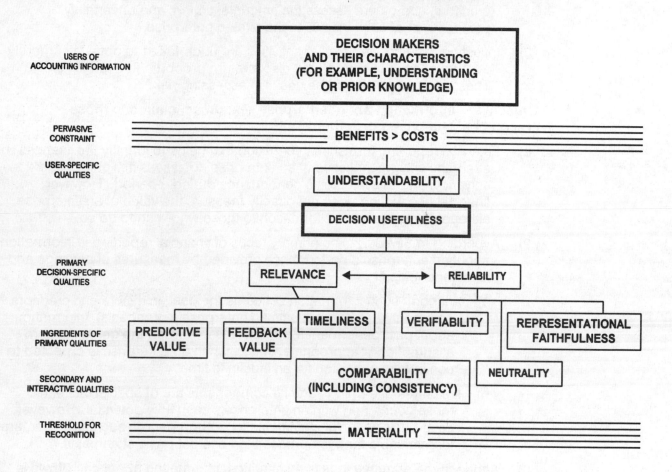

   b. **Decision makers.** Decision making has a central role in financial reporting, and decision makers must ultimately determine what information is useful.

      1) Information becomes more beneficial as it is understood by a greater number of users.

      2) **Understandability** (a user-specific quality) depends on both the characteristics of users (such as prior training and knowledge) and those of the information (reliability, relevance, etc.).

   c. **Relevance.** The primary decision-specific qualities are relevance and reliability. Relevance is "the capacity of information to make a difference in a decision by helping users to form predictions about the outcomes of past, present, and future events or to confirm or correct prior expectations."

      1)   The two principal ingredients of relevance are feedback value and predictive value.

          a)   **Feedback value** is defined as "the quality of information that enables users to confirm or correct prior expectations."

          b)   **Predictive value** is "the quality of information that helps users to increase the likelihood of correctly forecasting the outcome of past or current events."

      2)   SFAC 2 describes timeliness as an ancillary aspect of relevance.

          a)   **Timeliness** means "having information available to a decision maker before it loses its capacity to influence decisions."

d.   **Reliability.** The other primary decision-specific quality is reliability. Reliability is "the quality of information that assures that information is reasonably free from error and bias and faithfully represents what it purports to represent."

      1)   The first ingredient of reliability is **representational faithfulness**, which is "correspondence or agreement between a measure or description and the phenomenon that it purports to represent."

      2)   The second ingredient of reliability is **verifiability**, which is "the ability through consensus among measurers to ensure that information represents what it purports to represent or that the chosen method of measurement has been used without error or bias."

      3)   **Conservatism** is "a prudent reaction to uncertainty to try to ensure that uncertainty and risks inherent in business situations are adequately considered."

          a)   Conservatism does not mean a deliberate understatement of net assets and net income.

              i)   Thus, if estimates of future amounts to be paid or received differ but are equally likely, conservatism requires using the least optimistic estimate. However, if the estimates are not equally likely, conservatism does not necessarily require use of the estimate that results in understatement rather than the estimate that is the most likely.

e.   Secondary and interactive qualities

      1)   **Neutrality** is "absence in reported information of bias intended to attain a predetermined result or to induce a particular mode of behavior."

          a)   Neutrality interacts with the other ingredients of reliability.

      2)   **Comparability** is "the quality of information that enables users to identify similarities in and differences between two sets of economic phenomena."

          a)   Comparability interacts with the primary decision-specific qualities to enhance the usefulness of accounting information.

          b)   Comparability is not a quality of information in the same sense as relevance and reliability. Rather, it is a quality of the relationship among items of information.

          c)   Comparability includes **consistency**, which is "conformity from period to period with unchanging policies and procedures."

f.   **Materiality** is the threshold for recognition. Materiality is "the magnitude of an omission or misstatement of accounting information that, in the light of surrounding circumstances, makes it probable that the judgment of a reasonable person relying on the information would have been changed or influenced by the omission or misstatement."

   1)   The importance of materiality is emphasized by the exemption of immaterial items from the application of GAAP.

   2)   Judgments about materiality are primarily quantitative but are affected by qualitative concerns about the nature of particular items and the circumstances in which the judgments are made.

      a)   Because the unique circumstances affecting materiality judgments differ substantially, general standards of materiality ordinarily have not been promulgated.

g.   **Costs and benefits** is the pervasive constraint. Like other goods, financial information will not be sought often unless its benefits exceed its costs. However, these costs and benefits cannot be objectively quantified.

4.   **Elements of Financial Statements**. The elements of financial statements are defined in SFAC 6, which applies to business enterprises and not-for-profit entities. The elements defined are those that relate to measuring the performance and status of an entity based on information provided by accrual accounting.

a.   The following elements reflect resources and claims thereto at a moment in time:

   1)   **Assets** are "probable future economic benefits obtained or controlled by a particular entity as a result of past transactions or events."

      a)   A valuation allowance changes the carrying amount of an asset. It is not a separate asset or a liability.

   2)   **Liabilities** are "probable future sacrifices of economic benefits arising from present obligations of a particular entity to transfer assets or provide services to other entities in the future as a result of past transactions or events."

      a)   A valuation account, e.g., bond premium or discount, changes the carrying amount of a liability.

   3)   **Equity or net assets** is "the residual interest in the assets of an entity that remains after deducting its liabilities."

      a)   Equity of a business enterprise, in contrast with the net assets of a nonprofit entity, is changed by investments by, and distributions to, owners.

b.   The following elements describe transactions, events, and circumstances during intervals of time (the first three apply only to business enterprises):

   1)   **Investments by owners** are "increases in equity of a particular business enterprise resulting from transfers to it from other entities of something valuable to obtain or increase ownership interests (or equity) in it."

   2)   **Distributions to owners** are "decreases in equity of a particular business enterprise resulting from transferring assets, rendering services, or incurring liabilities by the enterprise to owners."

      a)   A distribution to owners decreases equity (the ownership interest).

   3)   **Comprehensive income** is "the change in equity of a business enterprise during a period from transactions and other events and circumstances from nonowner sources."

a) It excludes changes in equity resulting from investments by and distributions to owners.

b) Both comprehensive income and traditional financial statements are based on the financial capital maintenance concept; i.e., comprehensive income is a return on, not a return of, financial capital.

c) Comprehensive income differs from measures of net income in current practice because it encompasses certain changes in equity recognized in the equity section of the balance sheet but not in the income statement.

   i) These changes primarily include holding gains and losses, such as changes in the fair values of available-for-sale securities, adjustments arising from translating an entity's financial statements from its functional currency into the reporting currency, and the excess of an additional minimum pension liability over any unrecognized prior service cost.

d) Comprehensive income also differs from earnings as defined in SFAC 5. Moreover, adding to the terminological confusion, earnings is sometimes used in current practice as a synonym for net income. Earnings is similar to net income except that it excludes the cumulative effects of certain accounting adjustments of prior periods, e.g., the cumulative effect of a change in accounting principle.

4) **Revenues** are "inflows or other enhancements of assets of an entity or settlements of its liabilities (or a combination of both) from delivering or producing goods, rendering services, or other activities that constitute the entity's ongoing major or central operations."

5) **Expenses** are "outflows or other using up of assets or incurrences of liabilities (or a combination of both) from delivering or producing goods, rendering services, or carrying out other activities that constitute the entity's ongoing major or central operations."

6) **Gains (losses)** are increases (decreases) in equity "from peripheral or incidental transactions of an entity and from all other transactions and other events and circumstances affecting the entity except those that result from revenues (expenses) or investments by (distributions to) owners."

5. **Recognition and Measurement Concepts**. Recognition and measurement concepts are discussed in SFAC 5.

   a. Recognition criteria determine whether and when items should be incorporated into the financial statements, either initially or as changes in existing items.

      1) Four fundamental recognition criteria apply to all recognition issues. However, each is subject to the pervasive cost-benefit constraint and the materiality threshold.

         a) The item must meet the definition of an element of financial statements.

         b) It must have a relevant attribute measurable with sufficient reliability (measurability).

         c) The information about it must be capable of making a difference in user decisions (relevance).

         d) The information must be representationally faithful, verifiable, and neutral (reliability).

2)   According to the revenue recognition principle, revenue should be recognized when (1) realized or realizable and (2) earned.

    a)   Revenues are **realized** when goods or services have been exchanged for cash or claims to cash.

    b)   Revenues are **realizable** when goods or services have been exchanged for assets that are readily convertible into cash or claims to cash.

    c)   Revenues are **earned** when the earning process has been substantially completed and the entity is entitled to the resulting benefits or revenues.

    d)   The two conditions are usually met when goods are delivered or services are rendered, that is, at the time of sale, which is customarily the time of delivery.

    e)   As a reflection of the profession's conservatism, expenses and **losses** have historically been subject to less stringent recognition criteria than revenues and gains.

        i)   Expenses and losses are not subject to the realization criterion.

        ii)   Rather, expenses and losses are recognized when a consumption of economic benefits occurs during the entity's primary activities or when the ability of existing assets to provide future benefits has been impaired.

            • An expense or loss may also be recognized when a liability has been incurred or increased without the receipt of corresponding benefits; a probable and reasonably estimable contingent loss is an example.

3)   The following are exceptions to the basic revenue recognition rules:

    a)   Revenues from long-term contracts may be recognized using the **percentage-of-completion method**.

        i)   This method allows for revenue to be recognized at various stages of the contract although the entire job is not complete.

    b)   The **completion-of-production method** is an appropriate basis for recognition if products or other assets are readily realizable, e.g., precious metals and some agricultural products.

    c)   If the collectibility of assets is relatively uncertain, revenues and gains may be recognized as cash is received using the **installment sales method**.

b.   Different **measurement attributes** of assets and liabilities are used in current practice.

1)   **Historical cost** is the cash or equivalent actually paid for an asset and is ordinarily adjusted subsequently for amortization (which includes depreciation) or other allocations. It is the relevant attribute for plant assets and most inventories.

2)   **Historical proceeds** is the cash or equivalent actually received when an obligation was created and may be subsequently amortized. It is the relevant attribute for liabilities incurred to provide goods or services to customers. An example is a magazine subscription.

3) **Current (replacement) cost** is the cash or equivalent that would have to be paid for a current acquisition of the same or an equivalent asset. Inventory valued at the lower of cost or market may reflect current cost.

4) **Current market value (exit value)** is the cash or equivalent realizable by selling an asset in an orderly liquidation (not in a forced sale). It is used to measure some marketable securities, e.g., those held by investment companies, or assets expected to be sold at below their carrying amount. Certain liabilities, such as those incurred by writers of options who do not own the underlying assets, are also measured at current market value.

5) **Net realizable value** is the cash or equivalent expected to be received for an asset in the due course of business, minus the costs of completion and sale. It is used to measure short-term receivables and some inventories. Net realizable value is distinct from liquidation value, which is the appropriate valuation of assets and liabilities when the going concern assumption no longer holds.

6) **Net settlement value** is the cash or equivalent that the entity expects to pay to satisfy the obligation in the due course of business. It is used to measure such items as trade payables and warranty obligations. Net settlement value ignores present value considerations. The amounts that will be realized in a liquidation are usually less than those that would have been received in the due course of business.

7) **Present value** is in theory the most relevant method of measurement because it incorporates time value of money concepts. Determination of the present value of an asset or liability requires discounting at an appropriate interest rate the related future cash flows expected to occur in the due course of business. In practice, it is used only for long-term receivables and payables.

c. **Nominal units of money** are expected to continue as the measurement scale in current practice.

1) The use of monetary units unadjusted for changes in purchasing power is not ideal, but it has the virtue of simplicity and does not result in excessive distortion if inflation or deflation is relatively low.

6. Stop and review! You have completed the outline for this subunit. Study multiple-choice questions 7 through 30 beginning on page 393.

D. Limitations of Financial Statement Information

1. The measurements made in financial statements do not necessarily represent the true worth of a firm or its segments. The following are common limitations of financial statements:

a. The measurements are made in terms of money; therefore, qualitative aspects of a firm are not expressed.

b. Information supplied by financial reporting involves estimation, classification, summarization, judgment, and allocation.

c. Financial statements primarily reflect transactions that have already occurred; consequently, they are usually based on historical cost.

    d.   Only transactions involving an entity being reported upon are reflected in that entity's financial reports. However, transactions of other entities, e.g., competitors, may be very important.

    e.   Financial statements are based on the going concern assumption. If that assumption is invalid, the appropriate attribute for measuring financial statement items is liquidation value, not historical cost, fair value, net realizable value, etc.

2.   **Historical Cost Limitations**. As previously mentioned, most transactions on financial statements are recorded at their value on the date of the transaction. Many assets previously acquired are recorded on the balance sheet at their historical cost. When the values of these assets significantly change after the acquisition date, the balance sheet presentation of the assets becomes significantly less relevant in determining the company's worth.

    a.   Over time, discrepancies develop between the current and the historical values of a transaction or an asset. For example, the replacement cost and the book value of assets will diverge. Moreover, the value of the unit of measure (the dollar for U.S. firms) will also change. Accordingly, comparisons between prior years and between competing firms become less meaningful.

3.   Three major limitations exist in the reporting of a firm's segments.

    a.   The definition of what constitutes a segment is a subjective determination in some respects. What represents a segment is inconsistently applied among firms and industries.

    b.   Common cost allocations between related entities are subject to management manipulation. Many different allocation bases exist, allowing management to choose the one with the most benefits to a particular segment. Comparability of firms is again impaired.

    c.   Transfer pricing exhibits the same limitations as cost allocation. Transfer prices tend to be set to benefit particular segments and are also subject to management manipulation.

4.   Stop and review! You have completed the outline for this subunit. Study multiple-choice questions 31 and 32 on page 401.

E. Application of Public Reporting Standards

1.   **Generally accepted accounting principles** (GAAP) are the "conventions, rules, and procedures necessary to define accepted accounting practice at a particular time." They include both the broad guidelines and the detailed practices and procedures promulgated by the profession that provide uniform standards to measure financial presentations (**AU 411**, *The Meaning of "Present Fairly in Conformity with Generally Accepted Accounting Principles" in the Independent Auditor's Report*).

2.   AU 411 presents a GAAP hierarchy for both nongovernmental entities and state and local governments. The nongovernmental hierarchy is given on the opposite page. Conduct Rule 203 of the AICPA's *Code of Professional Conduct* provides that a member shall not express assurances about conformity with GAAP if the financial statements contain a material departure from a principle promulgated by bodies designated by the AICPA Council to establish such principles. However, in unusual circumstances, a departure may be permissible if literal application of a principle would be misleading. The FASB is the body designated by the AICPA Council, and the pronouncements in category 2.a. on the opposite page (officially established accounting principles) constitute principles as contemplated in Conduct Rule 203.

Established Accounting Principles

a. FASB Standards and Interpretations, APB Opinions, and AICPA Accounting Research Bulletins

b. FASB Technical Bulletins, AICPA Industry Audit and Accounting Guides, and AICPA Statements of Position

c. Consensus positions of the FASB Emerging Issues Task Force and AICPA Practice Bulletins

d. AICPA accounting interpretations, "Qs and As" published by the FASB staff, as well as industry practices widely recognized and prevalent

Other Literature

e. Other authoritative literature including FASB Concepts Statements; APB Statements; AICPA Issues Papers; International Accounting Standards Committee Statements; GASB Statements, Interpretations, and Technical Bulletins; pronouncements of other professional associations or regulatory agencies; AICPA Technical Practice Aids; and accounting textbooks, handbooks, and articles

3. **Comprehensive Bases of Accounting Other than GAAP.** The applicable pronouncement is **AU 623** (SAS 62), *Special Reports*. A comprehensive basis of accounting other than GAAP may be

a. A basis of accounting that the reporting entity uses to comply with the requirements or financial reporting provisions of a regulatory agency

b. A basis of accounting used for tax purposes

c. The cash basis, and modifications of the cash basis having substantial support, such as recording depreciation on fixed assets or accruing income taxes

d. A definite set of criteria having substantial support that is applied to all material items, for example, the price-level basis

4. Financial statements prepared in conformity with a comprehensive basis of accounting other than GAAP should be suitably titled.

a. Terms such as "balance sheet," "statement of financial position," "statement of cash flows," and similar unmodified titles imply that the statements were prepared in conformity with GAAP.

1) AU 623 suggests that cash-basis financial statements might be appropriately titled "statement of assets and liabilities arising from cash transactions" or "statement of revenue collected and expenses paid."

2) A statement prepared in conformity with provisions of a statutory or regulatory agency might be titled "statement of income -- statutory basis."

b. Suitable titles avoid the misrepresentation that the financial statements were prepared in accordance with GAAP.

5. Financial statements prepared on a comprehensive basis of accounting other than GAAP should include a summary of significant accounting policies, including

a. Discussion of the comprehensive basis used to prepare the financial statements and how that basis differs from GAAP.

6. **Financial Statement Disclosures**

   a. **APB 22**, *Disclosure of Accounting Policies*, requires that all significant accounting policies of a reporting entity be disclosed as an integral part of its financial statements.

      1) Disclosure of significant accounting policies is required when

         a) A selection has been made from existing acceptable alternatives.

         b) A policy is unique to the industry in which the entity operates, even if the policy is predominantly followed in that industry.

         c) GAAP have been applied in an unusual or innovative way.

      2) Certain items are explicitly listed in APB 22 as commonly required disclosures in a summary of significant accounting policies.

         a) These items include the basis of consolidation, depreciation methods, amortization of intangibles, inventory pricing, recognition of profit on long-term construction-type contracts, and recognition of revenue from franchising and leasing operations.

         b) APB 22 recognizes that financial statement disclosure of accounting policies should not duplicate details presented elsewhere in the financial statements. For example, the summary of significant policies should not contain the composition of plant assets or inventories or the maturity dates of long-term debt. Instead, the summary can refer to details about matters that are presented elsewhere in the financial statements.

      3) According to SFAS 95, an enterprise must disclose its policy for determining which items are cash equivalents.

   b. The basic segment reporting requirements are set forth in **SFAS 14**, *Financial Reporting for Segments of a Business Enterprise*. As amended, however, SFAS 14 now requires disclosure of segment information in annual financial statements of public enterprises.

      1) The information required by SFAS 14 relates to

         a) Operations in different industries
         b) Foreign operations and export sales
         c) Major customers

   c. **APB 28**, *Interim Financial Reporting*, requires certain minimum disclosures of interim data by public companies: sales, provisions for income taxes, extraordinary items, cumulative effect of accounting changes on net income, primary and fully diluted EPS, seasonal revenues, costs, expenses, significant changes in estimates or income tax expenses, disposal of a segment, contingent items, changes in accounting principles or estimates, and significant cash flows.

   d. **SFAS 57**, *Related Party Disclosures*, requires the disclosure of material related-party transactions other than compensation arrangements (officers' salaries and expenses), expense allowances, and other similar items in the ordinary course of business.

      1) According to SFAS 57, related-party transactions include transactions between

         a) A parent and its subsidiaries

         b) Subsidiaries of a common parent

    c) An enterprise and employee trusts managed by or under the trusteeship of the enterprise's management

    d) An enterprise and its principal owners, management, or members of their immediate families

    e) Affiliates

    f) An enterprise and its equity-based investees

    g) An enterprise and any other entity if one party can significantly influence the other to the extent that one party may be prevented from fully pursuing its own interests

    h) Parties all of which can be significantly influenced by another party

2) SFAS 57 requires disclosure of

    a) The nature of the relationship involved

    b) A description of the transactions for each period an income statement is presented and such other information as is deemed necessary to an understanding of the effects of the transactions

    c) The dollar amounts of transactions for each period an income statement is presented and the effects of any change in the method of establishing their terms

    d) Amounts due from or to related parties as of the date of each balance sheet, including the terms of settlement

    e) Certain tax information required by SFAS 109 if the enterprise is part of a group that files a consolidated tax return

e. **SFAS 105,** *Disclosure of Information about Financial Instruments with Off-Balance-Sheet Risk and Financial Instruments with Concentrations of Credit Risk,* requires the disclosure of information about the extent, nature, and terms of financial instruments with off-balance-sheet credit or market risk and about concentrations of credit risk for all financial instruments.

1) SFAS 105 (as slightly amended by SFAS 107) defines a **financial instrument** as cash, evidence of an ownership interest in an entity, or a contract that both

    a) Imposes on one entity a contractual obligation

        i) To deliver cash or another financial instrument to a second entity or

        ii) To exchange other financial instruments on potentially unfavorable terms with the second entity, and

    b) Conveys to that second entity a contractual right

        i) To receive cash or another financial instrument from the first entity or

        ii) To exchange other financial instruments on potentially favorable terms with the first entity.

f. **SFAS 107,** *Disclosures about Fair Value of Financial Statements,* requires all entities to disclose the fair value of financial instruments, whether or not they are recognized in the balance sheet, if it is practicable to estimate such fair values. If it is not, descriptive information relevant to estimation of the fair values should be provided. However, certain financial instruments are exempted.

g. **SFAS 119**, *Disclosure about Derivative Financial Instruments and Fair Value of Financial Instruments*, requires disclosures about futures, forward, swap, and option contracts, and other financial instruments with similar characteristics.

   1) SFAS 119 requires disclosures about amounts, nature, and terms of derivatives that are not subject to SFAS 105 because they do not have off-balance-sheet risk. It also distinguishes between instruments held or issued for trading purposes and those held or issued for purposes other than trading. Furthermore, it amends SFASs 105 and 107 to require that the above distinction be included in certain disclosures that they require.

   2) For entities that hold or issue derivatives for trading purposes, disclosure of average fair value and of net trading gains or losses is required.

      a) For entities that hold or issue derivatives for purposes other than trading, disclosure about those purposes and about how the instruments are reported in financial statements is required.

      b) For entities that hold or issue derivatives and account for them as hedges of anticipated transactions, disclosure about the anticipated transactions, the classes of derivatives used to hedge those transactions, the amounts of hedging gains and losses deferred, and the transactions or other events that result in recognition of the deferred gains or losses in earnings is required.

h. **SFAS 47**, *Disclosure of Long-Term Obligations*, requires that a company disclose commitments under unconditional purchase obligations that are associated with suppliers.

   1) Unconditional purchase obligations are commitments to transfer funds in the future for fixed or minimum amounts of goods or services at fixed or minimum prices.

   2) In addition to the disclosures required by other official pronouncements, SFAS 47 requires the disclosure of the following information for recorded obligations and redeemable stock for each of the 5 years following the date of the latest balance sheet presented:

      a) The aggregate amount of payments for unconditional purchase obligations

      b) The aggregate amount of maturities and sinking-fund requirements for all long-term borrowings

      c) The amount at which all issues of stock are redeemable at fixed or determinable prices on fixed or determinable dates

   3) If an unconditional purchase obligation is not presented in the balance sheet, certain disclosures are required, including

      a) The nature and term of the obligation

      b) The variable components of the obligation

      c) The amounts purchased under the obligation for each period an income statement is presented

      d) The amount of the fixed and determinable portion of the obligation at the latest balance sheet date and, if determinable, for each of the 5 succeeding fiscal years

7. **Reporting Issues for Multinational Companies**

   a. A U.S. corporation that operates a business through a foreign branch or division must report the income from that foreign operation on the company's U.S. income tax return. This foreign income will be taxed the same way as domestic income.

   b. A foreign subsidiary's income will not be taxed to the U.S. parent until it is distributed as a dividend to the parent.

   c. All U.S. companies doing business in foreign countries will be taxed by the foreign countries on their foreign income.

      1) Taxation may be upon dividend income, undistributed income, or value-added taxation.

      2) Many countries lower taxes on foreign companies to increase incentives to foreign investors.

   d. **SFAS 52**, *Foreign Currency Translation*, requires a foreign subsidiary of a U.S. parent company to determine a functional currency for its operations.

      1) If the foreign subsidiary has integrated its operations into the foreign country and stands alone, the functional currency is the local currency of that country.

      2) If a foreign branch or subsidiary is not operationally independent or does not stand alone, the functional currency is the U.S. dollar.

      3) If high inflation occurs in any country hosting a U.S. subsidiary, the U.S. dollar is the subsidiary's functional currency even if it stands alone.

      4) Foreign currency translation issues may affect the financial statements of a foreign subsidiary.

         a) Remeasurement gains and losses must be reflected in the subsidiary's income statement and may distort other financial statement numbers when the dollar remains the subsidiary's functional currency.

         b) However, if the subsidiary's functional currency is the local currency of the host country, the translation gains and losses are not reported in the income statement; they are reflected as a translation adjustment in shareholders' equity.

8. Stop and review! You have completed the outline for this subunit. Study multiple-choice questions 33 through 41 beginning on page 401.

F. The SEC and Its Reporting Requirements

1. The SEC was created by the Securities Exchange Act of 1934 to regulate the trading of securities and otherwise to enforce securities legislation.

   a. The basic purposes of the securities laws are to

      1) Prevent fraud and misrepresentation

      2) Require full and fair disclosure so investors can evaluate investments on their own

   b. Under the **Securities Act of 1933**, disclosure is made before the initial issuance of securities through registration (i.e., initial filing) and disseminating a prospectus to potential investors.

c.   Under the **Securities Exchange Act of 1934**, disclosure is made for subsequent trading of securities by requiring periodic reports to be filed that are made available to the public for review.

d.   The SEC requires the registration and the reports to comply with certain accounting standards and policies.

1)   **Regulation S-X** governs the reporting of financial statements, including footnotes and schedules.

2)   **Regulation S-K** provides disclosure standards, including many of a nonfinancial nature. Regulation S-K also covers certain aspects of corporate annual reports to shareholders.

3)   **Financial Reporting Releases (FRRs)** announce accounting and auditing matters of general interest.

a)   They provide explanations and clarifications of changes in accounting or auditing procedures used in reports filed with the SEC.

b)   These and **Accounting and Auditing Enforcement Releases (AAERs)** replace what used to be called Accounting Series Releases.

4)   AAERs disclose enforcement actions involving accountants.

5)   **Staff Accounting Bulletins (SABs)** are promulgated as interpretations to be followed by the SEC staff in administering disclosure requirements.

a)   SABs are not requirements to be followed by registrants.

2.   **Integrated Disclosure System**

a.   In 1982, a revised disclosure system became effective.

1)   Previously, disclosures were duplicative, i.e., required similar information in different formats under the 1933 and 1934 acts.

2)   To alleviate this problem, the integrated disclosure system

a)   Standardizes the financial statements

b)   Uses a Basic Information Package (BIP) common to most of the filings

c)   Allows incorporation by reference from the annual shareholders' report to the annual SEC report (Form 10-K)

b.   Standardized financial statements are required.

1)   They must be audited and include

a)   Balance sheets for the 2 most recent fiscal year-ends

b)   Statements of income, cash flows, and changes in shareholders' equity for the 3 most recent fiscal years

2)   They are required in the annual shareholders' report as well as in forms filed with the SEC.

3)   The accountant certifying the financial statements must be independent of the management of the filing company. The accountant is not required to be a CPA, but (s)he must be registered with a state.

c.   The **Basic Information Package (BIP)** includes the following:

1)   Standardized financial statements

2) Selected financial information

    a) Columnar format for the preceding 5 fiscal years

    b) Presentation of financial trends through comparison of key information from year to year

3) **Management's discussion and analysis** of financial condition and results of operations

    a) This information addresses such matters as liquidity, capital resources, results of operations, effects of tax legislation, and the impact of changing prices.

    b) Forward-looking information (a forecast) is encouraged but not required.

4) Market price of securities and dividends

    a) Principal market in which security is traded

    b) High and low sales prices for each quarter in the last 2 years

    c) Most recent number of shareholders

    d) Frequency and amount of dividends in the last 2 years

    e) Any restrictions on the payment of dividends

5) Description of business

    a) Fundamental developments for past 5 years, e.g., organization, reorganizations, bankruptcies, and major dispositions or acquisitions of assets

    b) Financial information of industry segments, and also foreign and domestic operations

    c) Narrative description including

        i) Principal products or services for each industry segment and principal markets for them

        ii) Total revenues of each class of products equaling or exceeding 10% or more of consolidated revenue (15% if consolidated revenue is not in excess of $50,000,000)

        iii) Other information material to the business on the basis of industry segments

6) Locations and descriptions of physical properties

7) Pending litigation, e.g., principal parties, allegations, and relief sought

8) Management

    a) General data for each director and officer

    b) Financial transactions with the corporation involving amounts in excess of $60,000

    c) Remuneration for the five highest paid directors and officers whose compensation exceeds $50,000 (including personal benefits)

9) Security holdings of directors, officers, and those owning 5% or more of the security

10) Matters submitted to shareholders for approval

11) Description of certain business relationships, such as those with related parties

3. **Registration (Initial Filing)**

    a.   The issuer must register new issuances of securities with the SEC.

        1) **Form S-1** is used for the registration statement for companies that have never registered securities.

            a) Incorporation by reference is usually not allowed, and all material must be included.

        2) **Form S-2** is a shorter form for companies that have been reporting to the SEC (Form 10-K, etc.) for at least 3 years and have done so on a timely basis.

            a) Form S-2 allows BIP to be incorporated by reference from the latest annual shareholders' report.

        3) **Form S-3** is another short form for companies that meet the requirements for Form S-2 and have at least $50,000,000 of stock held by nonaffiliates (or at least $100,000,000 with an annual trading volume of 3,000,000 or more shares).

            a) Form S-3 allows most information to be incorporated by reference from other filings with the SEC.

        4) Other forms

            a) **Form S-4** is a simplified form for business combinations.

               i) **Form F-4** is to be used by foreign registrants in business combinations.

               ii) **Form N-14** is to be used by investment companies to register securities in business combinations.

            b) **Form S-8** is for securities offered to employees under a stock option or other employee benefit plan.

            c) **Form S-11** is used by real estate investment trusts and real estate companies.

            d) **Form S-18** is for small companies not required to report annually to the SEC. The offering limit is now $7,500,000.

        5) Filings become public information.

        6) Securities may not be offered for sale to the public until the registration is effective.

            a) The registration statement is examined by the Division of Corporation Finance.

            b) Registration becomes effective 20 days after filing unless an amendment is filed or the SEC issues a stop order.

            c) A preliminary prospectus is allowed that contains the same information as a regular prospectus (prices are omitted) but is clearly marked in red (therefore called a **red herring prospectus**).

    b.   Registration forms requirements (especially Form S-1)

        1) Basic information package
        2) Plan of distribution, name of underwriter, use of broker, and commissions
        3) Use of proceeds and details of offerings other than cash

        4)   Description of the capital structure of the registrant
        5)   Risk factors
        6)   Signatures of

            a)   Issuer
            b)   Principal executive, financial, and accounting officers
            c)   Majority of board of directors

  c.   The **prospectus** is part of the registration statement.

      1)   Its purpose is to provide investors with information to make an informed investment decision.

      2)   However, it usually may be presented in a more condensed or summarized form than Form S-1.

4.   **Form 10** is used to register securities under the 1934 act.

  a.   Securities must be registered if they are traded in one of the ways listed below.

      1)   On a national securities exchange

      2)   Over the counter if the issuer has assets in excess of $5,000,000 and there are 500 or more shareholders

  b.   An issuer may voluntarily register its securities.

  c.   An issuer may deregister its securities if its shareholders decrease to fewer than 300 or if its shareholders are fewer than 500 and it had less than $5,000,000 in assets for each of the three most recent fiscal year-ends.

  d.   Banks must also register their securities, but they file with the appropriate banking authority, not with the SEC.

  e.   The required contents of Form 10 are

      1)   Basic information package
      2)   Other information required for Form S-1

5.   **Form 10-K** is the annual report to the SEC. It must be

  a.   Filed within 90 days of corporation's year-end
  b.   Certified by an independent accountant
  c.   Signed by the following:

      1)   Principal executive, financial, and accounting officers
      2)   Majority of the board of directors

  d.   Presented with the basic information package

      1)   Information contained in the annual report to shareholders may be incorporated by reference.

      2)   Information contained in proxy statements may also be incorporated by reference into Form 10-K because the proxy statement is a published source readily available to the shareholders and investing public.

6.   **Form 10-Q** is the quarterly report to the SEC.

  a.   It must be filed for each of the first three quarters of the year within 45 days after the end of each quarter.

  b.   Financial statements need not be certified by an independent accountant, but they must be prepared in accordance with APB 28, *Interim Financial Reporting*.

    c.   Also required are changes during the quarter, for example,

        1)   Legal proceedings
        2)   Increase, decrease, or change in securities or indebtedness
        3)   Matters submitted to shareholders for a vote
        4)   Exhibits and reports on Form 8-K
        5)   Other material events not reported on Form 8-K

7.   **Form 8-K** is a current report to disclose material events.

    a.   It must be filed within 15 days after the material event takes place. Also, a change in independent accountants or the resignation of a director must be reported within 5 business days.

    b.   Material events

        1)   Change in control

        2)   Acquisition or disposition of a significant amount of assets not in the ordinary course of business

        3)   Bankruptcy or receivership

        4)   Resignation of directors

        5)   A change in independent accountants, the reporting requirements for which are listed below:

            a)   Date

            b)   Disclosure of any disagreements in the prior 2 years

            c)   Disclosure of certain reportable events, e.g., the former accountants' concerns about internal control or the reliability of management's representations

            d)   Disclosure of prior consultations with the new accountants

            e)   Whether a disagreement or reportable event was discussed with the audit committee

            f)   Whether the company authorized the former accountants to respond fully to the new accountants' inquiries about disagreements

            g)   Whether the former accountants were dismissed, resigned, or refused to seek reemployment

            h)   Disclosure of any qualification of reports in the prior 2 years

            i)   Letter from the former accountant indicating agreement (or disagreement) with the above. The letter must be submitted within 10 business days.

            j)   Whether the decision to change was recommended or approved by the audit committee or the board of directors

        6)   Other events, e.g., major legal proceedings, default on securities or debt, write-down or write-off of assets, change of more than 5% of ownership of a security

8.   Stop and review! You have completed the outline for this subunit. Study multiple-choice questions 42 through 54 beginning on page 404.

MULTIPLE-CHOICE QUESTIONS

A. External Financial Statements; Users and Their Needs

1. Financial statement users with a direct economic interest in a specific business include

A. Financial advisers.

B. Regulatory bodies.

C. Stock markets.

D. Suppliers.

The correct answer is (D). *(Publisher)*
REQUIRED: The financial statement users with direct economic interests.
DISCUSSION: Users with direct interests include investors or potential investors, suppliers and creditors, employees, and management.
Answers (A), (B), and (C) are incorrect because financial advisers, regulatory bodies, and stock markets have indirect interests.

2. Which of the following is not a need of financial statement users?

A. Financial advisers and analysts need financial statements to help investors evaluate particular investments.

B. Stock exchanges need financial statements to set a firm's stock price.

C. Regulatory agencies need financial statements to evaluate price changes for regulated industries.

D. Employees need financial information to negotiate wages and fringe benefits.

The correct answer is (B). *(Publisher)*
REQUIRED: The item not a need of financial statement users.
DISCUSSION: Investors' purchases and sales set stock prices. Stock exchanges need financial statements to evaluate whether to accept a firm's stock for listing or whether to suspend trading in the stock.
Answer (A) is incorrect because financial advisers use financial statements for evaluating investments. Answer (C) is incorrect because regulatory agencies use financial statements for rate making. Answer (D) is incorrect because employees use financial statements for labor negotiations.

B. Development of Accounting Standards

3. Accounting standard setting in the U.S. is

A. Done primarily by the Securities and Exchange Commission.

B. Done primarily by the private sector.

C. The responsibility of the public sector.

D. Done primarily by the International Accounting Standards Committee.

The correct answer is (B). *(CMA 1295 2-12)*
REQUIRED: The source of U.S. accounting standards.
DISCUSSION: Accounting standards in the United States are set primarily by the private sector. The primary parties are the FASB and the AcSEC. The SEC and the IRS have the authority to set accounting standards, but neither has exercised that authority to any degree.
Answer (A) is incorrect because, although the SEC was granted the authority to establish accounting practices and procedures in 1934, it delegated this authority to the accounting profession. Accounting Series Release 150 acknowledged that the SEC would continue to look to the private sector for leadership in establishing and improving accounting principles. Answer (C) is incorrect because the public sector, through the SEC, has delegated accounting standard setting to the private sector. Answer (D) is incorrect because the IASC works to encourage uniform accounting principles worldwide, but it has no influence in a particular country.

4. When establishing financial accounting standards, the FASB

    A.   Issues an exposure draft as a final statement.

    B.   Holds a public hearing at least 60 days after the discussion memorandum is released.

    C.   Consults only with the SEC before the statement is released.

    D.   Delegates responsibility to the SEC or the IRS.

The correct answer is (B). *(Publisher)*

    REQUIRED: The true statement about standard setting by the FASB.

    DISCUSSION: After a group of experts has defined specific problems and a range of solutions for an agenda item, the FASB's staff conducts research and analysis and drafts a discussion memorandum. The FASB then holds a public hearing at least 60 days after the discussion memorandum is released.

    Answer (A) is incorrect because the exposure draft is usually amended following evaluation of public comment. Answer (C) is incorrect because all interested parties have an opportunity to comment. Answer (D) is incorrect because the SEC has effectively delegated standard-setting authority to the FASB.

5. In regard to accounting standards, the SEC

    A.   Has abdicated all responsibility to the FASB.

    B.   Does not require companies listed on the stock exchange to submit audited financial statements.

    C.   Continues to identify areas in which additional information should be reported.

    D.   Still establishes the principles to be followed by firms subject to the securities acts.

The correct answer is (C). *(Publisher)*

    REQUIRED: The SEC's role in standard setting.

    DISCUSSION: With the creation of the FASB, the SEC issued Accounting Series Release No. 150, which acknowledged that the SEC would continue to look to the private sector (through the FASB) for leadership in establishing and improving accounting principles. However, the release also stated that the SEC would identify areas for which additional information is needed and would determine the appropriate methods of disclosure to meet those needs.

    Answer (A) is incorrect because the SEC retains the ultimate power to set accounting standards. Answer (B) is incorrect because audited financial statements must be submitted by publicly traded companies. Answer (D) is incorrect because the GAAP, which are set primarily but not exclusively by the FASB, apply to firms subject to the securities acts.

6. The International Accounting Standards Committee (IASC)

    A.   Directly influences governmental legislation regarding accounting standards.

    B.   Develops binding pronouncements for its members.

    C.   Is composed of members from national standard-setting bodies.

    D.   Establishes uniform accounting standards to eliminate reporting differences among nations.

The correct answer is (D). *(Publisher)*

    REQUIRED: The correct statement about the IASC.

    DISCUSSION: The IASC was established to harmonize accounting standards used by member countries. Currently, 13 nations are voting members, and 31 standards have been issued. An affirmative vote by three-fourths of the IASC members is required to pass a standard. However, IASC pronouncements are not binding.

    Answer (A) is incorrect because the IASC has no direct influence on governmental legislation. Answer (B) is incorrect because the IASC authority is restricted to the willingness of participating and other countries to adopt its standards. Answer (C) is incorrect because the IASC is composed of members from various national professional accounting organizations, such as the AICPA.

C. Conceptual Framework Underlying Financial Accounting

7. An objective of financial reporting is to

A. Provide information useful for investor decisions.

B. Assess the adequacy of internal control.

C. Evaluate management results compared with standards.

D. Provide information on compliance with established procedures.

The correct answer is (A). *(CIA 1190 IV-27)*
REQUIRED: The objective of financial reporting.
DISCUSSION: According to SFAC 1, the objectives of financial reporting are concerned with the underlying goals and purposes of accounting. They are to provide (1) information useful to those making investment and credit decisions, assuming that those individuals have a reasonable understanding of business and economic activities; (2) help to current and potential investors and creditors and other users in assessing the amount, timing, and uncertainty of future cash flows; and (3) knowledge about economic resources, claims to those resources, and the changes therein.
Answers (B), (C), and (D) are incorrect because assessing the adequacy of internal control, evaluating management results compared with standards, and providing information on compliance with established procedures are functions of internal auditing, not financial reporting.

8. A publicly held corporation is required to have its financial statements audited by an independent external auditor. The three purposes of these financial statements are to provide useful information (1) for credit and investment decisions, (2) about the firm's resources, and (3) for

A. Determining the impact of inflation.

B. Long-lived asset replacements.

C. Assessing market values of assets.

D. Evaluating prospective cash flows.

The correct answer is (D). *(CMA 1286 4-24)*
REQUIRED: The third purpose of financial statements.
DISCUSSION: According to SFAC 1, *Objectives of Financial Reporting by Business Enterprises*, "Financial reporting should provide information to help present and potential investors and creditors and other users in assessing the amounts, timing, and uncertainty of prospective cash receipts from dividends or interest and the proceeds from the sale, redemption, or maturity of securities or loans. Since investors' and creditors' cash flows are related to enterprise cash flows, financial reporting should provide information to help investors, creditors, and others assess the amounts, timing, and uncertainty of prospective net cash inflows to the related enterprise."
Answer (A) is incorrect because the company is not required to present information about the effects of price level changes. Answer (B) is incorrect because such information will be communicated if the three broad purposes stated in SFAC 1 are satisfied. Answer (C) is incorrect because required financial statements for the most part reflect historical costs.

9. According to SFAC 1, *Objectives of Financial Reporting by Business Enterprises*,

A. External users have the ability to prescribe information they want.

B. Information is always based on exact measures.

C. Financial reporting is usually based on industries or the economy as a whole.

D. Financial accounting does not directly measure the value of a business enterprise.

The correct answer is (D). *(Publisher)*
REQUIRED: The true statement about the objectives of financial reporting.
DISCUSSION: Financial reporting furnishes information that helps to identify the financial strengths and weaknesses of an enterprise, to assess its liquidity and solvency, and to evaluate its performance during a period of time. However, financial accounting does not directly measure the value of an enterprise, although it may provide information to those who wish to do so.
Answer (A) is incorrect because some external users (e.g., taxing authorities) have the authority to obtain desired information, but most do not. The objectives are based on the needs of the latter class of users. Answer (B) is incorrect because financial information involves estimation and judgment. Answer (C) is incorrect because financial reporting is usually based on individual entities.

10. The accounting system should be designed

A. To meet external reporting requirements.

B. To balance management information needs with the cost of obtaining that information.

C. To eliminate fraud by accounting personnel.

D. By persons not directly involved with the system, such as consultants.

The correct answer is (B). *(CMA 684 4-1)*

REQUIRED: The true statement about the design of an internal accounting and reporting system.

DISCUSSION: One of the characteristics and limitations of the kind of information that financial reporting can provide is that the information is provided and used at a cost (see SFAC 1). All accounting information is subject to two quantitative constraints: materiality and cost-benefit. If a reasonable person relying on the information would not have changed his/her judgment as a result of an omission or misstatement, it is not considered material. The cost-benefit constraint states that the benefits of information must exceed the cost of obtaining it.

Answer (A) is incorrect because the first objective of the internal accounting and reporting system must be to provide relevant and reliable information for management decision making. Answer (C) is incorrect because the control of fraud is only an objective to the extent that the system is cost beneficial. Answer (D) is incorrect because those who best know the information needs should design the system.

11. Objectivity as used in accounting refers to

A. Determining the revenue first, then determining the costs incurred in earning that revenue.

B. The entity's giving the same treatment to comparable transactions from period to period.

C. The accountant's use of data that can be verified by other competent persons.

D. The disclosure of all facts that may influence the judgment of an informed reader.

The correct answer is (C). *(CMA 684 4-2)*

REQUIRED: The meaning of objectivity as the term is used in accounting.

DISCUSSION: If accounting information used by one accountant is objective, it can be verified by other competent persons. Statement on Management Accounting 2A, *Management Accounting Glossary*, defines objectivity as a trait of financial reporting that emphasizes the verifiable, factual nature of events or transactions and minimizes the personal influence of the measurer in the measurement process. SFAC 2 defines reliable information as verifiable, neutral, and representationally faithful.

Answer (A) is incorrect because it concerns the matching principle. Answer (B) is incorrect because it refers to the consistency principle. Answer (D) is incorrect because it refers to the full disclosure principle.

12. If the going-concern assumption is no longer valid for a company,

A. Land held as an investment would be valued at its liquidation value.

B. All prepaid assets would be completely written off immediately.

C. Total contributed capital and retained earnings would remain unchanged.

D. The allowance for uncollectible accounts would be eliminated.

The correct answer is (A). *(CMA 689 4-30)*

REQUIRED: The true statement about a situation in which the going-concern assumption is not valid.

DISCUSSION: Under the going-concern, or business continuity, assumption, a financial statement user is to presume that a company will continue operating indefinitely in the absence of indications to the contrary. The essence of this assumption is that liquidation values are not used in the financial statements because the firm is unlikely to liquidate in the near future. When the going-concern assumption is not valid, it is necessary to make appropriate disclosures and to report assets at their liquidation values. For instance, land would no longer be reported at cost but at its liquidation value.

Answer (B) is incorrect because some prepaid assets may have a liquidation value. For example, supplies can be sold and prepaid insurance can be redeemed. Answer (C) is incorrect because capital would change to equalize the write-downs and write-ups on the asset side of the balance sheet. Answer (D) is incorrect because the allowance would still exist because many of the accounts may never be paid.

Questions 13 and 14 are based on Statement of Financial Accounting Concepts No. 5, *Recognition and Measurement in Financial Statements of Business Enterprises*.

13. The concepts of earnings and comprehensive income have the same broad components, but they are not the same because certain classes of gains and losses are included in comprehensive income but are excluded from earnings. One of the items included in comprehensive income but excluded from earnings is

- A. A gain on discontinued operations.
- B. The cumulative effect of a change in accounting principle.
- C. A loss from the obsolescence of a material amount of inventory.
- D. An extraordinary gain.

The correct answer is (B). *(CMA 1290 2-19)*
REQUIRED: The item included in comprehensive income but not earnings.
DISCUSSION: SFAC 5 defines earnings as a measure of entity performance during a period similar to, but distinct from, present net income. It excludes certain accounting adjustments of prior periods that are currently recognized, such as the cumulative effect of a change in principle. Comprehensive income is "a broad measure of the effects of transactions and other events on an entity, including all recognized changes in equity (net assets) of the entity during a period from transactions and other events and circumstances except those resulting from investments by owners and distribution to owners." Certain gains and losses included in comprehensive income (referred to as "cumulative accounting adjustments" and "other nonowner changes in equity") are excluded from earnings.
Answers (A), (C), and (D) are incorrect because a gain on discontinued operations, a loss from the obsolescence of a material amount of inventory, and an extraordinary gain, are all included in both earnings and comprehensive income.

14. Revenues of an entity are normally measured by the exchange values of the assets or liabilities involved. Recognition of revenue does not occur until

- A. The revenue is realized and assured of collection.
- B. The revenue is realized and earned.
- C. Products or services are exchanged for cash or claims to cash.
- D. The entity has substantially accomplished what it agreed to do.

The correct answer is (B). *(CMA 1290 2-20)*
REQUIRED: The timing of the recognition of revenue.
DISCUSSION: Recognition is the process of recording an item in the financial records. Revenue should not be recognized until it is (1) realized or realizable and (2) earned. Revenues are realized in an exchange for cash or claims to cash. Revenues are realizable when "related assets received or held are readily convertible to known amounts of cash or claims to cash." Revenues are earned "when the entity has substantially accomplished what it must do to be entitled to the benefits represented by the revenues" (SFAC 5).
Answer (A) is incorrect because absolute assurance of collectibility is not required. Answer (C) is incorrect because an exchange is insufficient. The earning process must also be substantially complete. Answer (D) is incorrect because recognition also requires that revenue be realized or realizable as well as earned.

Questions 15 and 16 are based on the following information. According to Statement of Financial Accounting Concepts 5, *Recognition and Measurement in Financial Statements of Business Enterprises*, items currently reported in financial statements are measured by different attributes, depending on the nature of the item and the relevance and reliability of the attribute measured.

15. The appropriate attribute to use when measuring long-term payables is

- A. Historical cost.
- B. Current cost.
- C. Current market value.
- D. Present value of future cash flows.

The correct answer is (D). *(CMA 691 2-16)*
REQUIRED: The appropriate attribute to use when measuring long-term payables.
DISCUSSION: According to SFAC 5, the appropriate measurement attribute for long-term liabilities is "the present or discounted value of future cash outflows expected to be required to satisfy the liability in due course of business."
Answer (A) is incorrect because historical cost is an attribute of assets, not liabilities. Answer (B) is incorrect because current cost is an attribute of assets, not liabilities. Answer (C) is incorrect because current market value is an attribute of assets, not liabilities.

16. Refer to the fact pattern preceding question 15 on page 395. The appropriate attribute to use when measuring damaged inventory is

A. Historical cost.

B. Current cost.

C. Current market value.

D. Net realizable value.

The correct answer is (D). *(CMA 691 2-17)*

REQUIRED: The appropriate attribute to use when measuring damaged inventory.

DISCUSSION: Damaged inventory should be valued at its net realizable value, "which is the nondiscounted amount of cash, or its equivalent, into which an asset is expected to be converted in due course of business minus direct costs, if any, necessary to make that conversion" (SFAC 5). A markdown from cost is appropriate because the utility of the asset is not as great as when it was acquired. Also, because the company is not in the business of dealing in damaged inventory, there is no provision for a profit on the sale of such inventory. Thus, damaged inventory is valued at its expected selling price minus any costs of disposal.

Answer (A) is incorrect because the amount of cash or its equivalent paid to acquire an asset (historical cost) does not reflect the diminution of value caused by the damage to the inventory. Answers (B) and (C) are incorrect because damaged inventory should be recorded at net realizable value.

Question 17 is based on the following information. Randolf Castell opened a small general store in 1946. A cousin, Alfred Bedford, served as bookkeeper and office manager while Castell concentrated on operations. The business prospered and each of Castell's three sons joined their father in the business. In fact, as each son finished school, Castell opened a new store and put the son in charge. In time, each son began to specialize: one in hardware, another in dry goods, and the third in furniture. Further expansion took place, and the business was incorporated as Four Castles Inc. with all of the stock being held by the family. Castell closed his original store to serve as president and concentrate on administration.

As Four Castles prospered and more stores opened, the company needed additional capital. Bedford suggested "going public" but pointed out that this required accounting and reporting procedures with which he was unfamiliar. Therefore, a trained and qualified accountant was hired as controller. The new controller has had to provide explanations to Castell and Bedford on the accounting and reporting requirements of public companies.

---

17. Four Castles' records have been kept on the tax basis of accounting to eliminate the need to maintain a second set of records. When the tax basis allowed for a choice between cash and accrual bases of accounting, the firm employed the cash basis. Neither the tax basis nor the cash basis of accounting is generally acceptable for the financial statements of a publicly held corporation such as Four Castles. The accrual basis of accounting must be used so that

A. Specific expenses are related to specific revenues.

B. Expenses of a time period are related to revenues of the same time period.

C. Expenses and related revenues are expressed in terms of economic reality.

D. Necessary time-period allocations of long-lived costs are made on a systematic or rational basis.

The correct answer is (B). *(CMA 1286 4-25)*

REQUIRED: The reason the accrual basis of accounting must be used.

DISCUSSION: According to SFAC 1, "Accrual accounting attempts to record the financial effects on an enterprise of transactions and other events and circumstances that have cash consequences for an enterprise in the periods in which those transactions, events, and circumstances occur rather than only in the periods in which cash is received or paid by the enterprise."

Answer (A) is incorrect because perfect matching of expenses with revenues is often impossible. Answer (C) is incorrect because the accrual basis is principally used to match the occurrence and the effects of transactions. Economic reality is more difficult to express in historical cost/nominal dollar financial statements. Answer (D) is incorrect because it is a function of matching (depreciation is an allocation).

18. Accounting information that users can depend on to represent the economic conditions or events that it purports to represent best defines

- A. Relevance.
- B. Timeliness.
- C. Feedback value.
- D. Reliability.

The correct answer is (D). *(CMA 1292 2-2)*

REQUIRED: The term meaning that accounting information represents the economic conditions or events that it purports to represent.

DISCUSSION: Reliability and relevance are the two primary decision-specific accounting qualities. Reliability is defined as the quality of information that provides assurance that the information is reasonably free from error and bias and faithfully represents what it purports to represent. The ingredients of reliability are verifiability, neutrality, and representational faithfulness (SFAC 2).

Answer (A) is incorrect because relevant accounting information must be capable of making a difference in a decision. Answers (B) and (C) are incorrect because timeliness and feedback value are elements of relevance.

19. A company that sprays chemicals in residences to eliminate or prevent infestation of insects requires that customers prepay for 3 months' service at the beginning of each new quarter. Select the term that appropriately describes this situation from the viewpoint of the exterminating company.

- A. Unearned revenue.
- B. Earned revenue.
- C. Accrued revenue.
- D. Prepaid expense.

The correct answer is (A). *(CIA 1193 IV-30)*

REQUIRED: The classification of collected fees that pertain to a future period.

DISCUSSION: Under the revenue recognition principle, revenue is recognized (reported as revenue) in the period in which it is earned; therefore, when it is received in advance of its being earned, the amount applicable to future periods is deferred. The amount unearned (received in advance) is considered a liability because it represents an obligation to perform a service in the future arising from a past transaction. Unearned revenue is revenue that has been received but not earned.

Answer (B) is incorrect because the revenue is not earned. The exterminator has not performed the related services for the customer. Answer (C) is incorrect because accrued revenue is revenue that has been earned but not received. The exterminator has revenue that has been received but not earned. Answer (D) is incorrect because the customer has a prepaid expense (expense paid but not incurred); the exterminator has unearned revenue (revenue received but not earned).

20. An airline should recognize revenue from an airline ticket in the period in which

- A. Passenger reservations are booked.
- B. Passenger reservations are confirmed.
- C. Ticket is issued.
- D. Related flight takes place.

The correct answer is (D). *(CIA 593 IV-27)*

REQUIRED: The period in which an airline should recognize revenue from an airline ticket.

DISCUSSION: Revenue is recognized when it is realized or realizable and earned. The critical event in the earning process for the airline is the delivery of the service to the customer, which occurs when the related flight takes place.

Answers (A) and (B) are incorrect because the earning process is not complete when the reservations are booked or confirmed. Answer (C) is incorrect because the earning process is not complete when the ticket is issued.

21. On February 1, 1996, a computer software firm agrees to program a software package. Twelve payments of $10,000 on the first of each month are to be made, with the first payment March 1, 1996. The software is accepted by the client June 1, 1997. How much 1996 revenue should be recognized?

- A. $0
- B. $100,000
- C. $110,000
- D. $120,000

The correct answer is (A). *(CIA 1190 IV-28)*

REQUIRED: The revenue recognized in the year in which payments begin if delivery occurs in the next period.

DISCUSSION: Revenue is recognized when it is realized or realizable and the earning process is substantially complete. Delivery is the usual time at which recognition is appropriate. Because delivery occurred in 1997, no revenue should be recognized in 1996.

Answers (B), (C), and (D) are incorrect because no revenue should be recognized until realized or realizable.

22. A company provides fertilization, insect control, and disease control services for a variety of trees, plants, and shrubs on a contract basis. For $50 per month, the company will visit the subscriber's premises and apply appropriate mixtures. If the subscriber has any problems between the regularly scheduled application dates, the company's personnel will promptly make additional service calls to correct the situation. Some subscribers elect to pay for an entire year because the company offers an annual price of $540 if paid in advance. For a subscriber who pays the annual fee in advance, the company should recognize the related revenue

   A. When the cash is collected.

   B. Evenly over the year as the services are performed.

   C. At the end of the contract year after all of the services have been performed.

   D. At the end of the fiscal year.

The correct answer is (B). *(CIA 1192 IV-27)*
   REQUIRED: The appropriate timing of revenue recognition.
   DISCUSSION: In accordance with SFAC 5, revenues should be recognized when they are realized or realizable and earned. Revenues are realized when products, merchandise, or other assets are exchanged for cash or claims to cash. Revenues are realizable when related assets received or held are readily convertible to known amounts of cash or claims to cash. Revenues are earned when the entity has substantially accomplished what it must do to be entitled to the benefits represented by the revenues. The most common time at which these two conditions are met is when the product or merchandise is delivered or services are rendered to customers. In the situation presented, the performance of the service (monthly spraying) is so significant to completing the earning process that revenue should not be recognized until delivery occurs. At the time of performing the service (monthly spraying and any special visits), the revenue has been realized and earned and should be recognized.
   Answer (A) is incorrect because the revenue has not been earned when the cash is collected. Answers (C) and (D) are incorrect because revenue from services rendered is recognized when the services have been performed. A portion of the services is performed monthly. Thus, a portion of the related revenue should be recognized monthly rather than when the contract year or the fiscal year is complete.

23. One of the ingredients of the primary quality of relevance is

   A. Verifiability.

   B. Predictive value.

   C. Neutrality.

   D. Due process.

The correct answer is (B). *(CMA 1292 2-1)*
   REQUIRED: The ingredient of the primary quality of relevance.
   DISCUSSION: Relevance and reliability are the two decision-specific primary qualities of accounting information. Relevant information is capable of making a difference in a decision. The ingredients of relevance are predictive value, timeliness, and feedback value. Predictive value is the quality "that helps users to increase the likelihood of correctly forecasting the outcome of past and present events" (SFAC 2).
   Answers (A) and (C) are incorrect because verifiability and neutrality are the ingredients of reliability. Answer (D) is incorrect because due process is a nonsense answer.

24. SFAC 5, *Recognition and Measurement in Financial Statements of Business Enterprises*, indicates that for an event to be recognized in financial statements it must be

   A. Relevant, reliable, and measurable.

   B. Relevant, reliable, and useful.

   C. Relevant, reliable, and timely.

   D. Reliable, useful, and measurable.

The correct answer is (A). *(CMA 1292 2-3)*
   REQUIRED: The criteria that must be met for an event to be recognized in financial statements.
   DISCUSSION: SFAC 5 states that an item and information about the item should be recognized when the following four fundamental recognition criteria are met: (1) the item meets the definition of an element of financial statements; (2) it has a relevant attribute measurable with sufficient reliability (measurability); (3) the information about the item is capable of making a difference in user decisions (relevance); and (4) the information is representationally faithful, verifiable, and neutral (reliability).
   Answer (B) is incorrect because the information must be measurable. Answer (C) is incorrect because timeliness is an aspect of relevance. Answer (D) is incorrect because items must also meet the relevance criterion.

25. Although a transfer of ownership has not occurred, the percentage-of-completion method is acceptable under the revenue recognition principle because

    A. The assets are readily convertible into cash.

    B. The production process can be readily divided into definite stages.

    C. Cash has been received from the customer.

    D. The earning process is completed at various stages.

The correct answer is (D). *(CMA 1292 2-17)*

REQUIRED: The reason percentage-of-completion is acceptable as a means of revenue recognition.

DISCUSSION: SFAC 5 states that revenue should be recognized when it is both realized or realizable and earned. If a project is contracted for before production and covers a long time period in relation to reporting periods, revenues may be recognized by a percentage-of-completion method as they are earned (as production occurs), provided reasonable estimates of results at completion and reliable measures of progress are available. Thus, contractors traditionally use the percentage-of-completion method because some revenue can be recognized during each period of the production process. In a sense, the earning process is completed in various stages; thus, revenues should be recorded in each stage.

Answer (A) is incorrect because, depending upon the terms of the contract, the assets may not be readily convertible into cash. Answer (B) is incorrect because, on a large construction project, the production process often cannot be easily divided into definite stages. Answer (C) is incorrect because cash is sometimes not received until the project is completed.

26. The mining industry frequently recognizes revenue using the completion of production method. This method is acceptable under the revenue recognition principle for all of the following reasons except that

    A. Production costs can be readily determined.

    B. Sales prices are reasonably assured.

    C. Assets are readily realizable.

    D. Units are interchangeable.

The correct answer is (A). *(CMA 1292 2-18)*

REQUIRED: The reason that does not justify recognizing mining revenue at the completion of the production process.

DISCUSSION: Recognizing revenue at the time goods are produced is appropriate when the assets are readily realizable (convertible) because they are salable at reliably determinable prices without significant effort. Readily realizable assets are fungible and quoted prices are available in an active market that can rapidly absorb the quantity produced (SFAC 5). Examples include some agricultural products and rare minerals. That production costs can be readily determined is not a justification for immediate recognition. Production costs can be readily determined for almost any product manufactured.

Answers (B) and (C) are incorrect because recognition at the time of production is appropriate if assets are readily realizable, i.e., if they are salable at reliably determinable prices without significant effort. Answer (D) is incorrect because interchangeability (fungibility) is a requirement for recognition at the time of production.

27. Accounting information that enables decision makers to confirm or correct prior expectations is said to have

    A. Predictive value.

    B. Materiality.

    C. Representational faithfulness.

    D. Feedback value.

The correct answer is (D). *(CMA 1294 2-1)*

REQUIRED: The characteristic of accounting information enabling confirmation or correction of prior expectations.

DISCUSSION: One of the qualitative characteristics of accounting information is relevance. Relevant information is capable of making a difference in a decision. Relevance has three elements: predictive value, feedback value, and timeliness. Feedback value permits users to confirm or correct prior expectations (SFAC 2).

Answer (A) is incorrect because predictive value enables users to predict the outcome of future events. Answer (B) is incorrect because materiality is a constraint on the reporting of accounting information. Answer (C) is incorrect because representational faithfulness is the agreement between a measure or description and the phenomenon that it purports to represent.

28. The historical cost of assets and liabilities is generally retained in accounting records because this information has the qualitative characteristics of

- A. Neutrality, verifiability, and representational faithfulness.
- B. Reliability and relevance.
- C. Decision usefulness, reliability, and neutrality.
- D. Timeliness, verifiability, and relevance.

The correct answer is (A). *(CMA 1294 2-2)*

REQUIRED: The qualitative characteristics possessed by historical cost information.

DISCUSSION: The qualitative characteristics of accounting information include reliability. Reliable information is reasonably free from error and bias and faithfully represents what it purports to represent. According to SFAC 2, the three elements of reliability are verifiability, neutrality, and representational faithfulness. Verifiability means that the information can be verified by independent measurers using the same methods. Historical cost is a fixed amount arising from a past transaction and therefore is an objective measure. Neutrality means that information should be neutral; it cannot favor one statement user over another. Historical cost is neutral because it was determined by two individuals--a buyer and a seller--in an arm's-length transaction. Representational faithfulness means that financial statements accurately represent the events reported. Using historical cost results in an accurate depiction of the transaction that occurred.

Answers (B) and (D) are incorrect because some would argue that historical costs are not always relevant. Answer (C) is incorrect because historical costs may not possess decision usefulness.

29. Recognition is the process of formally recording and reporting an item in the financial statements. In order for a revenue item to be recognized, it must be all of the following except

- A. Measurable.
- B. Relevant.
- C. Material.
- D. Realized or realizable.

The correct answer is (C). *(CMA 1294 2-3)*

REQUIRED: The characteristic not required for recognition of revenue.

DISCUSSION: Recognition means incorporating transactions into the accounting system so as to report them in the financial statements as assets, liabilities, revenues, expenses, gains, or losses. When items meet the criteria for recognition, disclosure by other means is not a substitute for recognition in the financial statements. The four fundamental recognition criteria are (1) the item meets the definition of an element of financial statements, (2) the item has an attribute measurable with sufficient reliability, (3) the information is relevant, and (4) the information is reliable (SFAC 5). In addition, revenue should be recognized when it is realized or realizable and earned. Materiality is not a recognition criterion. An immaterial item that meets the criteria for recognition may be recognized.

Answers (A), (B), and (D) are incorrect because revenue is recognized when the item meets the definition of revenue, the item is measurable, the information is relevant and reliable, and the item is realized or realizable.

30. In Statement of Financial Accounting Concepts No. 5, *Recognition and Measurement in Financial Statements of Business Enterprises*, several alternatives have been identified for measuring items on the statement of financial position. Which of the following alternatives may be used?

	Present Value	Current Cost	Net Realizable Value
A.	No	No	No
B.	No	Yes	Yes
C.	Yes	Yes	No
D.	Yes	Yes	Yes

The correct answer is (D). *(CMA 1294 2-5)*

REQUIRED: The acceptable attribute(s) for measuring items in the balance sheet.

DISCUSSION: According to SFAC 5, items appearing in financial statements may, under certain circumstances, be measured by different attributes. The attributes used in current practice are historical cost (historical proceeds), current cost, current market value, net realizable (settlement) value, and the present value of future cash flows. For example, the present value of future cash flows is used to value long-term payables; current cost is the method used to measure and report some inventories; and net realizable value is used to measure short-term receivables.

Answers (A), (B), and (C) are incorrect because present value, current cost, and net realizable value are measurement attributes that may be used in appropriate circumstances.

D. Limitations of Financial Statement Information

31. Limitations of the statement of financial position include all of the following except

- A. The use of historical cost for valuing assets and liabilities.
- B. Inclusion of information on capital maintenance.
- C. Exclusion of some economic resources and obligations.
- D. The use of estimates in the determination of certain items.

The correct answer is (B). *(CMA 1294 2-4)*
REQUIRED: The item not a limitation of the statement of financial position (balance sheet).
DISCUSSION: The basic financial statements are prepared using the concept of financial capital maintenance. A return on financial capital results only if the financial (money) amount of net assets at the end of the period exceeds the amount at the beginning. Hence, inclusion of information on capital maintenance is a fundamental approach to financial reporting, not a limitation (SFAC 5).
Answer (A) is incorrect because historical cost may not be an accurate valuation of a balance sheet item. Changing prices and other factors are not recognized in the basic financial statements. Answer (C) is incorrect because not all assets and liabilities are included in the balance sheet; for example, certain contingencies and pension obligations are not included. Answer (D) is incorrect because measurement in financial statements tends to be approximate rather than exact. Estimates are commonly used to determine reported amounts, e.g., depreciation and present value.

32. The accounting measurement that is not consistent with the going-concern concept is

- A. Historical cost.
- B. Realization.
- C. The transaction approach.
- D. Liquidation value.

The correct answer is (D). *(CMA 684 4-3)*
REQUIRED: The accounting measurement inconsistent with the going-concern concept.
DISCUSSION: Financial accounting principles assume that a business entity is a going concern in the absence of evidence to the contrary. The concept justifies the use of depreciation and amortization schedules, and the recording of assets and liabilities using attributes other than liquidation value.
Answers (A), (B), and (C) are incorrect because each is part of the basic structure of accrual accounting.

E. Application of Public Reporting Standards

33. The Financial Accounting Standards Board has provided guidance on disclosures of transactions between related parties, for example, transactions between subsidiaries of a common parent. SFAS 57, *Related Party Disclosures*, requires all of the following disclosures except

- A. The nature of the relationship involved.
- B. A description of the transactions for each period an income statement is presented.
- C. The dollar amounts of transactions for each period an income statement is presented.
- D. The effect on the cash flow statement for each period a cash flow statement is presented.

The correct answer is (D). *(CMA 1290 2-24)*
REQUIRED: The related-party transaction disclosure not required by SFAS 57.
DISCUSSION: SFAS 57 requires disclosure of related-party transactions except for compensation agreements, expense allowances, and transactions eliminated in consolidated working papers. Required disclosures include the relationship(s) of the related parties; a description and dollar amounts of transactions for each period presented and the effects of any change in the method of establishing their terms; and amounts due to or from the related parties and, if not apparent, the terms and manner of settlement. The effect on the cash flow statement need not be disclosed.
Answer (A) is incorrect because disclosure of the nature of the relationship involved is required by SFAS 57. Answer (B) is incorrect because disclosure of a description of the transactions for each period an income statement is presented is required by SFAS 57. Answer (C) is incorrect because disclosure of the dollar amounts of transactions for each period an income statement is presented is required by SFAS 57.

34. SFAS 47, *Disclosure of Long-Term Obligations*, resulted in identifying disclosure requirements for long-term obligations as a group. The Financial Accounting Standards Board believed that a particular group of long-term obligations frequently was not disclosed adequately. Thus, this statement was specifically addressed to this group of items referred to as

- A. Loss contingencies.
- B. Noncancellable purchase obligations.
- C. Severance pay.
- D. Pension plans.

The correct answer is (B). *(CMA 1291 2-4)*

REQUIRED: The type of obligation specifically addressed by SFAS 47.

DISCUSSION: SFAS 47 requires disclosure of unconditional purchase obligations associated with suppliers' financing arrangements and future payments required by long-term debt and redeemable stock agreements. Unconditional purchase obligations are commitments to transfer funds in the future for fixed or minimum amounts of goods or services at fixed or minimum prices. SFAS 47 provides the standards of accounting for an unconditional purchase obligation that was negotiated as part of the financing arrangement for facilities that will provide contracted goods or services or for costs related to those goods or services, has a remaining term of more than 1 year, and is either noncancellable or cancellable only under specific terms.

Answer (A) is incorrect because loss contingencies are liabilities covered by SFAS 5. Answer (C) is incorrect because severance pay is a form of deferred compensation, a topic not addressed by SFAS 47. Answer (D) is incorrect because pension liabilities are covered by SFASs 87 and 88.

35. All of the following must be disclosed regarding financial instruments with off-balance-sheet risk of accounting loss except the

- A. Accounting loss incurred if any party to the instrument failed completely to perform, and the collateral proved to be of no value.
- B. Face or contract amount.
- C. Instrument's nature and terms, including credit risk, market risk, cash requirements, and related accounting policies.
- D. Amount by which earnings per share would change if the accounting loss were to occur.

The correct answer is (D). *(CMA 693 2-20)*

REQUIRED: The item not a required disclosure for financial instruments with off-balance-sheet risk of accounting loss.

DISCUSSION: SFAS 105 specifies the disclosure requirements for all entities with regard to the extent, nature, and terms of financial instruments with off-balance-sheet risk of accounting loss. An entity must also disclose the credit risk of financial instruments with off-balance-sheet credit risk and significant concentrations of credit risk for all financial instruments. The amount by which EPS will be affected if such loss were to occur is not required to be disclosed.

Answer (A) is incorrect because, in the financial statements or in a note, an entity must disclose accounting loss incurred if any party to the instrument failed completely to perform and the collateral proved to be of no value. Answer (B) is incorrect because the nature, extent, and terms of financial instruments with off-balance-sheet risk, including the face or contract amount, must be disclosed. Answer (C) is incorrect because disclosure of the nature and terms should include, at a minimum, discussion of credit and market risk, cash requirements, and the related accounting policy.

36. Which of the following should be disclosed in the summary of significant accounting policies?

- A. Valuation method used for work-in-process inventory.
- B. Interest capitalized for the period.
- C. Adequacy of pension plan assets in relation to vested benefits.
- D. Depreciation charges for the period.

The correct answer is (A). *(CIA 593 IV-26)*

REQUIRED: The item that should be disclosed in the summary of significant accounting policies.

DISCUSSION: APB 22 requires that all significant accounting principles and methods that involve selection from among alternatives, are peculiar to a given industry, or are innovative or unusual applications be specifically identified and described in an initial note to the financial statements or in a separate summary. The disclosure should include accounting principles adopted and the method of applying them. This summary of significant accounting policies should not duplicate other facts to be disclosed elsewhere in the statements. The valuation method for inventory is one example of an accounting method (policy) that should be disclosed.

Answers (B), (C), (D) are incorrect because the summary of significant accounting policies should not duplicate facts required to be disclosed elsewhere in the financial statements.

37. Publicly traded companies must report all of the following interim financial data except

A. Primary and fully diluted earnings per share for each period presented.

B. Summarized information on sales, income taxes, extraordinary items, effect of change in accounting principles, and net income.

C. A condensed balance sheet, income statement, and statement of cash flows for each interim period presented.

D. The disposal of a segment of a business, and extraordinary, unusual, or infrequently occurring items.

The correct answer is (C). *(CMA 693 2-27)*
REQUIRED: The item not a required disclosure by publicly traded companies in interim financial data.
DISCUSSION: APB 28 does not require presentation of interim income statements, statements of financial position, or statements of cash flows. Although interim financial statements may be presented, minimum disclosures required when a publicly held company does issue summarized financial information include

1) Sales or gross revenues, provision for income taxes, extraordinary items, cumulative effect of changes in accounting principles, and net income
2) Primary and fully diluted EPS
3) Seasonal revenues, costs, or expenses
4) Significant changes in estimates or provisions for income taxes
5) Disposal of a segment and extraordinary, unusual, or infrequent items
6) Contingent items
7) Changes in accounting principles or estimates
8) Significant cash flows

Answers (A), (B), and (D) are incorrect because PEPS and FDEPS; sales; income taxes; extraordinary items; the effect of a change in accounting principles; net income; disposals; and extraordinary, unusual, and infrequent items are disclosed.

38. The accounting profession has adopted various standards to be followed when reporting inventory in the financial statements. All of the following are required to be reported in the financial statements or disclosed in notes to the financial statements except for

A. Inventory detail, such as raw materials, work-in-process, and finished goods.

B. Significant financing agreements, such as product financing arrangements and pledging of inventories.

C. The basis upon which inventory amounts are stated.

D. Unrealized profit on inventories.

The correct answer is (D). *(CMA 695 2-23)*
REQUIRED: The item not a required disclosure about inventory.
DISCUSSION: APB 22 requires disclosure of accounting policies in a separate summary of significant policies or as the first footnote to the financial statements. The disclosure should specify accounting principles adopted and the method of applying those principles. Examples include inventory valuation methods; inventory details, such as the mix of finished goods, work-in-progress, and raw materials; methods used in determining costs; and any significant financing agreements, such as leases, related party transactions, product financing arrangements, firm purchase commitments, pledging of inventories, and involuntary liquidation of LIFO layers. Unrealized profit on inventories is not reported because the company usually has no assurance that the inventories will be sold.
Answers (A), (B), and (C) are incorrect because inventory details, financing agreements, and valuation methods should be disclosed in the footnotes.

39. SFAS 47, *Disclosure of Long-Term Obligations*, does not apply to an unconditional purchase obligation that is cancellable under which of the following conditions?

A. Upon the occurrence of a remote contingency.

B. With the permission of the other party.

C. If a replacement agreement is signed between the same parties.

D. Upon payment of a nominal penalty.

The correct answer is (D). *(Publisher)*
REQUIRED: The condition excluding unconditional purchase obligation coverage by SFAS 47.
DISCUSSION: SFAS 47 provides the standards of accounting for an unconditional purchase obligation that

1) Was negotiated as part of the financing arrangement for facilities that will provide contracted goods or services
2) Has a remaining term of more than 1 year
3) Is either noncancellable or cancellable only under specific terms

Excluded from these terms and from the provisions of SFAS 47 is a purchase obligation cancellable upon the payment of a nominal penalty.
Answers (A), (B), and (C) are incorrect because each is a condition indicating that the obligation is noncancellable.

40. If an unconditional purchase obligation is not presented in the balance sheet, certain disclosures are required. A disclosure that is not required is

    A. The nature and term of the obligation.

    B. The variable components of the obligation.

    C. The imputed interest necessary to reduce the unconditional purchase obligation to its present value.

    D. The amounts purchased under the obligation for each period an income statement is presented.

The correct answer is (C). *(Publisher)*
    REQUIRED: The item not required to be disclosed if an unconditional purchase obligation is not recognized in the balance sheet.
    DISCUSSION: When an unconditional purchase obligation is not recorded in the balance sheet, SFAS 47 encourages, but does not require, the disclosure of the amount of imputed interest necessary to reduce the unconditional purchase obligation to its present value.
    Answers (A), (B), and (D) are incorrect because each disclosure is explicitly required by SFAS 47 when an unconditional purchase obligation is not recorded in the balance sheet. SFAS 47 also requires disclosure of the amount of the fixed and determinable portion of the obligation in the aggregate as of the latest balance sheet date and the amounts due in each of the next 5 years.

41. Under SFAS 105, *Disclosure of Information About Financial Instruments with Off-Balance-Sheet Risk and Financial Instruments with Concentrations of Credit Risk*, which of the following is defined as a financial instrument?

    A. Merchandise inventory.

    B. Deferred subscriptions revenue.

    C. A note payable in U.S. Treasury bonds.

    D. A warranty payable.

The correct answer is (C). *(Publisher)*
    REQUIRED: The financial instrument.
    DISCUSSION: A financial instrument is cash, evidence of an ownership interest in an entity, or a contract that both (1) imposes on one entity a contractual obligation (a) to deliver cash or another financial instrument to a second entity or (b) to exchange other financial instruments on potentially unfavorable terms with the second entity, and (2) conveys to that second entity a contractual right (a) to receive cash or another financial instrument from the first entity or (b) to exchange other financial instruments on potentially favorable terms with the first entity. A note payable in U.S. Treasury bonds gives the holder the contractual right to receive, and imposes on the debtor the contractual obligation to deliver, bonds that are themselves financial instruments. Thus, it is a financial instrument.
    Answer (A) is incorrect because, although the sale of inventory could result in the receipt of cash, the holder of the inventory has no current contractual right to receive cash. Answers (B) and (D) are incorrect because these obligations will result in the delivery of goods or services.

F. The SEC and Its Reporting Requirements

42. The act that gives the SEC the ultimate power to suspend trading of a security, delist a security, and prevent brokers and dealers from working in the securities market is the

    A. Securities Investor Protection Act of 1970.

    B. Securities Act of 1933.

    C. Securities Exchange Act of 1934.

    D. Investment Company Act of 1940.

The correct answer is (C). *(CMA 1283 3-21)*
    REQUIRED: The statute providing the SEC ultimate regulatory authority in the trading of securities.
    DISCUSSION: The Securities Exchange Act of 1934 generally regulates the trading markets in securities. It requires the registration of brokers, dealers, and securities exchanges.
    Answer (A) is incorrect because the Securities Investor Protection Act of 1970 created a corporation to intercede when brokers or dealers encounter financial difficulty endangering their customers. Answer (B) is incorrect because the Securities Act of 1933 requires registration of securities involved in initial public offerings but does not apply to subsequent trading. Answer (D) is incorrect because the Investment Company Act of 1940 deals narrowly with the registration of investment companies.

43. Requirements not imposed by the Securities Exchange Act of 1934 and its amendments are

    A.   Proxy solicitation requirements.

    B.   Prospectus requirements.

    C.   Insider trading requirements.

    D.   Tender offer requirements.

The correct answer is (B). *(CMA 1283 3-22)*
    REQUIRED: The requirements not imposed by the Securities Exchange Act of 1934.
    DISCUSSION: Prospectus requirements are imposed by the Securities Act of 1933. Prospectuses are used to sell securities, and the Securities Act of 1933 regulates the initial sale of securities.
    Answers (A), (C), and (D) are incorrect because each is imposed by the Securities Exchange Act of 1934.

44. The SEC has issued Regulation S-K to govern disclosures in filings with the SEC of nonfinancial statement matters. It concerns descriptions of the company's securities, business, properties, and legal proceedings; information about its directors and officers; management's discussion and analysis of financial condition and results of operations; and

    A.   The form and content of the required financial statements.

    B.   The requirements for filing interim financial statements.

    C.   Unofficial interpretations and practices regarding securities laws disclosure requirements.

    D.   Guidelines for voluntary financial projections.

The correct answer is (D). *(CMA 1285 3-26)*
    REQUIRED: The item included under the disclosure requirements of Regulation S-K.
    DISCUSSION: In addition to those items mentioned in the body of the question, Regulation S-K also provides guidelines for the filing of projections of future economic performance (financial projections). The SEC encourages but does not require, the filing of management's projections as a supplement to the historical financial statements.
    Answers (A) and (B) are incorrect because financial statement disclosures are specified in Regulation S-X, not S-K. Answer (C) is incorrect because unofficial interpretations and practices, if codified at all, are made public through the issuance of Staff Accounting Bulletins (SABs).

45. An external auditor's involvement with Form 10-Q that is being prepared for filing with the SEC would most likely consist of

    A.   An audit of the financial statements included in Form 10-Q.

    B.   A compilation report on the financial statements included in Form 10-Q.

    C.   Issuing a comfort letter that covers stub-period financial data.

    D.   A review of the interim financial statements included in Form 10-Q.

The correct answer is (D). *(CMA 1286 3-21)*
    REQUIRED: The external auditor's most likely involvement with Form 10-Q.
    DISCUSSION: Form 10-Q is the quarterly report to the SEC. It must be filed for each of the first three quarters of the year within 45 days after the end of the quarter. It need not contain audited financial statements, but it should be prepared in accordance with APB 28, *Interim Financial Reporting.* A review by an accountant based on inquiries and analytical procedures would permit an expression of limited assurance that no material modifications would need to be made to the statements for them to be in conformity with GAAP. A review would help satisfy the SEC requirement of "accurate, representative, and meaningful" quarterly statements.
    Answer (A) is incorrect because audited statements are not required in quarterly reports. Answer (B) is incorrect because a compilation provides no assurance and would thus not satisfy the SEC requirement stated above. Answer (C) is incorrect because comfort letters are addressed to underwriters, not the SEC.

46. Form 10-K is filed with the SEC to update the information a company supplied when filing a registration statement under the Securities Exchange Act of 1934. Form 10-K is a report that is filed

A. Annually within 90 days of the end of a company's fiscal year.

B. Semiannually within 30 days of the end of a company's second and fourth fiscal quarters.

C. Quarterly within 45 days of the end of each quarter.

D. Monthly within 2 weeks of the end of each month.

The correct answer is (A). *(CMA 1286 3-20)*
REQUIRED: The true statement about filing Form 10-K.
DISCUSSION: Form 10-K is the annual report to the SEC. It must be filed within 90 days after the corporation's year-end. It must contain audited financial statements and be signed by the principal executive, financial, and accounting officers and by a majority of the board. The content is essentially that required in the Basic Information Package.
Answer (B) is incorrect because Form 10-K is an annual report. Answer (C) is incorrect because Form 10-Q is filed quarterly within 45 days of the end of each quarter except for the fourth quarter. Answer (D) is incorrect because no monthly reports are required.

47. SEC Form S-3 is an optional, short-form registration statement that relies on the incorporation by reference of periodic reports required by the Securities Exchange Act of 1934. Form S-3 offers substantial savings in filing costs over other forms since minimal disclosures are required in the prospectus. The SEC permits the use of Form S-3 only by those firms that have filed periodic reports with the SEC for at least 3 years and if the registrant

A. Has less than $150 million of voting stock held by nonaffiliates.

B. Is widely followed and actively traded.

C. Is seeking more than $150 million in funds.

D. Has not had to file Form 8-K during the most recent 2-year period.

The correct answer is (B). *(CMA 1286 3-22)*
REQUIRED: The requirement for use of Form S-3.
DISCUSSION: Form S-1 is used for a first registration. Form S-2 is used by companies that have filed timely reports for 3 years. Incorporation by reference from the annual shareholders' report of Basic Information Package disclosures is allowed in Form S-2. If a company meets the requirements for use of Form S-2 and at least $50,000,000 in value of its stock is held by nonaffiliates (or at least $100,000,000 is outstanding and annual trading volume is at least 3,000,000 shares), Form S-3 may be used. It allows most information to be incorporated by reference to other SEC filings.
Answer (A) is incorrect because the language of the requirement is that a company may use Form S-3 if nonaffiliates hold "at least $50,000,000" of the company's stock (not "less than $150,000,000"). Answers (C) and (D) are incorrect because neither is a requirement for use of Form S-3.

48. Regulation S-X disclosure requirements of the Securities and Exchange Commission (SEC) deal with

A. Changes in and disagreements with accountants on accounting and financial disclosure.

B. Management's discussion and analysis of the financial condition and the results of operations.

C. The requirements for filing interim financial statements and pro forma financial information.

D. Summary information, risk factors, and the ratio of earnings to fixed charges.

The correct answer is (C). *(CMA 1288 3-17)*
REQUIRED: The subject of SEC Regulation S-X.
DISCUSSION: The SEC requires registrations and annual reports to comply with certain accounting standards and policies. Regulation S-X governs reporting in the financial statements, including footnotes and schedules. Both annual reports and quarterly statements are covered by Regulation S-X.
Answer (A) is incorrect because Form 8-K is filed to report changes in, and disagreements with, accountants. Answers (B) and (D) are incorrect because Regulation S-X does not cover these matters. Regulation S-K governs required disclosures other than those in financial statements.

49. Form 8-K must be filed within

A. 90 days after the end of the fiscal year covered by the report.

B. 45 days after the end of each of the first three quarters of each fiscal year.

C. 90 days after the end of an employee stock purchase plan fiscal year.

D. 15 days after the occurrence of a significant event.

The correct answer is (D). *(CMA 1288 3-19)*

REQUIRED: The filing deadline for Form 8-K.

DISCUSSION: Form 8-K is a current report used to disclose material events affecting a company. It must be filed within 15 days after the occurrence of a material event that is required to be reported. However, the resignation of a director or a change in external auditors must be reported within 5 business days. An extension of up to 60 days may be obtained for filing financial statements and pro forma information required for an acquisition. Other material events include changes in control, bankruptcy, and acquisition or disposition of significant assets not in the ordinary course of business.

Answers (A), (B), and (C) are incorrect because the filing deadline for Form 8-K is 15 days after the occurrence of a significant event (5 business days after the resignation of a director or a change of external auditors).

50. In an effort to consolidate the registration process, the SEC has adopted a three-tier system of new security forms. However, these three forms do not cover all circumstances. Under which one of the following circumstances would a registrant use Form S-4?

A. Registering securities in connection with mergers and related business-combination transactions.

B. Registering securities in which the registrant does not qualify for Form S-1.

C. Registering securities when the registrant has not had to file Form 8-K during the most recent 2-year period.

D. Registering securities of real estate investment trusts.

The correct answer is (A). *(CMA 1288 3-20)*

REQUIRED: The circumstance under which a registrant would use Form S-4.

DISCUSSION: Form S-4 is a simplified form for business combinations, such as mergers. It is part of the integrated disclosure system established to simplify reporting requirements under the Securities Act of 1933 and the Securities Exchange Act of 1934. Thus, Form S-4 may incorporate much information by reference to other reports already filed with the SEC. The integrated disclosure system permits many companies to use the required annual report to shareholders (if prepared in conformity with Regulations S-X and S-K) as the basis for the annual report to the SEC on Form 10-K. Some may even use this report as the basis for registration statements.

Answer (B) is incorrect because Form S-1 may be used by any registrant. Answer (C) is incorrect because the filing of Form 8-K to report certain material events has no effect on the subsequent filing of the S forms. Answer (D) is incorrect because Form S-11 is used by REITs and real estate companies.

51. The SEC has adopted a three-tier system of forms in an effort to consolidate the registration process. However, these three forms do not cover all circumstances. A registrant would use Form S-8 when registering securities

A. When the registrant does not qualify for Form S-1.

B. To be offered to employees under any stock option or other employee benefit plan.

C. Of real estate investment trusts.

D. When the registrant has not had to file Form 8-K during the most recent 2-year period.

The correct answer is (B). *(CMA 1289 3-28)*

REQUIRED: The situation that would require a company to use Form S-8.

DISCUSSION: SEC Form S-8 is used when securities are to be offered to employees under any stock option or other employee benefit plan. It has become more commonly used in recent years because of the adoption of employee stock ownership plans (ESOPs).

Answer (A) is incorrect because Form S-1 is a long form than includes all possible required information. It can be used by any company. Forms S-2 and S-3 may be used as a substitute by companies that have been timely reporting to the SEC for 3 years. Answer (C) is incorrect because Form S-11 is used by REITs and real estate companies. Answer (D) is incorrect because the filing of Form 8-K to report certain material events has no effect on the subsequent filing of the S forms.

52. Regarding financial accounting for public companies, the role of the Securities and Exchange Commission (SEC) as currently practiced is to

A. Make rules and regulations regarding filings with the SEC but not to regulate annual or quarterly reports to shareholders.

B. Adopt pronouncements of the Financial Accounting Standards Board in all cases.

C. Regulate financial disclosures for corporate, state, and municipal reporting.

D. Make rules and regulations pertaining more to disclosure of financial information than to the establishment of accounting recognition and measurement principles.

The correct answer is (D). *(CMA 694 2-16)*

REQUIRED: The role of the SEC as it applies to financial accounting for public companies.

DISCUSSION: From its inception in 1934, the role of the SEC has been to promote disclosure rather than to establish accounting recognition and measurement principles. Its objective is to allow the accounting profession (through the FASB) to establish principles and then to ensure that corporations abide by those principles. This approach allows investors to evaluate investments for themselves.

Answer (A) is incorrect because the SEC regulates both quarterly and annual reporting. Answer (B) is incorrect because the SEC does not have to adopt FASB pronouncements. Answer (C) is incorrect because the SEC has no jurisdiction over state and municipal reporting.

53. Form 8-K ordinarily must be submitted to the SEC after the occurrence of a significant event. All of the following events would be reported by Form 8-K except

A. The acquisition of a major company.

B. The resignation of several directors.

C. A change in the registrant's certifying accountant.

D. A change from the percentage-of-completion method of accounting to the completed-contract method for a company in the construction business.

The correct answer is (D). *(CMA 694 2-17)*

REQUIRED: The event not reported on Form 8-K.

DISCUSSION: Form 8-K is a current report to disclose material events. It must be filed within 15 days after the material event takes place. Also, a change in independent accountants or the resignation of a director must be reported within 5 business days. Examples of material events that must be reported include a change in control, acquisition, or disposition of a significant amount of assets not in the ordinary course of business; bankruptcy or receivership; resignation of directors or independent auditors; or other events such as major legal proceedings, default on securities or debt, write-down or write-off of assets, or change of more than 5% of ownership of a security. A change in accounting principle does not require reporting on Form 8-K.

Answers (A), (B), and (C) are incorrect because bankruptcy, a major acquisition, the resignation of several directors, and a change in CPAs are events that must be reported on Form 8-K.

54. The SEC requires that Form 10-Q be filed within

A. 30 days after the occurrence of a significant event.

B. 45 days after the end of each of the first three quarters.

C. 15 days after the quarterly financial reports are issued.

D. 45 days after the end of each quarter.

The correct answer is (B). *(CMA 694 2-18)*

REQUIRED: The time when Form 10-Q must be filed.

DISCUSSION: Form 10-Q is a quarterly report to the SEC that includes condensed unaudited interim financial statements. It must be filed for each of the first three quarters of the year within 45 days after the end of the quarter. Form 10-Q need not be filed after the fourth quarter because Form 10-K is due within 90 days after year-end.

Answers (A) and (C) are incorrect because a registrant has 45 days after the end of each quarter to file Form 10-Q. Answer (D) is incorrect because Form 10-Q has to be filed for the first three quarters of the year.

APPENDIX A: ETHICS AS TESTED ON THE CMA/CFM EXAMS

6 pages of outline
14 multiple-choice questions

A. Ethics
B. Codes of Ethical Conduct
C. IMA Code of Ethics
D. Conflict of Interest
E. Legal Aspects of Social Responsibility

ETHICS

Questions containing ethical issues can appear on any part of the examination, presented within the context of specific subject areas. Candidates should be familiar with:

Statement on Management Accounting Number 1C (Revised), "Standards of Ethical Conduct for Practitioners of Management Accounting and Financial Management," Institute of Management Accountants, Montvale, N.J., 1997.

Current references to business ethics are also found in recent periodicals and newspapers.

A. Ethics

1. **Definitions**

   a. Corporate ethics -- an organization's policies and standards established to assure certain kinds of behavior by its members

   b. Individual ethics -- principles of conduct adhered to by an individual

2. **Increased Concern for Business Ethics**

   a. Electrical-equipment conspiracy cases in 1960 caused public concern and creation of the Business Ethics Advisory Council (BEAC) in 1961 under the Secretary of Commerce.

   b. BEAC pointed out areas needing self-evaluation by the business community:

      1) General business understanding of ethical issues

      2) Compliance with laws

      3) Conflicts of interest

      4) Entertainment and gift expenses

      5) Relations with customers and suppliers. Should gifts or kickbacks be given or accepted?

      6) Social responsibilities

   c. BEAC's recommendations generated business interest, especially from big business, in problems of ethical behavior.

3. **Factors That May Lead to Unethical Behavior**

    a. In any normal population, some people have less than desirable levels of ethics. If these people hold leadership positions, they will adversely influence subordinates.

    b. Organizational factors may lead to unethical behavior.

        1) Pressures for short-run performance in decentralized return on investment (ROI) centers may inhibit ethical behavior.

        2) Emphasis on strict adherence to chain-of-command authority may provide excuses for ignoring ethics when following orders.

        3) Informal work-group loyalties may subvert ethical behavior.

        4) Committee decision processes may make it possible to abstain from or dodge ethical obligations.

    c. External factors may lead to unethical behavior.

        1) Pressure of competition may compromise ethics in the interest of survival.
        2) Unethical behavior of others may force a compromise of ethics.
        3) Definitions of ethical behavior may vary from one culture to another.

            a) Bribes to overseas officials or buyers may be consistent with some countries' customary business practices, but such a practice is not considered ethical among U.S. purchasing agents.

                i) Bribes are now considered illegal under the Foreign Corrupt Practices Act.

            b) The propriety of superimposing our cultural ethical standards (by refusing to bribe) on another culture may be controversial.

4. **General Guides to Ethics**

    a. Golden Rule -- Do unto others as you would have others do unto you.

    b. Maximize good -- Act to provide the greatest good for the greatest number.

    c. Fairness -- Act in ways that are fair or just to all concerned.

    d. Maximize long-run outcomes -- Act to provide the best long-range benefits to society and its resources.

    e. General respect -- Act to respect the planet all humans share and the rights of others because corporate and individual decisions affect them.

5. **Simplified Criteria for Evaluating Ethical Behavior**

    a. Would this behavior be acceptable if people I respect knew I was doing this?

    b. What are the consequences of this behavior for myself, other employees, customers, and society?

6. Ethics are individual and personal, influenced by

    a. Life experiences (rewards for doing right, punishment for doing wrong)
    b. Friendship groups (professional associations, informal groups)
    c. Organizational pressures (responsibilities to superiors and the organization)

B. Codes of Ethical Conduct

1. An organization's code of ethical conduct is the established general value system the organization wishes to apply to its members' activities through

    a. Communicating organizational purposes and beliefs
    b. Establishing uniform ethical guidelines for members

        1) Including guidance on behavior for members in making decisions

2. Laws and written rules cannot cover all situations. However, organizations can benefit from having an established ethical code because it

    a. Effectively communicates acceptable values to all members

        1) Including recruits and subcontractors

    b. Provides a method of policing and disciplining members for violations

        1) Through review panels (formal)
        2) Through group pressure (informal)

    c. Establishes high standards against which individuals can measure their own performance

    d. Communicates to those outside the organization the value system from which the organization's members must not be asked to deviate

3. A typical code for accounting activities (note similarities to the Standards for the Professional Practice of Internal Auditing, GAAP, GAAS, etc.) holds that a financial manager must have

    a. Independence from conflicts of economic interest
    b. Independence from conflicts of professional interest

        1) Responsibility to present information fairly to shareholders/owners and not intentionally protect management

        2) Responsibility to present data to all appropriate managers and not play favorites with information or cover up bad news

        3) Responsibility to exercise an ethical presence in the conduct of professional activities

            a) Ensuring organizational compliance with spirit as well as letter of pertinent laws and regulations

            b) Conducting oneself according to the highest moral and legal standards

            c) Reporting to appropriate internal or external authority any illegal or fraudulent organizational act

    c. Integrity in not compromising professional values for the sake of personal goals
    d. Objectivity in presenting information, preparing reports, and making analyses

C. IMA Code of Ethics

1. The National Association of Accountants (now the Institute of Management Accountants or IMA), through its Management Accounting Practices Committee, issued a revised code of ethics for management accountants in April 1997. This code reflects the official position of the organization. Candidates are urged to study the provisions of the code closely because it is tested. The code is printed below and on the following page in its entirety. (Source: Statement on Management Accounting 1C (Revised), Objectives: Standards of Ethical Conduct for Practitioners of Management Accounting and Financial Management, April 1997, pp. 69-70). The mnemonic CCIO (competence, confidentiality, integrity, and objectivity) is useful. The final section, Resolution of Ethical Conflict, is especially significant.

STANDARDS OF ETHICAL CONDUCT FOR PRACTITIONERS OF MANAGEMENT ACCOUNTING AND FINANCIAL MANAGEMENT

Practitioners of management accounting and financial management have an obligation to the public, their profession, the organizations they serve, and themselves, to maintain the highest standards of ethical conduct. In recognition of this obligation, the Institute of Management Accountants has promulgated the following standards of ethical conduct for practitioners of management accounting and financial management. Adherence to these standards, both domestically and internationally, is integral to achieving the Objectives of Management Accounting. Practitioners of management accounting and financial management shall not commit acts contrary to these standards nor shall they condone the commission of such acts by others within their organizations.

Competence

Practitioners of management accounting and financial management have a responsibility to:

*   *Maintain an appropriate level of professional competence by ongoing development of their knowledge and skills.*
*   *Perform their professional duties in accordance with relevant laws, regulations, and technical standards.*
*   *Prepare complete and clear reports and recommendations after appropriate analyses of relevant and reliable information.*

Confidentiality

Practitioners of management accounting and financial management have a responsibility to:

*   *Refrain from disclosing confidential information acquired in the course of their work except when authorized, unless legally obligated to do so.*
*   *Inform subordinates as appropriate regarding the confidentiality of information acquired in the course of their work and monitor their activities to assure the maintenance of that confidentiality.*
*   *Refrain from using or appearing to use confidential information acquired in the course of their work for unethical or illegal advantage either personally or through third parties.*

Integrity

Practitioners of management accounting and financial management have a responsibility to:

*   *Avoid actual or apparent conflicts of interest and advise all appropriate parties of any potential conflict.*
*   *Refrain from engaging in any activity that would prejudice their ability to carry out their duties ethically.*
*   *Refuse any gift, favor, or hospitality that would influence or would appear to influence their actions.*
*   *Refrain from either actively or passively subverting the attainment of the organization's legitimate and ethical objectives.*
*   *Recognize and communicate professional limitations or other constraints that would preclude responsible judgment or successful performance of an activity.*
*   *Communicate unfavorable as well as favorable information and professional judgments or opinions.*
*   *Refrain from engaging in or supporting any activity that would discredit the profession.*

Objectivity

Practitioners of management accounting and financial management have a responsibility to:

- *Communicate information fairly and objectively.*
- *Disclose fully all relevant information that could reasonably be expected to influence an intended user's understanding of the reports, comments, and recommendations presented.*

Resolution of Ethical Conflict

In applying the standards of ethical conduct, practitioners of management accounting and financial management may encounter problems in identifying unethical behavior or in resolving an ethical conflict. When faced with significant ethical issues, practitioners of management accounting and financial management should follow the established policies of the organization bearing on the resolution of such conflict. If these policies do not resolve the ethical conflict, such practitioners should consider the following courses of action:

- *Discuss such problems with the immediate superior except when it appears that the superior is involved, in which case the problem should be presented initially to the next higher managerial level. If satisfactory resolution cannot be achieved when the problem is initially presented, submit the issues to the next higher managerial level. If the immediate superior is the chief executive officer, or equivalent, the acceptable reviewing authority may be a group such as the audit committee, executive committee, board of directors, board of trustees, or owners. Contact with levels above the immediate superior should be initiated only with the superior's knowledge, assuming the superior is not involved. Except where legally prescribed, communication of such problems to authorities or individuals not employed or engaged by the organization is not considered appropriate.*

- *Clarify relevant ethical issues by confidential discussion with an objective advisor (e.g., IMA Ethics Counseling Service) to obtain a better understanding of possible courses of action.*

- *Consult your own attorney as to legal obligations and rights concerning the ethical conflict.*

- *If the ethical conflict still exists after exhausting all levels of internal review, there may be no other recourse on significant matters than to resign from the organization and to submit an informative memorandum to an appropriate representative of the organization. After resignation, depending on the nature of the ethical conflict, it may also be appropriate to notify other parties.*

D. Conflict of Interest

1. Conflict of interest is a conflict between the private and the official responsibilities of a person in a position of trust, sufficient to affect judgment, independence, or objectivity in conducting the affairs of the business.

2. **Examples of Conflict of Interest**

   a. Having a substantial financial interest in a supplier, customer, or distributor

   b. Using privileged information gained from one's official position to enter transactions for personal gain

3. **Methods for Control**

   a. Provide a code of conduct provision applying to conflicts of interest.

   b. Require full financial disclosure by managers.

   c. Require prior notification of any transaction that may raise conflict of interest.

   d. Prohibit financial ties to any supplier, customer, or distributor.

   e. Encourage adherence to strong ethical behavior through corporate actions, policies, and public communications.

414 Appendix A: Ethics As Tested on the CMA/CFM Exams -- Legal Aspects of Social Responsibility

E. Legal Aspects of Social Responsibility

1. The **Racketeer Influenced and Corrupt Organization (RICO) Act** was passed in 1970 as an attempt to combat the problem of organized crime and its infiltration of legitimate enterprises.

    a. Its goals were to eliminate organized crime by concentrating on the illegal monies through the use of civil and criminal forfeitures.

    b. Criminal penalties can be levied up to $25,000 and 20 years in jail. Civil penalties include the awarding of treble damages and attorney's fees to the successful plaintiff.

    c. RICO specifically makes the following activities unlawful:

        1) Using income derived from a pattern of racketeering activity to acquire an interest in an enterprise.

        2) Acquiring or maintaining an interest in an enterprise through a pattern of racketeering activity.

        3) Conducting the affairs of an enterprise through a pattern of racketeering activity.

        4) Conspiring to commit any of these offenses.

    d. RICO has been used against white-collar criminals, terrorists, Wall Street insider trading, anti-abortion protesters, local law enforcement agencies, and public accounting firms -- none of which was intended by Congress when the law was passed.

2. The **Foreign Corrupt Practices Act (FCPA) of 1977** regulates payments by U.S. firms operating in other nations.

    a. The act is a reaction to publicity over questionable foreign payments.

    b. The FCPA makes it a criminal offense to make payments to a foreign government or representative thereof to secure or retain business.

    c. It prohibits payments of sales commissions to independent agents, if the commissions are knowingly passed to foreign officials.

    d. Corporations are required to establish internal accounting controls to assure that all overseas payments are proper.

    e. The FCPA applies even if payment is legal in the nation where it is made.

    f. The rationale for the FCPA is that the international reputation of the United States is affected by its international business conduct, which should reflect the best of the United States' ethics.

3. The SEC mandates that the composition of boards of directors include outside directors.

    a. To create diversity and broaden the overview of a company's place in the market and in society

4. Courts are increasingly willing to hold boards of directors and auditors liable for problems.

5. Stop and review! The following 14 multiple-choice questions cover the topic of ethics as it may be tested on the CMA/CFM exams. They are not divided by subunits. We anticipate some "case" questions that describe situations and are followed by one or more questions; e.g., to whom should the financial manager report an ethics violation?

MULTIPLE-CHOICE QUESTIONS

1. If a financial manager has a problem in identifying unethical behavior or resolving an ethical conflict, the first action (s)he should normally take is to

A. Consult the board of directors.

B. Discuss the problem with his/her immediate superior.

C. Notify the appropriate law enforcement agency.

D. Resign from the company.

The correct answer is (B). *(Publisher)*
REQUIRED: The proper ethical behavior by a financial manager.
DISCUSSION: The Standards of Ethical Conduct for Management Accountants state that the financial manager should first discuss an ethical problem with his/her immediate superior. If the superior is involved, the problem should be taken initially to the next higher managerial level.

Answer (A) is incorrect because the board would be consulted initially only if the immediate superior is the chief executive officer and that person is involved in the ethical conflict. Answer (C) is incorrect because unless "legally prescribed, communication of such problems to authorities or individuals not employed or engaged by the organization is not considered appropriate." Answer (D) is incorrect because resignation is a last resort.

2. Sheila is a financial manager who has discovered that her company is violating environmental regulations. If her immediate superior is involved, her appropriate action is to

A. Do nothing since she has a duty of loyalty to the organization.

B. Consult the audit committee.

C. Present the matter to the next higher managerial level.

D. Confront her immediate superior.

The correct answer is (C). *(Publisher)*
REQUIRED: The proper action when the financial manager's immediate superior is involved in an ethical problem.
DISCUSSION: To resolve an ethical problem, the financial manager's first step is usually to consult his/her immediate superior. If that individual is involved, the matter should be taken to the next higher level of management.

Answer (A) is incorrect because "financial managers have an obligation to the organizations they serve, their profession, the public, and themselves to maintain the highest standards of ethical conduct." Answer (B) is incorrect because the audit committee would be consulted first only if it were the next higher managerial level. Answer (D) is incorrect because if the superior is involved, the next higher managerial level should be consulted first.

3. If a financial manager discovers unethical conduct in his/her organization and fails to act, (s)he will be in violation of which ethical standard(s)?

A. "Actively or passively subvert the attainment of the organization's legitimate and ethical objectives."

B. "Communicate unfavorable as well as favorable information."

C. "Condone the commission of such acts by others within their organizations."

D. All of the answers are correct.

The correct answer is (D). *(Publisher)*
REQUIRED: The ethical standard(s) violated by failure to disclose unethical behavior.
DISCUSSION: A financial manager displays his/her competence and objectivity and maintains integrity by taking the appropriate action within the organization to resolve an ethical problem. Failure to act would condone wrongful acts, breach the duty to convey unfavorable as well as favorable information, undermine the organization's legitimate aims, discredit the profession, and violate the duty of objectivity owed to users of the subordinate's work product.

Answers (A), (B), and (C) are incorrect because each standard is violated by a financial manager who fails to act upon discovering unethical conduct.

4. Corporate social responsibility is

A. Effectively enforced through the controls envisioned by classical economics.

B. Defined as the obligation to shareholders to earn a profit.

C. More than the obligation to shareholders to earn a profit.

D. Defined as the obligation to serve long-term, organizational interests.

The correct answer is (C). *(Publisher)*
REQUIRED: The true statement about corporate social responsibility.
DISCUSSION: The concept of corporate social responsibility involves more than serving the interests of the organization and its shareholders. Rather, it is an extension of responsibility to embrace service to the public interest in such matters as environmental protection, employee safety, civil rights, and community involvement.

Answer (A) is incorrect because a perfectly competitive market was envisioned by classical economics. Answers (B) and (D) are incorrect because the concept embraces the public or societal interest.

5. A common argument against corporate involvement in socially responsible behavior is that

A. It encourages government intrusion in decision making.

B. As a legal person, a corporation is accountable for its conduct.

C. It creates goodwill.

D. In a competitive market, such behavior incurs costs that place the company at a disadvantage.

The correct answer is (D). *(Publisher)*

REQUIRED: The common argument against corporate involvement in socially responsible behavior.

DISCUSSION: Socially responsible behavior clearly has immediate costs to the entity, for example, the expenses incurred in affirmative action programs, pollution control, and improvements in worker safety. When one firm incurs such costs and its competitor does not, the other may be able to sell its products or services more cheaply and increase its market share at the expense of the socially responsible firm. The rebuttal argument is that in the long run the socially responsible company may maximize profits by creating goodwill and avoiding or anticipating governmental regulation.

Answer (A) is incorrect because such behavior may prevent governmental action. Answers (B) and (C) are incorrect because each is an argument for such behavior.

6. The IMA Code of Ethics requires a financial manager to follow the established policies of the organization when faced with an ethical conflict. If these policies do not resolve the conflict, the financial manager should

A. Consult the board of directors immediately.

B. Discuss the problem with the immediate superior if (s)he is involved in the conflict.

C. Communicate the problem to authorities outside the organization.

D. Contact the next higher managerial level if initial presentation to the immediate superior does not resolve the conflict.

The correct answer is (D). *(Publisher)*

REQUIRED: The proper action when organizational policies do not resolve an ethical conflict.

DISCUSSION: In these circumstances, the problem should be discussed with the immediate superior unless (s)he is involved. In that case, initial presentation should be to the next higher managerial level. If the problem is not satisfactorily resolved after initial presentation, the question should be submitted to the next higher level.

Answer (A) is incorrect because this course of action would be appropriate only for the chief executive officer or for his/her immediate subordinate when the CEO is involved in the conflict. Answer (B) is incorrect because the proper action would be to present the matter to the next higher managerial level. Answer (C) is incorrect because such action is inappropriate unless legally prescribed.

7. Financial managers are obligated to maintain the highest standards of ethical conduct. Accordingly, the IMA Code of Ethics explicitly requires that they

A. Obtain sufficient competent evidence when expressing an opinion.

B. Not condone violations by others.

C. Comply with generally accepted auditing standards.

D. Adhere to generally accepted accounting principles.

The correct answer is (B). *(Publisher)*

REQUIRED: The conduct required of financial managers.

DISCUSSION: The preamble to the IMA Code of Ethics states, "Financial managers have an obligation to the organizations they serve, their profession, the public, and themselves to maintain the highest standards of ethical conduct. In recognition of this obligation, the IMA has promulgated the following standards of ethical conduct for financial managers. Adherence to these standards is integral to achieving the objectives of financial managing. Financial managers shall not commit acts contrary to these standards nor shall they condone the commission of such acts by others within their organizations."

Answers (A), (C), and (D) are incorrect because each applies to external auditors. The IMA Code of Ethics does not expressly use such language.

8. Integrity is an ethical requirement for all financial managers. One aspect of integrity requires

A. Performance of professional duties in accordance with applicable laws.

B. Avoidance of conflict of interest.

C. Refraining from improper use of inside information.

D. Maintenance of an appropriate level of professional competence.

The correct answer is (B). *(Publisher)*

REQUIRED: The aspect of the integrity requirement.

DISCUSSION: According to the IMA Code of Ethics, financial managers must "avoid actual or apparent conflicts of interest and advise all appropriate parties of any potential conflict."

Answers (A) and (D) are incorrect because each states an aspect of the competence requirement. Answer (C) is incorrect because it states an aspect of the confidentiality requirement.

9. Under the express terms of the IMA Code of Ethics, a financial manager may not

A. Advertise.

B. Encroach on the practice of another financial manager.

C. Disclose confidential information unless authorized or legally obligated.

D. Accept other employment while serving as a financial manager.

The correct answer is (C). *(Publisher)*

REQUIRED: The action explicitly proscribed by the IMA Code of Ethics.

DISCUSSION: Financial managers may not disclose confidential information acquired in the course of their work unless authorized or legally obligated to do so. They must inform subordinates about the confidentiality of information and monitor their activities to maintain that confidentiality. Moreover, financial managers should avoid even the appearance of using confidential information to their unethical or illegal advantage.

Answers (A) and (B) are incorrect because the code does not address these matters. Answer (D) is incorrect because other employment may be accepted unless it constitutes a conflict of interest.

10. A financial manager discovers a problem that could mislead users of the firm's financial data and has informed his/her immediate superior. (S)he should report the circumstances to the audit committee and/or the board of directors only if

A. The immediate superior, who reports to the chief executive officer, knows about the situation but refuses to correct it.

B. The immediate superior assures the financial manager that the problem will be resolved.

C. The immediate superior reports the situation to his/her superior.

D. The immediate superior, the firm's chief executive officer, knows about the situation but refuses to correct it.

The correct answer is (D). *(Publisher)*

REQUIRED: The situation in which the financial manager must report to the audit committee and/or board of directors.

DISCUSSION: According to the IMA Code of Ethics, the financial manager should "discuss such problems with the immediate superior except when it appears that the superior is involved, in which case the problem should be presented initially to the next higher managerial level. If satisfactory resolution cannot be achieved when the problem is initially presented, submit the issues to the next higher managerial level. If the immediate superior is the chief executive officer, or equivalent, the acceptable reviewing authority may be a group such as the audit committee, executive committee, board of directors, board of trustees, or owners."

Answer (A) is incorrect because, in this situation, the chief executive officer is the next higher managerial level. Answers (B) and (C) are incorrect because the immediate superior has promised or taken action toward satisfactory resolution.

11. In which situation is a financial manager permitted to communicate confidential information to individuals or authorities outside the firm?

A. There is an ethical conflict and the board has refused to take action.

B. Such communication is legally prescribed.

C. The financial manager knowingly communicates the information indirectly through a subordinate.

D. An officer at the financial manager's bank has requested information on a transaction that could influence the firm's stock price.

The correct answer is (B). *(Publisher)*

REQUIRED: The situation in which a financial manager may disclose information to those outside the firm.

DISCUSSION: According to the IMA Code of Ethics, financial managers are responsible for observing the standard of confidentiality. Thus, the financial manager should "refrain from disclosing confidential information acquired in the course of his/her work except when authorized, unless legally obligated to do so."

Answer (A) is incorrect because the IMA Code of Ethics states that "except if legally prescribed, communication of [ethical conflict] problems to authorities or individuals not employed or engaged by the organization is not considered appropriate." Answer (C) is incorrect because the financial manager should inform "subordinates as appropriate regarding the confidentiality of information acquired in the course of their work and monitor their activities to assure the maintenance of that confidentiality." Answer (D) is incorrect because the financial manager is required to "refrain from using or appearing to use confidential information acquired in the course of his/her work for unethical or illegal advantage either personally or through third parties."

12. Which ethical standard is most clearly violated if a financial manager knows of a problem that could mislead users but does nothing about it?

A. Competence.

B. Legality.

C. Objectivity.

D. Confidentiality.

The correct answer is (C). *(Publisher)*

REQUIRED: The ethical standard most clearly violated when a financial manager does nothing about information that is misleading to users.

DISCUSSION: Objectivity is the fourth part of the IMA Code of Ethics. It requires that information be communicated "fairly and objectively," and that all information that could reasonably influence users be fully disclosed.

Answer (A) is incorrect because the competence standard pertains to the financial manager's responsibility to maintain his/her professional skills and knowledge. It also pertains to the performance of activities in a professional manner. Answer (B) is incorrect because legality is not addressed in the IMA Code of Ethics. Answer (D) is incorrect because the confidentiality standard concerns the financial manager's responsibility not to disclose or use the firm's confidential information.

13. The IMA Code of Ethics includes an integrity standard, which requires the financial manager to

A. Identify and make known anything that may hinder his/her judgment or prevent satisfactory completion of any duties.

B. Report any relevant information that could influence users of financial statements.

C. Disclose confidential information when authorized by his/her firm or required under the law.

D. Refuse gifts from anyone.

The correct answer is (A). *(Publisher)*

REQUIRED: The action required of the financial manager by the integrity standard.

DISCUSSION: One of the responsibilities of the financial manager under the integrity standard is to "recognize and communicate professional limitations or other constraints that would preclude responsible judgment or successful performance of an activity."

Answer (B) is incorrect because the objectivity standard requires the financial manager to "disclose fully all relevant information that could reasonably be expected to influence an intended user's understanding of the reports, comments, and recommendations presented." Answer (C) is incorrect because the confidentiality standard requires the financial manager to "refrain from disclosing confidential information acquired in the course of his/her work except when authorized, unless legally obligated to do so." Answer (D) is incorrect because the integrity standard requires the financial manager to "refuse any gift, favor, or hospitality that would influence or would appear to influence his/her actions."

14. The IMA Code of Ethics includes a competence standard, which requires the financial manager to

A. Report information, whether favorable or unfavorable.

B. Develop his/her professional proficiency on a continual basis.

C. Discuss ethical conflicts and possible courses of action with an unbiased counselor.

D. Discuss, with subordinates, their responsibilities regarding the disclosure of information about the firm.

The correct answer is (B). *(Publisher)*

REQUIRED: The action required of the financial manager by the competence standard.

DISCUSSION: One of the responsibilities of the financial manager under the competence standard is to "maintain an appropriate level of professional competence by ongoing development of his/her knowledge and skills."

Answer (A) is incorrect because the integrity standard requires the financial manager to "communicate unfavorable as well as favorable information and professional judgments or opinions." Answer (C) is incorrect because one of the suggestions from the "Resolution of Ethical Conflict" paragraph is to "clarify relevant concepts by confidential discussion with an objective advisor to obtain an understanding of possible courses of action." Answer (D) is incorrect because the confidentiality standard requires the financial manager to "inform subordinates as appropriate regarding the confidentiality of information acquired in the course of their work and monitor their activities to assure the maintenance of that confidentiality."

APPENDIX B: TAXES AS TESTED ON THE CFM EXAM

6 pages of outline
3 multiple-choice questions

A. Taxation
B. Fundamentals of Corporate Taxation

Taxes are tested in Parts 1, 2, and 4. The intended emphasis is on income taxes as an expense and the implications for business decisions. In general, the exam tests to determine whether CFM candidates understand the effects of taxes on investment decisions. Therefore, when reading the outlines in each of the CFM subunits, you must keep in mind the potential tax effects of financial transactions.

A.   Taxation

1.   **Two Principles of Taxation**

a.   Benefits received. Individuals should pay tax based on the benefits received from the services (e.g., paying for the use of a public park or swimming pool).

b.   Ability to pay. Consumers should pay taxes based on their ability to pay them (e.g., taxes on income and wealth).

2.   **Three Classifications of Taxes Reflecting Ability-to-Pay Principles**

a.   **Progressive**. With a higher income, individuals pay a higher percentage of their income in taxes (e.g., income tax).

b.   **Proportional**. At all levels of income, the percentage paid in taxes is constant (e.g., sales tax).

c.   **Regressive**. As income increases, the percentage paid in taxes decreases (e.g., payroll or excise taxes).

1)   EXAMPLE: An excise tax is regressive because its burden falls disproportionately on lower-income persons. As personal income increases, the percentage of income paid declines since an excise tax is a flat amount per quantity of the good or service purchased.

3.   Taxes also may be classified as either direct or indirect.

a.   **Direct taxes** are imposed upon the taxpayer and paid directly to the government, e.g., the personal income tax.

b.   **Indirect taxes** are levied against others and thus only indirectly on the individual taxpayer, e.g., sales and Social Security taxes paid by employers.

4.   **Incidence of Taxation** -- the parties who actually bear a particular tax. For example, the person who actually bears the burden of an indirect tax may not be the same one who pays the tax to the government.

a.   The incidence of taxation becomes important when a government wants to change the tax structure. Because taxation is a form of fiscal policy, the government needs to know who will actually bear the incidence of taxation, not just who will pay the tax.

b.   EXAMPLE: Taxes such as the corporate income tax and corporate property and excise taxes are often shifted to the consumer in the form of higher prices.

c.   EXAMPLE: Taxes such as windfall profits taxes are not shifted to the consumer via higher prices. This type of one-time-only tax levied on part of the output produced does not increase the equilibrium price of the taxed good.

5. In recent years, some authorities have supported a tax based on consumption -- a **value-added tax.**

   a. Many major industrial nations have already adopted a value-added tax.

   b. The tax is levied on the value added to goods by each business unit in the production and distribution chain.

      1) The amount of value added is measured by the difference between a firm's sales and its purchases.

      2) Each firm in the chain collects the tax on its sales, takes a credit for taxes paid on purchases, and remits the difference to the government.

      3) The consumer ultimately bears the incidence of the tax through higher prices.

   c. A value-added tax encourages consumer saving because taxes are paid on consumption only, not on savings.

      1) Because the value-added tax is based on consumption, people in the lower income groups would spend a greater proportion of their income on taxes.

      2) The value-added tax is thus regressive.

   d. Only those businesses that make a profit have to pay income taxes. Under the value-added tax, however, all businesses have to pay taxes, regardless of income.

6. **Taxes** as a business expense (federal, state, local, and foreign) are an important consideration because they are frequently 25% to 50% of all costs.

   a. They include income, use, excise, property, legal document, payroll, and others.

   b. Thus, governmental services (national defense, fire, police, etc.) are an important and costly factor of production.

   c. Tax planning is very important in investment and financing decisions.

      1) Investment tax credits have at times provided direct reduction of taxes when assets were purchased for use in the business.

         a) The net effect is to decrease the cost of the asset.

         b) The amount of the credit and limitations on the tax credit on used equipment affect investment decisions.

         c) Investment tax credit is currently available for solar and geothermal property (business energy credit), for rehabilitation of historic structures, and for certain reforestation property.

      2) Accelerated depreciation is permitted on many types of business assets.

         a) Accordingly, in the early periods of an asset's life, depreciation is higher, taxable income is lower, and the rate of return on investment is higher.

      3) Corporate capital gains are taxed at regular rates, and the capital gains of individuals are taxed at a maximum rate of 28%.

      4) Special loss carryforward and carryback rules permit businesses to deduct net operating losses incurred in one period against income earned in other periods.

      5)   A dividends-received deduction makes tax free 70% to 100% of dividends received by one company from investments in the stock of another company.

          a)   This prevents or reduces double taxation.

          b)   It also encourages one company to invest in the stock of another company.

      6)   Interest is a tax-deductible expense of the debtor company.

          a)   But dividends on common or preferred stock are not deductible by the issuer.

    d.   Federal tax policy is fiscal policy that affects the overall economy, which in turn affects production and the finished-goods markets in which the company deals.

    e.   Government monetary policy determines the availability and cost of capital, which affects financing (and in turn, investing) decisions.

      1)   Monetary policy also affects overall economic activity.

7.   Stop and review! You have completed the outline for this subunit. Study multiple-choice question 1 on page 425.

B. Fundamentals of Corporate Taxation

1.   A C corporation is subject to tax liability imposed on its income.

2.   **Gross income** means all income from whatever source derived (unless excluded by statute).

    a.   Income is considered realized when certain transactions occur.

      1)   Mere increases in value (appreciation) do not create income.

          a)   EXAMPLE: Land owned by a corporation increases in value from $5,000 to $20,000 per acre. There is no income until the land is sold or exchanged.

      2)   Transactions are normally in the form of a sale, an exchange, or the rendering of services.

      3)   Taxation of realized income may be excluded or deferred, for example, upon exchange of like-kind property.

      4)   The term "recognized" is used when income is realized and also taxed.

      5)   Nonresident aliens (including foreign corporations) are, generally, subject to federal income tax on U.S.-source income.

3.   **Deductions** are those expenses and other statutorily prescribed items that are subtracted from gross income to determine taxable income.

    a.   Deductions should be distinguished from **exclusions**. Exclusions are never included in gross income (e.g., interest on tax-exempt bonds).

4.   **Taxable income** is gross income minus deductions.

    a.   Taxable income is analogous to net income.

    b.   The tax rates are applied to taxable income to determine the tax liability.

5. **Credits** are subtracted from the tax liability.

   a. Credits directly reduce taxes, while deductions reduce taxable income upon which the taxes are computed.

6. **Book Income versus Taxable Income**

   a. CFM candidates are required to understand the difference between book income and taxable income. Problems may begin with book income, list numerous transactions, and require the adjustments necessary to arrive at taxable income.

   b. The following adjustments are necessary to adjust book income to taxable income:

      1) Add to book income

         a) Federal income tax

         b) Excess of capital losses over capital gains

         c) Taxable income not reported on books

         d) Expenses reported on books but not deducted on tax return (e.g., charitable contributions in excess of limit)

      2) Subtract from book income

         a) Income reported on books but not included on tax return (e.g., interest income from tax-exempt municipal bonds)

         b) Deductions on tax return but not reported on books (e.g., dividends-received deduction)

   c. These adjustments are the fundamental differences between net income for financial accounting purposes (book income) and taxable income. Therefore, the discussion of income and deductions in this study unit will concentrate on these differences and assume that candidates can already compute book (i.e., accrual accounting) income.

   d. According to generally accepted accounting principles (SFAS 109), accounting for income taxes (interperiod tax allocation) is based on the asset and liability method.

7. **Temporary Differences**

   a. Depreciation expense arises from using different methods for tax and book purposes.

   b. Bad debt expense. Direct write-off method is used for tax purposes and allowance method (estimating expenses) is used for book purposes.

   c. Warranty expense. For tax purposes, it is deductible only when paid, even if reserves based on estimates are used for book purposes.

   d. Charitable contributions exceeding 10% of corporate taxable income before charitable contributions and special deductions are deductible during the 5 succeeding tax years.

   e. Capital losses in excess of capital gains are not deductible in the current year. Instead, a net capital loss must be carried back 3 years (as a short-term capital loss) and applied towards any capital gains. Any loss remaining can be carried forward for 5 years. Capital losses can be used only to offset capital gains (i.e., ordinary income is unaffected).

f.   Prepaid rent income is included in taxable income when received. Prepaid rent expense is deductible in computing taxable income for the period to which it is attributable.

g.   The cost of certain intangibles (e.g., goodwill) acquired in connection with the conduct of a trade or business or income-producing activity is amortized over a 15-year period, beginning with the month in which the intangible is acquired.

h.   Organization costs are amortizable over not less than 60 months for tax purposes.

8.   **Permanent Differences**

a.   Life insurance premiums paid on key persons are not deductible if the corporation is the beneficiary. Proceeds from the policy are not taxed.

b.   Dividends-received deduction. 70% of dividends received from taxable domestic corporations are deductible by a distributee corporation that owns less than 20% of the stock of the distributing corporation. The percentage deductible is 80 if the distributee owns 20% to 80% of the distributing corporation. A 100% dividend-received deduction is permitted for dividends received among members of an affiliated group of corporations (80% ownership).

c.   Federal income tax expense is not deductible in computing taxable income.

d.   Tax-exempt interest is included in book income. Expense attributable to earning it is not deductible for tax purposes.

e.   Business gifts exceeding $25 are generally not deductible for income tax purposes.

f.   Compensation in excess of $1 million paid to the chief executive officer and certain other employees is not deductible in computing taxable income. Premiums, tax-free benefits, and compensation based on performance goals are excluded from the $1 million limit.

9.   **Tax Effects of Corporate Reorganization**

a.   A major consideration involving a business combination is whether it is a tax-free or taxable event.

b.   Study Unit 7 discusses the requirement for tax-free combinations, as well as the effects of a taxable transaction.

10. **Taxation on Multinational Corporations**

a.   Multinational corporations must deal with domestic parent taxes, foreign taxes, tax treaties, and tax agreements in the conduct of their foreign operations.

b.   See Study Unit 9 for the tax implications of multinational corporations.

11. Stop and review! You have completed the outline for this subunit. Study multiple-choice questions 2 and 3 on page 425.

MULTIPLE-CHOICE QUESTIONS

A. Taxation

1. Two examples of indirect taxes are

   A. Taxes on business and rental property and personal income taxes.

   B. Sales taxes and Social Security taxes paid by employees.

   C. Sales taxes and Social Security taxes paid by employers.

   D. Social Security taxes paid by employees and personal income taxes.

The correct answer is (C). *(CMA 686 1-20)*
   REQUIRED: The two forms of indirect taxes.
   DISCUSSION: Indirect taxes are those levied against someone other than individual taxpayers and thus only indirectly affect the individual. Sales taxes are levied against businesses and are then passed along to the individual purchaser. Social Security taxes are levied against both the employer and the employee. Those levied against the employee are direct taxes; those levied against the employer are indirect.
   Answers (A), (B), and (D) are incorrect because personal income taxes and Social Security taxes levied against the employee are direct taxes.

B. Fundamentals of Corporate Taxation

2. None of the following items are deductible as an expense in calculating taxable income except

   A. Estimated liabilities for product warranties expected to be incurred in the future.

   B. Dividends on common stock declared but not payable until next year.

   C. Bonus accrued but not paid by the end of the year to a cash-basis 90% shareholder.

   D. Vacation pay accrued on an employee-by-employee basis.

The correct answer is (D). *(CMA 1291 2-11)*
   REQUIRED: The item that is deductible in the calculation of taxable income.
   DISCUSSION: Sec. 162(a) states that a deduction is allowed for the ordinary and necessary expenses incurred during the year in any trade or business. A corporation may therefore deduct a reasonable amount for compensation. Accrued vacation pay is a form of compensation that results in an allowable deduction for federal income tax purposes.
   Answer (A) is incorrect because warranty expenses are not deductible until paid. Answer (B) is incorrect because dividends on common stock are never deductible by a corporation; they are distributions of after-tax income. Answer (C) is incorrect because amounts accrued by an accrual-basis taxpayer to be paid to a related cash-basis taxpayer in a subsequent period are not deductible until the latter taxpayer includes the items in income. This rule effectively puts related taxpayers on the cash basis.

3. All of the following are adjustments/preference items to corporate taxable income in calculating alternative minimum taxable income except

   A. All of the gain on an installment sale of real property in excess of $150,000.

   B. Mining exploration and development costs.

   C. A charitable contribution of appreciated property.

   D. Sales commission earned in 1990 but paid in 1991.

The correct answer is (D). *(CMA 1291 2-12)*
   REQUIRED: The item that is not an adjustment or preference item in calculating the alternative minimum tax (AMT).
   DISCUSSION: Taxable income is adjusted to arrive at alternative minimum taxable income. Some of the common adjustments include gains or losses from long-term contracts, gains on installment sales of real property, mining exploration and development costs, charitable contributions of appreciated property, accelerated depreciation, the accumulated current earnings adjustment, and tax-exempt interest on private activity bonds issued after August 7, 1986. A sales commission accrued in 1990 but paid in 1991 is not an example of an AMT adjustment.
   Answer (A) is incorrect because the gain on an installment sale of real property in excess of $150,000 is an adjustment to taxable income for purposes of computing alternative minimum taxable income. Answer (B) is incorrect because mining exploration and development costs are adjustments to taxable income for purposes of computing alternative minimum taxable income. Answer (C) is incorrect because a charitable contribution of appreciated property is an adjustment to taxable income for purposes of computing alternative minimum taxable income.

APPENDIX C: IMA MEMBERSHIP, ICMA APPLICATION, AND EXAMINATION FORMS

A. IMA Membership Application
B. Application for Admission to the ICMA
C. Examination Registration Form

You must apply and become an IMA member in order to participate in the IMA Certification programs. The cost is $135 per year for Regular or International membership; $45 for the first year and $90 for the second year for Associate membership (for those within 2 years of completing full-time studies and who reside in the U.S. or Canada); $67.50 per year for Academic membership (full-time faculty in the U.S. and Canada); and $27 per year for Student membership (must carry at least 6 hours per semester and reside in the U.S. or Canada). The IMA offers two member interest groups at $75 per year: the Controllers Council and the Cost Management Group. Everyone except students and associates must pay a $15 IMA registration fee. See pages 428 and 429, which can be photocopied and used to apply for IMA membership, or call the IMA at (800) 638-4427 and ask for a CMA/CFM "kit."

The application for admission to the ICMA is on pages 430 and 431. This form is required for participation in the IMA Certification Programs. Completion of the registration form on page 432 is required in order to take any and all of the five examination parts.

Photocopy the following 5 pages and fill them out and mail them today! It will take you less than 10 minutes!

IMA MEMBERSHIP APPLICATION

☐ Initial Application   ☐ Reinstatement   **PLEASE PRINT CLEARLY OR TYPE**

INSTITUTE of MANAGEMENT ACCOUNTANTS
CERTIFIED MANAGEMENT ACCOUNTANT PROGRAM

PERSONAL INFORMATION

☐ Mr. ☐ Ms. ☐ Miss ☐ Mrs. ☐ Dr.   ☐ Male ☐ Female   Send IMA Mail To: ☐ Home   ☐ Business

First Name	Middle Name	Last Name (Family Name)	Suffix	Nick Name (For IMA Badges, optional)

Social Security Number   Date of Birth   /   /   Professional Designations Earned: ☐ CPA   ☐ CFA   ☐ CIA   ☐ OTHER:

Home Street Address

City	State	Zip Code (9 digit)	Home Telephone Number ( )

Spouse's First Name	Middle Name	Last Name	Spouse's Professional Designation	Nickname for IMA Badges (Optional)

Part Time/School Address	Street	City	State	Zip Code (9 digit)	Telephone Number at part-time address ( )

COMPANY INFORMATION

Company Name

Street Address (Include room, suite and/or mail stop)

City	State	Zip Code (9 digit)	Business Telephone Number ( )	Extension	Fax Number ( )

SIC Code (See Reverse)   Job Title Code (See Reverse)   Responsibility Code (See Reverse)

Company Size (Check One)   ☐ Under $ 50 Million   ☐ $ 50 - $ 500 Million   ☐ $ 501 - $ 5 Billion   ☐ Over $ 5 Billion

CHAPTER AFFILIATION

Chapter Affiliation (Your Choice of Chapter/Student Chapter - see inside of booklet cover)   Chapter Number   ☐ Member-At-Large (Check here if no chapter affiliation desired)

EDUCATION HISTORY - BEGIN WITH CURRENT OR LAST SCHOOL ATTENDED

School Name	Major(s)	Date(s) attended or expected graduation date	Degree(s) or Expected Degree

ADMISSION CRITERIA FOR MEMBERSHIP

I affirm that I meet the criteria for membership which I have circled. (See Reverse. Check only one.) C: ☐ 1   ☐ 2   ☐ 3   ☐ 4   ☐ 5   ☐ 6

CPA Certificate Number: State: Year:

Have you ever been convicted of a felony? ☐ NO   ☐ YES (see reverse side)   Are you required to report CPE hours annually? ☐ NO   ☐ YES

MEMBERSHIP INFORMATION/DUES - FILL IN AS APPROPRIATE. ALL PAYMENTS MUST BE IN U.S. DOLLARS

☐ REGULAR MEMBERSHIP	☐ 1 Year - $ 130.00	☐ 2 Years - $ 250.00	☐ 3 Years - $ 360.00	$
☐ INTERNATIONAL MEMBER-AT-LARGE: (You must reside outside the United States and Canada.)			$ 130.00	$
☐ ACADEMIC: (You must be a full-time faculty member and reside in the U.S. or Canada.)			$ 65.00	$
☐ ASSOCIATE: (You must apply within 2 years of completing full-time studies and reside in the U.S. or Canada.)	☐ 1ST Year - $ 43.00	☐ 2ND Year -	$ 87.00	$
☐ STUDENT: (You must have not less than 6 equivalent hours per semester and reside in the U.S. or Canada.)			$ 26.00	$

MEMBER INTEREST GROUPS (IMA Membership Required):

☐ Controllers Council	☐ 1 Year - $ 75.00 ea.	☐ 2 Years - $ 140.00 ea.	☐ 3 Years - $ 200.00 each	$
☐ Cost & Financial Management Forum	☐ 1 Year - $ 75.00 ea.	☐ 2 Years - $ 140.00 ea.	☐ 3 Years - $ 200.00 each	$

OPTIONAL SERVICES (IMA Membership Required):

☐ Research Publication Service for 1 year (U.S. members)	$ 50.00	$
☐ Research Publication Service for 1 year (International members)	$ 60.00	$

REGISTRATION/REINSTATEMENT FEE:
Applies to Regular, Academic & International Members, ONLY. $ 15 00

PAYMENT INFORMATION   TOTAL DUE ➤ $

☐ Check enclosed. Make check payable to: Institute of Management Accountants, Inc.   ☐ Charge my credit card.: ☐ VISA   ☐ MasterCard   ☐ American Express

Credit Card Number: _____   Expiration date: _____ / _____

I affirm that the statements on this application are correct and agree to abide by the Standards of Ethical Conduct.

Signature: X _____   Date: _____

Sponsor's Signature (if applicable): X _____   Sponsor's Member Number: (if applicable) _____
      (Or Signature of Professor or Registrar for student)

STANDARD INDUSTRY CLASSIFICATIONS (SIC)

AGRICULTURE, FORESTRY, FISHERIES
01 AGRICULTURAL PRODUCTION
07 AGRICULTURAL SVCS / HUNTING / TRAPPING
08 FORESTRY
09 FISHERIES

MINING
10 METAL MINING
11 ANTHRACITE MINING
12 BITUMINOUS COAL / LIGNITE MINING
13 CRUDE OIL / LIGNITE MINING
14 MINING / QUARRY NONMETALLICS

CONTRACT CONSTRUCTION
15 BLDG. CONSTRUCTION - GENERAL CONTRACTORS
16 CONSTRUCTION - OTHER
17 CONSTRUCTION - SPECIAL TRADE CONTRACTORS

MANUFACTURING
19 ORDINANCE / ACCESSORIES
20 FOOD / KINDRED PRODUCTS
21 TOBACCO MANUFACTURERS
22 TEXTILE MILL PRODUCTS
23 APPAREL / FINISHED FABRICS
24 LUMBER / WOOD PRODUCTS
25 FURNITURE / FIXTURES
26 PAPER / ALLIED PRODUCTS
27 PRINTING / PUBLISHING
28 CHEMICALS / ALLIED PRODUCTS
29 OIL REFINING / RELATED INDUSTRIES
30 RUBBER / MISC. PLASTICS PRODUCTS
31 LEATHER PRODUCTS
32 STONE, CLAY, GLASS / CONCRETE PRODUCTS
33 PRIMARY METAL INDUSTRIES
34 FABRICATED METAL PRODUCTS
35 MACHINERY, NONELECTRICAL
36 ELECTRICAL MACHINERY
37 TRANSPORTATION
38 PROFESSIONAL , SCIENTIFIC, CONTROL INSTRUMENTS
39 MISC. MANUFACTURING INDUSTRIES

TRANSPORTATION, COMMUNICATION & UTILITY SERVICES
40 RAILROAD TRANSPORTATION
41 LOCAL AND SUBURBAN TRANSPORTATION
42 MOTOR FREIGHT / WAREHOUSING
44 WATER TRANSPORTATION
46 PIPE LINE TRANSPORTATION
47 TRANSPORTATION SERVICES
48 COMMUNICATION
49 ELECTRIC, GAS / SANITARY SERVICES

WHOLESALE & RETAIL TRADE
50 WHOLESALE TRADE
52 BUILDING / HARDWARE / FARM EQUIP DEALERS
53 RETAIL TRADE - GENERAL
54 FOOD STORES
55 AUTO DEALERS / SERVICE STATIONS
56 APPAREL / ACCESSORY STORES
57 FURNITURE / FURNISHINGS / STORES
58 EATING / DRINKING PLACES
59 MISC. RETAIL STORES

FINANCE, INSURANCE & REAL ESTATE
60 BANKING
61 CREDIT AGENCIES NOT BANKS
62 SECURITY / COMMODITY BROKERS, AND SERVICES
63 INSURANCE CARRIERS
64 INSURANCE AGENTS, BROKERS
65 REAL ESTATE
66 COMBINATIONS OF REAL ESTATE, INSURANCE, LOANS LAW OFFICES
67 HOLDING, INVESTMENT COMPANIES

SERVICES
70 HOTELS / ROOMING HOUSES / CAMPS, ETC.
72 PERSONAL SERVICES
73 MISC. BUSINESS SERVICES
75 AUTO REPAIR, AUTO SERVICES / GARAGES
76 MOTION PICTURES
79 AMUSEMENT / RECREATION SERVICES
80 MEDICAL / HEALTH SERVICES
81 LEGAL SERVICES
82 EDUCATIONAL SERVICES
84 MUSEUM / ART GALLERIES / GARDENS
86 NONPROFIT MEMBERSHIP ORGANIZATIONS
88 PRIVATE HOUSEHOLDS
89 PUBLIC ACCOUNTING

GOVERNMENT
91 FEDERAL GOVERNMENT
92 STATE GOVERNMENT
93 LOCAL GOVERNMENT
94 INTERNATIONAL GOVERNMENT

JOB TITLE
01 OWNER
03 CHAIRMAN OF THE BOARD
05 CHIEF EXECUTIVE OFFICER
06 CHIEF FINANCIAL OFFICER
07 PRESIDENT
09 GROUP PRESIDENT
11 CORPORATE SECRETARY
13 CORPORATE TREASURER
15 EXECUTIVE VICE PRESIDENT
17 SENIOR VICE PRESIDENT
19 VICE PRESIDENT
21 ASSISTANT VICE PRESIDENT
23 GROUP VICE PRESIDENT
25 DIVISIONAL VICE PRESIDENT
27 CORPORATE CONTROLLER
29 ASST. CORPORATE CONTROLLER
31 DIVISIONAL CONTROLLER
33 PLANT CONTROLLER
35 DIRECTOR
37 GENERAL MANAGER
39 MANAGER
41 GENERAL SUPERVISOR
43 SUPERVISOR
45 CHIEF ACCOUNTANT
47 ACCOUNTANT
49 ECONOMIST
51 ANALYST
53 SYSTEMS ANALYST
55 PROGRAMMER
57 ADMINISTRATOR
59 AUDITOR
61 BOOKKEEPER
63 ACCOUNTING CLERK
65 DEAN
67 PROFESSOR
69 ASSOCIATE PROFESSOR
71 ASSISTANT PROFESSOR
73 INSTRUCTOR
75 CONSULTANT
77 PRINCIPAL
79 PARTNER
99 OTHER

RESPONSIBILITY AREA
01 GENERAL MANAGEMENT
05 CORPORATE MANAGEMENT
10 PUBLIC ACCOUNTING
15 GENERAL ACCOUNTING
20 PERSONNEL ACCOUNTING
25 COST ACCOUNTING
30 GOVERNMENTAL ACCOUNTING
35 FINANCE
40 RISK MANAGEMENT
45 BUDGET AND PLANNING
50 TAXATION
55 INTERNAL AUDITING
60 EDUCATION
65 INFORMATION SYSTEMS
70 STUDENT
75 RETIRED
80 OTHER

Management Accounting Magazine
subscription rates per year:
★ Members $20.00
(included in dues, nondeductible)
★ Student members: $13.00
(included in dues, nondeductible)

ADMISSION CRITERIA FOR MEMBERSHIP:

All persons residing within the United States, its possessions, or Canada, and who are otherwise qualified for membership under the Bylaws, are eligible for membership as Regular Members, Associate Members or Student Members as defined in Article II, Section 2 of the Bylaws, provided they meet the following minimum criteria:

(b) Effective January 1, 1996, all new IMA members except CMAs, Emeritus Life Associates, Emeritus Life Members, Retired Members, and Student Members, will be required to meet a minimum standard for continuing professional education (CPE) of 10 hours per year as a condition of membership; that beginning January 1, 1998, the minimum standard of continuing professional education will increase to 20 hours per year; that all CPE hours must meet the qualitative specifications as set forth by the Institute of Certified Management Accountants; that CMAs will continue to meet a minimum standard for CPE of 30 hours per year; that the Board may adopt policies regarding CPE for volunteer leaders.

(c) (1) Have a full four-year college degree, or

(2) Have a two-year college degree with a minimum of 15 semester hours in accounting plus four years of experience in a management accounting position at the time of admission, or

(3) Hold a CPA certificate, or an international certificate comparable to a CPA or CMA certificate, or

(4) Have six years of experience in management accounting, or

(5) Agree to complete 18 Continuing Professional Education (CPE) hours in IMA-approved programs (local or national) in each of the five consecutive years from the date of admission. A member not fulfilling the commitment will automatically be dropped from membership, or

(6) Be a college student carrying a minimum of six undergraduate or graduate hours (or equivalent) per semester within a school, college or university in the United States.

NOTE: Prior felony conviction - This application, with a brief explanation of circumstances, should be sent directly to the Executive Director of IMA at the address on the reverse side of this form in an envelope marked "Confidential."

430

Institute of Certified Management Accountants
10 Paragon Drive • Montvale, New Jersey 07645-1759
(201) 573-9000 • 1 (800) 638-4427 • FAX: (201) 573-8438
Endorsed by the Institute of Management Accountants

APPLICATION FOR ADMISSION TO THE CERTIFIED IN FINANCIAL MANAGEMENT PROGRAM

PERSONAL INFORMATION

TYPE OR PRINT CLEARLY

☐ Mr. ☐ Ms. ☐ Miss ☐ Mrs. ☐ Dr.　☐ Male ☐ Female

Social Security Number ☐☐☐-☐☐-☐☐☐☐

Date of Birth ☐☐-☐☐-☐☐

☐ I would like my mail sent to my home address

Last Name (Family Name)	First Name	Middle Name	Suffix

Home Mailing Address

City	State	Zip Code (9 digit)

Home Telephone Number (include area code)
(　　　　)

☐ I would like my mail sent to my business address

Firm Name

Business Mailing Address

City	State	Zip Code (9 digit)

Business Telephone Number (include area code)	Extension
(　　　　)	

Are you a member of the Institute of Management Accountants?　☐ Yes　☐ No

If yes, please provide IMA Membership Number: ☐☐☐☐☐☐☐　　IMA Chapter Name: _____

If no, please note: IMA membership is required for acceptance into the CFM Program. You **must** complete and return the IMA Application. This application **must** include the appropriate dues payment.

EDUCATIONAL QUALIFICATIONS

A. College or University	Degree	Date Received/Expected
Undergraduate		
Graduate		

Name on transcript (if different than above)

State	Year	License Number
B. Candidates with CPA License:		

Check the appropriate box(es) and make arrangements for supporting documents to be forwarded to the ICMA.

☐ **College Graduate.** Submit official transcript showing university degree conferred and official university seal or arrange for university to send proof of degree directly to the ICMA. If you have more than one degree, submit only one transcript. Candidates with foreign degrees must have their degree evaluated by an independent agency. Contact the ICMA for details.

☐ **CPA.** Arrange to have proof of license sent directly from your State Board of Accountancy to the ICMA.

☐ **Applying as Student.** Be sure to provide, in the Character Reference Section on the reverse side of this form, the name of a professor who can verify student status. Upon graduation, be sure to arrange for an official copy of your transcript to be sent to the ICMA.

☐ **Applying as Faculty.** In addition to confirming your educational qualification, please provide a letter on school stationery affirming full-time teaching status.

PLEASE COMPLETE BOTH SIDES

11

CHARACTER REFERENCES

The names, addresses and telephone numbers of two character references must be supplied. One, your current employer, or current professor if you are a student; the other, a person neither employed by your firm nor a member of your family. The ICMA may contact the references as appropriate.

Name - Employer or Professor -(Circle one)	Name - Personal
Title:	Address:
Address:	Address:
City: State: Zip Code:	City: State: Zip Code:
Phone number:	Phone number:

Have you ever been convicted of a felony? ☐ Yes   ☐ No   If yes, please explain in an accompanying letter.

CFM EXPERIENCE REQUIREMENT

Appropriate experience is required before the CFM designation is awarded. The experience listed below will be used by the ICMA to identify candidates whose experience may not meet the requirements, making them ineligible for the CFM. For students and others who do not have the required experience, but who expect to be employed in the appropriate field, please check the following space: ☐ Not currently employed in the required field but expect to be in the future.

DATES (MONTH AND YEAR)	EMPLOYER	JOB TITLE	DUTIES & RESPONSIBILITIES
START DATE: END DATE:			
START DATE: END DATE:			

I agree to comply with the Standards of Ethical Conduct. I declare and affirm that the statements made in the foregoing application, including accompanying statements and transcripts, are true, complete, and correct. I authorize the investigation of all statements contained in this application.

Signature of Applicant*: **X**_____ Date:_____

*Original signature required; do not fax this form.

Please tell us how you obtained your CFM application.
☐ Employer   ☐ School   ☐ Chapter   ☐ Requested from IMA   ☐ Other: _____

NOTE: A SEPARATE EXAMINATION REGISTRATION FORM IS REQUIRED.

432

OFFICE USE ONLY	BATCH NUMBER	PAYMENT BY CHECK # _____ ☐ PERSONAL ☐ COMPANY	AMOUNT

Institute of Certified Management Accountants
10 Paragon Drive • Montvale, New Jersey 07645-1759
(201) 573-9000 • 1 (800) 638-4427 • FAX: (201) 573-8438
Endorsed by the Institute of Management Accountants

CFM
CERTIFIED IN
FINANCIAL MANAGEMENT

CFM EXAMINATION REGISTRATION FORM

PERSONAL INFORMATION
TYPE OR PRINT CLEARLY

☐ Mr. ☐ Ms. ☐ Miss ☐ Mrs. ☐ Dr.

Social Security Number ☐☐☐–☐☐–☐☐☐☐

Last Name (Family Name)   First Name   Middle Name   Suffix

Mailing Address

City   State   Zip Code (9 digit)

Daytime Telephone Number (include area code)

Please Specify ☐ Home ☐ Business

The separate Application for Admission to the CFM Program and an application to the IMA must accompany this CFM Examination Registration Form unless they have been previously submitted. These forms should be filed by March 1 for the June examination and September 1 for the December examination. If you are taking only Part 2CFM, the Registration Form should be filed at least six weeks before you plan to take the exam.

PLEASE COMPLETE THE FOLLOWING INFORMATION

☐ I wish to take the examination at the following site* _____ Site number: ☐☐☐☐
(see page 10 for site information)

☐ I wish to take the parts checked at the examination scheduled for* _____
(month/year)

*Not required for Part 2CFM.

PLACE A CHECK MARK IN THE BLANK SPACES BELOW FOR THE PART(S) YOU WISH TO TAKE AT THIS TIME

☐ PART 1
Economics,
Finance, and
Management

☐ PART 2CFM
Corporate
Financial
Management

☐ PART 3
Management
Reporting,
Analysis, and
Behavioral
Issues

☐ PART 4
Decision
Analysis
and
Information
Systems

TOTAL PARTS _____

X $ 60.00 Fee .... $ _____

Add $ 25.00 .... $ _____
International Site Fee
(if applicable)

Less Student/Faculty Discount...... $ _____
(if eligible)

AMOUNT DUE .... $ _____

PAYMENT INFORMATION

☐ I am enclosing a check payable to the Institute of Certified Management Accountants

☐ Charge my: ☐ VISA   ☐ MasterCard   ☐ American Express

Card Number: ☐☐☐☐☐☐☐☐☐☐☐☐☐☐☐☐   Expiration Date: ☐☐–☐☐

Signature: **X** _____   Date: _____

REFUND INFORMATION ON PAGE 9.   FEES SUBJECT TO CHANGE

13

CFM REVIEW CPE
CONTINUING PROFESSIONAL EDUCATION
FIVE SEPARATE COURSES

Courses Available	Course Level	Average Comp. Time	CPE Credit
* 1. Financial Statements	Basic	500 min.	5 hours
2. Long-Term Financing, Capital Markets, and Interest Rates	Basic	500 min.	5 hours
3. Investment/Commercial Banking and Financial Analysis	Basic	500 min.	5 hours
4. Business Restructuring and Risk Management	Basic	500 min.	5 hours
* 5. Accounting Standards and Financial Environment	Basic	500 min.	5 hours
*A&A Credit		**Total CPE Credit**	25 hours

1. Register to participate in this self-study CPE program by photocopying and completing the form below and mailing it, along with your $25 remittance, to:

    Gleim Publications, Inc.
    CPE Division
    P.O. Box 12848, University Station
    Gainesville, FL 32604

    a. If you are using a credit card, you can fax us at (352) 375-6940.

2. Gleim Publications will process your registration and send you one machine-readable answer sheet that you can use to submit up to five CFM CPE courses at one time. Should you decide to take fewer than five courses, you will need to purchase an additional answer sheet for $25 in order to submit additional courses.

3. Follow the specific instructions on the next five pages that describe exactly what must be done to earn CPE credit for each of the five courses.

Gleim's CFM CPE Registration Form

Name of Participant _____

Social Security No. (for recordkeeping purposes) _____

Mailing Address _____

_____

City _____ State _____ ZIP _____

Daytime Telephone _____ E-mail Address _____

Remit $25 registration fee by check, money order, or VISA/MC.

VISA/MC _____-_____-_____-_____ Exp. Date ____/____

Signature _____

NOTE TO GLEIM CFM-CPE CUSTOMERS
Twenty additional courses similar to those listed above are available to accompany the Gleim review materials for the CMA exam. Call (800) 87-GLEIM to order.

434

PROCEDURES TO OBTAIN CPE CREDIT

Follow the instructions presented at the opening of **each** course you have chosen. Also, read the rest of this Introduction carefully. In general, the procedure listed below is recommended.

1. Enroll in the program by photocopying and completing the form on page 433 and submitting it along with the $25 registration fee. We will send you a CPE answer sheet, which you must use to submit your final exam answers for grading.

2. Study the outlines in *CFM Review*. Make study notes in your book and work through all examples.

   a. Work through each multiple-choice question in the pertinent study units. Do not skip questions.

   b. Study the adjacent answer explanations for the questions you answered incorrectly or had difficulty answering.

3. When you complete the assigned outlines and study questions, turn to the appropriate course in this CPE section and take the open-book final exam.

   a. The best procedure is to answer the questions in the order they appear.

   b. If you are unsure of some answers, consult the outlines and answer explanations in *CFM Review*.

   c. Circle your answer for each CPE question. Wait until you have answered all the questions for a course before **carefully transferring** your answers to our machine-readable answer sheet.

      1) Do not make a mistake in this transfer (i.e., skip a line, start on the wrong line, etc.). Read the instructions at the beginning of each course and in the next section of this Introduction, and follow them carefully.

4. When you are ready to submit completed courses in this program, mail the machine-readable answer sheet in the special pre-addressed protective envelope accompanying your answer sheet to Gleim Publications, Inc., CPE Division, P.O. Box 12848, University Station, Gainesville, FL 32604. You may take one or more courses at a time using the answer sheet provided when you purchased this program. **Additional answer sheets are available for $25 and may be used for additional courses not submitted on the single answer sheet we send you upon registration in this program.**

   a. Complete the course evaluation sheet and send it with your answer sheet.

   b. **Same-day grading service** available Monday through Friday: Send your materials and $50 prepayment ($100 if out of the U.S.) (check, VISA, MC) via Federal Express (priority, so we receive it by noon) or UPS Next Day Letter Service to 4201 N.W. 95th Blvd., Gainesville, FL 32606. We will hand-grade your answer sheet and send the results back to you via UPS Next Day Letter Service the same day. Add $10 if you request Saturday delivery.

MACHINE-READABLE ANSWER SHEET

We have contracted with the Office of Instructional Resources at the University of Florida to read your answer sheet with optical scanning equipment that will record your responses. Computerization of the grading and grade analysis means that you must fill out the answer sheet carefully and correctly.

1. Fill out all of the required information on page 2 of the answer sheet completely. You must write in the required information **AND** darken appropriate circles. Note that the answer sheet is four pages long. On page 2, fill in the following data:

   a. Last name, first initial, middle initial. If your last name is over 15 characters long, use only the first 15 characters.

   b. Sex, so we can computer-generate a Mr. or Ms. in our correspondence

   c. Social Security number

   d. Course number(s)--**THIS IS VERY IMPORTANT**. Note the four-digit code in the following table for each CFM CPE course you will be asking us to grade on this answer sheet. "B" means leave that circle blank.

1) Financial Statements	B 7 B 1
2) Long-Term Financing, Capital Market and Interest Rates	B 7 B 2
3) Investment/Commercial Banking and Financial Analysis	B 7 B 3
4) Business Restructuring and Risk Management	B 7 B 4
5) Accounting Standards and Financial Environment	B 7 B 5
All Five Courses	B 7 B 1, 2, 3, 4, 5

   NOTE: If you wish to take all five courses, fill in 1, 2, 3, 4, and 5 in the fourth column.

   e. Total CPE credit hours for which you are applying on this answer sheet

   1) You may ignore this. Your Certificate of Completion will automatically reflect the proper amount of credit (see page 437).

2. **Sign and date** the self-certification statement on page 1 of the machine-readable answer sheet.

   - Self-certification: I confirm that I have studied all of the required material and answered all the required questions for the course(s) for which I am seeking CPE credit. I also have studied the answer explanations to questions I answered wrong or had difficulty understanding.

   _____   _____
   Signature   Date

3. If your answer sheet is not completed properly, it will be returned to you for correction.

4. Again, a single answer sheet may be used to take as many courses as you wish, but it may be submitted only once. CPE participants may **NOT** mix courses from different programs on the same answer sheet. If you decide to submit this answer sheet for grading of only one or a few courses, but you would like to take more CFM CPE courses in the future, simply enclose $25 with the answer sheet you submit for grading, and we will send you another blank answer sheet separately from the results of your CPE tests.

GRADING YOUR CPE EXAM FOR CPE CREDIT

After we receive the results from the machine grading,

1. We will send you a Certificate of Completion if you achieve at least a 70% score.

    a. For every question you answered incorrectly, we will send a synopsis of the concept tested.

    b. When you receive your results, take the time to read through these synopses to be sure you have no miscomprehension of basic concepts or principles.

2. If you do not get a score of at least 70%, we will return your answer sheet and a list of the question numbers incorrectly answered. A $25 regrading fee is payable upon resubmission of the corrected answer sheet. You cannot obtain credit until you obtain at least a 70% success rate.

RECORD RETENTION AND DUPLICATE CERTIFICATES

Gleim Publications, Inc. will retain your answer sheet(s) and a record of your course completions for 5 years. You must notify us within 60 days if you have not received your Certificate of Completion. After 60 days, we will charge $25 to send you a duplicate certificate.

You should retain your Certificate of Completion to document completion of your CPE course(s). You should also retain your *CFM Review* book containing this CPE section, which has your completed answers and notes.

ADDITIONAL INFORMATION ABOUT THIS CPE PROGRAM

Prerequisites and Advance Preparation -- A participant must have an undergraduate major in business or an equivalent.

Program Objectives -- Upon completion of this program, the participant will have knowledge of the basic principles in each area studied. More importantly, the participant will develop an "executive" or "managerial" point of view (as opposed to the more narrow, traditional accounting point of view). In addition, participants will be preparing to sit for the CFM examination, thus receiving continuing professional education credit while simultaneously expanding their professional horizons.

Change of Address -- Please notify us of any changes in your shipping and/or mailing addresses by writing to

> Gleim Publications, Inc.
> CPE Division
> P.O. Box 12848, University Station
> Gainesville, FL 32604

Time Limit on Completion of This CPE Program -- You have at least 1 year from the date of purchase to complete the courses in this CPE program. We will notify you at your permanent address (see the discussion on the previous page) when the program goes out of date and/or is superseded by a replacement program. You will have 30 days after our mailing to submit your final answer sheet. Thus, while we will allow you to use this CPE program until, in our opinion, it is no longer current, you should plan on completing the courses you desire within 1 year. Our intent is to serve you better than the competition; i.e., if a CPE program is not out-of-date in 1 year, why cancel it? We are committed, however, to provide up-to-date CPE programs, which requires us to retire out-of-date courses as we develop new (current) editions.

Limit on Amount of Correspondence Course CPE Credit -- We are concerned that some individuals may misuse our program (as is probably the case for all CPE programs). While we have not instituted limits on the maximum number of hours available through this CPE program, we ask that you do not misuse our programs. In addition, some state boards of accountancy have placed limits on the number of hours of CPE credit that may be fulfilled through individual study or correspondence course.

Additionally, our Certificate of Completion lists maximum credit for both formal self-study measurement principles: average completion time and one-half average completion time. Thus, if your time spent on any course is less than the "recommended maximum hours of CPE credit," we suggest that you **report your actual hours consistent with the rules and procedures of the agency or organization to which you are reporting**.

Our approach permits you to take simple courses or courses already familiar to you for review purposes "just to make sure." When you use less than the average time, you can so indicate. We have explained our approach to the various agencies/organizations requiring CPE.

FORMAL SELF-STUDY CPE PROGRAM CREDIT MEASUREMENT

The AICPA standard for measuring CPE credit for formal, noninteractive self-study CPE programs states that CPE credit should equal one-half of the average completion time, as determined by the program developer through pretesting. For example, a course that takes an average of 800 minutes to complete is recommended for 8 contact hours of CPE credit. The recommended credit we indicate is based on this AICPA standard.

Note, however, that about a third of CPE jurisdictions that require reporting of CPE credit will allow "full credit" for our programs; i.e., a course that takes an average of 800 minutes to complete is recommended for 16 contact hours of CPE credit. Thus, our Certificate of Completion lists both measures of credit, i.e., **average completion time** and **one-half average completion time**. We encourage you to verify the measurement standard (as it relates to Gleim's self-study courses) with your reporting jurisdiction(s) so you can properly report your credit.

Call us for assistance: **(800) 87-GLEIM.**

CFM CPE COURSE 1

FINANCIAL STATEMENTS

This CPE course covers Study Units 1 and 2 of **CFM Review**, First Edition. In addition to the introductory material, this course consists of 42 pages of outlines and text and 140 multiple-choice questions (16 of which constitute the final exam). As continuing professional education, 5 hours of CPE credit is recommended based on the AICPA's one-half the average completion time measurement principle. If any of the CPE agencies to which you report measures self-study CPE in terms of average completion time (rather than one-half average completion time), your certificate of completion will indicate 10 hours of maximum CPE credit.

Date Completed	Time (Minutes)		
_____	_____	**1.**	**Study Unit 1:**
_____	_____		a. Study the outlines on "Financial Statements and Annual Reports" on pages 31 through 49.
_____	_____		b. Work through questions 1 through 62 on pages 50 through 70 after covering the answer explanations on the right-hand side of the page. Answer each question and circle your answer.
_____	_____		1. Uncover the answer explanations and study the adjacent answer explanations for the questions that you missed or that gave you difficulty.
		2.	**Study Unit 2:**
_____	_____		a. Study the outlines on "Financial Statements: Special Topics" on pages 71 through 93.
_____	_____		b. Work through questions 1 through 62 on pages 94 through 116 after covering the answer explanations on the right-hand side of the page. Answer each question and circle your answer.
_____	_____		1. Uncover the answer explanations and study the adjacent answer explanations for the questions that you missed or that gave you difficulty.
		3.	**Final Exam:**
_____	_____		a. Take the final exam by answering questions 1 through 16 on the following pages.

               1. If you have difficulty, refer to **CFM Review**, or other sources. Remember, this is an open-book exam.

4. Carefully transfer your answers for these 16 questions to the CPE final exam answer sheet. Be sure you use the circles numbered 1 through 16.

5. Mark **B 7 B 1** (B means Blank) as the course number on page 2 of the answer sheet. See example at right.

    a. Refer to page 435 in this section for instructions on how to complete the remainder of the machine-readable answer sheet.

6. Please complete the accompanying course evaluation and submit it with your answer sheet.

Total Time _____ (Carry this amount to your CPE course evaluation form.)

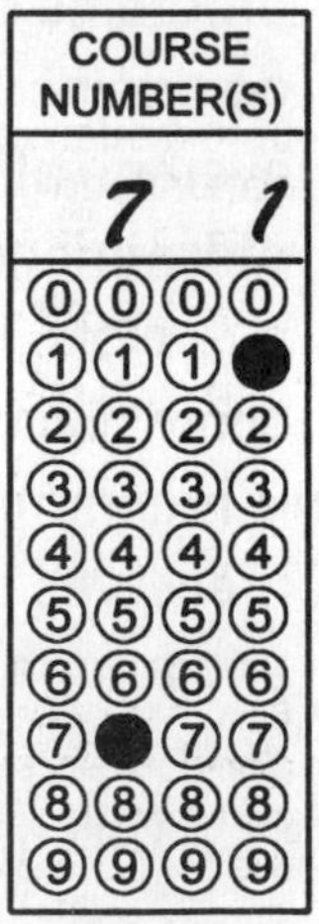

COURSE NUMBER(S)

7   1

(answer-sheet bubble grid showing course number with "1" filled in the second column and "7" filled in the first column)

1. Which of the following is NOT classified as an intangible asset on a balance sheet?

A. Patents.

B. Trademarks.

C. Oil and gas reserves.

D. Franchises.

2. Which of the following assets is reported on a balance sheet at cost net of accumulated depreciation?

A. Leased assets held under capital leases.

B. Land.

C. Land held for future plant site.

D. Deferred tax assets arising from interperiod tax allocation.

3. Which of the following accounts is reported as a current liability?

A. Unearned ticket sales revenue.

B. Bonds payable that are due in 3 months and are to be paid from a noncurrent fund.

C. Short-term obligation that management intends, and has demonstrated the ability, to refinance on a long-term basis.

D. An obligation due on demand after the longer of 1 year or the operating cycle.

4. Which of the following is NOT reported in the owners' equity section of a balance sheet?

A. Treasury stock.

B. Foreign currency translation adjustments.

C. Unrealized losses on available-for-sale securities.

D. Dividends payable.

5. If an item of income is classified as infrequent but not unusual, in which section of the income statement should it appear?

A. Continuing operations.

B. Discontinued operations.

C. Extraordinary items.

D. Cumulative effect of a change in principle.

6. Cost of goods manufactured appears in the cost of goods sold section of a manufacturer's income statement. What is the equivalent term appearing on the income statement of a retail department store?

A. Purchases.

B. Gross profit.

C. Beginning inventory.

D. Selling expenses.

7. Which of the following transactions is a financing activity reported on a statement of cash flows?

A. Receiving cash from sale of treasury stock.

B. Receiving cash from sale of equipment.

C. Converting convertible debt into common stock.

D. Entering into a capital lease.

8. The SEC requires that corporate annual reports include which of the following?

A. Balance sheets for the three most recent fiscal year-ends.

B. Income statements for the three most recent fiscal years.

C. Balance sheets for the five most recent fiscal year-ends.

D. Income statements for the five most recent fiscal years.

9. Depreciation in accounting can best be described as a(n)

A. Valuation process.

B. Allocation process.

C. Expense process.

D. Variable costing process.

10. An asset is acquired on January 2, 1997 at a cost of $5,000. The asset is expected to have a $500 salvage value at the end of its 5-year life. What is the depreciation for the first year under the 200%-declining-balance (DB) and sum-of-the-years'-digits (SYD) methods of depreciation?

	DB	SYD
A.	$2,000	$1,500
B.	$1,800	$1,500
C.	$2,000	$1,667
D.	$1,800	$1,667

11. An asset is acquired on January 2, 1997 at a cost of $5,000. The asset is expected to have a $500 salvage value at the end of its 5-year life. What is the depreciation for the second year under the 200%-declining-balance (DB) and sum-of-the-years'-digits (SYD) methods of depreciation?

	DB	SYD
A.	$2,000	$1,500
B.	$1,200	$1,200
C.	$2,000	$1,200
D.	$1,080	$1,333

12. Under which of the following depreciation methods is depreciation considered as a variable cost?

    A.   Straight-line.

    B.   Composite.

    C.   200% declining balance.

    D.   Units of output.

13. Under SFAS 109, which of the following is considered a permanent difference, as opposed to a temporary difference?

    A.   Operating loss carryforward.

    B.   Accelerated depreciation for tax purposes.

    C.   Dividends-received deduction.

    D.   Accrued warranty expense.

14. A lease must meet one of four criteria to be classified as a capital lease by a lessee. Which of the following is not one of these critieria?

    A.   The lease provides for the transfer of ownership of the leased property.

    B.   The lease contains a bargain purchase option.

    C.   The lease term is 75% or more of the estimated economic life of the leased property.

    D.   The discount rate used is the lower of the implicit interest rate or the lessee's incremental borrowing rate of interest.

15. Which of the following dividends may be distributed in excess of the balance in retained earnings?

    A.   Property dividends.

    B.   Liquidating dividends.

    C.   Stock dividends.

    D.   Cash dividends.

16. If the market rate of interest is <List A> the coupon rate when bonds are issued, then the bonds will sell in the market at a price <List B> the face value, and the issuing firm will record a <List C> on bonds payable.

	List A	List B	List C
A.	Less than	Greater than	Discount
B.	Greater than	Greater than	Premium
C.	Less than	Greater than	Premium
D.	Greater than	Less than	Premium

CFM CPE COURSE 2
LONG-TERM FINANCING, CAPITAL MARKETS, AND INTEREST RATES

This CPE course covers Study Units 3 and 4 of *CFM Review*, First Edition. In addition to the introductory material, this course consists of 28 pages of outlines and text and 140 multiple-choice questions (16 of which constitute the final exam). As continuing professional education, 5 hours of CPE credit is recommended based on the AICPA's one-half the average completion time measurement principle. If any of the CPE agencies to which you report measures self-study CPE in terms of average completion time (rather than one-half average completion time), your certificate of completion will indicate 10 hours of maximum CPE credit.

Date Completed	Time (Minutes)		
_____	_____	1.	**Study Unit 3:**
		a.	Study the outlines on "Long-Term Capital Financing" on pages 117 through 134.
_____	_____	b.	Work through questions 1 through 66 on pages 135 through 158 after covering the answer explanations on the right-hand side of the page. Answer each question and circle your answer.
_____	_____		1. Uncover the answer explanations and study the adjacent answer explanations for the questions that you missed or that gave you difficulty.
		2.	**Study Unit 4:**
_____	_____	a.	Study the outlines on "Financial Markets and Interest Rates" on pages 159 through 168.
_____	_____	b.	Work through questions 1 through 58 on pages 169 through 186 after covering the answer explanations on the right-hand side of the page. Answer each question and circle your answer.
_____	_____		1. Uncover the answer explanations and study the adjacent answer explanations for the questions that you missed or that gave you difficulty.
		3.	**Final Exam:**
_____	_____	a.	Take the final exam by answering questions 17 through 32 on the following pages.

3. **Final Exam:**

   a. Take the final exam by answering questions 17 through 32 on the following pages.

      1. If you have difficulty, refer to *CFM Review*, or other sources. Remember, this is an open-book exam.

4. Carefully transfer your answers for these 16 questions to the CPE final exam answer sheet. Be sure you use the circles numbered 17 through 32.

5. Mark **B 7 B 2** (B means Blank) as the course number on page 2 of the answer sheet. See example at right.

   a. Refer to page 435 in this section for instructions on how to complete the remainder of the machine-readable answer sheet.

6. Please complete the accompanying course evaluation and submit it with your answer sheet.

COURSE NUMBER(S)

7   2

⓪ ⓪ ⓪ ⓪
① ① ① ①
② ② ② ●
③ ③ ③ ③
④ ④ ④ ④
⑤ ⑤ ⑤ ⑤
⑥ ⑥ ⑥ ⑥
⑦ ● ⑦ ⑦
⑧ ⑧ ⑧ ⑧
⑨ ⑨ ⑨ ⑨

Total Time _____   (Carry this amount to your CPE course evaluation form.)

17. Which of the following is NOT an advantage to a corporation of issuing common stock as opposed to issuing bonds?

A. Dividends are not fixed.

B. There is no fixed maturity date for repayment of capital.

C. The sale of common stock increases the creditworthiness of the firm.

D. Dividends are an after-tax distribution to the firm.

18. Which of the following is a true statement with respect to preferred stock?

A. Transient preferred stock may be converted into common stock at the investor's option.

B. The dividends-received deduction for tax purposes does not apply to preferred stock dividends.

C. An 8% participating preferred stock could never receive more than an 8% annual dividend.

D. A call premium is an amount above par value that an issuer has to pay to redeem a preferred stock.

19. Major sources of intermediate term financing include all of the following except

A. Commercial paper.

B. Loans from banks.

C. Variable rate loans from insurance companies.

D. Floating rate loans from pension funds.

20. Following the concept of maturity matching, which of the following is the best source of funds to acquire a new building?

A. Commercial paper.

B. Bonds.

C. Term loan from a bank.

D. Floating rate loan from a pension fund.

21. Using a dividend growth model to estimate the cost of retained earnings, what would be the required rate of return if the dividend is $3 per share when the market price is $50 and the dividend is expected to grow at a constant rate of 10%?

A. 6%

B. 10%

C. 13%

D. 16%

22. Which of the following statements concerning dividends is INCORRECT?

A. Dividend policy refers to the policy of determining what portion of a corporation's net income is distributed to shareholders and what portion is retained for reinvestment.

B. A high dividend rate means a slower rate of growth.

C. A high growth rate usually means a high dividend rate.

D. Corporations normally try to maintain a stable level of dividends, even though profits may fluctuate considerably.

23. Which of the following is NOT one of the reasons that a corporation typically purchases treasury stock?

A. To meet employee stock option and bonus plan requirements.

B. To support the market for the company's stock.

C. To acquire stock to undertake a merger.

D. To decrease the debt-to-equity ratio.

24. A 25% stock dividend

A. Decreases the debt-to-equity ratio of a firm.

B. Increases future earnings per share.

C. Increases the size of the firm.

D. Decreases the market price per share.

25. Which of the following statements concerning financial markets is true?

A. The New York Stock Exchange is an auction market.

B. The issuer of securities receives the proceeds of sale in a secondary market.

C. Primary markets provide for trading of previously issued securities.

D. In money markets, an issuer raises new capital by making initial offerings of securities.

26. The over-the-counter market is best described as a(n)

A. Dealer market.

B. Organized stock exchange.

C. Primary market.

D. Money market.

27. Which of the following are not financial intermediaries?

    A. Commercial banks.

    B. Stock exchanges.

    C. Life insurance companies.

    D. Mutual funds.

28. Which of the following tends to stimulate stock market activity?

    A. A decrease in margin requirements.

    B. An increase in margin requirements.

    C. The elimination of short selling.

    D. Creation of new forms of capital by financial intermediaries.

29. Which of the following statements concerning international bonds is true?

    A. Foreign bonds are denominated in a currency different from that of the country where they are sold.

    B. Dollar-denominated bonds issued in France by a U. S. company are considered foreign bonds.

    C. Eurobonds are typically issued in bearer form, which makes them more desirable to investors who desire secrecy.

    D. Eurobonds are denominated in the currency of the country where they are sold.

30. Which of the following statements concerning foreign currency exchange rates is true?

    A. Spot rates are the rates at which currencies can be exchanged in the future.

    B. Forward rates are the rates at which currencies can be exchanged immediately.

    C. The current international monetary system is characterized by floating exchange rates subject to some management.

    D. If a foreign currency is expected to appreciate against the dollar, it will sell at a discount.

31. Assuming foreign currency exchange rates are allowed to fluctuate freely, which of the following factors will likely cause a nation's currency to trade at a discount in the forward market?

    A. A low rate of inflation relative to the rates in other nations.

    B. A high nominal domestic rate of interest relative to the rates in other nations.

    C. A low real domestic rate of interest relative to the rates in other nations.

    D. A currency that has appreciated relative to the currencies of other nations.

32. The term structure of interest rates is the relationship of yield to maturity and time to maturity. This relationship may result in different yield curves. Which of the following is not a possible explanation for a positive maturity risk premium (an upward-sloping yield curve)?

    A. Short-term securities may be preferred by investors because their liquidity protects against interest-rate risk.

    B. The market expects short-term inflation to be higher than long-term inflation.

    C. Borrowers prefer long-term funds to match the maturities of investments with the maturities of assets.

    D. Long-term borrowing avoids the expense of turning the debt over frequently.

CFM CPE COURSE 3
INVESTMENT/COMMERCIAL BANKING AND FINANCIAL ANALYSIS

This CPE course covers Study Units 5 and 6 of *CFM Review*, First Edition. In addition to the introductory material, this course consists of 29 pages of outlines and text and 126 multiple-choice questions (16 of which constitute the final exam). As continuing professional education, 5 hours of CPE credit is recommended based on the AICPA's one-half the average completion time measurement principle. If any of the CPE agencies to which you report measures self-study CPE in terms of average completion time (rather than one-half average completion time), your certificate of completion will indicate 10 hours of maximum CPE credit.

Date Completed	Time (Minutes)		
_____	_____	**1.**	**Study Unit 5:**
		a.	Study the outlines on "Investment Banking and Commercial Banking" on pages 187 through 198.
_____	_____	b.	Work through questions 1 through 50 on pages 199 through 214 after covering the answer explanations on the right-hand side of the page. Answer each question and circle your answer.
_____	_____		1. Uncover the answer explanations and study the adjacent answer explanations for the questions that you missed or that gave you difficulty.
		2.	**Study Unit 6:**
_____	_____	a.	Study the outlines on "Financial Statement Analysis" on pages 215 through 231.
_____	_____	b.	Work through questions 1 through 60 on pages 232 through 250 after covering the answer explanations on the right-hand side of the page. Answer each question and circle your answer.
_____	_____		1. Uncover the answer explanations and study the adjacent answer explanations for the questions that you missed or that gave you difficulty.
		3.	**Final Exam:**
_____	_____	a.	Take the final exam by answering questions 33 through 48 on the following pages.
			1. If you have difficulty, refer to *CFM Review*, or other sources. Remember, this is an open-book exam.

4. Carefully transfer your answers for these 16 questions to the CPE final exam answer sheet. Be sure you use the circles numbered 33 through 48.

5. Mark **B 7 B 3** (B means Blank) as the course number on page 2 of the answer sheet. See example at right.

    a. Refer to page 435 in this section for instructions on how to complete the remainder of the machine-readable answer sheet.

6. Please complete the accompanying course evaluation and submit it with your answer sheet.

COURSE NUMBER(S)

7 3

```
0 0 0 0
1 1 1 1
2 2 2 2
3 3 3 ●
4 4 4 4
5 5 5 5
6 6 6 6
7 ● 7 7
8 8 8 8
9 9 9 9
```

Total Time _____ (Carry this amount to your CPE course evaluation form.)

33. An investment banking firm assists an issuer in the sale of new securities. What provision in their agreement permits the investment banking firm to purchase more shares at the offering price?

A. A firm commitment to sell the securities.
B. A requirement that the offering be underwritten.
C. A Green Shoe option.
D. An undertaking to use its best efforts to sell the securities.

34. The disadvantages's of a corporation's going public include all of the following except

A. High costs of complying with SEC regulations.
B. Competing firms having access to some of the company's operating data.
C. Increased liquidity of the firm's stock.
D. Increased shareholder servicing costs.

35. When a firm makes an initial public offering of securities, it ordinarily must file a registration statement with the SEC. The purpose of registration is to

A. Insure investors against loss.
B. Provide adequate disclosure to potential investors.
C. Permit the SEC to express an opinion on the accuracy of the information.
D. Permit the SEC to determine the financial health of the registrant.

36. Under the Securities Act of 1933, tombstone ads are permitted during the waiting period between the filing of a registration statement and the time it becomes effective. A tombstone ad

A. Is an offer to sell.
B. Must not state the price of the securities.
C. Must identify the name and business of the issuer and the approximate date of the offering.
D. States that the SEC has approved the filing.

37. After a firm has filed a registration statement with the SEC, it may issue a red-herring prospectus. This document

A. Is a preliminary prospectus.
B. Must include a statement as to when the registration became effective.
C. Constitutes an offer to sell securities at a certain price.
D. Incorporates a bedbug letter from the SEC.

38. Shelf registrations

A. Is available to any issuer of securities.
B. Allows issuers to respond rapidly in volatile markets.
C. Typically increases flotation costs for securities.
D. Is effective for 3 years after the effective date.

39. The SEC promulgated Regulation D to govern private placements of securities. If an issuance qualifies as a private placement,

A. It is exempt from the normal process of registration with the SEC.
B. Sale is limited to nonaccredited investors.
C. General advertising is permitted.
D. Purchasers may include brokers, dealers, and underwriters.

40. Exemptions from SEC registration requirements are allowed for

	Intrastate Offerings	Small Offerings under Regulation A	Short-Term Commercial Paper
A.	No	Yes	No
B.	Yes	No	No
C.	No	Yes	Yes
D.	Yes	Yes	Yes

41. Given a quick ratio of 2.0, current assets of $6,000, and inventory of $2,000, what is the value of current liabilities if the only difference between current assets and quick assets is inventory?

A. $2,000
B. $3,000
C. $4,000
D. $6,000

42. What type of ratio is receivables turnover?

A. Profitability.
B. Asset management.
C. Cost management.
D. Leverage.

43. Which one of the following inventory cost flow assumptions will result in a higher inventory turnover ratio in an inflationary economy?

   A. FIFO.

   B. LIFO.

   C. Weighted average.

   D. Specific identification.

44. Using the data presented below, calculate the cost of sales for the Beta Corporation for 1996, assuming that inventory is the sole difference between current assets and quick assets.

Current ratio 12/31/96	2
Quick ratio 12/31/96	1
Current liabilities 12/31/96	$600,000
Inventory 12/31/95	$500,000
Inventory turnover	8.0

   A. $1,200,000

   B. $4,000,000

   C. $4,400,000

   D. $4,800,000

45. An increase in the market price of a firm's common stock will immediately affect its

   A. Return on equity.

   B. Return on assets.

   C. Debt-to-net worth ratio.

   D. Dividend yield.

46. Baylor Company paid out one-half of its 1995 earnings in dividends. Baylor's earnings decreased by 20%, and the amount of its dividends increased by 15%, in 1996. Baylor's dividend payout ratio for 1996 was

   A. 50%

   B. 53.1%

   C. 47.9%

   D. 71.9%

47. X Corporation computed the following items from its financial records for 1996:

Price-earnings ratio $\dfrac{Price}{EPS}$ 20

Payout ratio $\dfrac{Div}{EPS}$ .5

The dividend yield on Watson's common stock for 1996 is

   A. 2.25%

   B. 2.5%

   C. 4.5%

   D. 5.0%

48. The q-ratio equals the

   A. Shareholders' equity ÷ Shares outstanding

   B. Market price per share ÷ Book value per share

   C. Market value of all securities ÷ Replacement cost of all assets

   D. Dividend yield ÷ Capital gains

CFM CPE COURSE 4
BUSINESS RESTRUCTURING AND RISK MANAGEMENT

This CPE course covers Study Units 7 and 8 of *CFM Review*, First Edition. In addition to the introductory material, this course consists of 38 pages of outlines and text and 136 multiple-choice questions (16 of which constitute the final exam). As continuing professional education, 5 hours of CPE credit is recommended based on the AICPA's one-half the average completion time measurement principle. If any of the CPE agencies to which you report measures self-study CPE in terms of average completion time (rather than one-half average completion time), your certificate of completion will indicate 10 hours of maximum CPE credit.

Date Completed	Time (Minutes)		

1. Study Unit 7:

   a. Study the outlines on "Business Combinations and Restructurings" on pages 251 through 269.

   b. Work through questions 1 through 59 on pages 270 through 288 after covering the answer explanations on the right-hand side of the page. Answer each question and circle your answer.

   1. Uncover the answer explanations and study the adjacent answer explanations for the questions that you missed or that gave you difficulty.

2. Study Unit 8:

   a. Study the outlines on "Risk Management" on pages 289 through 307.

   b. Work through questions 1 through 61 on pages 308 through 326 after covering the answer explanations on the right-hand side of the page. Answer each question and circle your answer.

   1. Uncover the answer explanations and study the adjacent answer explanations for the questions that you missed or that gave you difficulty.

3. Final Exam:

   a. Take the final exam by answering questions 49 through 64 on the following pages.

   1. If you have difficulty, refer to *CFM Review*, or other sources. Remember, this is an open-book exam.

4. Carefully transfer your answers for these 16 questions to the CPE final exam answer sheet. Be sure you use the circles numbered 49 through 64.

5. Mark **B 7 B 4** (B means Blank) as the course number on page 2 of the answer sheet. See example at right.

   a. Refer to page 435 in this section for instructions on how to complete the remainder of the machine-readable answer sheet.

6. Please complete the accompanying course evaluation and submit it with your answer sheet.

Total Time _____ (Carry this amount to your CPE course evaluation form.)

COURSE NUMBER(S): **7 4**

49. Which type of merger involves two unrelated firms in different industries?

   A. Horizontal merger.

   B. Vertical merger.

   C. Congeneric merger.

   D. Conglomerate merger.

50. Which of the following is not a typical characteristic of firms that are candidates for leveraged buyouts?

   A. Considerable outstanding debt.

   B. An established business with proven operating performance.

   C. Stable earnings and cash flows.

   D. A quality asset base that can be used as collateral for a new loan.

51. Under federal tax law, a reorganization is taxable if one firm acquires

   A. All of the stock of another firm solely for cash and debt.

   B. All of the stock of another firm solely for its own stock.

   C. Substantially all of the assets of another firm solely for its own stock.

   D. Another firm through a statutory merger, the stock in the nonsurvivor is canceled, and its shareholders receive stock in the survivor.

52. Which of the following is a defense to corporate takeovers?

   A. Greenmail.

   B. Tax-free reorganization.

   C. Financial synergy.

   D. Operational synergy.

53. Which form(s) of accounting for a business combination may result in recognition of negative goodwill when the amount paid is less than the fair value of the identifiable net assets?

   A. Purchase only.

   B. Pooling only.

   C. Consolidation or pooling.

   D. Purchase or pooling.

54. A merger will be disallowed by the Department of Justice if the

   A. Acquired company is failing.

   B. Resulting entity is very large.

   C. Combination is vertical, not horizontal.

   D. Effect may lessen competition substantially.

55. A spin-off involves

   A. The creation of a new separate entity from another entity, with the new entity's shares being distributed to the shareholders of the parent entity.

   B. The sale of an operating unit to a third party.

   C. A liquidation of assets of an operating unit on a piecemeal basis.

   D. The sale of a portion of the firm through an equity offering of shares to outsiders.

56. Which of the following claims has the highest priority in the liquidation of a bankrupt's estate?

   A. Claims of tradespeople who extended unsecured credit after an involuntary case has begun but before a trustee has been appointed.

   B. Taxes due to federal, state, and any other governmental agency.

   C. Wages of up to $4,000 due to workers if earned within the 90 days preceding the earlier of the filing of the petition or the cessation of business.

   D. Claims of preferred shareholders, who may receive an amount up to the par value of an issue.

57. Reinvestment-rate risk and price risk are components of

   A. Purchasing-power risk.

   B. Default risk.

   C. Interest-rate risk.

   D. Systematic risk.

58. What measurement used in portfolio analysis measures the volatility of returns together with their correlation with the returns of other securities?

   A. Standard deviation.

   B. Covariance.

   C. Coefficient of variation.

   D. Variance.

59. Which of the following short-term instruments is a draft drawn on a deposit at a bank?

   A. A repurchase agreement.

   B. A bankers' acceptance.

   C. A floating lien.

   D. Commercial paper.

60. According to portfolio theory,

A. The relevant risk of a security in a portfolio is its contribution to the risk of the portfolio.

B. The variability (risk) of a portfolio's return is the weighted average of the standard deviations of the returns on the individual securities.

C. Unsystematic (investee-specific) risk is not affected by diversification.

D. Systematic (market) risk can be largely eliminated by diversification.

61. A measure that describes the risk of an investment relative to other investments in general is the

A. Alpha coefficient.

B. Beta coefficient.

C. Standard deviation.

D. Input price variability.

62. Which of the following is a European call option?

A. A right to sell an asset at a fixed price at any time before or on the expiration date of the option.

B. A right to buy an asset at a fixed price at any time before or on the expiration date of the option.

C. A right to sell an asset at a fixed price only on the expiration date of the option.

D. A right to buy an asset at a fixed price only on the expiration date of the option.

63. Duration hedging is intended to minimize interest rate risk by

A. Equating the duration of assets and the duration of liabilities.

B. Equating the total price change for assets with the total price change for liabilities.

C. Exchanging fixed interest and principal payments for a series of payments based on a floating rate.

D. Exhanging a series of payments based on a floating rate for fixed interest and principal payments.

64. A company has a $100,000 fire insurance policy on its building, which has a fair value of $200,000. The policy contains a standard 80% co-insurance clause. What amount will the company collect if it has a $120,000 fire loss?

A. $75,000

B. $100,000

C. $120,000

D. Some other amount.

CFM CPE COURSE 5
ACCOUNTING STANDARDS AND FINANCIAL ENVIRONMENT

This CPE course covers Study Units 9 and 10 of **CFM Review**, First Edition. In addition to the introductory material, this course consists of 47 pages of outlines and text and 124 multiple-choice questions (16 of which constitute the final exam). As continuing professional education, 5 hours of CPE credit is recommended based on the AICPA's one-half the average completion time measurement principle. If any of the CPE agencies to which you report measures self-study CPE in terms of average completion time (rather than one-half average completion time), your certificate of completion will indicate 10 hours of maximum CPE credit.

Date Completed	Time (Minutes)		

1. Study Unit 9:

  a. Study the outlines on "External Financial Environment" on pages 327 through 349.

  b. Work through questions 1 through 54 on pages 350 through 366 after covering the answer explanations on the right-hand side of the page. Answer each question and circle your answer.

   1. Uncover the answer explanations and study the adjacent answer explanations for the questions that you missed or that gave you difficulty.

2. Study Unit 10:

  a. Study the outlines on "Accounting Standard Setting" on pages 367 through 390.

  b. Work through questions 1 through 54 on pages 391 through 408 after covering the answer explanations on the right-hand side of the page. Answer each question and circle your answer.

   1. Uncover the answer explanations and study the adjacent answer explanations for the questions that you missed or that gave you difficulty.

3. Final Exam:

  a. Take the final exam by answering questions 65 through 80 on the following pages.

   1. If you have difficulty, refer to **CFM Review**, or other sources. Remember, this is an open-book exam.

4. Carefully transfer your answers for these 16 questions to the CPE final exam answer sheet. Be sure you use the circles numbered 65 through 80.

5. Mark **B 7 B 5** (B means Blank) as the course number on page 2 of the answer sheet. See example at right.

  a. Refer to page 435 in this section for instructions on how to complete the remainder of the machine-readable answer sheet.

6. Please complete the accompanying course evaluation and submit it with your answer sheet.

COURSE NUMBER(S)

7   5

```
⓪ ⓪ ⓪ ⓪
① ① ① ①
② ② ② ②
③ ③ ③ ③
④ ④ ④ ④
⑤ ⑤ ⑤ ●
⑥ ⑥ ⑥ ⑥
⑦ ● ⑦ ⑦
⑧ ⑧ ⑧ ⑧
⑨ ⑨ ⑨ ⑨
```

Total Time _____   (Carry this amount to your CPE course evaluation form.)

65. A corporation's articles of incorporation are not required to include

- A. The purpose of the corporation.
- B. The number of shares of stock the corporation is authorized to issue.
- C. The name and address of each incorporator.
- D. The corporate bylaws.

66. Which of the following statements is false with respect to the actions of corporate boards of directors?

- A. The board must hold its meetings in the state of incorporation.
- B. Actions taken by a board of directors are expressed in formal resolutions adopted by a majority of the board during a meeting at which a quorum is present.
- C. A director is not allowed to vote by proxy.
- D. Special meetings of the board can be held after proper notice has been given to all directors.

67. Which of the following statements regarding bond ratings is false?

- A. Corporate bond ratings are based upon the probability of default and the protection for investors in case of default.
- B. A corporation must pay to have its debt rated by an agency such as Moody's or Standard & Poor's.
- C. Higher ratings will raise the interest costs to issuing firms.
- D. A bond with a rating of D is already in default.

68. Which federal act placed restraints on unions that resulted in a more even balance of power between labor and management?

- A. The Fair Labor Standards Act of 1938.
- B. The Taft-Hartley Act of 1947.
- C. The National Labor Relations Act of 1935.
- D. The Norris-LaGuardia Act of 1932.

69. Which of the following statements is false with respect to the Occupational Safety and Health Administration (OSHA)?

- A. The objectives of OSHA are to protect the health and safety of workers by developing safety standards, preventing injuries, and promoting job safety.
- B. OSHA rules do not apply to businesses that operate only in intrastate commerce.
- C. OSHA encourages labor-management committees to formulate safety and health programs.
- D. OSHA is only an advisory group and cannot assess penalties against noncomplying companies.

70. Under the provisions of the Family and Medical Leave Act of 1993,

- A. Companies must provide employees paid sick leave (up to a limit) for child care needs.
- B. Companies must provide either parent up to 12 weeks of unpaid leave after the birth or adoption of a child.
- C. Eligible employees must have worked for the employer for at least 25 weeks.
- D. Only full-time employees are covered.

71. Federal antitrust regulation applies to organizations engaged in

- A. Interstate commerce.
- B. Regulated utilities.
- C. Agriculture and fishing.
- D. Major league baseball.

72. The Federal Reserve Board controls the money supply primarily through

- A. Manipulating reserve requirements.
- B. Changing the discount rate.
- C. Open-market operations.
- D. Holding deposits of member banks.

73. Which of the following is a currently active organization involved in setting accounting standards for business enterprises?

- A. Committee on Accounting Procedure.
- B. Accounting Principles Board.
- C. Governmental Accounting Standards Board.
- D. Accounting Standards Executive Committee.

74. Feedback value and predictive value are two principal ingredients of

- A. Relevance.
- B. Understandability.
- C. Timeliness.
- D. Reliability.

75. A prudent reaction to uncertainty to try to ensure that uncertainty and risks inherent in business situations are adequately considered is

- A. Neutrality.
- B. Comparability.
- C. Conservatism.
- D. Verifiability.

76. Which of the following financial statement disclosures is required under the provisions of APB 22 "Disclosure of Accounting Policies"?

    A.   Basis of consolidation.

    B.   Maturity dates of long-term debt.

    C.   Composition of inventories.

    D.   Composition of plant assets.

77. SEC Financial Reporting Releases

    A.   Govern the reporting of financial statements, including footnotes and schedules.

    B.   Announce accounting and auditing matters of general interest.

    C.   Contain interpretations to be followed by the SEC staff in administering disclosure requirements.

    D.   Cover certain aspects of corporate annual reports to shareholders and nonfinancial disclosure standards.

78. Under the Integrated Disclosure System, the SEC requires companies to submit which of the following financial statements?

    A.   Balance sheets for the 2 most recent fiscal year-ends.

    B.   Balance sheets for the 5 most recent fiscal year-ends.

    C.   Income statements for the 2 most recent fiscal years.

    D.   Cash flow statements for the 5 most recent fiscal years.

79. New public issues of securities ordinarily are registered with the SEC. If a company has not previously registered an issue of securities, it must use

    A.   Form S-1.

    B.   Form S-2.

    C.   Form 8-K.

    D.   Form S-X.

80. Which of the following material events should be reported to the SEC on Form 8-K?

    A.   Acquisition of significant assets in the ordinary course of business.

    B.   Reelection of directors.

    C.   Change in independent accountants.

    D.   Matters submitted to shareholders for a vote.

ADDENDUM: QUANTITATIVE PRACTICE QUESTIONS

65 multiple-choice questions   *Study these 65 quantitative practice questions carefully after you have finished Study Units 1 through 10. These questions were designed in response to candidate feedback. We are certain you will find them helpful in your preparation.*

Questions 1 through 10 are based on the following information. It was provided in a CMA computational question about a company that is preparing a single-step income statement and classified statement of financial position using the accrual basis. The company began operations on January 1, 1998.

Transactions for 1998

Cash sales	$232,000
Collections from credit customers	80,000
Payments on account for parts	80,800
Wages paid to employees	124,000
Payments to the utility company	22,000

- Uncollected customers' bills totaled $69,800 at December 31, 1998.
- On March 1, 1998, a supplier advanced the company $40,000 on a 1-year, 12% note payable with semiannual interest payments to be made on September 1, 1998 and at maturity on March 1, 1999.
- Unpaid bills to suppliers totaled $11,200 at December 31, 1998.
- Parts costing $8,000 were on hand at year-end.
- Wages owed at year-end were $5,600.
- Utility expense of $1,950 was unpaid at year-end.

- The $18,000 insurance premium was paid for a 1-year policy effective February 1, 1998.
- The rent of $3,000 was paid on the first of every month.
- The company's equipment, purchased at the time the company was founded, should be depreciated over its useful life of 10 years using straight-line depreciation with no residual value.
- The effective tax rate is 40%. No taxes have been paid.

Statement of Financial Position (Cash Basis)
January 1, 1998

Assets	
Cash	$ 49,600
Parts inventory	24,000
Equipment	220,000
Total assets	$293,600
Liabilities and shareholder's equity	
Purchase invoices outstanding	$ 28,000
Common stock	265,600
Total liabilities and shareholders' equity	$293,600

1. The total sales for 1998 were

A. $381,800
B. $312,000
C. $232,000
D. $80,000

The correct answer is (A). *(Publisher)*
REQUIRED: The total sales.
DISCUSSION: Sales on the accrual basis equal the sum of cash sales, ending receivables, and collections or $381,800 ($232,000 + $69,800 + $80,000).
Answer (B) is incorrect because $312,000 equals cash sales plus collections. Answer (C) is incorrect because $232,000 equals cash sales. Answer (D) is incorrect because $80,000 equals collections.

2. The parts expense for 1998 was

A. $88,000
B. $80,800
C. $80,000
D. $64,000

The correct answer is (C). *(Publisher)*
REQUIRED: The parts expense.
DISCUSSION: Parts expense equals beginning inventory, plus purchases, minus ending inventory. Purchases equals payments to suppliers, plus year-end accounts payable, minus beginning accounts payable, or $64,000 ($80,800 + $11,200 – $28,000). Consequently, parts expense was $80,000 ($24,000 BI + $64,000 purchases – $8,000 EI).
Answer (A) is incorrect because $88,000 assumes no year-end inventory. Answer (B) is incorrect because $80,800 equals payments to suppliers. Answer (D) is incorrect because $64,000 equals purchases.

3. Refer to the information preceding question 1 on page 453. The total of operating expenses other than taxes in the single-step income statement was

A. $339,950

B. $312,050

C. $304,500

D. $290,050

The correct answer is (B). *(Publisher)*

REQUIRED: The total of operating expenses other than taxes.

DISCUSSION: Operating expenses other than taxes included parts expense, wages, utility costs, insurance, rent, depreciation, and interest. Parts expense was $80,000 (see preceding question), wages were $129,600 ($124,000 paid + $5,600 owed at year-end), utility costs equaled $23,950 ($22,000 paid + $1,950 owed at year-end), insurance expense was $16,500 [$18,000 x (11 ÷ 12) months], rent was $36,000 (12 x $3,000), depreciation was $22,000 ($220,000 ÷ 10 years), and interest was $4,000 [$40,000 x 12% x (10 ÷ 12) months]. Thus, the total of operating expenses other than taxes was $312,050 ($80,000 + $129,600 + $23,950 + $16,500 + $36,000 + $22,000 + $4,000).

Answer (A) is incorrect because $339,950 includes income tax expense. Answer (C) is incorrect because $304,500 omits wages and utility costs owed at year-end. Answer (D) is incorrect because $290,050 omits depreciation.

4. Refer to the information preceding question 1 on page 453. The net income for 1998 was

A. $69,750

B. $55,050

C. $46,380

D. $41,850

The correct answer is (D). *(Publisher)*

REQUIRED: The net income.

DISCUSSION: The net income equals total revenues minus total expenses. Total revenues equal sales of $381,800 (see question 1), and total operating expenses were $312,050 (see preceding question), so income before income taxes was $69,750 ($381,800 – $312,050). Given a tax rate of 40%, net income was $41,850 [$69,750 x (1.0 – .4)].

Answer (A) is incorrect because $69,750 is income before income taxes. Answer (B) is incorrect because $55,050 results from omitting depreciation. Answer (C) is incorrect because $46,380 results from omitting wages and utility costs owed at year-end.

5. Refer to the information preceding question 1 on page 453. The total cash available during 1998 was

A. $401,600

B. $352,000

C. $232,000

D. $118,400

The correct answer is (A). *(Publisher)*

REQUIRED: The total cash available.

DISCUSSION: The total cash available equaled the beginning balance plus total receipts. Cash received equaled $352,000 ($232,000 cash sales + $80,000 customer collections + $40,000 proceeds from note). Hence, the cash available was $401,600 ($49,600 beginning balance + $352,000).

Answer (B) is incorrect because $352,000 equals total cash received. Answer (C) is incorrect because $232,000 equals cash sales. Answer (D) is incorrect because $118,400 equals the ending cash balance.

6. Refer to the information preceding question 1 on page 453. The ending cash balance was

A. $283,200

B. $154,400

C. $118,400

D. $68,800

The correct answer is (C). *(Publisher)*

REQUIRED: The ending cash balance.

DISCUSSION: The ending cash balance equals the beginning balance ($49,600), plus cash receipts ($352,000 as calculated in the preceding question), minus cash payments. The cash disbursed equaled $283,200 [$80,800 payments on account + $124,000 wages paid + $22,000 payments for utilities + $18,000 for insurance + (12 x $3,000 monthly rent) + ($40,000 x .5 x 12% interest)]. Thus, the ending cash balance was $118,400 ($49,600 + $352,000 – $283,200).

Answer (A) is incorrect because $283,200 equals the cash disbursed. Answer (B) is incorrect because $154,400 omits the rent. Answer (D) is incorrect because $68,800 omits the beginning cash balance.

7. Refer to the information preceding question 1 on page 453. The total current assets at year-end equaled

    A. $220,000

    B. $198,000

    C. $197,700

    D. $196,200

The correct answer is (C). *(Publisher)*

    REQUIRED: The total current assets at year-end.

    DISCUSSION: The ending cash balance was $118,400 (see preceding question), accounts receivable equaled the $69,800 (given) of uncollected customer bills, the parts inventory was $8,000 (given), and prepaid insurance was $1,500 [$18,000 annual premium x (1 ÷ 12)]. Consequently, the total current assets at year-end equaled $197,700 ($118,400 + $69,800 + $8,000 + $1,500).

    Answer (A) is incorrect because $220,000 equals the beginning equipment balance. Answer (B) is incorrect because $198,000 is the ending equipment balance. Answer (D) is incorrect because $196,200 omits prepaid insurance.

8. Refer to the information preceding question 1 on page 453. The total assets at year-end equaled

    A. $417,700

    B. $395,700

    C. $307,450

    D. $197,700

The correct answer is (B). *(Publisher)*

    REQUIRED: The total assets at year-end.

    DISCUSSION: The total current assets at year-end equaled $197,700 (see preceding question). The only noncurrent asset was equipment. After subtracting depreciation of $22,000 ($220,000 beginning balance ÷ 10 years, with no salvage value), its ending balance was $198,000. Accordingly, the total assets at year-end equaled $395,700 ($197,700 + $198,000).

    Answer (A) is incorrect because $417,700 omits deprecation. Answer (C) is incorrect because $307,450 equals total ending shareholders' equity. Answer (D) is incorrect because $197,700 equals ending current assets.

9. Refer to the information preceding question 1 on page 453. The total shareholders' equity at year-end was

    A. $395,700

    B. $335,350

    C. $307,450

    D. $265,600

The correct answer is (C). *(Publisher)*

    REQUIRED: The total shareholders' equity at year-end.

    DISCUSSION: Given no stock transactions and no dividends or other transactions affecting retained earnings except for the crediting of net income, the total shareholders' equity at year-end must have been $307,450 ($265,600 common stock + $41,850 net income as calculated in a preceding question).

    Answer (A) is incorrect because $395,700 equals total liabilities and shareholders' equity. Answer (B) is incorrect because $335,350 is based on pre-tax income. Answer (D) is incorrect because $265,600 equals common stock.

10. Refer to the information preceding question 1 on page 453. The total current liabilities at year-end equaled

    A. $90,650

    B. $88,250

    C. $60,350

    D. $48,250

The correct answer is (B). *(Publisher)*

    REQUIRED: The total current liabilities at year-end.

    DISCUSSION: Given that the company had no noncurrent liabilities, the sum of its current liabilities and shareholders' equity must equal total assets. Hence, the total current liabilities at year-end equal $88,250 ($395,700 total assets as calculated in a preceding question − $307,450 total shareholders' equity as calculated in the preceding question). This amount is the sum of accounts payable ($11,200 given), the note payable ($40,000 given), wages payable ($5,600 given), utilities payable ($1,950 given), interest payable [$40,000 x 12% x (4 ÷ 12) = $1,600], and taxes payable (40% x $69,750 income before taxes as calculated in a preceding question).

    Answer (A) is incorrect because $90,650 includes interest payable of $4,000. Answer (C) is incorrect because $60,350 omits taxes payable. Answer (D) is incorrect because $48,250 omits the note payable.

11. For the fiscal year ended September 30, 1997, Kooning Co. made two entries to retained earnings: a debit for a cash dividend and a credit to net income. The following information about balances is also available:

	Oct. 1, 1996	Sept. 30, 1997
Assets	$400,000	$500,000
Liabilities	200,000	250,000
Capital accounts other than retained earnings	100,000	100,000

Net income for the fiscal year ended September 30, 1997 was $75,000, so the dividend must have been

A. $150,000

B. $100,000

C. $50,000

D. $25,000

The correct answer is (D). *(Publisher)*
   REQUIRED: The dividend paid.
   DISCUSSION: Given that assets equal liabilities plus equity (other capital accounts + retained earnings), beginning retained earnings must have been $100,000 ($400,000 assets – $200,000 liabilities – $100,000 other capital accounts), and ending retained earnings must have been $150,000 ($500,000 – $250,000 – $100,000). Hence, the cash dividend must have been $25,000 ($75,000 net income – $50,000 increase in retained earnings).
   Answer (A) is incorrect because $150,000 is the ending retained earnings. Answer (B) is incorrect because $100,000 equals the total of the capital accounts other than retained earnings. Answer (C) is incorrect because $50,000 is the increase in retained earnings.

12. Auric Company's trial balance at its fiscal year-end included the following amounts:

	Debit	Credit
Cash	$ 20,000	
Net accounts receivable	40,000	
Inventory	60,000	
Trading securities	30,000	
Prepaid expenses	10,000	
Property, plant, and equipment	120,000	
Accounts payable and accruals		40,000
Common stock		30,000
Additional paid-in capital		120,000
Retained earnings		90,000
	$280,000	$280,000

Auric should have total current assets of

A. $60,000

B. $120,000

C. $150,000

D. $160,000

The correct answer is (D). *(Publisher)*
   REQUIRED: The total current assets.
   DISCUSSION: Current assets consist of "cash and other assets or resources commonly identified as reasonably expected to be realized in cash or sold or consumed during the normal operating cycle of the business" (ARB 43, Ch. 3A). Current assets include cash and cash equivalents, inventories, receivables, trading securities, certain available-for-sale and held-to-maturity securities, and prepaid expenses. Thus, total current assets equal $160,000 ($20,000 cash + $40,000 receivables + $60,000 inventory + $30,000 trading securities + $10,000 prepaid expenses).
   Answer (A) is incorrect because $60,000 omits inventory, trading securities, and prepaid expenses. Answer (B) is incorrect because $120,000 omits trading securities and prepaid expenses. Answer (C) is incorrect because $150,000 omits prepaid expenses.

13. For the year ended December 31, 1997, Reprop Co. appropriated $100,000 of retained earnings pursuant to a state law requiring that an amount equal to the cost of treasury stock be restricted. Reprop appropriated $2,000,000 for the construction of a new building. In 1998, Reprop sold the treasury stock for $150,000 and completed the building at a cost of $1,800,000. It also appropriated $400,000 for an estimated litigation loss and restricted $800,000 of cash for payment of certain debt instruments due in 1999. At December 31, 1998, Reprop should report appropriated retained earnings of

A. $2,500,000

B. $1,200,000

C. $600,000

D. $400,000

The correct answer is (D). *(Publisher)*
   REQUIRED: The appropriated retained earnings at year-end.
   DISCUSSION: The retained earnings balance is sometimes divided into appropriated and unappropriated amounts. Appropriations may arise from legal requirements, contractual agreements, or management decisions. They reduce the amount available for dividends. However, losses are not charged directly against appropriated or unappropriated retained earnings. When an appropriation is no longer necessary, the entry is reversed. Thus, the 1997 appropriation should have been reversed for the same amounts in 1998 after sale of the treasury stock and completion of the building. The cash restriction does not result in an appropriation but, if material, requires separate reporting, footnote disclosure, and reclassification of the item as noncurrent. Accordingly, the total appropriated at the end of 1998 is $400,000 for the estimated litigation loss.
   Answer (A) is incorrect because $2,500,000 assumes no appropriations were reversed. Answer (B) is incorrect because $1,200,000 assumes an amount was appropriated for the cash restriction. Answer (C) is incorrect because $600,000 assumes that $200,000 of the appropriation for the construction project was not reversed.

14. Hom Co. had adopted a plan to dispose of a business segment. The loss incurred by the segment from the start of this fiscal year to the date of adoption of the plan was $130,000. From that date to the date of disposal, an additional loss of $64,000 is anticipated. On the date of disposal, Hom estimates that it will sell equipment with a book value of $200,000 for $250,000. The estimated pre-tax loss on discontinued operations is

A. $194,000

B. $144,000

C. $64,000

D. $14,000

The correct answer is (B). *(Publisher)*

REQUIRED: The estimated pre-tax loss on discontinued operations.

DISCUSSION: The income or loss from operations of the discontinued segment up to the measurement date and the gain or loss on disposal should both be shown net of tax. The gain or loss on disposal includes estimated operating income or loss of the segment from the measurement date to the disposal date, any direct disposal costs incurred during the phase-out period, and the estimated gain or loss on the actual disposal. Thus, the estimated pre-tax loss on discontinued operations is $144,000 [$130,000 + $64,000 − ($250,000 − $200,000)].

Answer (A) is incorrect because $194,000 omits the gain on the actual disposal. Answer (C) is incorrect because $64,000 is the operating loss from the measurement date to the disposal date. Answer (D) is incorrect because $14,000 omits the loss prior to the measurement date.

15. For its recently ended fiscal year, a company reported the following material items that are unusual and infrequent in the environment in which it operates:

- A $100,000 loss caused by an earthquake
- A $50,000 loss from the writedown of inventory
- A $20,000 gain from an adjustment of the accruals on a long-term contract
- A $40,000 gain from translation of items denominated in a foreign currency

The pre-tax amount the company should report as the gain or loss from extraordinary items is

A. $60,000 gain

B. $40,000 loss

C. $90,000 loss

D. $100,000 loss

The correct answer is (D). *(Publisher)*

REQUIRED: The pre-tax amount the company should report as the gain or loss from extraordinary items.

DISCUSSION: Material items that are unusual and infrequent in the environment in which the company operates are extraordinary. However, APB 30 specifies certain items that are not to be treated as extraordinary gains and losses. These include write-downs of receivables and inventories, translation of foreign currency, disposal of a business segment, sale of productive assets, effects of strikes, and accruals on long-term contracts. Accordingly, the company should report as an extraordinary item the $100,000 loss caused by the earthquake.

Answer (A) is incorrect because a $60,000 gain assumes the losses are ordinary. Answer (B) is incorrect because a $40,000 loss assumes the gains are extraordinary. Answer (C) is incorrect because a $90,000 loss assumes all items are extraordinary.

16. During 1998, Gauche Co. sold its Droit Co. stock (not acquired specifically for resale) for $50,000. It also sold machinery used in its manufacturing operation for $100,000 and received cash dividends of $30,000. Cash payments included interest on long-term debt of $20,000. In its statement of cash flows for the 1998 fiscal year, Gauche should report a net cash inflow from investing activities of

A. $160,000

B. $150,000

C. $130,000

D. $80,000

The correct answer is (B). *(Publisher)*

REQUIRED: The net cash inflow from investing activities.

DISCUSSION: Investing activities include making and collecting loans and acquiring and disposing of debt or equity instruments and property, plant, and equipment and other productive assets, that is, assets held for or used in the production of goods or services (other than the materials held in inventory). Investing activities exclude transactions in cash equivalents and in certain loans or other debt or equity instruments acquired specifically for resale. Thus, the sales of stock and machinery are investing activities. However, dividend receipts and interest payments are cash flows from operating activities, so the net cash inflow from investing activities is $150,000 ($50,000 + $100,000).

Answer (A) is incorrect because $160,000 treats all items as flows from investing activities. Answer (C) is incorrect because $130,000 treats the payment of interest as an investing activity. Answer (D) is incorrect because $80,000 treats the sale of stock and the receipt of dividends as the only investing activities.

Questions 17 through 23 are based on the following information. It was provided in a CMA computational problem about a company that is preparing a statement of cash flows using the indirect method.

Statements of Financial Position

	Dec. 31, 1997	Dec. 31, 1998
Cash	$ 4,300	$ 5,100
Accounts receivable	3,700	4,200
Inventories	34,200	31,700
Prepaid expenses	1,800	2,100
Land	38,000	27,000
Buildings (net)	126,800	117,700
Equipment (net)	50,500	66,800
Leased equipment	---	7,700
Total assets	$259,300	$262,300
Accounts payable	$ 5,900	$ 3,400
Income taxes payable	2,600	2,100
Capital lease liability	---	7,700
Bonds payable	50,000	60,000
Deferred income taxes	2,200	2,400
Common stock, $10 par	125,000	135,000
Paid-in capital in excess of par	12,000	14,000
Retained earnings	61,600	37,700
Total liabilities and shareholders' equity	$259,300	$262,300

Supplemental Information

(a) Land costing $11,000 was sold for $14,500.

(b) A fire resulted in the complete loss of a building with a net book value of $8,400. The after-tax insurance cash proceeds were $5,800.

(c) Equipment was purchased for $17,500 in cash on January 2, 1998.

(d) On December 31, 1998, the company leased equipment and issued $10,000 of bonds payable at par.

(e) A stock dividend of 1,000 shares was declared and issued. The fair value on the date of issuance was $12 per share.

(f) Net income was $11,300.

---

17. The net cash flow from investing activities equaled

A. $13,200 used.

B. $11,700 used.

C. $3,000 used.

D. $2,800 provided.

The correct answer is (D). *(Publisher)*
REQUIRED: The net cash flow from investing activities.
DISCUSSION: Investing activities include making and collecting loans and acquiring and disposing of debt or equity instruments and property, plant, and equipment and other productive assets, that is, assets held for or used in the production of goods or services (other than the materials held in inventory). Thus, the equipment purchase, the sale of land, and the receipt of proceeds from the building destroyed by fire were investing activities. Hence, the net cash provided by investing activities was $2,800 ($14,500 land sale + $5,800 insurance proceeds – $17,500 equipment purchase).

Answer (A) is incorrect because $13,200 is the net cash outflow from financing activities. Answer (B) is incorrect because a net cash outflow of $11,700 omits the proceeds from the land sale. Answer (C) is incorrect because a $3,000 net cash outflow omits the proceeds from the insurance settlement.

18. The cash dividends paid equaled

A. $35,200

B. $23,900

C. $23,200

D. $12,000

The correct answer is (C). *(Publisher)*
REQUIRED: The cash dividends paid.
DISCUSSION: During 1998, retained earnings decreased by $23,900 ($61,600 – $37,700). Net income increased retained earnings by $11,300, and the stock dividend decreased it by $12,000 (1,000 shares x $12 fair value per share). Because these transactions account for only $700 ($12,000 – $11,300) of the net decrease during the period, the $23,200 remainder ($23,900 decrease in RE – $700) is most likely to be attributable to cash dividends.

Answer (A) is incorrect because $35,200 omits the stock dividend from the calculation. Answer (B) is incorrect because $23,900 is the difference between beginning and ending retained earnings. Answer (D) is incorrect because $12,000 is the stock dividend.

19. The net cash flow from financing activities equaled

    A. $23,200 used.

    B. $20,900 used.

    C. $13,200 used.

    D. $10,000 provided.

The correct answer is (C). *(Publisher)*
    REQUIRED: The net cash flow from financing activities.
    DISCUSSION: Financing activities include the issuance of stock, the payment of dividends, treasury stock transactions, the issuance of debt, and the repayment or other settlement of debt obligations. It also includes receiving restricted resources that by donor stipulation must be used for long-term purposes. Thus, the net cash used by financing activities was $13,200 ($23,200 cash dividends paid as calculated in the preceding question – $10,000 bond proceeds).
    Answer (A) is incorrect because a net cash outflow of $23,200 disregards the bond proceeds. Answer (B) is incorrect because a net cash outflow of $20,900 treats the lease obligation as a cash outflow. Answer (D) is incorrect because a net cash inflow of $10,000 ignores the cash dividends.

20. The depreciation expense for 1998 was

    A. $7,200

    B. $1,900

    C. $1,200

    D. $700

The correct answer is (B). *(Publisher)*
    REQUIRED: The depreciation expense.
    DISCUSSION: The net amount reported for buildings decreased by $9,100 ($126,800 – $117,700). Of this amount, $8,400 was attributable to the complete loss of a building in a fire. The remaining $700 ($9,100 – $8,400) is attributable to depreciation. The net amount reported for equipment increased by $16,300 ($66,800 – $50,500) despite a purchase of equipment for $17,500. The $1,200 difference presumably resulted from recognition of depreciation. Accordingly, total depreciation was $1,900 ($700 + $1,200).
    Answer (A) is incorrect because $7,200 is the combined increase in the buildings and equipment balances. Answer (C) is incorrect because $1,200 is the depreciation on the equipment only. Answer (D) is incorrect because $700 is the depreciation on the buildings only.

21. The indirect method calculates net operating cash flow by adjusting net income. The following are potential adjustments:

Bond interest expense	$4,000
Depreciation	1,900
Capital lease obligation	7,700
Increase in deferred taxes	200
Loss from fire (net of tax)	2,600

The amount of the adjustments to net income for the foregoing items is

    A. $16,400

    B. $14,500

    C. $8,700

    D. $4,700

The correct answer is (D). *(Publisher)*
    REQUIRED: The amount of the adjustments to net income.
    DISCUSSION: Bond interest expense is not a reconciling item because it is a cash outflow included in the determination of net income. The capital lease obligation recognized at year-end had no effect on net income or on cash flows. However, depreciation is a noncash expense that should be added to net income in the reconciliation. Similarly, the increase in deferred taxes (debit expense, credit deferred tax liability) is a noncash item that should be added to net income. The destruction of the building by fire resulted in a $5,800 cash inflow from an investing activity, but the loss should be added to net income because it entailed no cash outflow. Consequently, the listed items produce a net addition to net income of $4,700 ($1,900 depreciation + $200 deferred taxes increase + $2,600 fire loss).
    Answer (A) is incorrect because $16,400 includes the capital lease and the bond interest. Answer (B) is incorrect because $14,500 includes the capital lease and the bond interest but excludes the depreciation. Answer (C) is incorrect because $8,700 includes the bond interest.

22. Refer to the information preceding question 17 on page 458. The indirect method calculates net operating cash flow by adjusting net income. The adjustment for the difference between cost of goods sold and cash paid to suppliers is

A. $5,000 increase.

B. $2,500 increase.

C. $0.

D. $2,500 decrease.

The correct answer is (C). *(Publisher)*
REQUIRED: The adjustment for the difference between cost of goods sold and cash paid to suppliers.
DISCUSSION: To account for the difference between cost of goods sold (a deduction from income) and cash paid to suppliers, a two-step adjustment of net income is necessary. The difference between cost of goods sold and purchases is the change in inventory. The difference between purchases and the amount paid to suppliers is the change in accounts payable. Thus, the $2,500 inventory decrease should be added to net income because purchases are less than cost of goods sold. The $2,500 accounts payable decrease should be subtracted because cash paid to suppliers must exceed purchases. Accordingly, the adjustment for the difference between cost of goods sold and cash paid to suppliers is $0 ($2,500 inventory decrease − $2,500 accounts payable decrease).
Answer (A) is incorrect because a $5,000 increase assumes the accounts payable adjustment is an increase. Answer (B) is incorrect because a $2,500 increase ignores the accounts payable adjustment. Answer (D) is incorrect because a $2,500 decrease ignores the inventory adjustment.

23. Refer to the information preceding question 17 on page 458. The net cash provided by operating activities was

A. $11,300

B. $11,200

C. $5,100

D. $800

The correct answer is (B). *(Publisher)*
REQUIRED: The net cash provided by operating activities.
DISCUSSION: The net cash provided by operating activities is determined by adjusting net income. Depreciation ($1,900 as determined in question 20), the increase in deferred taxes ($200), and the fire loss ($8,400 − $5,800 = $2,600) are noncash items that reduced net income and therefore should be added. The difference between cost of goods sold (a deduction from revenue) and cash paid to suppliers ($0 as calculated in the preceding question) is reflected by adjusting net income for the changes in inventory and accounts payable. The $500 increase in accounts receivable is subtracted because it represents an excess of operating revenue over cash inflows. The $300 increase in prepaid expenses is also subtracted because it involves a cash outflow that was not expensed. The $500 decrease in income taxes payable also arose from a cash outflow that was not expensed. Finally, the gain on the sale of land ($14,500 − $11,000 = $3,500) was included in net income although it arose from an investing activity. Thus, the net cash provided by operating activities was $11,200 ($11,300 net income + $1,900 + $200 + $2,600 + $0 − $500 − $300 − $500 − $3,500).
Answer (A) is incorrect because $11,300 equals net income. Answer (C) is incorrect because $5,100 equals the year-end cash balance. Answer (D) is incorrect because $800 is the net increase in cash.

24. Felina Co., a calendar-year enterprise, reported the following information for its most recent fiscal year:

Inventory (January 1)	$100,000
Inventory (December 31)	150,000
Accounts payable (January 1)	50,000
Accounts payable (December 3)	60,000
Cost of goods sold	600,000

If payables are incurred solely to acquire inventory, Felina's cash payments to suppliers for inventory must have been

  A. $660,000

  B. $640,000

  C. $600,000

  D. $560,000

The correct answer is (B). *(Publisher)*
  REQUIRED: The cash payments to suppliers for inventory.
  DISCUSSION: Adjusting cost of goods sold for the changes in inventory and accounts payable is necessary to determine the cash payments to suppliers for inventory. The adjustment from cost of goods sold (an accrual accounting amount included in the determination of net income) to cash paid to suppliers requires two steps: from cost of goods sold to purchases and from purchases to cash paid to suppliers. Accordingly, purchases must have exceeded cost of goods sold because inventory increased, and cash payments to suppliers for inventory must have been less than purchases because accounts payable increased. Thus, cash payments to suppliers for inventory must have been $640,000 [$600,000 CGS + ($150,000 – $100,000) – ($60,000 – $50,000)].
  Answer (A) is incorrect because $660,000 results from adding the payables increase. Answer (C) is incorrect because $600,000 equals cost of goods sold. Answer (D) is incorrect because $560,000 results from adding the payables increase and subtracting the inventory increase.

Questions 25 and 26 are based on the following information. An asset acquired on January 2, 1998 costs $10,000 and has a 5-year estimated useful life with a $1,000 salvage value.

---

25. The double-declining balance (DDB) depreciation for 2002 is

  A. $1,800

  B. $1,296

  C. $864

  D. $296

The correct answer is (D). *(Publisher)*
  REQUIRED: The double-declining balance (DDB) depreciation for 2002.
  DISCUSSION: The DDB method applies a constant percentage rate to a declining book value that does not include the salvage value. However, the asset is not depreciated below its salvage value. The straight-line rate is 20% (100% ÷ 5 years), so the DDB rate is 40% (2 x 20%). Thus, fifth-year depreciation is $296.

Year	Book Value	Depreciation
1	$10,000	$4,000
2	6,000	2,400
3	3,600	1,440
4	2,160	864
5	1,296	296

  Answer (A) is incorrect because $1,800 equals straight-line depreciation. Answer (B) is incorrect because $1,296 results in depreciating the asset below its salvage value. Answer (C) is incorrect because $864 is the fourth-year depreciation.

26. The sum-of-the-year's digits (SYD) depreciation for 2002 is

  A. $1,800

  B. $667

  C. $600

  D. $296

The correct answer is (C). *(Publisher)*
  REQUIRED: The SYD depreciation for 2002.
  DISCUSSION: The SYD method multiplies a constant depreciable base (cost – salvage) by a declining fraction. It is a declining-rate, declining-charge method. The SYD fraction's numerator is the number of years of remaining useful life (n). The formula to compute the denominator is

$$n \frac{(n + 1)}{2}$$

The denominator is therefore 15 {[5 x (5 + 1)] ÷ 2}, and fifth-year depreciation is $600 [($10,000 – $1,000) x (1 ÷ 15)].
  Answer (A) is incorrect because $1,800 is the straight-line depreciation. Answer (B) is incorrect because $667 assumes no salvage value. Answer (D) is incorrect because $296 is the double-declining balance depreciation.

27. On January 2, 1997, Wright Corporation entered into an in-substance debt defeasance transaction by placing cash of $875,000 into an irrevocable trust. The trust assets are to be used solely for satisfying the interest and principal payments on Wright's 6%, $1,100,000, 30-year bond payable. Wright has not been legally released under the bond agreement, but the probability is remote that Wright will be required to place additional cash in the trust. On December 31, 1996, the bond's carrying amount was $1,050,000 and its fair value was $800,000. Disregarding income taxes, what amount of extraordinary gain (loss) should Wright report in its 1997 income statement?

- A.   ($75,000)
- B. $0
- C. $175,000
- D. $225,000

The correct answer is (B). *(Publisher)*
REQUIRED: The amount of extraordinary gain (loss) to be recognized on an in-substance defeasance.
DISCUSSION: SFAS 125, effective for extinguishments of liabilities occurring after December 31, 1996, prohibits the recognition of a gain (loss) from an in-substance defeasance, previously permitted by SFAS 76, *Extinguishment of Debt*.

Answers (A), (C), and (D) are incorrect because an in-substance defeasance does not result in the derecognition of a liability.

28. Simpson Corporation sells an 80% pro rata interest in a $1,000,000 note receivable to Bruns Company for $960,000. The note was originally issued at face value. Future benefits and costs of servicing the note are immaterial. If the provisions of SFAS 125 are followed, the amount of gain or loss Simpson should recognize on this transfer of a partial interest is

- A.   ($40,000)
- B. $0
- C. $160,000
- D. $200,000

The correct answer is (C). *(Publisher)*
REQUIRED: The amount of gain or loss to be recognized on a transfer of a partial interest in a loan.
DISCUSSION: The fair value of the note is $1,200,000 ($960,000 ÷ by 80%). The book value is $1,000,000. There is no servicing asset or liability. Given no servicing asset or liability, Simpson should record the receipt of the $960,000 as cash, reduce the carrying amount of the note receivable by $800,000 ($1,000,000 × 80%), and recognize a $160,000 ($960,000 – $800,000) gain.

Answer (A) is incorrect because a loss of $40,000 is equal to the $960,000 cash received minus the $1,000,000 carrying value of the note. Answer (B) is incorrect because a gain should be recognized equal to the pro rata (80%) difference between the fair value and the carrying value of the note. Answer (D) is incorrect because $200,000 is equal to 100% of the difference between the fair value and the carrying value of the note.

29. Goth Co. has decided to factor its accounts receivable. Assume a factor charges a 2% fee plus an interest rate of 18% on all monies advanced to the company. Monthly sales are $100,000, and the factor advances 90% of the receivables submitted after deducting the 2% fee and the interest. Credit terms are net 60 days. Assuming that the factor has approved the customer's credit in advance and that no sales returns and allowances are recognized, the cost to the company of this arrangement is

- A. $14,640
- B. $4,640
- C. $2,640
- D. $2,000

The correct answer is (B). *(Publisher)*
REQUIRED: The cost of factoring.
DISCUSSION: The amount to be received immediately is $85,360.

Amount of receivables submitted	$100,000
Minus: 10% reserve	(10,000)
Minus: 2% factor's fee	(2,000)
Amount accruing to the company	$ 88,000
Minus: 18% interest for 60 days (on $88,000)	(2,640)
Amount to be received immediately	$ 85,360

The company will also receive the $10,000 reserve at the end of the 60-day period given that it has not been absorbed by sales returns and allowances. Thus, the total cost to the company to factor the sales for the month is $4,640 ($2,000 factor fee + interest of $2,640).

Answer (A) is incorrect because $14,640 includes the $10,000 reserve. Answer (C) is incorrect because $2,640 omits the factor's fee. Answer (D) is incorrect because $2,000 omits the interest.

30. The only temporary differences for a calendar-year firm arise from a major lease, which is capitalized for financial reporting purposes and treated as an operating lease for tax purposes. At December 31, the temporary difference amounts to $600,000, and the related deferred income tax asset account has a $240,000 debit balance. What portion of this deferred tax asset should be classified as noncurrent if the firm, in its next year, expects to deduct $480,000 for rental expense in its tax return and to expense a total of $420,000 as depreciation and interest related to the lease in the income statement?

A. $0

B. $180,000

C. $216,000

D. $240,000

The correct answer is (C). *(Publisher)*
REQUIRED: The balance of the December 31 noncurrent deferred income tax account.
DISCUSSION: SFAS 37, *Balance Sheet Classification of Deferred Income Taxes*, states that, when a temporary difference is not related to a specific asset or liability, the related deferred tax account should be classified based on the expected reversal date of the temporary difference.

The temporary difference arising from the lease is not related to a specific asset or liability because it is related to both the capitalized fixed asset and the lease obligation. The temporary difference is being reversed because the expected tax deduction for the next year is greater by $60,000 than the expected financial reporting expenses. Given that the $60,000 reversing difference expected in the next year is 10% ($60,000 ÷ $600,000) of the temporary difference at December 31, $24,000 (10% x $240,000) of the deferred tax balance at December 31 should be classified as current, and $216,000 (90% x $240,000) should be classified as noncurrent.

Answer (A) is incorrect because $216,000 should be classified as noncurrent deferred tax asset. Answer (B) is incorrect because $180,000 results from the difference between the temporary difference and the amount of expense for depreciation and interest for next year. Answer (D) is incorrect because $240,000 is the total deferred tax asset.

31. The Grady Company acquired 100% of the Irwin Company for $1,000,000 in cash. The fair value of the identifiable net assets acquired is $600,000, and their tax basis is $450,000. Future recovery of the assets and settlement of the liabilities at their fair value will result in taxable and deductible amounts. If the enacted tax rate for the current year and all future years is 30%, the amount of goodwill to be recognized is

A. $355,000

B. $445,000

C. $555,000

D. $645,000

The correct answer is (B). *(Publisher)*
REQUIRED: The goodwill in a purchase business combination given a difference between the tax basis and the assigned value of the identifiable net assets acquired.
DISCUSSION: In accordance with SFAS 109, a deferred tax liability or asset is recognized for differences between the assigned values (fair values) and the tax bases of the assets and liabilities (except goodwill, unallocated negative goodwill, leveraged leases, and certain APB 23 differences) of an enterprise acquired in a purchase business combination. Because the difference between the assigned basis and the tax basis of the identifiable net assets acquired is $150,000 ($600,000 – $450,000), a net deferred tax liability of $45,000 ($150,000 x 30% tax rate) should be recognized. The assigned value other than goodwill is therefore $555,000 ($600,000 fair value of identifiable net assets acquired – $45,000 deferred tax liability). Goodwill of $445,000 ($1,000,000 purchase price – $555,000 assigned values) should be recorded.

Answer (A) is incorrect because $355,000 results from adding, not subtracting, the deferred tax liability to the fair value of identifiable net assets. Answer (C) is incorrect because $555,000 results from calculating goodwill as the fair value of identifiable net assets less the deferred tax liability. Answer (D) is incorrect because $645,000 results from calculating goodwill as the fair value of identifiable net assets plus the deferred tax liability.

32. Last year, before providing for taxes, Ajax Company had income from continuing operations of $930,000 and an extraordinary gain of $104,000. The current effective tax rate on continuing operations income was 40% and the total tax liability was $398,000 ignoring any temporary differences. The amount of the extraordinary gain net of tax effect was

A. $41,600

B. $62,400

C. $78,000

D. $104,000

The correct answer is (C). *(Publisher)*
REQUIRED: The amount of extraordinary gain net of the tax effect.
DISCUSSION: Given that the effective tax rate for continuing operations was 40%, the related tax expense was $372,000 ($930,000 x 40%). Because the total tax liability was $398,000, $26,000 ($398,000 – $372,000) was applicable to the extraordinary item. Accordingly, the extraordinary gain net of tax effect was $78,000 ($104,000 – $26,000).
Answer (A) is incorrect because $41,600 results from multiplying the extraordinary gain times the effective tax rate. Answer (B) is incorrect because $62,400 results from subtracting the extraordinary gain times the effective tax rate from the extraordinary gain. Answer (D) is incorrect because $104,000 results from not accounting for the tax effect.

Questions 33 and 34 are based on the following information. In Pitou Co.'s first year of existence, its pretax financial income is $520,000, and its taxable income is $500,000. The $20,000 difference is attributable solely to recognition of earned revenue from installment sales that will result in future taxable amounts when the receivables are collected. Pitou's applicable tax rate is 34%. In its second year, Pitou Co. has taxable income of $450,000, which includes the collection of $8,000 of installment receivables previously recognized in financial accounting income. There is no other difference between pretax financial income and taxable income.

33. The income tax expense for the first year is

A. $176,800

B. $170,000

C. $163,200

D. $6,800

The correct answer is (A). *(Publisher)*
REQUIRED: The income tax expense for the first year.
DISCUSSION: The deferred tax liability is $6,800 (34% x $20,000 taxable temporary difference), and the deferred tax expense is also $6,800 ($6,800 year-end deferred tax liability – $0 balance at the beginning of the year). Income tax payable (current tax expense) is $170,000 (34% x $500,000 taxable income). Accordingly, income tax expense is $176,800 ($170,000 current tax expense + $6,800 deferred tax expense).
Answer (B) is incorrect because $170,000 is the current tax expense. Answer (C) is incorrect because $163,200 results from subtracting the deferred tax expense from the current tax expense. Answer (D) is incorrect because $6,800 is the deferred tax expense.

34. The income tax expense for the second year is

A. $155,720

B. $153,000

C. $150,280

D. $2,720

The correct answer is (C). *(Publisher)*
REQUIRED: The income tax expense for the second year.
DISCUSSION: The taxable temporary difference is reduced to $12,000 ($20,000 – $8,000), the year-end deferred tax liability is $4,080 (34% x $12,000), and the decrease in the deferred tax liability (the deferred tax benefit arising from reduction in the liability) is $2,720 ($6,800 at the beginning of the year – $4,080 at year-end). Current tax expense (tax payable) is $153,000 (34% x $450,000 taxable income). Consequently, total income tax expense for the year is $150,280 ($153,000 current tax expense – $2,720 deferred tax benefit).
Answer (A) is incorrect because $155,720 results from adding the deferred tax benefit. Answer (B) is incorrect because $153,000 is the current tax expense. Answer (D) is incorrect because $2,720 is the deferred tax benefit.

Questions 35 and 36 are based on the following information. In its first year of operations, Miou-Miou Co. had taxable income of $400,000 and pretax financial income of $385,000. The difference is solely attributable to receipt of unearned subscription revenue (a liability) that was included as revenue in the tax return in the year of collection. The company will recognize $9,000 of this unearned revenue as earned in its second year of operations and $6,000 in the third year. The applicable tax rate is 34%. In its second year of operations, Miou-Miou had taxable income of $600,000. Taxable income and pretax financial income differ only in that $9,000 of unearned revenue collected in the preceding year is included in the determination of pretax financial income. Based on the evidence (taxable income), no valuation allowance is required for any relevant year.

35. The income tax expense for the first year is

A. $141,000

B. $136,000

C. $130,900

D. $5,100

The correct answer is (C). *(Publisher)*
REQUIRED: The income tax expense for the first year.
DISCUSSION: The deferred tax asset is $5,100 (34% x $15,000 deductible temporary difference), and the deferred tax benefit is also $5,100 ($5,100 year-end deferred tax asset – $0 balance at the beginning of the year). Income tax payable (current tax expense) is $136,000 (34% x $400,000 taxable income). Accordingly, income tax expense is $130,900 ($136,000 current tax expense – $5,100 deferred tax benefit).
Answer (A) is incorrect because $141,000 results from adding the deferred tax benefit. Answer (B) is incorrect because $136,000 is the current tax expense. Answer (D) is incorrect because $5,100 is the deferred tax benefit.

36. The income tax expense for the second year is

A. $209,100

B. $207,060

C. $204,000

D. $3,060

The correct answer is (B). *(Publisher)*
REQUIRED: The income tax expense for the second year.
DISCUSSION: At the end of the second year, the deferred tax asset is $2,040 [34% x ($15,000 – $9,000)], and the deferred tax expense (the decrease in the deferred tax asset) is $3,060 ($5,100 – $2,040). Total income tax expense is $207,060 [($34% x $600,000) current tax expense + $3,060 deferred tax expense].
Answer (A) is incorrect because $209,100 assumes the deferred tax expense is $5,100. Answer (C) is incorrect because $204,000 is the current tax expense. Answer (D) is incorrect because $3,060 is the deferred tax expense.

37. Mardi Co. has a $6,000 deductible temporary difference at the end of its current year. The applicable tax rate is 34%. However, after weighing all the evidence, Mardi Co. has decided that it is more likely than not (more than 50% probable) that $4,000 of the deductible temporary difference will not be realized. The amount of the deferred tax asset, net of any evaluation allowance, is

A. $6,000

B. $2,040

C. $1,360

D. $680

The correct answer is (D). *(Publisher)*
REQUIRED: The amount of the deferred tax asset, net of any evaluation allowance.
DISCUSSION: A deferred tax asset should be debited for $2,040 (34% x $6,000 deductible TD). To reflect the determination that it is more likely than not (more than 50% probable) that $4,000 of the deductible temporary difference will not be realized, a valuation allowance (a contra account) should be credited. The offsetting debit is to income tax expense. The amount of the valuation allowance should be sufficient to reduce the deferred tax asset to the amount that is more likely than not to be realized. Accordingly, Mardi should recognize a $1,360 valuation allowance to reduce the $2,040 deferred tax asset to $680 (34% x $2,000).
Answer (A) is incorrect because $6,000 is the amount of the deductible temporary difference. Answer (B) is incorrect because $2,040 is the deferred tax asset without regard to the valuation allowance. Answer (C) is incorrect because $1,360 is the valuation allowance.

38. The terms of a 6-year, noncancelable lease include a guarantee by Lessee of Lessor's 7-year bank loan obtained to finance construction of the leased equipment, a termination penalty assuring that the lease will be renewed for 3 years following the expiration of the initial lease, and an option that allows Lessor to extend the lease for 3 years following the last renewal option exercised by Lessee. The lease term as defined by current authoritative literature is

A. 6 years.

B. 7 years.

C. 9 years.

D. 12 years.

The correct answer is (D). *(Publisher)*
    REQUIRED: The number of years in the lease term.
    DISCUSSION: The term of a lease includes not only the fixed noncancelable lease term but also (1) any periods covered by bargain renewal options, (2) any periods covered by ordinary renewal options preceding the date at which a bargain purchase option is exercisable, (3) any periods covered by ordinary renewal options during which a guarantee by the lessee of the lessor's debt or a loan from the lessee to the lessor related to the leased property is expected to be in effect, (4) any periods for which failure to renew the lease imposes a penalty on the lessee in an amount such that renewal appears to be reasonably assured, and (5) any periods representing renewals or extensions of the lease at the lessor's option. In no case can the lease term extend beyond the date a bargain purchase option becomes exercisable. Here, the termination penalty covers the 3 years immediately following the initial 6-year lease term. The renewal option by Lessor at the end of the first 9 years covers an additional 3 years, resulting in a lease term of 12 years. The 7-year period of the bank loan is included in the 6-year term and the first 3-year renewal period.
    Answer (A) is incorrect because 6 years includes only the fixed term. Answer (B) is incorrect because 7 years is the debt term. Answer (C) is incorrect because the lease term includes both the period that would result in a penalty to the lessee and the period that is at the option of the lessor.

39. MacDunnell leased a new machine having an expected useful life of 30 years from Fiegull. Terms of the noncancelable, 25-year lease were that MacDunnell would gain title to the property upon payment of a sum equal to the fair value of the machine at the termination of the lease. MacDunnell accounted for the lease as a capital lease and recorded an asset and a liability in the financial records. The asset recorded under this lease should properly be amortized over

A. 5 years (the period of actual ownership).

B. 22.5 years (75% of the 30-year asset life).

C. 25 years (the term of the lease).

D. 30 years (the total asset life).

The correct answer is (C). *(Publisher)*
    REQUIRED: The proper amortization period.
    DISCUSSION: When a lease transfers ownership of the property to the lessee at the end of the lease or contains a bargain purchase option, the lessee will own the asset at the end of the lease. Hence, such a lease is capitalized and amortized over the expected useful life of the leased asset. If, instead, the lease meets either the 75% lease term test or the 90% fair value test, it will be accounted for as a capital lease and will be amortized over the lease term. Because the lease term is more than 75% of the expected useful life of the asset, the lease should be amortized over the lease term (25 years).
    Answer (A) is incorrect because the lessee's amortization period covers the entire period of the lease. Answer (B) is incorrect because, although it represents one of the four criteria for a capital lease, it does not reflect the proper amortization period. Answer (D) is incorrect because a lease is amortized over the expected useful life of the asset only when a bargain purchase option exists or ownership is automatically transferred at the end of the lease.

40. Equipment covered by a lease agreement is expected by the lessor to have a residual value at the end of the lease term of $20,000. As part of the lease agreement, the lessee guarantees a residual value of $12,000. In the case of excessive usage, the guaranteed residual value is $18,000. What is the amount of guaranteed residual value that should be included in the calculation of the minimum lease payments?

A. $0

B. $12,000

C. $18,000

D. $20,000

The correct answer is (B). *(Publisher)*
    REQUIRED: The amount of guaranteed residual value.
    DISCUSSION: The amount of guaranteed residual value to be included in the determination of minimum lease payments is the determinable amount the lessee is required to make good, even if that amount is materially lower than the expected salvage value. The $12,000 guarantee should be included. The additional guarantee of $6,000 ($18,000 – $12,000) is not included because it is contingent and thus nondeterminable.
    Answer (A) is incorrect because the guaranteed residual value is included in the determination of minimum lease payments. Answer (C) is incorrect because the additional guarantee of $6,000 ($18,000 – $12,000) is not included because it is contingent and thus nondeterminable. Answer (D) is incorrect because the minimum lease payments include only the amount of residual value that is guaranteed.

41. On January 2, a clothing store entered into a lease with a shopping mall for space to be used as a retail store. Terms of the 5-year, noncancelable lease require monthly payments of $600 plus 1% of sales. Sales have been averaging $15,000 per month and are expected to remain constant or increase. What monthly amount(s) should be included in minimum lease payments?

A. Only the $150 payment based on expected sales.

B. Only the $600 monthly payment.

C. Both the $150 and $600 payments.

D. Neither the $150 nor $600 payments.

The correct answer is (B). *(Publisher)*
REQUIRED: The amount(s) to be included in minimum lease payments on a lease containing a contingent payment term.
DISCUSSION: SFAS 29, *Determining Contingent Rentals*, defines contingent rentals as lease payments based on a factor that does not exist or is not measurable at the inception of the lease. Future sales do not exist at the inception of the lease and meet the definition of a contingent rental.
SFAS 13 excludes contingent rentals from minimum lease payments. Because the $150 based on expected future sales is a contingent rental, only the $600 periodic payment is included in minimum lease payments.
Answer (A) is incorrect because the minimum lease payment includes only those payments that are measurable at the inception of the lease. Answer (C) is incorrect because the $150 payment is not measurable at the inception of the lease. Answer (D) is incorrect because the $600 payment is included in minimum lease payments because it is measurable.

42. On January 2, a 5-year lease for a major piece of equipment is signed. Terms of the lease require a fixed annual payment of $12,000 plus $100 for each 1% of a specific bank's prime interest rate. If the prime interest rate is 14% on January 2, is expected to rise to 16% by July 1, and is expected to average 10% for the life of the lease, the total minimum lease payments for the life of the lease should be

A. $60,000

B. $65,000

C. $67,000

D. $68,000

The correct answer is (C). *(Publisher)*
REQUIRED: The total minimum lease payments over the life of the lease.
DISCUSSION: SFAS 13 excludes contingent rentals from the definition of minimum lease payments. SFAS 29 defines contingent rentals as the changes in lease payments resulting from changes occurring subsequent to the inception of the lease. But lease payments that are based on a factor that exists and is measurable at the inception of the lease are not contingent rentals. Thus, total minimum lease payments for this piece of equipment should include the five annual payments of $12,000 per year ($60,000) plus $7,000, which is the sum of the five annual $1,400 payments. This amount is based on the prime interest rate (14%) existing at the inception of the lease ($100 x 14 = $1,400).
As the prime rate changes during the lease term, the corresponding increase or decrease of $100 for each 1% of the prime rate should be charged or credited to income as appropriate. Minimum lease payments, however, should not be adjusted.
Answer (A) is incorrect because $60,000 excludes the $7,000 ($100 x 14 x 5) measurable at the inception of the lease. Answer (B) is incorrect because $65,000 is based on the average expected prime rate of 10%. Answer (D) is incorrect because $68,000 is based on the 16% prime rate in July.

Questions 43 through 46 are based on the following information. Lessee has entered into a direct-financing lease that requires 10 annual payments to Lessor of $1,000 each. The payments are due at the beginning of each year, and the first is payable immediately. Lessor's implicit interest rate of 8% is known to Lessee. Lessee's incremental borrowing rate is 9%. The present value of an ordinary annuity of $1 for 10 periods is 6.71008 at a rate of 8% and 6.41766 at a rate of 9%. The present value of an annuity due of $1 for 10 periods is 7.24689 at a rate of 8% and 6.99525 at a rate of 9%.

43. The liability recorded by Lessee at the inception of the lease is

A. $6,995

B. $6,710

C. $6,247

D. $5,995

The correct answer is (C). *(Publisher)*

REQUIRED: The liability recorded by Lessee at the inception of the lease.

DISCUSSION: The lease is a direct-financing lease, a type of capital lease, so Lessee should record an asset and an obligation. The applicable interest rate is 8% (the lower of Lessor's implicit rate or Lessee's incremental borrowing rate), and the payments are in the form of an annuity due. Accordingly, Lessee should record an initial liability of $6,247 [($1,000 x 7.24689 interest factor for an annuity due of 10 periods at 8%) – $1,000 initial payment made immediately].

Answer (A) is incorrect because $6,995 is based on a rate of 9% and does not subtract the initial payment. Answer (B) is incorrect because $6,710 is based on the interest factor for an ordinary annuity and does not subtract the initial payment. Answer (D) is incorrect because $5,995 is based on a rate of 9%.

44. The gross profit recognized by Lessor at the inception of the lease is

A. $2,753

B. $1,000

C. $937

D. $0

The correct answer is (D). *(Publisher)*

REQUIRED: The gross profit recognized by Lessor at the inception of the lease.

DISCUSSION: A lessor recognizes a gross profit in a sales-type lease. No gross profit is recognized in a direct-financing lease. The difference between a direct-financing and a sales-type lease is that the cost used in accounting for a direct-financing lease is ordinarily the fair value. For a sales-type lease, cost is less than the fair value (if a profit is to be recognized). This distinction is made by the lessor, not by the lessee.

Answer (A) is incorrect because $2,753 is the unearned lease revenue at the inception of the lease. Answer (B) is incorrect because $1,000 is the periodic payment. Answer (C) is incorrect because $937 is the lease revenue recognized by Lessor at the end of the first year.

45. The amount of the lease liability amortized by Lessee at the time of the second lease payment is

A. $1,000

B. $540

C. $500

D. $460

The correct answer is (C). *(Publisher)*

REQUIRED: The amount of the lease liability amortized by Lessee at the time of the second lease payment.

DISCUSSION: A periodic lease payment has two components: interest income or expense and the reduction of the lease receivable or obligation. Under the effective-interest method, the appropriate interest rate is applied to the carrying value of the lease receivable or obligation at the beginning of the interest period to calculate interest income or expense. Thus, Lessee's first-year interest expense is $500 (8% x $6,247 obligation at the inception of the lease as calculated in a preceding question), and the amount by which the second $1,000 will reduce the liability is $500 ($1,000 payment – $500 interest expense).

Answer (A) is incorrect because $1,000 is the periodic payment. Answer (B) is incorrect because $540 is the interest expense assuming an interest rate of 9%. Answer (D) is incorrect because $460 is the amortization assuming an interest rate of 9%.

46. The amount of lease revenue recognized by Lessor for the second payment is

A. $1,000

B. $540

C. $500

D. $460

The correct answer is (C). *(Publisher)*

REQUIRED: The amount of lease revenue recognized by Lessor for the second payment.

DISCUSSION: A periodic lease payment has two components: interest income or expense and the reduction of the lease receivable or obligation. Under the effective-interest method, the appropriate interest rate is applied to the carrying value of the lease receivable or obligation at the beginning of the interest period to calculate interest income or expense. Accordingly, Lessor should recognize lease revenue from the second payment equal to 8% of the carrying value (present value of the minimum lease payments – $1,000). Hence, lease revenue is $500 {8% x [($1,000 x 7.24689) – $1,000]}.

Answer (A) is incorrect because $1,000 is the periodic payment. Answer (B) is incorrect because $540 is the interest revenue assuming a 9% interest rate. Answer (D) is incorrect because $460 equals $1,000 minus the interest revenue assuming a 9% interest rate.

47. At the beginning of the year, the market-related value of the plan assets of Margie Company's defined benefit pension plan was $1,000,000. Margie uses a 5-year weighted-average method to determine market-related values. The company, however, had not previously experienced any asset gains and losses. The expected long-term rate of return on plan assets is 10%. The actual return during the year was $50,000. Contributions and benefits paid were $150,000 and $200,000, respectively. At year-end, the market-related value of Margie's plan assets is

A. $1,140,000

B. $1,040,000

C. $1,000,000

D. $950,000

The correct answer is (B). *(Publisher)*

REQUIRED: The market-related value of plan assets at year-end.

DISCUSSION: If market-related value is defined as fair value, the ending market-related value of the plan assets is the beginning value, plus the actual returns, plus the contributions, less the benefits paid. However, in this case, the company uses an alternative method to determine market-related value. This alternative includes 20% of the sum of the differences between the actual and the expected returns (asset gains and losses) over the last 5 years. The year-end market-related value is the beginning value, plus the expected return, plus the contributions, less the benefits paid, minus 20% of the difference between the actual return and the expected return for the current year only.

Beginning market-related value	$1,000,000
Expected return (10% x $1,000,000)	100,000
Contributions	150,000
Benefits paid	(200,000)
20% of $50,000 loss	(10,000)
Year-end market-related value	$1,040,000

Answer (A) is incorrect because it excludes the expected returns and benefits paid. Answer (C) is incorrect because it includes the entire loss. Answer (D) is incorrect because it excludes the expected return and 20% of the loss.

48. Janice, Inc. has a defined benefit pension plan. For the current year, the expected return on plan assets was $50,000. The actual return was $75,000. The increase in the projected benefit obligation was estimated to be $300,000. The amount of the projected benefit obligation determined at year-end reflected an increase of only $200,000. If no unrecognized net gain (loss) existed at the beginning of the year, the amount of net gain (loss) subject to required amortization for the current year is

A. $0

B. $(75,000)

C. $25,000

D. $125,000

The correct answer is (A). *(Publisher)*

REQUIRED: The amount of net gain (loss) subject to required amortization for the current year.

DISCUSSION: SFAS 87 does not require recognition of gains and losses as components of NPPC of the period in which they arise. The $25,000 asset gain ($75,000 actual return – $50,000 expected return) and the liability gain (the PBO at year-end was $100,000 less than estimated) are thus not required to be included in NPPC of the current year. The gain (loss) subject to amortization also does not include asset gains or losses not yet reflected in the market-related value of plan assets when market-related value is based on a moving average.

Answers (B), (C), and (D) are incorrect because SFAS 87 does not require recognition of gains and losses as components of NPPC of the period in which they arise. Also, gains (losses) subject to amortization do not include gains or losses not yet reflected in the market-related value of plan assets when it is based on a moving average.

49. Joe Company, with a final pay, noncontributory, defined benefit pension plan, settled its vested benefit obligation of $1,500,000 by purchasing participating annuity contracts for $1,650,000. Nonparticipating annuity contracts would have cost $1,500,000. The remaining unrecognized transition net asset is $180,000, the remaining unrecognized net loss since transition is $400,000, and the projected benefit obligation is $2,000,000. Prior service cost is $300,000. The settlement gain (loss) that should be recognized is

A. $135,000

B. $(165,000)

C. $(277,500)

D. $(390,000)

The correct answer is (B). *(Publisher)*

REQUIRED: The settlement gain (loss) that should be recognized.

DISCUSSION: The maximum settlement gain or loss is equal to the unrecognized net gain or loss arising subsequent to transition to SFAS 87 plus any remaining unrecognized net asset arising at transition. If the purchase of a participating annuity contract constitutes a settlement, the maximum gain is reduced by the cost of the participation rights, but the maximum loss is not adjusted. The maximum gain or loss is recognized if the entire PBO is settled. If only part is settled, a pro rata share of the maximum gain or loss is recognized equal to the percentage reduction in the PBO.

Unrecognized transition net asset	$ 180,000
Unrecognized net loss	(400,000)
Maximum loss	$(220,000)
Reduction % ($1,500,000 ÷ $2,000,000)	x .75
Settlement loss	$(165,000)

Answer (A) is incorrect because the $135,000 gain is the $180,000 unrecognized transition asset multiplied by the percentage reduction in the PBO. Answer (C) is incorrect because the loss should not be increased by the cost of the participation rights multiplied by the percentage reduction in the PBO. Answer (D) is incorrect because the prior service cost is not included in the calculation of settlement loss.

50. SFAS 88 defines termination benefits as benefits provided to employees in connection with their termination of employment. Termination benefits may be classified as either special termination benefits offered only for a short period of time or contractual termination benefits required by the terms of a pension plan only if a specified event occurs. The liability and loss arising from termination benefits should be recognized by an employer when the employees accept the offer and the amount can be reasonably estimated for

	Special Benefits	Contractual Benefits
A.	No	No
B.	No	Yes
C.	Yes	No
D.	Yes	Yes

The correct answer is (C). *(Publisher)*

REQUIRED: The termination benefits that should be recognized by the employer when the employees accept the offer and the amount is reasonably estimable.

DISCUSSION: The liability and loss arising from special termination benefits should be recognized by an employer when the employees accept the offer and the amount can be reasonably estimated. The liability and loss arising from contractual termination benefits should be recognized when it is probable that employees will be entitled to benefits and the amount can be reasonably estimated.

Answers (A), (B), and (D) are incorrect because the liability and loss arising from special termination benefits should be recognized by an employer when the employees can accept the offer and the amount can be reasonably estimated. The liability and loss arising from contractual termination benefits should be recognized when it is probable that employees will be entitled to benefits and the amount can be reasonably estimated.

	Historical Cost	Fair Value
Current assets	$250,000	$300,000
Fixed assets	350,000	500,000
Liabilities	100,000	100,000
Capital stock, $5 par	150,000	
Additional paid-in capital	150,000	700,000
Retained earnings	200,000	

Questions 51 through 54 are based on the following information. December 31, 1996 balance sheet items of the Star Company are presented in the opposite column on both a historical cost and a fair value basis.

51. On January 2, 1997, Planet Company issued 25,000 shares of its $10 par value stock in exchange for all of the outstanding shares of Star Company in a business combination that did not meet the criteria for pooling. If the market price of Planet's stock was $40 at the date of acquisition, which entry records Planet's investment in its new subsidiary?

A. Investment in subsidiary $500,000
   Capital stock $250,000
   Paid-in capital   250,000

B. Investment in subsidiary $1,000,000
   Capital stock $250,000
   Paid-in capital   750,000

C. Investment in subsidiary $500,000
   Capital stock $250,000
   Paid-in capital   50,000
   Retained earnings   200,000

D. Current assets $300,000
   Fixed assets   500,000
   Goodwill   300,000
   Liabilities $100,000
   Capital stock   250,000
   Paid-in capital   750,000

The correct answer is (B). *(Publisher)*
REQUIRED: The journal entry to record a stock investment accounted for as a purchase.
DISCUSSION: To account for a stock investment in a subsidiary accounted for as a purchase, the investment in subsidiary account should be debited for the $1,000,000 fair value of the stock issued (25,000 shares x $40). The capital stock account should be credited for $250,000 (25,000 shares x $10 par), and the remaining $750,000 should be credited to additional paid-in capital.
   Answer (A) is incorrect because fair value, not carrying value, is the appropriate value to be used in a purchase. Answer (C) is incorrect because it reflects a pooling of interests. Answer (D) is incorrect because it reflects a merger rather than a stock investment.

52. Assume that, in addition to the issuance of 25,000 shares of stock on January 2, 1997, the purchase agreement provides for the contingent issuance of 5,000 shares of Planet's stock to the previous shareholders of Star in 1996 if a certain level of earnings is attained. If the required level of earnings is attained and the 5,000 additional shares are issued when the market price of Planet's shares is $45, the journal entry to reflect this transaction is which of the following?

A. No entry is necessary.

B. Investment in subsidiary $225,000
   Capital stock $225,000

C. Investment in subsidiary $225,000
   Capital stock $ 50,000
   Paid-in capital   175,000

D. Investment in subsidiary $200,000
   Capital stock $ 50,000
   Paid-in capital   150,000

The correct answer is (C). *(Publisher)*
REQUIRED: The journal entry to reflect a contingent issuance of shares based on earnings.
DISCUSSION: APB 16 states that, when a contingency based on earnings is resolved and additional consideration such as stock is issued, the acquiring corporation should record the current fair value of the stock issued as an additional cost of the acquired company. This additional cost should usually be reflected as goodwill and amortized over the remaining life of the asset. Thus, Planet should debit investment in subsidiary for an additional $225,000 (5,000 shares x $45). The capital stock account should be credited for $50,000 (5,000 shares x $10), and additional paid-in capital should be credited for the $175,000 remainder ($225,000 − $50,000).
   Answer (A) is incorrect because an entry is necessary. Answer (B) is incorrect because the $225,000 must be allocated between capital stock and additional paid-in capital. Answer (D) is incorrect because the current fair value of the stock issued should be used, rather than the $40 fair value at the date of the original acquisition.

53. Refer to the information preceding question 51 on page 471. Assume that, in addition to the issuance of 25,000 shares of stock on January 2, 1997, the purchase agreement provides for the contingent issuance of additional shares necessary to pay a $1,000,000 purchase price if the market price of Planet's stock is not equal to $40 on December 31, 1997. If the market price of Planet's shares is $25 on December 31, 1997, which of the following entries is necessary to reflect the issuance of the contingent shares?

A. No entry is necessary.

B. Paid-in capital $150,000
   Capital stock $150,000

C. Investment in subsidiary $375,000
   Capital stock $150,000
   Paid-in capital   225,000

D. Investment in subsidiary $150,000
   Capital stock $150,000

The correct answer is (B). *(Publisher)*
REQUIRED: The journal entry to reflect the issuance of shares to resolve a contingency based on valuation of the acquiring company's stock.
DISCUSSION: APB 16 states that the cost of an acquired company recorded at the date of acquisition represents the entire payment, including any contingent issuance of securities based on security prices. For any additional shares distributed at a later date, the acquiring corporation should reduce the fair value previously allocated to the shares of stock issued. In this situation, Planet must issue an additional 15,000 shares of $10 par stock at a market price of $25; i.e., a total of 40,000 shares must be issued to pay the $1,000,000 purchase price. Thus, $400,000 (40,000 shares x $10 par) must be allocated to the capital stock account and $600,000 to additional paid-in capital. To adjust the existing capital stock balance of $250,000 and the paid-in capital balance of $750,000, the paid-in capital account must be debited and capital stock credited for $150,000.
Answer (A) is incorrect because an entry is necessary. Answers (C) and (D) are incorrect because the cost of the acquired company is not changed, so an adjustment to the investment account is unnecessary.

54. Refer to the information preceding question 51 on page 471. Assume that, in addition to the assets and liabilities among Star Company's December 31, 1996 balance sheet items, Star has brought suit against a competitor for an infringement of a patent. If sufficient evidence exists to indicate that settlement of the lawsuit in the amount of $75,000 is probable, the allocation of the $1,000,000 purchase price (25,000 shares x $40) should include goodwill of

A. $0

B. $225,000

C. $375,000

D. $425,000

The correct answer is (B). *(Publisher)*
REQUIRED: The determination of goodwill when a preacquisition contingency exists.
DISCUSSION: According to SFAS 38, *Accounting for Preacquisition Contingencies of Purchased Enterprises*, if the contingency is settled during the allocation period or if during this period information is obtained indicating it is probable an asset existed, a liability had been incurred, or an asset had been impaired at the date of the combination, and the amount of the asset or liability affected can be reasonably estimated, the preacquisition contingency must be included in the allocation of the purchase price based on that fair value. The fair value of the identifiable net assets is $775,000 ($300,000 current assets + $500,000 noncurrent assets − $100,000 liabilities + $75,000 contingent settlement). The excess of the $1,000,000 cost over the $775,000 fair value of the net identifiable assets is $225,000 of goodwill.
Answer (A) is incorrect because goodwill must be recognized when cost exceeds fair value of the net identifiable assets. Answer (C) is incorrect because $375,000 assumes that a contingent liability has been incurred by Star. Answer (D) is incorrect because $425,000 is based on historical costs, not fair values.

55. On July 1, the Prime Company acquired 90% of the Simple Company for cash in an amount equal to the carrying value of the net assets on Simple Company's books. During the year, Simple Company, a nonseasonal company, declared net income of $400,000, and it paid dividends of $50,000 on June 30 and December 31. The preferred presentation of the year-end consolidated income statement should contain which of the following amounts?

A. Minority income of $10,000.

B. Minority income of $20,000.

C. Preacquisition earnings of $180,000.

D. Preacquisition earnings of $200,000.

The correct answer is (C). *(Publisher)*
REQUIRED: The amount arising from a midyear purchase contained in a consolidated income statement.
DISCUSSION: ARB 51, *Consolidated Financial Statements*, states that, when a subsidiary is purchased during the year, the preferred method of presenting the results of operations is to include the subsidiary's operations in the consolidated income statement as though it had been acquired at the beginning of the year and to deduct from the total earnings the preacquisition earnings. The minority interest income for the entire year is also deducted. Preacquisition or purchased earnings are earnings of a subsidiary earned prior to the date of the acquisition of the subsidiary by the parent. These earnings are included in determining the purchase price. The minority income equals the year-end minority interest multiplied by the subsidiary's income for the annual period. Because the purchase of Simple Company occurred at midyear, the minority interest was 10% at year-end, and the subsidiary is nonseasonal, the preacquisition earnings are $180,000 [50% x ($400,000 total income – $40,000 minority interest income)].

Answers (A) and (B) are incorrect because minority income deducted is $40,000 (10% year-end minority interest x $400,000 annual net income). Answer (D) is incorrect because the preacquisition earnings do not include the minority income earned prior to the date of the acquisition.

56. Sorrento Company repurchased 10,000 shares of its outstanding stock for $600,000 on December 31. Sorrento's owners' equity sections immediately before and immediately after this treasury stock transaction are presented below.

	Before	After
Capital stock, $10 par	$1,000,000	$1,000,000
Additional paid-in capital	1,500,000	1,500,000
Retained earnings	2,500,000	2,500,000
Treasury stock	-0-	(600,000)
Total owners' equity	$5,000,000	$4,400,000

Assume that Sorrento repurchased this stock from the general public. By what amount should Palermo Company, which holds 75,000 shares of the outstanding stock of Sorrento, adjust its investment in subsidiary account because of Sorrento's treasury stock transaction?

A. $0

B. $83,333 debit.

C. $83,333 credit.

D. $366,667 debit.

The correct answer is (C). *(Publisher)*
REQUIRED: The investment in subsidiary account adjustment to reflect the repurchase of shares by the subsidiary from the minority interest.
DISCUSSION: Immediately before this treasury stock transaction, the parent's interest in the subsidiary was 75% (75,000 shares held ÷ 100,000 shares outstanding). Immediately after the transaction, it was 83 1/3% (75,000 shares held ÷ 90,000 shares outstanding). The parent's proportionate interest in the total recorded owners' equity of the subsidiary decreased from $3,750,000 (75% x $5,000,000) to $3,666,667 (83 1/3% x $4,400,000). Thus, the investment account should be credited (decreased) by $83,333 ($3,750,000 – $3,666,667). The carrying value of the investment account is not needed to calculate the adjustment because the adjustment relates only to the parent's proportionate interest in the subsidiary's owners' equity.

Answer (A) is incorrect because the investment account should be adjusted for the change in the parent's proportionate interest. Answer (B) is incorrect because the $83,333 decrease should be credited, not debited. Answer (D) is incorrect because $3,666,667 is the parent's proportionate interest in the subsidiary.

Questions 57 and 58 are based on the following information. Suwannee Company issued 20,000 additional shares of its common stock for $1,600,000. Suwannee Company's owners' equity sections immediately before and immediately after this issuance of stock transaction are presented below.

	Before	After
Capital stock, $10 par	$1,000,000	$1,200,000
Additional paid-in capital	2,500,000	3,900,000
Retained earnings	3,900,000	3,900,000
Total owners' equity	$7,400,000	$9,000,000

57. Assume that Suwannee Company issued this stock to the general public. By what amount should Palatka Corporation, the owner of 80,000 of the outstanding shares of Suwannee Company, adjust its investment in subsidiary account because of the issuance of stock by Suwannee Company?

A. $0

B. $80,000 debit.

C. $80,000 credit.

D. $1,280,000 debit.

The correct answer is (B). *(Publisher)*

REQUIRED: The investment in subsidiary account adjustment to reflect the issuance of stock by a subsidiary to the general public.

DISCUSSION: Immediately prior to the issuance of the additional shares of stock by Suwannee Company, Palatka's ownership interest was 80% (80,000 shares held ÷ 100,000 shares outstanding). Its proportionate interest in the subsidiary's recorded owners' equity was $5,920,000 (80% x $7,400,000). Immediately after the issuance of the shares, Palatka's ownership interest was 66 2/3% (80,000 shares held ÷ 120,000 shares outstanding), and its proportionate ownership interest was $6,000,000 (66 2/3% x $9,000,000). Thus, its investment in subsidiary account should be debited (increased) for the $80,000 difference ($6,000,000 after – $5,920,000 before). The corresponding credit is to paid-in capital.

Answer (A) is incorrect because the investment in subsidiary account should be adjusted for the change in the parent's proportionate interest. Answer (C) is incorrect because the increase should be debited. Answer (D) is incorrect because $1,280,000 assumes that the ownership percentage remained at 80%.

58. Assume that Suwannee Company issued the stock to Palatka Corporation, whose ownership interest thereby increased from 80,000 shares to 100,000 shares. If the carrying value of the identifiable assets of Suwannee is equal to their fair value at the time the additional shares are issued, the goodwill indicated in the purchase of the additional shares equals

A. $0

B. $20,000

C. $320,000

D. $1,580,000

The correct answer is (B). *(Publisher)*

REQUIRED: The determination of goodwill when the parent purchases additional stock issued by the subsidiary.

DISCUSSION: Prior to the issuance of the new securities, the parent company owned 80% of the outstanding stock of the subsidiary, resulting in a proportionate ownership in the subsidiary's recorded owners' equity of $5,920,000. Following the issuance of the 20,000 shares, the parent holds an 83 1/3% interest (100,000 shares held ÷ 120,000 shares outstanding), resulting in a proportionate ownership interest in the subsidiary's owners' equity of $7,500,000 (83 1/3% x $9,000,000). The difference is $1,580,000 ($7,500,000 – $5,920,000). Hence, goodwill of $20,000 results ($1,600,000 price paid – $1,580,000).

Answer (A) is incorrect because goodwill must be recognized. The purchase price exceeded the fair value of the identifiable net assets acquired. Answer (C) is incorrect because $320,000 assumes the ownership percentage did not change. Answer (D) is incorrect because $1,580,000 is the increase in the proportionate interest.

59. Sub Company had net assets according to its books of $1,000,000 on January 1, 1996. On the same date, Parr Company owned 9,000 of the 12,000 outstanding shares of Sub's only class of stock, and its investment in Sub Company account had a balance of $795,000. If, on January 1, 1996, Sub repurchased 2,000 shares from Parr for $200,000, the gain on the sale of the stock recognized by Parr was

A. $3,000

B. $7,000

C. $10,000

D. $23,333

The correct answer is (B). *(Publisher)*
REQUIRED: The gain on a purchase of treasury stock by a subsidiary from its parent.
DISCUSSION: The gain recognized by the parent will equal the difference between the amount received and the credit to the investment account. The latter has two components: (1) the decrease in the parent's equity in the net assets of the subsidiary and (2) the reduction in the unamortized differential (investment balance – equity in the subsidiary's net assets) attributable to the decrease in the percentage of ownership. Prior to the treasury stock transaction, Parr's equity in Sub's net assets was $750,000 [$1,000,000 x (9,000 shares ÷ 12,000 total shares)]. Hence, the unamortized differential was $45,000 ($795,000 investment balance – $750,000 interest in net assets). Parr's equity in Sub after the treasury stock transaction was $560,000 [(7,000 shares ÷ 10,000 total shares) x $800,000], and the decrease in the equity was therefore $190,000 ($750,000 – $560,000). Given a reduction in percentage stock ownership from 75% (9,000 ÷ 12,000) to 70% (7,000 ÷ 10,000), the reduction in the unamortized differential was $3,000 {[(75% – 70%) ÷ 75%] x $45,000}. Accordingly, the total decrease in the investment account was $193,000 ($190,000 + $3,000), and Parr realized a gain of $7,000 ($200,000 proceeds – $193,000 credit to the investment account). The journal entry in Parr's books was

Cash	$200,000	
Investment in Sub Company		$193,000
Gain on sale		7,000

Answer (A) is incorrect because $3,000 is the reduction in the unamortized differential. Answer (C) is incorrect because $10,000 ignores the reduction in the unamortized differential. Answer (D) is incorrect because $23,333 assumes that the investment balance is reduced by approximately 22.22% (2,000 shares ÷ 9,000 shares).

60. At January 1, Seacoast Company, an 80%-owned subsidiary of Plantation Corporation, had $1,000,000 face value of 14% bonds outstanding. They had been issued at face value. Market conditions at January 1 provided a 10% yield rate when Plantation purchased these bonds in the open market for $1,100,000. Which of the following amounts should be included in a consolidated income statement for the year?

A. Bond interest expense of $140,000.

B. Bond interest revenue of $110,000.

C. Constructive loss of $100,000.

D. Constructive loss of $80,000.

The correct answer is (C). *(Publisher)*
REQUIRED: The amount of an intercompany bond transaction in consolidated net income.
DISCUSSION: Because a consolidated financial statement should include both Plantation and Seacoast as a single (consolidated) reporting entity, the purchase of the $1,000,000 outstanding bonds of Seacoast by Plantation for $1,100,000 was in substance a retirement of debt for $100,000 more than the debt's carrying value. This transaction should be reflected in the consolidated income statement as a constructive loss (extraordinary) from the retirement of debt in the amount of $100,000.
Answers (A) and (B) are incorrect because each represents the intercompany interest reflected on the subsidiary's and parent's books that must be eliminated in the consolidated financial statements. Answer (D) is incorrect because ARB 51 requires an adjustment for the total loss, not just the parent's share.

61. The arbitrage pricing theory (APT) explains asset returns in terms of multiple macroeconomic factors. Assume that the macroeconomic variables are the gross domestic product, inflation, real interest rates, differences in yields of different grades of corporate bonds, and differences in yields on long versus short-term government bonds. The factor return or risk premium (k_i) and the factor sensitivity or beta coefficient (β_i) for each variable are given below:

Variable =	1	2	3	4	5
k_i =	.03	.04	.07	.05	.03
β_i =	.5	.3	.3	.4	.6

If the risk-free interest rate is .05, the expected rate of return according to the APT is

A. 13.6%

B. 10.3%

C. 8.3%

D. 5.0%

The correct answer is (A). *(Publisher)*

REQUIRED: The expected rate of return according to the APT.

DISCUSSION: Arbitrage pricing theory (APT) is based on the assumption that an asset's return is based on multiple systematic risk factors. In contrast, the CAPM is a model that uses just one systematic risk factor to explain the asset's return. That factor is the expected return on the market portfolio, i.e., the market-valued weighted average of all securities available in the market. Accordingly, APT provides for a separate beta and a separate risk premium for each systematic risk factor identified in the model. Examples of the many potential systematic risk factors are the gross domestic product (GDP), inflation, and real interest rates. The APT for a three-factor model may be formulated as follows:

$$R = RF + \beta_1 k_1 + \beta_2 k_2 + \beta_3 k_3$$

If: R = expected rate of return
RF = risk-free rate
$\beta_{1,2,3}$ = individual factor beta coefficients
$k_{1,2,3}$ = individual factor risk premiums

Thus, the expected return under the APT is 13.6% [.05 + (.5 x .03) + (.3 x .04) + (.3 x .07) + (.4 x .05) + (.6 + .03)].

Answer (B) is incorrect because 10.3% is based on the three factors with the highest betas. Answer (C) is incorrect because 8.3% is based on the two factors with the highest betas. Answer (D) is incorrect because 5.0% is the risk-free rate.

62. A company has unit sales of 300,000, the unit variable cost is $1.50, the unit sales price is $2.00, and the annual fixed costs are $50,000. Furthermore, the annual interest expense is $20,000, and the company has no preferred stock. Accordingly, the degree of total leverage is

A. 1.875

B. 1.50

C. 1.25

D. 1.20

The correct answer is (A). *(Publisher)*

REQUIRED: The degree of total leverage.

DISCUSSION: The degree of total leverage equals the degree of financial leverage (DFL) times the degree of operating leverage (DOL). The DFL may be stated as earnings before interest and taxes (EBIT) divided by EBIT minus interest and preferred dividends (before the tax effect). If EBIT is $100,000 [($2 x 300,000 units) sales – ($1.50 x 300,000 units) VC – $50,000 FC], the DFL is 1.25 [$100,000 ÷ ($100,000 – $20,000 – $0)]. The DOL may be stated as contribution margin divided by the contribution margin minus fixed costs. Hence, if the contribution margin is $150,000 [($2 unit price – $1.50 unit VC) x 300,000 units], the DOL is 1.5 [$150,000 ÷ ($150,000 – $50,000)], and the degree of total leverage is 1.875 (1.25 x 1.50).

Answer (B) is incorrect because 1.50 is the DOL. Answer (C) is incorrect because 1.25 is the DFL. Answer (D) is incorrect because 1.20 equals the DOL divided by the DFL.

63. Samoore Co. sponsors a defined benefit pension plan. Its service cost for calendar year 1998 was $450,000, and pension benefits paid for the year equaled $400,000. If the projected benefit obligation at January 1, 1998 was $1,800,000, and the company's assumed discount rate is 10%, the projected benefit obligation at year-end is

A. $2,430,000

B. $2,030,000

C. $1,850,000

D. $1,800,000

The correct answer is (B). *(Publisher)*

REQUIRED: The projected benefit obligation at year-end.

DISCUSSION: The PBO at the end of a period equals the PBO at the beginning of the period, plus service cost and interest cost, plus retroactive benefits (prior service cost) granted by a plan amendment during the period, minus benefits paid, plus or minus changes in the PBO resulting from changes in assumptions and from experience different from that assumed. Given no prior service cost, changes in assumptions, or experience different from that expected, the ending PBO is $2,030,000 [$1,800,000 + $450,000 + (10% x $1,800,000) – $400,000].

Answer (A) is incorrect because $2,430,000 disregards the benefits paid. Answer (C) is incorrect because $1,850,000 omits interest cost. Answer (D) is incorrect because $1,800,000 equals the beginning PBO.

64. M.C. Katt Co. sponsors a defined benefit pension plan. For its fiscal year ended December 31, 1998, contributions to the plan equaled $300,000 and benefits paid were $260,000. If the fair value of the plan assets increased from $1,200,000 to $1,600,000, the actual return on plan assets was

A. $700,000

B. $400,000

C. $360,000

D. $100,000

The correct answer is (C). *(Publisher)*

REQUIRED: The actual return on plan assets.

DISCUSSION: The actual return on plan assets is the difference between the fair value of the plan assets at the beginning and end of the accounting period adjusted for contributions and payments during the period. Thus, the actual return on plan assets was $360,000 ($1,600,000 – $1,200,000 – $300,000 + $260,000).

Answer (A) is incorrect because $700,000 is the sum of the increase in the fair value of plan assets and contributions. Answer (B) is incorrect because $400,000 is the increase in the fair value of plan assets. Answer (D) is incorrect because $100,000 is the excess of the increase in the fair value of plan assets over contributions.

65. Neue Co. sponsors a defined benefit pension plan. For the year ended December 31, 1998, the following information relevant to the plan has been accumulated:

Service cost	$120,000
Return on plan assets	30,000
Interest on the PBO	40,000
Amortization of actuarial loss	10,000
Amortization of prior service cost	5,000
Amortization of transition obligation	15,000
Accrued pension cost at 1/1/98	40,000

If the company's contribution to the plan for 1998 was $220,000, the prepaid pension cost at year-end was

A. $60,000

B. $40,000

C. $35,000

D. $20,000

The correct answer is (D). *(Publisher)*

REQUIRED: The prepaid pension cost at year-end.

DISCUSSION: A recognized pension liability (unfunded accrued pension cost recorded as a credit to the accrued/prepaid pension cost account) arises when funding is less than the NPPC. Prepaid pension cost (a debit to accrued/prepaid pension cost) results from funding the plan in excess of the NPPC. Accordingly, the prepaid pension cost at year-end was $20,000 ($220,000 contribution – $160,000 NPPC – $40,000 accrued pension cost).

Answer (A) is incorrect because $60,000 results from ignoring the accrued pension cost. Answer (B) is incorrect because $40,000 is the accrued pension cost. Answer (C) is incorrect because $35,000 omits amortization of the transition obligation.

INDEX

Gleim Publications, Inc.	TOLL FREE:	(800) 87-GLEIM	Customer service is available:
P.O. Box 12848	LOCAL:	(352) 375-0772	8:00 a.m. - 7:00 p.m., Mon. - Fri.
Gainesville, FL 32604	FAX:	(352) 375-6940	9:00 a.m. - 2:00 p.m., Saturday
	INTERNET:	http://www.gleim.com	Please have your credit card ready
	E-MAIL:	sales@gleim.com	

"THE GLEIM SERIES" OBJECTIVE QUESTION AND EXPLANATION BOOKS

AUDITING & SYSTEMS . . . . (760 pages • 1,784 questions) . . . . $16.95 $_____
BUSINESS LAW/LEGAL STUDIES . . . . . . (736 pages • 1,788 questions) . . . . $16.95 _____
FEDERAL TAX . . . . (800 pages • 2,524 questions) . . . . $16.95 _____
FINANCIAL ACCOUNTING . . . . (768 pages • 1,756 questions) . . . . $16.95 _____
MANAGERIAL ACCOUNTING . . . . (752 pages • 1,290 questions) . . . . $16.95 _____

CIA REVIEW (7th Edition)
VOLUME I: Outlines & Study Guides . . . . $27.95 $_____
VOLUME II: Problems & Solutions . . . . $27.95 _____

CIA TEST PREP Software (@ $35.00 each part) ☐ Part I ☐ Part II ☐ Part III ☐ Part IV _____

CMA/CFM REVIEW
Part 1, Economics, Finance and Management . . . . $22.95 $_____
Part 2CMA, Financial Accounting and Reporting . . . . 22.95 _____
Part 2CFM, Corporate Financial Management . . . . 22.95 _____
Part 3, Management Reporting, Analysis and Behavioral Issues . . . . 22.95 _____
Part 4, Decision Analysis and Information Systems . . . . 22.95 _____

CMA/CFM TEST PREP Software (@ $35.00 each part)
☐ Part 1   ☐ Part 2CMA   ☐ Part 2CFM   ☐ Part 3   ☐ Part 4

CPA REVIEW (1997-1998 Edition)

	Books	Audiotapes	**CPA Test Prep** Software	
Auditing	☐ @ $24.50	☐ @ $75.00	☐ @ $35.00	$_____
Business Law	☐ @ $24.50	☐ @ $75.00	☐ @ $35.00	_____
TAX-MAN-GOV	☐ @ $24.50	☐ @ $75.00	☐ @ $35.00	_____
Financial	☐ @ $24.50	☐ @ $75.00	☐ @ $35.00	_____

A System for Success (112 pp.) . . . . ☐ FREE with your order of any Gleim CPA Review book

The Complete Gleim CPA System (save 15%) . . . . $457.00 _____
   (5 books, 4 audio cassette albums (40 tapes), and 4 CPA Test Prep diskettes)

Shipping (nonrefundable): **1 item = $3; 2 items = $4; 3 items = $5; 4 or more items = $6** . . . _____

Add applicable sales tax for shipments within Florida. . . . . _____

Fax or write for prices/instructions for shipments outside the 48 contiguous states.   **TOTAL** $_____

1. We process and ship orders daily, generally one day after receipt of your order.

2. Please COPY this order form for others.

3. No CODs. All orders from individuals must be prepaid. Library and company orders may be purchased on account. Shipping and a handling charge will be added to the invoice, and to telephone orders.

4. Gleim Publications, Inc. guarantees the immediate refund of all resalable texts if returned within 30 days. Applies only to books purchased direct from Gleim Publications, Inc. Refunds or credit are not offered on software and audiotapes. Our shipping charge is nonrefundable.

NAME (please print) _____

ADDRESS _____ Apt. _____
   (street address required for UPS)

_____

CITY _____ STATE ____ ZIP _____

____ VISA/MC/DISC/AMEX ____ Check/M.O. Daytime Telephone (___)_____

Credit Card No. _____ - _____ - _____ - _____

Exp. ____ / ____   Signature _____
      Mo. / Yr.

Printed 9/97. Prices subject to change without notice.

☞ Visit our home page on the Internet at www.gleim.com.

Please forward suggestions, corrections, and comments concerning typographical errors, etc., to **Irvin N. Gleim** • c/o **Gleim Publications, Inc.** • **P.O. Box 12848** • **University Station** • **Gainesville, Florida** • **32604**. Please include your name and address so we can properly thank you for your interest.

1. _____

2. _____

3. _____

4. _____

5. _____

6. _____

7. _____

8. _____

9. _____

10. _____

11. _____

12. _____

13. _____

14. _____

15. _____

16. _____

17. _____

18. _____

19. _____

20. _____

Remember for superior service:	<u>Mail</u>, <u>e-mail</u>, or <u>fax</u> questions about our books or software. <u>Telephone</u> questions about orders, prices, shipments, or payments.

Name: _____

Company: _____

Address: _____

City/State/Zip: _____

Phone: (___) _____   FAX: (___) _____   E-mail: _____

GLEIM BOOKMARK

Dr. Gleim's Recommendation: Cover the answers and explanations in our book with this bookmark to make sure you do NOT cheat yourself. Answers will not be alongside questions when you take your exam.

SOFTWARE

If you don't have it - GET IT!
Gleim's **Test Prep** software is
the most effective tool for
passing the CPA, CIA, CMA, and CFM exams.
One disk for each section of each exam
contains hundreds of questions
not found in the books.
Call today or download a
demo from our website.

BOOKS ◆ SOFTWARE ◆ AUDIOTAPES

(800) 87-GLEIM
www.gleim.com

GLEIM BOOKMARK

Dr. Gleim's Recommendation: Cover the answers and explanations in our book with this bookmark to make sure you do NOT cheat yourself. Answers will not be alongside questions when you take your exam.

SOFTWARE

If you don't have it - GET IT!
Gleim's **Test Prep** software is
the most effective tool for
passing the CPA, CIA, CMA, and CFM exams.
One disk for each section of each exam
contains hundreds of questions
not found in the books.
Call today or download a
demo from our website.

BOOKS ◆ SOFTWARE ◆ AUDIOTAPES

(800) 87-GLEIM
www.gleim.com